INTO FILM

by

Laurence Goldstein and Jay Kaufman

New York
E. P. DUTTON & CO., INC.

Book Design by George H. Buehler

First Edition

10 9 8 7 6 5 4 3 2 1

Published simultaneously in Canada by Clarke, Irwin & Company Limited, Toronto and Vancouver.

ISBN: 0-525-13447-6 (cloth)
ISBN: 0-525-47315-7 (DP)

Library of Congress Catalog Card Number: 75-10080

To our wives, who made this book possible,
and to our children, who made it necessary.

Preface

The magic associated with motion pictures has made them one of the most immediate and powerful of the contemporary arts. Especially for the young, as Jean-Luc Godard has said, "Film is truth twenty-four times a second." Yet all too often even the most avid of today's film-goers knows little about the techniques used by film-makers to rivet the attention of an audience for ninety minutes or more.

However, the meanings embedded in a film, and the techniques used to elicit those meanings, are not things that ordinarily yield to learning from books. Film-making, like any other craft, is best understood when it is approached directly, either by working on a motion picture or by carefully looking at someone else's work. Still, for the vast majority of film-goers—even those with an abiding interest in film—neither of these approaches is readily accessible.

We have, therefore, attempted to re-create, by means of a book, the insights and the delight that result from carefully looking at a film, one frame at a time. Through still photographs taken from actual movie frames we have explored some of the most beautiful, powerful, compelling film sequences ever created. From Eisenstein's *Battleship Potemkin,* Griffith's *The Birth of a Nation,* Wiene's *The Cabinet of Dr. Caligari* to the films of such modern masters as Antonioni, Godard, Bergman, Ford, and Hitchcock we have taken critical sequences that illustrate and define not only the art of the motion picture but some of the most powerful thrusts of the artistic imagination.

Our interest, though, extends beyond the exploration of classic motion pictures. Film has become such a popular means of expression that between television, the schools, libraries, museums, and churches our lives are immersed in film. The result of all this exposure to the moving image is the creation of a vast audience to which the film-maker can appeal through a variety of shorter films—documentaries, experimental films, commercials, and student work. We have included segments from all these various types of film. They not only provide examples of important techniques, but they also give the reader the added advantage of checking our explanations and insights against everyday experience.

The analytical approach that we have chosen—the isolation of frozen bits of action—is in fact at the very heart of film-making. At the center of the film-making process stands a large and complex film editing machine called a Moviola. This machine allows the film-maker to slow down the film and inspect it frame by frame if necessary, an essential process in both the editing and close analysis of a motion picture. We have tried to reproduce this indispensable way of looking at films by including almost 1,400 frames from sequences taken from over one hundred movies. These still pictures are an integral part of the text and all the critical analysis in the book is keyed to these photographs. The effect is similar to looking over our shoulders as we analyze sequences from the films, a shot at a time, on a Moviola.

And for two very special sequences this Moviola approach is carried one step farther. Every other frame from the last twenty-five seconds of the memorable "Odessa Steps" sequence from Sergei Eisenstein's *Potemkin* is printed on the lower corner of page 9 through page 385. In the second section there is a ten-second segment from Jean-Luc Godard's equally important film, *Breathless*. By slowly flipping through the pages of either section, one of these sequences can be seen in motion. These flip sequences thus permit the close inspection of pictures in motion—a type of analysis usually available only to film students and scholars.

These analytical techniques should prove informative not only to film-goers, but also to a new and expanding generation of would-be film-makers. Because of the continuing revolution in the tools of film-making, particularly the development of high-quality super 8mm film and cameras, serious film-making has come within reach of both the budgets and the competence of beginning film-makers. As a result, those who, in the past, might have remained content simply to look at films are increasingly trying their hand at film-making.

This growing interest in film-making has in turn revived interest in books on film aesthetics, from the early writings of Eisenstein and Pudovkin through Arnheim and Spottiswoode to Bazin and a host of other contemporary writers on film. The same is true for how-to-do-it books on film, a large number of which have recently appeared. Almost invariably, though, these two subjects are treated separately. What we have done, through the careful dissection of actual sequences, is to combine what have been two separate areas into a comprehensive view of films and film-making. By focusing on specific frames we can clearly analyze the technical means used to produce a film. This understanding of the mechanics of film then allows us to spell out the effect of these film-making techniques on the meanings a sequence can create for an audience.

As is evident, our purpose is to reproduce, as nearly as is possible in a book, the original experiences of the writers, directors, cameramen, sound men, and editors who create and then manipulate the pieces of sound and picture that go into a film. And, since these jobs are progressively being combined into one and the same person—the film-maker—our theme is the indivisible nature of the film-making process as it unfolds in the mind of a film's creator. Film-making has begun to approach the status of Alexandre Astruc's *caméra stylo*—the camera that can be handled as easily as a writer's pen or a painter's brush—so it is this secret of the film-maker's art, the unbroken connection between the parts, that ultimately must be forced to reveal its mysteries.

No book, particularly one this size, is written without the help of many people. Although most of these contributions took the form of small assists and passing kindnesses, there were a number of major contributors without whose help this book could not have been completed.

Willard Van Dyke, former Director, Department of Film, The Museum of Modern Art, who made available to us all the extensive resources of the museum's film archives.

Mary Corliss, Film Stills Archivist, The Museum of Modern Art, who kept watch over our valuable collection of negatives, and who saw to it that we had study prints and a place to view them.

Richard Bailey, graphic artist, *Newsday,* whose incredible skill in the darkroom provided us with the prodigious number of photographic prints used in these volumes.

Rick Brown, interested student and critic who also helped organize the glossary.

Leo Dratfield, Vice-President, Phoenix Films, Inc., who, when President of Contemporary Films/McGraw-Hill, provided us access to nearly half the films used in this book.

A. William J. Becker III, Chairman of the Board, Janus Films, Inc., who made available to us almost the entire collection of Janus Films.

I must also acknowledge one last enormous and sorrowful debt to my friend, colleague, and coauthor of this book, Larry Goldstein. He died in February 1972, before the manuscript could be completed. The inspiration for this book was his and this volume represents a large part of the last three years of his life. The thoughtfulness, care, and excitement that he brought to writing created what are for me some of the finest passages and most vivid insights to be found in these pages. I will be forever grateful for having known and worked with him.

This is the first frame of a flip sequence from Eisenstein's Potemkin*—the last 25 seconds of the scene on the Odessa steps. Flip through it slowly; it is designed to be seen at eight frames per second. On page 395 another flip sequence begins—the killing in Godard's* Breathless. *That sequence runs to the end of the book.*

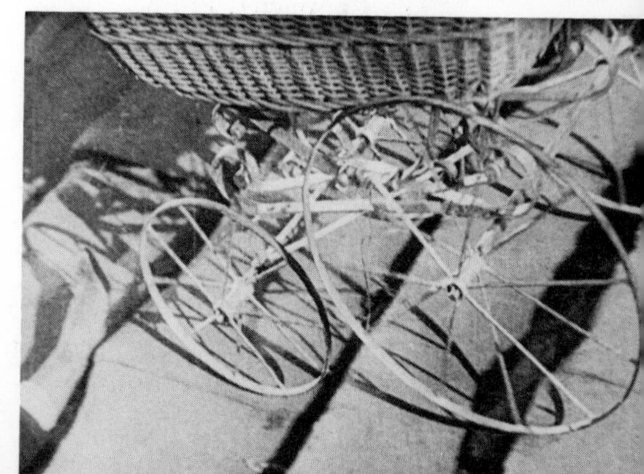

Contents

Section I

Section II

INTO FILM
SECTION I

Technique as Expression

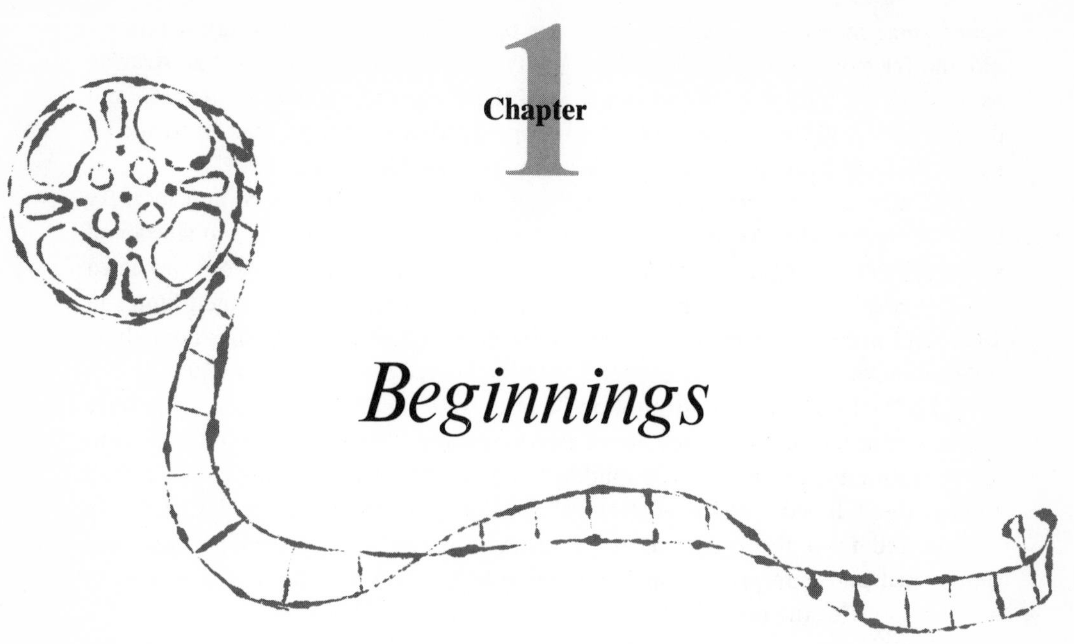

Chapter 1

Beginnings

One man sitting alone in a room can conceive a film. But between the inspiration and its realization stand an army of specialized technicians, complex equipment, and the need for a small fortune to mobilize both men and equipment in the service of his dream. Each step of the way his original ideas for the film will be mediated and compromised as they are filtered through this machinery and the ubiquitous hands at its controls. This alone should inhibit any reasonably intelligent film dreamer.

It wasn't always this way. There was a brief time in the earliest beginnings of motion pictures, for just a decade or so, when a film-maker could go out with his cameraman and make a film. But then films became popular, film-making became an industry, and the ideas of the film-maker became a product. He lost control of his films and became just an employee of the man who could buy the equipment, hire the technicians, and distribute the films. Once the film-maker was separated from the ownership of the equipment he used, the history of motion pictures was written on corporate profit sheets.

Let us go back briefly and see these patterns as they were first set. It has only been recently that the independent film-maker has reclaimed his equipment and

found some measure of distribution in this battle that is more than half a century old and far from over. The film-maker today is as much a product of this struggle as his films are a product of the influence of those films which won production and distribution. And the specific shape and scope of what he can produce is tempered by the kinds of equipment that have been made available to him.

Motion pictures emerged from that unique marriage of science and industry that summarized the sweep of nineteenth-century progress. After fits and starts and some delightfully ingenious experiments, the first motion pictures were projected simultaneously by different inventors in England, France, and the United States in 1895; and within just fifteen years there were film production companies flourishing in Scandinavia, Italy, France, England, and the United States.

The first big audience for motion pictures were the middle classes. They were initially so attracted by the novelty of moving images that films were offered them as the feature act in their stately vaudeville houses. But by 1902 this audience had tired of the dull and repetitious stories these films presented, and movies gradually disappeared from the program. As a result, the price of projection equipment plummeted and enterprising small businessmen could afford to set up makeshift movie houses for the poor.

Films opened a new world for the poor and illiterate, and the insatiable demands of this audience to fill their lives with bits of comedy and adventure not only kept film-making alive but swiftly turned it into an industry. The elusive promises of a democracy found a metaphor in cheap, often filthy, nickelodeons as tangible as that of the cathedrals of the Middle Ages. Movie houses gave the poor a place to go to take part in a society that was indifferent to them. Seated together in the dark, no seat more expensive than any other, their view of the world on the screen was intimate and compelling. Moving pictures had an immediacy, a vitality that made swift contact with an audience yearning to see beyond the confines within which they toiled.

Even the titles proved to be no barrier. There was always someone willing to shout them aloud in the crowded, communal, exuberant world of the early movie houses. And for the American immigrant, there was usually someone nearby who could translate the titles into a familiar language. Movie-going was a shared experience—a way into a new culture.

By 1909 films were already big business, expanding by more than twenty-five million dollars a year. They were in such demand that the largest film producer-distributors banded together to keep their hold on the market. The group called itself the Motion Picture Patents Company in early recognition that it was equipment upon which the industry was built. Among its members, this combine held sixteen patents on camera and projection equipment. To this they added an exclusive contract with the Eastman Kodak Company, the only major supplier of film stock in the United States. The Patents Company further tightened its grip on the American market by setting up a licensing system that attempted to force theaters to show only films made by the company.

What followed could have been scripted by those Hollywood writers who later immortalized gangland Chicago. Theaters were bombed. Gangs of toughs invaded the sets of independent producers, beating up actors and smashing equipment. Under the protection of court injunctions, sheriffs and police seized cameras and projection equipment. The independents in turn employed armed guards to protect their studios; and when this proved ineffective they shifted entire sets from location to location until they could finish their films. After ten years of warfare, the Patents Company monopoly was broken. Equipment became widely available, and independent producers like the Warner brothers, Carl Laemmle of Universal, Adolph Zukor of Paramount, and William Fox were on their way to becoming giants of the motion-picture industry.

With the destruction of the trust, the newly liberated independents changed the tide of motion-picture production by immediately launching longer and more expensive films. Up until that time the members of the Patents Company had been able to resist exhibitors' demands for longer films. It had been far more profitable for them to flood the country with cheap, fifteen-minute productions. Even when the fabled D. W. Griffith made a modest thirty-minute film, his studio immediately cut it in half and sent it out as two separate shorts. But with the independents in full swing and the American market open to foreign films, movies as long as two and three hours were given distribution. Productions became increasingly lavish and expensive. Film stars were developed and paid increasingly larger salaries. Advertising budgets increased and bigger theaters charging higher prices were used to recoup spiraling production costs. An affluent middle class was again attracted to motion pictures and the film companies built a multi-million-dollar industry to make successively bigger films to satisfy their demands.

In the heat of this expansion, the ardor of the film companies for the individualistic film director cooled. They could no longer afford his failures. He became just one more company employee and his imagination was just one more company asset. When that imagination failed to hold a large audience, it became a liability. On the ledgers of film companies across the world, the columns of red ink were written in the blood of directors fallen from favor. Early film-makers like Griffith, Stroheim, and Flaherty were all ultimately measured against the losses on their last picture. Creative imagination was a negotiable property and the tendency of the industry was to sell short.

Amateur Film-making

By the 1930's, cameras, projectors, and films had also been developed for the amateur, and the film audiences could then become their own film-makers. For this new amateur market, equipment was developed that was compact, rugged, and, above all, manageable. To be commercially successful, a camera had to be built

for the man who was not expected to know much about making films. Everything had to be simplified. And so as professional film crews and sound stages grew larger and more complex, the amateur was given an instrument that could minimize the complexities and still put a perfectly sharp image on the screen. It was assumed that the amateur was a one-man film crew, and each successful development in his market increased his ability to do as much as possible as easily as possible.

But film in the hands of amateurs took shape as home movies. Because professional films were so big, so glamorous, so perfect in their technical facility, it seemed the best an amateur could hope for was a credible reproduction of his own world. The aura of the old movie palace—its darkened majesty, its communal mystery, its limitless expectations—was a whole aspect of motion pictures that seemed too overwhelming to be manufactured in the home. And it seemed especially unlikely that the final product of the small amateur camera could compare in any way with the awesome films that filled those grand theaters.

Yet, even in home movies, much of the magic is preserved. The darkened room, images of people made larger than life size, pictures of real moments preserved in continually changing space and time—these are at the heart of all film-making. Shifting images seen in hushed darkness possess a beguiling fascination. Possibilities exist in every frame. An imagination open to those possibilities can manipulate the images into perceptions that cut deeply into our lives.

For more than three decades home movies have been an underground torrent of film-making, spilling forth millions of feet of film each year. But even though equipment has been devised that is sophisticated enough to enable the unskilled amateur to make creditable films, the results are rarely thought out or imaginative. It is even unusual for the films to capture a dramatic or interesting event. The people filmed are usually defined solely by their relationship to the film-maker. The flavor of their existence, the shadings in their personalities are normally lost in the self-conscious, mock theatrics of playing to the camera.

Purposeful Film-making

The motive for shooting home movies is mainly to preserve the simple fact of someone's existence. Yet even this can provide surprising insights, as the film-maker Andy Warhol has discovered in his long, existential odysseys. But unlike Warhol, who often lets his camera run until the film is gone, amateurs rarely let their cameras run long enough for the actions filmed to develop in any interesting ways. Nor does the amateur have a feeling for the flow of action from shot to shot. Each brief shot is a complete entity, and the shot that came before and the one that will follow usually have no connection. Because there is no overall design to the shooting, there is no necessary relationship between the shots, and there is no advantage to rearranging them. In other words, there is no need to edit the film.

The sense of drama and feeling that can turn home movies, or almost any other footage, into a film must begin with a purpose—any purpose with ambitions beyond merely wishing to preserve the existence of the people filmed. This purpose can either motivate the shooting of a film or be discovered in the process of trying to organize random footage. Obviously, if the film-maker knows why he is shooting, he has a better chance of controlling the meaning of his footage than if he waits until he edits it. But even random footage can be organized, given a purpose. Once events have been sealed as images on film, they have been wrenched from their original context and can be imaginatively reassembled into a new existence. Even such unplanned footage as a home movie can be made coherent and sometimes interesting by purposeful editing.

The following pages hold as good an example as any of unplanned footage.

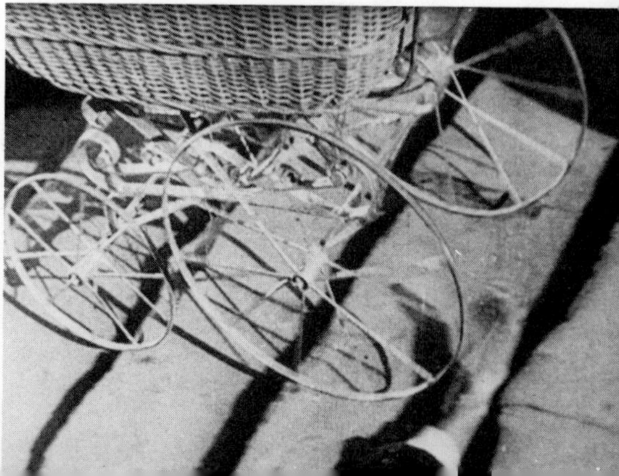

These pictures are eight frames from a home movie placed in the order in which they were filmed. Each frame represents a shot. Each shot was sufficiently brief so that any frame from it shows essentially what happened in the entire take. This then is the raw material. If you were given the film to edit, how would you change the order of the shots, even eliminating some of them if necessary, to make a coherent little film out of the scenes provided?

The possibilities, while not overwhelmingly intriguing, are still unbelievably varied. Just in terms of the mathematics, if all eight shots were used, there are an incredible 40,320 different combinations from which to choose in ordering the film. And given the additional options of eliminating some of the shots and varying the length of all of them, the possibilities for constructing a meaningful film from even this mundane home-movie footage are deceptively broad.

As a specific example, one way of ordering this footage would be to focus upon the experience of two small children getting to know one another through their common fascination for a pail. With this point of view controlling the editing, the children cease to be just the cameraman's son or daughter, whose mere presence upon a screen is enough to give the footage its interest. They become more representative of all children, and their actions can then develop into insights on the drama of childhood.

Once the footage becomes susceptible to a controlling idea, the relevance or irrelevance of each scene quickly becomes apparent. If the subject of the film is the tentative, delicate creation of a friendship between two very small children, the scenes with the mother (4 and 7) not only become irrelevant, they intrude. The mother exists in an entirely different world from the children playing alone, and her presence would radically alter the nature of that film. Obviously, given another point of view, the presence of the mother could be crucial to the meaning of a different film; but, for the sequence we are attempting, the takes that include her would be the first to go.

Next, the remaining shots have to be placed in a meaningful order. In this case, the shots would be arranged to show the children getting progressively closer to playing with each other, until they finally become friends by sharing the pail. The sequence would run: take 1; take 3; take 5; take 2; take 8.

A coherent sequence develops once there is a reason for ordering the shots. Here, the reason is a simple story idea that was discovered in the random uncut footage.

Simply rearranging these shots has created a new relationship between them. But the meaning inherent in this relationship is so fragile that the addition of just

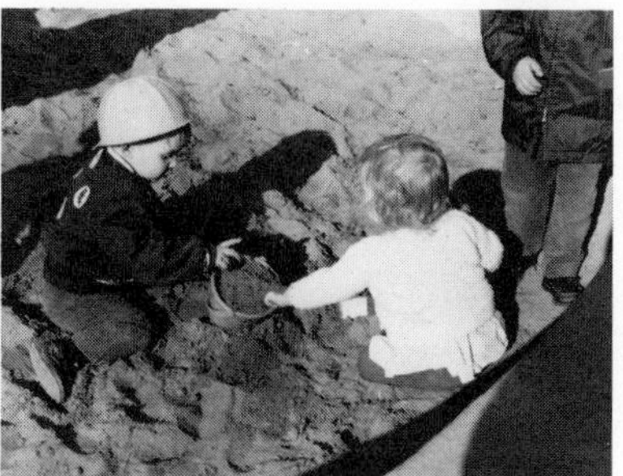

one more shot to the sequence can change the connection we make between all the shots. If take 6 were added to the end of the edited film, the sequence would no longer tell the story of the children's becoming friends. It would now show that these children are capable of playing together only briefly and that the possessiveness of one child can quickly end a tentative friendship.

The discovery of possibilities in the footage during editing that were not apparent when it was shot is by no means unusual in film-making. Bruce Conner has, in fact, made an incisive short film called *A Movie* that was culled from nothing more than stock newsreel footage of disasters and destruction. But it was so carefully thought out and so skillfully edited that it became a grimly ironic comment on the modern world.

If we go back to our home-movie example just once more, there is an additional lesson that can be extracted. Although the shooting of the home-movie footage was not consciously organized, each of its shots still ordered the space which it framed. Any time a camera is pointed toward a subject, the viewfinder frames just a fraction of the world that it is possible to film at that moment from that position. The film-maker selects the piece of the world that will be filmed and the particular angle from which it will be shot. This choice allows him to use the space within the frame in ways that will bring particular insight to the subject being filmed. And since all we see on a screen is what he included within the frame, the way he organizes this space is usually important, and sometimes critical, to our understanding of the actions that take place within it.

For example, the actions of the children in take 2 are seen from their level with a large amount of open sand in front of them. The very openness of this view provides an unrestricted environment in which their relationship can develop, and the atmosphere of the scene is created by the relationship of the camera to the chil-

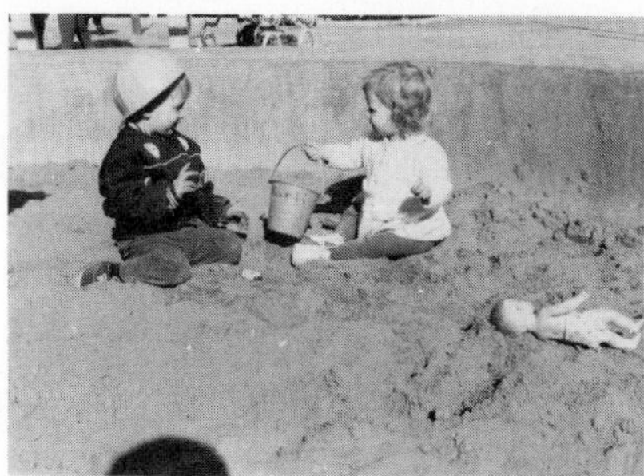

dren as well as by the children's actions. In other words, the way space is organized can create specific expectations for the actions which occur in that space.

In take 3 a different atmosphere is created. The children are shot from above and they are enclosed by their surroundings. They are dominated by the massive stone porpoise in the foreground, and the narrow space this allows them makes their connection with each other seem almost forced. But it is the high, downward camera angle which accentuates this feeling that the children inhabit a restricted environment.

There are now two ways of looking at the children's actions, an open view and a restricted one. The high-angle, restrictive view is as an adult would see the children from outside the sandbox, neatly placed together and expected to play nicely. The other way is the more open, lower-angle from within the sandbox, which shows the children at their own level as they would confront one another. With this difference in mind, an interesting sequence would begin to develop if take 3 were placed before take 2.

The film would begin with the actions of the children seen first from the adult viewpoint of take 3 and then from the open, child-level world of take 2. Each shows the children in a different context. Then, by alternating all the high, adult-level shots taken from outside the sandbox with the child-level shots taken from within, these two ways of seeing the children—restricted and free—are brought into contrast. It is through this contrast that a story can be told of the children slowly ignoring the expectations of the adult world so they can act on their own impulses. The sequence would run: take 3; take 2; take 8; take 5; take 1; take 6.

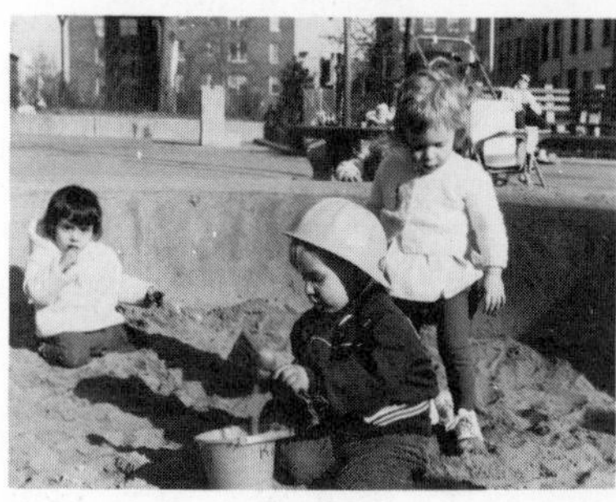

The meaning of the action in the sequence develops through the undulation between the adult- and child-level views. The child-level shots develop to show that the children, of their own accord, will respond to each other in the ways that are most natural to them—in this case with the boy finally taking the pail for himself. And as each succeeding adult-level shot drops toward the children's level, these shots gradually become less severe in their restrictive use of space. As a result, the children are made to appear as if they have increasing freedom to express their natural, self-centered impulses as the sequence progresses. Because the adult-level view is made to give way to a child's-level view of the action, we finally come to see the children acting as if the adult world didn't exist.

Our suggested editing obviously has more subtleties than the original footage can bear. Forced to confront the raw footage, we were able, with persistence and a lot of hard looking, to discover the visual elements that gave us our story. However, it would have been better had the sequence originally been shot with our scenario in mind. Then an adult actually could have been placed in the foreground of the first high-level shot. From then on we would have known that the high-level shots were clearly meant to signify the restrictions of parental supervision. This

way a much better film could have been made. But even without planning, this home-movie footage was shot from two naturally expressive points of view. Because the cameraman gravitated toward two distinctive views of the action, this use of space could later be emphasized through editing.

Organizing Space

The Japanese director Akira Kurosawa developed in *Yojimbo* a sequence somewhat similar to our home-movie example. He also alternated high shots with low-level shots. But he did it quite precisely in order to show the dramatic relationship between an authority figure and the characters who are swept into doing what is expected of them. In this case the "adult" is a wise and powerful samurai who is determined to destroy all the evil, childish inhabitants of a village. The town is divided into two warring factions, and the samurai contrives events so the two sides will confront and destroy each other in battle.

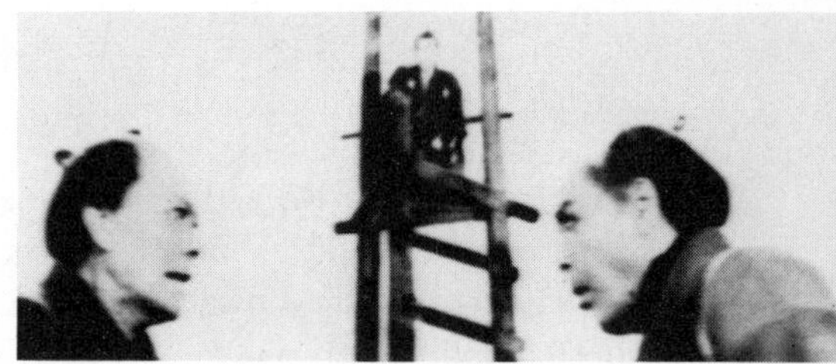

By looking down upon the villagers from the samurai's elevated vantage point, the camera makes the actions of the townspeople seem dominated by the massive form of the samurai in the foreground. They become small children under the control of the samurai's will. In contrast, the ground-level shots swell the villagers to almost heroic size. By alternating these two views, Kurosawa controls the ways in which his audience responds to the battle. When the ground-level action builds to a peak, he cuts to a high-level shot that gives the battle a fresh perspective. The steady contrast between the villagers as monumental-sized warriors and as tiny creatures under the will of the samurai gives the sequence its ironic distinction. Through these contrasting shots of the same action in the same location, it becomes apparent that each camera angle alters the space in which the action flows and so alters our feelings about the action itself. The difference in the camera angles of the two opening shots of the home-movie sequence worked to a similar effect.

In both the home-movie example and *Yojimbo,* space is not only expressively composed but it is also expressively developed from shot to shot so that the final meaning of each shot depends upon its context. The effectiveness of the two shots from *Yojimbo* is totally dependent upon their contrast. If they are shown singly there is no feeling for the flow of action and so we cannot see the film-maker's real purpose for framing each shot as he did. This relationship of one shot to the next is unique to films and no analysis of any one frame from a sequence can accurately or persuasively show how the film-maker used space in his film. We are not dealing with still pictures that are totally self-contained. A frame, after all, is ephemeral. It shows what filled the screen for just one twenty-fourth of a second and can rarely represent more than the single shot from which it was extracted. For this reason we will use a number of frames from each sequence to approach space in films as the film-maker has developed it.

The development of space is central to the meaning of a film. In films, reality exists only as images in space, and these images are constantly being redefined by the space they are allotted both within the frame and from shot to shot. As the physical dimensions of an object change with each new viewpoint, so its emotive, dramatic, and poetic attributes change. Seen up close the villagers in *Yojimbo* are brutal and menacing, while seen from the samurai's height they are merely absurd and petty. In this fact lie the beginnings of film-making as an expressive form.

The reality being photographed is so susceptible to interpretation, so dependent for its final meaning upon how it is filmed and edited, that it is in essence almost abstract. Reality thus becomes malleable, capable of holding a large variety of meanings and feelings. These meanings are born in the imagination that will tie the images together into a coherent film. This film imagination is really no more than the ability to shift one's vision of the world just enough to see expressive possibilities in everyday reality. It is, in Camus's phrase, "the revolt of the artist against the real." The objects which fill our world become the substance from which the film-maker extracts his story.

Moving the Camera

Thus far we have seen how two camera angles can be alternated to create a meaning that is not inherent in each. But in films it is also possible to move the camera and so transform the meaning of a scene within a single shot. We can see an example of this in a scene from Robert Flaherty's landmark documentary *Nanook of the North*. These three frames are from the beginning, middle, and end of one pan shot showing the Eskimos carrying their kayak to the sea and launching it. At the start of the shot the Eskimos are grouped domestically, with the dog and the children filling much of the foreground and the small fleet of kayaks almost playfully cutting through the water in the background. The arrangement of people and boats within the frame gives the impression of nothing more dangerous than a family outing. And this is precisely what Flaherty intended. But as the shot develops, the panning camera follows the boat being taken to the sea and the entire nature of the shot quickly changes. Their home on the shore and the boats in the background are soon omitted from our view, and we become aware of a bleak sea

washing against a desolate shoreline. The Eskimos are now primarily hunters who must challenge that sea. By the end of the shot the Eskimos are small figures in a barren landscape. They suddenly seem quite fragile as they enter a cold and empty expanse of water to hunt the food they need to survive.

With great economy Flaherty has shown in one shot the dramatic duality of the Eskimos' lives. Although they live in a happy, communal group, the Eskimos ultimately exist on the thin edge between survival and oblivion. These truths about their lives are presented spatially. The Eskimos are the substance of the film, but the film-maker has chosen to unfold from frame to frame the particular reality of their lives that he wished to penetrate. Without even changing the position of his camera, but simply by turning it, he shows us the band of Eskimos in dramatically different contexts. The space they occupy within each frame controls not only how we see them but also how we feel about them.

It is possible, of course, for the film-maker to use both camera angle and camera movement in the same shot to develop his meanings. There is a lovely moment in *Jules and Jim* when François Truffaut employs exactly this technique. The story is about a love triangle. Jules and Jim are close friends who both love Catherine. When Jules marries her, Jim unsuccessfully tries to content himself with another girl. Eventually Jim visits Jules and his wife, and, with Jules's consent, becomes her lover.

In this shot, when Catherine leaves Jules to sleep with Jim, Truffaut traces the line of the triangle from its base to its apex. We see Catherine give Jules a civilized kiss good-bye at the bottom of their narrow stairwell. Then the camera slowly tilts upward to follow Catherine's assent to Jim. In one shot the camera looks down upon the broken marriage, takes a close, hard look at the mercurial,

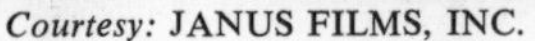
Courtesy: JANUS FILMS, INC.

egocentric wife, and finally looks up at the hopeful new lovers. The emotional effect of this continuous shot is also quite different than if the scene had been made with three separate shots. Here the close ties that bind the characters are dramatized by the thread of constricted, continuous space in which they are locked. The characters share an insanely closed world, where even a chance remark by one can set the other two vibrating. The irony and grotesque humor of this situation is given cohesion and emphasis when Catherine can leave her husband for the arms of another man without even leaving the frame.

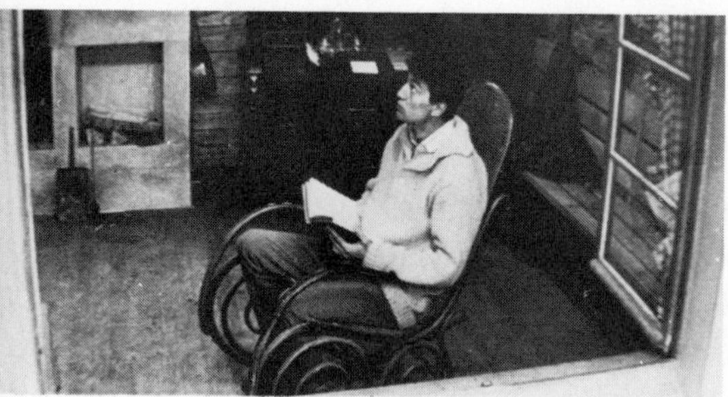

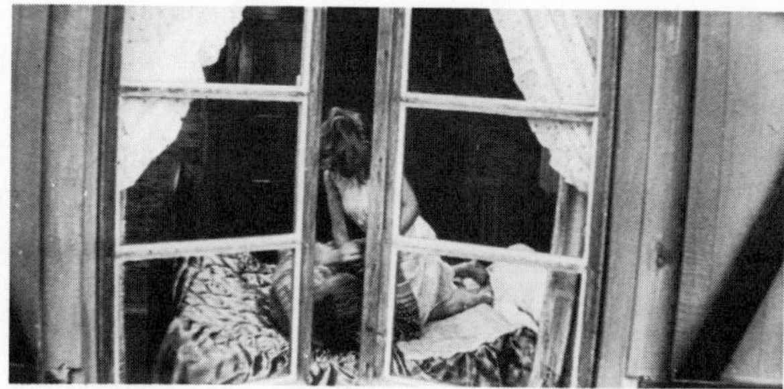

A few minutes later in the film Truffaut uses the same technique to show the instability of this particular triangle. Days have gone by since Jim claimed Catherine. We look down upon him through a window as he sits alone reading. When he hears strangely disturbing sounds above him, the camera cranes up the side of the house until we see husband and wife playfully wrestling in bed. Because we look down on the isolated figure of Jim at the beginning of the shot, we sense that he has been demoted from favor even before he knows it. This feeling is then confirmed as the camera moves up to reveal the cause of his discomfort. Although

the characters are in separate rooms, they are still connected within the same shot. And by keeping us outside the house, Truffaut makes us see his lovers at a sufficient distance to enjoy their game of musical beds without being involved in their pain. Also, because we stay outside, the house itself becomes a tangible reminder of their self-imposed isolation.

Cumulative Images

As we have now seen in several examples, objects in film derive much of their meaning from the changing spaces they occupy. The final meaning that emerges throughout these changes tends to be cumulative, and therefore symbolic. For instance, in *Jules and Jim* the symbiotic dependence of the characters is constantly objectified by the small house in which they live and the narrow rooms they inhabit. This confining view becomes a visible symbol of the suffocating nature of their relationship.

But another interesting thing can also happen. When the same object is seen in a number of different contexts, it is possible to impart a meaning to that object that is the sum of our changing views of it. It is in this complex of associated meanings that the object becomes transformed. It is no longer just itself. It is also the receptacle for our accumulated images of it. And since this vision is being successively constructed—built out of constant modifications and refinements—our knowledge of the object and our feelings about it are never fully solidified. What this finally means is that objects in films, since they constantly reappear in different spatial perspectives, have an unfinished quality to them. And since they are unfinished, they are susceptible to symbolic development. While most objects are usually what they seem at first, an object that is carefully chosen and even more carefully filmed can also be made to stand out from the other objects around it and carry a surprisingly heavy load of meanings.

An example of this, the use of space to develop an object symbolically, occurs in the center segment of *Yesterday, Today and Tomorrow*. Here Vittorio de Sica transforms a Rolls-Royce into a universe that houses and defines a pair of lovers. Since De Sica's use of space is cumulative and metaphoric, we have taken representative frames from the entire sequence to show how a director can control the meaning of his film through the precise use of space. The film is a tour de force that can be enjoyed as much for the director's skill as it can for the marvelous performances of its actors.

De Sica takes the old story of the bored, spoiled, rich lady and her poor,

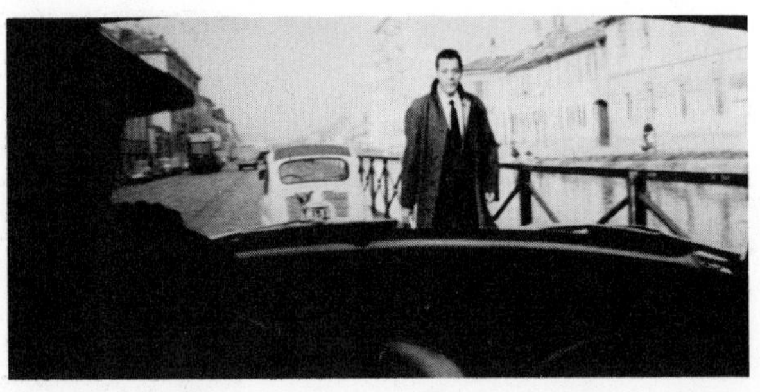

idealistic lover and gives it new meaning by having their affair played out within the confines of the lady's Roll-Royce.

We first see the young man—small and vulnerable standing next to his pathetic Fiat—through the majestic breadth of the windshield of the Rolls. The powerful outline of the woman rises almost organically from the comfortable massiveness of the car, and their relationship is immediately made visible by the space each occupies. She is the Rolls and he is a Fiat. That is the essential fact of their lives and it is given to us visually.

From the moment he enters her car he is enveloped in her world. As they drive off and talk, the dialogue merely fills in a few details—they met for the first time the night before, she is married, her husband is out of town. Then their talk begins to move in opposition to what we see. As she tells him how he has transformed her life, made her feel more compassionate toward the people who surround her, she casually bangs into cars and then shrugs off the minor collisions without even acknowledging them. There is no mention of the car or the road they are traveling.

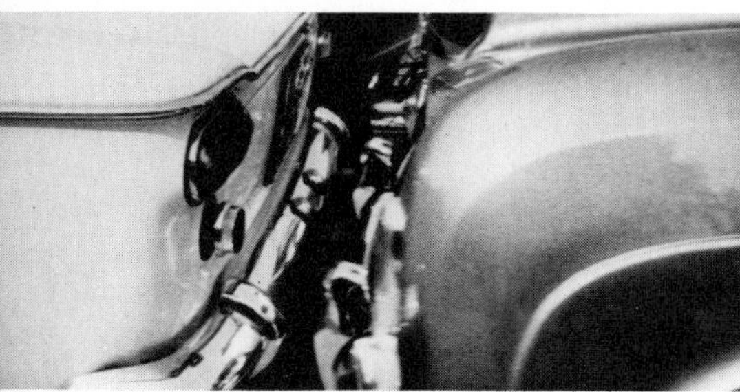

People keep getting in her way, and the distance between her and them is as great as the imperious sweep of the hood of her Rolls.

Her vision of the people in the oppressive outside world is contoured by the limits of the windshield through which she views them. They are really no more to her than changing specimens under glass.

Since she and the splendid automobile are one, for him to make love to her is to embrace them both. Yet, even as they gently hold hands, they bang into still another car. But the accident is of no importance next to the massive importance of their hand-holding. They are the center of the world, comfortably enclosed within the space of the car, and all the rest is no more than a petty annoyance seen at a distance.

And so it goes. She musing about these profound changes in her life, he listening in adoration, as they bang into cars and nearly sideswipe a truck. They ride the road as though it were a sea—a lovers' journey, enclosed, secure, buffeting the currents that dare move against their course. But the charming conceit of lovers blind to the world around them becomes chilling when the lovers move through space in a powerful car with the world at their mercy.

The metaphor is fully realized when she surrenders the car to him. They are so locked within the space of the car that her affection for him is climaxed by an exchange of places within that space. But even when she surrenders the car to him she rises above him. Their bodies touch and finally he is at the wheel. Then it happens. She puts her hand on his thigh and he is distracted.

He looks up too late to see a boy in the road and swerves at the last minute to avoid him. He misses the boy, but badly damages the car.

The ride and the romance are over. She gets out, caresses the car, and inspects the damage.

Her lover, by violating the car, has lost his claim upon her. Her affection is instantly transferred to the wounded automobile. He becomes irrelevant.

The story and metaphor reach their close when she is rescued by a fast, red Ferrari and drives off into the distance, leaving the poor lover with the wrecked car and romance to contemplate.

The relationship of the characters to each other and the world is constantly conditioned by the enveloping car. There is some view of the automobile in almost every frame of the film. Yet from their dialogue you would never know that the car was important. It is an assumption to them and too pervasive for comment. They are so fused with the car that by the end of the film it is difficult to imagine their lives outside it. The director can then play upon this by stepping back from the frame-filling shots of them inside the car to show us the car as just another object on the highway. He has led us into a world so heavy with specific meanings that just a standard cut from a close shot to a long shot becomes ironic. Through the car, a balance has been created between the lovers' attitude toward each other and our attitude toward them. De Sica can then manipulate these attitudes visually to enrich what could have been a pedestrian love story.

An even more subtle kind of extended visual metaphor occurs in the *Grapes of Wrath* where John Ford weaves successive shots of fences into the narrative of the film. Here it is not only the perspective from which we see the action but the unfolding inclusion of objects within the space of the frame that deepens the meaning of the film. As the story develops, the fences become stark signs of a

country whose people are separated from the land which must support them if they are to survive.

The plot is about a family of farmers who lose their property during the Depression and cross the country to find jobs as migratory workers in California. Ford symbolically carves the American landscape into the parcels of property which divide the have's from the have-not's. The fences at the beginning of the film enclose the farmers' land and signify their claim to a piece of the American dream. Once the farmers are dispossessed, the fences objectify their dislocation. They are set adrift upon a landmass carved up for other people. They are at the mercy of the men who own property and their journey becomes a quest to get past the gates. Nothing less than their survival depends upon it. The more imperative their need to be taken in, the more menacing become the fences and the fence-keepers.

Ford, with his almost tactile feeling for the land, also controls the growing estrangement of the farmers from that land by placing them in increasingly more constricted spaces. Surrounded by fertile fields and lush valleys, they cannot break through the ubiquitous membrane of wire-mesh fence that seems to wall off a

continent. Much of the frustration, anger, and deepening sense of injustice felt by the farmers as they travel through lands forbidden them is made visual by the narrow spaces allowed them, the seemingly limitless spaces controlled by the landowners, and the endless fences that separate the two.

An environment which objectifies the characters' essential place in the world needn't be woven throughout an entire film to be effective. Even just one scene can pierce to the center of their world and strip their lives to its basic condition. Quickly and surely, an immediate and lasting sense of recognition can be created by the objects which are chosen and the ways in which they carve up the space the characters inhabit. We can see this in a short scene from Ermanno Olmi's first feature film, *The Sound of Trumpets.* The film tells the story of an awkward, shy young man who leaves his poor home on the outskirts of Milan to take a test for a low-level job in a giant corporation. From the moment he appears for this examination, he is trapped in the erosive world of the company where he will spend the rest of his life holding successively more uninteresting jobs. In this new and strange environment his only familiar feeling is a wistful attraction he develops for a pretty young girl who is also taking the test. During a break in the exam, they meet by chance and share a pathetically brief walk through the streets of Milan.

Courtesy: JANUS FILMS, INC.

We see them here as they try to hurry back to the company but find themselves first caught in a construction project and then in a traffic jam. Olmi ironically treats the pair like archetypal film lovers. But instead of expressing their exuberance for one another in an athletically expressive run through wood and field, he has them running back to an interview for a dreary job through crowded streets filled with the litter of industrial progress. In shot after shot they are enmeshed by the ugliness of a world to which they are poignantly oblivious. Olmi never isolates them from this world. We not only see them in this environment, but we see that its objects constantly impede their progress and channel the directions in which they must move. As they run faster and faster, they blend more and more firmly into the grotesque shapes and limited spaces that anticipate what they can expect out of life. Once they have won their jobs they will become progressively enclosed by the corporation. Their paths will eventually cross only infrequently and accidentally, almost as if they lived in separate blocks of a giant penitentiary. It is only the youthful exuberance of their movements that seems to resist total enclosure, and we feel that the moment they stop moving they will be paralyzed.

Connected Images

The construction of spaces that create insights into the characters' lives need not even be woven into the same shot with them. Since meaning in film is cumulative and develops from shot to shot, visual material that is relevant but not physically connected with the characters in the same frame can be included in a sequence and so become fused with our impression of their lives.

An example of this can be found in this very brief sequence from Ingmar Bergman's *The Silence*. Two sisters, who both love and repel each other, are traveling together through a strange country whose language is totally incomprehensible to them. Essentially isolated from the world, they play out the delicate blend of hostility and concern which afflicts their lives in a semigenteel, slightly run-down hotel for transients.

In this sequence Anna has just debased herself in the sordid, cramped room of a waiter in the hotel. With her sister listening in shock outside the door, Anna draws release from the body of a man who is both beneath her station and totally incapable even of saying an understandable word to her. The lovemaking has been so depersonalized that, as the scene progresses, she is more responsive to her image of her sister at the door than she is to the man in bed with her. When the lovemaking is over, she escapes to the only window in the room—first looking

Courtesy: JANUS FILMS, INC.

down at the netherworld of hotel workers squeezed under a glass skylight and then looking up at a sky stifled by the soiled walls of the hotel's air shaft.

With her sister outside the door, a lover she despises on the bed behind her, we are suddenly given a subjective view of her world. For the first time we see precisely as she sees—a view from the window so bleak and confining that we share the impact of this difficult moment in her life. Bergman lets us look beyond the room in which the scene was played. He reinforces the effect of the room by expanding the location, adding new spaces to those he has already meticulously constructed. He has found additional objects and spaces which refract Anna's alienation and entombment. This ability to build a scene by fragmenting a location and then rebuilding it in pieces is one of film's major expressive advantages.

Perhaps the most classic example of building a scene through this accumulation of fragmentary perspectives is the "Odessa Steps" sequence in Sergei Eisenstein's *Battleship Potemkin.* This sequence has been called one of the most influential few minutes in cinema history. We have reproduced the last twenty-five seconds of this powerful scene as a "flip sequence" on the bottom of these pages. After flipping through it to gain some sense of the development of the action, go through it again slowly and see how Eisenstein is able to employ a multiplicity of isolated views of the events on the steps and still give us a solid impression of the space in which these events take place.

In the film the sequence begins with a joyous crowd assembled at the Odessa steps to welcome the crew that has mutinied and taken over the tsarist battleship *Potemkin.* Suddenly we see the relentless movement of Cossack boots marching down the steps. The crowd retreats. The Cossacks fire as they advance. Quick shots of men and women struck by the bullets. A mother with her dead child in her arms goes up the steps against the flow of the action. The Cossacks shoot her down and descend the steps over the bodies of the mother and child. Fleeing, panic-stricken crowds are cut off by Cossacks on horseback as they reach the base of the steps. Then the nurse in black is killed and the baby carriage she tried to protect plunges sickeningly down the steps. This is where the flip sequence begins. What we now see are flashes of all the elements in the sequence, none longer than two seconds, tied together and given force and cohesion by the journey of the carriage down the steps.

Eisenstein has shattered the original space of the Odessa steps and then rhythmically put the fragments together in a new cinematic whole. Although we never see any of the crucial events simultaneously in the same shot, we are finally left with a vivid impression of how they relate in space. We are very clear about the relationship of these events to each other, but we are never sure of exactly where they are located. For example, where is the young student in relation to the actions that fill him with such horror? One would be hard pressed to assign him an exact spot on the steps. And where exactly is the old woman? But we do know that all of them respond to the developing nightmare around them, and with their reactions

tie the scattered events on the steps tightly together. The world we have seen is entirely Eisenstein's creation. It never had a literal existence. The scene was shot in separate pieces and then assembled at the discretion of the director into purely filmic space. The people we see in the sequence are literally isolated from each other yet they are forever bound together by the vulnerable carriage during its famous descent.

Individual Spaces

There are few sequences in film that will stand up to the brilliant and innovative use of space that Eisenstein developed in the Odessa Steps sequence. By carefully breaking space apart he was able to exploit the full force of his camera angles and camera movements, and then, by the effectiveness with which he joined the pieces together again, to push the shots to their expressive limits. As is evident, space in films is an artifice, a construction which the film-maker develops as best suits his meanings. Although the people and objects he films have an essential identity of their own, the film-maker is empowered to place them in developing visual perspectives and relationships, and so give them a new life. But the technique for organizing the space in a film need not be complex to be effective. A simple film can be expressive in its own right.

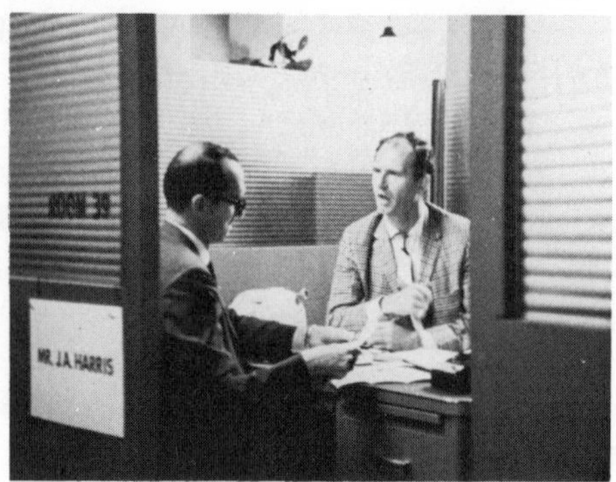

We can see this in this single frame from a one-minute Excedrin commercial. Here one frame shows the entire development of space in the film. The man on the right is being grilled about his rather expansive tax deductions by an Internal Revenue investigator. The men are framed within the frame—pushed together in their unhappy confrontation. We can see the spectrum of discomfort on the face of the tax delinquent as he sweats out the faceless, impersonally precise questions of the investigator. Since the film is a single unmoving shot, each expression and gesture swells in importance because it is the only variable in the frame. The meanings and humor are developed in a static space that immediately defines the delinquent's predicament and then serves to emphasize it through its relentless immobility.

As we have seen, there is no single formula for analyzing how the development of space gives meaning to a film. Because the visual elements in a film can vary so greatly, space can be organized in as many ways as there are films and film-makers. But the basic fact of all film is that information is given to us visually and sequentially. Once the film-maker has framed part of the world, he is able to force the world into new relationships that can be developed into coherent and expressive insights. The very act of filming is the act of coming to grips with the concrete nature of things. The act of film-making, however, begins when the concrete is made to bend and yield meanings that become the product of a distinctive vision.

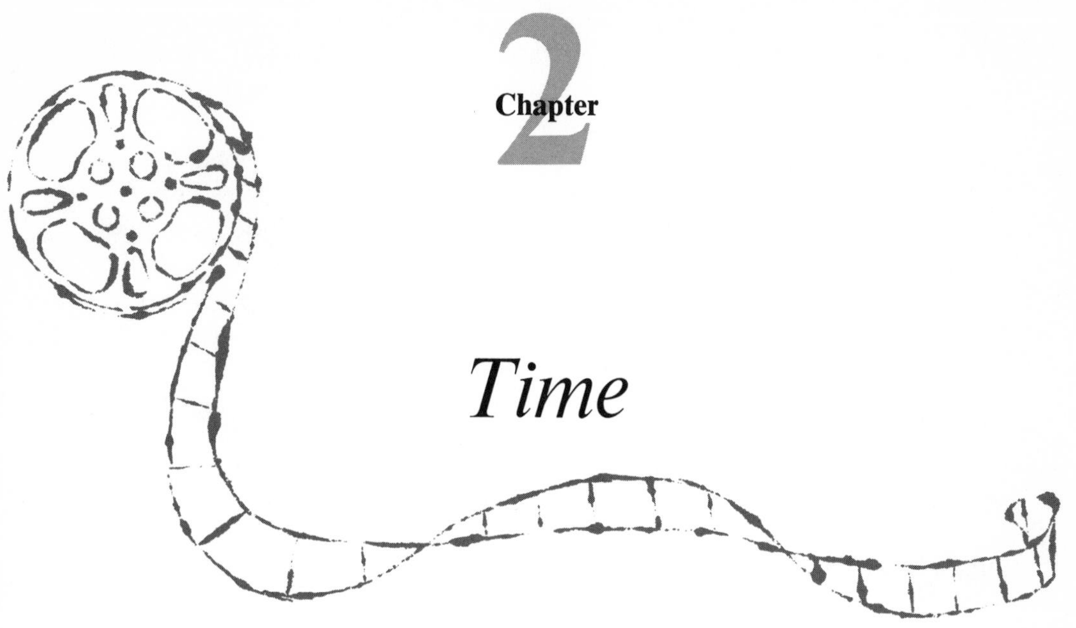

Chapter 2

Time

Thus far we have talked about space in films as though it was an entity unto itself. We have seen how the film-maker must continually reshape the physical world in which he works by creating and developing the visual relationships which are necessary to his story. But in film, as in life, action occurs simultaneously in time as well as in space. Both are inherent properties of motion pictures and both must be continually worked by each film-maker to develop the dramatic, emotive, and rhythmic structure of his film. An understanding of the unique fusion of these two dimensions is crucial to the understanding of both the craft of film-making and the nature of motion pictures as an art.

In our everyday lives the passing of time is too consistent with our world, too homogeneous for us to notice it under most circumstances. Yet time in our lives is as pervasive as the spaces which make such a constant claim on our attention. We confront those spaces directly. But our senses are too imperfect to perceive the steady flow of time; so, in countless practical ways, we shape our sense of time to the dimensions of the spaces we inhabit. For instance, when we are forced to rely upon it, we have a highly developed sense of the time it takes to cross the spaces which are familiar to us—the rooms in which we live, the distances we travel to

work, to shop, to keep regular appointments. Time, in fact, has become more convenient than space as a standard through which we finally conceptualize most distances. "It takes an hour by turnpike" is the usual, workable expression of a distance that might be fifty miles.

While we use time to measure distance, we also, quite literally, use distance to measure time. The primary way we have to objectify time is to translate it into movement across space. Although we think of the hands of a clock as somehow moving through time, it is their shifting positions in space which enable us to deal coherently with the passage of time. This interchangeable use of time and space merely reflects our everyday experience. In our lives time and space have a fixed relationship and we are intuitively able to calculate one from the other. For instance, if we speeded up a clock we could express what happens as a change of either time or space. The hands cover more space in a given time, or they take less time to cover a given space. Time is inextricably tied to space, and we can easily and interchangeably say that the hands go farther or that they go faster.

Filmic Time

This interchangeability works quite nicely for us in a world of clocks, but once we enter the world of motion pictures there is no longer an absolutely fixed relationship between space and time. Spaces are no longer continuous. Objects are isolated and severed from their location in reality. The regular ticking of a clock is

Courtesy: JANUS FILMS, INC.

replaced by the irregularly rhythmic flow of sound and picture. We are faced with nothing more concrete than a rectangular, two-dimensional screen and a sound track; and our means for relating time and space have been preempted by the filmmaker and placed totally under his control. Like the mainspring coiled within a clock deprived of hands, motion pictures unreel their images with an internal logic that can unfold an infinite variety of temporal worlds.

We can understand more easily what happens to time in films just by looking at how some films are put together. The simplest, most straightforward use of time we could find is this Volkswagen commercial. It is a complete film, lasting sixty seconds, made without interrupting the continuous run of the camera with a cut.

The action appears on the screen in exactly the same manner and same time as it would have appeared to someone watching in real life. There is only one

vantage point and our view of the action is not altered by moving the camera from this one position to any other. But, even if the camera had moved, either to follow the action or to get closer to it, this camera movement itself would have done no violence to the logical and necessary connection between space and time. We know that it takes a certain amount of time to get from one place to another, and we would have seen on the screen the space the camera traveled to reach each new view of the action. This is no more than an actual observer would have experienced in real life.

But it is extremely rare for a whole film, or even a scene within a film to exist in this kind of real time. Motion pictures are normally constructed by joining into a continuous roll pieces of film shot at different times and from different camera positions. As we saw in the first chapter, this process of intercutting film shot from a variety of perspectives reorganizes the space in which the action takes place. But such alterations of space become a reorganization of time as well. Only within the individual pieces do we encounter time in the same way as in real life. Once these

pieces are cemented together, time is freed of its conventional connections with space.

We can see an example of this in its most subtle and yet most common form in a simple dialogue sequence. This sequence from Jean Renoir's *Rules of the Game*

Courtesy: JANUS FILMS, I

is a typically filmic way of handling a conversation between two people. We chose this particular sequence because the action clearly stands out against its neutral background, because there are a large variety of camera positions, and because Renoir (wearing the hat) is a delight to look at.

The scene is three minutes of talk. If we just listened to the conversation with our eyes closed, it would exist in real time. But, as we have seen, motion pictures are essentially spatial and what we hear is irrevocably woven into what we see. And what we see are camera jumps through space. From the opening long shot and through the succession of close-ups, two-shots, reverse angles, and medium shots, we have been swept into a series of instantaneous jumps through space.

These jumps, however, are also movements through time—the time needed to get to each new position from which the action is seen. Since the camera is our eyes, each jump through space has moved us into a new position without regard for the actual time it would have taken us to get there in real life. But because we don't know how much space was eliminated, we have no way of judging how much time is also missing. All we have to gauge time is the smooth flow of the dialogue, the regular pace of the action, and cuts made almost invisible by their occurrence at natural breaks in the rhythms of the dialogue and the action. Since the action has been made seamless, time seems continuous. As a result, these instantaneous movements through space definitely and yet imperceptibly alter our sense of how time fits together.

The Significance of Cutting

In practical film-making terms the intercutting of a variety of camera angles allows a director to present a series of different visual perspectives without lengthening the scene to accommodate all of them. If this scene had been played without a cut so that both the camera movement and the conversation had occurred in real time, the length of time for the camera to move from the long shot to the close shot and then circle the characters to get reverse angles and reaction shots would have been interminable. Yet, even though the sequence has changed the flow of time by using cuts instead of camera movements, the audience is not consciously aware—and not meant to be aware—of how time has been altered.

In fact, time has been altered drastically. For once we have accepted the logic of these jumps through space, we can accept easily and without question a conversation that has been edited much more radically. In *A Thousand Clowns,* as just one example from many, there is a scene that shows a talk between an uncle and nephew that lasts three or four minutes. It is a complete, short conversation; but each time there is a cut, the scene shifts to an entirely different location. In the course of those few minutes the characters are seen talking in areas of New York that are miles apart.

We can even accept the cutting in Alain Resnais's *Je T'Aime, Je T'Aime.* Each individual shot in the main portion of the film takes place at a totally different time in the hero's life than the shots before and after it. The hero has been trapped in an experimental time machine and each cut propels him to a different moment in his past. Only within the length of each shot is time meant to be continuous. Every cut dramatizes the torturous mechanism in which he is enmeshed. His life has been broken into painfully discrete units and is revealed solely in those fragments of continuous space which reflect real time. When that space is broken by a cut, the hero finds himself pitched into a new location that can be anywhere along the length of his past.

The significance then of any cut is that, as long as that cut is unquestioned, spaces are no longer bound by their relationship to one another in time. Once the relationship of objects in space, and therefore in time, is no longer fixed, we are deprived of our usual associations between time and space. Each cut in a film instantly moves us through space to a new perspective that could be located anywhere and so could have been reached at any time. Because space is no longer continuous, time has become indeterminate. This indeterminacy is the key to time in the cinema because even the most "realistic" presentation of reality transforms that reality into

something new—a world that has little connection with the one we experience in our everyday lives. Time has been liberated from the weight of our normal assumptions, and it is finally capable of being perceived rhythmically and expressively, both adding to and even creating the drama in the scene before us.

The Conventions of Cutting

This extraordinary response to cutting is essentially conditioned. We have simply become accustomed to piecing together film shot from different camera positions. For those who have grown up with television, this conditioning started almost from birth. And even before television, the habit of regular movie-going gradually created the conditioning necessary for the acceptance of such an illogical technique as cutting.

For all their smoothly crafted flow of action, films force us to see quite differently than we normally see. The world on film is still essentially discontinuous. For example, in life if we focus in on a detail of a scene in front of us, the rest of the scene cannot change without at least our peripheral awareness of the fact. In films we can return from a view of the detail only to find that the action has been advanced by moving us to a new location. But we accept this change because we have been educated to accept the fact that films are constantly eliminating intervals and contracting time. This is a standard film convention.

Similarly, we never see a conversation in real life as it is presented us in shots 3 and 4 of Renoir's *Rules of the Game,* first from one side and then instantly from the other. But films do this all the time, and we have learned to interpret these abrupt changes as merely the equivalent of our constantly shifting attention in real life. But in life, when we momentarily look from one part of a scene to another, we are only shifting our vision, not the location from which we view the action. In film, however, each instantaneous change offers us not only another view of the action, but an entirely new viewpoint from which to observe that action. Yet we do not see the cut as a change in location, only as a slight change of emphasis. This too is part of the same convention.

Films have been with us so long that we forget that audiences didn't always accept cutting as natural. To find an audience unaccustomed to modern film techniques, we have to step outside our own culture. In his book *Film World,* Ivor Montagu mentions just such an audience in China. The Chinese know how to make quite sophisticated film, but in the films made for provincial audiences the action is still played out much as it would appear on a stage, with a minimum of cutting. "The man who enters the room will open the door, come through the doorway, cross the length of the room—and we will watch him till he reaches the other side." The cutting is purposely kept to a minimum because, "when you are making films for a public of 650 millions of whom only some 50 millions have ever seen films before, you are right to assume that the conventions now second nature to those who have acquired them will in others require a modicum of getting used to."

This problem is not limited to the uninitiated. Even within our own film-going generation audiences still have had to be educated to accept new techniques. Jean-Luc Godard's *Breathless* assaulted and dismayed audiences with its destruction of the conventional film unities of time and space when the film was released in 1959. But looking at the film after a generation of film-makers have seized its techniques, the radical cutting in *Breathless* now looks entirely logical and almost seamless.

Up until this time the convention which film-makers had developed into a nearly immutable law was that no matter how much time was contracted within a scene, the action must always preserve the illusion of occurring in that unbroken flow we call real time. Just as the Chinese provincial audiences demanded that once the actor entered a room he had to be seen crossing its entire length, so Western audiences demanded that the actor must at least seem to cross the room. In this convention a cut from one camera angle to another is permissible only if the illusion of continuous time is preserved. As long as the space in which the action occurs doesn't look illogically discontinuous, time appears continuous. The most heavily used device to accomplish this has been the reaction shot. An action begins, we cut away from that action to see the reaction it has produced, and then, when we return to the action, it has been advanced to a new location without calling attention to the time that has been eliminated.

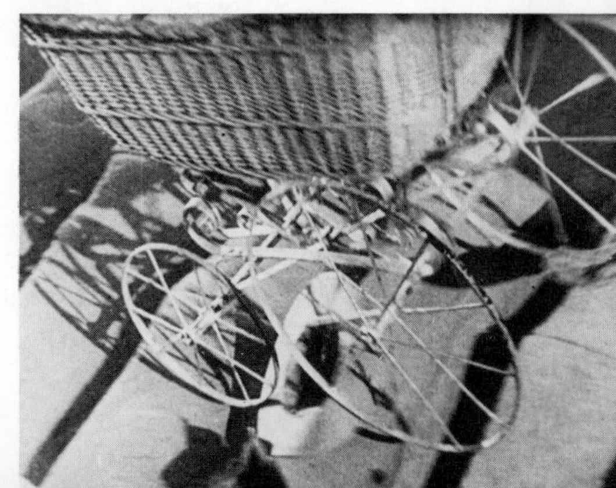

Look at the way this works in Jerzy Skolimowski's *Le Départ*. In this scene we see the young hero at a car show blowing up a paper bag and playfully bursting it behind a girl. We then cut away from the young man to see his girl friend's reaction. When we return to the young man, he is in a new location madly bursting paper bags. If the reaction shot had been eliminated, it would have been uncomfortably obvious that time had been unnaturally altered. The young man would have jumped instantly from one location to another. But since we cannot tell how far the young man had to travel from the first shot to the last, and we do not have a firm sense of exactly how long the girl's reaction took, we simply accept the fact that the time of the reaction was sufficiently long to cover his progress across the showroom floor.

The Contracted Present

It was this tradition which Godard challenged. Not only did he eliminate the conventional bridging shot, he eliminated everything that he felt inessential to the fast, random pace of his hero's life. In *Breathless* time is so contracted that even pieces of the same action are made visibly discontinuous. Individual actions are fragmented into discrete segments so that we might see the beginning of an action followed immediately by the beginning of another, followed by the middle of a third and the end of a fourth. These frames from *Breathless* show how this expressive condensation works.

The scene opens with a long shot of a car pulling up in front of Notre Dame. Cut to a close shot of the exterior of the car revealing Belmondo inside. Thus far we are still safely within the conventional ways we have been taught that films

bridge time. If the next shot had been a medium-to-long shot with the car in the foreground, he could have walked off into an entirely different part of Paris and this abridgment of the action would have passed unnoticed. But instead we cut from the view of Belmondo driving in the car to one of him suddenly installed inside a phone booth. From there we leap to a view of him walking down a street and immediately after to a view of him talking with the concierge of a small hotel. Then, without preliminaries, we see Belmondo inside the hotel keeping a careful eye on the concierge on the street. When he sees that the coast is clear, he reaches into the key box to steal a room key. But the second his hand is on the key, we are upstairs in the hotel room with Belmondo, who has just finished washing.

In this sequence time is not only contracted, it is distilled. All we see are those fragments of action absolutely necessary to advance the story line. Belmondo needs to see his girl friend and broods about it in the car. He calls her to find if she is in her room. She's not, but he must get to her; and, since he is wanted by the police, he can't wait for her in a public place. He quickly makes his way down the street, is seen by the concierge as he enters the hotel and makes some fast talk with him. He then immediately goes to the key rack, grabs the key while the concierge is still outside and goes to his girl friend's room, where he makes himself comfortable while he waits for her. Godard has shown us exactly what we need to know and no more. Although we seem to have leaped illogically from one place to the next, Godard has simply pushed the conventional logic of film condensation to an even more logical extreme.

But Godard has done more than just this. He has also welded time into an expressive force capable of summarizing the very nature of his hero's existence. These restless, nervous shifts in time strip each of Belmondo's actions to its essentials and so give every action a feeling of urgency and importance. Every moment is

severed from its comfortable place in the relentless flow of time. Since each moment is isolated from the next, his actions develop as a series of surprises. We literally see Belmondo as living from moment to moment, as free and rootless in time as he is in life.

Since its initial, doubtful reception, *Breathless* has been canonized for the relevance of its aesthetic and philosophic point of view. And jump cuts have since become as fashionable as the seamless transitions of earlier decades. Godard has created new temporal conventions which not only have been seized by other adventurous film-makers but have rapidly been incorporated in large numbers of conventionally popular films. The technique of joining together shots without regard to the unity of time and space between them is now, in itself, merely an acceptable device for advancing the action or increasing the tempo of a film. But it is only when style effectively distills its subject by creating incisive relationships with evocative rhythms that technique becomes art rather than embellishment.

The Expanded Present

We can see this in *Potemkin,* an even more radical film for its time, which exerted an enormous influence on the structure of succeeding motion pictures. For early film-makers the relentless unreeling of the action from beginning to end imposed an immutable chronology upon the events that were portrayed in a film. In *Potemkin* Eisenstein developed the idea that, even within that seemingly rigid structure, action could follow action, not necessarily in the order in which it had taken place, but rather in a series of dramatic revelations that would create a new temporal structure for the unfolding events in a film. As time could be artificially contracted, so it could be artificially expanded—stretched to include a profusion of images that are meant to be accepted as existing simultaneously in time rather than consecutively. In the execution scene in *Potemkin* Eisenstein demonstrated that, even in the fraction of a second between the start and the finish of a brief action, the action could be stopped and additional images inserted. These images would then change both the meaning of the action as well as its impact without doing violence to the audience's conception of the logical, progressive nature of the time in which the action occurred.

In this sequence Eisenstein takes the highly charged drama of sailors an

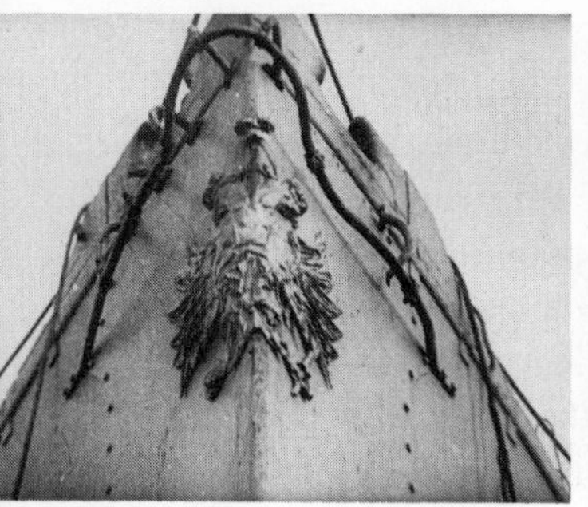

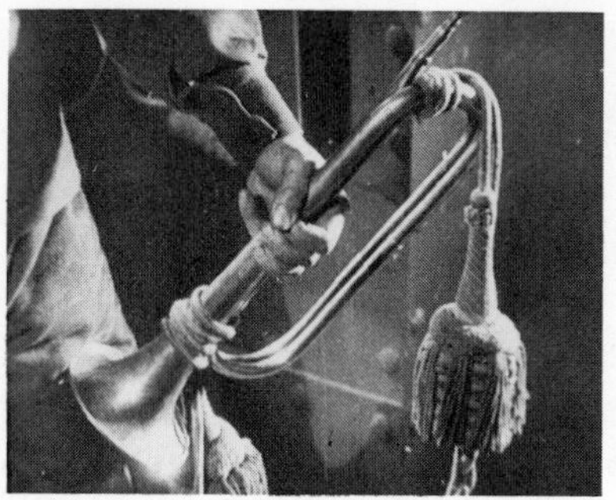

instant away from executing their mutinous comrades and brings the action to an abrupt halt by inserting shots of symbols between the shot of the firing squad and the shot of the victims huddled beneath a canvas waiting for their death. The continuous unfolding of time is stopped from the moment we last see the sailors to the moment we see the victims. Yet the scene drives forward as the symbols are revealed, sweeping each image into our developing conception of the moment.

Here the full meaning of the action depends upon the director's shrewd use of the indeterminate nature of the relationship in time between each shot. Just as the reaction shot in *Le Départ* was inserted to allow the film-maker to cut away from his hero and so condense the time until we next saw him, here the shots cut away from the action and so protract it in time. In both cases the shots sever the space in which the main action occurs. By introducing a new location that exists in its own realm of time, the film-maker allows his audience to lose track of the exact time in which the main action takes place. In *Potemkin* when we return to the action and it has not been advanced, then time has been imperceptibly expanded. Both the action and the symbols have been developed in an elastic present far more flexible than the continuous unrolling of the film would seem to permit.

This technique expands the moment into a realm of time that is purely expressive. Eisenstein has filled the screen with emotionally charged symbols suspended in time and then tied them into the unfolding action with the rhythm of his cutting. As a result the dramatic tension of the main action is stretched to the breaking point as the steady beat of these symbols keeps us from seeing the dramatic fulfillment of the scene. Thematically, the insertion of the symbols also serves to dehumanize the firing squad—to show the executioners as just another mute prop of the timeless tsarist autocracy. Eisenstein is telling his audience that, as feeling men, the sailors could not readily shoot their comrades. And so, when we

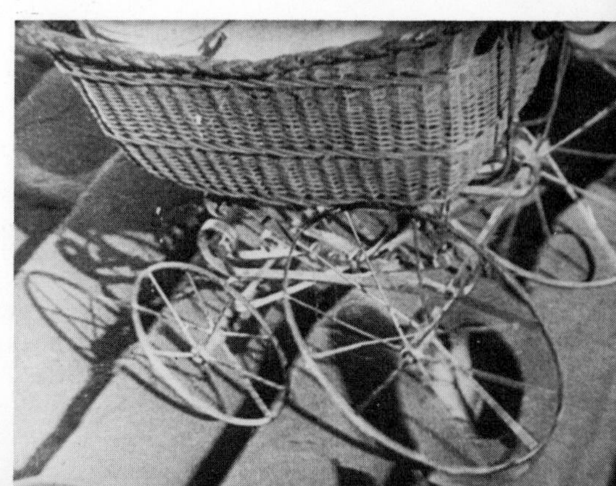

finally see the huddled victims, we no longer feel that it is men who are about to kill them. It is the State.

The insertion of the symbols thus offers a new perspective on the resolution of the scene because the time in which the action takes place is expanded to include them. By doing this Eisenstein accomplished something quite remarkable. With absolute economy he was able to extract from the action the last measure of suspense and tension while simultaneously drawing his audience *away* from their close involvement with that action so that they could view the scene with sufficient detachment to understand his polemic argument. This is no mean achievement.

The quintessential sequence that illustrates the expressive use of the expanded moment occurs during the closing portion of the "Odessa Steps" sequence, which comes a little further on in *Potemkin* and which we have reproduced as a flip sequence. Again go through the scene to get a feeling for the flow of action. The sequence was shot at sixteen frames a second and we have reproduced every other frame so that we could include as much as possible without doing too much violence to Eisenstein's use of time. If you flip through it at eight frames a second, it should take twenty-five seconds to complete the sequence—the same as Eisenstein intended.

Time here is an explosion of dramatic crises hurtling the audience from one part of the steps to another until the mind is saturated with images and the present is finally understood. Only the baby carriage inexorably descending the steps gives the scene a feeling of the literal passage of time. But, since the carriage is isolated in close shots, we have no way of knowing how far down the steps it has traveled each time we see it, and so we have no way of knowing exactly how much time has passed during the intervals between the shots. By building the rest of the action around the indeterminate descent of the carriage, Eisenstein is free to include as much action as he wants and still sustain the illusion that only a short period of time has passed. In the earlier part of the sequence he did much the same thing by keying the action to the descent of the Cossacks down the steps. By fixing on objects that have been severed from a specific location, he has been able to create an unfolding sequence of shots that expand the present. That present has been made to conform totally to the dramatic necessities of the scene. It envelops the fragmented action on the screen and welds it into a unified moment.

The Expressive Uses of Time

This use of time was a discovery, the culmination of Eisenstein's realization that films not only can but *must* alter real time to achieve clarity, insight, and emotional impact upon a screen. Eisenstein and the young Soviet directors of the 1920's had learned from the practical brilliance of D. W. Griffith that the narrative could be effectively manipulated by such time-loosening devices as flashbacks, crosscutting, close-ups, and dissolves. But Eisenstein saw even these innovations as no more than filmic equivalents of traditional literary conventions, and he and his revolutionary colleagues were determined to take the film-makers' control over their material even further.

The Soviet director and theorist—and Eisenstein's contemporary—Pudovkin argued, for example, that Griffith merely inserted close-ups to heighten long sequences essentially staged and shot from the theatrical medium distance that had been standardized by the first film directors. Pudovkin asserted that entire sequences could be built instead just from the accumulation of purely significant details. In his seminal work, *Film Technique,* he argued powerfully for film-makers to seize full control of their new medium and bend space and time freely to the forms of their emerging visions:

> The material of the film director consists not of real processes happening in real space and real time, but of those pieces of celluloid on which these processes have been recorded. This celluloid is entirely subject to the will of the director who edits it. He can, in the composition of the filmic form of any given appearance, eliminate all points of interval, and thus concentrate the action in time to the highest degree he may require.

Yet thirty years after these words were published, Jean-Luc Godard, cresting the New Wave from France, managed to startle and enrage film audiences by eliminating so many intervals in the action of *Breathless* that the picture looked to most film-goers as though it had been flung upon the screen with arrogant disregard for film conventions.

This battle with tradition for the expression of new realities has been fought by every generation of film-makers. Within the narrative form, the most disconcerting innovations have come from those film-makers who have seized upon the temporal and spatial discontinuities inherent in the structure of motion pictures and turned them into insights into both the nature of man and the nature of film itself.

A striking example of this is René Clair's brilliant, inventive silent comedy, *An Italian Straw Hat.* Clair emerged from that cluster of militantly idiosyncratic French avant-garde film-makers that invigorated motion pictures in the 1920's. Clair had learned early in his career that as time can be expanded and contracted in films, so it could be just as easily reversed, speeded up, slowed down, drawn into the future, or pushed into the past with no more effort than the sealing of a splice with cement. In *An Italian Straw Hat* he attacked both the conventional structure of motion pictures and the conventional pettiness and avariciousness inherent in the structure of the French middle classes with equal vigor. The scene we have chosen well illustrates the streams of temporal rhythms that can flow through a sequence to enrich it with the telling variety of relationships they create.

The film deals with a man who, on his wedding day, is threatened with having his house destroyed unless he replaces a damaged straw hat for a woman and her demonic lover. From this insane notion all the action in the film develops. In this

scene, the bridegroom is trapped at his own wedding celebration, caught between his obligation to remain, his need to end his troubles by finding another straw hat, and his uncontrollable fantasy about the destruction of all he owns.

The hero, whose anguish has been growing in direct proportion to the merriment surrounding him, senses disaster when his servant arrives and frowns, signaling his apprehension for the safety of his master's house. This does it. His anxiety for his vulnerable property is all he finally can focus on. His imagination and the screen are suddenly filled with images of the shutters of his windows being thrown open by the mad lover in the first step of an increasing and inevitable holocaust.

Momentarily he is spun away from his vision as he is ensnared into a dance. But as he moves faster and faster to the beat of the dance music (and his motion on

the screen is accelerated by a slightly undercranked camera), his mind dwells upon his house, where his precious chairs are floating, in painful slow motion, to graceful destruction—one after another.

Now he is almost completely isolated from the party by his nightmarish thoughts. He has a recurrent vision of his property being smashed by unseen forces, and when that ceases to be sufficiently horrible to him, he envisions his luxurious bed ambling from his house of its own malevolent accord.

His present is now so woven with his fantasy that each gesture and movement he makes is totally shaped by the carnage in his mind. Rapidly accelerated men flash to his doorway like animals of prey, quickly seizing everything they can find. And, as soon as they have stripped the street of his furniture, more chairs and tables race through his doorway to be grabbed. Even when his father-in-law takes him by the shoulder and tries to make him respond, his mind snaps away to the predatory men spiriting away their latest haul. He is caught in the agony of a moment of time distended to the limits of his destructive imagination.

The nightmare progresses. Once the vulturous men have grabbed everything in sight, the mad lover begins breaking off the windows themselves to appease his voracious appetite for revenge. Now even the very building in which the hero lives is in jeopardy.

The apocalypse is at hand. The mad lover races from the house and invites the scavengers in. Our hero, increasingly less able to focus upon anything but the climax of his fantasy, finally sees the walls of his building crumble and then collapse in a thick cloud of smoke. The fantasy is now so real to him that the dust not only covers the remains of his house but spreads out to the party and finally enshrouds him.

The present in this sequence has been expanded to include both an objective view of the hero and a subjective view of his fantasy. The orderly, sequential flow of events has been blurred in the undulation between these two perspectives. We have no way of knowing how much time has passed from vision to vision. In addition, since both the hero's life at the party and his imaginary life are fragments of two related but separate worlds, our feeling for the passage of time is structured differently in each. For example, at the beginning of the sequence his motions have been accelerated, giving us the impression that time is moving at a frantic pace. But his vision of the chairs falling from the window is presented in slow motion, protracting the moment in time. From shot to shot time has been speeded up and slowed down, placing us just a moment apart from two alien temporal worlds.

The effect of all of this is to dislocate us in time. As we shift from an objective to a subjective view of the action, from an accelerated to a protracted moment in time, we have lost all our normal ways of judging the passage of time and we are placed entirely in the hands of the film-maker. He now has complete control over our sense of time, and he can manipulate it with devastating effect. Clair has ensnared us in the very rhythms of his hero's life while masterfully controlling the way we respond to those rhythms. Through this use of time we are made to share the hero's growing anxiety while being jarred by the temporal discontinuity into sufficient distance so we can still laugh at this anxiety.

The Filmic Present

When worked in this way, time, like space, has been used to accumulate special meanings. As Clair's sequence progresses, thought has become as real as action not only because both are equally concrete upon the screen but because we perceive them with equal immediacy. The reason for this, as George Bluestone has pointed out, is because the present is the only tense that films have. "Unfolding in a perpetual present, like visual perception itself, [motion pictures] cannot express either a past or a future."

Pictures just don't have tenses. So no matter when any shot has taken place, we see the action it contains unfold before us with the same sensory impact as if it were happening now. And because, in effect, everything in the shot is happening now, each shot can be connected to the next to form one continuously developing action—an endless series of transient shots fused together by the flow of motion from one shot to another. "The transience of the shot falls away before the sweeping permanence of its motion. Past and present seem fused." As a result, the present can become a blend of action that occurred at any moment in the characters' lives. Their past and future, like our memory and fantasy, are freed from a fixed place in chronology and can be fused into an immediate and lively aspect of the developing present.

In *An Italian Straw Hat* the visualizations of both the hero's present and his thoughts are equally substantial, equally immediate, and therefore equally real to us. In fact, both are so real that Clair can finally drench both worlds in the cataclysmic dust at the end of the sequence without doing violence to the reality of either.

As in *Breathless* the present has lost even its semblance of uninterrupted continuity. It is deliberately stylized and made discontinuous. But Clair is using time in a much more complex way. When thought and action are woven together and made dependent upon one another for their full meaning, they begin to function like memory, which constantly reinterprets the past and so perpetually shapes the present. René Clair has used this insight to turn the solid, bourgeois present into an illusion. And this is his joke. Our dislocation in time allows us to see the present as just a fragment of consciousness. It is dependent for its full meaning upon impressions of what has gone before and anticipations of what lies ahead. What we are laughing at is the perilously insubstantial quality of that present which instantly transforms a celebration into a nightmare once time has ceased to be irreversible and thought has become just as real as action. These two realms of time have naturally and inevitably merged into an enveloping present that has been enlarged to encompass the totality of his hero's experience.

The Organization of Time

While the broad latitude with which time can be handled gives the film-maker enormous flexibility, it also demands that he manipulate time with skill and precision. Time can be organized in as many ways as the imagination can roam the universe, but it will be neither coherent nor illuminating if it isn't rooted in a logic that will structure that universe and give it form. It is imperative, for example, that

the film-maker let his audience know, from scene to scene and even from shot to shot, whether the action has been advanced into a new present or through flash-backs into the past and flash-aheads into anticipations of the future. But it is also imperative that each movement through time reveal the design of the film-maker, enlarging our knowledge of the characters and continually developing the film's meanings.

The Past as Memory

In *Wild Strawberries* Ingmar Bergman is meticulous in the way he leads his audience from the present into his hero's memory of the past. The story is about a seventy-six-year-old doctor, Isak Borg, who spends a day driving from Stockholm to a university town to receive an honorary degree. The day's ride becomes transformed into his life's journey through a series of confrontations with both the people who share his present and his memory of those who have shared his past. In this scene he visits the country house of his youth. Almost imperceptibly he slips into memories of the happy summers of his youth—of the girl with whom he once picked wild strawberries and whom he loved and lost.

Courtesy: JANUS FILMS,

We see Dr. Borg as an old man looking toward the empty, gray, boarded-up summer house. Then as he looks at us directly, his thoughts reach out to us and we hear his voice saying: "How it happened, I don't know, but the clear reality of day . . ." We hear the far-off playing of a piano and see the house again. This time it is open, clean and white in the sun, and surrounded by trees and plants in full bloom. Over this picture he continues: ". . . gave way to the still clearer images of my memory." In the background the piano blends with happy voices drifting through the open windows, laughter, footsteps, the cries of children, the squeaking of a pump, and finally a strong tenor voice singing. In spite of these sounds of activity, all we see is the house alone with not a human being in sight. Then we see Dr. Borg again, still facing us; and, as the camera slowly moves in on him, we hear him thinking: "I don't even know if it was a dream or memories which arose before my eyes with all the force of reality." Then three shots of objects as transient as they seem immemorial—a clump of young trees, clouds, and a patch of wild strawberries. Finally we see the girl he once loved kneeling among the strawberries—and we have been fully drawn into his memory of the past. When we next

see Dr. Borg, we are looking down upon him as a pathetic old man surrounded by the painfully fresh bloom of a world where he can only be an unwanted stranger.

Bergman takes us into the past with the caution and care of a man entering chilled waters. Each step of the way is delineated and tested before the next is taken. Using narration, sound effects, and picture in a meticulous blend, Bergman has not only taken us into the past without confusion but he has also dramatized the painfully cautious workings of a fearful memory in the process. His care as a craftsman is here used to make his point as an artist. The discreet, almost timorous,

way that Dr. Borg retreats into his past is captured by the obvious care with which Bergman has taken us there.

Courtesy: JANUS FILMS, INC.

Memory in this sequence becomes a confrontation rather than an immersion in the past. Dr. Borg never loses his identity as an old man, and he is never allowed to become totally involved with his memories. In most of the shots he is isolated or kept at a distance from the scenes that he remembers. But even when he is not in the picture and his past totally fills the screen, we do not feel we have been plunged back in time. The immediacy of the images that purely represent Dr. Borg's memory of his youth are constantly blended with our objective view of him as an old man. As a result, the present has become a hybrid, with the past and the present separately delineated in the same sequence of shots by lighting, makeup, and costume. Dr. Borg's world has become the visual embodiment of his lifetime of expectations and frustration. When he is set against his light-struck impressions of the past, like gnarled driftwood washed up on an untouched beach, he seems starkly old and pathetic. His cherished youthful aspirations have clung remorselessly to his life, and it is not his past, but his present, from which he is finally isolated. In the end it is the shadowy, transient, insubstantial nature of that present which is dramatized by his confrontation with the painfully solid images from his unremitting past. Finally that past has become a mirror held up to him with derision, locating him not in time so much as in time wasted, in moments discarded and unfulfilled.

Bergman has exploited the possibilities inherent in film's malleable present to engage the past, drawing from it only those elements crucial to Dr. Borg's life, and finally insinuating those elements into the structure of the doctor's consuming search for his identity. The past is made an inseparable aspect of the present, taking shape before our eyes with the freshness and uncertainty of a new and unexpected event. Not only do we feel that it is happening now—so does Dr. Borg.

Yet this illumination of the present through an evocation of the past need not be as elaborately structured as the scene in *Wild Strawberries* to be effective. Just a few seconds of film time can be used to call up the crucial past and so alter the nature of the present. In Alain Resnais's *Hiroshima Mon Amour,* the past is so close to the surface of the film's present that it can well up from the depths of the heroine's life, splash across the screen, and submerge again, altering the present by deepening our awareness of the unexpected elements that it contains.

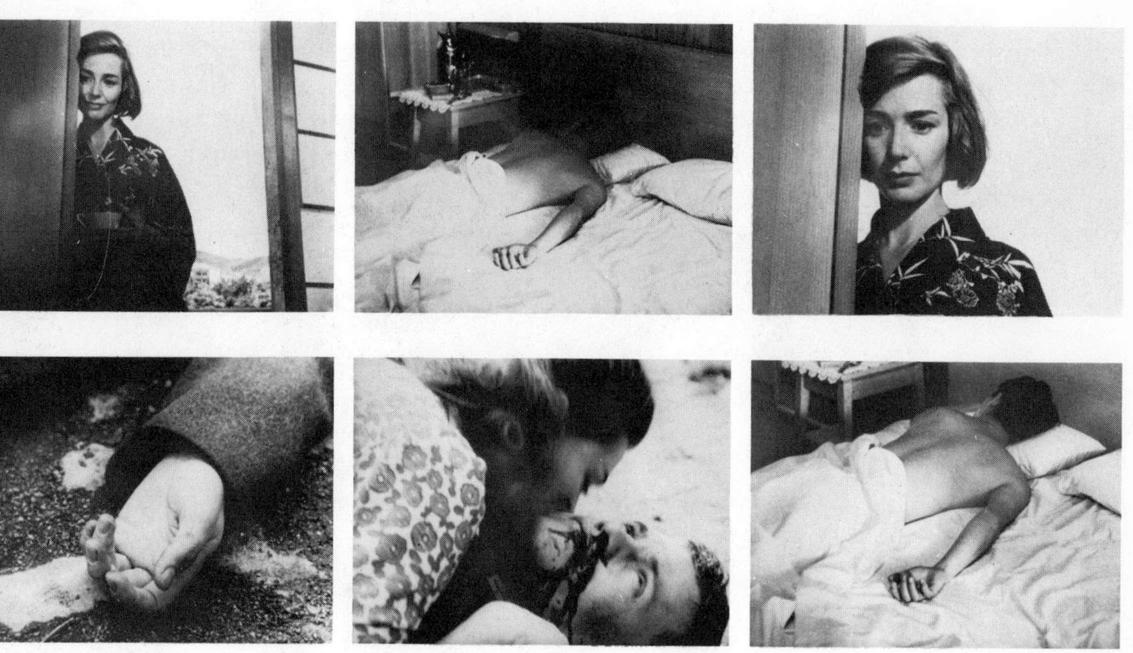

The heroine has come to Hiroshima to act in a peace film. She is not given a name since her identity is ultimately the sum of private memories dredged from the rubble of those public events that comprise mankind's knowledge of World War II. She meets and falls in love with a Japanese architect (also nameless) who served in the Japanese army during the war. Through their relationship she comes to terms with her youthful, tragic, wartime affair with a German soldier in her

occupied hometown of Nevers. This scene, early in the film, is the first of her excursions into her suppressed past. The position of her lover's hand—carefully lit so that our attention, like hers, is immediately drawn to it—evokes the memory of the dead German soldier. The flashback is sudden and unexpected—an involuntary nervous contraction triggered by the sight of the hand. The brutal images last a few seconds, but in those seconds her life has been opened. The past is palpable and raw. It has again become suffering flesh, and she must see each wound and bind it before she can recover her present.

Unlike in *Wild Strawberries,* we are thrown completely back into the past without an intermediary from the present to guide us. Yet we are not dislocated in time. The flashback works clearly, not only because it cuts from detail to analogous detail, but because the cutting rhythm of the scene encompasses the flashback in its structure. As the scene unfolds, it is absorbed in the beat of the cuts from her to her lover as she watches him asleep on their bed. Resnais also prepares us for this moment through his striking opening to the film: filling the screen with the

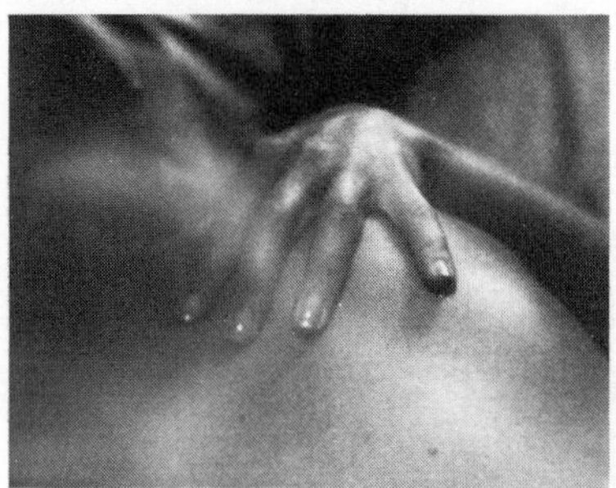

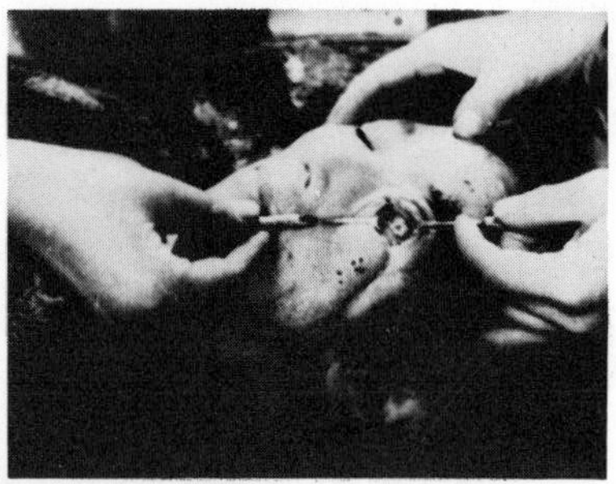

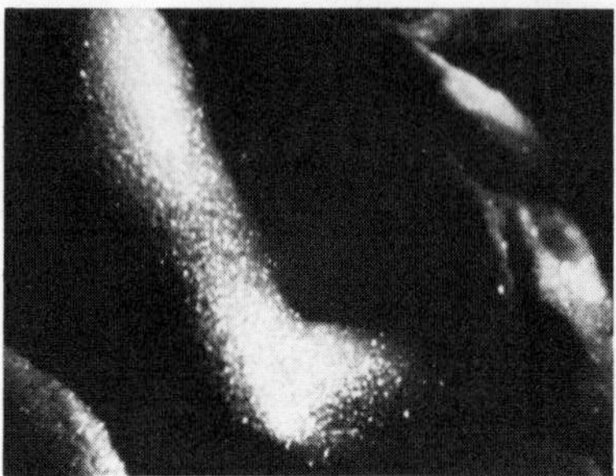

smooth naked flesh of the lovers, intercutting that flesh with documentary film of the actual torn, broken bodies of the people of Hiroshima after the atomic explosion, and finally dissolving and abstracting the flesh of the lovers under a fall of iridescent dust that violates and caresses them. And over these images the Japanese lover repeats: "You saw nothing in Hiroshima. Nothing." And each time she completes the litany, "I saw everything. Everything." The opening is monumental, sculptured, and timeless. The characters are fused together by memories that at the same time separate them. We begin to feel their identity exists in the fragments of their past. When we finally see that past emerge, we are not surprised. It arises organically out of the structure of the film.

The Objective Past

The past, of course, need not be memory in films. Countless films have used flashbacks as a simple narrative device to tell a story. But once the flashback is shown from an objective point of view, omnisciently advancing the story line, we tend to see the action in it as happening "now." After just a few moments, the past becomes the present, and we are usually jolted when the flashback ends and we find ourselves back in the future with a new present to deal with. For this reason the past as memory and the future as anticipation can be much more easily fused into the rhythm of a film. Both these subjective views are aspects of the immediate present and both enlarge our knowledge without severing us from the momentum of the characters' lives.

In the hands of a skilled film-maker, however, even an objective flashback can be organically joined to the progress of his characters' lives. During the superbly crafted opening to *The Fiancés,* Ermanno Olmi is able to call up the hero's past in an instant, present it with corrosive objectivity, and then continue the story without interrupting either the mood or the rhythm of the main action. This interruption is no different from the standard use of a flashback that enlarges our knowledge of the characters' lives without advancing the action in time. But, remarkably, Olmi has been able to fuse this information with the sense of loss and entrapment his hero feels at the moment we are thrown into his past. Instead of being severed from that moment in the present when we leave the character to join his past, the past has been made to objectify the powerful but mute impulses that are driving him on. The immediacy of both the present and the past on the screen is here being used to entwine two separate but related moments in the hero's life.

The film is about a betrothed couple who are too poor to marry. The man has accepted a construction job in the nether reaches of Sicily in order to earn the money they need. The couple must be separated for a couple of years and the girl is desolate because she fears that it will eventually mean the end of their relationship. The man knows that there is no other choice and that he must endure the loneliness of the separation. The film opens with the couple in a drab dance hall. As they talk and finally dance, they both reflect the strain of their impending separation.

Because he is leaving, the man has had to place his aged father in a home. The sequence recalls his conversation with an official of the home. Although the scene is triggered by the man's thoughts about his father, the flashback is handled objectively, in a semidocumentary style of film-making. We hear the official's first

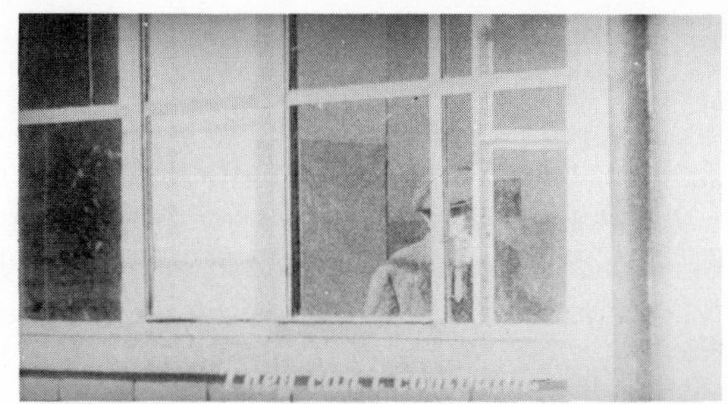

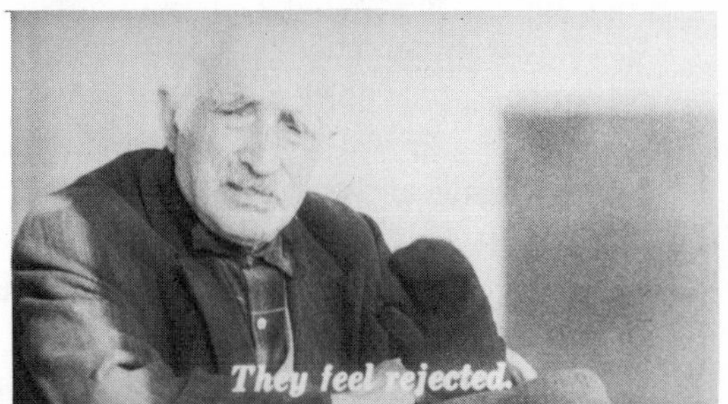

Courtesy: JANUS FILMS, INC.

soothing words to the man, but we see a series of contrapuntal images pointing up the hollowness of those words. These images do not correspond to what the man has seen. Rather they evoke his apprehensions and the guilt he feels in placing his father in the institution. The pictures of the inmates form a cool, distant, astonishingly elliptical study of the home's erosive atmosphere. The official's bland tone describing the final degradation and destruction of his charges lances the quiet images of the lonely old men and draws out the pain that the man must feel. Then suddenly we are back in the present for an instant as the girl asks, "What's next?" And just as abruptly we are hurtled into a new present as we see the man's plane taking off for Sicily. The rest of the film takes place with the man in Sicily and the girl in Milan.

The hero's past resides so close to the surface of the action, like a splinter under the skin, that it can be extracted without much preparation. The past is structured as if it were a separate world, complete unto itself, coldly analytical, more like a documentary than the embodiment of a memory. Yet the wound it leaves is organic to the story and our understanding of the characters. When we return to the present we linger for only a moment—just long enough to allow the implications of the past, the cruelty and loss that the man's abandonment will cause, to drench the moment. Then, with the impersonal whine of the jet engines, we are launched into the main body of the film.

The Historic Past

However, we not only accept footage that is *supposed* to be in the past as taking place in the present; we just as easily accept footage *actually* taken in the past in exactly the same way. The presentness of past footage is so powerful that even when we know that we are seeing objective, historical newsreel footage, we draw it into the present once it is thematically related to the life of a character in a film. In Truffaut's *Jules and Jim,* World War I newsreels were used to establish a feeling for the time in which the characters exist. The NBC documentary *Battle of the Bulge* goes even further. Its entire view of its narrator's past is confined to the impersonal documentation of newsreel footage. Yet we accept this too as a memory unfolding in the present.

Producers Frank DeFelitta and Joseph Mehan have told the story of the battle through the memory of some of its participants. Given only the faces and the voices of the combatants two decades after the event, and the objective, raw footage of the event itself, they were able to distill and dramatize a moment in

history by evoking the private experiences of the men who participated in that moment. In this sequence Lt. Robert Reppa revisited the American headquarters at Honsfeld and recalled what happened to him on the afternoon of 16 December, 1944.

CU = Close-up **MS = Medium shot** **LS = Long shot**

	PICTURE	SOUND
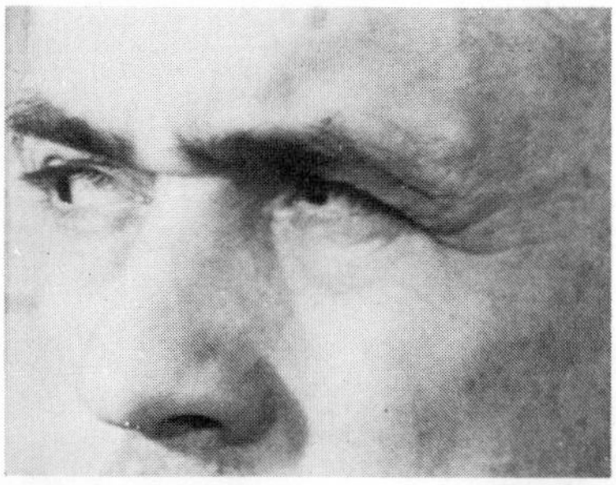	**1.** CU, Reppa's face looking toward window.	REPPA: And then out is where we heard the engi (Sound of tanks gradually creasing.)
	**2.** MS, view out of window in the present.	REPPA: First they were and then the tone chan (Sound of tanks.)
	**3.** CU, Reppa looking toward camera.	REPPA: The grating nois tank tracks. (Sound of tanks.)
	**4.** MS, camera slowly zooms in toward open window and goes out of focus.	REPPA: We looked out. could see the black ta coming to the door. (Sound of tanks increasi

	PICTURE	SOUND
	**5.** CU, window in focus through which can be seen actual film of the battle.	(Violent sounds of explosions and general sounds of tanks clawing the road and gunfire.)
	**6.** LS, general scene of troops moving during battle.	(General battle sounds.)
	**7.** MS, American soldiers being taken prisoner by Germans. Zoom in to . . .	(Sound of German saying "Raus! Raus!") REPPA: We looked around. There was no way to get out. That was the end for us.
	CU, freeze frame of American soldier taken prisoner with his hands on top of his head.	REPPA: It was prison camp.

The historical past in this sequence has been sculptured to the exact dimensions of Lt. Reppa's memory. After hearing Reppa's story, DeFelitta and Mehan designed the shooting so that the interview would end with the slow zoom toward the window's going out of focus. Then they searched through thousands of feet of actual battle footage until they found a war scene shot through a window. The result was a deft cut from the present to the past. With the steady pace of the narration and the sounds of battle bridging the transition, we slide twenty years into the past without disturbing the cadence of the scene. The footage was then excerpted and bent to the shape of Reppa's memory of the battle.

The documentary dramatizes the closeness of something as seemingly fixed as the remote past to the surface of the present in films. Even when that past is historical footage, it still can be easily subsumed by the present, offering its images to be woven into our view of the immediate consciousness of the narrator. All tenses have become totally the servant of the present, allowing the film-maker to make memory and its companion, history, elements in the film's structure without severing that structure from the force and impetus of the immediate present in which it exists for its audience.

The Simultaneity of Tenses

In effect, what we see on the screen is a compression of narrative into the tenseless impressions we usually associate with thought, memory, or dreams. No matter how literal the film's images and how simple its story, an audience is involved in a temporally impressionistic world. Images over time are disconnected from their surroundings, linger or rush by, and come to represent present, past, or future with the ease and fluidity of a random train of thought. Familiar images are abstracted in the process. They are broken into the hundreds of single shots within a film and then fused into a temporal experience that is unique for each motion picture. This is one of the enchantments of movie-going.

For example, on the surface Jean-Marie Straub and Daniele Huillet's film *Othon* is a straight, costumed rendition of Corneille's seventeenth-century verse tragedy set in ancient Rome. But it is constructed in a very special way so that the past, the present, and the future run simultaneously throughout the picture and the track, turning a slightly archaic drama into an extraordinary film experience.

In the opening shot we see two characters dressed in togas talking as they look out across a stone railing. As they talk to each other about the perils of court life in Rome following the death of Nero, the next shot reveals what they are looking at. It is a blatant high shot of automobile and truck traffic tearing through the streets of modern Rome. From this point on, Corneille's beautiful seventeenth-century Alexandrines are spoken by characters immersed in a tangle of ancient Roman politics above the familiar din of urban traffic congestion.

Three levels of time are presented simultaneously and with equal immediacy —the world of the plot, which unfolds in ancient Rome; the world of the language used to describe it, which is stylized seventeenth-century verse; and the world of the background environment, which is modern cacophonous Rome. The tense of each of these levels depends solely on how we interpret any one of them. If we are caught up in the plot, then the background noise exists in the future like an intimation of the impending brutalities and insensitivities that have marked the progress of mankind. But, if we accept the sounds of modern Rome as the present, the plot becomes the past and is ironically transformed into a prologue containing the roots of modern brutality. In fact, we constantly vacillate between both these views. We experience each moment of the drama with a temporal ambiguity that has collapsed all tenses into striking relationships and offers us a unique vantage point in time for understanding both the action and ourselves.

Present, past, and future are simultaneously fused into a single expressive moment. So entangled are these tenses with each other that, at any moment in the film, they are all perfectly interchangeable. Finally it is left to the members of the audience to work their way through the temporal worlds collapsed on the screen and individually label each on the basis of the relationships that any viewer wishes to make at any given moment. This, then, is the ultimate flexibility of how time can be used in a narrative film. In effect, the film-makers have given the audience the opportunity to create their own time schemes in order to deepen their involvement in the action.

Temporal Rhythms

Time then is not only an intrinsic element in the composition of a motion picture, it is a beautifully flexible tool which can fashion and distill a film's gross structure and major theses. But also within the large temporal currents that flow the length of a film, there is a constant wash of time, a subtle ebb and flow of time passing within each sequence and even each shot, that refines every action and gives it definition within the structure of the film.

Because a motion picture projected on a screen shows nothing but space, it is the rate of change and motion within that space that does much to give each sequence in a film its particular feeling of time's passing—its duration. This is our sense of how long it takes for events to occur regardless of their actual time on the screen. The rhythmic flow of cuts and movement within the scene control much of our sense of that duration and give each portion of a film its own interior feeling of time.

It is this aspect of film-making that comes closest to resembling the mathematical relationships and evocative rhythms throughout a musical composition. Changes in duration are the pulse of the action that result from the pace at which that action unfolds during the course of a film. Much of the cadence of a film, the

subtle variations in its melodic development, depends upon our sense of the changing rhythms which build the duration of each sequence.

There are ways of creating this sense of duration with both picture and sound, but the most basic way is visual, either by altering the space within the shot or by altering the spatial perspectives from shot to shot. We have chosen two short films which rely almost solely upon visually constructed pace to make their point in order to illustrate how pace is created.

The Canadian Film Board's documentary *Runner* builds its sensitive study of the commitment and endurance of a long-distance runner upon the variations of movement within the frame. The film begins with long, slow strokes picturing the runner as a small, lonely figure moving almost imperceptibly within a heavy, still landscape.

The enveloping monotony of his endless training and his iron discipline emerges through the opening shots and is then restated during the film's title shot. There, the track star runs toward the camera as the camera keeps pulling back, leaving the runner always the same distance away. Although he is moving at a fast pace, he does not move in relation to the camera. The only sense of motion in the shot comes from the receding planks of the boardwalk, which seem to unfold like an endless treadmill. The tension which the shot creates is built and sustained by an emerging sense of the track star's exertions set against his barely perceptible progress.

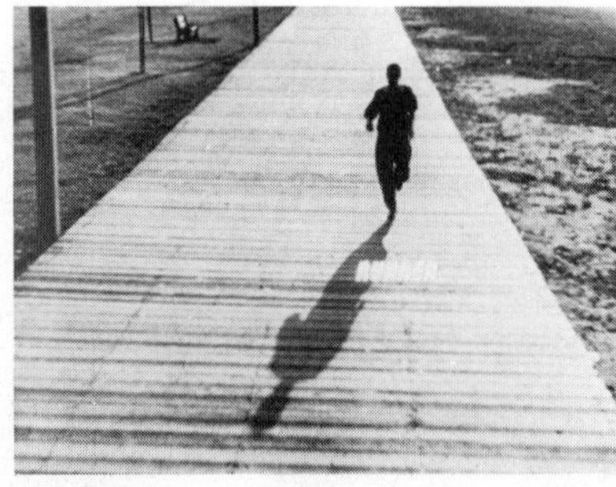

Although the film is about a swift runner, the cadence of the opening shots is slow and heavy. The shots are from a distance and the runner makes little headway across the frame. But as the film develops, the camera gets closer. Gradually we see the runner moving forward. Although the next shots run the same length as the opening shots, the pace of the film quickens with our sense of the progress being made by the runner.

Finally the camera moves in on the runner and the frame is filled with his speed. As he moves around the track, the camera must pan quickly to follow him. Even when he is moving directly toward the camera or directly away from it, the camera is so close that the frame is all motion. The speed of his churning feet and accelerating body is magnified by the quick movement of the camera attempting to keep up with him. The track seems to evaporate beneath him. Everything is in motion and the tempo of the scene is pitched to his speed.

By choosing camera angles that either intensified or diminished motion within the frame, the director of *Runner* built a medley of tempos that carried the weight of the film's theme. Our sense of the runner, his determination and his triumph, is keyed to our view of his motion. Each change in the film's pace reveals an insight into the nature of both the runner and his sport. Discipline, endurance, willpower, a sense of liberation and freedom, and finally triumph are all conveyed in the tempo of each shot. The film is almost pure rhythm structured from the movements within the frame.

These visual rhythms were also intensified by the sound track. The director used a poem by W. H. Auden, some music, and, in the closing sequence of the race, the sounds of the crowd at the track. These all contributed to the pace of the film, but the dominant rhythms were built from the meticulously constructed pictures of the runner's movements from his training to his triumph.

Roman Polanski's short film *The Lean and the Fat* also tells its story through carefully constructed rhythmic variations. Except that Polanski creates his basic rhythms with cutting. By choosing particular pieces of filmed action and then carefully joining them together in a sequence, he closely controls the dominant rhythms of his film. From the beat of these cuts emerges much of our sense of the nature of the characters, their relationship to each other, and their place in the world.

The film is about a servant (played by Mr. Polanski) and his blind, innocent devotion to an ungrateful, demanding master. For the first third of the film we are shown a catalogue of the servant's onerous duties. When the servant tries to escape, his master gives him a goat as an incentive to stay on. But the servant is soon overwhelmed by his only possession. The goat is shackled to his ankle, and this only frustrates his valiant attempts to do his duties. Up to this point the editing has been straightforward, with each action flowing quite naturally into the next. But in this final sequence, after the servant has been unshackled from the goat, Polanski wishes to capture a sense of frenzied, illogical, joyous release.

Courtesy: JANUS FILMS, INC.

He shows the servant racing through his routine activities; but unlike in the previous sequences, each new shot places the servant in a different location without regard for the appearance of continuous time. And so the servant seems to be everywhere, doing everything. We see him madly banging away on a set of drums, then, an instant later, dancing, then, in another, fanning his master—and so on through the scene.

This action is accompanied by a slow, plaintive jazz score and some sound effects. But it is the film's visual rhythms that weld it into a coherent and expressive work. Unlike most sound films, this one is essentially silent in its conception because the story is told entirely through pantomime. The sound track was then added to reinforce the rhythms of the action, just as a silent film was given added rhythmic impact by the playing of a movie-house pianist. Since there is no dialogue to amplify or explain the action, the music also serves as a reflection of the sadness of the characters' lives.

The visual rhythms of the film are contained in its pacing. This is most obvious in this final scene. Here the deft strokes of Polanski's caricature are drawn, like those of an animated cartoon, by an impossible acceleration of normal activities. But it is not just the extensive motion within each shot which creates this exaggeration. Our sense of hyperactivity also results from the awkward beat of an illogical succession of shots. Unlike the smooth, almost seamless, editing of the previous scenes, each unexpected jump in the servant's activities suddenly calls attention to the cut which made such a jump possible. It is simply our awareness of the abrupt, intrusive presence of these cuts which creates a rhythm that disrupts the flow of time within the film. Polanski ignores the time we had assumed it would take the servant to get from one location to another and so can place him anywhere and therefore make him seem everywhere. The rhythms drawn from this technique both capture the essential human drives of the characters and propel us through an otherwise chaotic scene.

Time and space have here been synthesized into a unique blend that allows us to experience the explosive rhythms which drive the characters on. These rhythms make visible that layer of feeling normally hidden just beneath the volatile outlines of the personality. Similarly, in *Runner* we were made to feel the pulse of the runner's personality in visual rhythms that distilled and intensified time.

Throughout the length of a film an audience is bathed in a wash of time. Its currents are felt in the variety of rhythms which bind together hundreds of discrete shots containing separate moments in time. These currents are also felt in the fluidity of our easy movements through the layered depths of a character's life—forward and backward in time—seeing reflections of his personality for varying lengths at different stages of his development. And even when the progression of time is resolutely forward, we are still propelled from moment to moment, sometimes in minute increments, sometimes in great gulps of time.

Our senses are alive to the passage of time. All tenses are collapsed before us into an immediate sweep of moments that carve out experience and force it into relief. Although the texture, shape, color, and volume of the screen images place a strong claim on our senses, it is their development within a self-enclosed temporal universe that discretely plays upon our nerve ends and organizes our sensual appreciation of their form. They are given meaning and proportion, discipline and variety as their carefully apportioned moments linger or rush before us.

These images are so nourished by their relationship to one another in time that both their substance and their meaning can be transformed, bloom, and flower into new shapes and associations before our eyes.

Norman McLaren's stunning *Pas de Deux* does not merely record a ballet, it creates one out of the temporal relationships discovered within the discrete movements that form the surface of a dance. Set within an enveloping blackness, the dancers are shaped only by their piercing outlines. Their bodies, compacted within these thin edges of light, slice through space as pure movement. First a movement sweeps the screen, fanning behind it those portions of the movement, fractions of a second apart, which mark its passage through time. At the peak of the movement,

when its arc through space has been completed, each instant of motion is visualized separately before finally collapsing back into the form that gave it birth.

Past, present, and future exist simultaneously on the screen, synthesized into pulses of expression. Motion, which usually structures our perception of time, has been abstracted and transformed, like time itself, into pure conception. What we see and feel is time made visible, stretched across a screen in sensuous combinations of movement and light.

The unique and distinct instants that comprise man's present are created, preserved, anticipated, and annihilated before our eyes. The wholeness of time—the total interdependence of past, present, and future—is objectified in this rhythmic assertion of movement. Memory, which gives the present its meaning and the future its existence, has been objectified and turned into the knowledge of this interdependence. And this knowledge has been transformed into expression and sensation. We have been moved toward the furthest reaches of a universe in which time progresses by bending back upon itself, creating new feelings, new forms of experience, and enriching the meaning and weight of those experiences familiar to us. This is inherent in the structure of all films. It is a powerful tool in the hands of a film-maker aware of its uses.

Chapter 3

Scripting Images

The story goes that at the 1966 Cannes Film Festival, during a public debate among the participating directors, the master storyteller, Henri Clouzot, asked, "Surely you agree, Monsieur Godard, that films should have a beginning, a middle, and an end?" To which Godard answered, "Yes, but not necessarily in that order."

Many modern film-makers no longer work just within a simple story line; and, even within the narrative tradition, scripting is more than the ordering process through which a plot unfolds from beginning to end. The script is the vessel which carries the film-maker's intentions from his initial impressions to their final realization. It is also his means for conceptualizing his world in terms of the craft he must employ.

While it is the function of a script to give a structure to a motion picture before it is shot, this is just the first step in a complex scripting process that also includes those hundreds of decisions along the way—the shift of a light, the composition of a shot, the choice of a microphone, a decision to leave in one shot and take out another—that give meaning and body to the initial structure. Scripting, then, is both the initial conceptualization and the sum of those insights discovered

each step of the way. Not only for Godard, but for most film-makers, the finished film—the seemingly immutable beginning, middle, and end—is ultimately a series of discoveries.

These discoveries are possible only from a vantage point sufficiently coherent that it permits the film-maker to explore his world with the sureness that will allow him to exploit each possibility along the way. This vantage point is embodied in the script, which charts the course of a film—a working outline that is unique for each film-maker.

The script can be a private document or a corporate effort; a few lines scratched on the back of a notebook or an intricate shot-by-shot breakdown complete with dialogue. The legendary *Breathless,* for example, had its origins in nothing more than a newspaper article discovered by Truffaut and offered to Godard, who reduced its theme to a few pungent notations. From this set of notations each day's shooting was improvised before a silent hand-held camera. The famous jump cuts that produced so much of the film's final effect were later discovered in the editing room.

Federico Fellini, on the other hand, in the tradition of many modern Italian directors, develops his films with the close help of the kindred imaginations of skilled writers. The basic idea for a film comes from Fellini, who then spends most of the scripting hours just discussing and refining those ideas with his writers, Tullio Pinelli and Ennio Flaiano. Finally Pinelli and Flaiano write the scenario and dialogue from which Fellini improvises his distinctive final shooting. In much the same way Antonioni has worked over the years with his two favorite writers, Tonino Guerra and Elio Bartolini; Luchino Visconti with Suso Cochi D'Amico; and Vittorio de Sica with Cesare Zavattini, who in his own right was one of the dominant forces in the postwar European cinema.

Sergei Eisenstein, who envisioned films with as much gusto and concern as he finally shot them, worked in yet another way. He filled entire notebooks with elaborate drawings and notations as a way of structuring his private vision of a film. For him the mere translation of an idea into a story was insufficient for both his artistic and his polemic purposes. Instead, he began the scripting process by seeking images so powerful and telling that the images themselves, alone and in combination, would carry the weight of his film and provide a means of awakening an emotional reaction commensurate with the stark revolutionary themes he composed.

For *Que Viva Mexico!,* for example, Eisenstein prowled the Mexican countryside and from what he saw extracted the framework for his final treatment. His major theme was built upon his observation that the entire history of the country was visually spread across the land in a present that tragically embraced the ancient with the new. Ernest Lindgren describes how Eisenstein scripted the film:

> Mexico gave him that which he needed above all, namely, not a ready-made story or even a story-idea for adaptation, but a rich exciting *milieu* in which his creative fancy could luxuriate and expand, and from the observation of which he could build the detail of his theme as he went along. What the script gives us is not the finished film, shot by shot, but merely the ground plan which might be varied, exceeded or rearranged, as the work went on.

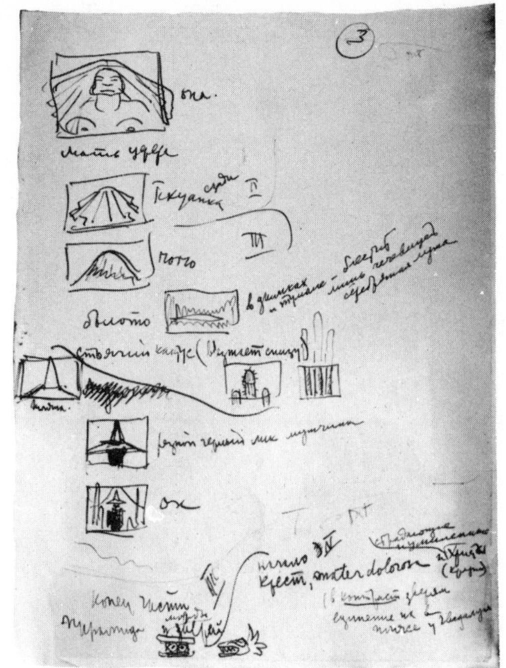

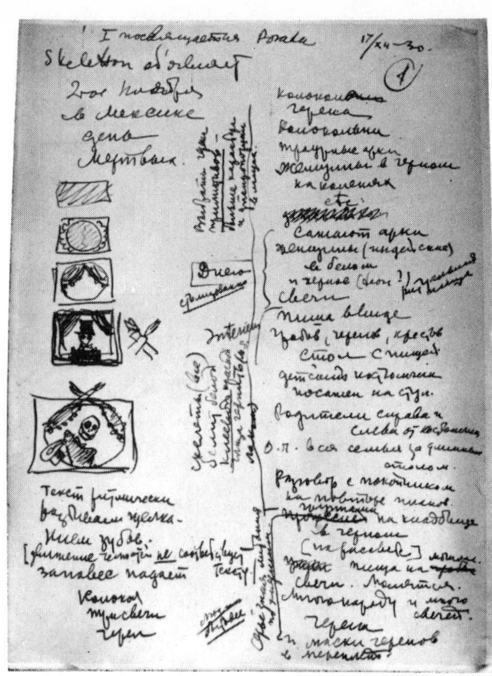

Compare this intensely personal approach to a film with Lindgren's description of the script-writing process for the typical Hollywood studio film:

> The associate producer begins his work by selecting a writer who can be trusted to take the story in its original synopsis form and follow it through the various drafts which will be necessary before it is ready for shooting. He may appoint one of the studio writers, or a free-lance: the one requirement is that his talents should suit the character of the story. In the course of work on the story, the associate producer may also call in other specialist writers, one to contribute new situations, another to add some light dialogue, a third to tighten up the continuity, and so on.

However, despite this collectivization of effort, we have come to find as much artistic vitality in an impressive number of Hollywood films as in the films sired (more or less) by a single author. As Richard Corliss has pointed out with that beguiling hyperbole that echoes the first salvo in a new critical attack, "This [group effort] doesn't diminish the validity of the Hollywood film as an art. Both Chartres and *Charade* were the work of a number of individuals who contributed their

unique talents to a corporate enterprise, but this fact doesn't necessarily make either work less appropriate for serious study. . . ."

Equally appropriate for study is the scripting process for that majestic procession of documentaries from *Nanook of the North* through *Woodstock;* here it is not a story but a process or chronology unfolding in a rhythmic play of images that structures the film—the monumental grace of the athletes' exertions in Leni Riefenstahl's *Olympiad;* the tragedy of a rich land being stripped bare, tree by tree, and laid open to waste in Pare Lorentz's *The River;* the impressionistic flow of everyday activity that marked the endurance of the British people during war and enlarged our concept of heroism in Humphrey Jennings's *Listen to Britain.*

The Nature of the Words that Structure a Script

For each film-maker scripting any type of film, the central problem is the translation of ideas and impressions into a coherent set of symbols (words) so that they can ultimately be transformed into another set of symbols (images). The script begins that tortuous movement from the inchoate impressions beneath the threshold of consciousness, out of which we draw our perceptions, to the concrete, often contrived, images which must transmit these perceptions. It is this complex process which is structured and anchored by the words which form a script. These word-symbols must formulate meanings drawn from the random, sensuous, illogical, imagistic play of the imagination in such a way that the core of each perception is understood sufficiently in words to be reworked again in terms of an analogous, but essentially different, symbolic representation—the images that will fill the screen.

Let us look briefly at the imagistic facility with which words first order our perceptions and then draw from these perceptions the initial meanings and feelings which eventually structure the script. This verbal language is above all rich in implications and subtle distinctions. It is capable of skittering along the imaginative impulses which gave it birth, continually yoking the disparate, ordering the illogical, claiming the irredeemable. It is our tool for both conceptualizing our world—bending it to our intellect—and remaking it over and over to please our fancies and satisfy our deepest needs.

The essential nature of verbal imagery lies in its remarkable ability to compact disparate images into layers of meaning that build a coherent impression. This process of joining words into symbolic images is, above all, cumulative. We continually superimpose the meanings of these words, one upon another, until they form a play of meanings which, in combination, force us to a new awareness. When carefully chosen and well structured, these words deftly prick at the imagination, jostle it to span new connections and then draw from these connections heightened perceptions.

To see how this process operates, look at the famous lines which open Shakespeare's seventy-third sonnet:

> That time of year thou mayst in me behold
> When yellow leaves, or none, or few, do hang
> Upon those boughs which shake against the cold
> Bare ruined choirs, where late the sweet birds sang.

The opening line sets up a comparison—a metaphor—that joins the object of the sonnet to the natural world and so charges each object in that world with a symbolic meaning. "Yellow leaves" become the embodiment of a quality of old age which "hangs" rather than "grows" upon boughs which "shake" rather than "stand" against the cold. The poignance of this conception of a worn and perilous old age is drawn from a succession of images, each of which refines and revitalizes the preceding one and all of which implicitly call to mind an opposite.

By the time we reach the last line we are prepared for the complete image conjured by just the word *bare*. But this immediately dissolves into *ruined* (pronounced "ruin-èd") and finally both merge into *choirs*. *Bare, ruined,* and *choirs* are rhythmically isolated—each word separately accented within the line so that we must pause, assimilate the image it casts, adjust to the previous image that it incorporates, and then move on to the next word. When we have reached *choirs,* the nature of the imagery, while retaining all of the feelings which have been accumulated, has been transformed. "Bare ruined choirs, where late the sweet birds sang" layers the basic sadness of a gray winter day under the inevitable dissolution of the human body and spirit. But it does even more. It questions man's sense of eternity by evoking the ultimate transience of even such a substantial institution as the Church. Finally it calls forth the perilousness of the age itself, in which revolutionary Protestantism has already loosened those uncontrollable forces that have led to the destruction of the churches and monasteries throughout the land. All this in one line.

The speaker's feelings—his overwhelming sense of abandonment—are objectified in a succession of images, each of which surprises us with an observation that enlarges our vision while moving us more deeply into the emotions that willed them. These images, while sufficiently complete to evoke an emotionally charged picture, are still fragments of the master image revealed in the last line. And it is not until these successive insights have merged into that final commanding image that the speaker's private vision of himself reaches out to embrace his world and his age.

The metaphorical construction implicit in all language depends upon this double view. Here we see man at once the center of his emotions and concerns and yet a distant fragment of a greater world. It is a view in which intellect heightens feelings, skepticism defines belief, and the polarities of human existence touch and spark those insights which renew man in each generation by making him account for the objects and beliefs with which he has filled his world. But like all metaphor, it is not a world that can be confronted directly. It is one seen out of the corner of

the eye so that the image and its afterimage blend, becoming at once object and symbol, real and imaginary. It is as though truths are hidden in the world. If they are looked at directly, they disappear.

The Nature of Visual Imagery

Yet in motion pictures, if nowhere else, the world is looked at with intense directness. Surrounded by darkness, our eyes riveted on the visual images that fill the screen before us, the literalness of the image is everything. We perceive directly what we see on the screen and respond to the world it portrays as an experience essentially different from that created out of a language that depends upon words. This is apparent. But what is deceptive is the fact that words and images can be worked in strikingly similar ways. The imagination that wrote the sonnet and lit the gathering forces of his century, in a later age, could have structured a film with similar economy and effect. The film-maker's effectiveness, as the poet's, grows out of his ability to visualize and then manipulate the potentialities of images in a rhythmically cumulative development, continually re-creating his world in surprising affinities.

We can see this kind of imagination brilliantly at work in just a short transitional scene from Fritz Lang's slick 1928 silent melodrama, *Spies*. It is a startling sequence conceptualized in many of the same ways as the opening lines of the Shakespearean sonnet.

The film details the exploits of a masterful international spy and is filled with numerous intrigues, deceptions, and, above all, disguises. This particular scene is

Courtesy: JANUS FILMS, INC.

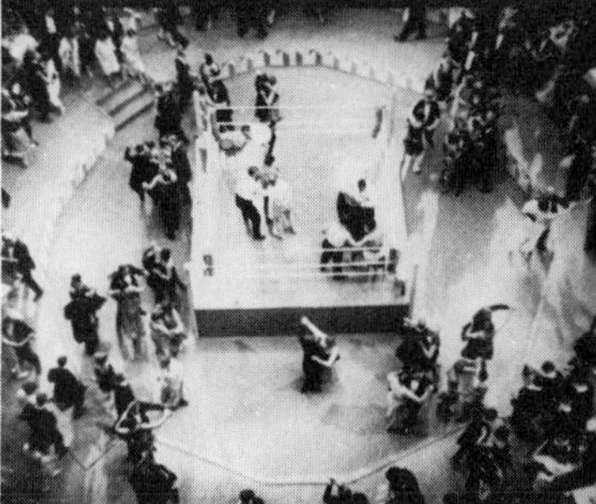

just a transition to get the spy from one place to another—in this case to the Café Danielle. But instead of a café filled with revelers, we see a stark overhead shot of a boxing ring lit as austerely as a surgical table. Then, as the boxers complete their prescribed exercise in violence, even as one of them lies sprawled upon the canvas, the orchestra bursts into music and the ringside is transformed into a dance floor. The camera never returns to the ring and the scene is never alluded to in the film again.

Although the sequence is not metaphoric, and, in fact, depends upon the specific literalness of the images for its power, it does derive its meanings from an accumulation of images that are constantly being redefined as the sequence progresses. The first image is of a boxing ring abstracted inside almost mystically concentric circles with its combatants miniaturized by the high angle. The image is severely mechanistic, both in its symmetry and in the depersonalization of the people within its space; and it is also ritualistic in its design of stylized violence. It is almost a work of art.

Next we see the fighters realistically, up close, fiercely intent on the brutality of their sport. The opening abstraction has given way to sweating flesh. But then we are surprised to see detached spectators enjoying their drinks and dinners in the background. Suddenly, with the flourish of the maestro's violin, the violent world of the arena and the refined world of the supper club coalesce, forming a dreamlike fusion of these normally abhorrent aspects of urban pleasure. Gladiator and diner have been joined in a congruent spectacle of awesome vulgarity. The sweat of the arena has become the spice for the meal. Then the violence is consummated, the band begins to play, dancing couples swarm across the ringside floor, and the café is again transformed—this time back to our conventional notions of a supper club. We are in a world buried deeply beneath the paths where civilized men walk.

As in the sonnet, a succession of precisely drawn evocative images continually modifies and expands the meaning of the sequence until these images cohere as statements that cut to the heart of the artist's universe. By the time we arrive at the last frame in the sequence—the couples tamely dancing on the nightclub floor—we have come to feel that the inhabitants of the club have been fused into a representation of their society. The lives of these club-goers have been abstracted in the grinding movement from impersonalized violence to disinterested pleasure. Like the speaker in the sonnet, they have been obliquely stripped to those elemental qualities that resolutely cling to the world they have fashioned. With a double perspective, we finally see them dancing to the beat of those nameless forces which have eroded their society.

We are, of course, in those painful transitional years of the Weimar Republic. As Siegfried Kracauer points out about the motion picture as a whole: "The film reflected the neutrality prevalent during that period—a neutrality which also manifested itself in the absence of any distinction between legal and illegal pursuits and in a prodigal abundance of disguises. No character was what he appeared to be. This constant change of identities was appropriate to denote a state of mind in which the paralysis of the self interfered with any attempt at self-identification." This scene then finally reaches out beyond the immediate pursuits of the characters to outline the world in which they exist. Their sense of dislocation, the dissolution of their moral values, their anesthetized response to pleasure and pain progressively emerge as the sequence unfolds. We are just four years from the rise of Hitler's Germany, and the scene plays as both a prophecy and an explanation. All this in about a minute of film time.

Yet in both this sequence and the sonnet, it is not the startling nature of the imagery nor the emotional pitch of the scene which gives them their distinction. Barren trees and a nightclub, even with a boxing ring inside it, hold no intrinsic dramatic interest, and both passages are rhythmically and imagistically low key. Rather it is the pressure of the artistic process itself which fuses the images into a deeply felt statement. It is this process which forms the cohesive, resonant tone from which emerge the feelings at work just beneath the surface of the images. When the surprising thrust of these feelings pierces the tightly woven images, the emotional topography of the scene is felt, and the sequence and the sonnet are brought alive in our imagination to make their final claim on our emotions and our intellect.

Lang's accomplishment in the sequence rests on his precise control over the meanings and feelings his images develop. It is his awareness of the possibilities, surprises, affinities, and resonances stored within each image, ready to burst the shape that holds them and spring alive in the excited imagination of an audience, that enables him to work the images with such effect. By contouring the hard edges of intractable reality—the tense literalness of things—to the shape of his vision, Lang, like all film-makers, informs the physical world with the play of his consciousness. From shot to shot he separates the objects he films from their loosely defined meanings, isolates them from their random associations, and reconstructs the world out of the hidden meanings he discovers layered within them.

The Qualities of the Image

It makes little difference whether the entire shape of a film derives from a plot which bends each image to support the activities of characters developing within a story line; or whether the film, or sequences in it, freely strike toward new associations, submerged likenesses, symbolic representations. The scripting of any film depends upon the selection and quality of the images that ultimately will give it substance.

Yet the nature of visual imagery is elusive. The images within the shifting contexts and internal designs that run the length of a film can either reveal and accent the meanings conceived by the film-maker, or they can unintentionally mute or be completely irrelevant to his purposes. It is very easy for the film-maker to find it difficult to realize the intentions of his own script. When this happens, it is essentially because his original ideas have been embedded and lost in verbal language. The problem is that the language he uses to structure his film stands poised between his perceptions and the impact of their symbolic representation, while in visual language his perceptions are themselves encoded within the very images.

An understanding of the nature of that code—its energy, diversity, and possibilities as well as its limitations—is central to a study of scripting. It is crucial for the film-maker to understand those inherent properties of the image which he can draw upon to create the effect he is trying to achieve. These elemental qualities can be roughly divided into three basic categories: the *representation,* the *assertion,* and the *symbol.* These are flexible aspects of the image that the film-maker will draw upon again and again to transpose his impressions onto the fixed surface of the motion-picture screen.

Aspects of the Image: Representation

The basic task for the film-maker is to make his images look like the objects he wants represented. Whether he is reproducing reality as he finds it or creating a whole new reality, the film-maker must first know clearly how he wants things to appear; and then he must be sure that these things conform to this appearance. The play of the camera, the lighting, the exposure, and the editing can all easily alter the appearance of things. Since the beginnings of motion pictures, sets and costumes, carefully lit and photographed, have created powerful illusions of reality that were effective because they were meticulously constructed.

This propensity for illusion is so built into film-making that it can even be

realized with a small, but well-controlled, flourish of imaginative sleight of hand.

F. W. Murnau in his horror classic *Nosferatu* needed a cemetery overlooking the ocean's edge. Just by planting some crosses in a sand dune he was able to transform an ordinary beach, in broad, flat daylight, into an ominous graveyard. Despite the fact that a shifting hill of sand is about the last place one would want to bury a loved one, and despite the lack of individualized burial mounds and all those embellishments we associate with a graveyard, a few crosses in the sand fully realize the cemetery for us.

But for the most part, it is sufficient for objects in films simply to look like what they are supposed to be. Filmic images, unlike verbal language, accomplish this reality so effortlessly that to state the fact almost seems absurd. Still, this representation of the world provides the level of our first contact with an image and the first way in which we understand it. It is also on this level that so much of the joy of a film is expressed.

Beautiful people and beautiful objects have been caressed by the camera since the earliest days of film-making. The value of cameramen around the world has depended upon their remarkable ability to make leading men and women continually fascinating in their beauty, and to make the rooms in which they lived, the streets on which they walked, the landscapes which stretched behind them to infinity, rich in texture and pleasing in outline. To accomplish all this the motion-picture industry went to the seemingly bottomless well of twentieth-century science to draw out new film stocks, better lights, and a variety of cameras and lenses so that they could be marshaled in the service of a representation of life that would make us hunger from one film to the next for the truth the beauty of this life seemed to convey.

In *Jules and Jim* François Truffaut sculpted his images out of the romance that lies at the heart of this tradition. Jules and Jim first encounter Catherine as the embodiment of the mystery that resides on the surface of things. During a slide show at the house of an artist friend, they see a representation of a woman's head carved in stone. They are fascinated as the planes and curves of the face are abstracted in a procession of cinematic close-ups taken from every possible angle. The lips, the eyes, the delicate curve of the cheek, and, above all, the tranquil smile

Courtesy: JANUS FILMS, INC.

that has been teased out of the stone fill them with a yearning that is a summation of their youthful idealization of beauty. They are so moved that in the next shot we see the friends on the Adriatic island where the statue rises like Venus shimmering in the bright, hot sun. As the camera lovingly circles the statue, they are lost in primitive wonder. Shortly after, when they finally see Catherine walking down a flight of steps, a living incarnation of the statue, it is, of course, love at first sight.

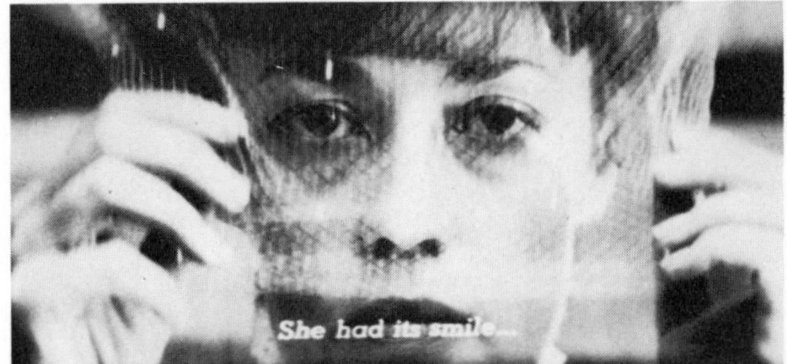

Truffaut offers us Catherine out of the depths of boyhood hours spent in movie houses lost in wonder and love at the shapes of beauty that move upon the screen. Catherine descends the staircase, much like Duchamps's nude, fragmented, in a series of close-ups (only the first few of which are reproduced here) that have torn apart her features and reassembled them into a portrait of desirability that is pure distillation.

She is an idealization constructed out of a playful but reverent extension of those stylized camera movements, angles, and close-ups designed over the years to tease a quality of yearning into a sense of love. Her beauty is timeless, not only in the way that a photograph or a work of art is timeless, but in the special ways that films have of isolating objects in space and so disconnecting and freeing them in time. Jules and Jim are excited by her in exactly the same way we are: as the embodiment of a cinematic language that has taught us to respond in ways that didn't exist before the invention of the motion-picture camera. She is Garbo, Dietrich, Harlow, and, of course, Moreau; an object uniquely formed upon the motion-picture screen to be loved in the darkest corners of the theater and later in the memory, where her image will linger and blend with our lives.

Aspects of the Image: Assertion

The second aspect of the image is its *assertive* quality. As the markings on a road sign instantly call to our attention the specific nature of the road that it is imperative we be aware of, so the assertive nature of the image shortcuts its random associations and draws us only toward those qualities we must instantly comprehend to understand its existence as a given time in a given place.

Picture a small boy, fists clenched tightly at his side, each of hundreds of muscles separately taut, and a face screwed into an immobile mask of petulant defiance. The quality of the image instantly asserts the bond between itself and the meaning of a specific moment in its existence. The outlines of the image immediately embody its meaning.

Similarly, this same assertive quality can focus the individual parts of the image into an assertion of the object's general place in existence. A man wearing a white jacket and a stethoscope is immediately recognized as a doctor. Here the essential quality of the individual is stated through those assertive aspects that identify him with a type. But whether the image asserts the importance of its individuality or its type, the camera is used to abstract the reality before it, implanting meanings and implications that exist primarily because they were isolated on film in a way that rammed home their significance.

This humorously contrived opening shot of a sequence in Theodore J. Flicker's comedy *The Troublemaker* was framed to tell us instantly the quality of life enjoyed by a crooked lawyer. Although heavy-handed and self-conscious, the shot serves both to introduce and to define the lawyer within seconds. The very speed of this revelation is part of its humor.

But the assertive composition serves one more function. It sets up visually our feelings for that crucial balance between the lawyer's sense of self and his overwhelming ambitions. And it is humorously obvious that the scale has long since been tipped in the direction of those ambitions which will hurtle him headlong into

Courtesy: JANUS FILMS, INC.

his comically imbalanced pursuits throughout the film. A bond has been created between audience and image that has defined the audience's relationship to that image. Whether the assertion is obvious or subtle, it is the clarity of this relationship that is keenly felt. Viewer and picture are suddenly brought into a dynamic equilibrium that draws the viewer to the center of the film-maker's intentions.

The Assertiveness of the Unexpected

The assertive quality of images, though, is more than just a function of their composition. In the earliest days of film, when the camera was essentially immobile and the images that filled the screen tended to work themselves out in a series of tableaux, stagy compositions drove home the meaning of each scene in classical arrangements that would have made a member of the French Academy blush. But as soon as styles of editing were developed that fused self-contained moments into rhythmic sequences, the film-maker could unravel his meaning within a cohesive dramatic structure. While the images still tended toward the melodramatic and the sentimental, their thrust was felt in the interplay between groupings. A quality of dramatic necessity developed from one shot to the next and from this emerged single images of unexpected strength.

In a very famous sequence from D. W. Griffith's *Birth of a Nation,* the defeated hero home from the war slowly makes his way down an empty street toward his ravaged home. His little sister greets him with a boundless, uncomprehending joy that seems to cleanse his spirit of the dirt and blood of the battlefield. But the scene doesn't reach its conclusion until the soldier ascends the steps to his house, where his mother's arms emerge from the doorway to encircle him and offer him rest. Those disembodied welcoming arms abstract and summarize a mother's

strength, courage, and love: possibly those of all mothers in all wars. When they emerge after the increasingly poignant images of the empty street, the slow walk, the exuberant sisterly greeting, these frail arms come to hold a quality of endurance and a stately offering of love that is all the more moving because of the unexpected discretion of the image.

The assertive force of the mother's arms grows out of the dramatic construction of the scene. For an audience sensitized by the almost bathetic images that comprise the soldier's welcome, the arms unexpectedly emerge like hoops of steel pinning us to the meanings they enforce. Where we expected the screen to be filled with a crescendo of emotion to top off the scene, we instead received a subdued image that we can infuse with the pitch of the feelings that have swept us down the street and into those waiting arms.

Over and over in films, the assertive use of the unexpected unsettles our expectations and drives home, in small shocks, meanings that might otherwise evaporate within the film's larger dramatic structure.

Courtesy: JANUS FILMS, INC.

In *The Troublemaker* its hayseed of a hero has come to conquer the big city only to be taken by just about everyone he meets. He moves into an apartment with all the paraphernalia of sophisticated living—modern paintings, sculpture, and furnishings. As he moves about the small apartment, we are dimly aware that the woman in the apartment across the way is watching his every move. Eventually he goes to the window, and we see that the prying neighbor is no more than a painting on the window shade—a representation that is a funny reminder of the insufferable closeness of existence in the city. Finally he releases the shade and reveals behind the painting—the neighbor in all her inquisitive splendor actually looking into his

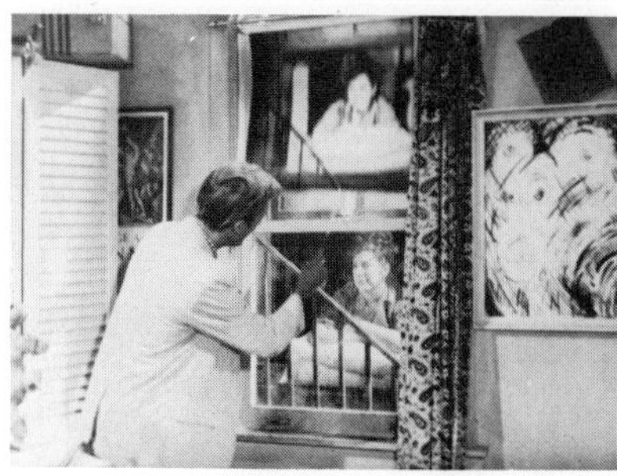

room. The film-maker's point about his hero's entrapment in a world that is slightly beyond his grasp is felt in this deft, comical assertion that has capsulized his existence in the unexpected thrust of the joke.

In Akira Kurosawa's *Yojimbo* the humor is unexpectedly drawn from the dark well of repugnance the director feels toward those driven aspects of man that make him bestial in his violence and corruption. Yet Kurosawa maintains the film's lightness through his disciplined and imaginatively assertive imagery. The hero of the film wanders into a village with a population that seems to have been born out of the imagination of an Oriental Hieronymus Bosch. He is a rootless, amoral samurai whose inherent rationality nevertheless slices through the twisted pretensions of this world with a force more swift than his sword. Two opposing factions, each incredibly more deformed and avaricious than the other, bid to hire him to establish their mastery over the town. In the end he manages to decimate both sides by turning them against one another, leaving the town piled with corpses in an act of judgment so final it almost seems like the last.

Yet out of this a comedy has been built. The humor as well as the plot depends on Kurosawa's resources in developing a line of action that weaves its way through horrible acts of violence, countless betrayals, lies, slanders, and intrigues while anesthetizing the pain and cauterizing the evil just at the point when it seems to overwhelm the creatures in the film. He accomplishes this by meticulously constructing a succession of images that precisely reflect the olympian sensibilities of his hero while rhythmically sweeping us into the action that he is holding up for our inspection.

Look at how carefully he introduces us to the town. As the samurai first walks down its deserted streets, not knowing what to expect, he sees a dog in the distance. He is bemused by the leisurely tread of the animal until it comes just close

enough for him (and us) to see that the tidbit it carries in its mouth is the remnant of a human hand. Just at that startling moment Kurosawa cuts away from the ani-

mal. We are first shocked by the unexpected discovery of the severed hand, and then we are surprised again that it is revealed for just an instant and then blithely ignored by both the film-maker and the samurai. What could have been merely a macabre image becomes instead an assertion that keys us into the world we are about to enter—one that is bestial in nature but humorous in construction. In this town the toads are very real, but the garden is distinctly imaginary.

Very quickly we learn that we are at the rotting heart of a corrupted humanity redeemed only by the surgical grace of the samurai's sword, which heals with every cut. Since the samurai is an agent of pure rationality in a world devoid of reason, each of his actions grows out of a moral certainty which forms the basis for the ironic humor which fills the film.

Kurosawa establishes the metaphorical weight of the samurai's position in the opening shot of the film. Immediately he appears to us a monolith. With the camera to the back of his mountainous figure, which weaves to the rhythm of a samurai's distinctive gait, he is set in careful opposition to a mountain that rises majestically in the distance. We are watching him walk down a nameless road on what appears to be an endless journey. We are in the presence of an archetypal hero swelled by the wide screen into monumental proportions. But within seconds Kurosawa transforms this assertion into another. Instead of striding toward the

distance, the samurai pauses and scratches his head. It is a gesture so human and so unexpected that we begin to see him with a double vision—one that will enable us to take pleasure in his quizzical humanity while understanding that his actions are idealized by a rigid sense of rightness that never allows him uncertainty. The thrust and counterthrust of Kurosawa's imagery have set up a film of delicate oppositions in a brutally explosive world. Its humor, meanings, and impact are formed in a precise blend of images that will tease a comedy out of the morality play that follows.

Inconspicuous Assertions

In the previous examples we've seen assertions develop out of dramatic compositions or dramatic surprises all of which brought us up short in the same way and called nearly as much attention to themselves as they did to the meanings they created. But the assertive quality of the image—its ability to sharpen and fix meanings in precise ways at specific points in the film—can emerge so subtly from the flow of action as to pass almost unnoticed. Still, the effect can noticeably pull a scene together and strengthen the film-maker's hold on the meanings and feelings that he is trying to develop.

Andrzej Wajda's *Kanal* details the desperate heroism of a small, worn group of Polish soldiers and patriots upon whose decimated ranks has fallen the impossible task of resisting the German army's final destruction of Warsaw. After waging a heroic resistance in the sewers, they regroup in front of a bombed-out hotel, uncertain of whether to continue the fight or to flee. As the frightening sound of the German tanks draws closer, a young boy picks up a pair of boots that had been worn by a slain comrade. He is oblivious to everything but the task of getting

Courtesy: JANUS FILMS, INC.

the boots on his feet. The sounds of the German advance grow louder, but the boy is still absorbed in his task. By the time he has managed to put the boots on, the enemy is so close that they must be fought, and he turns to pick up his gun with less emotion than he expended in getting the boots on his feet.

The historic destiny of this small band of fighters grows out of a casual sense of inevitability that marks the actions of each man. By isolating the force of the entire drama and absorbing its impact in a poignant moment in the life of one of its smallest combatants, Wajda can reduce the march of history to the sounds in the distance. The focus of the story as well as the powerfully restrained feelings that give it strength are summarized in the image of the boy, hopefully, patiently, determinedly putting on the boots while his civilization is being blasted from around him.

Aspects of the Image: Symbol

The third aspect of the image is its potential as a symbol. It is this quality of the image that engages our feelings by connecting the surface of an object with a body of experience filled with values and meanings that exist quite independently of that object. The symbolic aspect of the image in films usually develops meanings unexpectedly, almost imperceptibly, within controlled contexts that draw out and eventually condition our response to the image.

Symbols develop through a process that is analogous to the one that transforms a representation into an assertion. This process isolates aspects of the image and amplifies them in a way that drives home the meanings that the film-maker wants to convey. Except that, when a symbol is developed, we experience the image in two very different ways. Our visual perception directly comprehends the image as a physical object while our intellect simultaneously dismisses its shape and recognizes its affinities with a system of ideas. Within the gap between the two kinds of perception, tensions are created that touch our emotions. The range of feelings that these tensions evoke blurs the literalness of the image—expands its possibilities—so that it can hold a large store of meanings without destroying the integrity of the object it is supposed to represent. It is under the pressure of these feelings that the highly charged but often inconsistent meanings of the image are firmly bonded to physical reality. What emerge are insights formed through an awareness that has suddenly fused our senses and our intellect into a perception of striking new relationships. Quickly, an example!

This brief State Farm Insurance commercial illustrates the precariousness of automobile travel by shrewdly using eggs to represent the automobiles. We first see an egg mounted on wheels slowly moving across the frame. Next we see another mobile egg heading on a collision course for the first. And finally we are left with the smashed shell of the first egg mournfully at rest. The story is told succinctly and with immediate effect.

It is the representational aspect of the image that first engages our interest. An egg does not belong on wheels, and this unlikely, even charming, association of egg and wheels piques our curiosity. But as soon as we see one egg-vehicle hurtling toward another, the image becomes predominantly assertive. Instantly the screen reverberates with the essential fragility of the egg. Its thin-shelled vulnerability grips our attention. Finally, after the egg has been smashed, what we respond to is not the representational anomaly of an egg on wheels nor even any longer the powerful assertion of its fragility. The vehicular egg has come to symbolize the perilousness of a life that continually risks itself on the road.

In its journey from anomaly toward annihilation, the wheeled egg has become a vehicle which carries the assertive qualities that expand into an abstraction. The egg is now firmly the misshapen wreckage of an automobile. It is the bills that must be paid and the troubles that must be endured. And since the film was made to sell insurance, it is also, at its furthest limit, the embodiment of the essential vulnerability of modern life. The feelings loosed by the closing shot still sensually play upon its basic "eggness," but now intimations of mortality hover about its shape. Still, all this film has taught and made us feel about a perilous aspect of modern existence rests entirely upon the thin and brittle shell of an ordinary egg.

The force of the symbolic development of objects in films emerges from this tension between their physical, sensual representation and the abstract world that has gradually come to adhere to their surface. Possibilities curl in and around the planes and curves of real things, drawing out highlights, deepening shadows, twisting outlines back upon themselves like the fantastical Möbius strip, where inside and outside blend in an illusive form that has at once both one and two distinct surfaces, depending on the point in place and time at which it is comprehended. Like the world of the lovers we saw in *Yesterday, Today and Tomorrow* (Chapter One, pp. 28 to 32), whose constricted emotions were defined, then paralleled, and finally symbolized by the deformed space they inhabited inside the Rolls-Royce, symbols in films emerge with a logic of their own from a prismatic view of reality that has bent the surface of that reality to discover and then shape its meanings.

Integrating Symbols into the Flow of Action

Robert Flaherty drew *Nanook of the North* to its conclusion by capturing the terrible power of the north wind sweeping through the lives of his Eskimos with the relentlessness of death itself. He shows us the Eskimos fleeing the wind and finding shelter in an abandoned igloo carved out of the frozen waste. Then he concentrates on their dogs waiting in the snow outside the igloo. As the wind becomes more savage, the dogs draw themselves deeply within their protective fur. Like an ancestral memory borne across the bitter years, these dogs hold the same patient, mute, immovable quality of endurance that has been stamped upon the lives of the Eskimos themselves. These stark images are the final repository for the shafts of insight into the lives that Flaherty's camera has recorded. The Eskimos' awesome communal isolation, their buried loneliness, their stubborn instinct for survival in a brutal world—all have been expressed, felt, and summarized in the shape of the dogs curled against the wind and the snow.

The effectiveness of these dogs as a symbol depends upon their organic relationship with the lives of the Eskimos they come to represent. Their value as a symbol emerges from the way in which they can objectify crucial aspects in the lives of the Eskimos while still supporting the structure of the narrative. As with the most powerful symbols in films, an audience is not meant to be aware of the symbolic weight they have come to carry. Their impact must be felt, not stated.

When a symbol becomes detached from the flow of action from which it has surfaced, the quantity of meanings and feelings that it is meant to carry is usually too much for it to hold. Unless its relation to the characters and the action can be sustained so that it will blend into the surface of the film while developing those attributes that will probe for deeper meanings, it becomes a contrivance. It loses that wonderful ambiguity that keeps us from neatly categorizing its function in the film and its effectiveness is diminished.

This is why one of the most famous of all American film symbols, the legendary sled "Rosebud" in Orson Welles's *Citizen Kane,* ultimately disappoints. Its monumental importance is thrust upon us within minutes of the opening from the full-screen lips of the dying Kane, who breathes the word "Rosebud" as his life is extinguished. A crystal globe containing an artificial snowstorm swirling within it falls from his hand, rolls across the floor, breaks, and instantly refracts the distorted image of his nurse rushing into the room. End of opening.

From this point on the picture is structured around a reporter's quest to discover what or who "Rosebud" is—the mystical key to the life of an extraordinary man. But until the ending, the only time we see the sled is when Kane, as a boy, is playing on it while his mother signs him over to a guardian because he has inherited

a fortune. It is a memorable event that will draw him from the arms of his mother and into the bitter world of adulthood. As his mother introduces Kane to the man who is to become his guardian, the young boy, instantly recognizing the threat to

something crucial in his life, typically lashes out at the banker with his sled. The banker leaves, and the boy and his mother retreat into their home as the sled is abandoned and buried in the swirling snow.

As all this happens, we have no way of knowing that "Rosebud" and the sled are one and the same. Immediately after, we are plunged into the gargantuan Kane career, and it isn't until the closing minutes that the carefully withheld revelation is literally burned into our consciousness. We are in Kane's opulent mansion with the spoils of his avaricious life piled, like a fantastic ruined city, in endless rows of clutter. We see the reporter as he acknowledges his failure to penetrate the mystery of "Rosebud"; and then, in one splendid crane shot, the camera rises majestically above this city of the dead—the unearthly remains of an appetite so vast, insatiable, and corrupt that in death it has disgorged this empire of junk—

and slowly moves across the mounds of tasteless artifacts until it rests upon two workmen feeding the incinerator with this trash. The sled is thrown onto the center of the pyre; and finally the camera, drawn to it like a moth to light, moves in through the fire to reveal the word *Rosebud* just seconds before the sled is consumed by the flames.

Magnificent! A *tour de force!* We are pinned to the backs of our seats by the wonderment of this shot that links, in one sweeping motion, the search for "Rosebud" with the essential hollowness of Kane's life and finally the revelation that explains it all. But once the force of the shot has cooled in our memory, all that we are left with is the emptiness of the symbol. "Rosebud" seems to convey everything, but it means nothing. It is amorphous without being ambiguous. Instantly we are meant to feel that, if only Charles Foster Kane had been allowed to remain in the heartlands, he would have been happy; if only he hadn't been wrenched from his mother and assaulted, at a tender age, with a fortune, his small-town soul would have been fulfilled. But after nearly two hours of watching Kane stride through life like a colossus, we know this supposition isn't even remotely true.

"Rosebud" is, of course, a clever device used to structure the film—something like Hitchcock's famous "MacGuffin," that bit of nothing so crucial to his characters that it serves to motivate them on their carefully plotted course throughout his films. Rosebud's symbolic intensity grows in importance only when the characters are speculating about its meaning. Since it has no developing relationship to Kane's life as it is revealed upon the screen, the meanings for Kane that it finally conveys are imposed upon it in a burst of sentimentality that describes nothing more than a grown man sighing over his lost childhood.

How different this is from Eric Rohmer's equally unlikely transformation of a very ordinary object into a symbol of monumental importance in the life of his hero. In *Claire's Knee,* even before we enter the movie house we know from the engaging title alone that this sensually unlikely portion of the anatomy is going to be an object of unusual interest. The film begins by detailing, with almost Jamesean refinement, the hero's flirtation with a cheeky sixteen-year-old just a fortnight before he is to be married. He confesses each nuance of his tentative relationship

to a full-blooded old flame who is resting from a series of romantic adventures. It is during these talks that his flirtation swells in importance, gaining in conversational resonance the life it lacks in the tender but limp reality.

It is not until midway through the film that the hero finally encounters Claire, the pretty, lithe half sister of the girl with whom he has been flirting. Claire has a neolithic, but sexually adequate young boyfriend and is scarcely aware of the hero's presence. But he is irresistibly drawn to her and, out of self-preservation, focuses his desire, his conversation, and his delicate sense of adventure on her charming but undistinguished knee. He plans a stratagem—as imaginative and deceitful, if not quite as intricate, as the peregrinations of an eighteenth-century bedroom comedy—that will enable him to satisfy his timorous lust by finally managing to touch that beguiling knee.

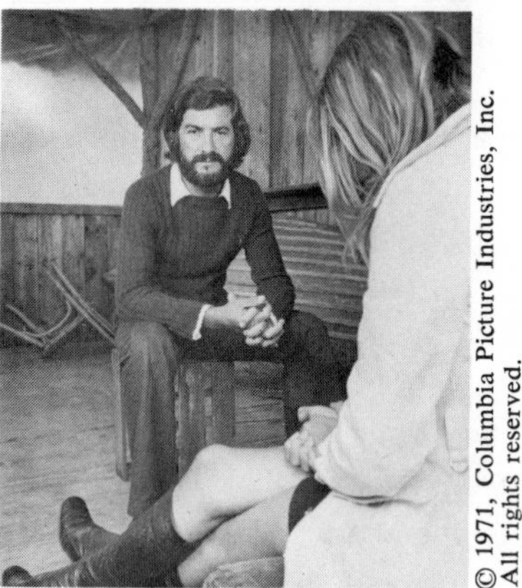

For the hero, then, Claire's knee has become a movable feast, a sort of portable grail enlarging expectations with each retreat. It has become, in Andrew Sarris's phrase, "sensuality transformed into sensibility," with each random movement on the screen dancing private visions in public places. With the suppleness inherent in all symbols, Claire's knee forms a double-layered world that objectifies a state of mind while resolutely playing out its literal function in a corporeal universe. The knee supports both an indifferent Claire and the hero's intimate, yet solitary, relationship with her.

From this point on, we continue to shift between the hero's vision of the knee and its objective place in the world. Each time the knee is intimately locked within the same frame as the hero, we are driven deeper into his obsession. But when Claire is freed to walk about in the warm summer world of Lake Geneva, we see her with a stranger's eyes—pretty, yet very young, unformed, and not overwhelmingly interesting. The humor of the hero's entrapment emerges from the ludicrous refinement of his pitiful ambitions for this humble object. A knee, whatever else its attributes, is still a knee. Yet, with the double vision that symbols evoke, we are at once charmed by the poetic and psychological pressures absorbed by the knee, while never forgetting for an instant the possibilities of real pleasure conjured by visions of the thigh above on the grass below.

In Jean Renoir's carefully measured antiwar drama *Grand Illusion,* it is a small potted geranium that develops into a surprisingly effective symbol. Except that here the plant depicts more than just an individual state of mind. Over the length of the film the plant comes to represent man's small but fierce impulses toward life as it is carefully tended in the barren confines of an impregnable stone prison by the prison keeper, a German officer played by Erich von Stroheim. His loving care of the plant, carefully placing it in the little sun that reaches the prison and each day patiently watering it, enables the plant to flower into unexpectedly forceful meanings. They are especially poignant when set against Stroheim's brutish, impassive appearance locked within a uniform that signifies man's obsession with heroism and death.

Courtesy: JANUS FILMS, INC.

Aspects of the Image: Emblems

The flower in *Grand Illusion* becomes a symbol that eventually surprises us with its importance; the uniform is an emblem that solidifies our feelings the moment we see it. Emblems are an aspect of symbols. They are, in effect, symbols whose meanings have been predetermined. Like symbols, they evoke a conceptual universe that bears little relation to their shape. But unlike film symbols, the nature and the limits of that universe are defined the instant we see an emblem. Emblems, such as the stars and stripes, the hammer and sickle, the Christian cross, to name just a few in a world thick with these visual insignia, instantly call forth neatly prescribed feelings and meanings to a large, homogeneous audience.

That is why emblems in films tend to be more assertive than symbolic, quickly locating the essential qualities that must be perceived and so ordering specific responses. The famous white-hatted cowboy is not so much a symbol of goodness

as he is easily recognized as being good. In their most obvious form these filmic emblems comprise those wonderfully blatant clues—white and black cowboy hats, sinister moustaches, slinky dresses—that have guided generations of film-goers along those glorious paths of adventure, comedy, and romance that still make movies a staple for families around the world.

Courtesy: JANUS FILMS, INC.

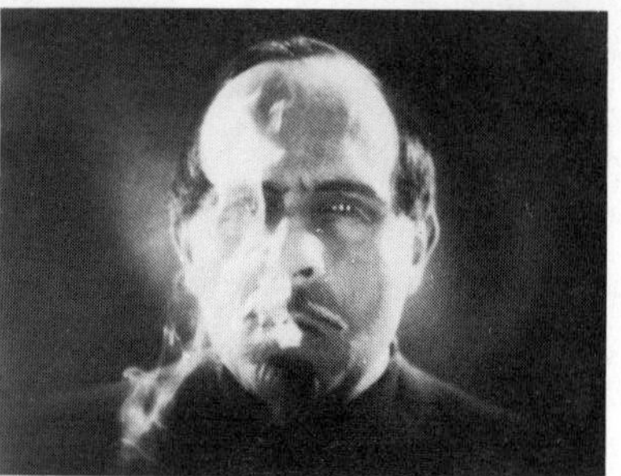

But, of course, the integration of emblems into the structure of a film story can achieve much more complex results. They are a flexible tool in the scripting process. As we saw in *Battleship Potemkin* (Chapter Two), Eisenstein was able to dehumanize the horror of sailors in the act of executing their comrades by inserting emblems of tsarist tyranny between his shot of the firing squad and the shot of the terrified victims huddled under a canvas. By the time the sequence is complete, the images of the sailors have been swept into the procession of emblems so that they are finally seen as one more impersonal standard of tsarist authority. We no longer feel ambivalent about their actions as men. They are merely functionaries of the hated State, and so our unsettled response to the sailors has finally been comfortably secured.

Courtesy: JANUS FILMS, INC.

Ingmar Bergman constructed his entire film *The Seventh Seal* out of the emblems which structure and secure allegory. Set in fourteenth-century Sweden, the film dramatizes the literal search for God by a knight who has returned to his homeland from a ten-year Crusade to the Holy Land. The world evoked by the flow of Christian emblems sharpens the focus of Bergman's moral concerns. Each of the many characters represents an aspect of man's consuming but unsatisfactory relationship with God. But unlike the hero in the prototypal medieval allegory, this hero is haunted by doubts. He inhabits a very modern world of uncertainty, where his most cherished assumptions are constantly challenged. Because the knight's doubts are set in dramatic relief against these stark emblems of traditional moral certainty, they become particularly poignant. For in a world in which man must search for God, the only certainty is death.

In this case it is death made manifest, living flesh—an active, human competitor for his soul. As an emblem, Death quickly draws us into the depths of a world where each action reverberates with moral implications. His shrouded presence embodies the force of centuries that have twisted morality into a rigid code. But as an adversary made increasingly human, his depiction as the cunning but fallible opponent of the knight permits the drama to be played out in a world where little is fixed and nothing is irredeemable. His flawed, dogged competitiveness widens the knight's possibilities for action and response beyond the limits of allegory but still within the heightened spell of its tense contrasts. This structure creates a world in which we can understand, with a self-contained logic, the troubled journey of a knight who is driven on a medieval quest armed only with the skepticism that is the burden of modern man.

Bergman has used emblems to create visual symbols with which to explore private moral questions. The shapes of these emblems possess the force of the moral certainties which anchor the corners of Bergman's beliefs. But the further

toward the center we move, the more we see these beliefs obliquely—distensions, occasionally parodies, of their original majesty. During the course of the film these emblems come to refract the medieval religious world they are supposed to re-create. Expectations go unfulfilled; limits are pushed to the breaking point. While the emblems remain powerful, immutable in shape, they become increasingly ambiguous and personal in meaning. The knight can even distract Death by overturning the magical chess game and so save the lives of a young family. All the rules can be broken as the emblems are absorbed into the knight's personal vision. It is here that the emblems finally come to symbolize the heavy burdens imposed by belief in a world in which the human spirit can be measured only by the extent of its blasphemies.

Where Bergman built a private vision out of the public meanings that emblems convey, René Clement in *Forbidden Games* developed his story by showing us the two worlds in parallel. He describes the lives of two children who escape the brutality of World War II by creating an exquisite private world out of the artifacts of death that surround their lives. First methodically and then passionately, they search for dead animals and proudly scavenge for crosses to celebrate the graves. In time they created an intricate, splendid, almost Byzantine cathedral of the dead to give meaning to their lives and protect themselves from any knowledge of the random horrors of the world.

Courtesy: JANUS FILMS, INC.

For the children the world of the cross is comprehensible only in terms of the dignity of their fantasy. But for the adults among whom they live, the cross is incomprehensible without the weight of the remote traditions attached to it. The adults understand only the emblem, while the children have discovered within its shape a symbol as enduring and perishable as childhood.

In this scene the two worlds of the cross finally collide and illuminate the limits of each in the afterglow of a comical explosion. The boy, Michel, is the youngest child of a family of farmers who adopted the girl, Paulette, when her parents were killed by the Germans in a senseless air attack. With earthy gusto the family is engaged in a bitter rivalry with their nearest neighbors. Here both families come together to attend the burial of the neighbors' eldest son.

The children, who have looted the cemetery of some of its finest crosses for their animal burial grounds, come to the funeral fearful that their thefts will be

exposed. As the heads of the two families walk among the graves, they notice that the crosses marking family plots are missing. Instantly they are at each other's throats, hurling accusations at one another. With growing apprehension Michel watches as the fury of the two men quickly reaches a pitch of anger. They grab and beat at each other, fall to the ground and roll over and over until they plunge abruptly into the dead boy's freshly dug grave.

Courtesy: JANUS FILMS, INC.

Their response to the desecration of the cemetery has been an act so gross that next to it the stolen crosses seem insignificant. Their private passions have relegated the cross to an emblem and forced it back to its remote corner of their lives. And even as they pound each other senseless in the hallowed ground, the remaining members of each family take up the war cry at full pitch, shouting insults across the open grave, until the village priest, in full ceremonial garb, scurries to the chaotic grave site.

His presence begins to restore order among the families, but it still hasn't reached into the grave, where the heads of the families continue to whack away at each other, utterly lost in the joyous violence of their own world. Finally we notice, at the feet of the bewildered priest, the little Paulette, who, with monomaniacal persistence, is equally oblivious to everything—except for the splendid crosses that dangle temptingly before her like a vision from heaven.

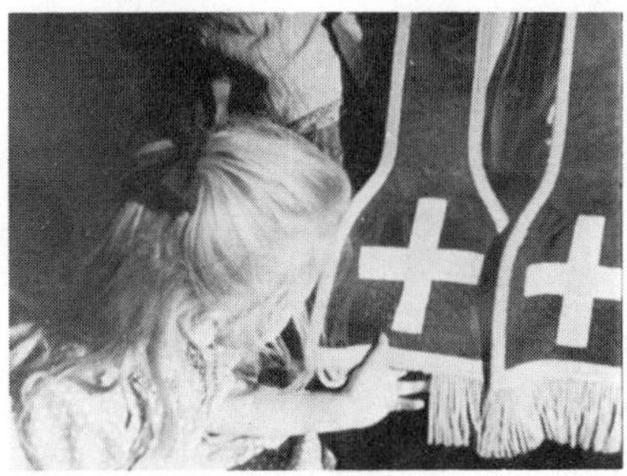

Clement scripted this scene out of the explosive potential held by a highly charged but normally stable emblem as it becomes increasingly volatile. The secure public world of order and respect which anchors the opening of the scene quickly dissolves into a disorderly procession of private responses to the cross that tear apart that world, revealing the passions, the deeply felt concerns, that surge just beneath the surface. The cross has become the point of interaction between the world of the adults and that of the children. Our understanding of the nature of each of these worlds is measured in relation to their actions involving this enveloping emblem. It is a dramatic, funny, and succinct way of getting at the

poignant disparity between life as it is seen and life as it is felt. Where the adults operate at the visible poles of deepest reverence and gross blasphemy, the children have found a secure course in between—fusing the poles so that their most blasphemous acts most completely express the fullness of their belief.

The Effect of Words on Images

The point about these central aspects of the image—representations, assertions, and symbols—is not that they are an immutable trinity, separate and hierarchic properties that once identified can be placed with loving care into some tight classification that denotes their intrinsic value. All images are, of course, representational. Many are assertive. Occasionally some well up over a period of time to become symbolic. Each image contains a full range of possibilities. What is important is that the script should be attuned to the flow of these possibilities. It is the workings of a script which set up a film's initial situations, encounters, juxtapositions, and elisions. These eventually funnel the images into those assertive and symbolic compressions that locate us within the film-maker's prismatic representation of the world.

But scripts are composed of words; and, as we have seen, words and visual imagery achieve their effects in related but still quite different ways. Thus in the making of a film there is a pressure exerted in the continual tension between the conception of a scene as it is first visualized and its structure when it is then written. These pressures are further intensified when a camera must also realize the thrust of the words as images, only to have them eventually shaped once again on an editing-room bench.

It is the script which orders all these aspects of the film. Yet the film itself is brought to fulfillment only under the pressure of a perpetual reconciliation between the words which captured the vision and the succession of images which give it expression. Because verbal language is governed by its own rules, the original visualization is often inseparable from the written language that molded it into consciousness. That visualization, when filtered through the rough abstractions that comprise language, quickly loses its shadings and textures in the string of words that have called it into existence. Inevitably physical realities must be filmed which conform to linguistic images. And so the visual images that eventually flow across the screen carry along with them the sediment of their verbal origins.

Yet this process can work surprisingly well for the film-maker. We can get a feeling for it as it is revealed in Carl Dreyer's tight production notes from his script for *The Passion of Joan of Arc*.

Each representation is a noun or a simple verb clearly realized. *Hair, beard, feet, laughs* are stated upon the screen in a declarative flow that follows the outlines of the trial. Dreyer has created a world in which the forces of its universe gather and form in aspects of its isolated inhabitants. While the role of each character has been designed by history, the drama itself exists in the kernel of their most minute responses to the pressures that have forced them into a tense series of explosively shifting relationships. Through his spare notations, Dreyer could seed that world with words that narrow and sharpen his meanings, continually shaping his universe

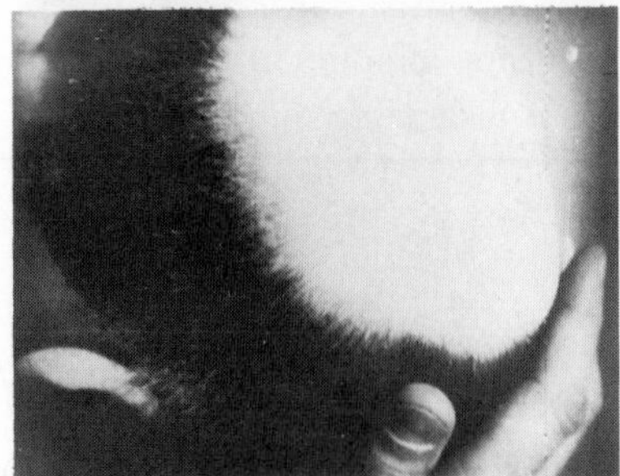

Maillard 1. in profile against floor, shouts at her.
2. contemplating.
Pilotte, hair
Gitenet, beard
Nikitine, feet
Ridez laughs.
Jean Ayme shouts traitor at Houppeville.
Ridez laughs so that his belly bounces.
Polonsky 1. soothes, 2. looks at her mildly. . . .

. . . .

Maillard panorama (cold silence)
Ridez — —
Groups cold silence
A clenched fist
Two hands raised in the air
A quick movement of the hand.
Dacheux hand to forehead
Argentine profile
Bac hand under cheek
Peritz hand in ear, looks at fingers. . . .

in terms of the precise images that must finally carry his intentions. From this succession of nouns he was then able to use his camera and his editing bench to recreate and refine these images by drawing out their specific emotional and dramatic content.

In cinema all images go striding through a film as tumescent nouns displaying their existence. When they suddenly curl into modifiers, teasing their shape into an assertion, their specific place in the film-maker's world is immediately riveted, and pressures are created in the transformation. And when an assertion occasionally uncoils and springs alive as a symbol—a dynamic verb crying not only the range of its existential possibilities but also its active place in a larger cosmology—these pressures boil over in waves of implications, currents of affinities that bring the visual aspects of film as close to conceptualization as it is capable.

Scripting Visual Conventions

The mystery itself, however, resides in the appearance of objects. Whether they are shaped into an assertion or abstracted into a symbol, it is the surface of things—the wonder of contours, shadings, colors, and movements—that makes a world cohere for us. That crystalline ability of film to represent objects as lucid shapes also gives the film-maker the power to attack his world by piercing the surfaces that seem to hold it together. For at the heart of the matter are the unreconcilable ambiguities that extend our senses, turn the familiar into the intimate, and make the intimate dissolve into unpredictable mixes. This is the rich soil in which visual conventions germinate and grow, ready to be reaped by the film-maker who will use them to organize and define his world.

Cesare Zavattini, scenarist, theoretician, and one of the dominant forces in the postwar European film, was entranced by the promises held in the surfaces that films nourish: "The cinema was our original meaning; from the first lens that opened to the light, everything was equal to it, this was its utmost uncontaminated and promising moment, the reality buried under myths was slowly reemerging: a tree, an old man, someone eating, sleeping, weeping; but then they preferred plots, to avoid too-surprising equations: the close-up of a poor man's eye might have been mistaken for a rich man's, and vice versa."

Zavattini, of course, was writing after the first flush of the postwar Italian neorealists lit the screen with the joy of objects bathed in their inherent mysteries. He passionately abandoned the conventions of his immediate past so that he could discover the meaning of that past. It was as though, after years in the dark, just to look around at the world freely was a privilege. Strangers before the camera became actors in the sense that their presence was sufficient to assert the importance of their lives at a particularly fragile point in history. Their faces, their bodies, the unique ways in which they walked, spoke, played, loved, and suffered were blended with the wreckage of their world to project the interior life of a people painfully building a civilization after the holocaust. Centuries of humanism had decreed that every man was responsible for his actions; but, in a world that had randomly flung the acid that marked each of these faces, the ability to act independently, even in small measures, was a triumph sufficient to lay the foundation for the dramas from which these films were made.

Scripting Visual Conventions: The Star

While the neorealists built a cinema out of hundreds of faces and hands set against shattered backgrounds lovingly filmed, the American cinema was still caressing the faces of its stars, giving them a life that moved freely from film to film: a journey of personality that was a triumph over circumstance and location. It was really no more than the other side of the coin. For the realist the mystery that inheres in a stranger's face is the discovery of a personality molded out of the rich clay of his type. Any humanity we can find beneath the flesh sculpted by the years to his intractable position in the world strikes us with the force of a revelation. But for the star, who if nothing else is an imperishable personality to begin with, it is the bits and pieces of self clinging to each type he plays that formulate the tensions which enliven his films.

The star is, and has been since the early days of motion pictures, the primal representation in a medium that represents everything. His (or her) face and body are formed to refract the longings of an audience come to watch in the dark for clues to existence. And because we see him through the years, and are able—especially through television—to jumble the early with the late, the hard lines of his development are continually tender and palpable. His age and youth are poignantly, even cruelly, inseparable. The force of his flesh has been subject to pressures inconceivable when he first ascended through a density of roles to that height which made him a star and so transformed everything that came before and redeemed everything that followed.

Take Bogart, who came to us in 1923 as, of all things, a romantic juvenile and left us a mystical thirty-three years later the quintessence of the gutsy, hard-shelled, softhearted, fiercely independent master of the American ideal of grace under pressure. Follow him on either side of the law, tender or tough, rich or poor, respectable or living in the shadows: there was always the essential Bogart, somehow slightly out of phase with his role—just sufficiently independent of it so that he and his part bounced echoes off each other, created an aura loaded with reverberations that connected both part and personality in a way that gave us something to work with when we left the movie house, blinked away the comfortable darkness, and refocused the world.

Unlike an actor who blends into his role, the star is first a representation of himself. But this representation is so powerful that he is not just a man, but Bogart-man, Wayneman, Brandoman—the assertive sum of those unique values that he has accumulated, focused, and projected over the years. He need only enter the

frame for a scene to be charged with meanings that could not be duplicated by any other actor playing the same role. Indeed, so primal is the star in our world that we can see him only across the distance of our expectations so that what we finally respond to is a lonely figure isolated from his surroundings and inseparable from ours.

In all films the casting of actors to flesh the bones of a script is a skill so central to the film's final structure that at critical points it is impossible to separate the actor from the distant imagination that envisioned the role. The blend is seamless. Each actor brings, within the possibilities of his appearance, personality, skill, and range, a force that spins each part off into small but unique directions. But for the star, whose distinctive power lies in his uncanny ability to represent that image of self he has projected over the years through the formidable pressure of the parts he has played, the entire importance of a role is altered the moment he is named to play it.

In *The African Queen* John Huston and James Agee banished Bogart to one of those way stations on the edges of our civilization where endurance fulfills the requirement that heroism would demand in any other place. There he is thrust, soiled, slightly craven, a spongy shell of a creature, into the path of Katharine Hepburn, an awesome presence on the edge of whose fine temper the likes of Spencer Tracy had been brought to manhood. Bogey, cast against the grain, is set adrift down turbulent African waters with Hepburn the master of his fate. And seeping through his part, like the waters battering upon his frail craft, is the surge of those forces that brought him to us a star. His ultimate courage and strength wash through his characterization each timid step of the way so that his eventual transformation, which structures the film, is given the inevitability of an ancient Greek drama. We can only watch with the quiet satisfaction of seeing a ritual work its way through to its ordained conclusion. With more than an ordinary being in the role, what would have been simply an adventure has been turned into a parable on the final resilience of the human spirit.

Scripting Visual Conventions: The Star as Symbol

The mythic qualities of the star have so infused our culture that they both nourish our fantasies and make us hunger for more with an appetite as voracious as our deepest yearnings. This is the stuff of legends: each generation finding the meat in some secret place. Jean-Luc Godard, whose instincts prowl through our culture with the circuitous step of the hunter weaving for the kill, discovered Bogart two years after his death in the tough bramble of his gangster films and drew him into the traps of the 1960's—a wild and beautiful incarnation of a mournfully depleted stock.

Breathless canonized Bogart. It was a stylish reliquary for that idea of Bogart as a naturally independent agent in a world where independence seemed to have been martyred in the womb. In the bruised softness of Belmondo's face lined with nameless, angry battles that made his twenty-five years ageless, Bogart became a symbol. With a fierce nostalgia a generation brought to films unsatisfied—eager to see the vacancies in their lives justified, their restlessness given meaning, their unformed aspirations given structure—claimed their parents' dreams for themselves, tore them apart and reworked them with dazzling energy. At the center, a sensibility that saw the link between father and son as the thread which could make their natural hostility comprehensible. Bogart spanned the memory of two generations. But where his fearsome independence flickered and danced shadows in the dreams of the father, it was hauled into the light and tested as a possibility for the son.

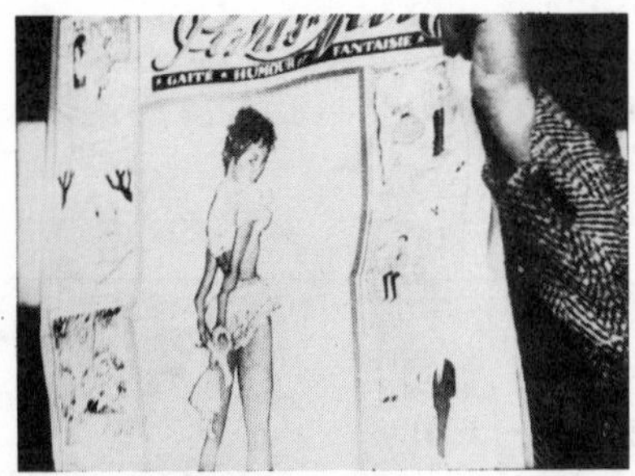

To be successful the Belmondo/Bogey role had to be developed obliquely. Any other way would have smacked of moralizing. So Belmondo literally appears to us out of the comic pages—those serialized fantasies that diffuse the headlines by cartooning the throb of violence and sex and so connect them to our lives with a heightened impersonality that we can handle. We soon learn that this is the way Belmondo has desensitized his world. Throughout the film he will move through a procession of action-packed tableaux stylized by his movie-struck sensibilities and bordered by the limits of his aspirations.

The film opens with the screen filled with a comic section that is lowered

to introduce the posturing Belmondo testing the rootless, tough-guy images that have sketched a stance toward life since the films of the 1930's. It is a neat piece of scripting that instantly asserts Belmondo's cautious sense of self and his wary feelings toward his society. With his thumb rubbing a tense upper lip, self-consciously evoking the Bogey aura of a wily disinterestedness coiled to challenge an irrational world in direct combat, we are hurled into his sprint through life. Soon after, he steals a car and shoots a cop, with the camera cartooning the act by working out the murder in a tableau of close-ups of the gun (see the flip sequence in Section 2). Then he meets up with the girl he will love after the cool fashion prescribed in a gangster film, and who will finally betray him in the same cool fashion.

Each step of the way Belmondo will test his actions against those of an image that he is re-creating by molding his face into a parade of grimaces that march from movie-anger to movie-joy and always end with the thumb testing a tightened upper lip. Quite early in the film he passes a movie house playing *The Harder They Fall* with a larger-than-life-size picture of Bogart on a poster advertising the film. With the cigarette strutting from his lips dancing in imitation to the pull of his movie hero, Belmondo, lovingly, reverently, mists the Bogey picture with an exhalation of smoke that seems to well up out of the fumes of his modern, city soul. Then he turns from the poster to re-create the Bogart image in the touch of his thumb against that archetypically tightened lip. From acts with less love and need than this, religions have been built.

In the end, when he has made his final dash down an alley, betrayed by his girl and mortally wounded by the police, even as he lies dying in the street, he

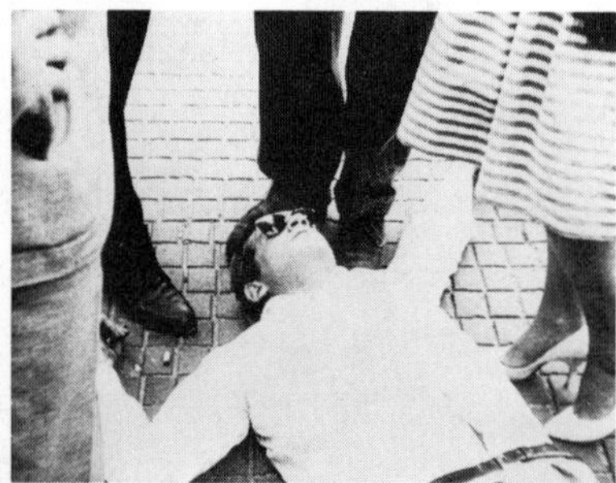

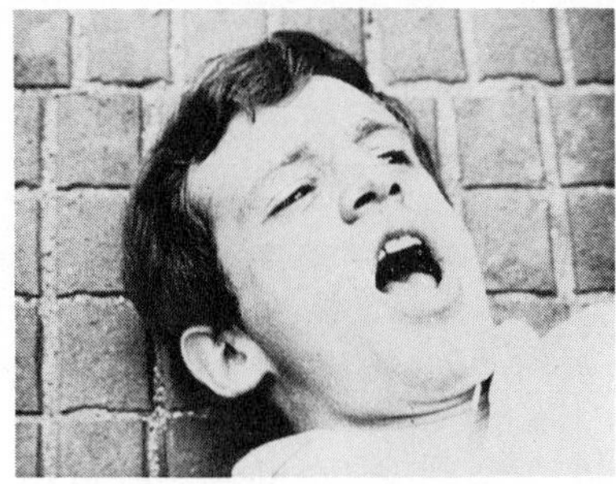

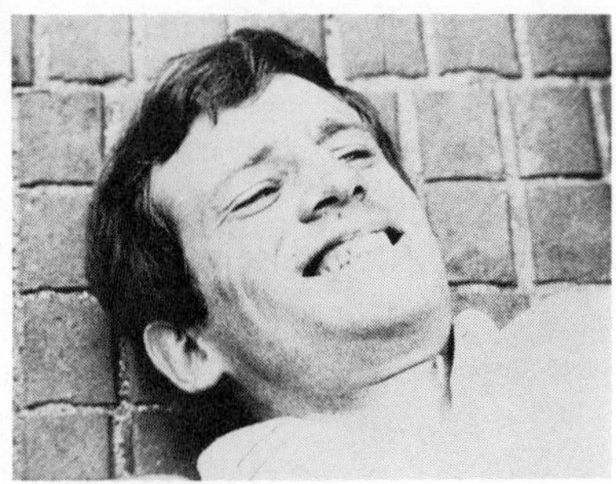

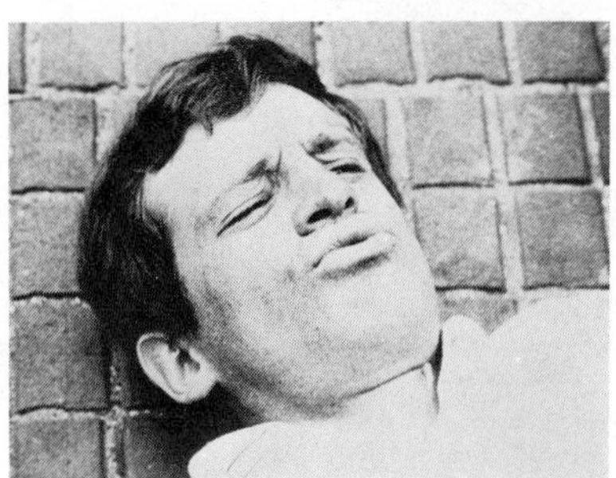

asserts his courage, his values, the importance of the few seconds that have become his lifetime by exhaling his last breathful of cigarette smoke and going once more through his ritual of grimaces before he dies. A last amen is formed by the girl as she completes the litany with the move of her thumb across her lips—then she turns away and the film ends.

Scripting Story Conventions

By evoking the Bogey aura and resurrecting the world of the gangster films of the 1930's and 1940's, Godard found a way into the structure of those myths of our immediate past that sensitized the dreams of our youth. Each evocation, by asserting the fragile connection between longing and aspiration, fills the image with a poignance, a lost sense of romance, that both enlarges and focuses the world of its hero. Through this use of film convention, Godard has given his images a resonance from which he can shape those melodies that force his film into our lives with unexpected energy.

By drawing upon such film conventions, the film-maker can swell even his sparest image with feelings and implications that might otherwise be unavailable or, at least, take elaborate construction to achieve. It is a quick way of creating an assertion because it draws upon aspects of a common language to tap those shared experiences that bind a people to their culture. This is not so much the reconstruction of a myth as it is an evocation of the language that houses the myth. And even when that language has grown and changed in the imaginations of succeeding generations that felt the need to use and test it, what still remains is the unalterable core of emotion at its heart wrapped in just the minimal images needed to bring it to life. Armed with this language, the film-maker starts out with a primal resource that he can use—if only in occasional phrases—in the construction of both his thoughts and his films.

This Whirlpool commercial cleverly uses a cinematic story convention to make one simple point: the company has set meticulous standards for its servicemen in the repair of its products. But the message we get has enormous strength. We are immediately placed in one of those timeless courtyards in which unspeakable brutalities seem to rise from the stones like a cold, damp mist. There we look down on three figures waiting—until a half-expected black limousine pulls into view. Out of the car slithers a figure whose cruelty and authority we understand the instant we see the taut contours of his face. He has come to us out of the swamp of half-remembered barbarities that we have witnessed and felt in films whose names we have long forgotten. From first view he is inquisitor, Gestapo chief, subtle torturer—so closely woven to our anxieties that just his appearance makes our hearts beat faster.

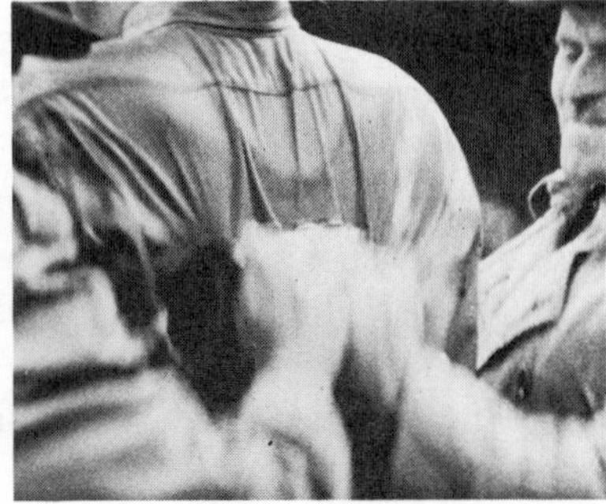

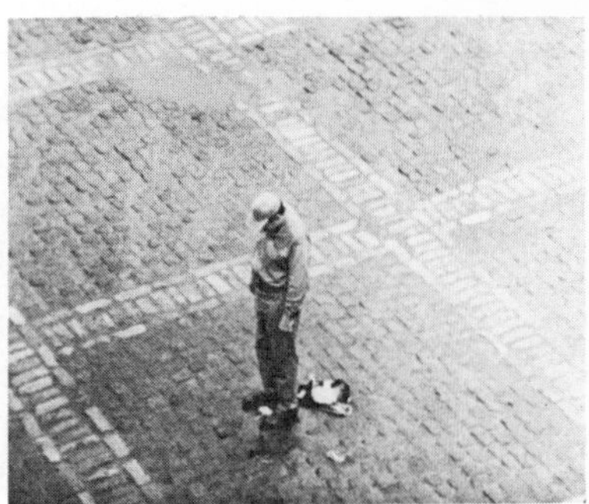

And then the ritual ceremony of disgrace. The fallen Whirlpool repairman, looking so strongly middle American and caught in nightmares given flesh by two generations of film-makers, passively accepts his punishment for sins more felt than understood. Finally, to our relief, the convention is turned back upon itself in an image that parodies the fearful world that has entrapped us. Here the commercial shifts to an older convention telling of dishonor instead of death. But instead of epaulets and insignia of unquestioned value being torn from the repairman, his tormentors rip off his Whirlpool emblem and leave him to stand in mock shame while we smile at the absurdity of his condition and the frightening vulnerability of ours.

Here a film convention was used to evoke and then parody a world that exists purely in a shared language of images created and elaborated upon by a succession of film-makers. While the fears and anxieties stored within the images are as real as our dreams, the visual language that makes them accessible is real only within the

contrivances that have come to objectify these elusive emotions. Without our cultural awareness of their implications much of the meaning of these images is lost. We have become like tribes that have learned their culture from campfire stories woven from phrases and characters that have gradually come to represent the complexities of their fears and hopes. The film-maker has these images, which are instantly recognizable, powerfully felt, at his command to spin into stories for an audience grown to maturity on their meanings.

Scripting with Locations

But these conventions need not dominate the film-maker's frame to be effective. Those objects and shapes that enclose the characters in a film story in themselves form a considerable part of the film-maker's visual language. They are not merely an arbitrary succession of locations in which events happen during the course of a film, but a series of precisely controlled environments that often complete the meaning of the action and occasionally even create that meaning.

It is no accident that John Ford shot all or part of nine films in the powerfully sculptured Monument Valley, where the red buttes rise from the mesa with a lonely grandeur and persistence. These shapes project a sense of man's unconquerable determination while humbling the transiently ferocious activities played out within their shadows. From film to film the repetition of this background gives it an accumulation of meanings. By *Cheyenne Autumn,* when it bore witness to the flight of a small tribe of Indians instead of the heroic escapades of the United States cavalry, its looming presence endowed the film with such a close feeling for the textures of history that the plight of these Indians became bitterly inseparable from our sense of the easy triumphs of the cavalry pursuing them.

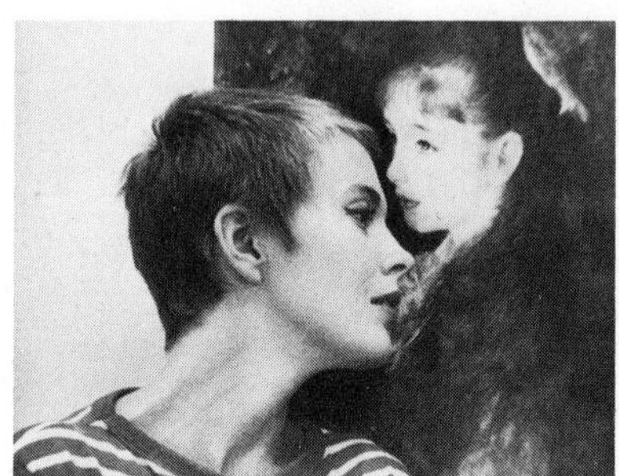

And on a smaller scale, it is more than just whim that possessed Jean-Luc Godard, in *Breathless,* to frame Belmondo's mercurial, evanescent Patricia in graceful, haunting contrast against the fragile permanence of a Renoir girl. Or made François Truffaut, in *Jules and Jim,* enclose, for a memorable instant, the hot tragicomical pursuit by the two rivals of the illusive woman they love within a tightly caged stretch of a narrow bridge, thus summarizing the inflexible borders that bound the three together. These are decisions that go to the very structure of a film.

Similarly, through the masterful use of a cavernous building Federico Fellini, in *The White Sheik,* captured the growing anxiety of a young husband from the

Courtesy: JANUS FILMS, INC.

provinces who has lost his wife during their honeymoon visit to Rome. With some

trepidation the husband has gone to the police to ask for their help in finding her. They disbelieve his story and, for a moment, he is left alone in the massive office. When he looks out the window, he sees a jeep full of police pull into the courtyard. As the squad jumps from the jeep, it is just too much for him. His village soul feels naked. He is vulnerable in their presence and he turns to flee. But, in escaping the window, he knocks over a bundle of documents. As it crashes to the floor with a frightening thud, he bolts down the long room. Piles of anonymous documents con-

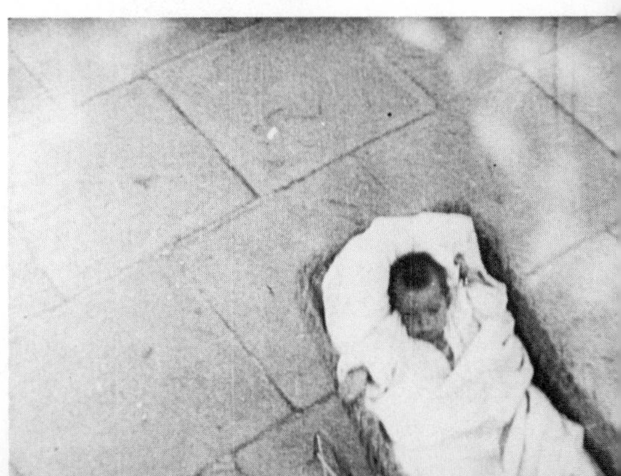

taining god-knows-what on god-knows-whom litter the office. As a faceless bureaucrat enters the room carrying another armload of the mysterious files, the now absolutely terrified husband charges past him into a narrow hallway that holds even more of the eerie documents piled against its walls. He dashes down the corridor,

charges through a door, and immediately confronts still another faceless transporter of these endless files. He cautiously edges around him and his ominous load and finally makes it to the stairwell, where, on each level of his descent, he sees more and more dossiers piled in increasingly alarming numbers.

Fellini has made the building and the documents conspire against the miserable husband. Although not a word is spoken nor a real threat even implied, we see this absolutely guiltless man absorb the guilt suggested by the very existence of the building with its wretched files. Fellini is carefully working the labyrinthian ways that tunnel our fears, and within these drear walls he has entombed the dreadful mounds of files and reports. Seizing his images out of the fragments of our most anxious moments, he has entrapped us in a setting that speaks to us directly. He knows our vulnerability and he has expressed it clearly in a language that is as precise as a set of detailed instructions.

The intense interrelationship between the setting and the action, in which the distinction between foreground and background is obliterated under the spell of their intricate involvement, has been scripted out of an available visual language molded by our cultural awareness. The dreamlike spaces of the offices and hallways can mean something to us only when they have been controlled by an intelligence that has recognized the submerged universality of the drama and then has been able to find the touchstone images to express it. In this sequence Fellini defines the spaces of the building—gives a specific meaning to their emptiness—by anchoring them with the ubiquitous piles of paperwork. The meaning of the unspecified bundles of documents gradually becomes apparent, and with it the nightmare of the rooms that hold them. They are assertions about our culture that have been formed by sharply focusing the scattered images produced by that culture. Once we can feel as a people that we are drowning in a sea of paper, then the moment the film-maker allows us to recognize that paper, we begin to drown.

Yet, even when the lives of the film characters exist in a fiercely personal world, the images that support and develop that world must be drawn from publicly recognizable associations. In *Hiroshima Mon Amour* Alain Resnais crafted a tortured love story between a French woman, who loved and was punished for loving a German soldier in Nevers during the occupation, and a married Japanese architect living in Hiroshima after the war.

Much of the film exists in the twitches of memory that torment and explain the woman. Resnais brought the story to its painful conclusion by inflicting the Nevers of memory on the Hiroshima that is soon to become a memory. The woman knows she must leave her lover; he knows she must leave. As she walks through the neon-lit streets of Hiroshima, followed at a distance by her lover—their impending separation exquisitely unfolding into physical reality—she broods about the end of their love:

> I meet you.
> I remember you.
> This city was made to the size of love.
> You were made to the size of my body.
> Who are you?
> You destroy me.
> A time will come. When we'll no more know what
> thing it is that binds us. By slow degrees the
> word will fade from our memory.
> Then it will disappear altogether.

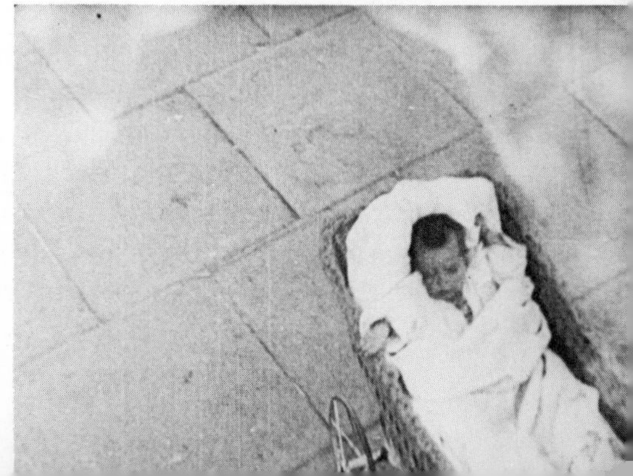

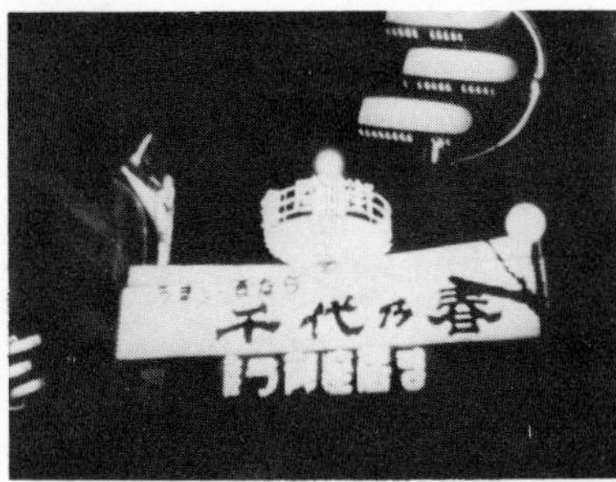

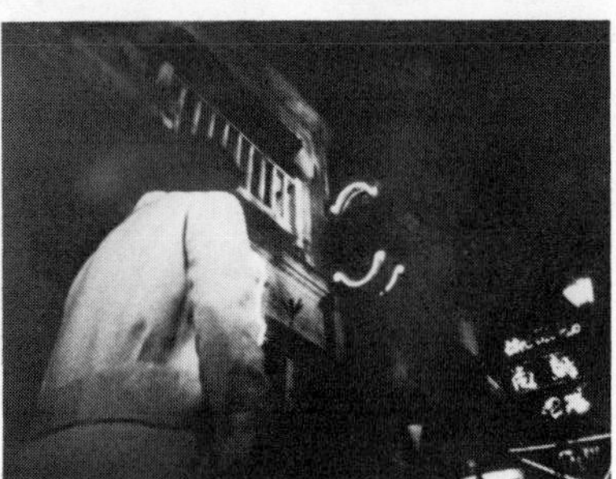

During this passage we see the thin, bright, gaudy lights of Hiroshima set in counterpoint to the gray, heavy stone of Nevers. Her reality is a dream gliding through the flickering night world of the reborn Hiroshima while her memories are anchored in the solid stone that has become a mausoleum entombing her past. The feverish strands of her life that stretch directly from the twisted streets of Nevers to the shallow avenues of Hiroshima have been made palpable in the splay of textures that penetrate our senses with the raw authority of their relentless associations.

While the significance of the images that form Hiroshima and Nevers are carefully developed during the course of the film, it is still our learned feelings about neon and stone, darkness and dawn, newness and age that complete our understanding of the depth of the woman's emotions. The tacky, insubstantial promise of the malformed Hiroshima makes her decision to flee the present not only comprehensible but felt. Set against the enclosed solidity of the inescapable Nevers, we know from our sense of the stone that she must return there again and again until it grows too heavy for her to bear its weight. Eventually she will be crushed.

It is out of the force of these learned feelings that Marcel Carné was able to work the bleak, dehumanizing shapes of the industrial world to contour the spirit of the troubled hero of *Le Jour Se Lève*. François, played by Jean Gabin, is an orphan, raised by the state and brutalized by it at every point of contact. When the film opens, he has walled himself into a room after murdering a man during a passionate argument about a woman. As he waits for the inevitable arrival of the police—and his death, which must follow—he thinks about the events that have entrapped him in his small room. His first memory is of his meeting with the girl who finally penetrated his isolation, redeemed his life, only to ensnare him accidentally in the events which have led to the murder.

Courtesy: JANUS FILMS, INC.

In this memory Carné first shows us the factory—an ugly silhouette against the hopeful morning sky—that forms François's sole point of contact with the narrow society he inhabits. Then we see him enchained inside his grotesque protective suit brutishly laboring in the workshop of the sandblasting factory. Without elaboration the setting has rigorously defined François's world and his unhappy place within it.

Carné has resurrected the industrial nightmare that has fascinated film-makers since the 1920's to drive toward his portrait of a unique man afflicted with familiar wounds. François's temperament, strength, his need to love and suffer, to continually challenge a world he despises are all set in sharp relief against Carné's evocation of the common horrors of an urbanized world. Just the presence of that summation of independence, Jean Gabin, toiling in a factory is sufficient to fill the screen with enough tension to pitch us headlong into the drama of a man stubbornly at war with a world he will not allow to destroy him.

Courtesy: JANUS FILMS, I

At this point we see the girl—a stranger to this ugliness—almost a vision in her light, flowered dress, carrying a pot of azaleas—surrounded by the inhuman shapes of the factory and its laborers. In a particularly lyrical shot the camera recedes before her soft steps outside the nether reaches of the workshop; pauses as she reaches its brink—her world still separated, for a final instant, from the grotesques within; and then turns with her as she enters—a breath of air; an absurd, fragile loveliness expanding the room with the unexpected possibilities she contains.

Once the girl has entered the factory with her silly flowered dress and potted plant, Carné has made us aware, without belaboring the fact, that we are in the presence of two outcasts, severed from the world and destined for each other and tragedy. Later in the film Carné will extend their symbolic estrangement from society by setting the consummation of their love in the artificial warmth of a greenhouse, where beauty survives only in careful isolation.

The setting in which a scene exists need not just complement the action to extend its meanings. The ambience of the setting can phrase a language so powerful that the location, even more than the action, becomes the vessel carrying the filmmaker's full intentions.

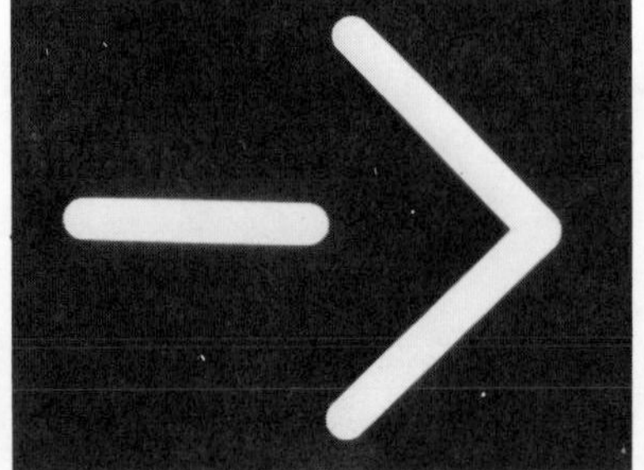

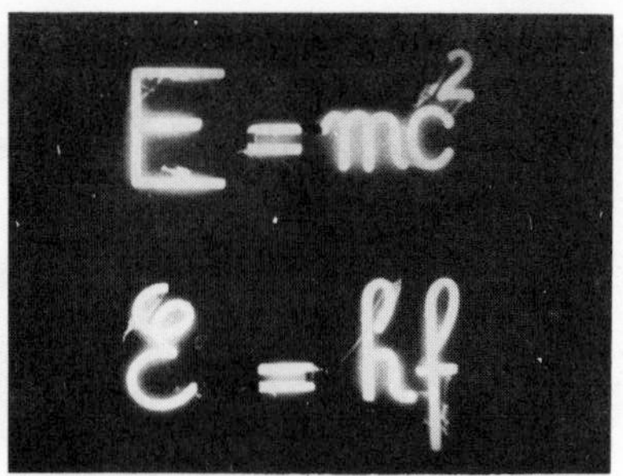

Jean-Luc Godard, who continually discovered small beauties in the corners of Paris his camera explored during his early films, abstracted that same Paris in *Alphaville* and transformed it into a nightmarish city of the future where emotion, instinct, and spontaneity have become enemies of a state whose chilling slogan reads: "ALPHAVILLE. SILENCE. LOGIC. SAFETY. PRUDENCE." The locations in the film: "Deserted lobbies, parking lots, shopping plazas, cloverleaf intersections, curtain wall buildings, self-service elevators, hotel bathrooms, phone-booths, circular staircases, highways around large cities, a bedroom with a juke box." This is Paris lobotomized; but it is, nonetheless, full on the screen, Paris.

In a particularly striking scene Godard turns a large swimming pool into a place where political prisoners are executed in large groups. The prisoners, wearing street clothes, line the side of the pool patiently awaiting their turn for death. As officials of the State watch from the spectators' balcony, each prisoner is led to the edge of the diving board, is allowed a few moments to make a last impassioned oration on freedom, love, and human solidarity, and then is mechanically cut down in a burst of machine-gun fire. As the victim falls into the pool, a line of girls—

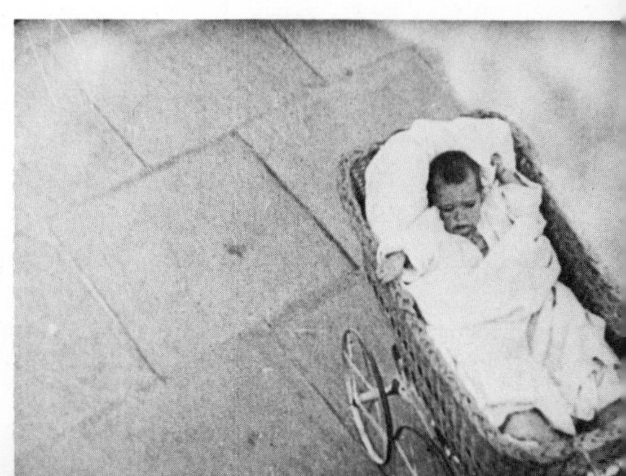

dressed and choreographed out of the inane water ballet short films of the 1940's—dive into the pool, and with knives as shapely, sleek, and antiseptic as their cool, long legs they draw for the State the last blood of each prisoner in as graceful a *coup de grâce* as one could expect to see.

Godard has exploited every conceivable aspect of the swimming pool to draw us into his dream of Alphaville. It is the large, hollow, pristine, echoing spaces of the pool that are the conduit for the crucial details that form the passionless, frightened world of this wretched city whose limits skirt the edges of our consciousness. This is no bleak courtyard to tear at the heart with its ugly, pitted walls stained with the blood of martyrs and waiting to receive its victims in the dread first light of dawn. Here everything is antiseptic—polished tile, shadowless fluorescent lighting, and precise racing lines reflected in the chlorinated waters of the pool. Even the defiant speeches of the condemned are hollow echoes in this chamber. They are finally as inhuman as the echoing gunfire that abruptly cuts them off. This is not a place for passion. Its dimensions comfortably hold the mindless aquatic dance whose rigid grace already speaks of death. Within these waters that have no currents, the flash of a knife and the flash of a limb are barely distinguishable. The horror is not in the killing; it is in the death drained of meaning by the setting in which it occurs.

Scripting with Props

Even a detail within a setting can speak to an audience with a clarity and strength that pierces both the action and its environment with the force of its meanings. It is this transformation of the ordinary into major assertions about the nature of the lives explored on the screen that provides the film-maker with a vocabulary as rich in intricacies as the tightly woven lines of a poem.

Fritz Lang, in his classic study of a psychopathic child murderer, *M,* gathers the separate threads that form the comfortable middle-class world and the world of criminals that feeds off it to stitch a picture of society that coheres at the seams where the facing and the backing join to form the garment. The murders are so horrifying that the shape of society itself is threatened, and both criminal and police are charged to find and exterminate the killer so they can restore their comfortable balance.

The child murderer is embodied by Peter Lorre, in—and there is really no other word for it—a breathtaking performance, as a mentally atrophied, physically immature mutant born to the solid petty bourgeoisie. Lang continually asserts this connection between the murderer and the class he has betrayed. The murderer wears the overstuffed suits, coat, and stylish hat of his class as he wanders the streets in search of prey. As pressure mounts for his capture, Lang, with painstaking care, describes his angered bourgeois brothers behind screens of expensive bric-a-brac placed upon their tables like articles of faith expressing their pos-

Courtesy: JANUS FILMS, INC.

sessions, achievements, and place in life. But when we next see the murderer, now firmly established as an outcast, he is seated on a café terrace—not surrounded by the intricate cups and vessels that are his birthright—but through a bramble-covered trellis, his comfortable coat and hat hidden in the darkness and his face, isolated from all connection with his world, glowing like that of a cunning beast hidden in the forest.

The murderer, visually, has been defrocked. He has been severed from the

Courtesy: JANUS FILMS, INC.

prerogatives of his class. But he is also anathema to the criminal world, which is equally horrified by his crimes. In their way these criminal outcasts form an identically structured society. Lang takes great pains to show this parallel and through it a chilling conception of man in which his irrationality, his uncontrollable impulses, must be chained at all levels, even the lowest, by this rigid need for order.

At those lofty points of authority, where these two worlds merge, both bourgeois and outlaw carry the formal weight of their society distilled in their garments. Here, the chief police investigator conducts his inquiry with his formal hat and cane prominently resting like an insignia beside him in the foreground. From this shot Lang cuts directly to an investigation held by the criminals, presided over

by their chief with an identical hat and cane stabilizing the screen with the implicit authority and respectability they offer their owner. Nothing could tell us more so quickly about the bond between these worlds that have become a mirror image of each other.

In the end, when the murderer is finally captured by the outcasts and brought to their parody of a trial, it is a rumpled, hatless creature that is presented to them.

It is as though, with the loss of his hat, the murderer has finally been stripped of his last connection with civilized society. Frightened and dislocated he is brought to judgment before his superiors, each of whom is armed and shielded by his

covered head. The impact of this ominous wave of covered heads, waiting, poised at its crest ready to smash him, is terrific. He is broken. While an appointed "lawyer" argues his defense—with a hat securely resting by his side—the murderer, totally isolated, crouches against a barricade hiding his naked head in shame and despair.

This use of the traditional, ritualistic, evocative, and symbolic elements attached to a covering for the head was later employed by John Ford in *The Informer* as a running signal to key his audience into his hero's state of mind. George Bluestone points out that when Gypo (a man who has betrayed his friend in the Irish rebellion to the British for twenty pounds) "is cocky and sure of himself, the cap sits on his head at a jaunty angle. When he is nervous and unsure, as in the Tan headquarters, or at the court of inquiry, he twists it nervously in his hand, or uses

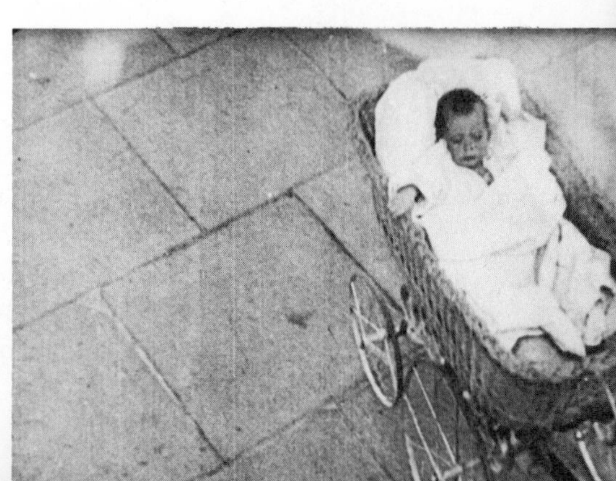

it to wipe the perspiration from his face. Toward the end, from the time of his imprisonment to his death, Gypo goes bareheaded."

Courtesy: JANUS FILMS,

The cap is more than just a prop that works as a security blanket for the hero in good times and in times of stress. Gypo, as played by Victor McLaglen, is a simple, brutish hulk of a man who puzzles his way through the intrigues of the bitter Irish revolt with a primitive inarticulateness. He can comprehend and express so little that the way he uses his cap in response to the complexities of life continually describes, to a large extent, his limited emotions. And because this simple device is so fully descriptive, it helps draw for us that crucial, moving picture of Gypo, dumb and ape-necked, at odds with a world just beyond his grasp. It is this careful portrait that opens the well of sympathy that must be drawn from again and again to make his actions appear pathetic, eventually even tragic, rather than despicable. And it is from this delicate response to him that the film succeeds as a poignant study of a simple man, an innocent, for whom the fierce demands of the world are just too much.

Scripting a Conception of the World with Editing

The elements which combine to form film art give rise to assertions not only about the characters in a film but also about the nature of the universe in which they are enclosed. The continuous flow of action that transmits the film-maker's story is carved out of a thousand and one separate shots, each of which tells its own tale. The camera position, lighting, setting, costumes, and sound that combine within the shot only to be modified, altered, transformed, even violated, in succeeding shots give the film both a pulse and a point of view unique in the narrative arts.

In each film we are strangers in the house of the film-maker. Even if the furniture has a relation to our own, the sliding walls, the changing heights and depths, the expanding and contracting dimensions of each room, thrust us precipitously upon each leg of a tour conducted along paths made familiar only by the associations that cohere to form the film's structure. Yet this strange house is built to hold an image of man, and from its form emerges a picture of him singular in its construction. These images impress themselves upon us out of the substance of dreams, ordering our impressions through a succession of tantalizing individual glimpses of man's relationship with the world. We are in the presence of nothing less than a conception of man crafted out of the necessities of an art that has brought him to us in a new life.

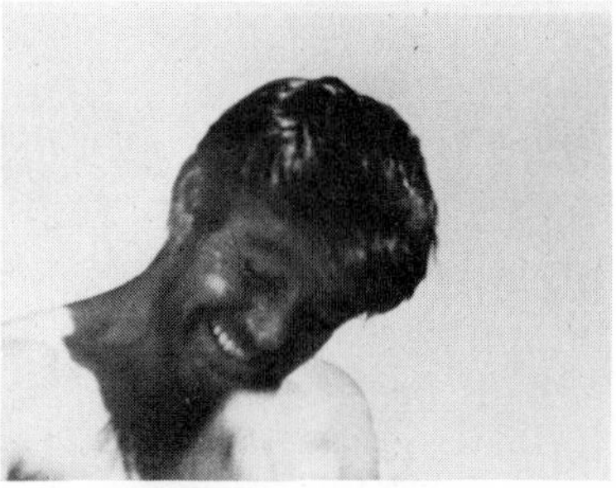

Cy Endfield's *Sands of the Kalahari* details the adventures of a group of plane crash victims as they struggle for survival in the African desert. In the scene excerpted on these pages, three members of the starving group must attack and kill a desert animal if they are to survive. From the moment the beast charges into

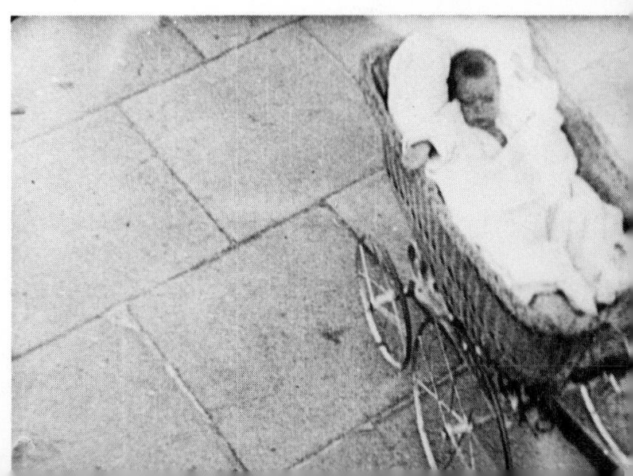

their midst, they are forced into a cohesive unit. They have become predators. The arguments that have marred their heroic attempt to escape the African wastes are forgotten. But even as a unit, where the survival of each totally depends upon the actions of the others, they are separated by the film-maker, isolated in their individual struggles, and severed from the surrounding world. We look down upon them, up at them, and straight across at them. During the course of the sequence we see each alternately framed either by the relentless sand from which there is no escape, or against the high, arcing, clear African sky. In most of the shots there is only a hint of the beast, and in many we don't see it at all. Each man is essentially alone.

Within seconds each is shown a hero and a coward, a man who can master his destiny and one who has fallen prey to it. It is, in short, a brutally existential projection of man that shows him separated by his individual needs from the rest of the world and yet forced to respond intimately to its demands. He is clearly isolated, judged in terms of his own resources, made the measure of his own responses, even while at the center of an encounter that has made his life fully contingent upon the actions of other men.

The scene is a pounding progression of close shots relieved only by one ironic long shot that shows the men as infinitesimal creatures whose struggle is no more than the churning of sands that will quickly shift and leave no memory.

It is this cut to the long shot, at the climax of the action, that joins two disparate views of man and makes them immediately congruent. Once the image of man's easy perishability becomes entwined with his heroic, self-important struggle to survive, we have begun to follow Sisyphus up the mountain.

This is no easy irony imposed upon the action. It flows logically from the structure that makes the sequence work. For the action to be comprehensible each cut must first move that action forward, with each new angle clarifying the shots before and setting up the ones that will follow. The long shot does exactly that; and, in the process, offers a needed pause after the succession of driving close-ups. But, in addition, with each cut we are forced to piece together, bit by bit, a view of that action which also gives us a shifting perspective of the men involved in it. It is from the unraveling of all these shots that the essential relationship of each man to the other and each to his world is developed and clarified.

Out of the inherent drama and excitement of the battle—brought to a fever pitch by its presentation—Endfield has constructed a coherent and moving picture of man fashioned out of the very materials that brought him to us as a mere function of his adventures. It is the variety of angles, rhythmically intercut to emphasize the force of the struggle, from which this picture is drawn. This is not a probing work of art made to send its audiences back into the streets overflowing with philosophic notions. It is an adventure picture, and a very good one. But it is in the nature of cinema itself, which allows both for man's isolation in close-ups and for

shots that can be continually angled to make his world a function of his presence in it, from which this existential conception of man has emerged.

Each camera position is a statement. And each bit of film joined to another is a statement. But the flow of action that draws its meaning from this flood of perspectives and associations is as much a statement about the nature of man as it is about the drama of the particular men who happen to fill the screen. As in this scene from *Sands of the Kalahari,* many of the final impressions of a film cut through the action and come to reside in the technique. The lives in romantic conflict here bear not the slightest connection to our own, and yet a picture is drawn that tells us a good deal about ourselves. It is the imprint of that picture that finally rests in the memory, allowing us those movie-house dreams that have charged our lives with their strangely persistent relevance.

Because we have it available to us and are already familiar with it, let's look at how this works over the extended sequence of the Odessa Steps from *Battleship Potemkin.* If we just casually flip through it, it quickly becomes apparent that Eisenstein built his vivid impression of the massacre out of the individualized details of fear and suffering. Although the fluid inevitability of the action, keyed to the relentless descent of the Cossacks down the steps, fuses the events into a seamless blend, we experience this tragedy only through the horror of a score of separately personalized events. While the Cossacks are always seen together, undifferentiated, an animal stalking on a hundred legs, spewing forth death at random, it is the masses who are given a soul in the slices of agony peeled from their number. Here a close-up of an individual is a revelation of his humanity.

In a revolutionary world in which the hero ultimately must be the group from which an individual only briefly emerges, a critical aspect of the drama exists in the picture of the individual strands and fibers that go to form the group. Eisenstein used his camera to separate and differentiate the components that comprise his masses and then went to his editing room to reassemble them as a collective force, an inevitable moment in the progress of the world. This tension between the world recorded by the camera and the world assembled in the editing room allows us to feel each shock while understanding the historic imperatives that make each man we see part of a fixed revolutionary design.

It is because of Eisenstein's discovery of the capability of film to resolve events in this fashion that he was able to place his art so effectively at the service of his politics. A world that can move men to pity at the plight of the individual and still blend the individual into a portrait of his society is a world that is perfect for expressing the ontology upon which the propaganda of that society can flourish. The artistry of Leni Riefenstahl in the service of the Nazis, Humphrey Jennings in the service of the British, Frank Capra in the service of the United States during World War II brilliantly exploited this aspect of film to arouse a people by giving them a heroic sense of their country while also showing them their necessarily small but organic place within it.

In the two films we just looked at, the careful camera work and editing served to create an extensive picture of man which existed independently of the story line and yet served to complement it and give it additional power. In the hunt scene from *Sands of the Kalahari* the isolation of the characters asserted their essential responsibility for their own actions. In the "Odessa Steps" sequence it dramatized their fragmentary role in the large rhythms of history. The effectiveness of both scenes grew from these philosophic positions, which gave the action the stature of an insight into the human condition. The importance of this susceptibility of film to ordering man's place in the universe with the effortlessness of a cut or a close-up lies in the control this gives the film-maker over the final effect of his script. Within the basic techniques which he must employ to make his film lie those same elements which he can use to summarize his feelings on the elemental nature of the universe his characters will inhabit.

The close-up and the rhythmic use of cuts, of course, do more to tell the film-maker's story than just to define his speculative attitudes toward the nature of his characters. On the most accessible level they move his story on by building a mood and place while emphasizing the details that are crucial in its telling.

In this brief moment from John Ford's *My Darling Clementine* Wyatt Earp first meets the leading members of the powerful and evil Clanton family, who will

eventually force him into that life-and-death shoot-out at O.K. Corral immortalized in a number of films. At this point we know little about them when we see the Clantons framed in the first two-shot. Ford then cuts to a lingering close-up of Old Man Clanton (Walter Brennan), who fills the screen with his ominous power behind the clenched hand of his eldest son. He then cuts directly to Earp (Henry Fonda), framed against the skies of his Tombstone, and we know that it will be man-to-man, these two antagonists kept apart in space but entwined, set against each other to the death. The cutting rhythm, the camera angles, the juxtaposition of shots have combined to set up the film's basic oppositions succinctly and with clarity and force. The technique used here has been used in so many films that it is needless to belabor the point.

Scripting with Continuous Space

It is well worth detailing, however, the importance to each script of the decisions that control the kinds of space that the characters inhabit. Space in films need not always be fragmented to be effective. Montage is just one of a number of film conventions, even though its power was discovered by some of the earliest film-makers, who saw that individual shots are given their life and meaning from the shots that come before and the ones that go after. In this process, though, the immense and unique power of motion-picture photography to preserve accurately actions occurring in real space and real time is lost. This ability has been replaced by an artifice that continually loosens the bonds of space and time that hold the real world together. A new reality has been created. It may be thoroughly compelling and moving, but it has lost the effect of its organic connection with the physical world it seems to describe.

Thus the cut that separates parts of a continuing action is a decision to stylize that action radically. It is the creation of something new built from slices of space and increments of time seized from the world. By constructing the contrasts, affinities, ironies, and tensions that form the totality of a film from a succession of single images, the relationship of the action on the screen to the world has become more imaginary than real.

The great French film theorist André Bazin developed this insight into a concerted approach toward film-making. He argued that while all films are basically edited in this fashion (montage), the film-maker must be aware of the effect produced by this violation of reality.

> All that matters is that the spectator can say at one and the same time that the basic material of the film is authentic while the film is also truly cinema. So the screen reflects the ebb and flow of our imagination which feeds on a reality for which it plans to substitute. That is to say, the tale is born of an experience that the imagination transcends. Correspondingly, however, what is imaginary on the screen must have the spatial density of something real.

As an example, Bazin points to what he calls an unforgettable sequence in an otherwise mediocre English film, *Where No Vultures Fly*. A child has wandered away from her parents' camp in the South African bush and has found a lion cub. The lioness, alerted to the threat to her offspring, follows the child and cub back to the camp. As they approach the camp, the child's parents see their child with the lioness close behind ready to spring on her. Bazin explains that up to this point everything has been shown in parallel montage. We are given alternating views of the child and the lioness. "Then suddenly, to our horror, the director abandons his montage of separate shots that has kept the protagonists apart and gives us instead parents, child, and lioness all in the same full shot. This single frame in which trickery is out of the question gives immediate and retroactive authenticity to the very banal montage that has preceded it." Bazin points out that, despite the concrete nature of each shot, the total effect of this intercutting is to produce a story rather than a real event. But once all the participants are fused in one shot, the force of its reality "carries us at once to the heights of cinematographic emotion." He concludes that the power of the realism here "resides in the homogeneity of space."

The decision, then, to allow the characters in a scene to share contiguous space argues for the reality of that scene. When this occurs within a structure that has fragmented that space with impunity, isolating its characters from shot to shot, its effect also becomes an assertion of the meanings that can be drawn from the simple physical relationships that combine to fill the frame.

Alfred Hitchcock recognized this by introducing, in *The Lady Vanishes,* the comedy team of Basil Radford and Naunton Wayne as an archetype of the provincial English mentality that places the importance of a cricket match ahead of any disaster that does not affect the playing of it. Caught in an avalanche and surrounded by murderous spies, their only concern is in reaching England in time for the Test Match. Each man is an echo of the other. So in the comic opening third of the film, Hitchcock seals them together within the frame, shot after shot, scene after scene, almost like a pair of Siamese twins, each of whom can have no life without the other by his side. As the plot develops, the Englishmen eventually get

Courtesy: JANUS FILMS, INC.

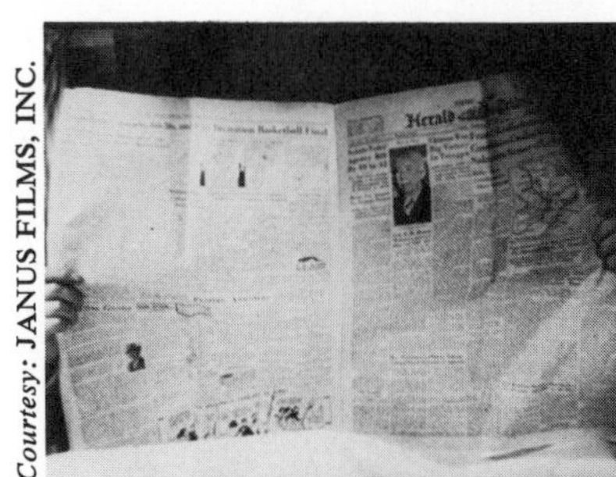

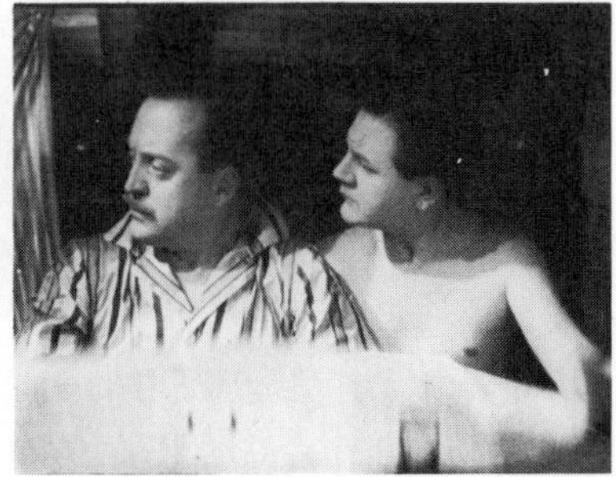

involved with the lives of the imperiled people around them. They act, and so are seen, as individuals finally separated from one another as if they had emerged from the cocoon of comforting space that had nourished their insularity.

The most dramatic technique for combining actors and objects in assertive relationships within the frame is called *deep focus*. Here all the details of the setting that run from the foreground to the furthest reaches of the background are carefully lit and sharply defined. The action no longer skims across the surface but extends to the limits of the space in which it occurs. Instead of cutting from detail to detail to build a scene, one extended shot is created. This permits the actors to move freely within the frame and develop a fluid series of significant relationships among themselves, and also between themselves and each part of their setting. The world is seen with a force drawn from its continuous unfolding in the uninterrupted space and time that we associate with reality.

With the extraordinary camera and lighting techniques of Gregg Toland at his command, in his first film, the landmark *Citizen Kane,* the twenty-five-year-old Orson Welles exploited composition in depth with the ferocity of a caged imagination compulsively pushing at the inhibiting boundaries of expression itself. The characters in the film are enveloped in a succession of assertive environments that both instantly pinpoint the significance of each scene and also enlarge our feeling for the scope of the drama by extending their lives to fill the entire space within view. Thus every inch of the screen has been made to conform to the dramatic structure of the moment.

In this scene Kane has just lost his race for governor. For him it is the end of a cherished personal ambition. As he stands alone in the great composing room of his newspaper, the walls littered with the bitter reminders of his campaign, his close friend, Jedediah Leland, enters drunk and angry to tell Kane that he has betrayed the principles for which he so glibly campaigned.

In this meticulous shot we see in the foreground the hulking figure of the great man as he listens to the only man who will tell him the truth carefully placed in the depths of the background, while between them lies the monumental space that will soon separate them forever. What we see is the essence of their relationship beautifully designed on the screen: Charles Foster Kane, a flawed monolith rising large out of the wreckage of his ambitions, battered yet always heroic in scope, listening to the gentle, uncertain voice in the distance offering him the honesty and conviction which is nothing less than the love Kane needs to be complete but which will always be just beyond his grasp. There they are held, in the embrace of the newsroom where they shared their dreams, now emptied of everything except the reminders of a failure that they both share. There they are bound, in that terrible distance which so eloquently separates them.

By sculpting the scene out of the large block of space he constructed at the opening of the shot, Welles provided himself a particularly expressive material with which to work the dramatic and emotional intricacies of his story. When Kane moves to Leland to offer him his friendship, he must walk the length of the room, and we are physically aware of the great man's efforts to establish contact with one of the few true friends he has. Kane diminishes in size with each step toward Leland, becoming more human and more vulnerable during what we can see has become a journey of reconciliation. And when Leland rejects him, Kane returns to the foreground and to the brutish size it grants him. But now the camera follows Kane's movement, isolating him by severing Leland from the space of his world. Good friend Leland has been reduced to a nagging voice in the prophetic distance.

Both the physical depth and the temporal continuity of the shot have been used to project each small shift in the emotional balance of Kane and Leland's volatile relationship. What is apparent on the screen is a translation of the basic emotions the characters feel just beneath the surface. Because they are joined in space through most of the scene, it is the essential congruence of their lives, and not the dramatic hostility of their words, that carries the meaning of their confrontation.

It is this inclusive use of continuous space that allows the film-maker both to conceive and realize relationships of enormous complexity and to have them understood with clarity and feeling. It is an admission that the physical world, which has been reduced to images, is still of such magnitude that the actual relationship of its parts has a force worth reckoning with. It is an understanding that the literal flow of time, which binds a series of actions, is, in itself, an assertion of the essential relevance of the continuity of those actions.

Although deep focus has influenced a whole style of film-making, it is still rare for it to be exploited to the extended limits used by Welles in *Citizen Kane*. But composition in depth is just one way of realizing the possibilities of continuous space. More common and equally effective, though usually less spectacular, is the expressive unification of space through the use of a camera moving freely within it.

Laurence Goldstein opened his short film about a radical poverty program in West Virginia with one shot that ran 20 percent of the film's length. We first see the outside of a flourishing coal mine from which millions of dollars of coal are extracted yearly; then the camera pulls back to reveal an enormous train yard with thousands of fully loaded coal cars taking the state's wealth beyond its borders; the camera then pulls back still further and tilts down to show a solitary man raking leaves (the man had been a miner for fifteen years before his job was eliminated by automation, and now he is on the county's welfare rolls, assigned to do this mindless work); and finally the camera traces the path of the raker and moves beyond him to discover a house in the process of being built by a small group of men (these men are also on welfare, but they are part of a radical new program in which they are learning construction skills while building a house for one of their fellow poor). All this was filmed in one continuous take with narration laid over the picture to explain the significance of each portion of the shot.

The opening could have just as easily been conceived in the more typical fashion of cutting together bits of the mine with pieces of the rail yard, added to a few angles of the raker, and then attached to a number of shots of the men working on the house. Ostensibly the content of these shots fused together would have been the same as the carefully designed long take. Certainly the same narrative information could have been read over each version. But the essential information given in the continuous shot is markedly different. It speaks directly to the powerful fact that the wealth flowing from the mine each day exists in the same small portion of space as the discharged worker forced by the state to rake leaves.

What is described, then, is not so much the obvious irony of wealth and poverty existing in the same world as it is the fact that this world has been created out of the obscene proximity of unemployment to the source of wealth. This proximity, forged by the simultaneity of what we see, is the basic content of the shot; and the shot is strengthened by its obvious believability. In a medium in which one can cut from anything to anything else, everything here is terribly real. Even the flatness of the images becomes a dry statement created out of their evident authenticity. Punchy flashes of close-ups and dramatic angles would have worked to deny the elemental connection in space and time between the productive coal mine and the wasted raker. Equally, in a fragmented world the fact of the new poverty program would not have been a revelation—just another piece of film added to the ones that came before. In a continuous shot this image comes after we first see the organic and inevitable connection of mine, rail yard, and raker. That this radical program is truly tied to the same insensitive, acquisitive world can come as nothing less than a revelation.

However, scripting with continuous spaces offers more than the authenticity of connecting things together. It also develops a dramatic unity by allowing the world before the camera gradually to accumulate impact and emotion as the critical elements within the setting are revealed to build the action. Jean Renoir, who is a master of the incisively moving camera, created one of film's small, splendid moments with a trucking shot in *Grand Illusion*.

Courtesy: JANUS FILMS, INC.

The French prisoners in a German prisoner-of-war camp are rehearsing for a show. A crate containing women's costumes has just arrived and one of the officers enters dressed in one of the outfits. These men have not seen a woman in years and a number of them gather around him just to stare. He can't quite comprehend their reaction, but he feels sufficiently uncomfortable to try and make light of his dress. At this point Renoir cuts to a close-up of one of the prisoners totally entranced by

Courtesy: JANUS FILMS, INC.

the costumed officer. Then the camera slowly begins a long trucking shot backward down the length of the hall. One man after another, the camera picks out the intense, stunned silence of each man it passes. The room, now absolutely still, is threaded with a succession of hungry, caged men, where just moments before they had been a crowd of high-spirited soldiers. Finally the camera reaches the end of the room and slowly turns to encompass its breadth. Every man in the large hall is staring intently at the awkward, embarrassed officer, who has suddenly become for his fellow prisoners the incarnation of femininity.

Once again the scene could have been made with a series of cuts, but its impact would have been quite different. Each cut would have arbitrarily fragmented the men in the hall, individualizing and isolating their reactions. The cadence of the scene would have been drawn from the tattoo of cuts that formed its structure, and the hesitant eloquence of the men's unexpected reaction would have been lost.

By understanding that these men are an inseparable group bound to each other through their common deprivation, Renoir was able to move his camera through their midst with the lyric slowness of a dream, binding them together in the parched stillness of their need. Each moment of the camera's long move progressively strips these soldiers of the gay and courageous masks they have worn to survive and leaves them, at its conclusion, trembling and terribly human. What had been simply soldiers at the beginning of the shot have become men by its end—men sealed together, inextricably linked, by the artificial world in which they exist. And because their powerful reaction to the costume would have been ludicrous in any other circumstance, the reality of the shot—catching each man exactly where he stands in the room, seizing his feelings and passing them on to the next man in the camera's line of movement—gives their emotions a comprehensibility drawn purely from the compelling rhythm and logic revealed in the shot's design. By respecting the dramatic unity of the space which holds these prisoners together, Renoir turned what easily could have been merely an amusing digression into a poignant description of his characters' vulnerable humanity.

Jean-Luc Godard worked continuous space with equal virtuosity but with a quite dissimilar effect in his stylized opening of *My Life to Live.* A husband and a wife are seated with their backs to the camera at the bar of a café. As they talk, we gradually learn that the wife has left her husband to try and become an actress; and the husband, angry and increasingly hostile, wants her to return to him and their child. The husband does not understand his wife's behavior, and the wife is revolted by her husband's insensitivity. All this has the makings of an explosive domestic crisis. But Godard filmed the entire five-minute conversation from behind the man and the woman using just two shots. In the first the camera stays on the woman, and in the second all the camera does is continually pan slowly from the back of one to the back of the other. As the conversation builds in intensity, the characters become increasingly depersonalized.

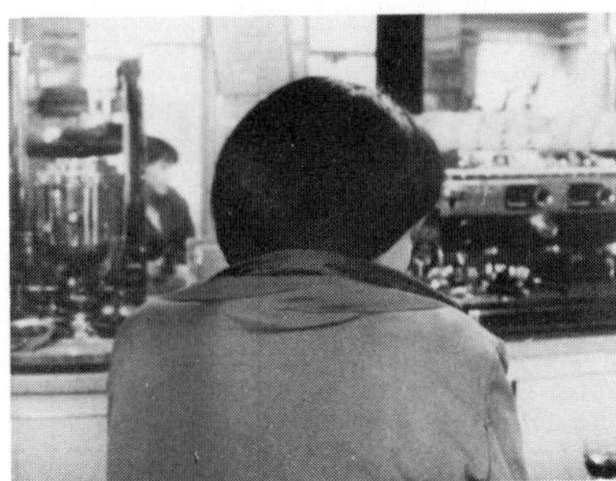

The effect of the scene is to deprive the audience of the usual ways that films allow them to get to know characters quickly—through a varied succession of views. Instead Godard selected an emotionally neutral vantage point to show the

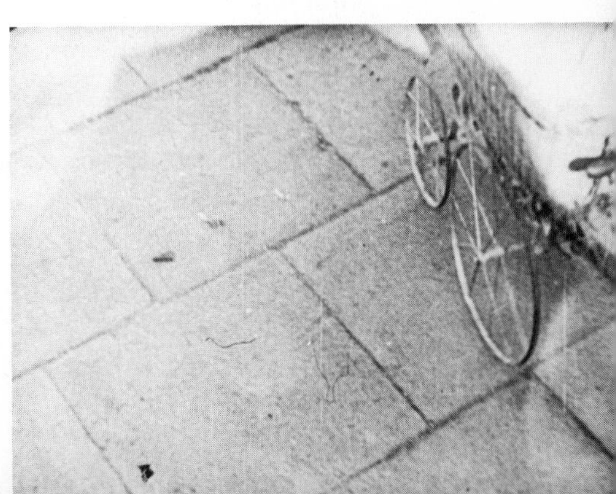

dramatic confrontation and then neutralized the shot further by refusing even to vary it to any degree. Like casual eavesdroppers, we are put at a distance, held there, and kept from getting involved in the tangled lives of the people on the screen.

Since the audience has little to see, about all it can do is hear—and then try to understand the growing estrangement between the emotional words and the faceless man and woman who speak them. As the scene builds, it is not the complexity of the characters' lives that holds our interest. Rather, the drama finally unfolds in this curious separation of the words from the feelings which come to envelop them. Godard has visualized the troubling fact that there is a natural distance between language and meaning—a theme he tenaciously pursues throughout the film. For his opening, which sets up that theme, it is as though he has enclosed us in a room containing a radar scope through which we search for the characters, trying to get a fix on them with each sweep of the camera. The way we finally come to know them is through this relentless device, which measures one thing only—the telling distance between the monotonous flow of words and the shifting emotions which sent them spiraling toward us.

The basic attribute of scripting with continuous spaces is that it allows the people and the objects in the film-maker's universe to gather the weight of their dramatic importance as the scene develops. It is as if we were allowed to see the formation of that universe from its creation, with each object in it gaining, as we watch, the mass sufficient to hold its dramatic place in a self-contained world. As we have seen, this technique offers great satisfactions. Yet, it must be remembered, a good deal of the effectiveness of continuous space emerges from its surprising inclusion in a world basically structured from bits of space and time. The process of fusing these pieces has become our usual source for receiving the film-maker's insights. By varying this root structure of the film, by playing upon this elemental means we use to understand the action unfolding before us, the film-making is able to endow our perceptions of that action with an intensity drawn not only from the progress of his drama but from our basic expectations about the way films are made. This capability permits him to work within the foundations of film-making itself to conceptualize and express his ideas about the inner nature of the world that contains his story.

Scripting with Time

The choice of building action with either continuous or discontinuous space within a film is also a choice which affects the nature and quality of the time in which that action occurs. As we have seen, each cut loosens the run of time that binds actions together. Each movement through space is simultaneously a movement in time, so the progression of cuts allows the film-maker the opportunity to choose his moment to condense or expand time to suit the purposes of his script. All this falls comfortably within film's narrative traditions. These movements in time essentially go unnoticed.

But a great part of the effectiveness of this time structure lies in the potentiality of the cuts to alter time in more discernible ways without doing violence to the credibility of the action. The film-maker can work with time as he works with space to build assertions that embody the meaning of his story at those critical moments when his audience must be specifically located to understand his intentions fully.

Until the middle of Ermanno Olmi's *The Sound of Trumpets,* the story of a young man searching for a job in a large corporation unfolds in a quiet, straightforward, almost documentary, fashion. We see the boy leave his working-class home, enter the ugly reaches of Milan, take the mandatory examination for the coveted job, meet and tentatively flirt with a girl who is also seeking a job, and finally win the job. He becomes an assistant porter and is assigned to a desk outside one of the many gray offices containing the bleak rows of jobholders who, in their youth, also won a lifetime job in this enormous firm.

Until this point Olmi has caught us up with the boy's determination to win the job. Now that it is his, Olmi shows us the world the boy has become heir to. We see the boy hopefully groomed and attired in his best suit, sitting with the porter outside the office. And then we enter that office. In shot after shot we see these corporation drones, laboring within their appointed niches, each isolated from the com-

Courtesy: JANUS FILMS, INC.

Courtesy: JANUS FILMS, INC.

panionship of his neighbor in the enveloping silence that fills this unhappy room. Suddenly, with a noisy flourish that speeds along the line of desks, one of the clerks

makes a triumphal show of emptying his desk. In this world that exists without even the warmth of words, he is telling his colleagues that his years have passed, that he is free. They respond with a calculated indifference that phrases their hatred so

completely that it echoes through the room like a diatribe. Then quickly and silently they are back at their work again. We see them in a long shot—the stifling

walls (the room is much smaller than we expected) holding the warren of desks with each man at his narrow task.

It is here that Olmi breaks the relentless procession of shots that have shown us what is left of the personalities that have been worn away in this erosive atmosphere. A messenger enters the room and pauses at one of the desks to share a bit of gossip. The clerk with whom he talks repays him with a gratuitous comment about one of his fellow workers. He explains that the man, hunched over his papers,

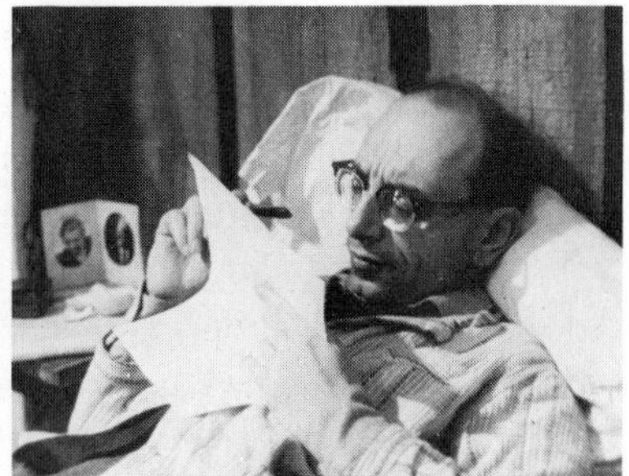

is woefully nearsighted. The next instant we see that man in the comforting stillness of his home reading, with the same intensity he displayed in the office, a manuscript that consumes most of his free hours. This moment merges with a succession of glimpses into the home lives of the other clerks that sadly parallel their existence in the office.

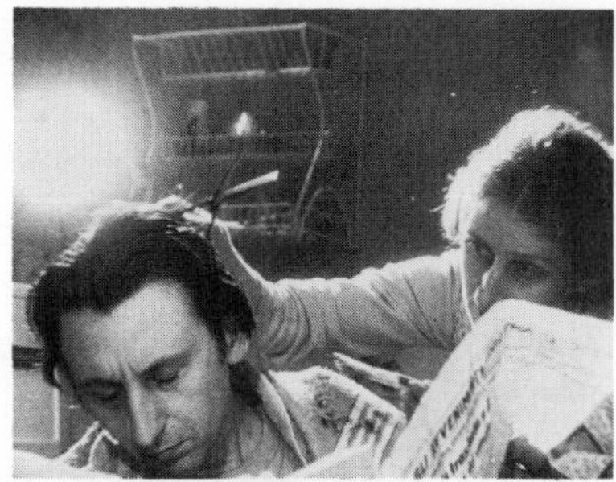

Courtesy: JANUS FILMS, INC.

We see the vain young man who continually combs his hair during the day being given a loving haircut by his wife at night. We see another, the office dandy, asserting this conception of himself at home by carefully cutting a cigarette into two pathetic pieces and then ostentatiously placing one of those pieces in a cigarette holder and luxuriously puffing upon it in the contrived elegance of his small living room. And we see still another, the most gregarious man in the office, gaily singing an aria among friends in a club. In each glimpse, the man set free at home is no different from the man confined at the office.

Finally Olmi shows us a fragment from the life of the woman in the office that is a little more jagged than the rest. We see her returning from work, only to

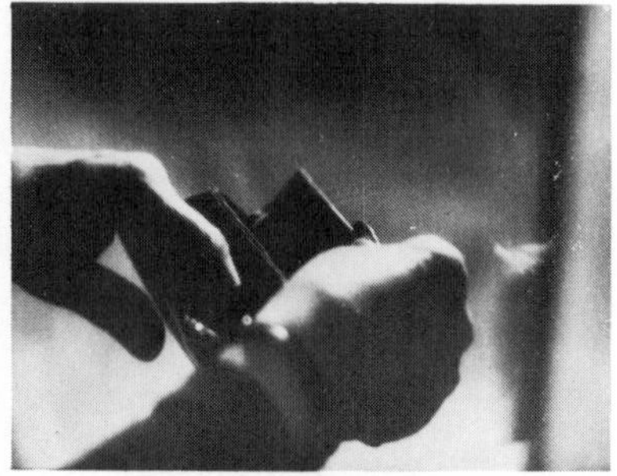

learn from her housekeeper that her son has stolen money from her purse. At first she finds this impossible to believe, but when she is confronted with the empty purse, she breaks into tears. Her life at the office, endured for the sake of her child, has been a waste.

We watch her cry and then hear her sobs over the faces in the office for whom her expression of feeling is a disturbing intrusion. We have returned to the office, where it is, as it always has been, the morning after the life that has been touched. Any residue of that life still clinging to the worker resides there like an embarrassing stain. So we watch her sob and understand the indifference of her fellow workers as they try very hard to bury themselves in their tasks. And outside the room, while all this goes on, the newly hired boy sits at the desk waiting for the

opportunity that will place him in the rear of that office, where he will spend the rest of his life slowly working his way toward the front.

Olmi has carved out of the discrete spaces which enclose each worker a picture of despair that grows in intensity until even the look on a clerk's face fills the screen like an anguished cry. Each shot separates the workers, not only from one another but from any part of themselves they might see in the others. They are bound together only in their isolation.

When Olmi suddenly slices into time, he has not really done anything radical to the structure of his narrative. He has only carried the slow beat of the characters' lives into an additional dimension. The spaces of the office have been designed as impenetrable blocks, each enclosing a clerk at his desk. Each cut from worker to worker in the office has built the barriers between them. So when Olmi moves through time away from the office, he only transports these blocks of space to a new location. The structure of the clerks' lives and the mournful rhythms that express this structure remain intact. Only now the potentiality of a movement through space to become an equally definitive movement through time has been tapped. Olmi uses this inherent possibility to deepen our knowledge. But he does not do it to alter our perception of time. The world of the characters is of one piece. By slowly turning this piece for our inspection in time as well as space, Olmi shows us the deadening completeness of the characters' isolation. In the process he effectively obliterates the significance of time in their lives.

Because space and therefore time in films is discontinuous, each shot offering short strands which are woven into a coherent picture of the time the film represents, motion pictures actually abstract the physical world they seem to represent with such overwhelming literalness. The film-maker is always working in a unique temporal universe in each of his films. Even the simple present is made elusive—expanded or contracted at will to develop its meanings by expressing time in a play of cadences. These constantly alter our feelings for the nature of time passing and so give its passing a texture that embodies its meanings. In addition, past and future reside so close to the surface of the present that they are ready, at the edge of any of its hundreds of pieces, to be called up to deepen or explain the relationship between the present and the world that surrounds it. These temporal possibilities are finally an assertion not only of the singular nature of the present we see but also of the intricate forces that have exposed it to view. By scripting images in space, the film-maker has simultaneously scripted those images in a powerful flow of time. This force constantly moves through his characters' lives with an energy sufficient to chip away the physical reality that protects each life, exposing the elements that form the core. In one way or another all films must be scripted with this in mind.

In all these examples we have concentrated on the image as the vehicle for the communication of the film-maker's ideas and vision. We have dealt with the scripting of these images as the primal method that moved the film-maker from his original conception to the completed film. But it is obvious that in sound films dialogue, music, and sound effects also contribute mightily to the finished product, and there are numerous examples in which each of these aspects of the sound track have dominated the film's initial conception and produced remarkable results in its finished version. Hearing is, of course, a sense as rich and complex as sight.

In films it embodies our connection with the thoughts and emotions expressed in language, with the rhythms and harmonies contained in music, with the qualities inherent in the raw sounds of our world, all distilled to complete the meanings of the image. Because of the importance of sound we have dedicated three chapters of the second section to a long look at how this aspect of film-making is conceived and produced and how it harmonizes with the totality of the finished motion picture.

But in this chapter what we have attempted has been an inspection of the nature and uses of images—that primary sensory information which films offer in their unique ability to move us visually through space and time in such a way as to create a new picture of the world that encloses us. Next, with the actual construction of that picture through camera and lighting techniques, we shall look even more closely at the possibilities of cinema. It is finally through carefully mastered techniques that films reach their full potential. And it is upon these techniques that the film-maker builds that intricate construction, rising out of thousands of small technical decisions, from which will emerge a film that is the repository of his vision, intellect, and artistry.

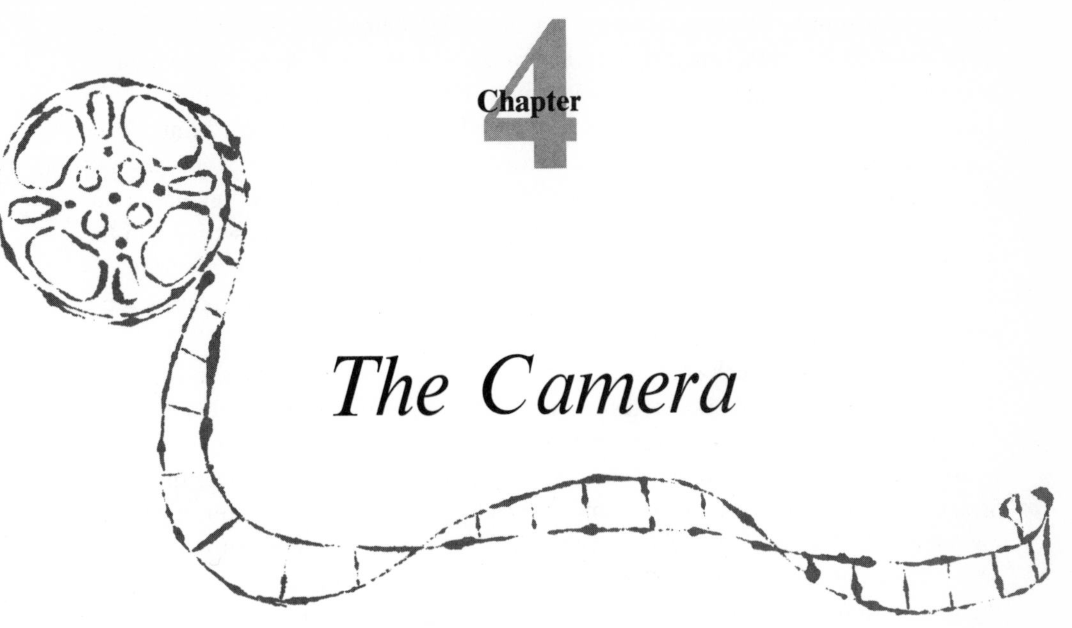

Chapter 4

The Camera

The image first springs to life in the camera. It is here that space and time, isolated in the viewfinder, are seized from the world and transformed into consciousness and meaning within the vision of the film-maker. The camera becomes an extension of his senses: an infinitely responsive mechanism capable of ordering the world in fragments of insight that distill the chaotic flow of events with a private logic tuned to the impulses feeding the central nervous system.

Eventually a completed work will be created in the editing room; but by then the potential meaning of every shot will have been sealed on film. The judgments of the cameraman—the objects included within the frame, their size and arrangement, their sharpness, color, brightness or shading, the details of their movements—are stamped on each frame. Thus the camera becomes the primary means for organizing the film-maker's perceptions, and eventually those of his audience, by allowing him to control within the rigorous limits of the viewfinder each nuance that will give the image clarity and meaning.

The intricate process of constructing each shot essentially begins when the cameraman decides where to place the camera. Every shot contains an aspect of the world that he wants to convey, and he must determine how that fragment will

fit into the frame. He must decide whether the action will occur across the foreground or in depth, whether the camera will remain stationary or move, and, if it moves, in what direction and how much. Depending upon the nature of the film, each camera position can either be worked out in detail ahead of time or be improvised by the cameraman as the action occurs; but no matter how it is arrived at, camera placement is not just a mechanical decision—it is also an important aesthetic judgment. It determines the relationship of the action to its setting and the perspective from which the audience will see both the action and the setting develop. It is a deceptively complex decision, and we will treat it in considerable detail in the first part of this chapter.

The contents of each shot are also affected by the nature of the camera itself. The camera is composed of a series of interrelated and quite sophisticated mechanisms which allow the cameraman to choose a variety of means for recording the image. But these too are more than just mechanical choices. The lens, the viewfinder, the frame shape, and the camera speed all play a part in determining the meanings which that image will convey, and all these components must be subtly adjusted to the requirements of each shot. The nature of these mechanisms, and the degree to which they can be controlled, is the subject of the second part of the chapter.

Finally, the shooting must be organized so that the shots will eventually fit together. One of the most effective ways to do this is to reorganize the script so that the large number of shots in the film can be made as efficiently as possible. It also means developing a sense of where the camera should be placed from shot to shot so that the vast amount of detailed information in each shot is coherently developed. This is a monumental task that depends upon a number of what have become highly standardized shooting procedures, procedures which both expedite the shooting and lay the groundwork for lighting each sequence. Although, over the years, they have been enshrined into rules, these procedures are still quite helpful whether followed or observed in the breach. So they will be covered in the last section of this chapter, while the problems of lighting and exposure will be discussed in the following chapter.

Part 1:

The Nature of Camerawork

There are no set ways of using the camera. There is only a multitude of techniques which can be used in as many different ways as there are directors and cameramen interpreting different kinds of visual material. Each confronts the script in his own way, bringing to it his particular sense of how the action should be developed by means of the numerous techniques at his disposal. The result is an endless variety of shots, each combining techniques in various ways to create segments of the action that are then built into still more complex combinations by editing.

But no matter how they are made, all shots have one thing in common. The techniques used to create them indelibly structure the action within each shot and fix the limits within which the editor must work. He can build the action in the film only around the shape of the action contained in each shot. This, in turn, means that the cameraman must construct each image around some idea of how the shot will interact with the shots on either side of it. These are not still pictures he is framing in the viewfinder. Each image contains action that will be joined to a sequence of other actions.

Building Action in a Static Frame

At its simplest, building the action can mean nothing more than just firmly anchoring the camera in place and then arranging and moving the actors in front of it. This is how many silent films were made before more sophisticated shooting and editing techniques were invented. The camera was treated as if it were set in the middle of a theater; and as long as the action developed as it would within the confines of a stage, just putting a frame around it was enough to hold the viewer's attention. This was not a simpleminded approach to making films, just limited, and it eventually gave way to a moving camera and a variety of shots made from different angles. But placing the action within a static frame remains one of the most basic ways to make a shot.

However, even within a static frame there is more to building the action than simply putting a frame around it. This is because the action in a shot is not just the movement on the screen. The viewer's own visual activity plays an important part in creating a coherent impression of that action. As Stephenson and Debrix have succinctly stated in *The Cinema as Art,* ". . . in the real world, vision is controlled by attention, but in the cinema it is the other way round: attention is controlled by vision. In everyday life we see what we attend to; in the cinema we attend to what we see—that is, what the film director chooses to show us."

It's not that we see a movie differently than we see everything else. Just as in our everyday experience, while we are generally aware of the vast amount of detailed information on the screen, our continually shifting attention concentrates on only a part of this complex image at one time. What is different, though, is that we see the image the way the director and the cameraman want us to see it. They organize our perceptions by using the shape, size, arrangement, and movement of the objects on the screen to form patterns that control the movements of our attention. These patterns form a structure that molds our awareness throughout the film.

They not only focus our attention from moment to moment, but by giving a rhythm to what we have seen, help us anticipate what is about to come. In effect, the movements of our attention become beats in a rhythm of expectations, and it is this rhythm which helps tie together the essentially discontinuous pieces of space and time that are used to build the action in the film.

For the cameraman this means that he must continually re-create the world he films. This is true even in a shot that does nothing more than show us a relatively immobile figure in a static frame. Take, for instance, this shot of Joan in Robert Bresson's *The Trial of Joan of Arc*. It is relatively simple in terms of its contents and any experienced cameraman would instinctively frame it in this way. But because the camera has been used to distill a unique world, the way the shot works is quite complex.

The first thing the shot does is focus our attention on Joan's face. This is done in several ways. One is by making her face the lightest part of an otherwise dark, dimly lit setting. This automatically reduces the competition for our attention. The focus of our attention is then reinforced by how she is placed in the frame. She dominates the space both by being the largest shape in the frame and by being placed almost, but not exactly, in its center. Although she is equidistant from the sides of the frame, her head is in the upper third (dividing the frame into thirds is a rule of thumb generally followed by professional cameramen). In addition, her body is turned slightly so that it has a more nearly triangular shape. This arrangement shows enough of her figure to give it a sense of weight or gravity; it also gives it a shape with a broad, firm base that holds her in place and an apex that draws our attention up to her face.

Because her figure is firmly set in the frame we have no expectation of movement or any other change. This expectation is fully satisfied and she seems imprisoned in her role as defendant throughout the shot. But even though she remains immobile, we can still sense her involvement in the action around her. For one thing, we are immediately aware that she is not alone in the frame, that there are people in the background whose subdued presence represents a fragment of a much larger setting. They serve to connect her to the rest of her surroundings and thus reinforce our expectation of significant action outside the frame. And because our attention is really quite volatile, her slightly turned head and persistent offscreen stare cause us to shift uneasily back and forth along her line of sight in anticipation of what she sees beyond the frame. So, while the shape and placement of her figure initially direct our attention to her face, this interplay between her figure, her gaze, and her surroundings creates a pattern of attention that makes her part of the developing action.

The film itself is a reconstruction of the heresy trial of this medieval French heroine by her English captors. As most of the action takes place in a courtroom, what we see and hear is largely restricted to the measured exchange of questions and answers between accuser and accused. Bresson has purposely flattened the dramatic quality of these exchanges to the shape of the historical document from which they are taken, but he gives them immediacy by building tension visually. Our attention is never simply held on a figure seated in the middle of the frame; instead, each person's gaze creates expectations that continually tug our attention in the direction in which they are looking.

These movements of our attention are then used to build the action from shot to shot. This can be seen in the short sequence which contains the previous shot. In the first four shots Joan is asked questions, which we then see her answer. During this exchange the editing progressively intensifies the action by rewarding the movements of our attention in each shot with a shot that first answers our

search and then forces us to search back again. Halfway through the last of these shots Joan turns, in silence, to look in the opposite direction. In the following shot (5) we see another man, a priestly counselor who can give her advice and comfort only by meeting her gaze. But then he lowers his eyes. Like a period at the end of a sentence, this gesture momentarily interrupts the flow of our attention by drawing it inward to rest on his figure. The result is a pause in the action that both breaks the visual tension and underlines the brief silence which marks an impasse in the questioning.

The editing of this sequence is typical of that in the rest of the film and is a direct result of Bresson's use of the camera to isolate his characters from each other. Although we know that they cannot be more than a few feet apart, we never see Joan and her interrogators in the frame together. This technique immediately establishes their relationship, a relationship predetermined by their place in history. They are each locked in a separate ideology and inhabit such morally different worlds that Joan cannot give her inquisitors an acceptable answer and they cannot ask her a meaningful question.

Only the editing joins the give-and-take of their questions and answers; it permits our shifting attention to connect figures that confront each other only by looking offscreen. But this tenuous connection of isolated spaces is so coherently structured by Bresson that we are able to re-create the space in the courtroom for ourselves. We build it in our heads as we would if we were reading a transcript of the trial, thus intensifying our involvement in the action by transforming the setting into an abstraction, an archetypal courtroom of almost mythic proportions in which their irreconcilable conflict can be played out to its inevitable conclusion.

Bresson also abstracts the setting by using the camera to isolate his characters from what little of their surroundings we see in each shot. Although we are aware of the people and objects around them, by building the action back and forth across the frame, he purposely restricts our attention to a space that seems no deeper than the surface of the screen. This shallowness reduces everything in the setting to simply a veiled suggestion: a thin, uncomprehending tapestry that offers his characters neither solace nor protection.

While Bresson purposely creates this shallow image, it is possible, by constructing the action toward or away from the camera, to create an image that seems to stretch back into the frame. However, the image itself is only two-dimensional, so a sense of depth is an illusion in film. But exactly because it is an illusion, depth can be created in a number of ways. For instance, the sense of depth in the following shot is created by nothing more than converging lines. The shot is from the opening scene of René Clair's *The Italian Straw Hat*. In this scene the hero of the film is riding through a park when he loses his buggy whip. As he goes to retrieve it, his horse wanders off and he is left to search down the road for his buggy.

Here the extreme sense of depth is used to emphasize the man's predicament. As we look at his face staring plaintively into the distance, the vast emptiness behind him conjures up a vision of an equally lonely and endless road ahead of him. We use the background to mirror that part of the landscape which is never revealed; and because the emptiness we envision is fashioned by our imagination,

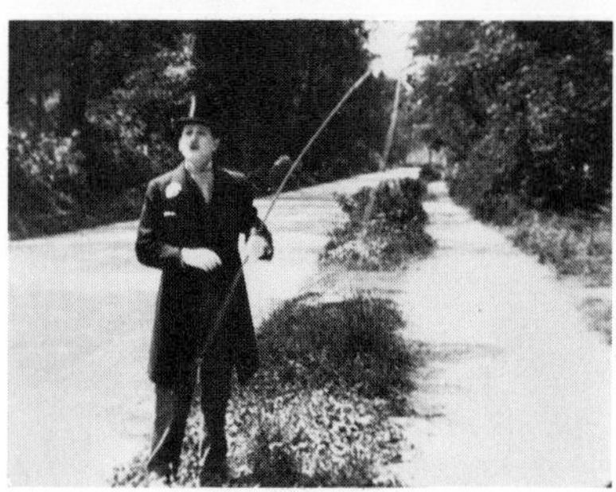

it is easily exaggerated into hopeless isolation. This is both momentarily terrifying and slightly ridiculous, and until Clair cuts to a shot showing the horse just down the road, we are left to laugh apprehensively at our own illusion.

The comic power of this illusion is the result of Clair's clever manipulation of the sense of depth in the shot. This depth is created by the converging pairs of parallel lines formed by the sides of the road. These lines interact with the immobile figure staring out of the frame to move our attention first up the screen to where the lines intersect, then across the horizon in the direction of the hero's gaze, and finally back by the same route to the bottom of the screen. It is really only movement in two dimensions; but the illusion of depth makes it seem a search forward and back along the road—and it is not much of an extension to protract that search beyond the screen itself into a lonely countryside that exists totally in our imagination.

Depth is also indicated by the decreasing size of objects as they get further from the camera. This can be seen in a shot from Akira Kurosawa's *Rashomon.*

Courtesy: JANUS FILMS, INC.

The film consists of four different versions of a rape and a murder. This shot is from the story told by a woodcutter who has secretly witnessed these events. He evokes an image of the participants as victims of vanity and pride, each playing upon the weaknesses of the others to provoke a cycle of betrayal and revenge. In this shot the woman lies on the ground after the rape, caught between her assailant in the foreground and her husband to the rear. They must fight a duel to clear her name or she will have to commit suicide, but now both of them have rejected her as a shameless whore.

The agony of her abandonment is instantly caught in the pattern formed by the shapes in the frame. They move our attention up and down the screen from figure to figure in an unending cycle, while the sense of depth created by the decreasing size of their figures makes it seem as if our attention is wavering forward and back between the two men. But this suspended moment also foreshadows its own resolution. The decreasing size of their figures allows the man whose legs fill the foreground to dominate both the husband and the wife. Once she has goaded the men into dueling, it is foreordained that he murder her husband and then desert her.

When any object extends toward the camera, the part nearest the lens is disproportionately enlarged. This effect, called *foreshortening,* becomes especially noticeable when the object is quite close to the camera, and it can be used to create a pronounced sense of depth. For instance, the only source of depth in the following shot is the extreme foreshortening of the man's arm as he reaches out to ring a

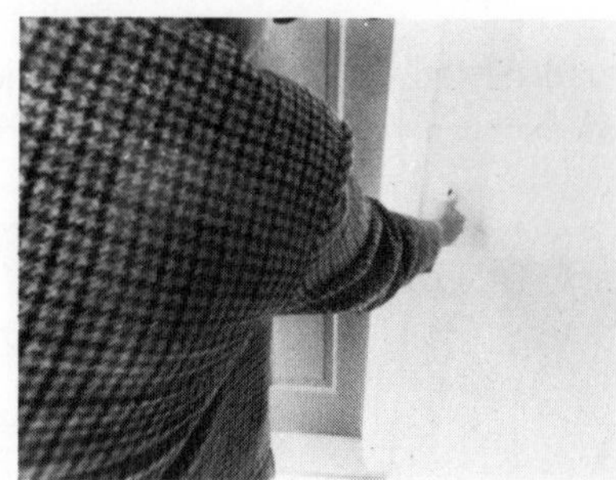

doorbell. The shot is part of a short sequence entitled "Singing Salesmen," produced by Dave Schmerler for Eliot Frankel's NBC magazine show *First Tuesday.* In this sequence shots of a door-to-door vacuum-cleaner salesman demonstrating a machine in a woman's home alternate with shots of a company sales meeting. This is almost a revival meeting, with the salesmen being inspired to new heights of success by animatedly singing a rallying song in praise of positive thinking and aggressive salesmanship. Their singing furnishes the background for all the shots in the sequence.

The sequence opens with a short speech followed by several shots of the men clapping and singing. These are cut to the beat of the music and establish a rhythm in the editing. Then, right on the beat, instead of men singing, we see this shot, the first shot made outside the meeting, and on the next beat we return to the singing. In a single thrust, the extreme foreshortening of the salesman's arm shoves our attention toward the finger stabbing at the button. A successful salesman even rings the doorbell aggressively, and it is this sense of zealous determination that sets the tone for all that is to follow.

Although depth seems to occur automatically, it is really a quite fragile illusion. Our common sense tells us that the image we are seeing is only two-dimensional; but from our long involvement with painting, photography, movies, and television we have learned a sense of visual perspective and have unconsciously come to accept converging lines and diminishing size as indicators of depth. Because these are learned responses, however, they can be manipulated by the filmmaker to emphasize or reduce the sense of depth. For instance, in this shot from

Robert Wiene's *The Cabinet of Dr. Caligari,* the converging lines painted on the walls of the set, and the canted walls of the set itself, accentuate the feeling of depth and height within the limited space in which the set is built.

Ingmar Bergman also trades upon the basic instability of the illusion of depth in this shot from *The Silence.* In this case he uses an optical trick to convey the subtly ambiguous relationship of his characters. Because the woman doesn't speak

Courtesy: JANUS FILMS, INC.

the same language as the waiter in her hotel, she cannot tell him she wants more whiskey. As a result, she is reduced to holding up an empty bottle and making some gestures. However, Bergman emphasizes the fact that they are just barely in contact by having the waiter react to her image in a mirror. This makes them seem face to face even though we see the frame of the mirror and know that she has to be off to one side and looking beyond him. The result is that, when our attention shifts between the two of them, we are fleetingly uncertain if we should interpret it as movement in depth or simply as movement across the foreground. This quite literally reflects their ambiguous relationship.

A special problem arises when depth is created by pointing the camera up or down. While depth increases the feeling of height in a shot, it is not the depth itself but the angle from which we see some familiar object that tells us whether what we are seeing is supposed to be above or below us. This is because, no matter whether the camera is pointed up, down, or straight ahead when a shot is made, the footage ends up projected on a screen directly in front of us. That means that we don't have to tilt our head to see things the camera had to tilt up or down to record, and this deprives us of the usual clues, the pulling of the muscles in our head and neck, that tell us we are looking at things from other than eye level. As a result, we tend to assume that any depth in the image indicates something extending directly away from us unless there is some indication to the contrary in the position of some familiar object.

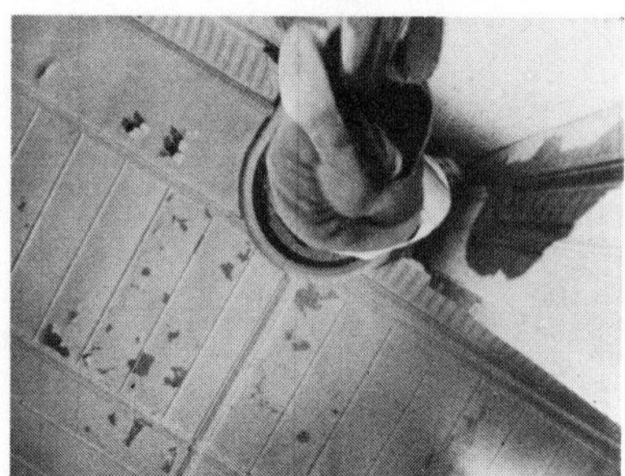

The ease with which our sense of up and down can be confused can be seen in this shot from the NBC documentary *Fire Rescue,* produced by Fred Freed. The shot is an extreme up-angle of a fireman sliding down a pole. It is easy enough to tell that we are looking toward the ceiling, but not because of the depth in the shot —only because we know which end of a fireman is up. Without the fireman, though, we couldn't be sure whether the camera was pointed at the ceiling, the floor, or even at something as unlikely as a wall with a pole running through it. Because of this possible confusion, the editor was very careful to use only that portion of the shot in which there is a fireman actually descending the pole.

The assumption that what we see on the screen is at eye level sets quite a powerful standard. Normally, when we look out on the world, things that are below us seem subordinate and under our control, while things that are above us seem dominant and, if not in control of us, at least beyond our control. This is the norm by which we judge what we see and it is a standard that is built into our culture. In a movie theater, however, we substitute the omniscience of the camera for our own limited vision. Instead of judging objects relative to our normal eye level, we judge them according to whether they are above or below the level of the camera.

This means that the film-maker can determine the meaning of objects by carefully selecting the level of the camera. We have already seen how this works (in Chapter One) in the ironic alternation between upward and downward angles in two shots from Kurosawa's *Yojimbo.* In the first of these shots the samurai, high in a tower in the center of the village, looks down on and dominates the gnomelike figures of the villagers below him. In the other shot the leaders of the warring

factions loom above us as if they were the masters of their fate, while the samurai's figure towers over them in the background.

A similar use of camera angle can be seen in this shot from *Corral,* a short documentary made by the National Film Board of Canada. The film is about the breaking of a wild horse. This shot, in the opening of the film, introduces us to the

cowboy who finds and eventually tames the animal. Heroic shots like this have been with us, in one form or another, almost since the beginning of films. It is the general before the battle, the Indian brave surveying the plains: a tradition that reinforces our expectations in every new context in which such a shot is placed.

But it is the camera position which creates these expectations. The foreshortening of the figures not only makes the horse seem to stretch back into the frame, but also makes the cowboy tower over him. This angle shapes the horse into a broad, firm platform, a solid base from which the cowboy can look out over the horizon; and it gives a tapering shape to the cowboy's figure that draws our attention up to his face, where it tends to rest. We are caught in a moment of tranquillity, a pause before the action that gives us a sense of timeless patience. And the upward tilt of the camera, by asserting his dominance, creates a feeling of power and determination. These expectations then slowly develop over the following shots into the tough persistence needed to break the horse while retaining its trust.

All the techniques discussed so far, by directing the movements of the viewer's attention, give meaning to an immobile subject in a static frame. But in motion pictures the subject can also move about, and when this movement occurs in an otherwise immobile setting, it then becomes the dominant means for controlling attention. This can be seen in a shot from Marcel Carné's *Le Jour Se Lève.* In the film the hero is confronted by a man whom he suspects has had an affair with his fiancée. When the man tries to play upon these suspicions the hero becomes enraged. He grabs the man by the lapels, and in a series of shots that show his mounting anger, first shoves the man to the window and then pushes him out over its ledge.

The horrible possibilities inherent in this action are then frighteningly intensified because the final shot in the series is made from outside the building. This

Courtesy: JANUS FILMS, INC.

allows Carné to use every technique for creating depth—the foreshortened building, the converging lines, the tiny figures on the sidewalk below. Our attention is drawn sharply up and down the face of the building, and with each movement our awareness of its height increases, pulling taut our sense of the hero's by now almost homicidal rage.

At the peak of suspense, as the man hangs immobilized on the ledge hoarsely pleading for his life, a pedestrian carrying a white newspaper rounds the corner

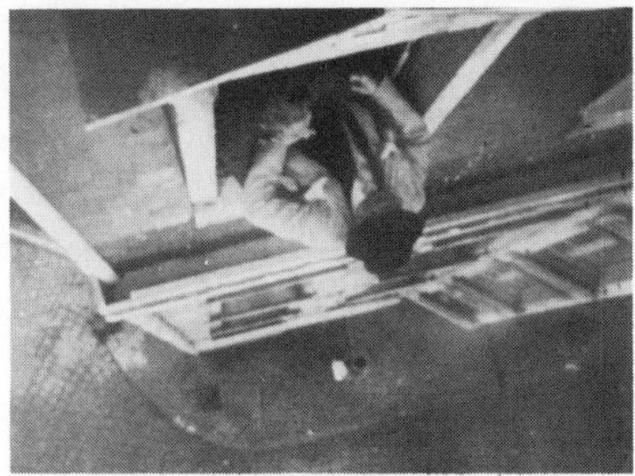

and casually crosses the sidewalk. This apparently meaningless diversion breaks the tension, and by suddenly broadening the action to include the world in which it is set, it makes us realize, as the hero must, that the people on the street below don't know and probably don't care about what is happening above them. The feelings of futility and indifference that result seem to blunt the hero's anger and sap his resolve. Carné then cuts to a shot from inside the room as the hero pulls the man back and releases him.

While our attention is initially attracted by any movement in an immobile setting, the impact of that movement will quickly diminish unless the placement of objects and the nature of the movement form a pattern that reinforces the hold motion has on our attention. This can be seen in a simple shot from Robert

Flaherty's *Nanook of the North*. Flaherty builds the meaning of an Eskimo family's spring migration by using a wide, static shot of a hill to focus our attention solely on their movement across the horizon.

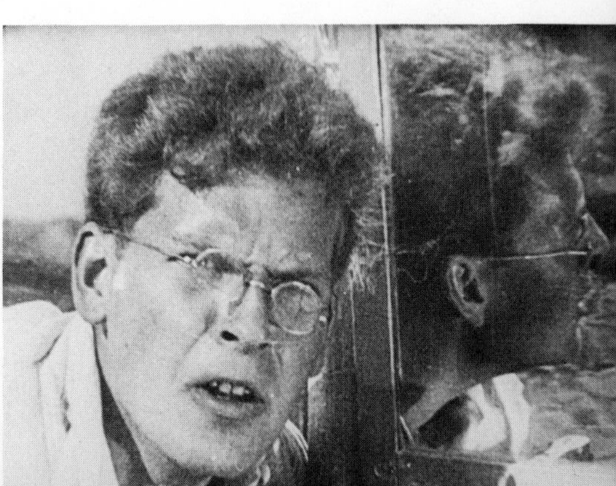

By placing the brow of a low hill high in the frame, he creates a large, dark shape that sets off and defines the Eskimos' movements. This massive form seems to restrict their trek to the narrow band of light at the top, a horizontal space whose very width seems to extend their journey and slow its pace. And since there is nothing in the flat perspective to divert our attention, it is their movement along the horizon which rivets our gaze throughout the shot, creating an expectation of slow but continuing motion from right to left, an expectation that is used in the editing to build a sequence of shots all tending in the same direction.

It is also possible to focus our attention on a particular movement even when other objects in the frame are in motion as well. Here is an example from Godard's *Breathless*. The shot is part of a sequence in which Jean Seberg is followed by a

police detective who hopes that she will lead him to Belmondo; and Belmondo is following both of them to make sure the police are led astray. In this shot the three of them pass, one after the other, through the fringes of a restless crowd watching a parade. The frame is dotted with aimless motion, so by having the three central figures move quickly and purposefully on a diagonal along the margin of the crowd, Godard separates their movements from that of their surroundings. In fact, even in the frozen action of this single frame it is possible to pick out Belmondo (almost in the center) by the forward thrust of his hurrying figure.

In these last two examples all the movement was across the frame; but again, there is much more room in which to build the action when the movement is toward or away from the camera. Here, for example, is a shot from Charlie Chaplin's *The Gold Rush* in which movement in depth is used to create the meaning of the shot. In the first part of the shot Chaplin wanders into a Klondike dance

hall and disappears among an aimlessly milling crowd. He has no particular reason for being there, but the rest of the crowd doesn't appear to have any either, so he doesn't seem so terribly alone. Suddenly all the men take partners and step off onto

the dance floor. Now our expectations are completely reversed. His large, still figure is placed in sharp contrast with the small, active figures behind him. This movement isolates him from their gaiety, and by focusing our attention on him, makes him seem more alone than he was before he entered.

Movement can also be used to reveal depth a layer at a time so that each change of depth alters the meaning of the action. One example is the opening part of this extraordinary shot from Orson Welles's *Citizen Kane*. The story of the film and the character of Kane roughly follow the life of millionaire publisher William Randolph Hearst. In this shot we learn that Kane has lost control over his newspaper empire in the stock market crash of 1929. But this revelation is built up slowly as the action develops. At first we see only Mr. Bernstein, Kane's managing editor and business confidant, reading a legal document setting out the new terms

under which the newspapers must operate. As he reads he lowers the document to reveal Mr. Thatcher, Kane's childhood guardian and present adversary, seated on

the far side of the table. Bernstein continues reading thoughtfully, almost to himself, as Thatcher patiently waits for him to finish; then, a moment later, Bernstein leans back and we see Kane at the far end of the room. Kane now interrupts, and with casual bravado just shrugs off the whole proceeding.

At the beginning of this shot we are not sure how Kane will avert complete ruin. We have just been shown an animated map from which, in quick succession, most of his properties have disappeared. Then Bernstein reads the abject terms of surrender, only to reveal Thatcher, whose prudent counsel Kane has made a career of rejecting. But as Bernstein leans back to reveal Kane, we can instantly perceive Kane's iron resilience. His figure is so far in the background that he seems completely disengaged from what is happening around him; and as he speaks he turns his back in disdain and stares out the window. He is Charles Foster Kane, and in Kane's gargantuan world disaster is only temporary. Thus, through a series of revelations, Welles has enveloped us in the lofty arrogance that is central to the development of Kane's character.

Another way to reveal depth is to move the viewer's attention a bit at a time by changing the point of sharpest focus. That is what happens in this shot from Jean Renoir's *Grand Illusion*. The shot is the last part of a scene in which a German army officer is conducting his French prisoners of war on a tour of the castle in which they'll be held captive. At the beginning of the shot the men are being shown the view from a parapet. However, while we hear the officer telling them about the surrounding countryside, all we see are their figures parading past

Courtesy: JANUS FILMS, INC.

the camera and the landscape out of focus in the background. Then, after the last man leaves the frame, Renoir holds the shot a moment longer and refocuses it so that we can clearly see what they have been looking at. But instead of focusing on the distant landscape, he moves our attention no further than the middle ground of the shot by focusing on the machine gunners who normally occupy the parapet. The irony of the shot instantly becomes apparent because it reinforces what we already know the Frenchmen are intent on seeing. They are trying to estimate the strength of their prison, and it is this one last detail that deflects our attention from the German's glowing descriptions of the beauties of the castle to the Frenchmen's mute search for possible escape routes.

Let's pause for a moment and look at a few of the basic pieces of equipment needed to make these shots. The camera itself will be dealt with later on in this chapter, but it is enough to know that any standard camera and lenses could have been used. And since the frame remained static, the camera needed only to be firmly anchored in place. In most cases this is done by mounting the camera on a tripod. A standard motion-picture tripod has three sturdy wooden legs that are

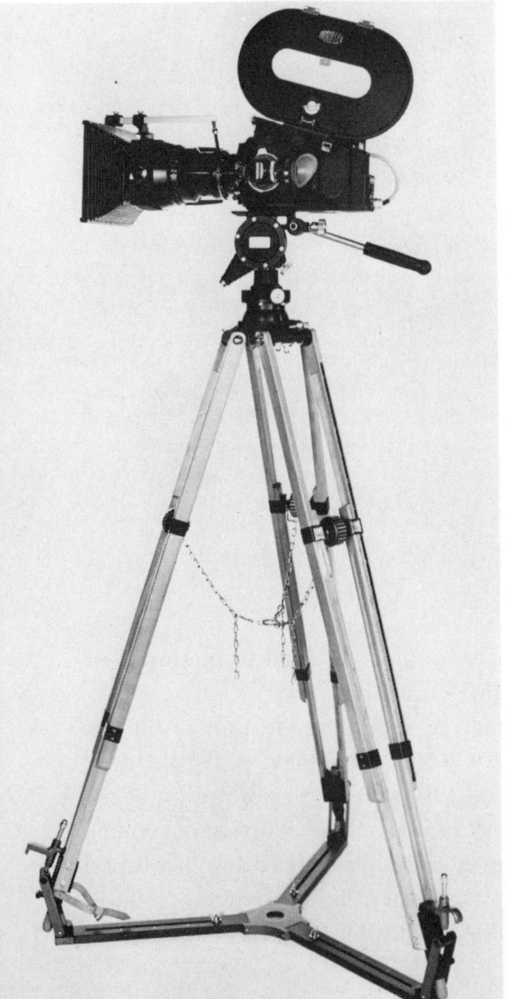

Standard wooden tripod. The Y-shaped device attached to the bottom of the tripod legs is called a spider, it connects the legs together so they won't slide apart when the tripod is set up on a hard, smooth surface.

pivoted from a small platform on their upper end. On their lower end are pointed metal spurs that dig into the ground, or other soft surfaces, and keep the legs from sliding apart. The camera is mounted on a tripod head fastened to the platform of the tripod. The head permits the camera to be moved about freely while the shot is being lined up and then to be locked in place so that the alignment won't change.

The tripod legs are usually forty-eight inches long and can be extended to half again this length. This permits the camera to be positioned at eye level or higher. For shots made from somewhat below eye level the legs can be spread further apart, while for shots made from much lower than that there are "shorty" and "baby" legs. These are progressively shorter sets of legs that permit the camera to be set up at heights as low as two feet. Below this height the camera and head are mounted on a "hi-hat." A hi-hat has a fixed height of from four to six inches. It

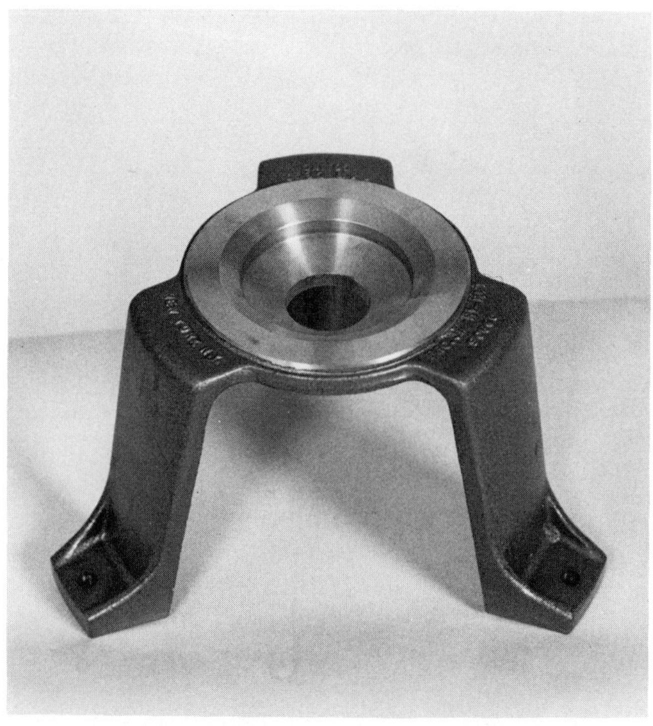

Hi-hat. A tripod head is attached to the level top surface and the camera mounted on the head.

can be placed on the ground for very-low-angle shots or fastened to platforms or risers of various sizes to make shots at any height.

Static shots are also quite commonly made by mounting the camera on one of the small, metal, telescoping tripods used for still photography. And of course, if necessary, the camera can simply be placed on any level, stable surface or, at the other extreme, firmly locked in place on one of the more complicated mobile mounts that will be described later in this chapter. But the standard wooden tripod has been used in almost its present form since the earliest days of motion pictures, and it remains one of the most stable, portable, and flexible camera mounts available.

Building Action in a Moving Frame

Camera movement, like editing, was a revolutionary discovery for the early film-makers. It changed the camera from a passive observer comfortably watching from the best seat in the house to an active participant in the unfolding action. The camera was no longer restricted to showing what happened in a set space in front of its lens; now space could be continuously varied to accommodate or even create the action. Like editing, this movement permitted the film-maker to build the action within complex spaces related in time, spaces that were not available before the camera was moved.

Camera movements can be as complex as necessary. At their simplest they include nothing more than pivoting the camera horizontally (*panning*) or vertically (*tilting*); or they can include freeing the camera and its mount from their fixed position on the floor and moving them toward or away from the subject (*dollying*), parallel to the subject horizontally (*trucking*), or parallel to the subject vertically (*craning*). *Zooming* is also included in camera movement even though, strictly speaking, it is a movement of the lens and not the camera. But the effect of zooming is similar to that of the other camera movements since it too changes the space included in the shot.

One of the most basic ways to move the camera is simply to pan and/or tilt it over an immobile subject. These movements build the action by directing our attention as much to the dramatic relationship between objects as to the intrinsic importance of the objects themselves. This effect can be seen in a shot from *The Birth of a Nation,* D. W. Griffith's silent classic about the Civil War. The shot starts on a southern woman and her family hiding among some barely sheltering branches, then slowly pans right and tilts down slightly to reveal a northern army

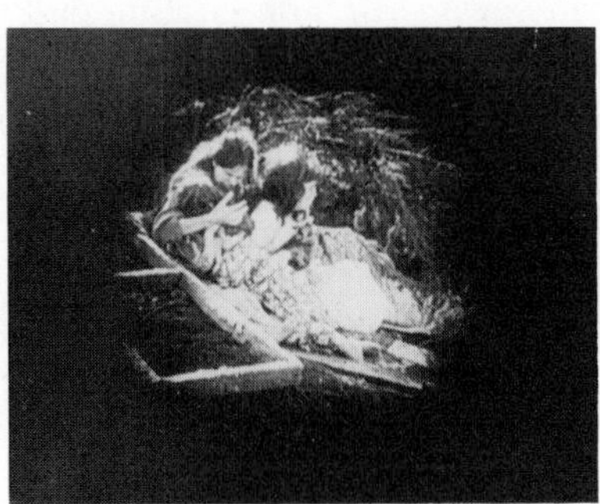

marching through the valley below. In this case the cameraman further focuses our attention at the beginning of the shot by using an *iris,* a small circular opening placed just in front of the lens. This was a standard optical effect in silent films. As the camera pans, the opening in the iris increases in size until the iris is completely gone by the end of the pan.

What Griffith is trying to do in this shot is to show the awesome power of an invading army in terms of its impact on the people whose land is invaded. He does this by slowly expanding the action within the continuously developing space of a pan. The shot at first isolates the reaction of a huddled group of fearful victims by showing them in medium shot. This creates an expectation of some immediate cause by directing our attention out-of-frame along the apprehensive gaze of the oldest daughter. Our expectation is then fulfilled, and the fear directly connected to its source, by a pan in the direction she is looking to show a column of soldiers that stretches beyond the confines of the frame.

While the meaning of each group depends upon the presence of the other, it is the moving camera directing our attention across the intervening space that intimately joins them together within a continuously developing flow of action. This is not a relationship that can be created within a static frame. At the very least, that would require using several different shots, and then the action would have to be carefully built from shot to shot in order to preserve the spatial connection between the groups.

But a sequence of shots would have none of the unfolding drama of a single pan. Because each cut totally changes the image, the cuts themselves would intrude upon the flow of action, imposing a rhythm that is distinctly their own. A pan, however, can be minutely adjusted so that the changing image subtly controls the rhythm of our developing awareness. Like the pull of a painter's brushstroke, the movement of the camera draws our attention along, building tension and suspense until the purpose of the movement is finally revealed. For Griffith this meant narrowing the shot at first, and then carefully, almost imperceptibly, expanding the space in the frame until we are involved in the far wider world marked by the passage of an army.

A pan or tilt can also be used to create a sense of movement in an immobile setting. For instance, in these two shots from Godard's *Breathless,* Belmondo ascends to the top floor of an apartment house simply through the rapid upward tilt of the camera. First we see him run into the back entrance of the building. Then, just as he disappears from sight, the camera sweeps sharply up the face of the building, quickly blurring it into vertically descending streaks as the movement

accelerates. This effect re-creates the compulsive pace which characterizes everything Belmondo does in the film, including his frenzied dash up several flights of stairs to borrow some money.

The camera movement itself is almost pure anticipation. Since there is no way to judge the nature of the intervening space, all we can do is wait for what we see at the end of the shot and connect it to what we saw at the beginning. In this case the movement ends in an abrupt cut to a close-up of a woman answering her

door, and we instantly know that her apartment is on the top floor and that she is responding to Belmondo's knock.

This effect, called a *swish* pan or tilt, is caused by the rapid movement of the camera past stationary objects. Beyond a certain point the camera shutter cannot freeze the rapidly changing image and only a blur is registered. A similar effect can also be created by following a rapidly moving object. Then the moving object stays sharp because it remains fixed in the frame, while the immobile surroundings pass rapidly through the frame and blur. Here is an example, a running shot from

Courtesy: JANUS FILMS, INC.

Kurosawa's *Rashomon.* In this shot the rather egocentric assailant is triumphally celebrating a rape and murder by running whooping through the forest. The movement of the camera increases our sense of his joy and abandon; the rapid camera movement blurs the branches and leaves, and these seem to accelerate and lighten his movements by racing past him.

There is a difference, however, between a pan or a tilt that moves over static objects and one that follows a moving object. When only the camera moves it connects objects in space, but when the camera follows a moving object, that object is connected instead to the changing spaces through which it travels. This is not very apparent in *Rashomon* because the setting is blurred, though even here, by anticipating a change, the blurred surroundings serve to connect the runner's previous setting to the new location in the following shot. But when the movement is slower, the nature of the changing space becomes quite important. Then we can see every subtle change in the setting and this change continually alters our perception of the characters' relationship to their surroundings. This technique can be seen in a shot from Ingmar Bergman's *Monika.* The film is about a socially alienated adolescent who defies his father by running off with a rather wild girl to seek sexual pleasure and total freedom. We see them here as they take his father's boat and head up a fjord into a thinly populated rural area.

The shot begins with just the front of the boat nearly filling the frame, but we don't really see it because we are forced to shift our attention between her

supple figure sunning on the deck and his halting efforts to start the engine. Thus, by dividing our attention the shot quickly delineates the totally different role each expects the other to play. Then, as the engine starts and the boat pulls away, the camera tilts up to reveal the placid, dark water and the barely visible shore toward which they are heading. This movement opens up the space in the frame, giving them seemingly unlimited room in which to move; yet as the camera holds on this foreboding gray setting, their separate figures coalesce in the solitary image of the receding boat. Now our attention focuses on the boat itself. As it shrinks in size it seems to bind them together inexorably, a bleak expectation that dominates all the rest of their journey.

Executing Simple Camera Movements

There are two factors that must be considered when panning or tilting the camera: the speed of the movement and its smoothness. These factors are interrelated because it is very difficult to move the camera smoothly and slowly at the same time. But particularly when the camera is moving past a static subject, or when the direction of the camera movement is not related to any movement of the subject, the pan or tilt must be very slow if the viewer is to see the changes in the shot clearly. Otherwise objects will pass through the frame too fast to be recognized, or in extreme cases will blur or skip across the screen.

Exactly how slow the movement must be depends upon the field of view (*focal length*) of the lens. With a telephoto lens only a small movement of the camera is needed to make an object jump across the narrow field of view, so the camera movement must be extremely slow. With a wide-angle lens just the reverse is true; but even then the speed of the pan or tilt cannot be as fast as our normal head movements because even this speed is too fast for the image to register.

However, the speed at which the camera can be moved past an immobile subject can be increased if the frame rate is increased from the standard 24 frames per second (fps) to 32 or 48 fps. (This can only be done when sound is not synchronously recorded along with the picture—the reasons for this are covered in Section 2, Chapter Six). This increase helps smooth out the camera movement, especially when a telephoto lens is used; and later, when the film is projected at a standard 24 fps, the footage will be slowed down and, therefore, also the speed of movement of the pan or tilt.

The speed at which the camera moves is less of a problem when the camera is following a moving object. Although the speed of the object controls the speed of movement of the camera, any skipping or blurring in the background is rarely noticed because the object fixed in the frame becomes the focus of attention. But there is a threshold beyond which these problems again become noticeable. As we saw in the running shot from *Rashomon,* following very fast action can make the background unrecognizable. In addition, the amount of blurring and skipping also increases with the focal length of the lens; since the narrow field of view of a telephoto lens includes a smaller area of the background, background objects cross the screen quite rapidly.

A higher frame rate will help eliminate these problems; but this is not always feasible because the increased frame rate makes the subject move in slow motion. When that is undesirable, the only other way to freeze the background is to increase the shutter speed without changing the frame rate. On most amateur cameras this is not possible because shutter speed is entirely dependent upon frame rate. However, most professional cameras, and an increasing number of the more expensive amateur cameras, have a "variable" shutter. This permits the normal

exposure time of 1/50 of a second to be increased all the way up to 1/400 of a second without a change in the frame rate.

All panning movements also require one special precaution. If the horizon or other horizontal lines in the shot are to remain level throughout the pan, the camera must be made perfectly level beforehand by means of a spirit level built into the tripod head. The tripod is leveled either by adjusting the tripod legs or by using a "ball leveling mount." With a ball mount, the tripod head, instead of having a flat bottom, has a bowl-shaped base that fits into a similarly shaped platform on top of the tripod. This makes it possible to tip the camera and head quickly and easily in any direction until they are level; then they can be locked in place.

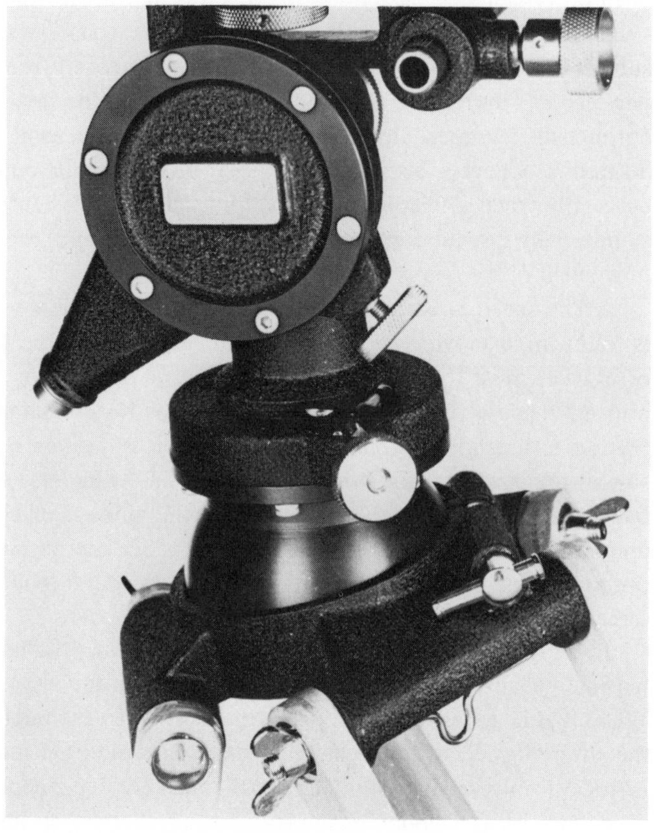

Ball-leveling mount. A right-angle spirit level is just above the shiny round knob in front.

Because of the relatively slow speed of most pans and tilts, it is extremely difficult to smooth out these movements. Again, this is not as difficult a problem when the camera follows a moving object, both because the movement is usually faster and because we attribute any jerkiness in the movement to the object itself; but it is always a problem when the camera moves past an immobile setting because we don't expect the objects to jerk across the frame without apparent reason. In either situation, however, the problem can't be solved simply by the use of a wide-angle lens and a faster frame rate. These will help, but the best solution is to mount the camera on a good-quality *pan head*. This is a tripod head which is designed to control the movements of the camera.

There are several types of pan heads, each somewhat larger and more expensive than the next. The lightest and least expensive is a *friction* head. This type of head smooths out the movement of the camera by retarding the speed of a pan or tilt with the friction between the moving and stationary parts of the head. The degree of friction is adjustable. A friction pan control is also sometimes combined with a spring-counterbalanced tilt control. As the camera is tilted it pushes against this spring, and the further it is tilted, the greater the resistance offered by the spring. This is a better arrangement than friction alone since the spring keeps the camera from dumping forward or back and possibly tipping the tripod over.

A friction head, however, does less to smooth out the movement of the camera than a *fluid* head. In a fluid head every movement of the camera forces a viscous liquid through vanes in drums located in sealed chambers to the side and at the bottom of the head. The damping action of this fluid retards the movements of the camera and, by forcing the cameraman to exert a strong, constant pressure in order to move the camera at all, greatly smooths its motion. In the larger fluid heads there is also a spring-loaded counterbalance in the tilt mechanism; this has the same effect as the spring in a friction head.

For larger, heavier cameras there is also the somewhat larger, heavier *gyro* head. Instead of working against the resistance of a fluid, the gyro head uses the resistance of a heavy, whirling flywheel, or gyroscope. Every movement of the camera causes the flywheel to turn, and it is the inertia of this flywheel that smooths the movement of the camera. This type of head provides a particularly nice kind of motion because it not only tends to retard an accelerating movement, but also maintains the speed of a decelerating movement, giving a very smooth feeling to the end of a pan or tilt by causing the camera to coast to a stop.

Building Action with a Mobile Camera

Once the camera was free to move there was no reason why it should remain fixed on a tripod and restricted to moving through a simple arc. So the camera and the pan head were fastened instead to a mobile platform. At first these platforms were mounted on rails which only permitted the camera to move in a straight line; but this soon gave way to complex rail systems and then to rubber-tired vehicles that allowed the camera to be freely steered across any smooth, level floor. Finally, boom arms were added so that the camera could be raised and lowered as well. And these were only the devices used in the studio. On location almost any wheeled vehicle could become a camera mount, though eventually special dollies, camera

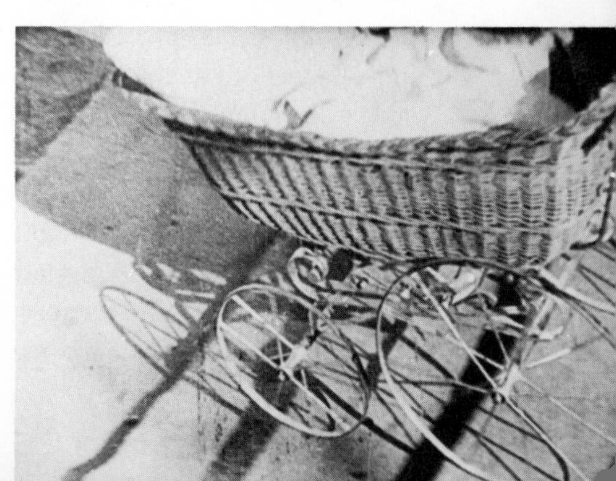

cars, and mobile cranes were designed for use on location. While some of these mounts are more flexible than others, they all remain in use because each serves some special function in dollying, trucking, or craning the camera.

Dollying the camera toward or away from an immobile setting has a unique visual effect. Unlike any other camera movement (except zooming), it does not build the action a piece at a time by substituting new spaces for the part of space originally in the frame. Instead, a dolly holds a part of the space constantly in the frame while expanding or contracting the total space in which the part is set. This effect builds the action either by showing a general setting and then focusing our attention on an isolated part of it, or, as in the following shot from Josef von Sternberg's *The Blue Angel,* by showing a part and then slowly revealing the place that the part occupies in the whole.

This is the final shot in the film. The aging professor, reduced to servitude by his young wife and dishonored by his tawdry part in her sleazy nightclub act, is finally betrayed by her and returns in desperation to his former classroom. He forces his way into the school in the middle of the night, and the caretaker, unable to stop him, follows him as he stumbles to his old desk and collapses across it. We see him here, at the beginning of the shot, caught in the light of the caretaker's flashlight. He is sprawled on the desk, grasping its corners as if to steady himself.

Then, as the clock on the school tower strikes midnight, the camera slowly pulls back to reveal row upon row of dark, empty seats.

The gradual expansion of the space—from the desk to which he clings as a last firm anchor in a reeling world, to the empty classroom devoid of humanity or light—sums up his life in terms of his role as a teacher. He had never needed his students, only the neat rows that they filled; they merely provided a perfectly ordered world in which he stood at the apex, ruling them from his podium. He considered this his place by right, not by obligation, and we see it at first as he does, in isolation. But as the fixed rows of seats methodically recede past the camera, the space slowly opens around him to show that the room bears no mark of his former awesome presence. Layer upon layer, the empty rows build a sense of the rigidity and limitations of his cherished past, until we finally see him as his students did—small and insignificant. By the end of the shot we know that he is as empty as the room; that there is nothing left for him and that he has given up and died. This expectation is then confirmed as the clock ceases tolling.

A short, quick dolly can also be used to direct our attention to small movements in an otherwise static setting. A dolly out, for instance, can suddenly broaden the context of a gesture; or a dolly in can be used, as it is in this shot from Ingmar Bergman's *The Seventh Seal,* to isolate a movement and build its meaning. The shot is part of a scene in a medieval church. A knight returning home from the Crusades has encountered Death, in the form of a black-hooded monk, and they have made a pact that Death will not take him if he can beat Death in a game of chess. Now he is in a monastery church seeking comfort and strength; and because he believes that his confession is being taken by one of the monks, he lets slip his strategy to win at chess. But what the knight cannot see is that it is Death that is concealed behind

KNIGHT: By a combination of bishop and knight I will break his flank.

the confessor's hood. At this point Bergman cuts to a medium shot from the knight's point of view as Death turns and reveals his identity.

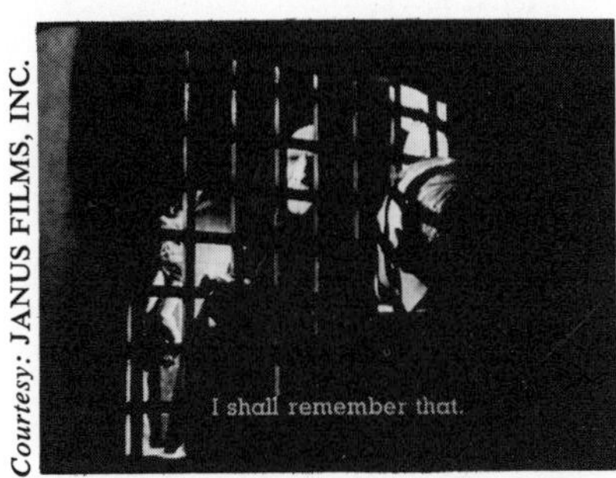

Courtesy: JANUS FILMS, INC.

DEATH: I shall remember that.

The knight clutches the grate that separates them and the camera suddenly dollies in and tilts up as he rises in the frame. This leaves the two of them in medium close-up, confronting one another in stunned silence.

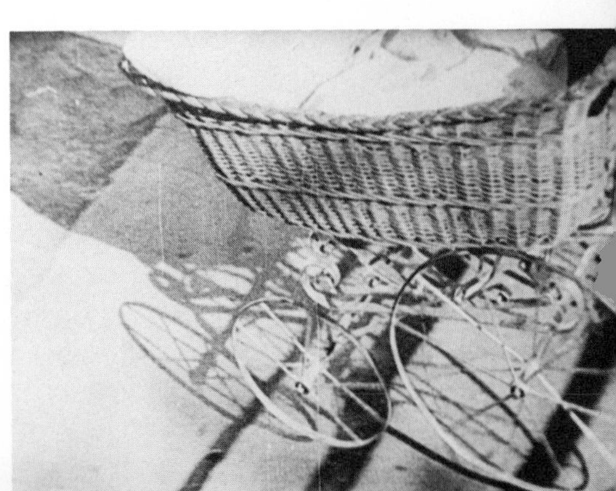

This short dolly is an important dramatic device. We have been aware of Death's presence throughout this whole rather static, long scene, so the revelation is no shock to us, only to the knight. The important point then is to show the effect on the knight, and Bergman chooses to do this indirectly. He uses the quick inward and upward movement of the camera both to emphasize the sudden tensing of the knight's body and to isolate the look of disdainful triumph on Death's face. But this abrupt movement does more than just underline the unexpected reversal of circumstances. It sharply constricts the space in the frame, making it seem as if the knight is suddenly forced to look into a mirror that confronts him with an image of his own mortality. His sin of pride has been swiftly rewarded with an irrevocable promise of death, and our only expectation from then on is to see how this reward will be played out in the rest of the film.

A very similar kind of movement can be created by the use of a zoom lens. This long zoom from Pierre Schoendorffer's documentary *The Anderson Platoon* is a typical example. The film explores the conditions under which a U.S. Army platoon must live and fight in Vietnam. Here we see them on a search-and-destroy

mission. At the start of the shot they are seemingly bunched near a tree line, waiting for an order to move out. Then, at the signal to move, the cameraman zooms the

lens as wide as he can. Now we see that the shelter of the trees was an illusion created by the initial telephoto effect of the lens; actually the men are crossing an open field and are in an extremely dangerous position. This is the first indication of the trouble that is soon to engulf them when they are pinned in the open by an enemy ambush.

Obviously a zoom rather than a walking dolly shot is the only possibility under these difficult circumstances. But even though the effect of a zoom is similar to that of a dolly, in some ways they are quite different. Since a zoom lens can be varied between the collapsed sense of depth of a telephoto lens and the extended depth of a wide-angle lens, the spatial relationship of the objects in the frame is altered throughout the shot. In the first part of the shot both the trees in the background and the rifle barrel in the foreground seem close to the soldiers in the center of the frame; but as the shot widens we see that the trees are more distant from and the soldier holding the rifle is much nearer to the camera than either originally appeared. This effect is quite different from that of a dolly since in a dolly the trees would always seem about the same distance from the camera, and only as the camera moved back would the closer soldier appear in the frame.

There is also a striking difference in the relative speed at which a zoom can take place without seeming to wrench our attention into a wider context. If a dolly had tried to move as rapidly as the zoom, the camera would seem to be hurtling along, adding a sharpness and urgency to the shot. But the zoom could be completed in the short time it took for the soldier in the foreground to take two or three steps because, during most of the zoom, the telephoto effect of the lens col-

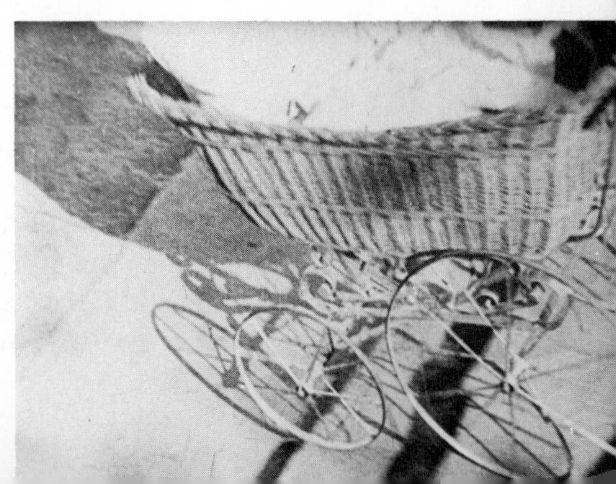

lapses the depth in the shot and the ground doesn't seem to rush by as fast as it would if the camera were dollying at the same speed. As a result, we tend to equate zooming with an instantaneous shift in our attention rather than with actually moving through space, and so we accept a relatively short, rapid zoom as almost equivalent to a cut.

Trucking the camera in an immobile setting is similar to panning in that the camera moves past the subject horizontally. The only difference is that trucking can be infinitely more varied and therefore tie space together in more complex combinations. This can be seen in an extensive trucking shot from John Ford's *The Grapes of Wrath.* In this case the shot is literally meant to show the view from inside a truck—the broken-down, overloaded truck that has brought a family of Okies to a camp filled with other migrants also heading for California. In the shot that immediately precedes this view of the camp we see the truck as it enters the gate. Then Ford cuts to a shot made from the point of view of the driver as his truck winds its way down a narrow, dusty road lined with ramshackle huts, broken automobiles, suspicious adults, and pinch-faced children. Finally, we see the truck again as it pulls into the frame before a shack indicated by one of the guards in the camp.

The space within the frame unfolds like a series of tableaux, discrete images merged by the movement of the camera into a picture of hostility born from the desperate circumstances these people are forced to share. And since we are seeing the camp from the point of view of the people on the truck, the twisting movements of the camera make it seem as if, no matter which way they turn, there is no escape from the problem none of them made—the Great Depression. They are caught in a seamlessly unrolling coil of misery, and even before the truck has lurched to a halt we know that, in a place where savage competition is a necessity of life, they can expect to find little help or comfort.

As we have seen, trucking in an immobile setting has an effect quite different from that of dollying. But when these movements are used to follow a moving object they are practically identical. At least theoretically, dollying with a moving object means moving the camera before or behind the object in order to keep it in frame, while trucking means keeping the object in frame by moving alongside it. But any difference in speed between the subject and the camera will convert a truck into a dolly, and vice versa. Because they are so similar, the effect of either movement is almost the same as that of panning with a moving object. The major difference is that a truck or a dolly not only holds the object in frame, it keeps it the same size throughout the shot, permitting the camera to show a movement develop from about the same perspective for a much longer period of time.

This is also true of craning. Craning is simply raising or lowering the camera —trucking done vertically rather than horizontally. When the camera is craned to follow a moving object the effect is similar to tilting except that the camera maintains its perspective—it doesn't shift from looking down to looking up, and vice versa. But when craning is done independently of the movement of the subject, or past an immobile setting, this movement also gives the camera a new vantage point, one from which it can look up, down, or straight ahead, depending upon the meaning of the shot. Both this use of craning to get a changed point of view and the effect of trucking with a moving object can be seen in this extraordinarily complicated and effective moving camera shot from Jean Renoir's *Grand Illusion*. Renoir is a master of these kinds of shots, and in this one he pulls together and orchestrates several different types of camera movement.

The shot climaxes a scene in which some French officers are giving a Christmas variety show for the other prisoners and the German officers in charge of the camp. About half the performers act as a chorus of female dancers, so they are dressed in women's clothing. Shortly after their dance number starts, one of the leading characters in the film, Jean Gabin, steps from the wings with a copy of a newspaper and announces that the German army has failed to hold a critical position. In a flash of pride, one of the female impersonators tears off his wig and commands the orchestra to play the French national anthem. The long moving camera shot starts on a medium close-up of this performer as he is joined in singing by the rest of the audience, and it is the sound of their voices that creates an emotionally charged background for the entire shot.

First we see the performer looking offscreen toward the stage. Then, in a

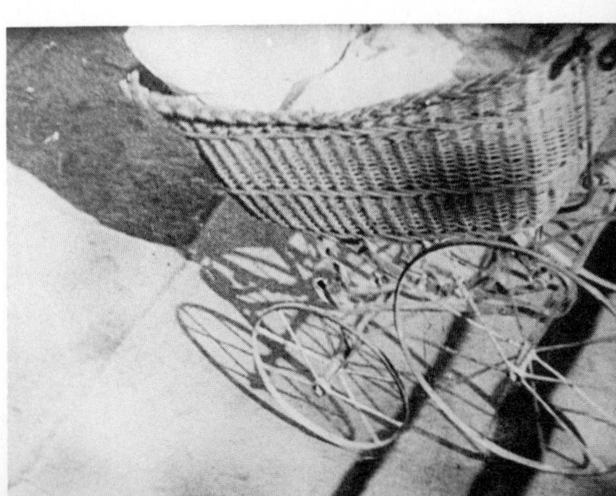

single, complex movement the camera begins to truck back and crane up as it simultaneously pans and tilts in the direction he is looking to show Gabin onstage

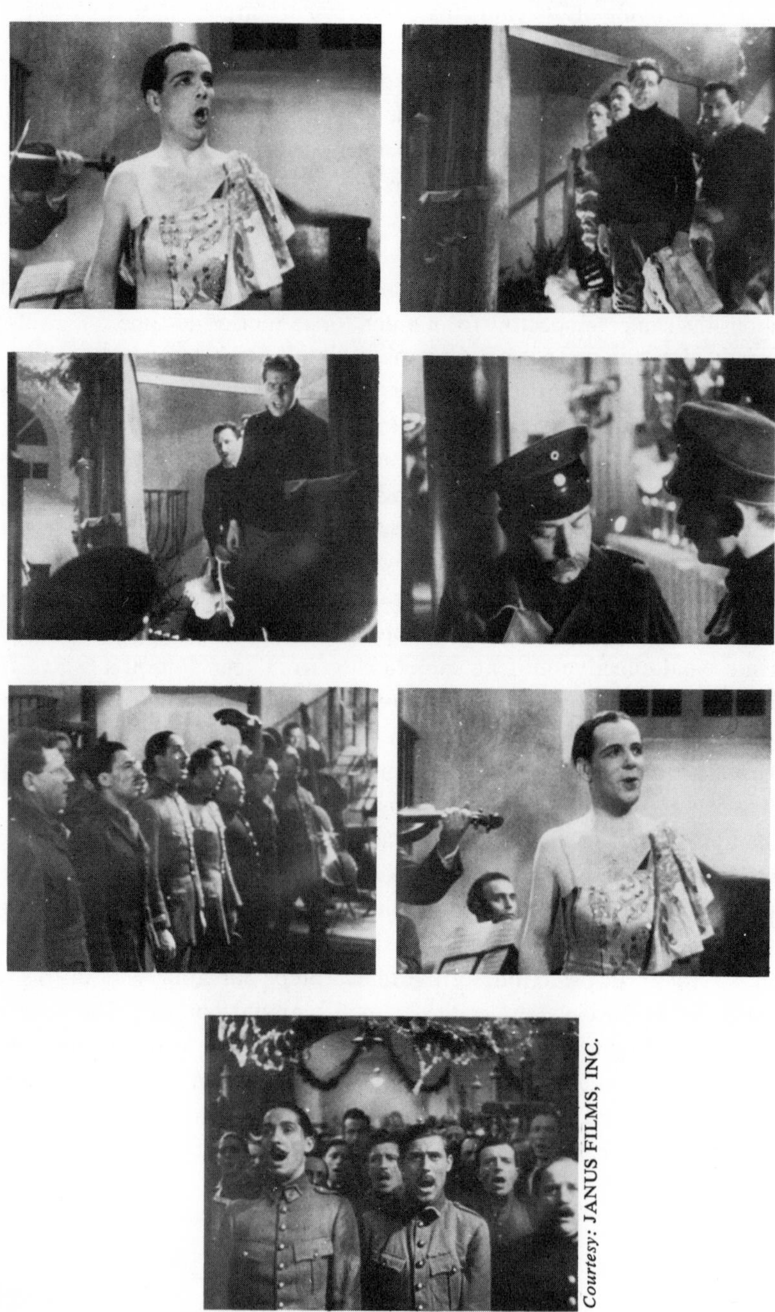

Courtesy: JANUS FILMS, INC.

in the midst of the other performers. When Gabin starts walking across the stage, singing loudly at the German officers seated in the front row, the camera trucks with him until the officers' heads appear in the foreground of the shot. Next, the camera tilts down and holds on them briefly, as they exchange a few words, and then pans left to follow them as they turn to leave. But it pans only as far as the front row of the audience, and when the officers leave the frame we see a long row of prisoners fiercely singing the "Marseillaise." Now the camera slowly cranes down as it trucks back in the direction from which it came, passing along the row of prisoners. At the end of the truck the camera pans right to return to the shot with which it began, a medium close-up of the lone performer, now with a slight smile of accomplishment on his face. Finally, the camera slowly pans left until it is looking straight back into the hall to show the entire group of prisoners singing. This is the closing chorus, and as the song ends the shot dissolves to another of boots running across the darkened courtyard. A squad of German troops has been sent to disband the rebellious prisoners.

With little more than the moving camera Renoir has gradually built an impulse into an insurrection. Each of the various camera movements is designed so that it interacts with the movements of the actors, and together they build the action in stages. But the meaning of this action is cumulative because the continuous movement of the camera links the defiant gesture of one man to the actions of successively larger groups of men until the prisoners are tied together in a sublime act of solidarity and pride. And because the speed and direction of the camera movements are coordinated with a series of progressively faster actions, the pace of the action is imperceptibly matched to the rising intensity of the music so that both music and action reach a crescendo during the final chorus of the song.

The song begins with only one man looking toward the stage in search of support. Then, as the camera slowly begins to truck back, it pans along his line of sight and tilts up until we see the men onstage responding to his lead. This upward camera angle also establishes Gabin's commanding position overlooking the audience; and when the trucking movement quickens to fix him in the frame as he crosses the stage, it both accelerates the pace of the action and holds him in a dominant perspective until he has deliberately insulted the German officers.

But the craning movement was also necessary or the camera would have had to look up at the German officers as well, giving them a towering, almost heroic appearance. Instead, Renoir created just the opposite effect by having the camera elevated slightly so that it could look down upon them, letting us see them as Gabin does: vanquished and slightly diminished.

When the officers abruptly turn to leave, the camera quickly swings about to follow them. The brusqueness of this movement gives the camera its final thrust. It sweeps back past the front row of prisoners, showing their intense involvement, and returns to the performer who started it all just as he savors a brief feeling of

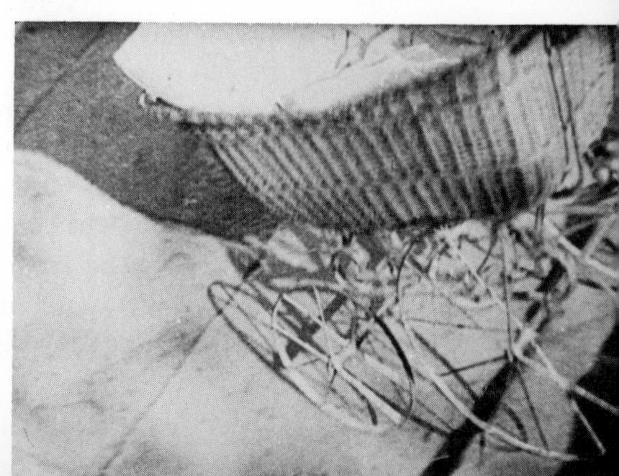

revenge. Then the triumphal closing chorus begins and the camera completes its movement with a long pan to the hall full of prisoners. What began as simple defiance has now swelled to full-scale revolt. Through a carefully plotted series of movements, the force of their singing has risen to a threatening pitch, and the camera lingers on their passionate faces for one last moment before the Germans return to break up the performance and punish its leaders.

Executing Mobile Camera Movements

Now that good-quality zoom lenses are widely available, it is possible to make moving camera shots without actually moving the camera. Even in feature filmmaking zooms are increasingly being used to replace simple dolly movements because they save time in setting up a shot. A zoom also makes it possible to create camera movement in situations where dollying would be extremely difficult, such as across a body of water, over a large object, or up a staircase. And when a zoom is made while the camera follows a moving object, it is hard to tell whether it is a zoom or an actual camera movement because the changing depth of the image is less noticeable.

However, a zoom lens operates so effortlessly that there is always a strong temptation to zoom rather than move the camera. This is especially true now that many cameras come equipped with only a zoom lens. But the constant, arbitrary use of zooming not only becomes monotonous and boring, it can also eliminate many of the important effects created by actual movement of the camera. A zoom just goes straight in or straight back; but even a simple camera dolly permits the camera to be moved about in a variety of ways so that the cameraman can always show the subject from the most meaningful angle.

In trucking or craning the restrictions are the same as those that apply to panning or tilting. The speed of these movements past an immobile setting must be very slow if the viewer is to be able to see the changes in the shot, while the movement can be much faster when the camera follows a moving object. And since the same problems are encountered—skipping and blurring—the remedies are the same: a wide-angle lens and a higher frame rate or faster shutter speed. Dollying, however, is an exception: the objects don't move across the screen, they simply get larger or smaller as they approach or recede from the camera. Because this change is quite gradual, there is no blurring or skipping even during quite rapid dolly movements and therefore no limit on the speed of a dolly. Smoothness too is a problem in all these movements, but unlike the case of panning or tilting, smoothness decreases as the speed of the movement increases. Most mobile mounts are bulky enough to absorb bumps in a slow movement; but as the mount moves faster it hits the bumps harder.

The most basic mobile camera mount is a three-wheeled *tripod dolly*. At its simplest it consists of nothing more than a triangular frame with a wheel at each corner. Each tripod leg sits next to one of the wheels, and the tripod is held in place by a rope or chain stretched between the top of the tripod and the frame of the dolly. Because the wheels are all permanently mounted pointing in the same direction, the dolly can only roll in a straight line. While this makes the dolly rather inflexible, it is sufficient for most camera movements and makes it easy for the dolly to *track*. That means that the dolly follows exactly the same path each time a shot is repeated.

There is also a type of tripod dolly that has wheels mounted on castors. This arrangement permits the dolly to move in several different ways. The wheels can be left to swivel about freely for ease in moving the camera from one setup to another; or two of the wheels can be locked so that they both point in the same direction. These locked wheels are then placed ahead of the camera so that it moves in a straight line until pressure on the rear wheel steers the mount in a new direction. In addition, all three wheels can be locked in the same direction so that the camera tracks in a straight line.

While tripod dollies are extremely light and portable, they have a number of disadvantages that can be overcome only by the use of a type of larger, heavier dolly that completely eliminates the tripod. The big advantage of these more sophisticated dollies is that all the wheels can be turned simultaneously by means of a steering wheel. This kind of movement is called *crabbing* since it permits the dolly to make sharp, angular changes in direction, crablike movements that are particularly useful when the filming is being done in cramped quarters. Because of their larger size these dollies also allow the cameraman, and sometimes an assistant, to ride along with the camera, a necessity with many cameras because the cameraman must keep his eye to the viewfinder eyepiece in order to see the image. Riding the dolly also permits the cameraman to concentrate on framing the shot while a stagehand, called a *grip,* pushes the dolly along a prearranged path.

Another disadvantage of the tripod dolly is that it is cumbersome to change the height of the camera. This is not a problem with most larger dollies, however, because they have an elevator column or a boom arm on which to mount the camera. These permit the camera to be raised or lowered either manually or automatically, and most are designed to work smoothly and quietly enough so that they can be used to crane the camera up and down during the shot. The largest of these cranes can carry a cameraman, his assistant, and the director forty feet above the floor; and because of the great horizontal as well as vertical flexibility of the crane arm, there is little need to move the rest of the unit during a shot. However, some of these cranes are also self-propelled, permitting them to be easily moved in place for a shot, while those on a jeep or a truck chassis can be taken on location.

Because of their size, most studio dollies and cranes also accommodate the largest, most sophisticated pan heads. These are called *cradle* heads. Instead of simply tipping the camera forward or backward, a cradle head rocks the bottom out from under the camera, thus keeping the weight of the camera centered over

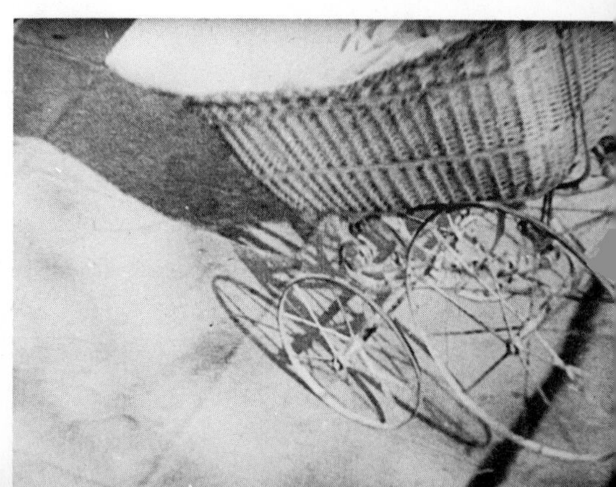

Cradle head mounted atop the boom arm of a 4-wheeled crab dolly.

the mount—something which is particularly important with a large, heavy camera. Otherwise its great weight would be hard to control and would put a tremendous strain on the pan head.

The movement of a cradle head is controlled either by friction, or even better, by means of two cranks, one for pans and the other for tilts. These cranks work on the principle of a large number of turns for a small movement of the camera; this automatically smooths out any irregularities in the cranking and gives the cameraman very close control over the speed of the movement. The cranks are geared so that they can be set at two different speeds, one for slow and the other for faster movements. The cranks can also be completely disengaged so that the camera can be moved freely.

The techniques and camera mounts used on location are somewhat different from those used in the studio. While most rubber-tired studio dollies can be used on indoor locations, they can be used outdoors only if the ground is level enough to lay a floor of plywood sheets. However, if this process is too expensive or inconvenient, a *track dolly* can be used: a four-wheeled dolly that runs on wooden or metal rails. These rails can be laid and leveled over all but the roughest terrain; and while the tracks themselves restrict the complexity of the camera movement, they can be designed to support a relatively large dolly with a boom arm, adding to the freedom of movement. There are also monorail systems. Like tripod dollies, these single-track systems permit only simple, straight-line movements. Their great advantage, however, is that the rails and the mount are quite light and portable.

A car or a truck can also be converted into an extremely flexible camera platform, to which any silent comedy auto chase will attest; but there must be a relatively smooth road on which to travel, and the springs and shock absorbers must be in good condition if the shot is to be free of a lot of bounce and jiggle. In addition, the camera must be firmly mounted or it will vibrate. If the camera is inside the car or truck, it can be mounted on a low tripod firmly fastened to the floor of the vehicle, or on a hi-hat fastened to a plank running between the rear windows. If the camera is outside the vehicle, it can be fastened to a car-top mount, the simplest of which is a hi-hat with suction-cup feet.

The smoothness of the camera movement will also be affected by the speed of the car or truck. The faster it goes, the bumpier the ride. However, if a high speed is necessary, the illusion of speed can be created without an actual increase in the speed of the vehicle by simply using a slow frame rate and closing down the variable shutter so that the image won't blur. For instance, if the car travels at 10 mph and the camera runs at 12 fps, when the film is projected at 24 fps the effect is the same as if the car were traveling at 20 mph. Of course, this technique works only if there are no people moving in the shot, since the speed of their movements will also be doubled. Still, this is such a useful technique that there is a table in the *American Cinematographer Manual* which gives the speed that will result from various combinations of car speed and frame rate, and also the shutter opening necessary to prevent blurring.

Because of their extreme maneuverability, helicopters too have become an important means for moving the camera. They can be used both for aerial shots and as a kind of supercrane that permits the camera to start at ground level and then smoothly pull up and away, either slowly or quickly, and in any direction. At one time the bone-jarring shake of their whirling blades had ruled out helicopters as a

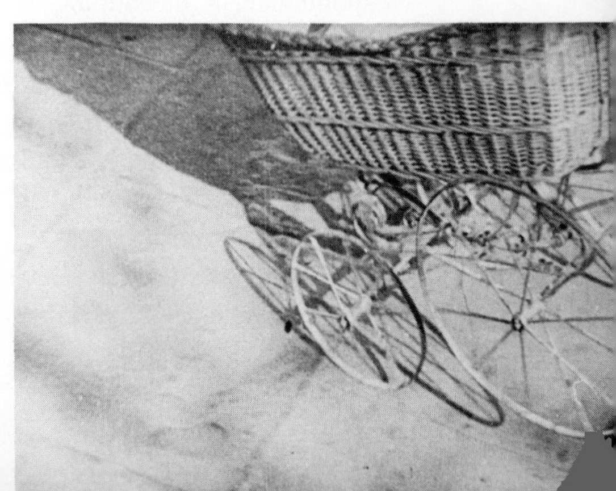

camera platform, but this problem has been overcome by means of specially built suspension mounts. These work so well that helicopter shots are now widely used in all kinds of film-making, even for wide-screen feature films, giving rise to a corps of cameramen who specialize in this kind of cinematography.

The Freely Moving Camera

As is evident by now, with each increase in the range and complexity of the camera movement, the paraphernalia needed to move the camera become heavier and more cumbersome. This inconvenience was long accepted as a necessary condition for making films (with a few notable exceptions in documentary film-making); but it became a problem of immediate and pressing concern in the early days of television news because the requirements 16mm news film had to meet were almost the opposite of those for 35mm films designed to be shown on a theater screen. In television the camera had to be able to move about freely and quickly in order to capture the often fast-paced and unpredictable events unfolding before it; and if the image was a little unsteady as a result, this was no problem because the television screen was so small.

The only solution, and it was not a new one, was to use a hand-held camera. However, the few small cameras that could be used in this way were not adaptable for filming with synchronously recorded sound, and those used for sound were too big to carry about. The next step, then, was to design not only a small camera that could be used to film with synchronous sound, but also a good-quality zoom lens so that the actual movement of the camera could be minimized. Up to that time the image quality of zoom lenses had been mediocre at best and the zoom range quite limited. Within a short while, however, zoom lenses were developed with exceptional sharpness and an extreme zoom range, and more recently, with focusing that extends to within inches of the lens. These lenses have also been made considerably smaller and lighter than their predecessors, so as to keep up with camera designs that have progressively reduced the size and weight of the camera from over fifty pounds to ten pounds or less.

Television news film not only created the impetus for lightweight, highly portable camera and sound equipment, it also showed what could be done when such equipment was available. Once the camera was free to move about it could engage reality in a completely new way. Since there was now no restriction on how sound and picture could be synchronously recorded (the details of this problem are discussed in Section 2, Chapter Seven), the cameraman could immediately respond to a spontaneously developing flow of action. And because this response was usually instantaneous and intuitive, it functionally combined the jobs of director, cameraman, and crew in the one person who had control of the camera. Thus, portable equipment, plus the use of naturally available light, allowed the film to be shot by just a cameraman and a sound man; and the smallness and mobility of this production unit in turn permitted more complete involvement in the action they were filming.

The nightly flow of television news film and documentaries spurred the interest of documentary film-makers, who had long desired more flexible, less obtrusive means for interpreting their subjects. And the audience, because of their experience with television, were now both more familiar with and accepting of the less polished techniques that marked the use of the hand-held camera. They tended to ignore the unsteadiness, the sudden movements, the searching for focus that might otherwise have intruded upon the developing action by calling attention to the technical means needed to capture the image.

This combination of equipment, audience, and artistic interest was catalytic, and it inevitably led to the development of a whole new style of experimental and documentary film-making which received the French title of *cinéma vérité*. In this type of film-making the camera and the sound recorder attempted to capture a slice of life by continuously following one subject. The assumption was that the film-making process was now so unobtrusive that what was recorded on film was perfectly spontaneous and natural, and therefore truthful. This quality of unadorned honesty was then stylistically reinforced by shooting in long takes so that editing need play only a minimal role in shaping the reality caught by the camera.

Very little pure *cinéma vérité* is done now, however, because the form is too restricted without editing. The material had to be shaped in the editing room to make it both more interesting and more meaningful for the audience. As a result, in recent years film-makers have reverted to styles and techniques reminiscent of earlier documentary film-making, but now they are using a formidable array of equipment that still permits them to become intimately involved with their subject in a way only dreamed of by their predecessors. And the equipment itself, while smaller and more manageable than ever, is now so complex and sophisticated that a hand-held 16mm camera can be used to produce wide-screen images for projection in a theater.

Hollywood was never unmindful of these developments, even though they went against the grain of traditional feature-film-making practice, and were occurring at a time when the feature film was being enlarged to cover a bigger, wider screen than ever before. The fact is, a hand-held camera had always found specialized uses in certain types of action-oriented feature films. The cameraman James Wong Howe had even achieved a degree of recognition for shooting a boxing sequence in *Body and Soul* by hand-holding a studio camera while roller-skating around the fighters. But recently, as the economics of film-making have slowly forced Hollywood films out of the studios and onto locations, what had always been viewed as the necessary exception to the rule of a rock-steady camera has increasingly become an expressive tool in its own right, and the lightweight, portable camera is now a necessary part of feature film-making. This fact, in turn, has led to

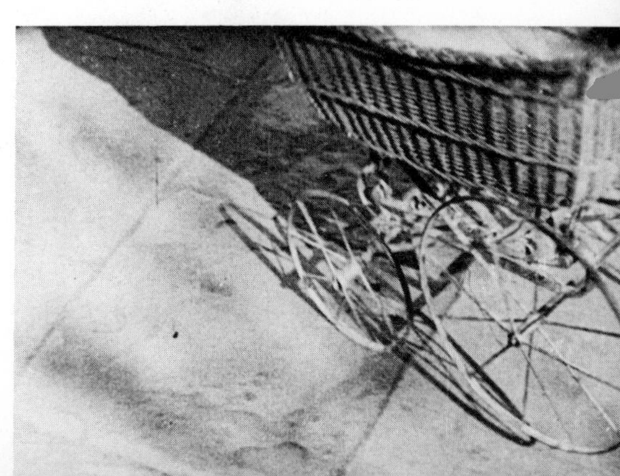

the development of a whole new breed of 35mm and even 65mm cameras specifically designed for hand-held operation.

While a hand-held camera can make all the various movements that have been discussed so far, they can't be made as slowly and steadily as from the simplest camera mount. On the other hand, a hand-held camera can make complex movements quickly and spontaneously and can readily move about in places where a standard mobile mount can't be used without elaborate preparations, such as up and down stairs, through dense crowds, and over rough terrain. A hand-held camera can also be moved in ways that would be next to impossible for even the most flexible camera mount. For instance, in the following shot from *The Anderson Platoon,* the uneven quality of what might loosely be called a trucking movement deeply involves us in the meaning of the action.

In this shot the men are pinned to the ground by enemy gunfire, and as they scramble for cover, the cameraman shows their tortuous progress by holding the camera in front of him while crawling alongside them. Here the camera not only captures the scene in the only way possible but adds to the meaning of what we are seeing. Its jagged, bumping motion makes us feel as if we too are caught under fire and gives us a very real sense of imminent injury and death by making us see the horizon jerk and the ground heave just as these soldiers do.

It is even possible to create movements that are uniquely the result of hand-holding the camera. That is the case in this shot from a prize-winning student film, *The Trip,* by John Dentino. The film is a re-creation of the experiences of an adolescent on LSD, and in this shot we see his morbid hallucination of being run over by a car.

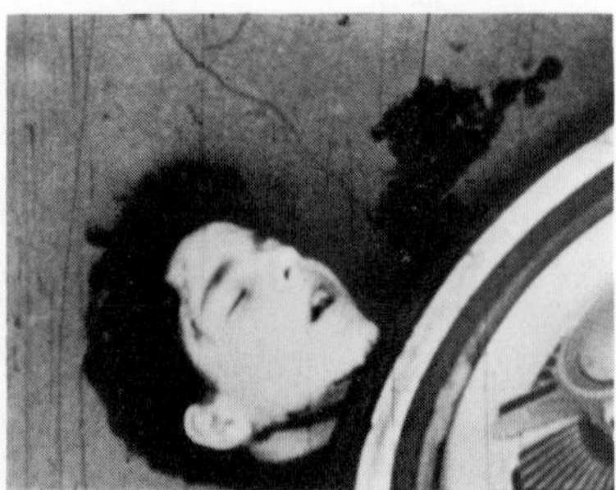

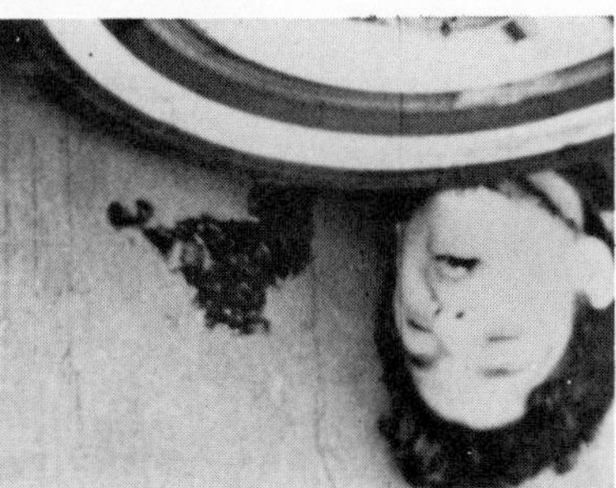

While a simulation of a wheel actually running over the boy's body would not have been hard to stage, it would have had little impact compared to the feeling of distended and irresistible motion created here by the movement of the camera. The movement itself, however, was quite simple. It consisted of nothing more than pointing the camera straight down at the victim, and then slowly rotating it about the axis of the lens so that the frame turned through a full circle. The result is an illusion that the wheel itself is actually turning when in fact it only revolves around the periphery of the frame.

Executing Hand-Held Camera Movements

As the use of the hand-held camera has increased, a number of techniques have evolved which make it easier to steady the camera and support its weight for long periods of time. One of the most important of these is a redesign of the camera itself so that most of its weight is toward the rear of the body. This elongates the body and makes it possible for the cameraman to balance the camera on his shoulder rather than having to brace it in front of him. However, when the camera is of the more traditional, top-heavy design, added support can be obtained by the use of a body brace. This is a metal tube that is bent into a right angle, with one end fastened to a belt around the cameraman's waist and the other hooked over his shoulder. The camera rests on top of the angle with the viewfinder level with the cameraman's eyes. In either case, whether braced or balanced, the camera is partially supported so that only one hand is needed to steady it while the other is free to zoom and focus the lens.

There are, in addition, several techniques that can be used to smooth the movement of the camera during the hand-held equivalent of a dollying or trucking

shot. Since these hand-held movements involve the same problem of steadiness as has been previously mentioned, the remedies are again the same: use a wide-angle lens, and if possible follow a moving object. Also, when walking slowly with the camera it is better to walk on the balls of the feet than to put each foot down as we normally do, heel first. Each time the heel strikes the ground, it jars the camera. And just as a matter of caution as well as steadiness, it is best to have someone guide the cameraman when he is walking backwards in front of a moving subject. It would take nerves of steel and suicidal instincts for a cameraman to walk smoothly in one direction while looking in another.

Like James Wong Howe on roller skates, the camera can also be moved smoothly by putting the cameraman on wheels. At its simplest this can mean nothing more than just pulling him in a child's coaster wagon, or pushing him on a bicycle, in a swivel chair or on a furniture-mover's dolly. Or if there is time for more elaborate preparation, a wheelchair makes a good mobile mount. In fact, Haskell Wexler, who often prefers working with a hand-held camera, designed what he calls a *paraplegic dolly* for the shooting of *Who's Afraid of Virginia Woolf?* This is a low, rolling platform with tall side rails in which he can stand or kneel while being pushed about.

There are times when it is even preferable to hand-hold the camera. For instance, when shooting from a fast-moving vehicle, a hand-held camera can be supported out in front of the cameraman, free of his body, so that his arms and shoulders absorb the bumps, jiggles, and vibrations caused by the high speed. Handholding the camera is also the only means for making the fluid action shots needed in surfing, skiing, sky-diving, and other sporting films. However, as the demand for such footage increases, cameramen are devising shoulder harnesses or head mounts. These keep the camera pointing straight ahead of them while freeing their arms and hands so that they can become active participants in the action.

Probably the ultimate freedom of camera movement, though, is achieved when the camera alone participates in the action. An early example of this is a shot from John Grierson's *Granton Trawler*. While he was filming fishermen heaving in nets during a heavy storm, an abrupt lurch of the boat sent the camera, still running, hurtling to the deck. This toppling, spinning effect was so expressive of the men's exertions that it was later included in the film. A similar effect is also created when footage from fighter-plane gun cameras is used to show an air battle; or, as was done in Jack Nicholson's first feature, *Drive, He Said,* a small combat camera was sealed inside a styrofoam sphere and pitched through a basketball hoop. In all these examples the movement itself is the meaning of the shot, but it is movement that can be produced only if the camera is made part of the action.

Part II:

The Nature of the Camera

We have been on an odyssey through a world in which the film-maker's vision is distilled by camera placement and movement. Yet this is just the first step in realizing those very special relationships between objects that plunge us deeper and deeper into the intensely personal image of the world each film-maker develops throughout a film. The fragments of this world must still be captured by means of the camera. The light reflected from the objects that make up the image must be gathered, bent through the camera's mechanism, and impressed on a strip of film, a complex optical and mechanical process that has a definite effect on the quality of the image. It is this aspect of camerawork that we will look at next.

The Basic Qualities of Lenses

In *The 400 Blows,* François Truffaut uses lenses to manipulate space in especially precise ways. They are his means for indicating the increasing alienation of the young hero, Antoine, as he tries to find his place in the world. Throughout the film the places Antoine lives and visits—his school, the streets of Paris, a reformatory—are shown as larger and larger spaces in which he becomes hopelessly lost. Eventually these spaces engulf his small figure and cut him off not only from those around him, but from his own past, making it impossible for him to find his way back to the relative safety of his childhood.

During the early part of the film Antoine's impending isolation is first suggested by the changing perspective from which we see the two rooms that delimit his existence. First we see the tiny combination living-dining room which Antoine shares in cramped familiarity with his mother and father; then an equally small room in which he hides after he runs away from home. These are the widest views shown us in the sequence of shots from each room. While both shots had to be made from about the same distance, how different each room appears. With just the change of a lens and a slight change of angle, it is as though Antoine has entered a different world. By using a wide-angle lens to show the room to which Antoine has escaped, Truffaut has literally expanded the space around him.

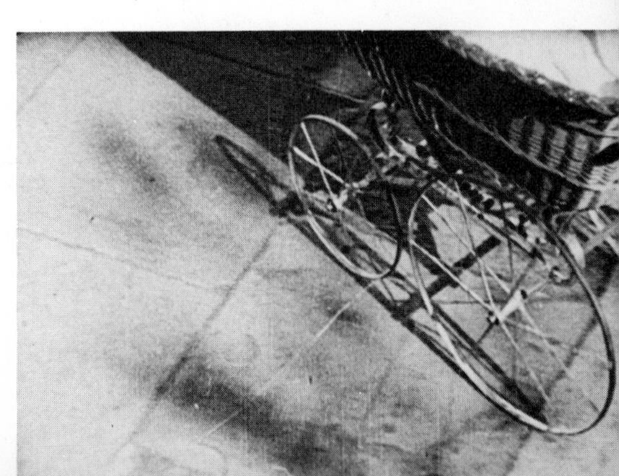

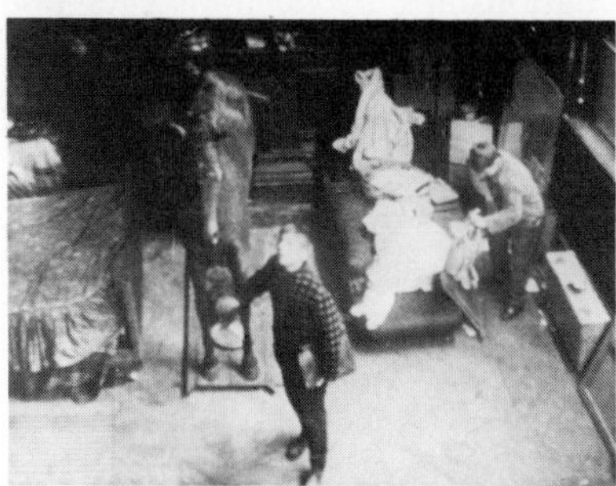

Courtesy: JANUS FILMS, INC.

This change of lens controls our perception of Antoine. It alters both the size of the rooms and his size in relation to them. As a result, whenever we see him in his home he seems relatively confined—but the space is his, he dominates it by filling it. And whenever we see him in his hideout he seems less enclosed and therefore almost free—but also much smaller, more lost in his surroundings.

The ability of different lenses to expand or contract the field of view, that is, to see a wider or narrower area in front of them, is referred to in terms of the *focal length* of the lens. This is an optical characteristic of the lens, a measure of the distance between its optical center and the film when the lens is focused on a very distant object. Put very simply, the shorter the focal length of the lens, the wider its field of view. This rule holds true for both regular and zoom lenses since a zoom lens is nothing more than a lens in which the focal length can be continuously varied.

But a change of focal length does more than just produce a wide or a narrow shot. It also affects the apparent depth of the shot. The shot in Antoine's hideout is not only wider than that in his home, it also seems deeper. If, however, instead of changing lenses, Truffaut had made the shot in Antoine's hideout simply by moving the camera farther away, the objects would become smaller as more of the room was included in the shot, but the room itself wouldn't seem to recede as far into the distance. It is the shorter focal length (wider angle) of the lens which creates this sense of greater depth. Or looked at in reverse, in his home the back wall of the room seems quite close behind the figures because of the longer focal length of the lens.

Thus, in these two shots, the change of focal length alters both the area included in the shot and its apparent depth. But even when focal length is not used to change the field of view, the film-maker can still use different focal lengths to control the sense of depth. This technique, in turn, also affects the shape of objects and the way in which they seem to move. These effects can all be seen in three shots from the NBC documentary *Confrontation,* produced by Fred Freed. The shots are close-ups of college professors involved in the student-faculty strike at San Francisco State College. While each of these heads almost fills the frame, each was shot from

a different distance with a lens of a different focal length. This use of different focal-length lenses alters our perception of each of these characters and helps delineate the different role each plays in the strike.

The man in the first shot is in sympathy with the goals of the strike but is opposed to the strike itself. He is shown here as he crosses a picket line of chanting, hostile students and faculty, who are blocking access to the campus. His estrangement from these activities, and the frustrations of his role as an unwilling antagonist, are quickly summed up by his isolation in the narrow view of a long-focal-length lens. The collapsed sense of depth created by this lens slightly flattens the entire scene, thus making him seem rather two-dimensional and stiff by making his ear and nose appear to be in almost the same plane. This lens also makes the light posts appear almost immediately behind him, even though they stretch back along the path, and this effect makes his surroundings seem to press in upon him. And it retards his movements. He doesn't seem to get very far because his image becomes only slightly larger as he approaches the camera. He is caught and held by the qualities of this lens, unable to bend, or turn, or escape from the strike.

The man in the second shot is one of several faculty members involved in a heated discussion at union headquarters. He is both deeply committed to the strike and greatly concerned about its consequences. Here the expanded depth of a short-focal-length lens is used to emphasize the emotional agitation of the situation in which he finds himself. This lens distends his features and makes his slightest move-

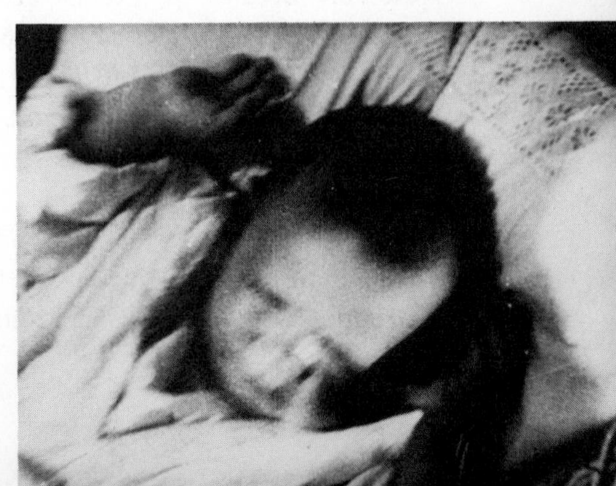

ment seem unnaturally large and quick. His nose juts from his face while his ear recedes almost to the back of his head; and even the slightest inclination of his head toward the camera makes him seem to lean precariously forward. The lens also expands his surroundings to include the activities going on around him, activities which add to the intensity of his feelings by placing him in the organizational center of the strike.

The third shot is of one of the faculty strike leaders. He is at home listening to doubts voiced by his wife. But at least temporarily he is outside the action with a moment to think, and the choice of an intermediate-length lens reflects his situation. His features are neither flattened nor expanded. A normal distance seems to separate his nose and ears, and the hand in front of his face isn't exaggerated even though it extends toward the camera. His movements are completely natural, and his comfortable setting doesn't either push up against him or extend so far back as to leave him exposed in the middle of the room. Here the lens provides a kind of benign neutrality in which he can sort out his thoughts and consider alternatives.

The sense of depth created by each of these lenses is a result of their focal length—but only indirectly. All lenses expand or collapse space, depending upon the distance between the lens and the subject. It is focal length, however, which determines how close to the lens an object must be placed to fill the frame. For instance, the first close-up was made with a long lens, one of approximately 100mm focal length. As a result, the subject had to be at least twenty-five feet from the camera for his head to fit in the 16mm frame. The second shot, on the other hand, was made with a wide-angle lens of about 12mm focal length, so the subject had to be no more than three feet away to get the same result. And in the last shot, made with approximately a 25mm lens, the lens-to-subject distance was about six feet. In other words, as the focal length decreased, the object had to be moved closer to the lens in order to fill the frame, and it was this change of distance which caused the apparent change of depth.

Of course, the size of the frame affects the lens-to-subject distance as well. If the same 100mm lens used in shot 1 is used to fill a 35mm instead of a 16mm frame, the subject must be moved to within twelve feet in order to fill the larger frame. But moving closer would nullify some of the inherent distortion of distance. So, to create the same effect by maintaining the needed lens-to-subject distance with the larger frame, a proportionately longer, or 200mm lens must be used. Similarly, if the same shot were to be made on 8mm film, the focal length of the lens would have to be reduced to 50mm.

How any particular-length lens will work with a particular frame size is predictable, because for every frame size there is a normal-length lens. This is a lens which is twice as long as the diagonal dimension of the frame. With 65mm film, a normal lens has a focal length of 100mm; with 35mm film, 50mm; with 16mm film, 25mm; and with 8mm film, 13mm. It has been found through long experience that for each frame size lenses of these focal lengths produce image qualities that approximate those of the human eye. This fact also means that lenses that are longer than this normal length will have a telephoto effect, while those that are shorter will have a wide-angle effect. As a result, a 25mm lens is a normal lens in 16mm, a wide-angle lens in 35mm, and a telephoto lens in 8mm.

Focal length is also used to measure the amount of light which can pass through a lens. The maximum amount of light that can enter the lens is determined by the diameter of its front element, and how large an area this light will be gathered from is determined by its focal length. Therefore, the light-passing ability of a lens is expressed by a fraction composed of these two numbers. The top part of the fraction is the lens diameter and the bottom part is the focal length. In other words, the light-passing ability of a 25mm lens with a front element 12.5mm in diameter is 12.5/25, or 1/2. This fraction is then abbreviated into an *f* number or *f stop,* and the lens is known as an *f*2 lens. Similarly, if the front element of another 25mm lens is 20mm in diameter, the light-passing ability is 20/25, or 1/1.2. This, then, is an *f*1.2 lens, and because we are dealing with the weird world of fractions, this smaller *f* number means that a greater amount of light can pass through the lens.

Since it is rarely necessary to use a lens at its maximum *f* stop, inside every lens there is some device for reducing the amount of light reaching the film. This device is usually an *iris diaphragm,* a circular opening located at about the middle of the lens that can be increased or decreased in diameter by the rotation of a ring on the outside of the lens. This ring is marked off in *f* stops. The smallest *f* number on this ring is the largest possible opening in the iris. This is the maximum light-passing

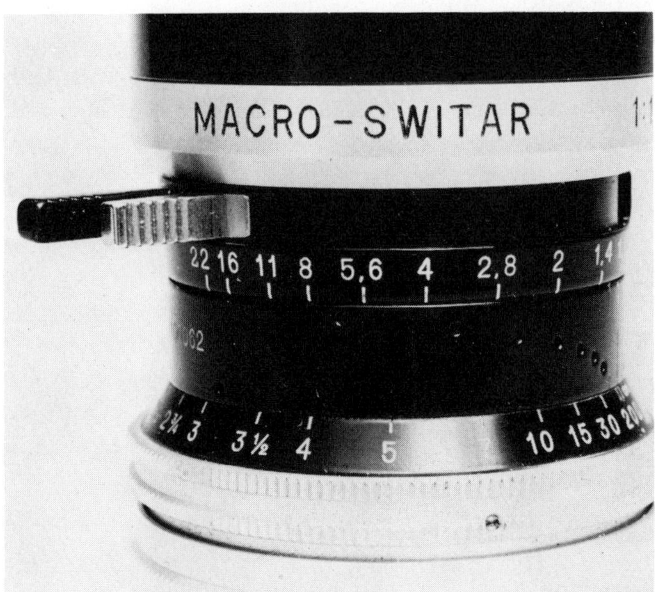

Aperture ring (upper scale) marked off from f 1.4 to f 22. This ring is rotated by means of the handle projecting to the left.

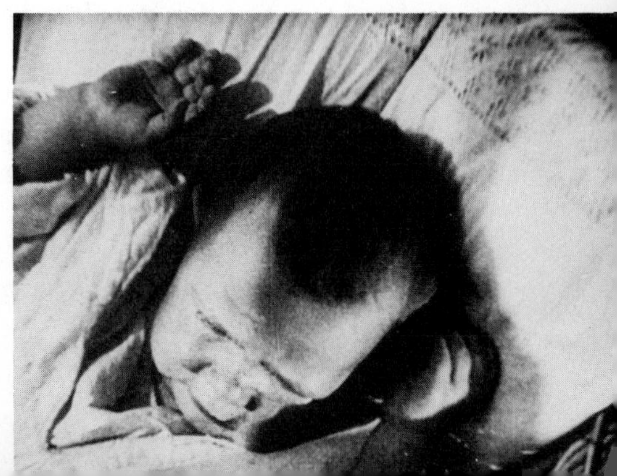

power of the lens. All the other numbers represent progressively smaller openings in the iris, so the *f* numbers get increasingly larger. Each number represents half the light-passing power of the smaller number immediately preceding it, or twice the power of the larger number immediately following it. These numbers have now been standardized and most modern lenses have *f* stops of 2, 2.8, 4, 5.6, 8, 11, 16, and 22. Some *faster* lenses open up farther than *f*2, and some wide-angle lenses cannot be *stopped down* further than *f*16.

There is, in addition, a relationship between focal length and another important function of the lens: controlling focus. The point of sharp or *critical* focus changes as the lens moves toward or away from the film. The closer the object that has to be critically sharp, the further the lens has to be moved from the film. Focus, however, can either drop off sharply, or it can be made to fall off slowly. When it falls off slowly, other points in the frame, while less than critically sharp, are still sharp enough not to appear blurred. This zone of acceptably sharp focus is called the *depth of field.* It is the distance between the closest and the farthest points that still appear sharp, and it is controlled by the focal length of the lens, the *f* stop, and the point of critical focus.

The role that focus and depth of field play in directing our attention within the frame can be seen in two shots from Ingmar Bergman's *The Silence.* The film is about the brief stay of three travelers—a young woman, her son, and her older sister —in a nameless foreign country. Since they cannot speak even the simplest phrases in the local language, they are totally isolated and forced in upon themselves. This isolation and the conflict it generates is one of the principal themes of the film, and it is developed at least partly by the control of focus.

Courtesy: JANUS FILMS, INC.

In the first shot the older woman, seated in the foreground, is trying to occupy herself by listening to the radio, while her sister, in the background, is dressing to go out by herself. The great depth of focus in this shot forces us to watch both of them at once, and the tension of having to alternate our attention between their divergent activities creates a sense of the estrangement that is growing between them.

In the other shot the boy's mother has now left him alone in the hotel room. He lies down on the bed, and all we see are his hands describing arcs through the air as he makes them into dog-fighting warplanes. Here the shallow depth of field

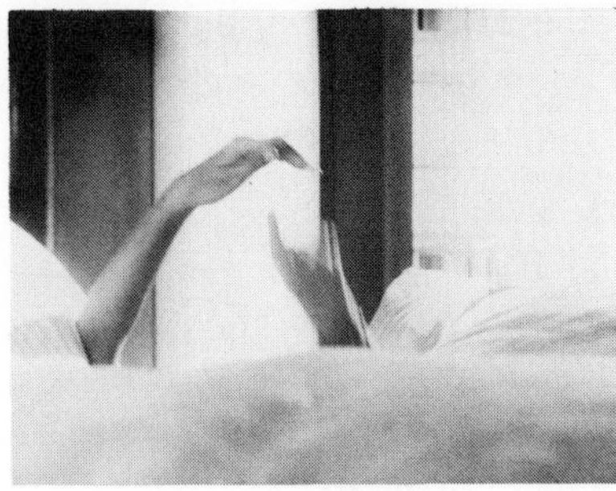

focuses our attention on his hands by isolating them in a blurred field of bedclothes and lace curtains. And by the isolation of his motions, his feeling of separation and loneliness, of being cut off from the only other person to whom he can speak—his aunt—is made poignantly apparent.

Because depth of field increases as the opening in the iris diaphragm of the lens gets smaller, the larger the *f* number, the greater the depth of field. However, *f* numbers are fractions of focal length, so as the focal length gets longer, the diameter of the actual opening in the iris at any particular *f* stop gets larger. This means that at the same *f* stop, a long-focal-length lens has less depth of field than a short-focal-length lens. Depth of field also changes with the focus of the lens, becoming shallower as the point of critical focus gets closer. For instance, a 100mm lens set at *f*8 will have thirty-three feet of depth when focused at fifty feet, but only one foot, three inches of depth when focused at ten feet.

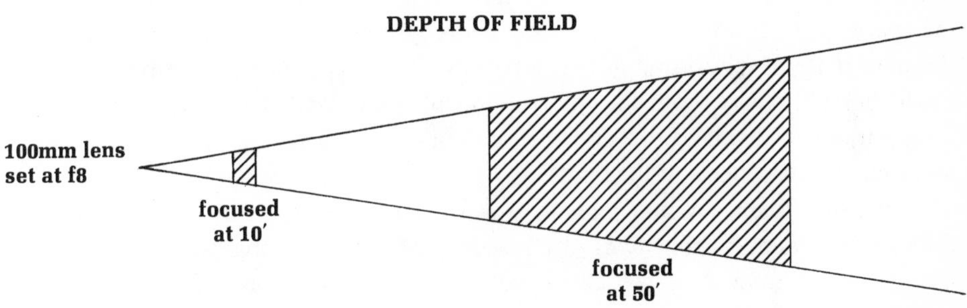

In addition, depth of field doesn't extend an equal distance on either side of the point of critical focus. It is shallower in front than behind. For example, when a

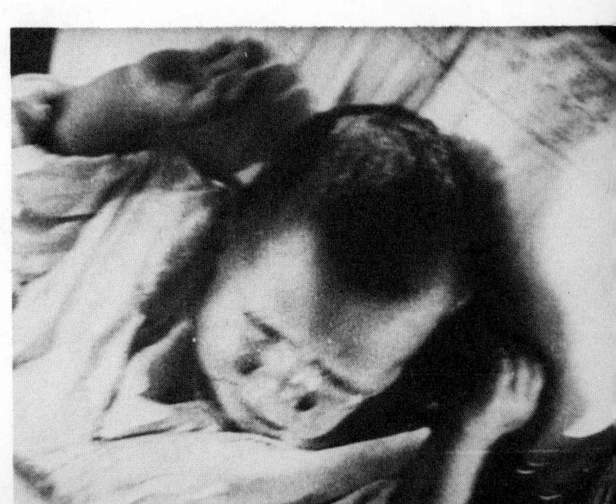

100mm lens set at *f*8 is focused at fifty feet, the depth of field extends only eleven feet in front of the point of critical focus compared to twenty-two feet behind it.

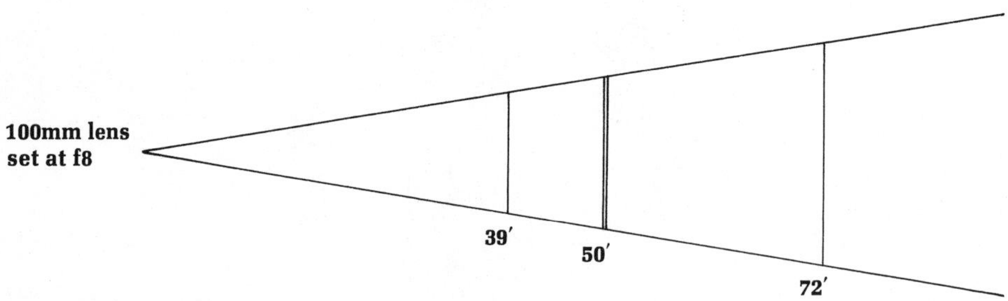

As a result, if two objects at different distances from the camera must both be sharp, the point of critical focus has to be closer to the nearer object. This characteristic also produces what is called the *hyperfocal distance,* a combination of critical focus and *f* stop that will create an acceptably sharp image extending from half the distance of critical focus to as far as the eye can see (called *infinity*). For instance, a focus setting of ten feet will produce an image that is sharp from five feet to infinity, when shooting in 16mm with a normal lens set at *f*8.

Since the hyperfocal distance provides the greatest possible depth of field, it is particularly useful in uncontrollable situations in which there is a great deal of action and no time to focus. Hyperfocal distance is also the basis for a whole style of feature film-making. In this visual style, called *deep focus,* everything from the immediate foreground to the distant background is extremely sharp. This opens up the space in the frame so that carefully choreographed actions can occur in several different parts of the setting at the same time. It also permits the action to develop for longer periods without the interruption of a cut; and this, in turn, gives great weight to every detail of the setting since our attention has more time in which to focus on minute aspects of the image.

We have seen how this technique was used to develop the action a layer at a time in the example from *Citizen Kane* in part 1 of this chapter. But depth can also be used to develop an entire pattern of simultaneous actions throughout a setting. This can be seen in a deep-focus shot from Orson Welles's *The Magnificent Ambersons.* During a formal dress ball at the Amberson home, the young heir of the family has taken a liking to the daughter of his mother's former beau. We see

them here, sitting quietly and talking while the dance continues in the background. As they converse, the boy's mother and the girl's father break away from the festivities and, behaving as if the years had never separated them, interrupt the conversation with irrelevant pleasantries. At the same time, the boy's father, always a shadowy figure in the marriage, stands behind all of them, tolerantly examining the developing relationships from which he is excluded. This all takes place against a background of the gaiety and splendor that marks the zenith of Amberson family power, affluence, and social prominence. Thus, during the span of just one shot, all the principal characters in the film are pulled together into a complex spatial arrangement that shows their personal relationships, develops the connections between these relationships, and ties them to the world in which they exist.

There are times, however, when even the hyperfocal distance is not enough to include all the action in a shot, or conversely, when the director wants to use a shallow depth of field to direct our attention to parts of the action that are different distances from the camera. Then the lens must be focused first on one point and then another if each part of the action is to come to our attention as it becomes important. This technique, called *follow focus,* can be seen in another, slightly earlier shot from

The Magnificent Ambersons. Here the two youngsters are isolated in medium close-up before an out-of-focus background. They have paused between dances, so she asks him if he plans to be a doctor or a lawyer. When he answers with a rather distasteful "No!," she asks him, "Well, what will you be?," and he replies, "A yachtsman." Then, before she can do more than just register startled surprise, the music strikes up. As he sweeps her onto the dance floor, the camera tilts down slightly and is refocused to the hyperfocal distance so that they are back once again in a bright, carefree world that makes even that answer seem reasonable.

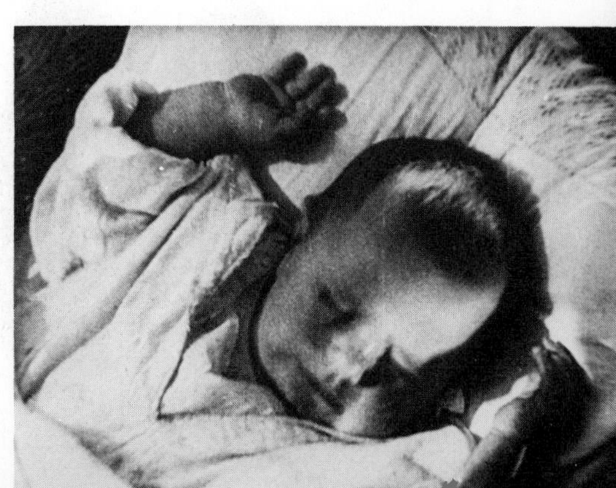

Exactly what the depth of field and hyperfocal distance is for every lens and *f* stop combination is too complex to figure out or memorize, so there are depth-of-field and hyperfocal-distance tables. These can be purchased separately for each lens, or they can be looked up for standard-length lenses in the *American Cinematographer Manual.* These tables are subject to interpretation, however, because acceptable depth of field is entirely dependent on how greatly the image will be magnified on the screen. When any image with shallow depth of field is projected on a small screen, everything in it will appear sharp because the out-of-focus areas are not magnified enough to appear blurred. But if a small image, even one with good depth, is shown on a large screen, whatever is blurred will be greatly magnified, and therefore quite apparent. That is why films shot in 65mm, even though they must be made with relatively long-focal-length lenses, don't seem to lack depth. The image area is so large that it doesn't have to be magnified enough to make the blurred areas very noticeable.

Extending the Image Quality of a Lens

It is possible to extend the normal range of image qualities a lens can produce —to soften, deepen, or enlarge the image—by putting glass elements or certain translucent materials in front of the lens. This is such a common practice that most professional cameras are equipped with a combination sunshade-matte box, which is used to hold these supplementary elements in place. The matte box is named after the opaque cardboard cutouts, or *mattes,* used to produce optical effects in the early days of film-making. It is simply a set of slots behind the sunshade into which can be slid the various elements used to modify the image.

One of the most common limitations of a lens is that it cannot focus closely enough for really large close-ups. Normal and wide-angle lenses will commonly focus down to about two feet, and telephoto lenses to about five feet, but this range is not always sufficient. Take, for instance, the tight close-ups used to depict this

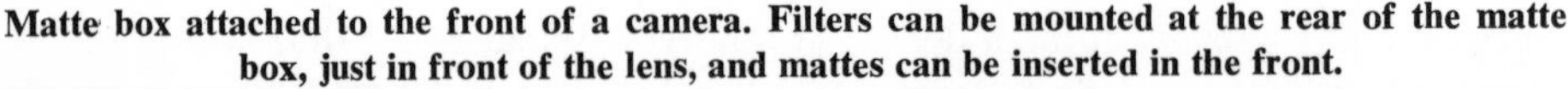

Matte box attached to the front of a camera. Filters can be mounted at the rear of the matte box, just in front of the lens, and mattes can be inserted in the front.

killing in Godard's *Breathless*. (This scene is also reproduced as a flip sequence on page 395 through page 607.)

XCU = Extreme close-up **CU = Close-up** **MS = Medium shot**
MLS = Medium long shot **SFX = Sound effects**

PICTURE	SOUND
1. LS, motorcycle cop turns down country road.	SFX: Motorcycle
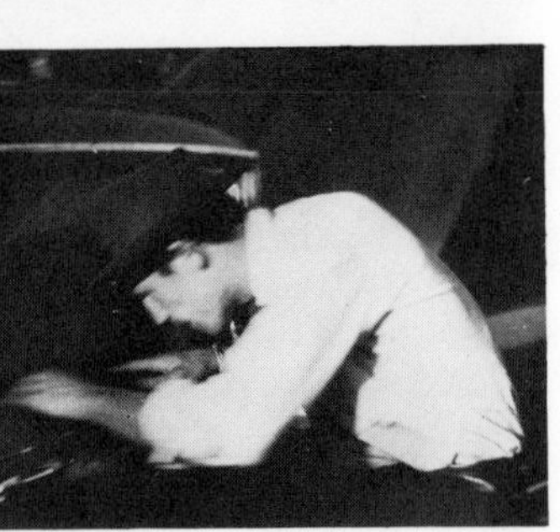 **2.** MS, Belmondo rushes to car to get gun.	SFX: Motorcycle stops.
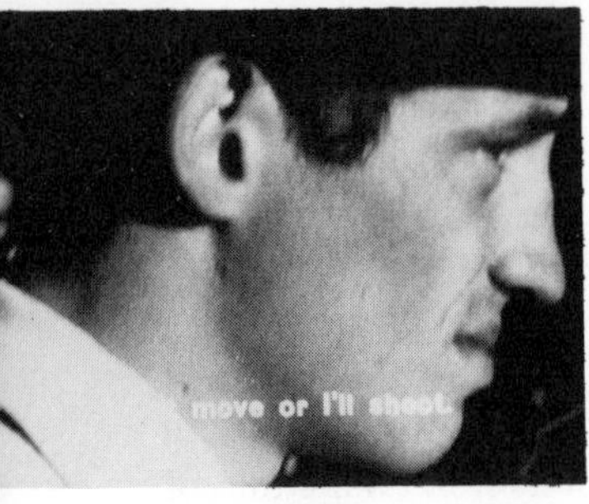 **3.** CU, camera tilts down Belmondo's face to his shoulder.	COP: Don't move or I'll shoot.

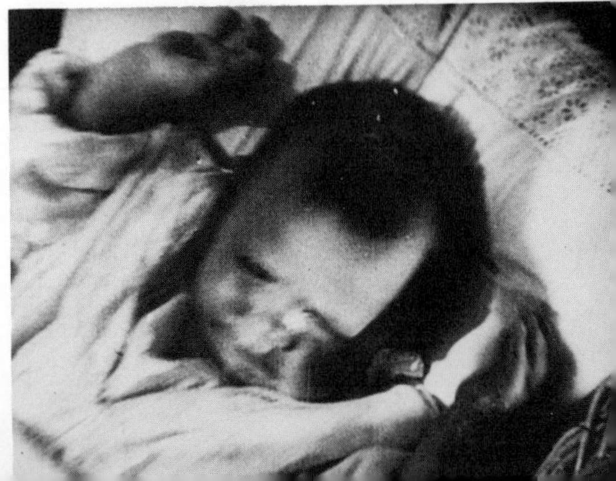

	PICTURE	SOUND
	**4.** CU, camera pans along arm to hand holding gun as Belmondo cocks it.	
	**5.** XCU, chamber revolves and then fast pan along gun barrel.	SFX: Single shot just bef chamber moves.
	**6.** MLS, policeman falls into bushes.	SFX: Crunch of break branches and then lence.

This scene appears in some form in almost every gangster picture ever made. But Godard gives it heightened impact and suspense, while still retaining a great deal of emotional distance, by showing only the mechanical details of the gun's going off. There is nothing personal in this killing, no passion or even real conflict. The victim is just a cop who has inadvertently and unfortunately crossed paths with a man who thinks so little of his own life that he has no hesitation in taking that of another.

There are a number of ways to make extreme close-ups, including lenses that focus more closely than normal lenses (*macro* lenses) and devices, such as bellows and extension tubes, that mount the lens further than its normal distance away from the film. But these can be used only on cameras with interchangeable lenses. So the only way to make extreme close-ups when the lens is permanently mounted to the camera body is to use what are called *plus, diopter,* or *closeup* lenses. These are simple glass supplementary lenses that are mounted in front of the regular camera lens. They are supplied in values marked +½, +1, +2, etc., on up to +10. The larger the number, the closer the plus lens permits the camera to focus. These lenses can also be used in combination so that a +1 and a +2 can be mounted together to create a +3. However, unless these lenses are up to the highest optical standards, they will degrade the quality of the image.

A special kind of plus lens, called a *split-field diopter lens,* can be used to extend the range of sharp focus beyond the maximum depth of field allowed by the *f* stops and the focal length of the regular camera lens. The use of this kind of lens is often necessary when an extremely close object and a much more distant one have to be in frame and in sharp focus simultaneously. Here, for example, is a shot that might have been made as easily with a split-field lens as by any other means. It is another deep-focus shot from Welles's *The Magnificent Ambersons.* In the fore-

ground is the young scion of the Amberson family. In the background, through a window, we see the old and adored suitor of his now-widowed mother leaving the house because the servants have been instructed to refuse him entrance. As we see both of them together for the only time in the scene, the younger man is willfully and sternly hovering in close-up over the distant figure of the man who is his mother's last chance for personal happiness.

The split-field lens used to make this kind of shot is something like the bifocal lenses used in eyeglasses; it is ground so that half is a plus lens and the other half is simply flat glass. Like regular diopter lenses, these lenses come in values ranging between +½ and +10. When they are used, the regular lens is first focused on the more distant object and then the proper value split-field lens is placed in front of it to bring the closer object into focus. Because there is an abrupt shift in focus where the plus part of the lens ends and the flat glass begins, this transitional area must be camouflaged by lining up the transition with some background object, such as a tree, the corner of a room, or the edge of a tabletop. The transitional area will also be

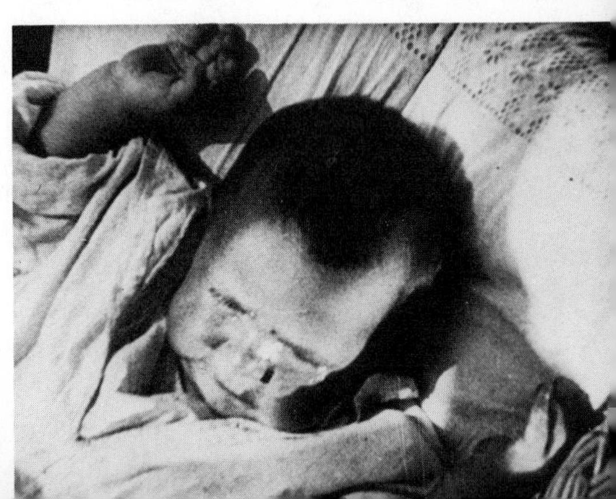

unnoticed if it extends across a flat, even, out-of-focus background area. In addition, the actors must stay within their area of the split field or they will go out of focus as they cross the transitional zone.

There are also times when the image normally produced by a lens is too brilliant and sharp, and the film-maker must tone it down by resorting to what is called *soft focus*. Soft-focus techniques, in fact, were quite the vogue during the late 1920's and the early 1930's, but they were used so indiscriminately that they fell into disrepute. These techniques are revived from time to time, however, to fulfill a specific purpose. For instance, George Cukor had the whole of *Gaslight* shot in soft focus. He did this both to reproduce the soft, flickering light cast by the lamps of that period and to create the aura of unreality in which the heroine believes she is losing her mind.

Because soft focus also smooths out wrinkles and takes the edge off angular features, it has always been associated with close-ups of female movie stars. This has created the conventional soft-focus image of the female heroine that is exploited in this close-up from Marcel Carné's *Le Jour Se Lève*. This is the hero's view of the

Courtesy: JANUS FILMS, INC.

girl he worships. She is his ideal love object, and we see her as he does, in soft focus, flattered by the light, lovely, and unattainable. No matter, as he becomes involved in her life, that he is led to murder a man with whom she has seemingly had an affair.

Soft focus can be created by the use of either a supplementary diffusion lens or a fine-mesh net. Both of these produce an image with softer edges, a slight flaring or starring of the highlights, and a decrease in contrast. However, the principal problem when using any of these devices is to match the image quality from long shot to close-up. This match is generally achieved by the use of little or no diffusion on long shots, and then just enough in successively closer shots to soften the image gradually without making the change intrusive.

The amount of diffusion is controlled by the use of more or less diffuse filters or by a change in the coarseness of the netting. And on a moving shot, part of which is a long shot and the other part a close-up, the amount of diffusion can be smoothly altered by the use of a long, graduated diffuser. This is slowly slid through the matte box so that the most diffuse part of the filter is in front of the lens during the closeup portion and the least diffuse part during the long shot. In addition it is possible to diffuse just part of the frame by using a partially diffuse filter or by simply cutting a hole in a coarse (less diffuse) net. The result is a partial change in sharpness that subtly directs the viewer's attention where the director wants it.

Another kind of diffusion lens, called a *fog filter,* is used, as its name implies, to create fog effects. These lenses are valuable because using a fog filter is much easier than waiting around for the right amount of naturally occurring fog. These filters also permit, in conjunction with artificial fog machines, the creation of fog effects in a studio, a setting in which every aspect of the shooting can be closely controlled.

While fog is often used to set the mood of a scene, it can also contribute to the meaning of the action. Look, for instance, at the subtle shift in meaning conveyed by the fog in these studio-made shots from Kenji Mizoguchi's Japanese classic *Ugetsu.* In this scene the fog plays a dual role. At first it simply hides the boat that

Courtesy: JANUS FILMS, INC.

holds two peasant families fleeing under cover of darkness from an invading army. They have chosen to go by boat because it seemed safer than traveling overland, and the fog seems to affirm this decision both by giving the setting an idyllic tran-

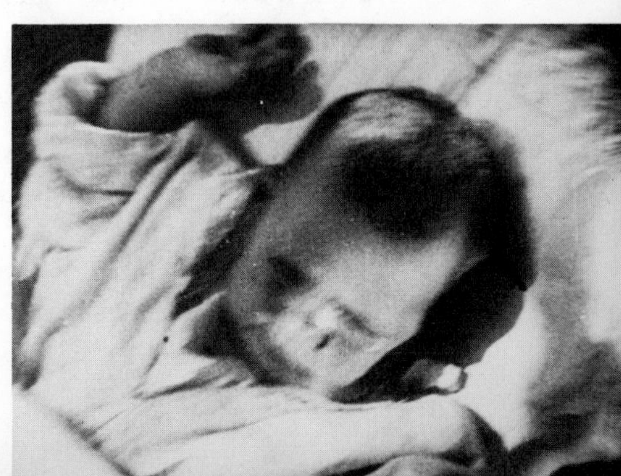

quillity and by providing a protective cloak for their journey. Within seconds, however, they cross paths with another boat, plundered and adrift, and they realize that they are in as much danger from pirates as they would have been from bandits. Now the fog changes into an ominous shroud that obscures the presence of unknown dangers. This swift reversal of circumstances, as the refugees' lack of worldly experience makes each seemingly wise decision change into a nightmare, is a theme running throughout the film. Here the change is reflected in the mood and meaning they, and we, attach to the fog.

Although both shots were made in a studio with the use of artificial fog, fog filters were needed to complete the effect. In the first shot the boat emerges from a bank of artificial fog and slowly glides toward the camera. Without a fog filter the image of the boat would have become unnaturally sharp and clear as the boat approached the lens; with a fog filter the image remained soft and veiled, just as it would in a real fog. The filter has a similar effect in the second shot, plus creating a slight halo around the glints of simulated moonlight bouncing off the water.

Fog filters come in ten steps and two types—regular and double fog filters. The regular fog filters create a halo around the highlights and decrease the contrast of the image by softening and diffusing it, effects that increase as the higher number filters are used. The double fog filters create less of a halo and merely decrease the contrast of the image without softening it as the higher number filters are used. They give a more natural effect with color film than do the regular fog filters.

The trick when using these filters with either black-and-white (*B&W*) or color film is to match the fog effect from shot to shot. This matching can be accomplished by the use of a lower number filter on more distant or less contrasty shots than is used on close-ups or contrasty shots. The filter is thus kept from obscuring the finer detail in the long shots while softening the edges in close shots. Although this technique contradicts what happens in reality—in a real fog things get softer as they get further away—it does give a more convincing continuity to the images.

The Qualities of the Frame: Frame Shape

One of the most basic qualities of the image is the physical shape of that image on the film. This rectangular area, called the *frame,* is crucial to the structure of the film because its shape determines the shape of the real spaces within which the film-maker can build the action. In all films except those currently made for theaters, the frame is the same shape, a rather squarish rectangle four units wide for every three units of height. This shape was originally created by Thomas Edison when he decided that a frame one inch wide by three quarters of an inch high was most convenient for his purposes. To this day this 1.33 to 1 ratio of width to height, technically called the frame's *aspect ratio,* is standard for all 8mm and most 16mm and 35mm film-making.

Since about 1950, however, this standard frame shape has coexisted with a number of 35 mm and 65 mm wide-screen processes in which the image is considerably longer than it is high. These elongated frame shapes were not developed out of any widespread unhappiness with the older frame but out of the movie industry's need for some spectacular new way to differentiate its product from that of its TV competition. The result was a 35mm frame shape with an aspect ratio as large as

1.85 to 1, and a whole new 65mm film size in which the aspect ratio is 2.21 to 1. It also led to the development of the special lenses used in Cinemascope and Ultra Panavision 70 that produce an image as wide as 2.75 to 1.

FRAME SHAPES

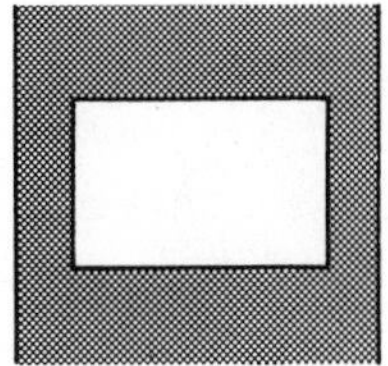

Standard 35mm

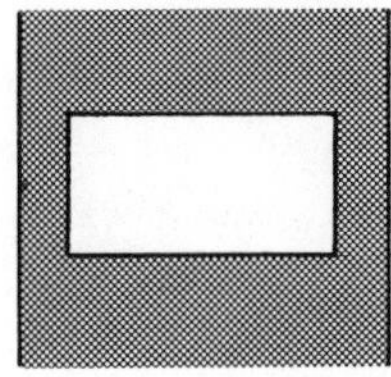

1.85 to 1 on 35mm

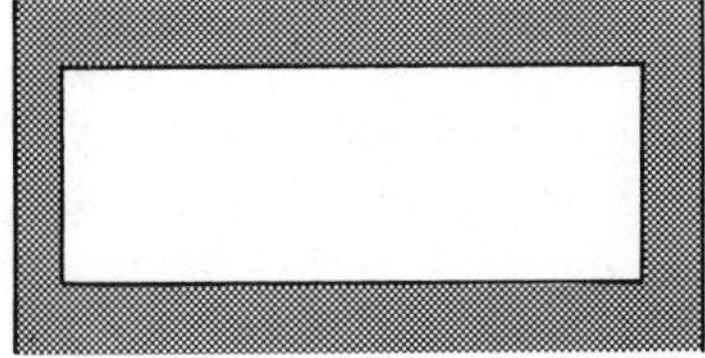

2.21 to 1 on 65mm

Although these new frame shapes were adopted for economic reasons, and are still restricted mainly to feature-film production, they have had an impact on how films are made. For example, the wide screen makes long shots broader, more panoramic, and therefore more impressive than was possible with the older frame shape. This new shape can also affect the pace of a scene because the wide horizontal area permits complex actions to develop back and forth across the screen for long periods of time. As with deep focus, the action can unfold without the interruption of a cut, or the changes of angle caused by camera movement.

Exactly how this new ratio works can be seen in these two frames from the *Yesterday, Today and Tomorrow* sequence discussed in Chapter One. These frames are from the same shot, except that one is from the original wide-screen version of

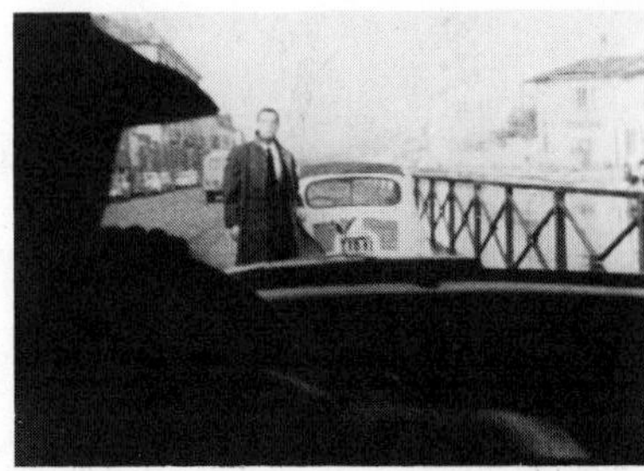

the film and the other is from the standard frame print used on television. Here the

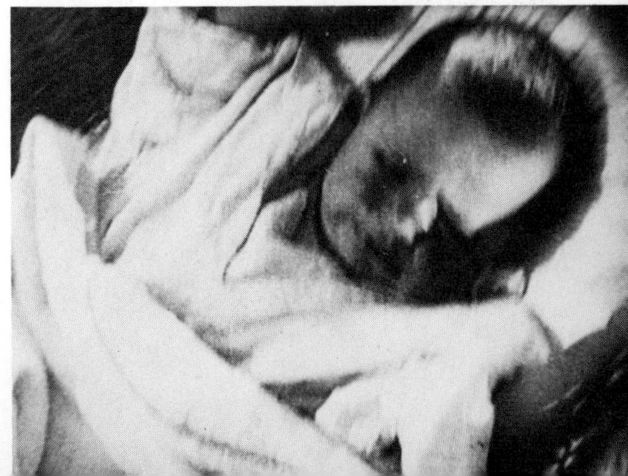

broad sweep of the wide-screen image allows us to see what cannot be shown within a standard frame shape—a single, stationary shot that holds on both a close-up of the woman and a more distant view of her lover as he approaches and enters the car.

If, in this case, the full width of the windshield were to be fitted into a standard frame, the top and bottom of the frame would show so much of the interior of the car that these large black areas would absorb the powerful effect of the woman's silhouette. And if the start of the shot were to be framed as it is in the television print, the camera would either have to pull back or pan right, or there would have to be a cut to another angle, to keep the man in frame as his figure passes across the full width of the windshield. In the television print itself he simply walks out of frame, leaving a gap in the action.

Any of these changes would alter the means used to shape the space in the wide-screen shot and thus in turn would affect the shot's pace and meaning. In the wide-screen version her imposing silhouette fixes our attention along the line of sight between her and her lover, creating a tension that is never broken by any movement other than his long, rather hesitant walk toward the camera. This dominant rhythm, plus her immobile figure poised in the foreground, forces us to see him just as she does. He is another victim framed in her windshield, slowly but inexorably coming under her control.

There are several different systems used to produce wide-screen films. Most of them, however, require special equipment because they each use a different frame shape to create the wider image. The one exception is a system that retains approximately the same three-by-four frame shape but alters the image itself by means of an *anamorphic lens.* An anamorphic lens squeezes the image horizontally while leaving it unaffected vertically. This means that a normal frame shape can be used to record an area in front of the camera that is more than twice as wide as it is high. Later, when the film is projected, an anamorphic projection lens reverses the process, unsqueezing the image so that the objects on the screen regain their normal proportions.

Squeezed 35mm image

2.35 to 1 unsqueezed screen image

The big advantage of this anamorphic process is that the lens is a separate unit that fits in front of any regular camera or projector lens. This means that any camera and projector can be used to produce wide-screen images, even 8mm equipment. Wide-screen 8mm is not currently produced, however, because the image isn't sharp enough yet to fill even a moderately wide screen. As a result, anamorphic lenses are not now available for use with this size of film. But each improvement in the quality of film stock brings low-cost, wide-screen 8mm production closer to realization.

The Size of the Frame

Regardless of the shape of the frame, its size is normally determined by the width of the film the camera is designed to use because the longest dimension of the frame is usually placed across the width of the film. As a result, the wider the film, the larger the frame. But there is one major exception—8mm film. In 8mm film there is now both a standard and a super-size frame. In super 8 mm the sprocket holes are narrower than in standard 8mm, providing enough space for a 50-percent larger image without the use of wider film. The improvement in image quality has been so significant, in fact, that the concept has also been extended to super 16mm, a professional format used for wide-screen production.

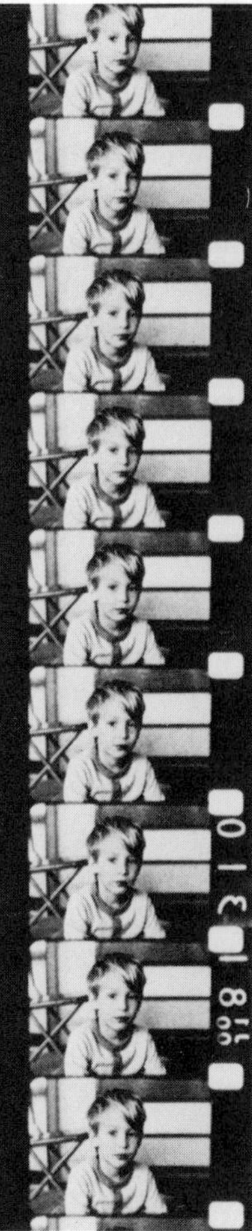

Frame size increases L-R, from standard 8mm to super 8mm, 16mm, and super 16mm. The frame in super 16mm extends almost all the way to the left edge of the film.

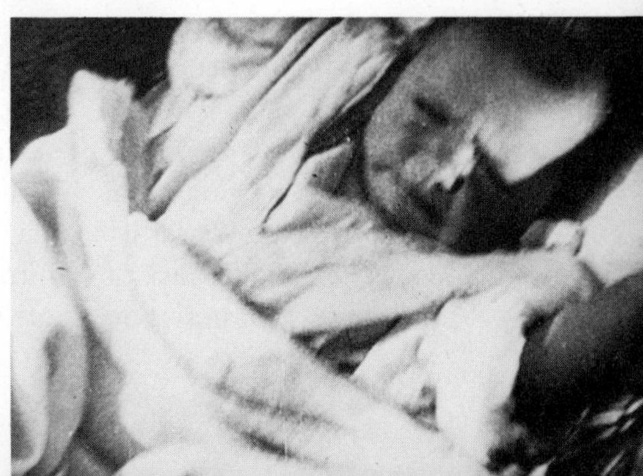

Frame size is as important a consideration as frame shape because it determines the largeness, sharpness, and brightness of the image projected, and these factors in turn dictate where the film can be shown. If the film is going to appear only on a small screen, such as in a classroom or on television, 16mm or even 8mm film will produce an adequate image. But if the film must be projected on a large theater screen, a 35mm or 65mm image size is preferable.

There are, however, other factors besides screen size which help decide the size of the film to be used. One of the most important of these factors is whether or not the camera and editing equipment available for a particular film size is up to professional standards. These standards will be discussed in some detail later in this book, but for now it is enough to say that standard and super 8mm equipment is not yet as accurate and flexible as that available for the wider films. As a result, films to be released in 8mm are often shot on 16mm or 35mm film and then reduction-printed onto the smaller size (the details of this process are covered in Section 2, Chapter Ten).

Another consideration is the ease with which the equipment can be handled. Because of the physical size of the film itself, equipment designed for large-sized film has to be considerably bigger and heavier than that designed for 8mm or 16mm film. Also, 35mm and 65mm cameras require sturdier mounts and are harder to move about or hand-hold than smaller cameras. For this reason 16mm film has become the preferred size for highly mobile documentary and news-film production, and even some scenes for feature films are being shot in this smaller film size. These shots are then blown up during printing to the same size as the rest of the footage.

Finally, the wider the film, the more expensive it is to use. This cost is normally not an important part of the total cost of a film with a large budget; but in low-budget film-making, film stock and processing may represent a major part, or even the entire cost, of the project. As a result, 16mm film is a very popular size for educational, industrial, and experimental film-making—and for low-budget feature films. The entire feature film is then enlarged to 35mm for theatrical distribution, since very few commercial theaters have 16mm projection equipment.

Framing and Focusing the Image

There are various kinds of viewfinder systems, but they all serve the same purpose—to determine which objects fall within the field of view of the lens and where the lens is focused. While these may seem like fairly simple requirements, we've already seen how important they are in building the action. Just how critically accurate a viewfinder system must be, however, can be seen in this shot from *The Fiancés* by Ermanno Olmi. The film is about a northern Italian worker who has had to go to Sicily to find work. While there he continually searches back through memories of his home. One of these flashbacks includes a dalliance with another woman and the ensuing argument with his fiancée. He had gone swimming with a group of friends and afterwards had gotten involved with one of the women in the party. The seduction, and his lack of any strong personal feeling toward the woman, is quickly and simply told in this one shot. The woman reaches up and pulls him down. As he

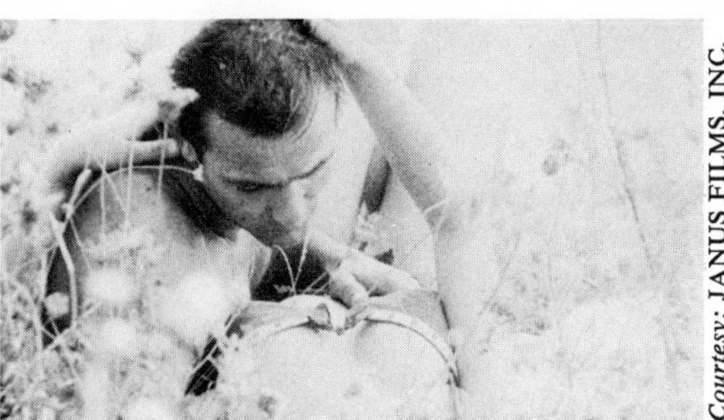

Courtesy: JANUS FILMS, INC.

lowers himself onto her the camera sinks down slightly and tilts up so that just her head is out of frame. This leaves only her body on the screen and it is this body alone to which he responds.

Because of the great need for accuracy in the viewfinder system, the history of the development of professional motion-picture cameras is largely one of increasingly accurate and more flexible viewfinders. In the earliest movie cameras framing and focusing were quite accurate because the shots were lined up by the use of a focusing tube that worked directly through the lens itself. This tube looked through the back of the film, and the film, functioning as a kind of ground-glass focusing screen, made the image cast by the lens visible to the eye. Although this image was relatively small and dim, and was both upside down and reversed left to right, just as the lens projected it onto the film, it was still exactly the image recorded on the film itself.

But this system became inadequate once more sensitive, or *faster,* film was invented. Because faster film needed less light to record an image, there was less light for viewing. And faster film also required an *anti-halation backing*. Halation occurs when the light that forms the image bounces off the back of the film and into the light-sensitive material. The older, slower film stock was relatively insensitive to this small amount of reflected light, but in the faster film these reflections grayed out the shadows and formed a halo around the brighter highlights. Since this softened the quality of the image, the stray light had to be absorbed by covering the back of the film with a dark-gray anti-halation coating. This backing, however, reduced to zero the light available for viewing.

The successor to direct viewing was the *rackover* and the side viewfinder, a system still in use today. This system uses the same focusing tube except that the tube is next to the film path instead of behind the film. In order to line up the shot

the whole camera body is slid, or racked-over, to the right past the lens so that the focusing tube instead of the film is behind the lens. This shift allows the cameraman to frame and focus as before, directly through the camera lens. Then, to make the actual exposure, the camera body has to be moved back into position behind the lens.

Of course, the focusing tube alone fails to offer the cameraman any means for checking the framing during the actual filming. This deficiency is overcome by the use of a side, or *monitor,* finder, an optical viewing system mounted on the side of the camera. The field of view of this monitor finder is matched to that of the camera, or *taking,* lens so that the cameraman can see that the action stays accurately framed and can monitor the changing field of view if the camera is moved during the shot.

A rackover system is standard on many professional studio cameras, and just the side finder, without the focusing tube and the rackover mechanism, is found on many inexpensive amateur cameras. When there is no focusing tube, however, the lens must be focused by measuring the lens-to-subject distance with a tape measure and then setting the lens to this distance using the scale engraved on the barrel of the lens. While this system may seem arduous compared to focusing directly through the lens itself, it is still the most accurate means for focusing, especially with a wide-angle lens. Because short-focal-length lenses have an inherently great depth of field, and because their wider field of view produces a more finely detailed image, focusing directly through a short lens is often difficult. Therefore, even with professional studio cameras, the point of critical focus is usually determined by means of a tape measure.

A similar procedure is used to *follow focus* when the lens-to-subject distance changes during the shot. First the various distances between the camera and the different points of sharp focus are measured. These points are next marked on the studio floor, or when shooting outdoors, indicated by pounding in stakes just out of camera range, and the sequence of distance settings is noted by the first assistant cameraman. Then, as the subject, or in the case of a moving camera, the camera dolly, moves between these marks the focus is shifted by the assistant from one setting to the next so that the movement and the focus both reach the same point at the same time. This is a skilled operation that requires careful rehearsal and good coordination between the actors and the camera crew.

While a monitor finder is the easiest type of viewfinder to use, it is not absolutely accurate. Because it must be mounted either above or to the side of the taking lens, it cannot include exactly the same field of view as the lens itself. This discrepancy, called *parallax,* is minimal when the subject is distant, but increases as the subject gets closer. Parallax is also more of a problem with a long-focal-length lens since the lens's narrow field of view allows less room for error. On studio cameras parallax is compensated by linking the monitor finder to the focusing mechanism. Then, when the lens is focused more closely, the whole finder tilts so that its field of view converges with that of the taking lens. A similar tilt is accomplished on simpler cameras by means of a rotating distance scale that alters the position of the viewfinder eyepiece. In either case, this correction is good down to about two feet with normal and short lenses and to about six feet with moderately long lenses.

Because of parallax, it is extremely difficult to use a monitor finder to make a close-up of a moving object or to frame a close shot accurately with a long lens. Therefore, yet another finder system was invented. Called *reflex viewing,* it uses a mirror between the lens and the film to divert the light from the taking lens into a focusing tube mounted on the side of the camera. This mirror is not stationary, however, but mounted on the front surface of the shutter. As a result, when the shutter is open the light goes directly to the film, and when the shutter is closed it is reflected into the viewfinder.

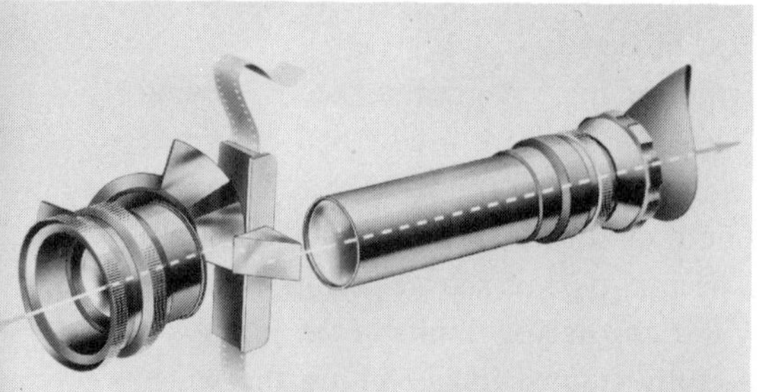

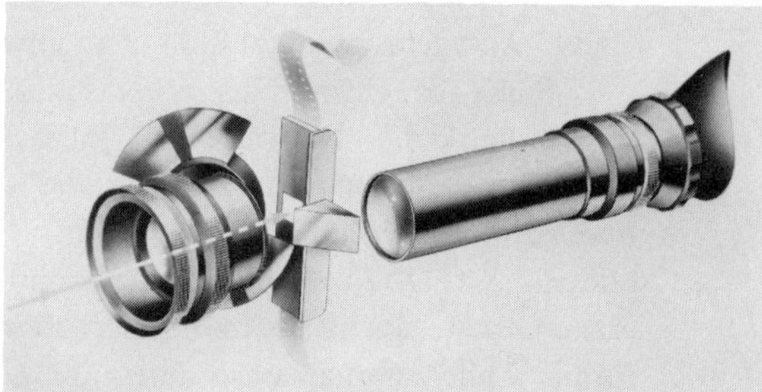

Mirror shutter system. On the left the shutter is closed, diverting all the light from the lens into the viewfinder; on the right the shutter has rotated 90°, permitting the light to strike the film.

Of course, every time the shutter opens the viewfinder image is interrupted, but this happens so quickly (twenty-four times per second) that the blank periods are perceived only as a slight flicker in the image. Even this flicker is eliminated, however, in the most recently developed reflex viewing systems. These use a partially silvered mirror or prism permanently mounted between the lens and the shutter. This partial mirror reflects a small amount of light from the lens (between 8 and 12 percent) into the viewfinder while the rest passes through the mirror to expose the film. The only drawback to this system is that it can't provide as bright an image in the viewfinder since the more light diverted for viewing, the greater the exposure compensation required to make up for what is lost.

The most obvious advantage of reflex viewing is that it permits highly accurate framing and focusing even during filming. Another advantage, however, is that it is the easiest finder system to use with a zoom lens. The great strength of a zoom lens is that its field of view can change as the shot is being filmed. But it is complicated

and expensive to design a monitor finder that can synchronize its field of view with that of a zoom lens. One answer is to build a reflex viewing system into the lens itself, but even this is unnecessary if the camera has built-in reflex viewing.

As reflex viewing becomes more common, it is taking on many of the refinements long associated only with the monitor finders on professional studio cameras. One of the most important of these refinements is a viewfinder image that is somewhat larger than the area actually being filmed. The area filmed is then indicated by a black outline just inside the edges of the viewing screen. This larger image permits the cameraman to see what is entering the frame without taking his eye away from the finder. It also helps prevent accidental panning beyond the edge of the set or inadvertent inclusion in the shot of an unwanted object.

Some reflex viewfinder systems also permit the interchangeable use of viewing screens marked with a variety of outlines. These screens are used when only part of the standard 16mm or 35mm frame is going to be used for wide-screen projection, or when the same footage is to be used both on a wide theater screen and on a television set. The multiple markings on this second type of screen permit the cameraman to include all the important action within the narrow limits of the television format while simultaneously obtaining a carefully framed image within the wider area to be shown in the theater.

There is, in addition, a type of hybrid viewfinder that includes a small television camera as part of the reflex viewing system on a standard motion-picture camera. As the image is recorded on film, this television camera transmits it to a TV set and video tape recorder so that the director can watch the action develop and then instantly replay the tape for evaluation before retaking the shot. These electronic viewfinders have also speeded up production of the vast amount of motion-picture film used on television. If two or three motion-picture cameras equipped with electronic viewfinders are used simultaneously, the director can monitor the images and direct the camera operators just as if he were directing a live television show. And as he watches, he can make notes for the editing of the footage or even make a video tape recording in which he switches between cameras, thus providing a visual record for the editor. This procedure keeps shooting time to a minimum and reduces editing to just the mechanical assembly of the pieces of film.

The Illusion of Motion

Frames are also the basis for the motion in motion pictures. Frames are created when the camera mechanism divides the continuous motion of the real world into minute segments of time that can be frozen on film as a series of still pictures. The motion in these still pictures can then be put back together after the film is processed by the use of a similar mechanism in the projector that quickly flashes the frames on a screen.

The camera mechanism used to create the frames is called a *shutter* and an *intermittent movement*. Each time the shutter opens the film stands still for an instant while it is exposed to light; and each time the shutter closes a claw enters a sprocket hole and quickly pulls down fresh film for the next exposure. Thus the shutter and stop-start, or intermittent, movement of the film produce a long strip of frames, still pictures that each record a slightly altered image of the moving objects viewed by the lens.

This process is then reversed by means of a shutter and an intermittent mechanism in the projector. Each time the shutter opens the frame stands still while the light shining through it is focused on the screen; and each time the shutter closes the next frame is pulled into place, ready to be projected. Here, the shutter and the intermittent movement quickly replace the image from each frame with the slightly altered image in the next, thus creating the illusion of continuous motion.

This illusion, however, is based on a physiological fact, a peculiar characteristic of our eyesight called *persistence of vision.* To see how this works, slowly flip through the frames from *Potemkin* printed on the lower right-hand corner of these pages. These are frames from a strip of film reproduced so that they can be viewed without a projector. Slowly flipping the pages will permit you to see the slight changes from frame to frame; but flipping them more rapidly will make these changes seem continuous. This is the result of persistence of vision. The image of one frame persists until we see the next, bridging the gap between the frames so that these small, discrete changes fuse into the illusion of continuous motion.

Frame Rate

This characteristic holds true whether we flip quickly through frames printed on the pages of a book or see these same frames projected on a screen. During projection, however, the frames must be replaced on the screen at a rather rapid rate or the image flickers, that is, the audience becomes aware of the dark periods between frames. This flicker can be eliminated only if the frames change at least sixteen times per second.

A *frame rate* of 16 frames per second (fps) was used as early as 1895 by the Lumière brothers in one of the first movie projectors invented. There were a number of advantages to this speed, and because there was a need for standardization, 16 fps was soon universally adopted for the projection of all silent films. The speed itself was the slowest used to that time. Edison, in fact, ran his peep show films at 40 fps without the slightest improvement in image quality, so the slower speed saved film. Sixteen also happened to be the number of frames in a foot of 35mm film, so 16 fps made it quite easy to convert shooting time into footage and vice versa. Every second filmed equaled a foot of film, and every foot of film equaled one second on the screen.

Standardization, however, was even more important than the speed itself. It

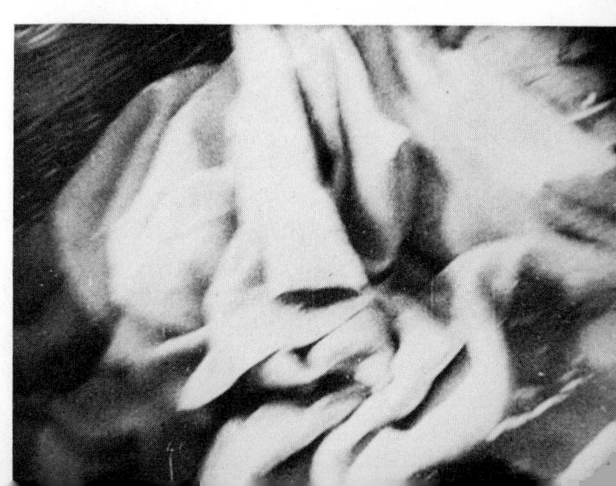

assured the cameraman that if he cranked the camera at 16 fps, the motion in the image would appear normal no matter who showed the film. This then became the standard *camera speed* as well. Silent cameras were geared so that sixteen frames of film were propelled through the camera with each complete turn of the crank. That way, if the cameraman turned the crank through one revolution per second, he was shooting at 16 fps.

But the cameraman was not required to crank only at this particular speed, and it became part of his art to decide at exactly what camera speed each shot should be filmed. If he wanted to speed up the action he would turn the crank more slowly than normal, or *undercrank.* This would run the film through the camera more slowly than it would eventually pass through a projector running at a standard 16 fps, and this relatively faster projection speed would accelerate the action. The reverse was also possible: turning the crank faster than normal, or *overcranking,* which would slow down the action by running the film through the camera faster than it would later run through the projector.

However, changing the camera speed is more complicated than it sounds because a change of frame rate is also a change in exposure. The higher the frame rate, the less time the shutter can remain open for each frame. At least theoretically, computing this change is not very difficult. When the camera speed is twice normal the shutter remains open half as long, so twice as much light must be allowed through the lens. This is an increase of one *f* stop. And when the camera speed is cut in half, half as much light must be allowed through the lens, requiring a decrease of one *f* stop. But practically speaking, making these adjustments while shooting required great skill and dexterity on the part of a silent cameraman. Since there was no time to look at the lens setting or even the dial that showed how fast the camera was running, he had to know intuitively both how fast he was cranking and how far he had to reset the lens. That way he could keep his eyes on the action so that it would always be accurately framed.

These changes in camera speed often exerted a subtle control over the pace at which the action developed. As Kevin Brownlow remarks in his long and loving book about the silent film, *The Parade's Gone By . . . ,* "If an actor took a long time to mount a horse, the cameraman could slow down. The actor would then appear to leap nimbly into his saddle. As the horse galloped away, the cameraman would then return to normal, adjusting the exposure so that the density of the shot would remain even."

More obvious undercranking was also very much part of the silent comedy. For instance, in this undercranked shot from Charlie Chaplin's *The Gold Rush,* Chaplin's fast, jerky movements are used to convey his desperate situation while making fun of it at the same time. Chaplin, a city boy cast loose in the Alaskan gold rush, is contending with a fur trapper for the last morsel of food in the trapper's cabin—a dry old bone. When he sees that he is going to lose the argument, Chaplin drops his civilized manner, seizes a gun, and chases the man from the cabin. But now he must try both to chew on the bone and to keep on guard in case the trapper returns, forcing him alternately to lower the gun to eat, raise it whenever he thinks he hears something, and then aim it first at the front door and then at the side door. The result is a typical Chaplinesque ballet, in which his desperate resort to arms is made even more hopeless and ridiculous by the speeding up of his actions.

Sound Speed

With the coming of sound in the late 1920's the standard frame rate was increased to 24 fps. This increase in speed was needed to produce adequate sound quality and in itself was no great change for the cameraman. But this was not the only change required for sound. Now the camera had to run at exactly 24 fps throughout every shot in which sound and picture were recorded simultaneously. Otherwise the quality of the sound would change disastrously (the reasons for this are discussed in Section 2, Chapter Six). Since the majority of the early sound films were composed almost entirely of synchronously recorded dialogue, most of the time the camera could run at only one fixed speed. This fixed speed was maintained better with a motor than a crank, and the crank disappeared from film-making.

However, even though the camera speed is fixed as long as we hear what someone on the screen is saying, if we see something other than someone speaking there is no need to record sound and picture at the same time. Then the footage can be shot without sound, and the sound—music, narration, or sound effects—added later, during editing. This permits a great deal more flexibility in the shooting of sound films; and once the early infatuation with synchronous dialogue had waned, a changing frame rate, controlled by a variable-speed motor, again became an important means for controlling the pace of certain shots.

Here, for instance, is a slow-motion shot from Jean Cocteau's sound film of the classic fairy tale *Beauty and the Beast.* In this shot Beauty is exploring the magic castle in which she is being held captive. Although there is sound behind the shot, the shot itself was filmed without sound. As a result, Cocteau was able to use slow motion to create a majestic, billowing effect in the windblown curtains, and a

Courtesy: JANUS FILMS, INC.

slow, dreamlike, gliding motion as Beauty was pulled along the corridor on a hidden dolly.

Undercranking is also possible when making a sound film, but it has become a rarity, perhaps because audiences no longer find it funny, or because it became so closely associated with comic effects that it is no longer possible to use it as a serious technique. The effect of undercranking always occurs, however, when an old silent film is shown on a projector operating at sound speed. This is because these old films were shot at 16 fps, while projectors now normally operate at 24 fps. The result is the unnaturally speeded-up action that we have long erroneously associated with all silent pictures.

Time Lapse and Animation

Another kind of undercranking is quite common, however: time-lapse photography. Time lapse is used both to collapse a long process into a shorter period on the screen and to make apparent any process that happens so slowly that it can't be perceived unless it is accelerated. It is a technique that has long been associated with marvelous shots of flowers blooming or crystals growing; Edward Steichen has even used it to show the natural growth cycle of a young tree over the four seasons of the year. It has also been used to show the stage being built at the beginning of Michael Wadleigh's *Woodstock,* and the sun slowly rising over the desert in the opening of David Lean's *Lawrence of Arabia.*

Time lapse depends upon what is called *single framing,* the ability of a movie camera to expose one frame at a time. In single framing the shutter opens and closes, and the film advances one frame, each time the shutter is released. Since this process permits the cameraman to expose the frames over any interval he chooses, it results in frame rates that are usually measured in frames per minute or hour, or even per day, depending upon the speed of the process and the time it is supposed to last on the screen.

Unlike ordinary undercranking, in single framing changing the frame rate doesn't affect the length of time the shutter stays open. The single-frame mechanism is so designed that the film receives the same exposure each time the shutter is activated. The need to calculate the frame rate itself, however, is not eliminated. The interval between exposures is arrived at by the division of the length of the process, in seconds, by the time it should remain on the screen, also in seconds, multiplied by 24, the number of frames per second. If, for instance, a flower which blooms over twenty-four hours is to be shown in twenty seconds, the figures are as follows:

$$\frac{24 \text{ hrs.} \times 60 \text{ min.} \times 60 \text{ sec.}}{20 \text{ sec.} \times 24 \text{ frames}} = \frac{86{,}400}{480} = 180 \text{ seconds between frames, or one}$$

frame every three minutes.

This sort of photography would be quite onerous and difficult if the cameraman had to stand by the camera and release the shutter without fail once every three minutes for twenty-four hours. As a result, this work is usually done by means of an *intervalometer,* a device that automatically trips the shutter at predetermined intervals. Intervalometers usually have a range of from several frames per second to one frame every twenty-four hours. Some intervalometers also permit a variable frame rate so that sequences which stretch over several days won't be recorded during dormant periods or at night. In addition, a heavy-duty intervalometer can also turn on lights just before each exposure and shut them off until the next exposure.

Single framing is also used in animation, but with the big difference that in animation the motion is created and controlled by the film-maker. Animation, in fact, means taking any normally immobile object, such as a drawing, a puppet, a clay figure, or a cutout, and changing its position between each single frame exposure so as to "bring it to life" when the frames are projected. This, for instance, is the process used to make all the great Disney animation features and all short cartoons—the photographing of thousands of drawings, each representing a slightly altered position of the objects and figures that eventually move on the screen.

However, animation needn't be this complex. Here is an example of a particularly simple piece of animation that was used in a television commercial. Every time

there is a cough on the sound track, these squiggly lines expand and subside. Then a box of Luden's Cough Drops slowly squeezes the lines off the screen and the cough disappears. But as simple as this device is, not even this much artistic skill is needed to create animation. Just about any movable object can be animated, including such animate objects as people and animals, by simply moving the object slightly between each single-frame exposure.

The calculation of these movements and the frames needed to record them is somewhat different from that used for time-lapse photography. In animation there is no frame rate in the sense of frames per unit of time because the animator trips the shutter whenever he has completed moving the objects in front of the lens. There is, however, a rate at which the frames will be projected—24 fps—and this is the basis for determining the number of frames that must be shot for any particular screen time. As a result, this frame rate is used to calculate the amount of movement between each frame so that the action can be completed within an allotted period of time; or working the calculation in reverse, the frames needed to complete an action can be determined and this much screen time allotted in the finished film (these calculations and the other requirements of animation are treated in greater detail in Section 2, Chapter Ten).

These, then, are the elements common to all movie cameras—a lens, a frame, a viewfinder, a shutter, and a film transport. However, there are many different types of even these basic components, plus a large number of other, auxiliary features that are now built into cameras to make them either more flexible or easier to operate, or both. These variations are designed to meet the needs of the increasing numbers of independent and amateur film-makers who want to use the same camera to do a wide variety of filming.

But it is just this range of features that has made the camera equipment now available so diverse that most people become confused when it comes to choosing a camera. This confusion is then compounded by the fact that there are no simple answers to the two questions that must be asked when one is evaluating a camera: (1) Will it meet my needs? and (2) Will it produce an acceptable quality of work? However, even the complex information needed to answer these questions can be handled in a systematic manner. Just such a methodical approach is included in Appendix A at the end of Section 2. It treats all the variables involved in choosing and testing camera equipment, so there is no need, at this point, to go into these details; but they should be of invaluable assistance to those who wish to go on into film-making.

Part III:

Placing the Script Before the Camera

Once the locations and actions in the script have been translated into specific shots, there are well-developed means for organizing the shooting so that the material in the script can be efficiently placed in front of the camera. For some sorts of films, such as standard Hollywood feature films, this procedure is usually quite detailed and elaborate; for other, less easily scripted films, the procedure is often quite general. But shooting a film is too long and involved a process to be done haphazardly; in order to be filmed with any degree of efficiency, every script must first be broken down into its component parts and then reassembled for shooting.

Script Breakdown

This reassembly procedure is called the *script breakdown*. It means grouping the shots so that those with similar requirements can all be made at one time. The first step in the breakdown is to separate those shots made in a studio from all the rest. These studio shots are then grouped according to the separate settings in which they must be made. Then the remaining shots, those made outside the studio "on location," are grouped into exteriors and interiors. This grouping separates those shots that depend upon sunlight from those that must be made by artificial light. And finally, the location shots are grouped according to the various interior and exterior settings in which they must be filmed.

These groupings by setting are the basis for any further breakdown according to such factors as the time of day required for certain shots; particular weather conditions (rain, clouds, high winds, etc.); the cast members needed in certain shot sequences; and whether or not sound will be synchronously recorded along with the picture. This last is a particularly important consideration. It determines the kind of equipment needed both to shoot the picture and to record the sound and the size of the crew needed to do the shooting.

Separating shots according to their settings is the simplest kind of break-

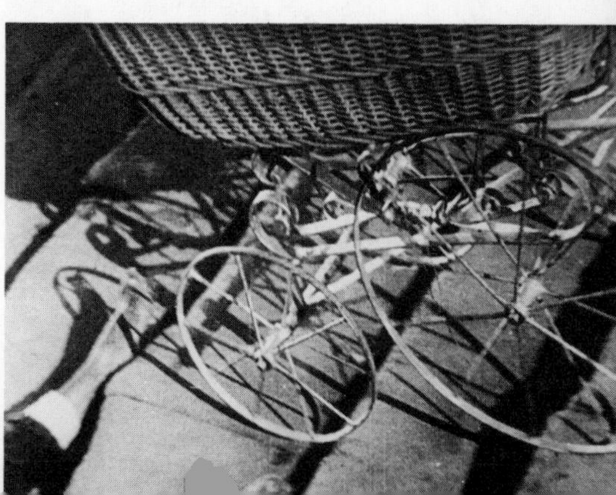

down that can be made; but it is basic to every type of film-making, from shorts to full-length features. As can be seen in a breakdown of even as uncomplicated a film as *Almost,* a prize-winning film made by Joseph Goldman, a sixteen-year-old student, it is the most efficient way to organize the shooting. *Almost* takes only seven minutes, and a minimum of locations, to tell its simple, poignant story.

1

2

3

A young boy leaves his drab, tenement home and wanders the streets looking for something to do. Eventually he arrives at a construction site where he discovers a long piece of drainage pipe. Since there is nothing else of much interest here he decides to crawl through the pipe. When he crawls out the other end though, the

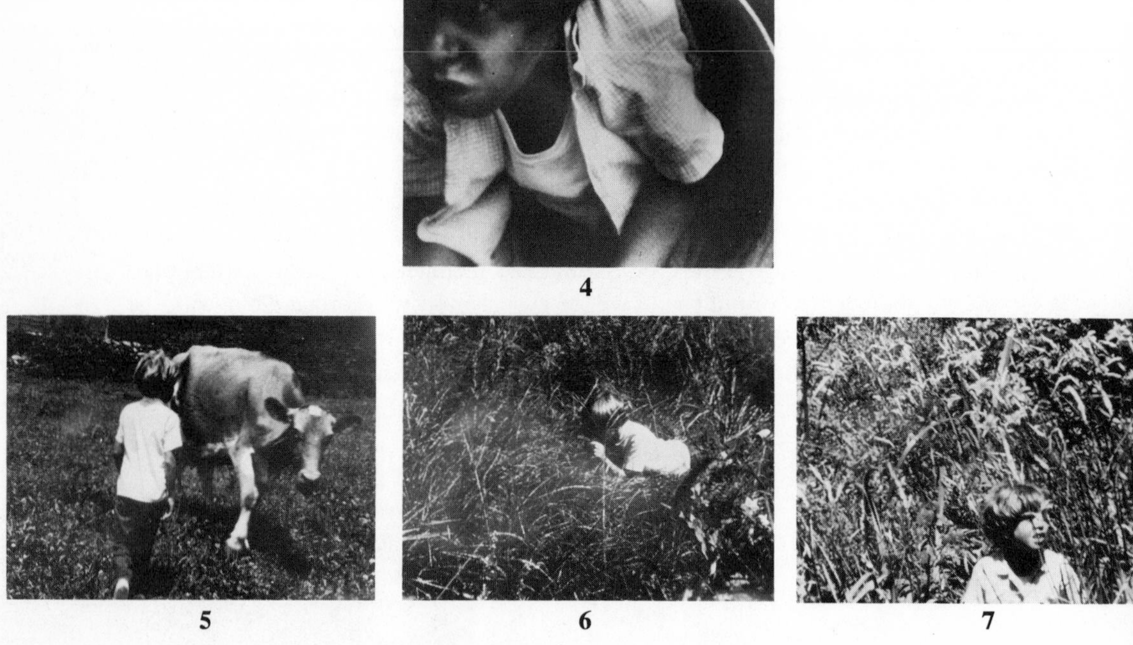

4

5 6 7

film has switched from B&W to color, and he discovers that he is now in the country. Without a sidelong glance or any hesitation, the boy joyfully explores his new surroundings, chasing cows, catching grasshoppers, and watching birds as he wanders through fields of lilies. He decides that this is so much better a life than that in

8 9

10 11

the city that he crawls back through the pipe, rushes home to pack his few belongings, and returns to the construction site. This time, however, there is no magic

12 13 14

countryside when he exits from the pipe. After looking around in disbelief, he slowly turns and starts back toward home.

In order to group these shots by location, the script would have had to be broken down as follows:

1. City streets	exterior, day—B&W	1,2,14
2. Construction site	exterior, day—B&W	3,9,11,12,13
3. Boy's home	interior, day—B&W	10
4. Countryside	exterior, day—color	4,5,6,7,8

These groups can then be shot in any order, and the shots within each group can be filmed in any convenient sequence. But it is easy to see that as long as the shots are filmed in groups, the shooting is much more efficient than if the film-maker ran from one location to the next in order to make the shots in the same sequence as they appear in the film.

Building Continuity

No matter what order the shots are filmed in, however, the necessity of making a film one shot at a time imposes a great burden on the film-maker's imagination. Because the flow of action is interrupted every time the camera stops, each shot must be designed so that it can eventually be connected to the one before it and the one to follow. This means that the director and the cameraman must constantly visualize shots that are yet to be made, keep a firm grasp on the details of those shots already completed, and anticipate the effect of each cut.

The need to construct each scene mentally before it can be shot makes a detailed shooting script quite valuable, since a script provides a conceptual framework within which to fit each shot. But the interruption between shots also creates some purely mechanical problems that cannot be dealt with by means of a script alone. Especially in scenes in which the action in each shot is supposed to represent the uninterrupted continuation of the action in the previous shot, time and space must be made to seem continuous even though the shots used to create this illusion are often filmed hours, or sometimes days, apart. This need for continuity means that, if the shots are eventually to join together into a seamless whole, a number of special procedures must be followed during shooting.

These procedures are based on the requirements of the editing technique that is used to create an uninterrupted continuity of action from shot to shot. This technique, called *match-action cutting,* can best be illustrated by a short sequence from *Ecstasy*. The film, a low-budget feature made in 1933 by Gustav Machaty, is now almost legendary for showing a very young Hedy Lamarr in a long, nude bathing sequence. The story is a classic love triangle; in this sequence the heroine is taking leave of her clandestine lover. The frames are arranged in pairs, each pair representing the action immediately on either side of each of the four cuts in the sequence. In each case a movement starts in one shot and is completed in the next. On the cut between shots 1 and 2 she is stepping in front of him, from 2 to 3 he pulls her to him, from 3 to 4 she is pulling away, and from 4 to 5 their hands separate.

Even though these cuts fall at quite specific points in the action, very little had to be done during the shooting to provide each cutting point. All that was needed

1

2a

2b

3a

3b

4a

4b

5

was to make the action in each shot overlap the action in the shots on either side of it. Then, during editing, this overlap was eliminated so that an action started in one shot exactly matched its continuation in the next. Of course, the cuts needn't fall in the middle of an action. The shots could just as easily have been overlapped at points where there was no movement at all. Cutting on movement, however, smooths over the interruption caused by the cut by changing the shots while our attention is focused on the movement. It also diverts our attention from slight mismatches in the position of the actors. For instance, on the cut from shots 4 to 5 the man's hand goes from his hip to his side. Such mismatches are quite common but usually go unnoticed as our attention follows the continuous flow of action.

The amount of overlap needed for match-action cutting depends upon the nature of the sequence. In most cases it is enough just to run each shot a few seconds beyond the cutting point and then restart the action a few seconds before the cutting point in the next shot. This kind of overlap is most easily done when the shots are made in sequence so that the overlapping movements can be duplicated while they're still fresh in everyone's mind. In the previous example, however, because the same long shot and medium shot occur at both the beginning and the end of the sequence, it would have been easier to make each of these shots as a *cover shot*. That means that the whole scene would first be filmed in long shot, then most of it repeated in medium shot, and finally just the central piece of action done in medium close-up. This technique minimizes the number of times the camera must be moved and permits the closer shots to be made in any convenient sequence once the "master" long shot is completed. But it does require that the action throughout each shot be as similar as possible to the action in the master shot so that there are definite points at which to make match-action cuts.

Another requirement of match-action cutting is that each cut represent a definite change of *angle,* that is, that each shot be made from a quite perceptibly different camera position. This change is necessary because, if the change of angle is too small, instead of a smooth cut to a new view of the action, the cut will look like just a jump in the action (a *jump cut*). An example of this occurs in even as fine a film as Truffaut's *The 400 Blows.* Since this was his first feature, it was shot on a low budget and a tight schedule with nonprofessional actors. As a result, this jump cut was probably caused by his having to join parts of two takes of the same shot in

Courtesy: JANUS FILMS, INC.

order to get the desired performance. Although the action is continuous, the change of angle is so small that instead of a cut, it looks as though the camera was suddenly knocked slightly to the left. This seemingly unnecessary jerk of the camera momentarily interrupts the action, but in this case Truffaut smooths over the break by using the unrelenting flow of dialogue to maintain our attention.

Screen Direction

There are also, however, certain situations in which too great a change of camera angle can disorient the viewer. Whenever the action flows back and forth across the screen, moving the camera beyond a certain point to the right or the left of the subject will reverse the position and direction of everything on the screen. This problem, called *screen direction,* can best be seen by looking at an example of just such a reversal from *Ecstasy*. In these two shots the woman's lover quite unknowingly asks her husband for a ride and the two of them drive off together.

In the first shot the car is headed screen right, and unless it moves or we see the camera move, we would expect to see it headed in the same direction in the next

shot as well. But when the camera was moved back for the second shot, it was also moved around to the opposite side of the car. As a result the camera crossed the *axis,* an imaginary line drawn through the dominant action that is used to determine its screen direction. Here is how the axis would look in the first shot (camera 1):

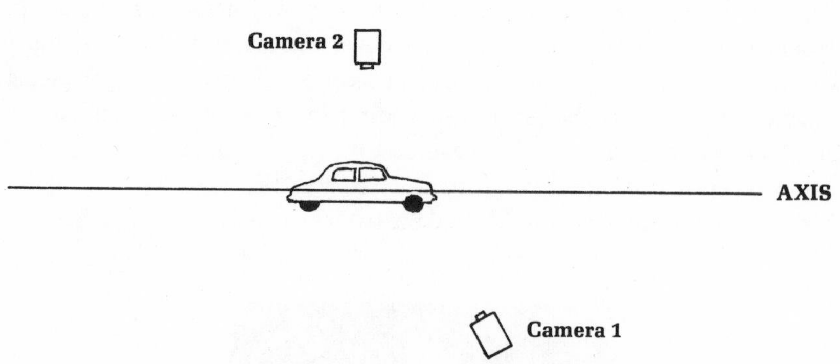

Had the camera stayed on the same side of this axis for the next shot, the screen direction would have remained the same. For some reason, however, the camera was moved to the other side of the axis (camera 2), reversing the position and direction of both the actors and the automobile and creating a momentary disorientation that disrupts the illusion of continuous action.

It is possible to cross the axis smoothly, however, as long as the film-maker is careful to ease the transition from shot to shot. A good example is this reversal of screen direction in *A Day in the Life of Two Hoods,* a prize-winning film made by a student, John MacKenzie. One of the strengths of this film, in fact, is that even this beginning film-maker had a firm grasp of screen direction and used it to develop a sense of continuous action. In these three shots, two young hoods get into an argument with a high school student, and then suddenly knock him down and leave him lying in the gutter.

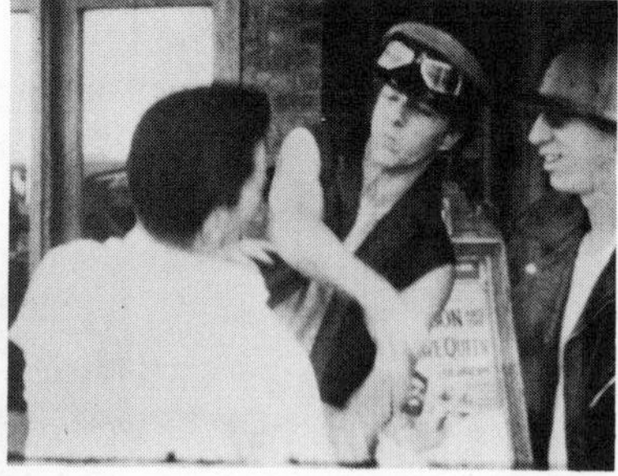

Here the student is first toward the right side of the screen and then on the left. But in this case the film-maker cut on the movement of the fist so that the reversal actually helped maintain the direction in which it was moving. In the first shot it initially moved left to right; then, just as it began to swing away from the camera, the cut to the next shot continued its movement from left to right. This second shot also just barely crossed the axis. That way we see the action almost from a *neutral* angle—a camera angle in which the action has no screen direction since it takes place directly toward or away from the camera. As a result, when the student is hit, instead of changing screen direction, his fall toward the camera simply becomes directionless. This neutral angle is then the basis for the hoods' right-to-left movement in the third shot, counter to their screen direction in the first shot. But this movement is no longer seen as a change in direction because their screen direction has been neutralized by the intervening shot.

The Cut-away

Since it is not always possible to duplicate accurately the action from shot to shot or to maintain screen direction, match-action cutting also requires the cameraman to shoot what is called a *cut-away*. One form of the cut-away, a reaction shot from *Le Départ,* has already been described in Chapter Two. There it was used as a means for imperceptibly shortening the time required to show a piece of action. But a reaction shot, or any other shot of someone or something not directly involved in the ongoing action, can also be used by the editor to cut away momentarily from the main action so that shots which don't match, or change direction, aren't cut directly together.

A cut-away, however, interrupts the flow of movement in a scene and can destroy its pace unless, like a reaction shot, the cut-away maintains the thrust of the action by amplifying its meaning. An example of this expansion of meaning is a cut-away in René Clement's *Forbidden Games.* It is a shot of an owl that is used to

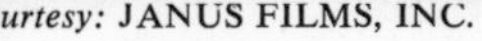
ourtesy: JANUS FILMS, INC.

intensify the sadness of a scene in which a young boy is feverishly destroying a collection of crosses he has painstakingly accumulated throughout the film. The crosses are the secret collection of the boy and a younger girl, a war orphan who found temporary refuge in his remote farm home. Now his companion has been taken away by the authorities, and in a fit of rage and desperation he is attempting to destroy the last vestige of their relationship. In this context the shot of the owl is more than just a means for bridging a gap in the action. It has appeared in previous scenes as the lone witness to the children's activities. As a result, when we see it here, it is both a reminder of all they have been through together and a silent observer who is helpless to alter events or mitigate the pain that a distant war has eventually brought even to the isolated childhood of this lonely farm boy.

Instead of shooting separate cut-aways, there is also a technique for incorporating a cut-away into the beginning and the end of each shot. This is done by starting and stopping the action out of frame so that the camera holds on the setting for several moments before the action starts and after it ends. Like a cut-away, this extra footage can then be used by the editor to divert our attention momentarily from the ongoing action. The same technique is also used to smooth the flow of action across a cut between a moving camera shot and one made when the camera is still. When the camera moves everything in the frame is in motion, so a cut to or from a static shot will cause everything in the frame either to spring into motion or to come to an abrupt halt. This kind of jarring cut can be avoided, however, if the camera is held still until the action begins and after it ends.

Settings and Costumes

One last problem is the continuity of settings and costumes. At its simplest this means that if a character wears a hat in a scene, he should always be wearing a hat —unless he is shown taking it off—even though the various shots in the scene are made hours or even days apart. The same thing is true of the rest of the clothing worn by the actors and the details of the setting. These can add up to a tremendous number of minute details; but in most cases the overwhelming complexity of this problem can be alleviated if the shooting is arranged so that all the pieces of what is to be continuous action are filmed at one time. That way there is less chance that even small changes will go unnoticed. However, in longer, more involved films, keeping track of all the settings and costumes can become quite time consuming, so this is made the special responsibility of a *script girl.* This is someone who makes detailed notes on each day's shooting and may even keep a file of still pictures of each setting and change of costume in case some detail must be checked at the last minute.

Slating and Logging the Shots

Every shot in the script is usually numbered in sequence, and each time a specific shot is repeated during the shooting it is given a *take number*. These numbers are written on a small chalkboard, or *slate,* along with the date, the name of the film, and sometimes the names of the director and the cameraman. This slate is then held in front of the lens and filmed at the beginning or the end of each take so that every piece of film is clearly numbered and identified. These numbers, and all the other information on the slate, are also noted on a *camera log,* by either the second assistant cameraman or the script girl, and the number of each take that is acceptable to the director is circled. The accumulated logs from each day's shooting then tell the director what shots in the script have been filmed so that nothing is missed.

Each roll of film is also given a number, and the log sheets are made out so that there is one for each roll. When the processing laboratory is requested to sort the footage before printing, a copy of the log sheet is sent to the laboratory along with the film. Then, after the film is processed, the laboratory compares the slates to the logs and pulls out and prints only the circled takes. This print, called the *rushes* or the *dailies* because it is usually ready the next day, is first screened by the director and the cameraman so that they can check their work as they go. Then the print is used in the editing of the film.

It is not possible, however, to follow this elaborate slating procedure when shooting unscripted footage, such as news film or a documentary. Then a *dope sheet* is usually kept by the sound man or an assistant. The dope sheet simply lists the roll number, a short description of each shot in the order in which the shots appear in the roll, and the number of takes of each shot. If the shooting is not terribly rushed it is also possible to slate the beginning or the end of each roll with the name of the film, the date, and the roll number; and the cameraman can indicate the takes by holding the appropriate number of fingers in front of the lens at the start of retake. Later, the dope sheets are used by the editor to sort out the rolls, separate the takes, and identify each shot.

These procedures—overlapping the shots, changing the camera angle and observing the axis, providing cut-aways and holds, keeping track of settings and costumes, and logging and slating the shots—can all be applied to any sequence of shots. But these are only the mechanics of shooting. While they help ensure that all the pieces will cut together smoothly, they do not create the whole film. Continuity and meaning also depend upon how the pieces are fit together by means of lighting and editing. There are important aspects of both continuity and meaning that are controlled in the lighting and exposure of each shot, a complex area that will be discussed next. And beyond this there is a vast array of editing techniques that will be discussed in Section 2, Chapters Eight and Nine. Editing, too, affects the meaning and continuity of the shots and therefore how each shot is scripted

and filmed; but the effects of these editing techniques can be understood only in terms of the role editing itself plays in building the action. Thus camerawork, while the first step, and probably the most important one, in producing the footage, is only the beginning of the long process that is required before that footage can be projected in front of an audience.

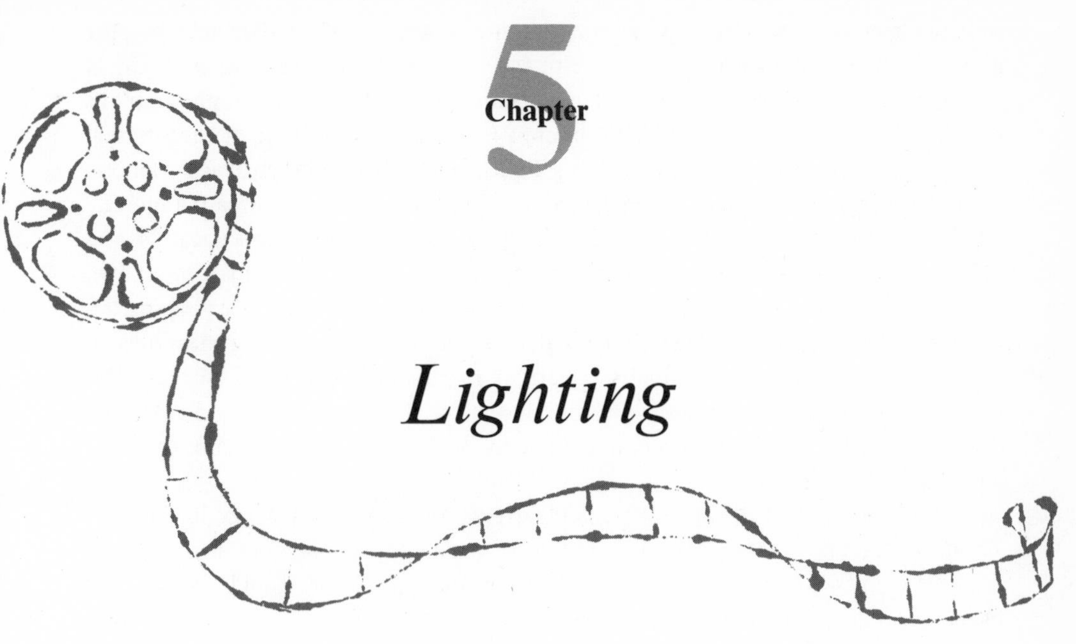

Chapter 5

Lighting

Part 1:
Creating the Light

The making of films consists of seizing light from the physical world, registering its impression on a sensitive emulsion, and then projecting that impression in clear and occasionally even beautiful and powerful images. The whole process depends upon the film-maker's understanding of the qualities of the light that illuminates the objects he films and the effect these qualities will have on the meanings he is trying to convey.

It is this aspect of motion pictures that is most responsible for those illusive impressions of reality that seem as hard and firm as truth itself, and yet, on closer inspection, come to us out of rays and beams no more substantial than the memories that linger briefly after the images leave the screen. Siegfried Kracauer,

in his *Theory of Film,* tells about a photographer he knew in the 1930's who had for a model a young man with a nondescript face. Just by subtly varying the light in each of a hundred shots, he produced astonishing results. "None of the photographs recalled the model; and all of them differed from each other. Out of the original face there arose, evoked by the varying lights, a hundred different faces, among them those of a hero, a prophet, a peasant, a dying soldier, an old woman, a monk."

In motion pictures this quality of light becomes both more evocative and more complex because our comprehension of the film-maker's world is cumulative. Lighting values, often changing from second to second, are definitive in shaping the objects and movements on the screen—defining, modifying, creating meanings in a tumble of impressions that finally cohere as rhythmically unfolding images. The lighting of each scene becomes a melodic line in the dramatic, tonal, and compositional harmonies that form to become our sense of the film. And each shot becomes a phrase in that melody.

Josef von Sternberg knew this as clearly as any director. He saw in the possibilities of studio lighting the culmination of a quality of imagination that could cradle dreams whole from the shooting to the watching. He once said about a film of his, *Morocco,* that he purposely chose a fatuous story so that his audience would not be distracted from the play of light and shade in the photography. Here, then, is Sternberg, lighting the corners of his characters' most private needs with his skill at modeling and working their flesh until it no longer conforms to their bones but to the substance of their innermost thoughts. Watch the magic at work in *The Blue Angel.*

Professor Rath (Emil Jannings), repressed, middle-aged, protected from his needs and the demands of the world by his tyrannically ordered high school classroom, ventures forth blindly into the dressing room of the devastating Lola-Lola (the quintessential Marlene Dietrich). His students frequent her rooms backstage in the tavern where her small company performs; and there he has come, fierce and vulnerable, to save them from corruption. He is, of course, smitten. Instantly, irrevocably, tragically. He is now bound to her—a poor bearish plaything to strut for her amusement and then be discarded when his driven awkwardness no longer pleases.

We see the good professor here, upon his return to Lola-Lola's dressing room, now fully the servant of her charms. He has fumbled and dropped a packet of her cigarettes and has plunged beneath the table to recover them. For the first time we see him as the new beast he has become, half bearish animal and half timorous professor. His full chest is in shadow so that the light burning the edges of his face reaches its stark conclusion in the short, professorial beard that seems to glow with self-mockery, ridiculing the needs of the massive dark body behind it. Next to his head, the incandescent Dietrich thighs light his way among the shadows. And beneath them, the exquisitely formed calf, ankle, foot, shaped to their perfection in long, warm, teasing shadows edged with a hot white light that sears to preserve the outline of the leg. The professor gropes for the cigarettes for a second or two, then finds them and rises, his large body drawing its shadow up with him, as we remain below watching those legs, now in full light, burn the screen with their splendor.

This, then, is a pivotal moment in the film. Its relationships, attitudes, and themes are defined by their abstraction in a reworking of the haunting opposition of beauty and beast. Only beauty here is both complete and incomplete in those marvelously sensual legs cherished by the perfect, loving lights which form them. And the beast is a man whose tragic contradictions are brought to a tense reality by the lighting that instantly draws this critical flaw to our attention.

Light was also a plaything in the hands of Orson Welles, whose fun-house Gothic, all mirrors and lights, continually surprises and enchants. This frame is from a turning point in the narrative of *Citizen Kane*. We see the reporter, seeking the identity of the elusive Rosebud, granted admission to the central vault of the Thatcher Memorial Library. Thatcher is the old banker who administered the fortune of the young Kane; and the papers, under lock and seal, are the key to the flashbacks that will follow and finally will make us a witness to the epic career of the legendary Charles Foster Kane. The vault, then, is not just a moment in the

progress of the film, but the repository of Kane's childhood and his beginnings as a publisher—seeds of his personality and source of his power.

The vault is thus a way station between heaven and hell. Shafts of burning light cut through the room like a message from heaven, the heavy marble walls etherealized in their shadows. In this light the guard becomes a divine messenger bringing the fiercely glowing documents out of the darkness into the light as an offering at least as majestic as the tablets offered Moses; and the hard mahogany table that will receive the documents burns with the glint of a sacred altar. Over all this the librarian, guardian of the trust, presides: a silhouette without weight or substance; severe, inhuman, judgment itself. All of this accomplished with lighting effects. It is trickery and hokum; still, it is conceived out of a kind of primitive wonderment that has embraced, with large feelings, not only the life of Kane but that quality of the magical which touches all of cinema.

More often than not the magic is worked with invisible wires, hidden doors, false bottoms. We are not meant to know that we are in the presence of an illusion. The lights which play upon the surface of every object lightly coat that surface with a special sense of reality. Much of what we see, what we think we see, and what we need to see are conjured together under the spell of these lights. Their effect lies so intimately upon everything revealed before us that this effect becomes each surface, bearing it into the film-maker's world infused at once with both form and meaning.

We can see this at a critical moment in *Wild Strawberries*. Ingmar Bergman finally brings the journey of Dr. Isak Borg to a rest after the old man has retreated once more to his past to work out his heavy sense of failure. He has just seen, with terrible clarity, his wife commit adultery, reaching out not for passion (which is forgivable) but merely for warmth; and he has finally seen himself, within the chill surface of this dream, a macabre specter walking the world in ignorance of the dread and pain his unfeeling life has inflicted on those who have come close to him.

Courtesy: JANUS FILMS, INC.

Now he has awakened from this nightmare. He sits in the car next to his daughter-in-law—during a pause in this drive that has taken him to each of the tortured stations of his life—and he tells her that he is dead. His face is lit with the death suffered each of his frightened years, the left side of his face washed a bloodless white, the right side in soft shadows molding enough of the flesh to show us the hollow old man.

Then we see the daughter-in-law, Marianne, saying his son had pronounced the same sentence upon himself, sitting in the same place, in the same car, just a few months before. She is a window between father and son, and between both and the outside world. Her flesh is not born of the cursed old man's and so it is kept alive even in this close contact with him. Yet she is carrying his flesh, a new generation, a grandchild.

Here her image contrasts with that of the old man. The skin of her face is touched lightly and evenly by a light that models the sensual, gentle curves without denying the strong angularity of a face that has lived with and triumphed over the death inherited by the son. Yet, among the sensuous lines also lie hints of her needs, her contribution to the bonds that have limited and hurt all three. She explains how, in anger and desperation, she told the son about the life she was carrying and how he, sitting where the father now sits, so feared that life, and his own, and his father's that he rejected her, cutting himself loose from the steady buoyance of their marriage, so he could sink.

Last we see the son as he was when he heard the news, lit like the father, but more intensely, painfully in darkness; one side of his face bleached the same bloodless white, the other side hidden and lost in deep shadow. The sins of the father have been clearly visited upon the son; and we see the mark, lit so we cannot miss it, in the dreadful similarity between the appearance of the old man, whose life is behind him, and that of the son, whose life has vanished somewhere in the wake of the old man's receding past.

These faces, molded and defined by the film-maker's lights, draw together the accelerating insights propelled by the story. We are meant to pause at each face, see who each is, understand where each has been, and finally know how each is bound to the others. What has been lit is the inescapable responsibility of each of these faces for the suffering of those they have touched.

The film-maker is lighting for clarity. He has reached behind the words his characters speak to their thoughts, to their feelings, and to a statement of their place in the world. But this clarity of expression depends upon a firm sense of the physical world to bring it into relief. Because it is the canons of reality which give the film-maker's story shape and limits, each moment first had to be tested against the hard laws of plausibility. A quality of reality had to be meticulously simulated. Since each person in the car was lit in a studio, each light first had to capture an aspect of the natural world. But that same world has also been freely bent to the film-maker's will, refracted and extended in the lights that fall upon these faces.

This is the central function of lighting. On the one hand it must clearly reveal the physical world, but it must also reveal that world in terms of the film-maker's private vision of it. Every object on the screen is potentially a revelation of the film-maker's insights and can be infused with a spectrum of meanings. This is one of those powerful but unstated assumptions from which narrative films draw their energy and specialize their insights. In these films every surface in the corporeal universe is ultimately anthropomorphized—with man as the controlling intelligence and his nature as the infusing spirit—to become an indication of his meaning on earth.

Man becomes a summation of the physical world, formed of its clay, the perfect embodiment of its elements. Yet, even without man, when just those elements are seen as a landscape, they are strong, beautiful, or expressive because they reflect the spirit of man. Each portion of the physical world has been selected to express the story of the men who inhabit it, so the face of a mountain and the face of a man can both yield equal insight into the human condition.

It is the lighting, however, that makes this pliable universe first cohere. Every

surface is defined—shaped and emphasized—by the light that brings it to us. So it is primarily under the pressure of light that the hard, intractable surfaces of the world are made to yield and comply until they conform to the film-maker's particular conception of mankind. The way light plays upon and molds every object on the screen finally insinuates itself into our perception of the lives unfolding before us.

Courtesy: JANUS FILMS, INC.

An example of this so nearly perfect that it has become a cinematic archetype of the extension of man into the landscape which surrounds him is the island sequence in Michelangelo Antonioni's *L'Avventura.* To this barren, isolated, crumbling speck of volcanic rock surrounded by the fearsome sea comes a group of bored, aimless, nomadic people from the shrinking, arid island that has become the Italian upper class. Almost like mythic voyagers, they have been swept toward a place that is a terrible summation of the land they have fled. If not quite a symbol, every aspect of the island comes to assert the brittle emptiness of these reluctant explorers who have discovered and claimed its surface. We can fully understand these people—feel their isolation, their rootlessness, the cold, inhospitable plains

of their lives—only in their association, shot after shot, with the malformed island they have been drawn to.

It is this conception that is pulled together by the lighting. Antonioni chose his days to film with care. The light actively conspires with his script to force his sense of man into every object framed by his camera. The ice-cold gray light which spills across the island, smoothing the texture between man and rock, draws out our sense of the weakly driven flesh set against the petrified volcanic ash crumbling under the whip of the elements. This sunlight, straining through heavy clouds, is just sufficiently bright and even to set off the surface of each jagged edge of rock, each of the broken boulders that litter the island, every dangerous swirl and break of water isolating the island and wearing it away. And in this light each of the faces we encounter is molded to the expectations formed by this piece of rock severed from the world—cold, vulnerable, empty.

Lighting thus becomes the medium through which these objects are fully realized as they flow through the illuminated pool of each shot and into the torrent of separately lit shots that forms the course of the film. Light, of course, is the elemental means—the medium—through which the world impresses itself on film. But simultaneously, its values, carefully gathered or created, separate the world into fragments, call attention to some, depress interest in others, and mold its surfaces into rich and fluid dimensions. All this happens equally in the sweep of a long shot and in a close-up of a detail. From the light that discreetly controls the appearance of each surface, a procession of landscapes forms and then combines to set a tone for each scene that expresses many of the film-maker's most subtly conceived meanings.

Hard Daylight

Since the earliest days of film-making, sunlight has been a primary source of illumination. Not only is it cheap and on most occasions plentiful, but, as we saw in *L'Avventura,* it is capable of yielding remarkably expressive results under a skilled and watchful eye. It naturally varies in direction, intensity, and qualities of diffusion depending upon the time, the season, and the particular cloud formations of the day. But with the aid of a few reflectors, the knowledgeable choice of a camera angle, or just patience in choosing a day or waiting a particular day out, the broad sweep of this light can be bent to conform to the film-maker's most exquisite designs.

All these techniques were common knowledge almost from the beginning, when lenses and film stocks were not nearly so responsive as they are now to the film-maker's demands. Two examples from the silent films of the early 1920's, a feature and a documentary, point up how a film-maker, without sophisticated equipment, could skillfully exploit hard, bright sunlight and the sharp, deep shadows it casts to give an expressive, coherent tone to his film and then draw from that tone his basic meanings.

John Ford's first great western, *The Iron Horse* (1924), captured the spirit of danger and adventure of the pioneers as they crossed the continent and brought with them, in an act of supreme strength and will, the long steel tracks that would stretch the nation. This was not a world of subtlety or ambiguity. A sense of either would have been both unmanly and inappropriate. Ford pictured his pioneers with a lusty sense of the task at hand, men capable of meeting head-on the endless series of disasters that seemed to conspire against them each mile of the way. Success and failure were all too easily put in the same stark balance with life and death. It was a world in which everything was clearly defined.

Ford used bright sunlight to make this encounter with the Indians tangible evidence of the strength and rightness of his heroes' cause. Under a sun that broiled

the flatlands white, he sent his black iron horse into battle. In this attack the barricade and the Indians, like all the dangers in the film, are instantly laid before us by a hard light that throws their shapes into bold relief. These shots are from the driving prelude to that great action dance of the mythic West—the pitched battle—in which, in the firing of each arrow or gun, the pleasure of the kill on each face, the fall of each body, lived the spirit of the Republic these men were building. The key to the scene is that Ford has not merely made us a witness to an intense sense of

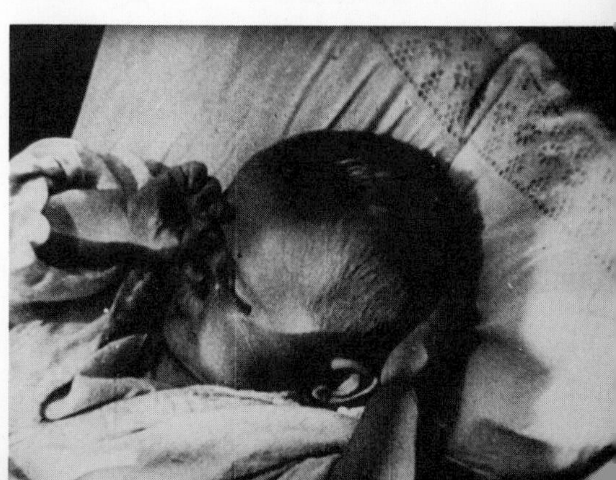

history's being revealed. Rather, he has also made us intimate participants in a ritual of life and death. And so everything is made wondrously clear and precise under the high sun, which sets deep blacks against brilliant whites. Clear and abstract.

Three years earlier Robert Flaherty brought an equally keen sense of ritual to his documentary on the lives of a small band of Eskimos, *Nanook of the North.* What we see is not life captured on the run. The heavy equipment and slow film would have just about made that impossible. Besides, after Flaherty completed the shooting, his negative was ruined and he had to restage and refilm everything. So, instead of spontaneity, we are led with care into the stately but fragile lives of the Eskimos in scene after scene that captures their majestic assault on the treacherous Arctic cold.

The brilliant white, frozen plains of snow, the bitter, beautiful cold and ice

are the stage on which the Eskimos confront the dangers and challenges which shape their lives. In this scene describing one of the long, nomadic treks that Nanook and his family must endure to survive (and representative of many of the descriptive long shots in the film), Flaherty records the Eskimo family as it carefully makes its way across the ice by tracing the shadow line thrown by the low sun. He has chosen his time of day carefully to make this shot. The sharp white snow, the distinct gray shadows, the deep black specks that are the Eskimo procession hugging the edge of the trail cast by the sun speak to the world of simple clarity. There is death a thousand times over waiting for the slightest mistake.

As in John Ford's West, there is a quality of wonder at lives that can express themselves so fully in precise actions whose sum means nothing less than survival. It is as though the meaning of life is only truly revealed in its reenactment, in the rationalization of its impulses into a stylized drama whose narrow stage is the sharp line between death and life.

Nowhere in film is this stark vision more dramatically stated than in the "Odessa Steps" sequence from Eisenstein's *Battleship Potemkin.* Just flipping through the sequence and pausing at random, one can see Eisenstein working the bright, sharp sunlight to draw together his fervent sense of history. Everything in the sequence is clearly delineated in this light. Toward the beginning the sunlight creates the ominous, deep shadows of the Cossacks as they slowly descend the steps, while it shines brightly upon their victims. In the sun the white face of the mother whose baby will hurtle down the steps is transformed into a memorial death mask against the deep black of her clothing. Later on, the sun pours into the ferocity of a Cossack's face, gouging its features into a personification of evil, as he strikes at an old woman; and then the sun rims the blooded head of the woman as she receives the blow. In the long shots, where hundreds of lives are tangled in this clash of historic forces, the hard sunlight throws each of the participants into clear relief. For Eisenstein this is a reenactment of a critical moment in the progress of mankind. Nothing less than the future of civilization rests upon this summation of the barbarities of the past. It is as if a pivotal instant has been lifted from the heart of man's travail on earth and held out for his close inspection. And, in the crisp sunlight, each detail is registered with such precision that the clarity of each action then becomes the clarity of Eisenstein's truth.

Hard, bright sunlight also enables the film-maker to break down his image into planes of light, and so divide the screen into expressively interrelated units that can capture and then unify a range of feelings. Toward the beginning of Andrzej Wajda's *Kanal,* the Polish patriots take shelter in a bombed-out building to decide what they should do in the face of the German destruction of Warsaw. We are meant to linger with them during this painful moment of intense uncertainty. In the distance the ugly rumble of the German guns grows louder and louder. Their impulse tells them to fight, to resist to the last man. But their intelligence and their training tell them there is nothing significant they can do to stop the inevitable German advance.

Courtesy: JANUS FILMS, INC.

It is at this moment that we see them. Bright sunlight slices through the building, bringing the wall shattered by the heavy German artillery into sharp relief. The same hard sun also falls upon the soldier intently listening to the German progress and upon the soldier above him who has just come in from the danger

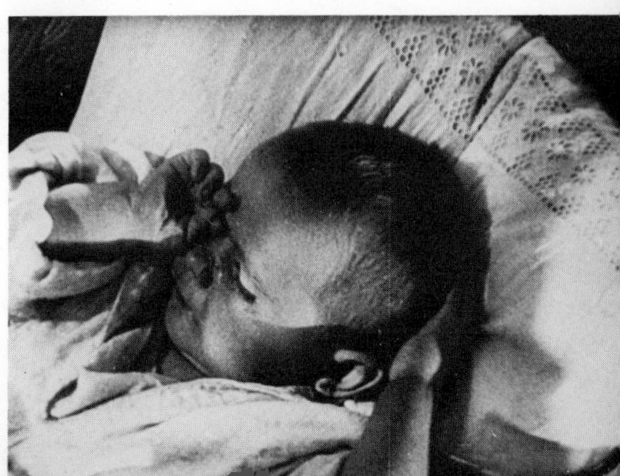

zone. The bright sun is the immediate thread connecting them with and exposing them to the advance of the Germans, and they are particularly vulnerable in its sharp light. Beneath these soldiers, in the merciful, almost safe, shadows, is their commander, trying to work out a plan of action. Soon he will lead them into the sewers of Warsaw, into the permanent darkness that is their only hope for fighting without being detected. The world of bright sunlight has become enemy territory; the shadows, the only possible domain for resistance. The premise of the film has been established, and with it a sense of the intense dedication of these men, whose faces, caught between shadow and light, are molded into that awesome mask of grim determination that will become the sole badge of their eventual martyrdom.

Soft Daylight

When softer, more diffuse light falls evenly across the image, reducing shadows and gently shaping each surface, the realities of war are defined quite differently. In Pierre Schoendorffer's documentary on the Vietnam war, *The Anderson Platoon,* the film-maker is getting at the quiet, daily erosiveness of war. Life-and-death encounters exist only in bright, brief flashes of action. But for the most part the soldiers' lives are embedded in the leaden, numbing, perpetual discomforts that mark the texture of the war for the American platoon we see. There are no heroes, only young men doggedly performing their duty as they have been instructed.

In shot after shot we see these men in the faded grayish light that filters through the web of jungle in which they operate. It would have been easy enough for Schoendorffer to ravage these faces with expressive patterns of light and shade. But this is not a world of high drama, with stark highlights and shadow needed to drive home the intensity of battle. It is a world of frightened young men, of the monotony of discomfort, of the enervating confusion between expectation and reality. And the diffuse, even light, by gracefully resting on the gentle contours of these soft, unformed faces, emphasizes their untried youthfulness until the youthfulness itself becomes a collective, anonymous presence in the film. It is at this point that we begin to feel the obscenity of this war fought by the young without purpose and without passion.

One reason for the softening effect of this light is that diffuse daylight molds every contour and fills and balances even the roughest surfaces. As a result, it mutes differences in shape and texture and gives the total image a sense of evenness and calm. These are qualities that are most apparent and easiest to capture in those still moments just after daybreak and just before nightfall. Then, with fast film stocks and even faster lenses, the film-maker can exploit each nuance of the light, subtly changing in value by the minute, to give his scenes a special feeling of quiet and equilibrium that can be invaluable in working out the tensions of his script.

Alain Resnais used the stillness of nightfall descending to quiet the tormented shapes of Hiroshima and absorb the raw edges of a crisis in the lives of his lovers. The woman in *Hiroshima Mon Amour* has just begun to relive the horror of her wartime memories and she is filled with overwhelming anxiety at the nerve ends that will be rubbed raw in this plunge into her past. She now knows that she must make that journey, but not right away, not until she is better prepared. As for her lover, he is painfully aware that there are only sixteen hours until she must leave his country and his life forever.

At this point Resnais breaks from the lovers and shows us the city under the

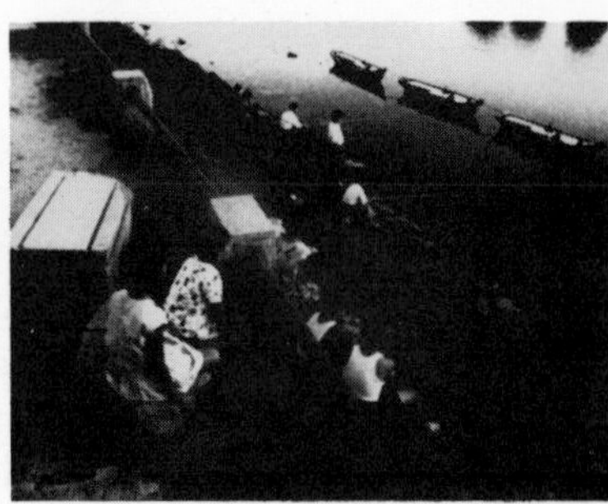

peaceful, steadying approach of night. Here the empty new buildings, the sullen canal, even the twisted remains of the Palace of Industry, the last visible reminder of the atomic holocaust, seem at rest, suspended in the translucent fall of light that bathes Hiroshima in its warm glow. Water, people, stone, and steel cohere in the dying light and fill the screen with a calming quality of balance, a sense that each of the fragments forming the world can lengthen and meld, hold together, if only for a moment. When we return to the lovers they are at peace, within themselves and with each other. There is no word of explanation for their change in mood. Simply, the soft light of nightfall has cushioned the shock of the last scene and set the tone for the next.

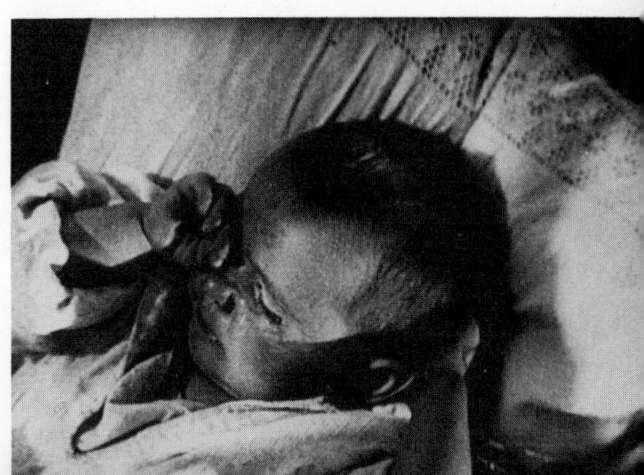

In *Young Aphrodites* Nikos Koundouros also exploited the qualities of soft daylight. He sensitively moved the pivotal events in his reworking of the Daphnis and Chloë legend out of the bright, hard Grecian sun and into the quiet, even shadows. It is a film whose substance exists in the tremulous, uncertain feelings brought to each action rather than in the inevitable performance of that action. So the gentle moods revealed through carefully sought locations and a decorously placed camera subdue the passions of the legend by capturing the soft light in which it could find fresh significance.

The story plays upon the sexual awakening of two children. They live on the periphery of a nomadic tribe of shepherds come down to the sea in search of new pastures two centuries before the birth of Christ. The ten-year-old Skymnos idealizes twelve-year-old Chloë and follows her everywhere. They are at playful peace with each other until they discover an older couple making love in a cave. The children are numbed by the discovery, caught between a growing desire and their ignorance of the source of that desire. Soon after, a mute shepherd finds Chloë alone by the water's edge and assaults her. Even as she struggles against his brute strength, the growing warmth of her desire for a man fills her body until she responds willingly to his attack. In the rocks above them Skymnos watches. When it is over, he looks at her and sees that she is looking back at him with the distant eyes of a stranger. He wanders to the ocean, on his way eradicating every remnant of his joyful memories of Chloë, then working deeper and deeper into the water until it surges over him and claims him and every trace of his brief love.

The tragic ending is ordained. The theme is as stark and clear as the fierce sunlight that strikes and intensifies the hard edges of rock and the violent boil of ocean waters. So Koundouros worked instead in the shadows, in the caves and grottoes where the light is softened, where the edges blend and merge, to make the myth more human. These are children—tentative, unformed, learning life in secretive, dark draughts. Koundouros used the dark gentleness of subdued light to hide the eagerness of their bodies from each other and clothe the full extent of the passion they are beginning to feel. He also used the shadows to give them something to cling to. Away from the hard light of the sun, in which everything is clearly defined, Koundouros provided the children a sense of mystery to sustain the incompleteness of their world and still keep it tenderly alive.

For this reason the physical liberation of love they witness is also carefully placed in the dark, private hollows of a cave, where the curves and angles of flesh can lose their individual identity. They see it as if in a dream. And the rape, too, is hidden from the sun. The light plays off the violent surface of the water, but the

Courtesy: JANUS FILMS, INC.

act and its consummation are buried in the shadows. Throughout the film this dark, even light calms each burst of passion and emphasizes only the groping uncertainties that define the children's lives.

Even when they are in the sun, during the long, lyrical courtship ritual in which Skymnos mutely follows Chloë over bright rocks and across open beaches, hungrily watching her beauty from a distance, Koundouros keeps the sun behind

them, maintaining their young faces and bodies in a gentle, even wash of shadow. The drama and its beauty exist in the darkened hollow of each tentative action, in the longing for expression rather than in the inevitable response. In the quiet, even shade each action softens and blends with the next, forming the intricate succession of moods that will find their eventual meaning in Skymnos's ordained death in the bright surge of ocean waves.

So far we have seen this soft, pliable light at dusk and daybreak (*Hiroshima Mon Amour*), in locations casting long, open shadows (*Young Aphrodites*) or in those capable of filtering the direct rays of the sun (*Anderson Platoon*), and in carefully chosen camera angles that mask each subject from direct light (again *Young Aphrodites*). There is, in addition, one other major source of this light: those gray, overcast days that harbor high, evenly clouded skies. The particular effectiveness of this soft light, diffused by layers of clouds, lies in its tendency to separate evenly and clearly the varying shapes under its fall. The action can be set in bold relief against the backdrop formed by this sky, and each object can be etched upon the screen with sharpness and precision.

F. W. Murnau, in his silent horror classic *Nosferatu,* used the evenness and clarity of this light to help build and then sustain his compelling projection of evil. The film is a retelling of the Dracula story, only instead of the urbane, sensually

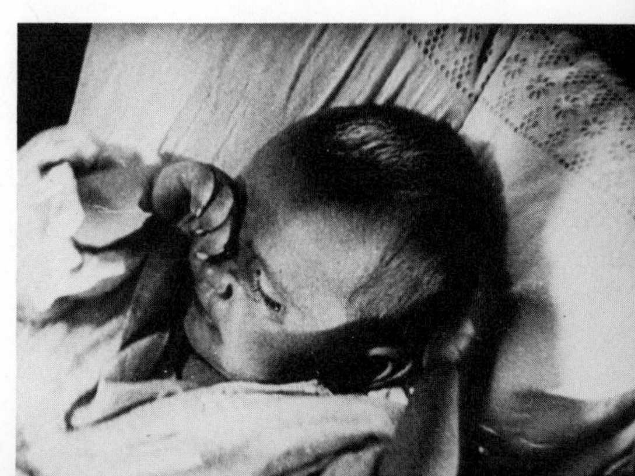

bloodsucking Count Dracula that we have come to associate with that most immortal of vampires, Bela Lugosi, the Nosferatu figure here is the raw incarnation of an evil so great that, when he enters the world of men, he brings pestilence wherever he walks.

In this shot we see Nosferatu at the height of his corrupt journey into that world, on board a ship to which he has brought death, and just seconds before he frees the ship of the rats that will bring the plague to the world. Up to this point Murnau has defined the extent of this creature's demonic powers by portraying the inside of his lair with shrill lighting effects that filled the screen with ghostly whites and ominous black shadows. But now that Nosferatu is loose upon the world, his evil has become so complete that overly dramatic lighting effects would be superfluous. In stalking the world he has become the perfection of horror. Daylight, the mythic limit of the vampire's domain, has been overcome; and the very plainness of the light he has conquered calls up a greater terror than the familiar pools and slashes of light and shadow that have defined his private kingdom. It is our world which he has entered, the calm of ordinary affairs which he will destroy with his evil, and it is this awesome fact that the soft, steady light helps bring home.

This light from a high overcast sky captures the familiar shapes of sail, rope, and wood and throws them into clear relief as a frame and a backdrop for the sinister glide of the monster across the deck that he has decimated. Against this sky Nosferatu stands out sharply. From the horrible, shadowy pockets of his face to his severe black dress, the light curls cleanly around each aspect of the demon, bringing him to us in the full range of his terrors. But the still, even light gives Murnau an additional opportunity. He builds an impression of a ghostly silhouette stalking the world by setting the dark form of Nosferatu against the high, gray sky so that the shot eventually echoes the monster's lethal prowlings in his own castle. Murnau has mastered and claimed for his creature the still, even light of the world, widening the boundaries of his power in order to intensify our sense of growing dread.

Interior Daylight

There is a limitless variety of subtle uses for soft, natural light, as many uses as there are imaginations that will develop them to illuminate a conception of the world. And the effectiveness and charm of this light are not limited just to outdoor filming. Diffused daylight, even trapped indoors, can provide a full range of evocative and beautiful lighting effects.

Soft, luminous, womanly beauty has rarely been captured in films more effectively than in this shot of Anna Karina in Jean-Luc Godard's *Alphaville.* Yet the only light that brings her to us is daylight coming through a window. She is standing opposite the window and the light from such a broad, frontal source tends to fill in the shadows cast by her features. This light gently rounds those features until they fit perfectly into the mask of desirability that we see. And since there are no shadows, the only contrast in the image is the natural blackness of the hair that frames her face and the eyes that have been given the mystery of darkness.

However, if the actress is turned slightly away from the source of light, shadows can be formed to mold the contours of her face to give it a stronger and

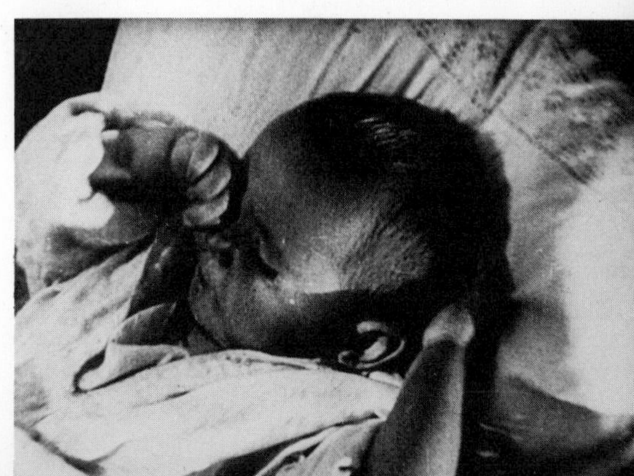

in this case, a more playful character. This is the winning, mercurial Jean Seberg in *Breathless*. The source of light, the window, is now at a steep angle to her head and so the light softly edges her face. Because of this angle the gamine hair, the pixie dimple, the cute, sharp nose are brought into relief. Yet the face is simultaneously washed in a gentle shadow that almost hides the puckish smile and makes it seem more fleeting and mysterious. Note also how, with just this elementary light source, Godard (with his cameraman Raoul Coutard) has also skillfully used the crosslight on her hand to catch the delight of each finger stolen from the shadows. Given just enough bright light entering the window, a range of lighting possibilities floods the room.

A dramatically different mood can also be evoked if the camera is simply turned around toward the source of the light. Then every object in the room becomes backlit, turning both actors and furnishings into graceful silhouettes. Victor Nunez, in *Fairground,* used this back lighting to capture effectively the poignance of a young woman's isolation. The film is a compassionate study of an attractive young couple trapped on a farm away from friends and comforts and slowly sinking toward age and death. This is the empty attic floor of their large, austere farm-

house. During the stillness of the day, while her husband is at work in the fields and her child is asleep, the wife slips up here to escape the cramped sameness of her existence and let her mind wander across those bright but unfulfilled hopes for her life that she once treasured.

Where the lighting downstairs was even and flat, here everything is in languorous contrast. The house has been transformed by the graceful urgency of her formless expectations. But Nunez has also placed his camera just far enough back to include the stairwell and a large expanse of walls; and the light, slicing across those bare walls at a sharp angle, raises the texture of the wood, brings it into relief, and dramatizes its roughhewn sameness. While we feel the rush of her dreams evoked by the almost ethereal light entering the window and her lovely silhouette rising up the stairway and into the room, there is still enough of the bare, confining hallway clearly visible to remind us of the world she has been driven to flee. With nothing more than daylight, Nunez has worked the light into a complex rendering of the fragility of a woman's dreams that also embodies the quality of life that forced her to those dreams.

Naturally Occurring Artificial Light

There is one further and complete world of lighting that the film-maker can exploit without going to the expense and elaborate construction of studio lighting effects. At night the world is filled with expressive hard lights that fall in a score of different ways, altering textures and shapes and creating a unique atmosphere for each location. And even during the day there are windowless corridors and rooms that are expressively defined by the quality of the light that fills them. In addition, it is not only the fall of this artificial light, but often the very source of illumination itself, from the tangle of neon to the poignance of a bare bulb, that contributes to the feeling of a scene. As with sunlight, the quality of artificial light in each location determines to a large extent the effectiveness with which that location will draw out the insights devised by the film-maker's script.

Godard and Coutard, who in *Breathless* had been so good at exploiting the lyrical possibilities of a city romance in daylight, prowled the sunless world of artificial light in *Alphaville* to create their brutal, antiseptic city of the future. The film

is almost a textbook for these locations. This is another close look at the beautiful Anna Karina, but how different she appears when taken out of soft daylight. Here she is sitting in a car with the hard glare of a streetlight defining her face. The flesh that had been translucent earlier is now bruised by the harsh light. Where she was contained and mysterious, now she is vulnerable. Our entire impression of her and the world she brings with her has been altered by the light that falls upon her. And as if this wasn't enough, Godard hammered at her face with the very source that altered it. The bright ball striking her face is the reflection of a passing streetlight. Throughout the scene these reflections sweep across the windshield in a pounding

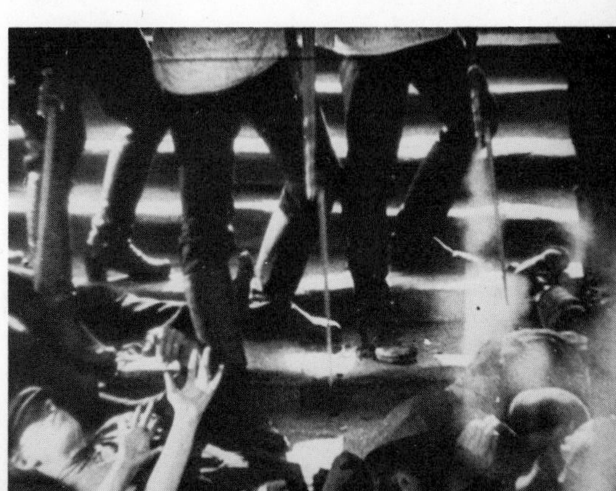

procession that continually draws her from the merciful shadows into the brutal glare of the watchful Alphaville world.

In another shot from *Alphaville,* the film's hero, Eddie Constantine, is framed in the hard light of a telephone booth. Under the single overhead bulb his skin looks unusually coarse as its pitted surface is thrown into relief. Unlike the effects of daylight, the illumination comes more nearly from a small, single point and, as it cuts across his face, there is no scattering of light that can fill in the shadows. The result is a sharp, harsh black shadow beneath every craggy mark and line on his face. Under this light he has been given the worldly, worn, beat-up exterior that forces home his role as the tired, tough private detective at cynical and losing odds with his world.

Later in the film, Constantine ascends one of the innumerable stairwells that lead to one of the seemingly endless number of windowless corridors that form the geography of Alphaville. Again the artificial light captures the shadowy, worn quality that marks his passage through the film, while picking up and emphasizing the empty, soiled walls that project the shabby, inhospitable world the hero has been forced to inhabit.

At the top of those stairs Godard created this striking portrait of an outcast, Akim Tamiroff, a seedy humanist who has no place in the sterile Alphaville structure and who has become Constantine's first contact with its underworld. He is

lit by just a single light bulb hanging from the ceiling. Robin Wood, in his essay on *Alphaville,* describes the importance and the effect of the light cast by the bulb to the meaning of the film.

> As Lemmy (Constantine) and Henri Dickson (Tamiroff) talk on the stairs of Dickson's shabby hotel, a single naked light bulb swings between them. The emotional effect of the scene derives primarily from our sense of a small circle of light—the unguarded bulb seeming very precarious and vulnerable—surrounded by an enclosing, menacing blackness. At the same time the light shining into Dickson's face has a merciless quality, as if it were cruelly exposing his weaknesses

> and decay. The scene movingly epitomizes a mood basic to the whole film: the sense of Lemmy and Dickson representing a last, and perhaps inadequate and crumbling survival of humanity in a civilization becoming increasingly dehumanized. Dickson talks of the inability of some people to adjust, and Godard cuts in suddenly a shot of the illuminated exterior of a vast office building with

> thousands of identical anonymous windows. Light, like everything else, is equivocal in Alphaville: there is the naked light bulb, there is also the glare of Alpha 60 during the interrogations, light that helps you see and light that blinds.

In this same sequence, Godard not only cuts to the façade of the office building, where the light from each window speaks to the darkness of the lives within, but he also inserts, during the conversation, shots of neon tubing curled around an

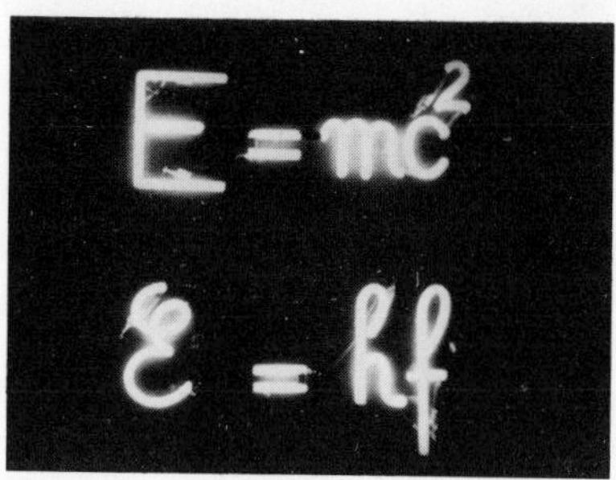

essential truth, and so reduces the truth to neon tubing. The light source itself tells us we are in a world where the speed of light is man's final constant—a proto-medieval assurance of order and certainty. This is a truth not sufficiently powerful to build a cathedral, but more than adequate for an office building.

With both the building and the equations, it is the source of light that fills the screen and carries the thrust of Godard's message. He has even turned the bare bulb, which so evocatively lit the conversation, into an expressive object in its own right. When the men finish talking, Dickson strikes at that insufficient bulb and, as

it arcs across the hallway dancing their shadows against the squalid hotel walls, we are left with the bulb orbiting the screen, a final glimmer of light as the men disappear into the blackness.

The energies of the modern world have been so fully employed in bringing all kinds of light to soothe or amuse our night world that locations of varying expressive density form with every city block we walk after dark. In *Hiroshima Mon Amour,* Resnais fastened onto the neon excess of a modern city and used it to describe his heroine's aversion to the present. In shot after shot he flooded the screen with these deformed lights, and with them he caught the elusive impulse of

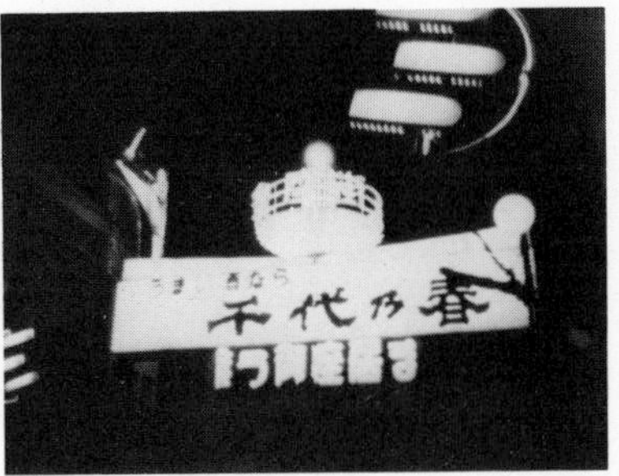

his heroine to flee the city, and her love—a present which had become no more to her than the irrelevant and convoluted cry for gaiety of these sadly twisted lights.

François Truffaut, in *Shoot the Piano Player,* saw the city quite differently.

Courtesy: JANUS FILMS, INC.

He found, in the streetlights of Paris sweeping past the thrust of a moving car, an invigorating source of energy to sustain his characters in their mock-heroic exploits. The lights, given movement by the car, dazzle and pound at us and provide that sense of urgency and abandon, that feeling of drugged unreality that is relentlessly impelling his hero to the tragically violent conclusion of the film.

The source of these expressively bare lights is not, of course, limited to the city. They are just more abundant there. Wherever it is found, a light orders and defines the darkness it penetrates, and with care it can come to reflect some quality

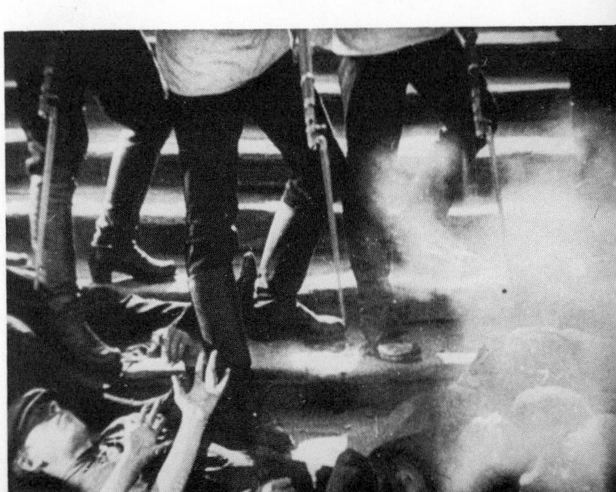

of the lives it serves. Victor Nunez, in the concluding shot of *Fairground,* found in a single light straining through the heavy darkness around the isolated farm a way of indicating the fragile but determined hope of his young couple to make the best of their future. The light shines in the distance from a barn where the couple

is helping in the birthing of a calf. This light cuts through the darkness, becoming a sign for the renewal of life that it illuminates. The light is a signal that there is hope, that the darkness can be pierced.

Studio Lighting

All the various kinds of light we have discussed so far exist ready-made, there to be seized from the real world by a film-maker with the imagination to use them. But to a large extent these kinds of light can also be created in the studio. In some cases studio lighting is used as a matter of convenience: there are too few shots in a particular setting to justify the expense of taking a crew, equipment, and actors on location, or there might be lip-synchronous dialogue in the scene that is much easier to record in a studio (the reasons for this are discussed in Section 2, Chapter Six). In addition, studio lighting effects are often easier to create and control than their naturally occurring counterparts. Especially in feature films, this flexibility permits scenes requiring a specific quality of light to be neatly fitted into a complicated production schedule.

However, when shooting in a studio, the film-maker is not restricted to simulating various kinds of naturally occurring light. There are also types of light peculiar to the studio that are without direct counterpart in our everyday surround-

ings. The best illustration is an example that goes back to the very beginnings of studio lighting, an interior setting used in D. W. Griffith's silent feature *The Birth of a Nation* (1915). Because the early film stocks were relatively insensitive to light, a great deal of light was required to produce an adequate exposure. So, while electric lighting was available, it was extremely expensive to use compared to the ever-present California sun. As a result, the film studios of that period were constructed like huge greenhouses. They had roofs and walls of glass through which daylight could enter and adjustable opaque and translucent shades that could be used to control the quantity and quality of light hitting the various parts of the set.

As this example demonstrates, the result was a very flat style of light, because the light entering the studio was not mainly direct sunlight but the indirect light reflected from the sky. It was impossible to use direct sunlight because the angle of the sun, and therefore the length and direction of the shadows, would change from moment to moment throughout the day. That is why some of the early, small studios had been built on turntables and rotated to follow the sun. But larger studios had to be fixed in place, so they faced away from the sun. Then only the relatively constant *skylight* would illuminate the action.

Skylight, however, is rather scattered and diffuse, and when it enters through large banks of windows, it strikes objects from several directions simultaneously, filling in any shadows. As a result, relatively smooth objects, especially faces, had little gradation from dark to light across their surface. Without such shading figures and faces lose their sense of texture and volume, because in a two-dimensional medium like photography, it is this gradation that gives us a feeling for an object's three-dimensional shape. This type of lighting also did little to distinguish the faces when they were shown in close-up and added almost no sense of depth to the sets. Some separation between the figures and the background was achieved, however, because a certain amount of direct sunlight was allowed to strike the characters from above and behind, creating a bright rim of light that outlined their heads and shoulders, particularly when they stood before a dark backdrop.

This light is thus peculiar to the studio because it is only rarely found in ordinary homes or other buildings. But it is a style of light with a long tradition. It was used to make photographic portraits for over half a century, and before that to illuminate the studios of painters and other graphic artists. This light, then, was not just a necessity but an artistic convention, one that a film-maker like René Clair could later exploit for the memories it evoked. In *The Italian Straw Hat* Clair graced his comedy with a gentle aura of the *fin de siècle* by using his lights to call

forth the photography of that period: an even, almost shadowless lighting from the front to the back of the set, and a bright rim of light around the figures.

Electric Lighting

At the time *The Birth of a Nation* was released, other directors were already exploring the use of carbon-arc and mercury-vapor lamps to light their sets. These alone gave off the tremendous amounts of light needed to expose the film of the period. But later, when film became more sensitive, these lights were supplemented by a wide variety of smaller, lighter, less expensive units using "mazda" or tungsten filament lamps. And as the technology developed, so did the expressive possibilities of studio light. As a result, the early, daylight style of studio lighting became just another, less and less used convention in an expanding repertoire of studio lighting techniques.

By now there are over a hundred different kinds of studio lights, called *luminaires,* each providing a somewhat different quality or intensity of light. They permit the film-maker to use lights in combinations that create an almost infinite variety of lighting effects. But no matter how these lights are used, the quality of light they produce is governed by three basic factors: the amount of diffusion in the light source (how focused or scattered the light is), the direction from which the light hits the subject, and the intensity (brightness) of the light from each of the various lighting units. Of course, all three factors operate simultaneously to create the final effect of the light, but each must be considered separately, and in this order, when the lighting is designed.

Types of Lights

In the argot of the Hollywood film studios every luminaire has a nickname. For instance, in the Mole-Richardson line, one of the oldest and biggest suppliers of studio lighting units, there are such interesting items as the *mini-mole, broads, deuces, "big eye" tener, super softlite, brutes, titans,* etc. These names are more than just colorful additions to the language—they are also ways of identifying some of the unique qualities of each lighting unit according to the light it produces.

First of all, luminaires are divided into two broad categories according to whether or not they diffuse the light. If the light produced is hard, the unit is called a *spot,* and if the light is soft, it is called a *flood.* The difference is determined by the construction of the luminaire. A spotlight has a single lamp, a small reflector that gathers the light, and a front condensing lens that focuses the light into a beam.

This arrangement concentrates the light into a small area (a spot); on most of the small and medium-sized units the diameter of this spot can be changed by moving the lamp and the reflector toward or away from the lens. The result is light which is much like direct sunlight—it has little tendency to scatter so it creates dense, hard-edged shadows.

A floodlight, on the other hand, has a large reflector and one or more lamps that are either clear or frosted. These lamps may also be positioned behind a small metal shield. Therefore, floodlights have varying degrees of softness since different amounts of direct light are mixed in with the reflected light. But it is the large reflector, rather than the lamp itself, that becomes the principal source of light; and, because the light originates from across a broader area than in a spotlight, it acts more like skylight—it scatters into darker areas and creates a soft gradation between the highlights and the shadows. Also, because the reflector tends to spread rather than concentrate the light, it covers (floods) a wider area.

Within these two broad classifications of spot and flood, luminaires are then rated according to the amount of light produced by the lamp, measured, as with household light bulbs, in watts—the more watts, the brighter the lamp. In studio lighting, however, the smallest lamps start at about the level of the brightest household bulbs, 100 watts, and then continue up to as many as 10,000 watts in the largest units. The names of the units then tend to reflect the increasing wattage of the lamps—a *baby* (spot or flood) is from 500 to 1,000 watts, a *junior* is from 1,000 to 2,000 watts, and a *senior* is 5,000 watts. Smaller or larger units have more specialized uses and are given their own separate names, such as *mini* (50 to 250 watts), *"big eye" tener* (10,000 watts), or *super softlite* (up to 16,000 watts).

Some of these individualized names also derive from the special uses to which the lights are put. *Nooklites* are small units that can be fit into tight corners, *cyc strips* are long bands of lights that are used to illuminate the background (called the *cyclorama*), and *single* or *double broads* are lights that create a rectangular rather than a circular pattern of light. Arc lights are also named according to the power they use; however, their power consumption is so large that the bigger arcs are called *brutes* and *titans*.

Building the Lighting

There is thus a wide variety of luminaires to choose from when lighting a set, but this choice quickly narrows once the quality, the direction, and the intensity of the light for a particular scene is decided upon. This decision is made systematically,

one step at a time. First, an overall layer of *base* illumination is put down so that there will be a certain amount of detail in even the darkest areas of the set. Then a second layer of *key* lighting is added to indicate the dominant light source. If the scene must simulate some type of natural lighting, it must be decided how diffuse the key light must be, and from what direction it should come, to imitate this light. Or, if there is no apparent source of light in the scene, some arbitrary point is chosen as the principal direction from which a particular quality of key lighting will originate.

This second layer is important because it begins to get at the film-maker's concerns. It adds those highlights and shadows that call attention to certain objects, or parts of objects, while at the same time subordinating everything else. It also describes the objects on the set, giving them varying degrees of shape and texture, depending upon the diffuseness of the light and the steepness of the angle from which it hits an object. In addition, it is the relative brightness of this light compared to the level of base lighting that makes the overall lighting seem contrasty or flat. And finally, this dominant light source also governs the lighting of all the shots in a scene. As long as they have a similar key, they will have a common appearance, creating a continuity of time and place from shot to shot.

Once the key lighting is in place, a third, cosmetic layer of light is applied. This consists of *fill* light, used to lighten the shadows, and *back* light, used to rim the figures. The effect of these lights is either to suppress or to amplify the key lighting. A soft, bright fill, for instance, can open up the shadows and smooth out the highlights, while a dim, hard fill can add minor highlights that make the key seem harsher. Or no fill at all, just a back light, will leave the key the same but separate objects from their surroundings. These small alterations are important because they can significantly shift the mood of a shot without greatly changing its general appearance, thus helping to maintain the continuity of the lighting from shot to shot.

Last of all, there is a fourth layer of *background* lighting. As the name implies, this is added to the background to create a stronger sense of the setting. It is used both to highlight certain areas and to form patterns of light that reinforce a feeling for the time at which the action occurs.

To understand the lighting process clearly, it is first necessary to see how each of these layers of light works. It is possible to do this, even though we rely upon frames from actual films, because, while base, key, fill and back, and background lighting are usually all used in every scene, they are not necessarily used in every shot. So, by looking at shots in which only a limited combination of lights was used, we can see the effect of just one or a couple of these types of light.

It must be recognized, however, that these descriptive terms are rather slippery when applied in practice. The principal light source in a shot is always referred to as the key, even if in another shot, or another part of the same shot, it is used as base, fill, or back light. For instance, when the heroine turns off the light to go to bed, the moonlight streaming through her window suddenly becomes the key light for the rest of the shot. Similarly, the spill from the key lighting can simultaneously serve both to backlight one of the characters and to illuminate the background.

Base Lighting

Base lighting is usually created by a number of large, diffuse floodlights that throw a soft, flat light throughout the set. These lights are normally placed overhead and toward the front of the set so that any shadows they might cast fall behind objects and onto the floor. This placement of the base lights keeps these unwanted shadows out of camera range so that the important shadows will be created by the next layer of light. The effect of base lighting can be seen in this example from Fritz Lang's *Spies*. It is a shot of the master spy's headquarters. While the light

Courtesy: JANUS FILMS, INC.

here is quite diffuse and generalized, it has been restricted to a wash of light across just the background, making the base lighting a key light that effectively simulates daylight entering through an overhead skylight.

In this shot Lang has used a flat-on view of the staircase to create a strong geometric pattern that emphasizes the rigid efficiency of the place. But it is the light which creates a sense of spaciousness. Because the light is limited to the background, the stairway becomes a silhouette. The image then progressively grays out as it recedes in space because the diffuse light increasingly scatters into the shadows. This same effect can be seen in a hazy landscape, where the increasing density of the haze makes objects appear lighter as they get further away. Here, the effect of the lighting is more complicated than that of most base lighting, but it is still base light because it is a soft, even light that fills the set.

Key Lighting

Because key lighting creates the dominant play of light and dark on the set, it is the angle from which this light originates that controls whether highlights or

shadows will be most prominent. This angle, in turn, also affects the *modeling* of objects, that is, our sense of their dimensionality, and the apparent texture of their surfaces. The first step, then, in establishing the quality of the key lighting, is to determine where the highlights and the shadows should fall. This is usually done by taking a single luminaire and placing it at an angle to the camera. When it is near the camera the shadows will be small, and as it gets further to either side the shadows will lengthen. However, when the light is from 60 to 90 degrees to either side, the amount of light and shadow is about equal, so there is maximum contrast between them, thus giving objects their greatest modeling and making their texture most pronounced. Moving the light up and down also has a similar effect. But the key light is rarely placed below camera level. Because everyday light normally strikes objects from above, low-angle light gives objects an unnatural appearance.

Of course, the effect of the key lighting is also controlled by the diffuseness of the luminaire. When the key light is hard, the shadows are sharp and dense, and this minimizes the dimensionality of objects by reducing the highlights and the shadows to hard-edged planes of light and dark. However, a hard key light also creates maximum contrast between the highlights and the shadows and that emphasizes textures. Soft light, on the other hand, strongly shapes objects by gently molding the shadows into the highlights, but it smooths over textures by filling in the shadows.

The effect of a single, soft, carefully placed key light can be seen in this shot from John Ford's *The Grapes of Wrath*. The shot is of an Okie farmer. In this scene the hero of the film has returned home, only to find many neighboring farms deserted. When he goes to one to see what has happened, he finds this man huddled in a dark corner, fearfully hiding from the sheriff and foreclosure. Here the key

lighting seems just to imitate the candlelight. But by softly hitting the face from slightly below and to the far side, it helps capture the man's feeling of fear and desperation. Because of its low angle it fills in his eye sockets and gives an eerie glow to his eyes. And by cutting across his face, it picks out the rough texture of his overgrown beard and rumpled clothes while throwing large shadows on and around his face. The softness of the light then molds these shadows so that the contours of his face gently blend into that surrounding darkness from which he seems to have only reluctantly emerged.

A quite different effect is produced by a hard key light, even when used from a similar angle, as can be seen in an example from Ingmar Bergman's *Wild Straw-*

berries. The shot is in an early part of the film, a dream sequence in which Dr. Borg sees himself in a coffin. Bergman has flooded the coffin with bright sunlight to

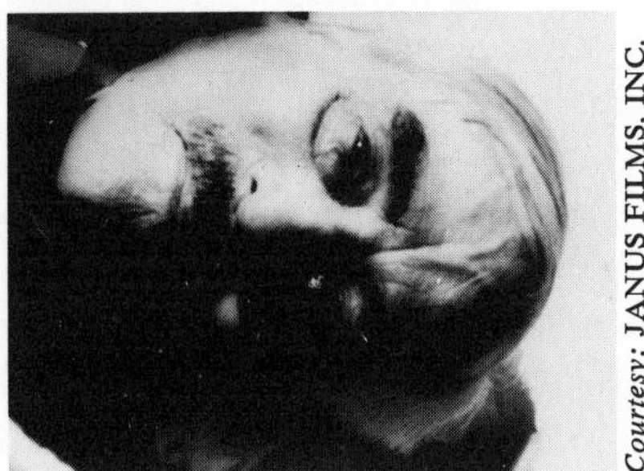
Courtesy: JANUS FILMS, INC.

emphasize the clarity with which Dr. Borg confronts his own death. But at the same time he also uses the stark quality of the light to turn Borg's face into that of a corpse. Bergman got this effect by simulating direct sunlight with a single spotlight placed level with Borg's head and at a right angle to it. The result is the reduction of his face to two strongly contrasting planes. On the shadow side there is almost nothing, while on the other side, the light, penetrating beneath the brow, gives his eye a malignant stare and makes a sharp black welt of every bump and wrinkle. His face has become a death mask chiseled in stone, and we instantly recognize the horror he must feel when he sees himself in this light.

Fill and Back Lighting

Once the key lighting is set, fill and back light can be added. These lights are used to emphasize or subdue the effect of the key lighting without changing the basic pattern of light and shadow created by it. There are two ways to do this. One is to position a luminaire so that it throws light into the shadows without casting any noticeable shadows of its own. This type of lighting, known as fill light, is usually created by placing a light very near the camera so that the shadows it casts fall straight back behind the subject. The other way to alter the key lighting subtly is to throw the subject into silhouette by pointing a light toward the camera from behind the subject. Then the subject becomes one big shadow upon which the key lighting is imposed. This is known as back light.

Because fill and back lighting so expand the variety of effects that can be

created in the studio, this stage of the lighting process can become quite complex. For instance, while fill lights are ordinarily placed near the camera and back lights directly opposite it, these points are really the extremes on a continuum. With a little care it is also possible to place these lights in various other positions around the subject to produce any number of fill and back lighting effects. These effects can then be expanded still further by moving the lights up or down, using harder or softer lights, and varying the relative intensity of each light. Finally, all these fill and back light combinations interact with an equal diversity of key lighting. The result is an almost infinite variety of possible studio lighting effects.

Obviously, this is a greater range of lighting effects than it is possible to discuss in one book, so we will look at only those basic combinations that characterize most studio lighting. Here, for example, is a typical combination of a hard key and a soft fill. It is used to light the face of Dr. Borg in another shot from *Wild*

Courtesy: JANUS FILMS, INC.

Strawberries. Now, however, instead of seeing him at the nadir of his life, as he was in the previous example, we see him at the peak of his career, as he is awarded a prize and a medal for distinguished service to his profession.

Again, a hard key cuts across his face, only now from an even steeper angle than before to simulate the direct sunlight streaming through the window behind him. This light has pursued him throughout the film. In the beginning it turned him into a corpse, and then, as we saw in the example used earlier in this chapter, became an assertion of the death that haunted not only him, but his son as well. However, at this point in the film he has completed both his physical and metaphoric journey and has reached a reconciliation with his past that gives him a degree of peace and inner freedom. It is this renewed sense of himself that is reflected in the very pronounced change in the lighting.

The normally harsh effects of the strong key are here greatly mitigated by a diffuse fill light which, placed near the camera, unobtrusively penetrates all the shadows. As a result, instead of deadening his features, the key lighting picks out his profile and makes him look almost heroic. And even though the key still reaches under his brow to light his eye and casts massive shadows that catch the weathered texture of his skin, the fill light, by softening and molding these salient features, gives his face a warmer, more sensual roundness. The effect of this lighting is to make the shot faintly ironic because the hardness of the key still calls up all we know about his past. But it is a hardness tempered with a new humanity that asserts itself in the quality of the shadows.

In this case the soft fill light subdues the otherwise sharp-edged shadows and harsh textures of a hard key. But the same fill, when used with a soft key, builds up the shape and texture of the shadows. This effect can be seen in an example from Murnau's *Nosferatu.* It is a shot of a hunchbacked bookkeeper, one of

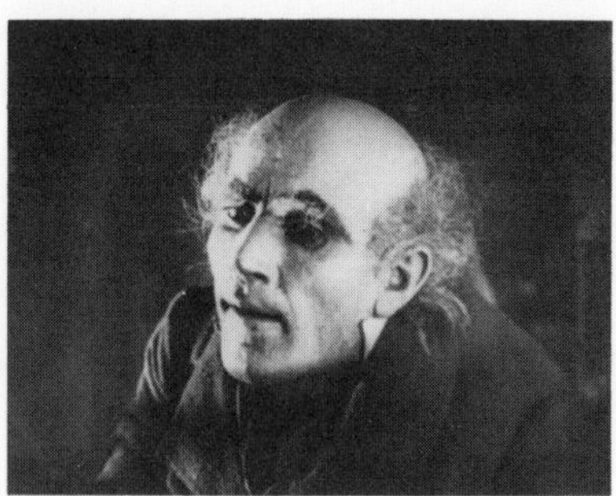

the vampire's disciples, who goes berserk as soon as he senses the evil count's impending arrival.

While we don't yet know that he is falling under his master's spell, the light helps us sense that something is wrong with him by giving his head and face a slightly misshapen appearance. He is lit by a soft key that simulates the diffuse light entering a window to our left. Like the key in the previous example, this light cuts across his face from a steep angle, but because it is a soft light it rounds his features and gives a bulbous fullness to his bald head. It also penetrates beneath his deep brow, but doesn't sharply catch his eye. Because it is such a diffuse source, it is reflected off the corner of the pupil as a broad, dull glare that makes his eye look glazed and slightly askew.

His odd appearance is then further accentuated by the bright, soft fill light. This light originates from slightly to the right of and well above the camera. Because of its intensity, and the sharp downward angle, it bounces gentle highlights off his head, cheekbone, and nose that add to the roundness of these features. But the steep tilt of the fill also keeps it out from under his brow so that his left eye is almost obscured by darkness. This shadow is then emphasized by its contrast with the highlights on the nose and cheek, making his eye seem clouded over. In addition, these highlights, by nearly eliminating the shadows thrown by the key, give his face a faint, unnatural glow. It is thus the interaction of these two steeply angled lights that vaguely twists his features and gives his eyes an unfocused, distracted

look—our first warning of his incipient madness and the powerful imminence of the count.

Back Lighting

While fill lighting is usually done with soft light, because it casts weak, diffuse shadows, back lighting is done with hard light in order to create a bright rim of light that strongly contrasts with a sharp, definite shadow. However, there are also technical reasons for using hard light. Because a back light faces toward the camera there is always the possibility of light's hitting the lens and causing flare. This appears either as a milky haze over the whole image or, in extreme cases, as bright spots that are actually an out-of-focus image of the light source itself. But flare is minimized with hard spotlighting, both because the focusing mechanism on a spotlight permits the light to be restricted to just the area to be backlit and because the light has little tendency to stray beyond the area toward which it is aimed. The possibility of flare is then further reduced if the luminaire is placed either well above or directly behind the subject so that the light is either angled away from the lens or blocked by the subject. Flare is also controlled by the use of a sunshade to shield the lens from stray light. All these elaborate precautions are necessary because only extreme flare can be detected before the film is processed.

Here is an example of back light alone. It is a shot from Jean Cocteau's

Courtesy: JANUS FILMS, INC.

Beauty and the Beast. The only illumination is provided by a light directly above and behind the Beast and another coming through the doorway to his right. In this scene Beauty faints with fright when she first encounters the Beast, a man with the fierce head of a lion. He then picks up her limp figure and, in this shot, carries her into the bowels of his castle. At this point in the film we know very little about the Beast except that he has awesome magical powers. Since we can't be sure how he intends to use these powers, the darkness heightens the aura of evil and mystery that surrounds his magic.

This quality of darkness is created by the nature of the light. The back light, by just barely picking out his figure, leaves an enveloping blackness that makes him a shadowy presence in even more obscure surroundings. These surroundings are then made to seem still more threatening by the light streaming through the doorway, which casts the shadow of a prisonlike iron grille across the foreground. Finally, the light itself is weakened and diffused by a small amount of smoke that fills the air. This smoke gives a veiled substance to the shafts of back light that emphasizes their inability to dispel the darkness. It is as if the Beast is taking Beauty from the last vestiges of beneficent sunlight that enter the castle and carrying her into an unknown and impenetrable darkness—an ominous portent of his intentions for his now helpless victim.

Back lighting can also be added, in varying degrees, to key and fill light. When it is kept at a relatively low level, the back light simply produces a slight highlighting around the rim of an object that helps to separate it from the background. This is a standard lighting technique that is, as we saw in the example from *The Birth of a Nation,* almost as old as motion pictures. However, as the back lighting becomes more intense, it begins to add highlights that are as important as those created by the key light. This effect can be seen, most typically, in the back lighting that is used to glamorize Hollywood's female stars. Particularly when the back light passes through a diffusion lens, it creates highlights in a woman's hair that give it a rich sheen and make it look thick and soft.

However, in the hands of Josef von Sternberg, this conventional style of light became a lighting signature. He used it on Marlene Dietrich to create an air of svelte sophistication that marked her appearance in all the films they made together. Here, for instance, is the shot from *The Blue Angel* in which he first lit her in this

way. She has just defied her shambles of a husband, the once proud Professor Rath, by bringing another man into her dressing room. When Rath reacts with little more than a drunken stare, she returns his gaze with this distant look of scornful disdain.

Her appearance in this shot is different from that in any previous shot in the film. Instead of the soft pudginess that had been created by the use of very diffuse

light, she is suddenly made quite strong and determined looking. This new look is accomplished by the use of a hard key that cuts across her face, and a low level of fill so that the shadow remains half dark. But Sternberg also sets off her head and shoulders with two back lights, above and to either side of her. These lights give an iridescence to her hair and draw bright lines along her face and neck that detail the slender structure of her fine-boned face, adding a refined beauty to her anger which makes her seem more desirable than ever just as she is openly rejecting her husband. She is still young and full of life, while he is sunk in age and dissolution, and this disparity so enrages him that he first attempts to murder her and then goes off alone to die.

Because back light is such a standard part of studio lighting, there is a shortcut for creating the back lighting used in that most common piece of studio business —a conversation between two people. Called *double key* or *X* lighting, it is created by placing the lights as shown in the following diagram.

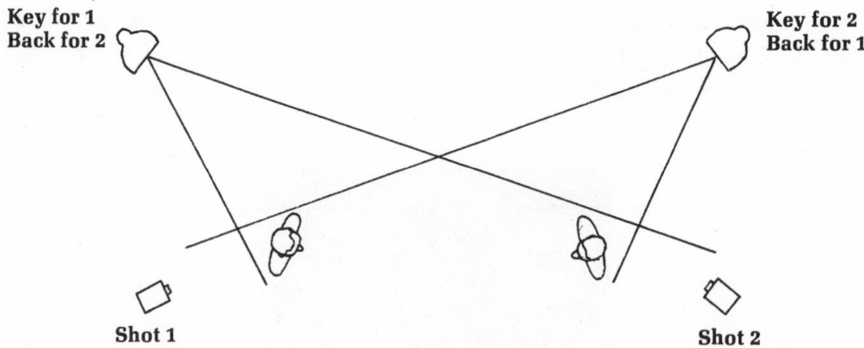

The effect of this ingenious lighting arrangement can be seen in two shots of a conversation between the knight and his wife in Bergman's *The Seventh Seal.* When the camera looks over her shoulder at him (shot 1), the key for shot 2 becomes his

Courtesy: JANUS FILMS, INC.

back light, and both lights backlight her. And when we see the reverse angle over his shoulder (shot 2), the role of each light is automatically reversed. This technique not only reduces the number of lights needed for the sequence, it also simplifies the shooting since just the camera, and not the lights, has to be moved.

In most cases the stark quality of basic X lighting is greatly softened by the addition of a fill at or near the camera. But here Bergman wanted just the bare key and back lights to simulate the illumination of a torch hanging from the wall behind the two characters, a light that hardly penetrates the shadows of their huge castle. This is their first meeting upon his return home, and the intense darkness and hard light are used to point up the reserve with which they confront each other. They know that they are doomed by the plague which is stalking the countryside; this knowledge tempers the warmth of their greeting and prevents them from feeling much comfort from being together once again.

Background Lighting

The final layer of light is the background lighting. This kind of lighting includes all those seldom-noticed highlights and shadows that, by giving a stronger sense of time and place, help elicit the meaning of the setting. This can be seen in another example from *The Seventh Seal,* a shot of a corridor in the knight's castle. The knight has just left the frame, after pausing before the statue of Christ,

Courtesy: JANUS FILMS, INC.

and the camera holds for a moment on the seemingly empty setting.

Here, only two sharply focused spotlights illuminate the background, just enough light to pick out its two salient features, the statue and the immobile figure of Death. Our sudden awareness of Death's presence immediately changes the castle from a sanctuary to a place of surrender. But it is the shadowy simulation of torchlight, its brightness barely touching the intense darkness of the castle wall, that

conveys the inevitability of this surrender. By isolating Death in a niche of light similar to that holding the statue, Bergman turns Death into a companion piece to the Christ figure. This makes Death as necessary a part of the setting for the knight's life as any of the frescoes, tapestries, and statues that decorate the knight's quest for salvation throughout the film.

Jean Renoir also used background lighting to create a sense of the setting in the following example from *Grand Illusion*. The shot is part of a scene showing Jean Gabin's deterioration while in solitary confinement. At first Gabin tries to escape; but when he fails he abandons hope, lapsing into a staring, insolent, but passive kind of madness. Gabin's state moves one of his guards to pity, and he tries to cheer Gabin with a few kind words and some small gifts.

We see Gabin here, sitting despondently on his narrow bed as the guard leaves the cell. When the door bangs shut the background suddenly goes dark, except for a slit of light admitted by the viewing port. Renoir created this lighting

Courtesy: JANUS FILMS, INC.

effect by covering one of the background lights with a card that had a small rectangle cut out of it; later, this effect was synchronized with the sound of a door closing. But the lighting effect does more than just reinforce the sense of confinement contained in the sound of the closing door; it also captures the feeling of suffocating control exercised over even Gabin's light and air. What little contact is left him with the outside world, and therefore with his sanity, can easily be cut off by the simple shutting of that tiny port.

Background lighting can also create a sense of time that adds to the meaning of a setting. Early in the film *Beauty and the Beast,* Jean Cocteau uses a pattern of light on the background that not only conveys the fact that it is daytime, but that his heroine lives in virtual servitude. In this scene a young suitor, a friend of her brother's, interrupts Beauty while she is polishing the floor. He offers to take her away from this drudgery if she will marry him. But she refuses because she feels it her duty to remain with her father until he has fulfilled his obligation to the Beast.

In the background of the scene is a crosshatched pattern of daylight entering through a small, paned window. This effect is created by placing a wood or metal

Courtesy: JANUS FILMS, INC.

cutout of this pattern, called a *cookie,* in front of a spotlight. In this case, the pattern of sunlight, by starkly contrasting with her dim surroundings, emphasizes the dreariness of the life that is forced upon her by her evil sisters. She is kept enslaved in darkness, while they enjoy the lazy, bright sunlight, because they know that in the light of day her simple beauty would easily overwhelm their gaudy pretense of wealth and fashion.

In *Suspicion,* Hitchcock too uses the patterned play of light on the background to convey the mood of a particular time, only here the light is used to evoke a feeling of evil. The film is about a woman who suspects that her husband intends to murder her for her money. At this point in the film she is convinced that he is going to poison a glass of warm milk he is about to bring her to calm her frayed nerves. After her husband leaves to prepare the milk, we linger with her for a moment of tense anticipation. Then Hitchcock cuts to the following long, panning shot.

First we see a darkened vestibule, the dim light of a full moon marking the pattern of an overhead skylight across its floor. Suddenly a door swings open and a slash of light crosses the vestibule. This light is quickly filled by the shadow of the

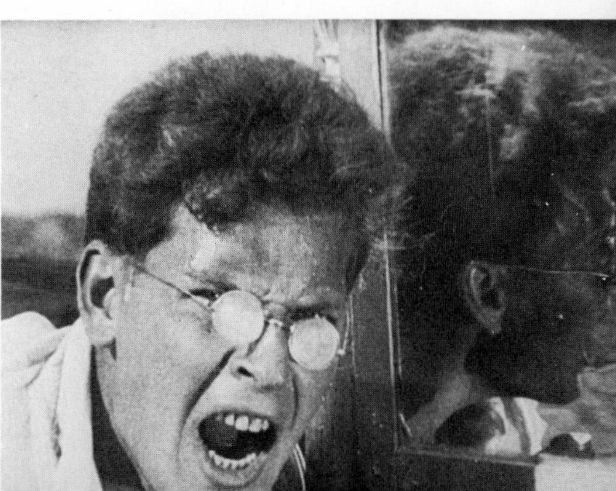

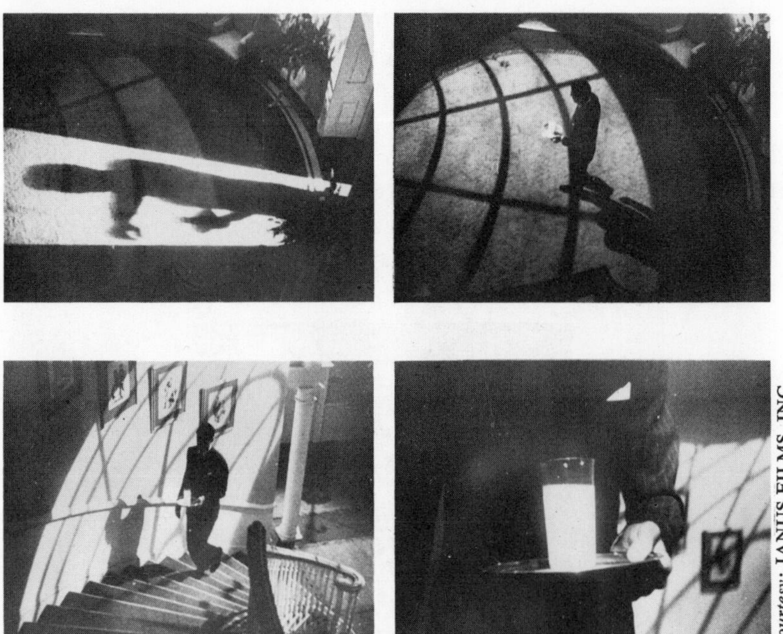
Courtesy: JANUS FILMS, INC.

husband carrying a tray holding the glass of milk. He stops, turns off the light, and proceeds toward the stairway. As he carries the innocently plain glass up the stairs, the camera follows him. Then it holds as he brings the glass directly toward the lens.

The shot would seem to leave little doubt about her husband's intentions. Hitchcock has used every nuance of the light to convince us of the threat inherent in his actions. He has invoked all the ominous feelings we associate with the dark loneliness of a moonlit night, and then intensified these feelings by first showing the husband as a hovering shadow and then as a silently ascending presence. And to make the darkness seem even more threatening, he has illuminated the glass by putting a light inside it. This gives it a dim, malevolent glow that rivets our attention to it as the husband slowly, deliberately carries it toward us. However, as unmistakably evil as all this is made to seem, in the end it remains ambiguous. His wife will not, of course, drink the milk, so the film must proceed to the next stage of her homicidal imaginings. Yet, with little more than light, Hitchcock has made her fears seem plausible by forcing us to share them with her.

Lighting Intensity

The last factor to be considered when building the lighting is the relative brightness of the various lights. As we have already seen in many of the previous examples, it is this *lighting balance* that determines the intensity of the highlights and shadows. In other words, when there is a large difference in the brightness of the various lighting units, the scene appears contrasty; and when the difference is small, the lighting appears flat. This difference, in turn, affects not only the appearance, but the meaning of a scene.

The effect lighting intensity has on both appearance and meaning can be seen in two shots in which the only major difference is in the balance of the lights. One is

Courtesy: JANUS FILMS, INC.

from Jean Cocteau's *Beauty and the Beast;* it is another part of the same shot just discussed in background lighting. The other is from Fritz Lang's *Spies.* It is a shot of the lady spy beginning the seduction of her only too willing victim.

Each of these shots is lit with X lighting, yet the difference in the overall balance of the lighting makes them appear quite dissimilar. This difference is partly due to the fact that in the shot from *Beauty and the Beast,* the difference in level between the foreground lighting (key, fill, and back) and that on the background (base lighting) is quite large, while in the shot from *Spies* the reverse is true. Also, the difference between the level of the key and the fill lights is greater in the shot from *Beauty and the Beast* than in the shot from *Spies.* As a result, both the background and the shadows are darker in the first shot than they are in the second, making the scene from *Beauty and the Beast* seem dark and heavy, while the flatter lighting in *Spies* gives a feeling of sun-washed lightness.

Strictly speaking, however, the different appearance of these two shots results from more than just the lighting balance alone. How the light acts when it is recorded on film finally determines the quality of the image. This is true whether it is studio lighting or naturally occurring light that must be recorded. As a result, creating a particular lighting effect is a rather complicated process that depends as much upon technical knowledge of the interdependence of light and film as it does upon the quality, direction, and intensity of the lights. It is these technical considerations—the nature of film and the processes it must undergo to achieve a specific effect—that are the subject of the second part of this chapter.

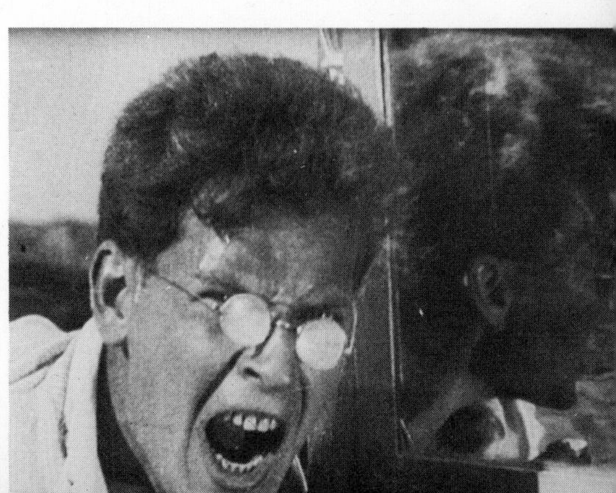

Part II:

Capturing the Light

Thus far we have talked about the wondrous effects that are created with light. In motion pictures, however, these effects cannot exist independently of the film on which they are impressed. This wouldn't matter if film responded to light in the same way our eyes do; but film can record only imperfectly a small part of what we see. As a result, what we see and what the film records are often radically different. For instance, because the sensitivity of our eyes to light can vary over a wide range, with only the slightest subconscious adjustment of our eyes we can easily see first in bright sunlight and then in deep shadow. Film, however, has a relatively fixed sensitivity and will work well only with a certain level of illumination.

Film also registers only a limited range of contrasts. Unlike the human eye, it cannot record details in both the brightest and the darkest parts of a contrasty scene. If film is correctly exposed for the brightest parts of the scene it will record the darkest parts as an undifferentiated black mass; and if it is exposed for the shadows the brightest parts will become equally undifferentiated white areas. Also, if the film is exposed halfway between the brightest and darkest areas, the shadows will be darker and the highlights lighter than they seem to the eye, and there will be fewer intermediate tones.

Because of these differences, no matter how a scene looks to our eyes, it won't look the same way on film. As a result, the effect of the lighting can be gauged only in terms of the film's response to light. But adjusting the light to get the desired effect on film requires more than just manipulating the lighting. It actually starts with the choice of film and includes how that film is exposed, developed, and duplicated. Since each of these steps plays a part in determining how the light is recorded, each also helps control the quality of the image that eventually appears on the screen.

Film Speed

The first thing the film-maker must choose is the sensitivity of the film he will use. Because the intensity of light can vary so widely, one of the principal differences between the various types of photographic film is in their sensitivity to different light levels. This is known as the *speed* of the film. Film which requires a great deal of light is called *slow,* while film which requires very little light is called *fast.* Therefore, either a slower or a faster film stock is used, depending upon the lighting conditions under which the film will be shot.

However, film speed also affects two other essential qualities of the film. For one thing, it has an important effect on the sharpness of the image the film can record because speed is directly related to the nature of the image-forming material

—infinitesimal grains of silver which are blackened by being exposed to light and then developed. In slow film these grains are so small that they are barely visible; but as the film speed increases the grains tend to form clumps that become progressively more noticeable. In a faster film this graininess diffuses the edges of objects so that, as the projected image gets larger, the grain is more greatly magnified, making the image look increasingly softer. Grain also makes it impossible to project both 8mm and 35mm film of the same speed on the same size screen and have the 8mm look as sharp. Since the smaller frame must be magnified four times as much as the larger one to fill the screen, the grain is four times as large, and so the image is inevitably softer.

The other quality affected by film speed is the inherent contrast of the image. As the film increases in speed, it can handle a wider range of contrasts and so will show more details in both the brighter and the darker areas of the picture. This increased range also gives faster film more *latitude,* that is, it can tolerate a greater degree of overexposure before the highlights will cease to show details and more underexposure before the dark areas will go black.

Grain and contrast affect not only the image quality of the *original,* that is, the film exposed in the camera, but they also have a cumulative effect on the quality of each succeeding copy made from that original. The reason is that each copy, called a *generation,* superimposes its own graininess and limited contrast range on that of the previous copy. As a result, by the third or fourth generation the image is quite harsh and coarse unless the grain and contrast in the original are kept to a minimum.

Negative and Reversal Film

The film-maker must also choose between two very different kinds of film stock—*negative* and *reversal.* These differ according to the chemical process used to form the image. On negative film the image becomes the exact opposite of what we see. A bright area is recorded as a dark image and a dark area as a clear image. In addition, color negative also records each color as its opposite or complementary color. This negative image must then be printed onto another, similar piece of film, or *positive,* so that the tonal values (and colors) are again reversed to their normal relationship. In the reversal process, however, the film is developed directly into a positive, eliminating the need to print the film before obtaining a normal image.

The choice between these two types of film is based on the different image quality each produces. Negative films, as a whole, are faster than reversal films but

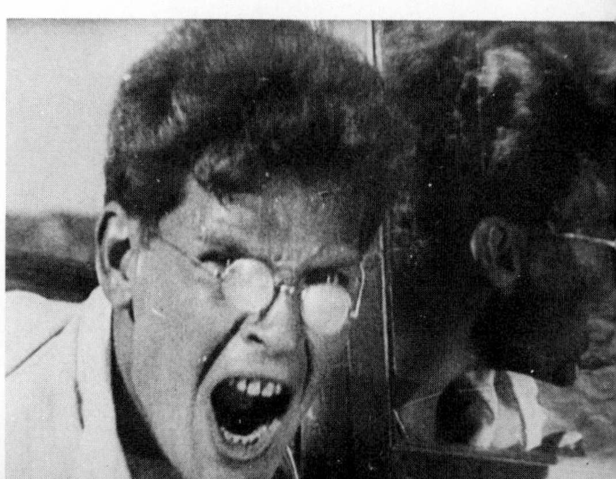

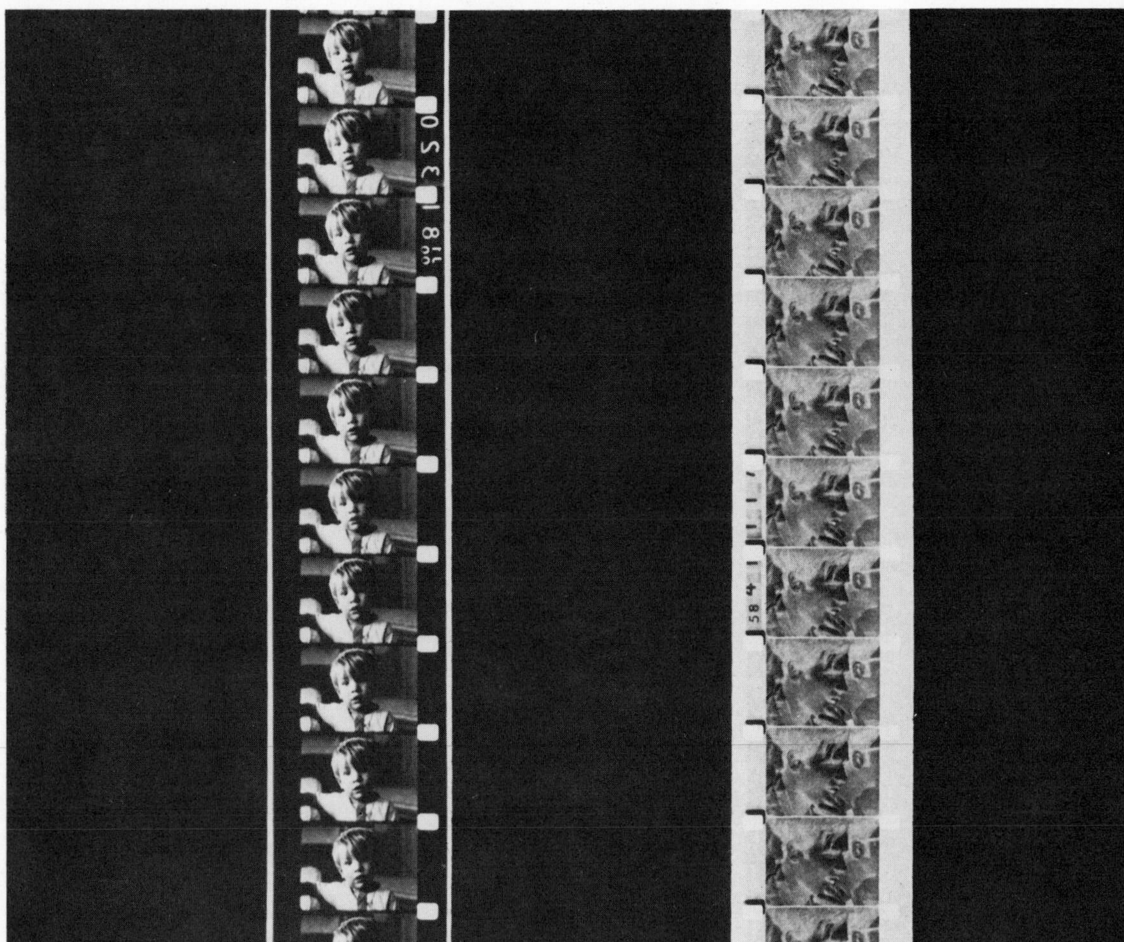

Reversal original, L, and negative original, R. On the negative the facial tones are reversed: the face is black and the hair, white.

produce more grain for a comparable speed. And because they are faster, negative films also have less inherent contrast and more latitude. As a result of these differences, negative stock is generally preferred when shooting in 35mm or 65mm. Because of the larger frame size, the grain isn't as greatly magnified as it is in 8mm or 16mm; and the extra speed permits the cameraman to use a smaller *f* stop. This smaller *f* stop is particularly important with the longer-focal-length lenses used in 35mm and 65mm filming since these lenses have less inherent depth of field than those used in 8mm and 16mm (see Chapter Four, pp. 204–205).

However, in the smaller film sizes reversal stock is preferred, both for its tighter grain pattern and because dirt is less noticeable on prints from a reversal original. When a negative is printed, black becomes white, so dirt—which is black—prints white. These dirt marks then show up as tiny white flashes on the screen. But dirt on a reversal original prints black, which is much less noticeable than a white flash, and that is particularly important in 8mm and 16mm since dirt marks are so greatly enlarged upon the screen.

With color reversal film stocks one other consideration enters into the choice. There is one type of color reversal stock which is designed for immediate projection without making prints, and another type that is used when prints are made. The first type includes the high-speed color reversal films used in television news and the slower color films used for home movies. These films produce an original that looks normal when put directly on a TV or projection screen; but a print made from this type of film has a harsh contrast range and dense, muddy colors, because, with color film, printing not only builds up grain and contrast, but also the intensity, or *saturation,* of the colors. For this reason, a second type of color reversal stock is used when prints are needed. It produces an original with low inherent contrast and low color saturation, image qualities that are then built back up to normal through printing.

Color Sensitivity

There is one other choice which must be made when the movie is to be shot in color and that is the color sensitivity of the film. Put more simply, this means that the film must be matched to the kind of light to which it will be exposed—there is one kind of color film for daylight, and another for artificial illumination. These two kinds of color film are necessary because each type of light source produces light composed of a different blend of colors. We perceive this light as white, or colorless, because we psychologically compensate for shifts in the color blend, or *color balance,* of the light. But color film has no such psychological mechanism, and even small changes in the color balance of the light will give an overall cast to the colors on the film.

This shift in color balance is most pronounced between daylight, which tends toward the blue end of the spectrum, and incandescent lighting, which is mainly reddish. As a result, each type of color film is designed to match one of these major sources of light. The artificial light, or *indoor,* film compensates for the lack of blue in tungsten lighting by means of a built-in bluish cast, or *mask,* while the daylight, or *outdoor,* film has no such internal masking. But either type of film can be used both indoors or out as long as a *color-conversion filter* is used to compensate for the changing color balance of the light. The proper filter for use with each type of film is listed in the instructions packed with the film.

However, any conversion filter cuts the amount of light reaching the film, so using a filter requires an increase in exposure. As a result, most professional filming, both indoors and out, is done on indoor film. For very practical reasons, shooting

indoor film outdoors is less of a problem than doing the reverse—using outdoor film indoors. While the conversion filter used with indoor film requires half again more exposure, daylight is free and plentiful; but the filter used to convert outdoor film requires three to four times more exposure, and every increase in indoor illumination costs money. In addition, indoor film with a filter produces somewhat better results outdoors than regular outdoor film because the filter automatically absorbs the large amounts of ultraviolet light found in sunlight. This type of light is invisible to our eyes, but it is not invisible to the film, and it can give a scene shot on outdoor film an unexpected and unwanted bluish cast.

Color sensitivity also used to be a problem with black-and-white (B&W) film. The earliest types of B&W film, for instance, were sensitive only to the green-blue-violet end of the spectrum, totally excluding red, orange, and yellow. This exclusion meant that a blue sky would end up being rendered as pure white and red lips would become black. This older type of film, called *orthochromatic,* is still widely used in processing laboratories to make B&W prints because it is slow and therefore fine grained. Also, this film doesn't need to be handled in total darkness. Since it is not red sensitive, a dim red *safelight* can be used to illuminate the printing and processing rooms. But ortho film is now only rarely used to make an original. By the end of the silent era it had been almost completely replaced by *panchromatic* film. This film is equally responsive to every color in the spectrum and therefore gives a more natural rendition of the tones in a scene.

Narrowing the Choice

Because there is such a wide variety of film stocks to choose from, choosing the right one would seem fairly complicated. But there are several limiting factors that narrow the choice and therefore simplify it. For instance, while the movie can be made in either B&W or color, this decision depends not only upon aesthetic considerations, but also upon budget. Since it is markedly more expensive to make a movie in color than in B&W, the expressive potential of color must be weighed against the added costs involved. The choice of negative or reversal film is also more or less determined by film size, even though either type of film is available in both 16mm and 35mm. And if the movie is shot in color, the choice of indoor or outdoor film is largely controlled by the lighting conditions under which the movie will be made.

There is, however, one basic decision which serves as the starting point for controlling image quality, and that concerns the speed of the film. Regardless of whether the movie is shot in B&W or color, negative or reversal, indoors or out, there is still a range of film speeds from which the film-maker can choose. In effect, this choice is a compromise between a film's sensitivity and its grain; while a faster film extends the range of lighting conditions under which the movie can be shot, increased speed means increased graininess. As a result, unless a grainy effect is desired, as slow a film is used as the light level will allow so that the sharpest, clearest possible image will be produced.

The choice of film speed is made in terms of the ASA (American Standards Association) number given the film by the manufacturer. The lower the ASA number, the slower the film. Slow films will typically have numbers between 16 and 50, while medium-speed films have numbers up to 100, and fast films are rated at 100 or more. These numbers have a direct mathematical relationship to the sensitivity of the film. A film with a speed of 50 requires twice the exposure of one rated at 100, or four times the exposure of one rated at 200, etc. This number also serves to predict the graininess of the film, since an increase in the ASA number means an increase in grain size.

Varying Film Speed and Contrast

The next step in controlling image quality is to decide upon how the film will be processed. This decision is necessary because both film speed and image contrast are more than just inherent properties of the film itself. They are actually the result of processing the film in a particular developer for a specified amount of time. As a result, variations in the processing of the film give the film-maker a means for altering film speed and an important method for matching the contrast range of the film to the requirements of the lighting. In other words, changes in processing permit even a contrasty scene to be captured within the limited range of the film or the contrast range of the image to be increased when it is recorded on film. In addition, changes in the processing of color film also change the color saturation so that the contrast between the colors is either emphasized or muted.

These changes in both speed and contrast are directly related to how long the film spends in the developer. Put simply, the longer the developing time, the higher the film speed and the greater the image contrast. This, in turn, means that when the film is *underdeveloped* in order to decrease contrast, film speed is also decreased, so the film must be given more exposure. And when the film is *overdeveloped* to increase contrast, the speed is increased and the film must be given less exposure.

Underexposing and overdeveloping the film is also a useful means for making a fast film even faster. In addition, this technique allows a slow film to be used under poor lighting conditions (the reasons for doing this will be discussed shortly). The process is called *pushing* or *forcing* the film. While it increases the contrast of the image, it permits the speed of B&W film to be increased by two or three times. And in color, the speed can be increased from two to as much as four times the normal speed, depending upon the film stock and how great an alteration in color fidelity is acceptable.

In order to determine exactly how much of a change in both exposure and contrast will give the best results, a test roll is shot before filming begins. This test

is made by first shooting the film at a variety of speeds under lighting conditions which are typical for that motion picture. Next, the laboratory that will do all the rest of the processing develops the roll to a specified degree of contrast and makes a print of it. Finally, the film-maker picks out that section of the print that looks best for his purposes. The film speed used to produce this section is then known as the *exposure index,* or EI. This is an upward or downward adjustment of the ASA number that becomes the standard for determining exposure throughout the filming.

Controlling Exposure

Once the EI is arrived at, it is used to determine the *f* stop which must be used for each shot. In some cases this calculation is very simple. For instance, the same *f* stop may suffice for every shot lit from in front with bright sunlight. In fact, in the early days of film-making, when the film was so slow that almost everything was shot outdoors in bright sunlight, few cameramen used an exposure meter. Instead, they became intimately familiar with one particular film stock under standardized lighting conditions and set the exposure by eye. As a result, the camera department of one major studio posted a sign saying, "When in doubt, use *f*5.6." In those days, though, the cameramen also worked in the laboratory, inspecting the film as it passed through the developer. They would "read" the negative under the dim glow of a safelight and regulate the processing time to achieve the proper negative quality.

But this kind of visual control over exposure and processing has disappeared with the advent of faster film, faster-working developers, and more varied types of lighting. So, cameramen have had to learn how to work blind. Since they can no longer watch the image as it develops, they have had to standardize the processing and, instead, control the image while it is being exposed onto the film. They do this by setting an exposure meter for the film's EI. Then the meter, by converting the EI into an *f* stop, determines how much of the light hitting the subject should be used to register an image on the film.

Types of Exposure Meters

An exposure meter is thus one of the cameraman's primary tools for controlling image quality; but the degree of control he can exercise depends upon how he uses his exposure meter and the type of meter he uses. Exposure meters fall into two classes—*reflected* and *incident.* The reflected type measures the amount of light reflected from the subject toward the camera, while the incident type measures the amount of light falling on the subject. The big advantage of a reflected meter is that, since it is held at the camera and pointed toward the subject, it can be used quickly. Thus it is most useful when the cameraman must stay behind the camera, when the action changes rapidly, or when the subject is distant. The advantage of an incident meter is that, since it is held near the subject, it tells exactly how much light is hitting any particular part of the scene. This meter is also most helpful in a studio, or wherever studio lights are used, since the meter tells how the various lights should be manipulated to achieve a particular result.

However, both types of meter suffer from the same disability. Because they average the amount of light reaching them, they don't register the difference between the lightest and the darkest parts of the scene, that is, its contrast range. A reflected meter, for instance, gives an exposure reading in which an object reflecting light equal to the average for the whole scene records as a medium tone on the film. This is fine as long as the most important areas in the scene reflect an average amount of light. If, however, there is a great deal of sky in the shot, its inherent brightness will push up the average and even a normally lit face will tend to be underexposed. Or if the background is dark, just the reverse will happen.

One way to remedy this disadvantage is to move close to the subject and just read the light reflected from the most important area. This area will then be a medium tone. Another alternative is to use a *spot meter*. This is a reflected meter that has an extremely narrow *angle of acceptance,* that is, it reads only a small area

Reflected light meter. The meter is held near the camera and pointed toward the subject; it averages the light reflected from the subject.

Incident light meter. The meter is held near the subject with the light-gathering hemisphere pointing toward the camera; the hemisphere averages the light illuminating the subject.

in front of it, usually a circle only one or two degrees wide. This restricted angle permits the cameraman to stand at a distance and still choose the areas he wishes to read. He then strikes his own average. A similar metering system is also used in cameras that include a reflected light meter as part of the optics. Instead of reading the whole scene equally, these built-in meters are now *center weighted*. This means that the exposure reading is principally based on the central part of the frame since this is where the most important part of the picture usually falls.

Incident light meters, on the other hand, work on the theory that it is easier and more accurate to read just the light hitting the scene. This reading is taken by means of a meter with a hemispherical light-gathering device. The hemisphere gathers all the light hitting each part of the scene, no matter from what direction it comes, and then averages this light so that an object of average reflectance will produce a medium tone on the film. But, instead of depending on just the meter reading, the cameraman also calculates the exposure by using his past experience to make allowances for the lightness or darkness of the subject. That way, the meter reading isn't based on any large, but relatively unimportant highlights or shadows.

Depth of Field

One other factor which must also be considered when determining the *f* stop is depth of field. As we mentioned in the previous chapter, depth decreases as the lens is opened up and increases as it is stopped down. As a result, if the *f* stop which will provide the necessary amount of depth isn't the same as that required for the proper exposure, some other means must be used to control exposure.

If, to achieve shallow depth, the lens must be opened wider than is required for the correct exposure, the amount of light reaching the film can be reduced in one of two ways. Either the variable shutter can be closed down, or if that is not possible, a *neutral-density filter* can be used. These neutral gray filters cut down the amount of light without changing its color, and so they can be used with both B&W and color film. They come in thirteen grades, or densities, that represent from ¼ to 13¼ *f* stops less light; but the most widely used ones reduce the light an even 1, 2, or 3 *f* stops.

If, however, the lens opening must be smaller than that which will give the proper exposure, there is no simple way to increase the light reaching the film. Of course, it is always possible to force the film, or even change to a faster film. But because faster film means more grain and forcing produces more contrast, both of these alternatives cause image quality to deteriorate. It is usually preferable, therefore, to increase the level of illumination. But this too presents problems since the light level must be doubled for each *f* stop that the exposure is reduced. It is also possible to decrease the frame rate, or undercrank, since reducing the number of frames per second increases the amount of time the shutter remains open. However, because undercranking speeds up any movement in the scene, it is restricted to those shots in which there is little or no motion.

Variations in Exposure

While accurate exposure is an important step in the control of image quality, there is a margin for error built into both the film and the processing that permits a certain amount of variation in exposure. First, and most importantly, film has latitude, that is, it will tolerate a degree of under- or overexposure without losing all detail in either the shadows or the highlights. But, as we said previously, there is less latitude in slow film than fast, and less in reversal than in negative film. In addition, there is less latitude in color than in B&W, not only because color films are relatively slow, but because the colors change with changes in exposure. Underexposure makes the colors dense and muddy, and overexposure makes them thin and washed out. As a result, in a slow color reversal film the latitude is as small as ± ½ *f* stop, while a fast B&W negative has as much as ± 2 *f* stops of latitude.

Even the broadest possible latitude, however, is not always sufficient to cover the extreme variation in exposure that occurs when the camera pans, tilts, or trucks from a bright to a dark area. Then it is necessary to *follow-f-stop*—to change the *f* stop during the shot. This is usually done by an assistant cameraman; but it can also be done by the cameraman, without his interrupting the filming, if the lens has

click stops, that is, if each *f* stop clicks into place so that the cameraman can feel the changes without looking. The clicks make it easy to shift any number of whole *f* stops.

Exposures that fall within the latitude of the film can be further evened out during printing by *timing* the print, that is, by varying the amount of light used to expose the original onto a duplicate. If a reversal original is too dark, a brighter printing light will make the image lighter; and if the original is too light, less printing light will darken the image (just the reverse procedure is followed with an original negative). In fact, if the original is properly exposed, timing permits quite sizable shifts in the overall tonality of the print. But timing cannot compensate for *blocked-up* areas: shadows or highlights that fall outside the latitude limits of the film. If the brightest or darkest areas in the original lack color and/or detail, no manipulation of the printing lights can alter their contents.

Contrast Control

Another extremely important consideration is the contrast range of the scene. Once this range from light to dark is recorded on the original there is almost no way to change it. Unlike exposure, which can easily be varied from shot to shot during printing, contrast can be altered only when the original is processed, and this means changing the contrast in every shot on the roll. As a result, the contrast range in the shots on each roll should, whenever possible, be controlled at the time of the original exposure. This control involves adjusting the brightness range of the light falling on the scene so that the density of the shadows has a certain relationship to the intensity of the highlights.

This relationship, called the *lighting ratio,* is simply a mathematical comparison of the light falling in the shadows to the light hitting the highlights. With B&W film this ratio is usually kept within 4 or 5 to 1; and with color film, which has greater inherent contrast, the range is usually never more than 3 to 1. Therefore, with B&W film the intensity of the key and fill lights together should be no more than five times the intensity of the fill light alone; and with color film, key plus fill should be kept within three times the level of the fill alone. Otherwise, when the film is printed, by the third or fourth generation it would be impossible to obtain details in both the highlights and the shadows; one or the other would block up.

The lighting ratio is normally calculated by the use of an incident light meter with a flat-faced light-gathering device that reads only the light coming from one direction at a time. First the cameraman determines the level of the key light, or if outdoors, the sun. Then he points the meter at the fill lights and adjusts them until the lighting ratio falls within the particular limits he is using. He can then switch back to a reflected meter, or an incident meter with a hemispherical light collector (incident meters often accept both flat and hemispherical collectors), to obtain his overall exposure.

Reducing Contrast

Obviously, setting the lighting for a particular ratio presupposes a certain amount of control by the cameraman over his light sources. But even when the sun is the principal light source, sufficient control is not hard to achieve. It is not difficult, for instance, when shooting in bright sunlight, to use a reflector to bounce a small amount of sunlight back into the shadows. While such reflectors are commercially available, it is easy for the film-maker to build his own, since all they normally amount to are strips of aluminum foil glued to the face of a large, thin sheet of plywood. The degree of reflection is controlled by putting foil with the shiny side up on one side of the board and rumpled foil, dull side up, on the other: then, one side will give a bright, hard light and the other a duller, more diffuse light.

Of course, if electric power is available, the shadows can be filled in with artificial light. But while this is a relatively straightforward procedure in B&W, it is more complicated in color. Unless the artificial lighting is the same color as the daylight, the shadows will turn reddish. One way to prevent this is to use a carbon, xenon, or metallic arc light, since arcs produce very bluish light. Another is to use a *color-balancing filter* over a regular tungsten studio light. These filters are of two types. One, made of blue plastic, simply absorbs the red and yellow part of the light; the other, called a *dichroic,* is made of a special glass that transmits only blue and blue-green light while reflecting all other colors. This process also keeps the dichroic cooler and prolongs its life. With either type of filter, however, the amount of light is drastically reduced.

The lighting ratio can also be reduced, and the direct sunlight softened, by a large white sheet, stretched, out of camera range, between the subject and the sun. This technique became a fine art during the silent era, when the only light source then available, harsh sunlight, was reduced and diffused with large, finely woven sheets of various thicknesses of silk. Now, even though these diffusers are also made of muslin, fiber glass, or plastic, they are still known as *silks*.

Control over the lighting ratio in long shots presents a somewhat different problem. Since it is more difficult, because of the distance, either to fill the shadows or to diffuse the sunlight, the contrast can instead be reduced by overexposing and then underdeveloping the original. This applies only to B&W, however, since with color film variations in developing time affect the fidelity of the colors. But a similar effect can be obtained with color film by the use of a light fog filter. This slightly diffuses the image rather than the illumination, but in the process it lightly grays out the deepest shadows, making them less opaque. This technique has become especially useful with wide-screen color since longer long shots are so effective in that format, and there is now available a set of five graded *low-contrast screens,* a type of fog filter that cuts the contrast without diffusing the image.

Contrast can also be selectively reduced in long shots, in both B&W or color,

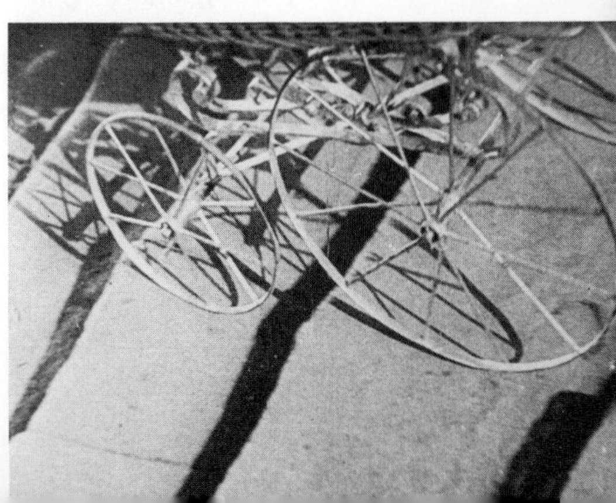

by the use of either a graduated or a half-neutral density filter. The graduated filters are used mainly to reduce the brightness of the sky, so they are most dense at the top, grading down to clear glass by the middle of the filter. This gradation matches the characteristics of the sky, which becomes most intensely bright toward the top of the shot. The half-neutral filter, on the other hand, is used to tone down evenly any large, bright area. However, since there is an abrupt change between the two halves of the filter, the cameraman must hide this dividing line by aligning it with the edge of some straight object that extends all the way across the frame.

Contrast control techniques similar to those used outdoors are also used indoors when working with artificial light. Indoors, of course, if a light is too bright it can simply be moved. But if this is not possible, either because of the size of the space or because the light is permanently mounted, the intensity of the light can be reduced by placing a piece of metal window-screening in front of it. This *scrim* reduces the light without changing its character from hard to soft. And if one layer of screening is not enough, two or three layers can be used to form a double or triple scrim. Or if the light is both too bright and too harsh, a fireproof silk can be used to reduce the light and soften it simultaneously.

With artificial light there is also the problem that light aimed into one area may spill over into another and make it too bright. This spill can be controlled by means of *barn doors,* thin, black metal wings attached to the front of the lighting unit that look like blinders for a horse. These doors swing into the light path and

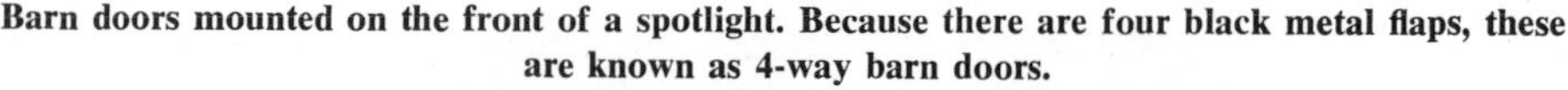

Barn doors mounted on the front of a spotlight. Because there are four black metal flaps, these are known as 4-way barn doors.

restrict the light to just the desired area. A similar function is also served by a square metal *flag* or a circular *target*. These too can be used to block the light, but they are somewhat more flexible than barn doors since they can be used to keep the light from selected sections within the total area covered by the light.

When artificial light and daylight are mixed on an indoor location, the high level of daylight often requires an extraordinary amount of artificial lighting if the difference between the two is to be brought into balance. The amount of artificial light needed can be minimized, however, if the daylight is filtered through large sheets of neutral-density plastic placed over the windows. These sheets come in many of the same grades as neutral-density camera filters, thus permitting the sunlight to be reduced by known amounts. In addition, when shooting color in mixed light, the daylight can be rebalanced to match the color of the tungsten illumination by covering the windows with plastic sheeting the color of a conversion filter. And when both the level and the color of the daylight must be altered, a type of sheeting is used that combines the conversion color and one of a number of neutral densities into a single sheet.

Increasing Contrast

The reverse situation, too little contrast, can also pose a problem. Particularly in B&W, in which objects appear only as shades of gray and cannot, therefore, be separated by their color differences, a broad range of tones is required to differentiate and shape the parts of the image. Lack of contrast in a B&W image arises from a number of sources. One of the most common is naturally occurring flat light, such as cloudy daylight, open shade, or the light from banks of evenly spaced fluorescents. Under these lighting conditions a B&W image will have a long scale of middle grays but will lack the clear separation of crisp blacks and whites. This situation can be remedied in one of two ways. The overall contrast of the entire scene can be increased by underexposing and then overdeveloping (forcing) the original; or the contrast in only certain parts of the image can be increased by the addition of small amounts of artificial light to selected areas, such as a face. This second technique has the advantage of leaving an overall flatness to the image while still clearly separating and shaping the most important details in the shot. (It is also the best technique to use with color since changes in processing affect color fidelity.)

Another cause of low contrast in a B&W image is the inability of B&W film to render adjacent areas of a different color, but similar brightness, as different shades of gray. Then the color sensitivity of the film must be altered by the use of one of a

number of differently colored *contrast filters.* These filters transmit light that is the same color as the filter and strongly absorb light of the opposite, complementary color. The effect is to lighten objects of the same color and darken objects of the complementary color.

A typical example of the use of a filter in B&W are the billowing white clouds in a blue sky that occur in this shot from Gustav Machaty's *Ecstasy.* This herd of wild

horses is used in the film as a symbol of the animal vitality that is struggling to express itself through the sexual urges of the film's heroine. In order to stress the beauty and naturalness of these urges, Machaty filmed the horses from a low angle against the grandeur of a sky full of high, drifting clouds. But, since even panchromatic film is still very blue-sensitive, both the clouds and the sky would have been recorded as white unless a yellow filter was used. This filter absorbed its complement, blue, and so darkened the sky without darkening the clouds, making them stand out in strong relief.

Because contrast filters come in a variety of colors, the choice of filter depends upon the color of the objects to be separated and the degree of separation. A blue sky, for instance, can be darkened only slightly with a light yellow filter, can be darkened appreciably with an orange filter, and can be made almost black with a red filter. The rendition of other colors can also be changed with other filter combinations.

However, since any contrast filter absorbs some of the light used to expose the film, the exposure must be increased according to a *filter factor.* This factor, which varies with the filter and the type of film, indicates how many times more light must be used to obtain a normal exposure. For instance, a factor of 2 means twice as much exposure, or an increase of one *f* stop. Similarly, a factor of 6 indicates an increase of 2½ *f* stops (because each *f* stop gives twice the exposure of the next, opening up the lens one *f* stop doubles the exposure, two *f* stops gives four times as much, three *f* stops eight times, etc.). Filter factors can be looked up in a cameraman's handbook or in the instructions packed with either the filter or the film.

There is also a type of contrast filter than can be used to increase the contrast in part of the frame while simultaneously decreasing the contrast range of the entire image. Called a *sky filter,* it comes in a variety of colors, with the color slowly graduating to clear glass by the middle of the filter. When it is used outdoors, the colored upper half makes the clouds stand out by darkening the sky and at the same time reduces the amount of light coming from the sky so that its brightness is closer to that of the foreground objects.

Haze and Reflections

A source of decreased contrast that is common to both B&W and color is atmospheric haze. This haze is a combination of water vapor, smoke, and dust particles that is most noticeable in long shots and shots made with a telephoto lens. It can appear in a shot even when the air seems relatively clear and will increasingly obscure objects as they get further from the lens. Haze has the same effect as a fog filter since it scatters light into the shadows, graying them out. Haze is also highly reflective of the blue and the ultraviolet light from the sky; this light increases the density of the haze in a B&W image and adds to the blueness of the haze in a color image.

When shooting in B&W, haze is automatically minimized by the use of one of the contrast filters in the series that goes from light yellow, through orange, to deep red. Since each of these filters progressively absorbs more of the blue light, they both darken the sky and increase the overall contrast of the image by absorbing the light reflected by the haze. Of course, these colored filters cannot be used with color film without giving a cast to the image, so with color a *skylight filter* is used instead. This is a pale pink, almost colorless filter that absorbs ultraviolet light without visibly changing the rest of the colors in the image. This filter can also be used with B&W film when there is no need to darken the sky. With either type of film the filter absorbs so little visible light that it isn't necessary to increase the exposure.

A particular problem when shooting in color is the direct reflection of light off the surface of objects, especially on a bright, clear day. This reflected light forms a white sheen that coats everything and cuts down the color contrast. While this sheen is visible to the eye, we are so used to it that we aren't really aware of it until we put on a pair of Polaroid sunglasses. These eliminate the glare, that is, the direct reflections of the sun, and make all the colors look rich and saturated. This same effect can also be obtained by the use of a *polarizing filter* with color film. These filters eliminate surface reflections, and because they are neutral in tone, they don't add any color of their own to the image. They also serve the same purpose with B&W film and, in addition, they darken the sky in the same manner as a deep yellow-orange filter. The one drawback of a polarizer, however, is that it requires 2½ *f* stops more exposure.

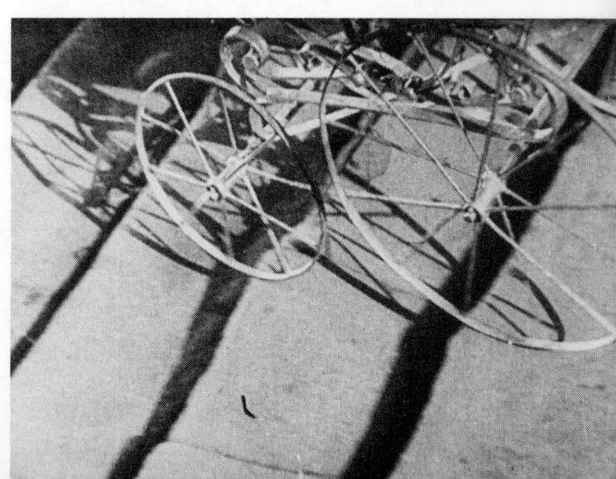

Estimating Contrast

Because of the increase in contrast between what we see and what is recorded on film, it is impossible for the unaided eye to judge how the contrast in the original scene will appear in the finished print. This is true, even when the lighting ratio is carefully controlled, because different parts of the scene reflect differing amounts of light. It is possible, however, to estimate the eventual contrast of the scene, and then adjust the lights to even out any noticeable discrepancies, by the use of a *contrast viewing glass.* These viewing glasses, one for color and the other for B&W, are really nothing more than two specific grades of neutral-density filter. When a viewing glass is held in front of the eye it reduces the amount of light so that the eye responds to light more closely to the way film does. Then, if the contrast is too great, the shadows become opaque, while if there is not enough contrast, the highlights and shadows tend to blend together.

Low- and High-Key Lighting

The fact that a film stock's contrast range and latitude are restricted permits the film-maker to use both light and exposure to push the image toward the extremes of a film's usable limits. The result is an image that is not quite like anything in the real world. This peculiar image quality can be seen in the following examples. They are all taken from films by Ingmar Bergman because his movies are a particularly fertile source of images that produce their effect through the expert use of light on film. Look, for instance, at the opening scene from *The Seventh Seal.* In the first part of this scene the knight and his servant ride through the sun-bleached countryside and into a seemingly deserted farming village. When they receive no greeting, the servant dismounts and enters the village to look around.

Courtesy: JANUS FILMS,

This is a *high-key* image, one in which there are broad, bright areas, usually lit from in front, that in the extreme highlights go pure white. This effect is created by simply overexposing the original but still developing it normally. Then, when the original is printed, the exposure is timed to produce any degree of darkness in the shadows without greatly increasing the detail in the blocked-up highlights. In this example the high-key effect gives a sun-washed blankness to the image that subtly instills a sense of emptiness and desolation.

Next the servant enters one of the houses and finds a plague victim sprawled on the floor. Once he enters the house he is immersed in darkness. This effect is

known as *low key,* or just the reverse of the previous effect. It is accomplished by using only light that comes from behind the subject so that the highlights rim objects and set them off from the background. The shadows are then emphasized by underexposing the original and developing it normally. Because little detail is recorded in the shadows, when the original is printed, the exposure can be timed to give any degree of brightness to the highlights without greatly affecting the shadowy quality of the dark areas. In this case the darkness maintains the blank emptiness of the previous shots while adding an ominous note to the scene that foreshadows the discovery of the body.

A similar kind of lighting is used to simulate the qualities of a dimly lit interior. A typical example is this shot of the inside of a movie theater from Bergman's *Monika.* This effect was produced by simply rimming the subjects with back light and then using a much lower level of key and fill light, in the ratio of about 10 to 1. The original was also underexposed about 1½ stops, just enough exposure to produce some detail in the dimly lit shadows while still letting the strongest high-

Courtesy: JANUS FILMS, INC.

lights go pure white. This technique thus permits us to see the action at the same time that it creates the effect of the projection light on the backs of their heads.

Limbo

Carried to an extreme, low-key lighting produces what is known as a *limbo setting;* that is, a well-lit figure against an unlit and therefore pure black background. Since a limbo background is totally lacking in the details that tell us where the characters are located, they are really nowhere. This setting is most often used when a narrator appears on camera. Since he or she is usually not part of the action but is only commenting upon it, a limbo setting both isolates the narrator from the rest of the film and concentrates our attention on the narration.

Bergman, however, has taken this limbo technique one step further. He has used it to sum up a character's predicament. In this scene from *Wild Strawberries* we see the old man, near the end of his journey, seated inside a car. Outside are

Courtesy: JANUS FILMS, INC.

several young hitchhikers who have been riding with him. They have just thanked him for the ride by giving him a bunch of wild flowers and then good-humoredly serenading him. Because this scene was made in a studio, Bergman could control every nuance of the lighting, and at the end of the song all but one light is extinguished. This leaves the old man in limbo, caught up in his own thoughts. As the

lights dim his expression becomes pensive, and we know that his passengers' simple pleasure in life has reawakened feelings in him he had thought long gone. So, for an instant, he is held in the dark, suspended between his bitter memories of the past and the vivid new possibilities of life in the present.

Night Scenes

A special case of low-key lighting occurs when shooting at night. Because, even when there is a full moon, nighttime shadows are quite opaque, only an extraordinary amount of exposure will produce any shadow details. As a result, the original can be exposed only for the highlights, usually the lights and their reflections that appear in the shot. That is what was done in this night scene from Jerzy Skolimowski's *Le Départ*. In these shots the young hero of the film is searching Paris for a Porsche he can steal to drive in a race being held the next day.

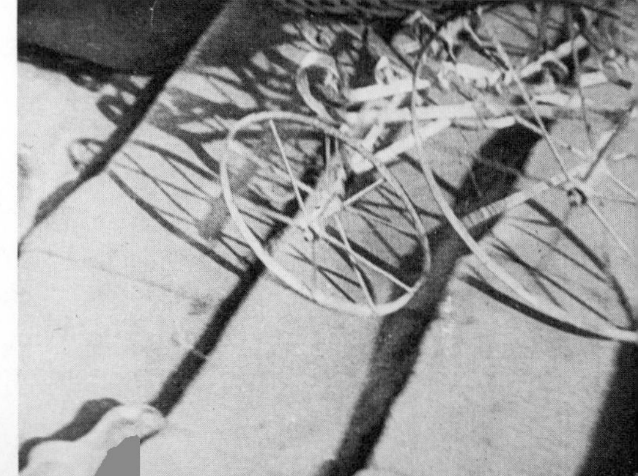

Skolimowski was able to shoot this scene at night because it takes place in a city and so there are plenty of lights around to produce an image. But since there is just barely enough light to illuminate the action, all we can see of the hero is his silhouette as he interrupts these highlights—a shadowy figure hopelessly flitting from Porsche to Porsche in a futile search for a car he can drive to victory.

Night-for-Night and Day-for-Night

However, when a night scene occurs in a setting that has little or no naturally occurring light, the action must be illuminated. This is done in one of two ways. One is to shoot at night and light the scene as if it were a dimly lit interior, that is, with crosslighting and back lighting to rim the figures and a low level of fill so that there is a minimum of shadow details. Then, if the scene is slightly underexposed, the barely lit figures will move against a black background. Obviously, this is easier to do in close and medium shots than in long shots, especially when there are no places to hide lights within the shot. Therefore, keeping the lights outside of camera range on a long shot requires light that can reach across a long distance without scattering: in other words, the light provided by huge arc lamps.

The other, somewhat simpler procedure for illuminating a night scene allows the film-maker to simulate a moonlit night by shooting in normal daylight. This *day-for-night* technique involves backlighting the subject and then underexposing by 1½ to 2 *f* stops. The result can be seen in this shot from Bergman's *The Seventh Seal.* It is a shot of a cart bearing a young girl, an alleged witch, to a forest clearing

Courtesy: JANUS FILMS, INC.

where she is to be burned at the stake. The scene takes place at night in order to emphasize the clandestine nature of the summary justice being meted out by a plague-frightened populace. But Bergman had the scene shot day-for-night so that there would be enough light to show the details of the action while still retaining a shadowy, nighttime effect.

To be convincing, however, day-for-night shooting should be done under certain conditions. In B&W, for instance, day-for-night should be shot on a bright, clear day in order to create a contrasty backlit effect. And if there is any sky in the shots, the scene should be heavily filtered, usually with a deep red filter. Otherwise, despite the underexposure, the sky would be quite light, while a night sky is dark even when the moon is out. It is also important to illuminate some of the windows in any houses that appear in the scene (unless the action is supposed to occur so late that no one is awake), and to boost the light level of any streetlamps or other lights, called *practicals,* that appear in the shots. This added illumination, by keeping these spots of light bright even when the scene as a whole is underexposed, makes the dark surroundings seem even darker.

Most of these same techniques also apply when color is shot day-for-night, though in some ways convincing color is easier to shoot. Color, for instance, can be shot on an overcast day. The light is closer to the actual quality of night-time illumination, yet even in this flat light, the contrasting colors will separate objects from the dark background. Of course, a contrast filter isn't used with color film since it would only color the image. Instead, a nightlike effect is created by underexposing indoor color film without a conversion filter. This technique gives the image a shadowy, bluish cast that approximates our normal loss of color discrimination outdoors at night. It also gives all window illumination and practicals a normal, warm tone because the film is color-balanced for these artificial light sources.

Continuity of Image Quality

All the techniques discussed so far can be used in varying degrees to shape the contents of each shot. Yet, in motion pictures, there is also a need for continuity of image quality so that shots that are often made at different times and under a variety of lighting conditions can be smoothly cut together. This uniformity is especially important in scenes in which time and space are meant to be continuous: nothing is more disconcerting than a sudden shift of image quality in a series of shots that represent a seemingly uninterrupted flow of action. As a result, there are a number of general techniques and specific precautions that are used to control the shooting throughout a scene and, in some cases, through the whole film.

Uniformity of Film and Processing

The simplest and most obvious step that is taken to maintain uniform image quality is to use the same film and processing throughout the shooting, or at least in all the shots that must be cut together without a transition (that is, without a fade or a dissolve). Of course, this uniformity depends upon a high degree of standardization in both the manufacture and the processing of the film, but motion-picture technology has become quite stable in that regard. In some ways, however, uniform standards are harder to meet in the production of color film, so film manufacturers

have assigned a *batch number* to each lot of film produced at one time, thus permitting the cameraman to use the same batch throughout a scene, or even the whole film. Then, any manufacturing errors remain constant from shot to shot. In addition, where small errors are within the manufacturer's tolerances, correction information is provided that can be uniformly applied to all the shooting with that batch.

Processing is a somewhat different problem since it is largely outside the control of the cameraman. There are, however, a number of precautions that can be taken. One is to adhere to the same exposure index (EI) throughout each scene so that all the film can receive the same processing. With color film it is also useful to process all the footage for one scene at the same time, usually by special arrangement with the laboratory. This procedure ensures that any processing errors will be uniform throughout the scene and therefore both less noticeable and easier to correct during printing. In addition, if there are any peculiarities in the lighting, and no time to shoot a test roll, the whole scene should be shot at some arbitrarily chosen exposure index and a twenty-foot test section included at the tail end of one of the rolls. This extra footage can later be processed as a test and the processing of the rest of the footage adjusted according to the results.

Another problem, one which is peculiar to color reversal films, is that the extremely slow professional film stock cannot be forced sufficiently to compensate for especially low levels of natural light. But, as was pointed out previously, switching to a faster film means using a stock intended for projection and not duplication, resulting in a jump in image contrast and color saturation as well as an increase in grain. The contrast and saturation differences can be minimized, however, if the faster film is *flashed,* that is, exposed to a small amount of light sometime before processing. This procedure is usually carried out by the laboratory under carefully controlled conditions, but the film should be tested before actual shooting begins. When done properly, this preexposure, or reexposure, to light cuts contrast and saturation by adding a slight fog to the image.

Continuity of Exposure

The second step in maintaining uniform image quality is continuity of exposure. At its simplest this just means using the same *f* stop for every shot in a sequence that has the same background. This precaution is necessary because changing the *f* stop to adjust for changes in the brightness of foreground objects doesn't alter the brightness of the foreground relative to that of the background. As a result, if the shots are printed so that the background is the same brightness throughout the scene, the foreground will become just as dark or light as it was before the exposure was changed.

This subtle problem can best be understood by a look at two shots from a simple dialogue sequence in *Breathless.* Here Jean Seberg returns a box of cigarettes to Belmondo and then lights a cigarette as he continues to talk. Because these shots were made using only the light coming through the window, the cameraman had to use an exposure that kept some details in the shadowy faces while not overexposing the windows and making them go blank white. The result is semi-

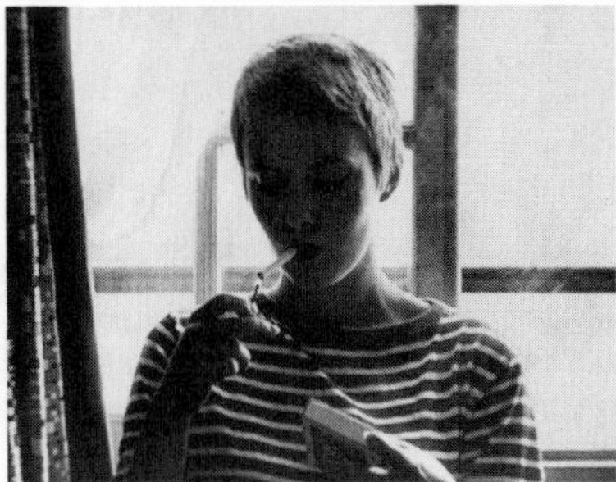

silhouettes that work fine in the longer shot because all we need to see is the general shape of their figures. But when the camera moves closer, Seberg's features dominate the frame, and if we are to see them they must be made lighter.

However, simply opening up the lens an *f* stop or two would make the background go pure white and the cut would be jarring. The same thing would also happen if the exposure were left the same and just this one shot made lighter by a change in the brightness of the printer light. Here it was acceptable to leave her face dark in the close-up since her reactions at this point in the film are meant to be obscure and rather enigmatic. But if this had not been the case, rather than changing the exposure, the cameraman would have had to bounce a small amount of light into her face. This light would illuminate her features but still keep the exposure constant so that the background would stay the same from shot to shot.

Matching Lenses

Another factor affecting continuity of image quality is the differences between the lenses used. This problem is now less prevalent because a zoom lens permits the film-maker to use just one lens for the majority of shots. But when specialized ultra-wide-angle and telephoto lenses are used to augment a zoom lens, or when several different fixed-focal-length lenses are used to shoot a scene, the quality of the light may be altered from lens to lens. One such alteration is in the amount of light transmitted by each lens. Even at the same *f* stop, a very complex lens like a zoom lens doesn't pass as much light as a simple, fixed-focal-length lens. This discrepancy means that, unless the cameraman compensates for the difference, a complex lens will consistently underexpose the film. This problem has been remedied in professional lenses, however, by the calibration of the lenses in *transmission,* or

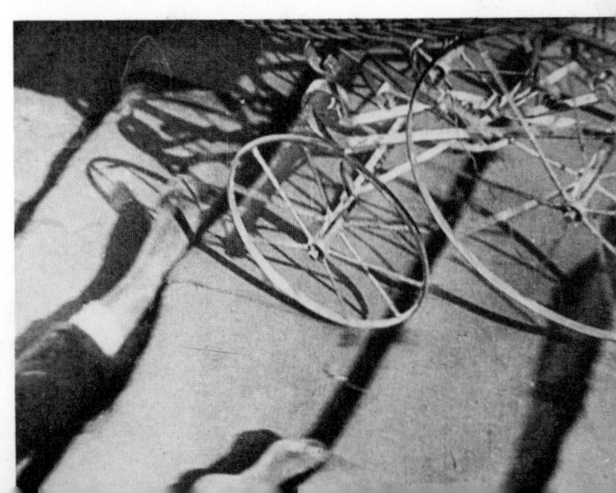

T, stops. These indicate the true light-passing ability of the lens according to an absolute standard, thus standardizing the exposure from lens to lens. But one word of caution. The T stops cannot be used to determine depth of field since that is a physical property of the lens which is based on the *f* stop. As a result, T-stopped lenses also have an *f* scale, which permits depth-of-field calculations.

T stops marked on an aperture ring. The numbers reflected in the mirror, rear, are f stops marked on the opposite side of the same ring.

Lenses also have to be matched for sharpness, a subjective quality of the lens which is composed of its *acutance*—that is, its ability to define very fine details—and its *contrast,* or its ability to render black and white without graying them out. In addition, sharpness is affected by a number of other optical aberrations that have to be minimized to produce a good-quality lens. As a result, when several different lenses are used to shoot a film, they have to be carefully matched for sharpness. There is also a need, when shooting in color, to match the lenses according to their ability to transmit various colors of light. Because of their construction, and the nature of the glass used to form their optical elements, some lenses tend to absorb more blue light than others. This absorption produces a warmer (redder) or cooler (bluer) image, depending upon the lens; so professional cameramen now handpick their lenses for *color match* as well as for sharpness.

Continuity of Lighting

Continuity of image quality also complicates motion-picture lighting. While every shot in a sequence needn't have exactly the same lighting, shots that are related in time and space must usually have a similar overall appearance. This kind of continuity is especially a problem when shooting in daylight. It is difficult to control the quality of the light, yet we easily sense the subtle changes in sunlight that tell us a great deal about time, place, and weather conditions. We use the length of the shadows cast by the sun to tell us the approximate time of day—long, oblique shadows occur early and late, while shorter, more vertical shadows mark the middle of the day. The sharpness of the shadows also tells us if the day is bright, hazy, or overcast; and very soft, almost directionless shadows tell us that the subject is in the shade.

Because each of these aspects of sunlight gives a specific quality to the images, shots that have to be cut together to form continuous action should all be shot in the same kind of light. This is most easily accomplished by confining the shooting to a period from about 9:00 A.M. to 4:00 P.M. on days that are uniformly bright, hazy, or overcast. And all the shots should be made either in or out of the shade unless we see the characters change from one to the other. There is nothing more disorienting than to see the light unaccountably change from hard to soft from one shot to the next.

Problems are also created by those big, drifting clouds that typically provide such a spectacular background for most westerns. These clouds intermittently cover the sun, both softening the light and reducing it by as much as two *f* stops. This change in the light makes continuity nearly impossible since, when the shots are cut together, the dark patches in the medium and long shots will rarely match up with those in the close-ups. As a result, it is best to shoot only when the sun is in the open. This procedure not only simplifies editing but makes it easier to calculate the exposure since the sunlight on the foreground will balance more closely with the bright sky in the background.

Time of Day

The continually changing angle of the sun also plays an important role in determining the order in which the shots in a scene must be filmed. This can best be illustrated by analyzing a sequence from John Ford's *The Grapes of Wrath.* It is a flashback in which one of the hero's neighbors describes how the land company, once it had bought up his foreclosed farm, forcibly incorporated it into a far larger commercial farming operation. The sequence is composed of twelve different shots (shots 1 and 3 are different parts of the same shot), all of which are characterized by the hard, bright crosslight of early morning. Although these shots were probably

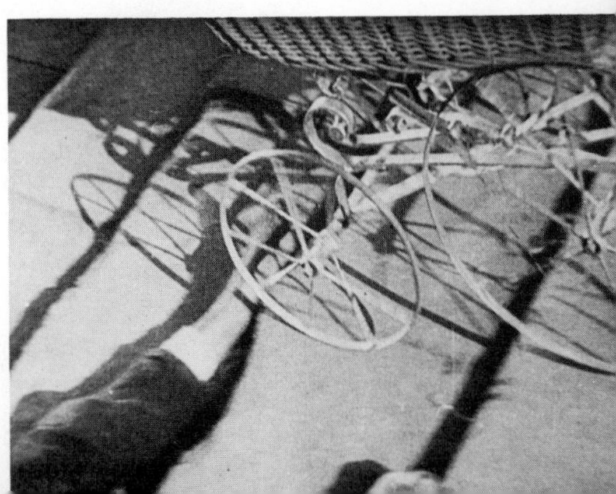

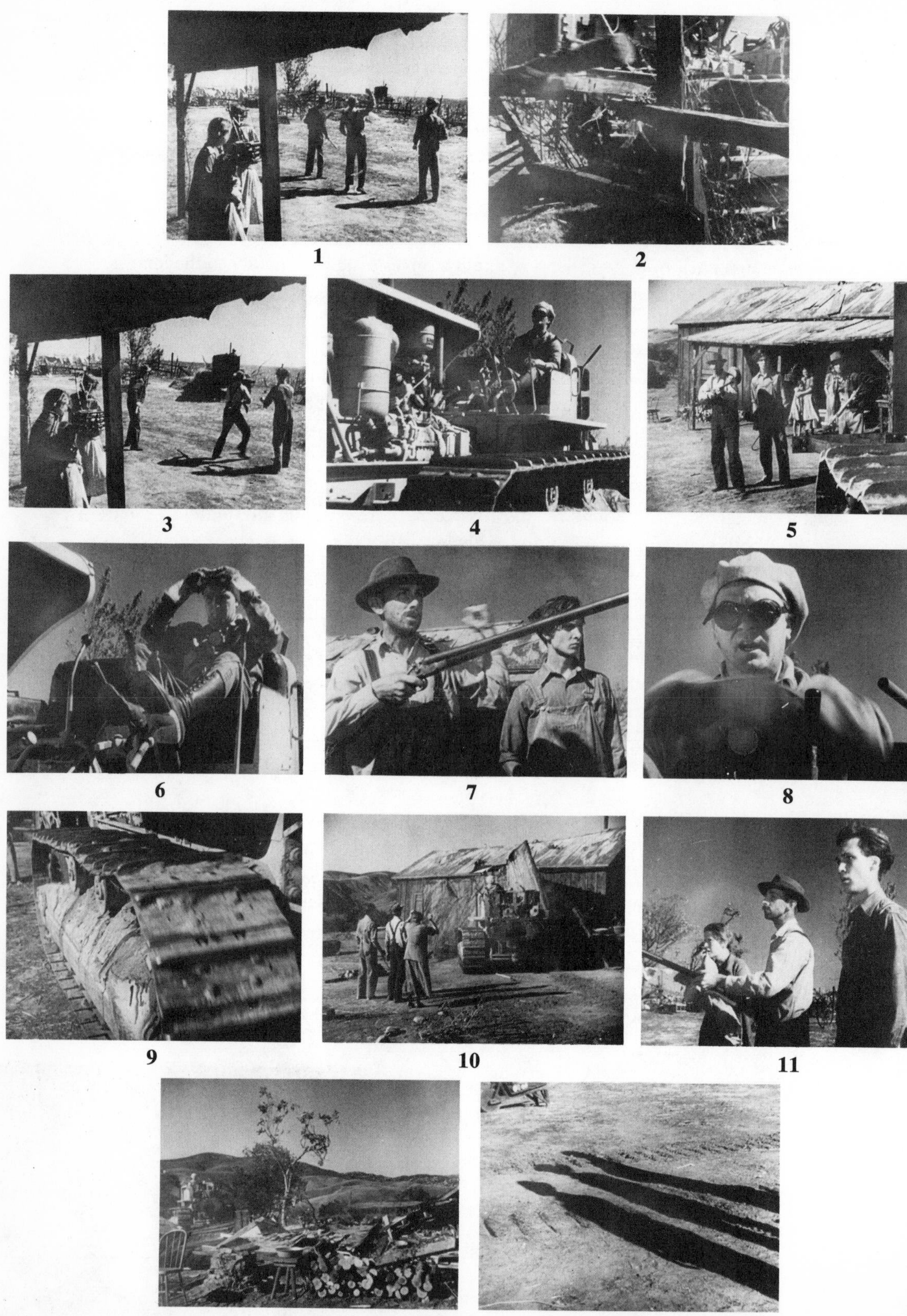

1 2

3 4 5

6 7 8

9 10 11

12 13

made over a period of a day or more, the light changes very little from shot to shot, and the scene seems to unfold on the screen as it would in real life.

This sense of continuity is created by Ford's first filming all those shots in which we see the long shadows of early morning, or in which we clearly see the relationship of the characters to their background. That includes shots 1, 3, 5, and 10, in other words, those long shots in which we see the farmer and his family. However, shots 2, 4, 6, 7, 8, 9, 11, 12, and 13 could have been made late in the day, when the sun is at an equally low angle, or even during the middle of the day. This schedule is possible because in these shots the characters' relationship to the background is indeterminate, so the actors can be *cheated around* until they receive the proper quality of crosslight without the change in time or position becoming apparent.

The Color of Daylight

The changing time of day also affects the color of daylight. Early and late in the day the sunlight must pass through more of the earth's atmosphere, which filters out more of the blue light and makes the sunlight reddish-orange. And at noon just the reverse is true, so the light is most intensely blue. This change in the color of the light changes the film's rendition of the tones in a scene, a change that is especially noticeable in the skin tones. We know how those should look even if we aren't certain how any other objects in the scene should appear. And, no matter how the settings may change, we also expect the characters' skin tones to remain about the same from scene to scene. As a result, the tonal response of both B&W and color film must be kept relatively constant over the course of each day's shooting.

In B&W this tonal correction is made by the use of a series of yellow filters. The process has been succinctly described by Charles Clarke (ASC), a Hollywood cameraman since 1915, in his short, highly personal book on camerawork, *Professional Cinematography*.

> I have found in practice that when we started filming exteriors early in the day, say 8:00 A.M., because there was little blue light, I would use the Aero 1 (light yellow) filter on the camera. About 9:00 A.M., as the blue radiation increased, I would change to the Aero 2 with its more blue absorption. Around 10:00 A.M. the #12 (heavy yellow) would be used, and from 11:00 A.M. to 2:00 P.M. the "G" or #21 (medium to heavy orange) would be used at the time when the maximum blue radiation occurs. After that time the same filters would be used in reverse order until the end of filming in late afternoon, when I would end with the Aero 1.

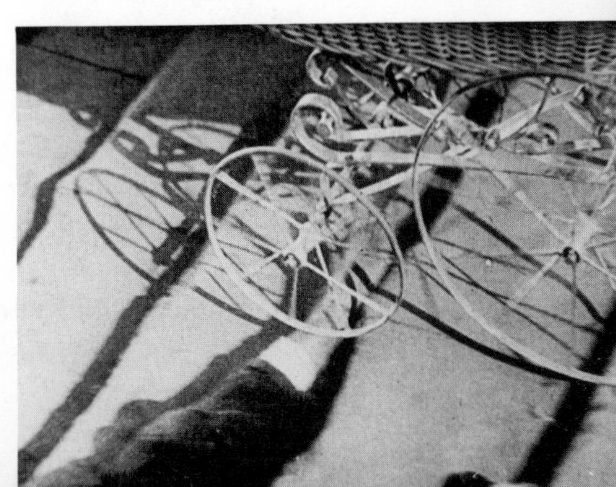

> This was for a sequence of scenes which cut together and where normal correction was wanted.

Clarke further notes that, while he did this to maintain the tonality of the image, the increasing filter factor also nicely balanced with the increasing intensity of the light so that the *f* stop stayed about the same all day long.

The process of correcting for the changing blueness of daylight is quite a bit more complicated in color. Because the response of the film to even subtle changes in the color of light is so much more apparent, correction is accomplished by means of a *color temperature meter* in combination with a series of from 40 to over 120 different, finely graded *color compensating,* or *CC, filters.* A color temperature meter measures the relative balance of the various primary colors in the light and reads out this balance in terms of one or more CC filters. These meters, however, are quite expensive and, until recently, were not terribly accurate. In addition, even the most precise color temperature reading can be thrown off by small differences in the quality of the film stock, and by color shifts that occur during processing and printing.

The result is that color correction is more an art than a science since it largely depends upon the experience of the cameraman with each particular color film. Fortunately, though, there is some room for error when shooting color. Color shifts that occur throughout a scene can be evened out during printing; and, if the film-maker can afford the higher printing costs, some corrections can even be made from shot to shot. But while these printing corrections can compensate for minor color shifts, there are certain extreme situations that are more difficult to correct.

For one thing, the reddish quality of sunlight for an hour after sunrise and an hour before sunset cannot be satisfactorily filtered out during either shooting or printing. So these hours should be avoided when shooting color unless the scene is supposed to occur either early or late in the day. Shooting color in the open shade is also a problem since the opposite effect, a very bluish image, is produced. The reason for this is that there is no direct sunlight in the shade, only the extremely blue light reflected from the sky. While it is possible to remove some of this blueness during printing, a better-balanced result can be obtained if a skylight filter is used on the camera. The same thing also occurs when shooting color on an overcast day. Although the clouds filter out light of all colors equally, the result is still bluish compared to what we normally see. As a result, unless the scene is supposed to seem quite cold in tonality, it should be warmed slightly by the addition of the pinkish color of a skylight filter.

Balancing Artificial Light

Color balance is also an important consideration when shooting color indoors by existing artificial light. This light is usually too red even for indoor color film and must be rebalanced by means of a deep blue filter. But the use of such a filter means an exposure increase of several *f* stops, which may be impossible under the normally low levels of existing light. When that is the case, one alternative is to replace some or all of the bulbs that furnish the existing light with photoflood lamps. These high-intensity lamps are brighter and bluer than ordinary bulbs. They get quite hot, however, and should be kept away from lampshades and other flammable materials. Another alternative is to increase the brightness of ordinary bulbs by plugging the light fixtures into a transformer that, by boosting the power, makes the light both brighter and bluer. These booster transformers are commercially available and quite easy to use, but they can be dangerous to use for extended periods with ordinary fixtures since these fixtures are not designed for the higher power.

Fluorescent lights are a special case because they don't produce the same color of light as ordinary incandescent lamps. Rather, they provide light rich in blue and green and will produce a greenish image unless a filter is used. One way to filter this light is to use a combination of CC filters. But since this *filter pack* varies with the type and make of lamp, this technique is cumbersome if a lot of shooting is done under a number of different fluorescent light sources. Then a universal fluorescent light filter is easier to use. This filter automatically rebalances the light regardless of the type of fluorescent light available. Although not always perfect, this balance is close enough so that any further compensation can be provided during printing.

Color Balance of Studio Lights

The color of the light from studio lighting units, whether used in a studio or on location, poses little problem since the lamps are designed to work at the proper color temperature for indoor film. This color temperature is expressed in *degrees Kelvin* (°K), terminology which is borrowed from the physical sciences. Studio lamps usually operate at 3,200°K, the same rating as all Type B professional indoor color films. There are also 3,400°K lamps designed for use with Type A indoor films, usually amateur color films. This 200°K difference simply means that the 3,400°K lamps are bluer; but since a change in color temperature of as little as 100°K is noticeable, the two types of lamp shouldn't be mixed except for special effects.

Maintaining the proper color temperature of studio lamps used to be a problem because the light would slowly become redder as the lamps got older. But this problem has been all but eliminated by the invention of *tungsten-halogen lamps.* These lamps are more expensive than the older type because their design is quite sophisticated. However, this expense is justified because they remain at the same color temperature for most of their useful life and then drop off sharply so that the change is quite apparent. They are also cheaper to operate than the older lamps

since they produce two or three times as much light from the same amount of power.

Continuity of Studio Lighting

Because of the large variety of lighting effects that can be created in the studio, continuity of lighting from shot to shot also becomes a problem. However, the object with studio lighting, like that with daylight, is not identical lighting for each shot, but only an overall appearance that remains the same when the shots are cut together. The latitude this gives the cameraman in setting lights so as to evoke particular feelings in each shot can be seen in three shots from a brief dialogue sequence in *Citizen Kane*. The scene takes place in the evening. Kane has just met

his mistress-to-be, Susan Alexander, and in the first shot we see the two of them in the parlor of her rooming house, talking. This shot is followed by a closer shot of Kane turning on his charm and then a close-up of Susan responding.

In the first shot the key light is from directly in front and is somewhat flat in its effect. But there is a strong back light that simulates the bright street light entering a window to the right, and this light both rims her head and highlights his profile. There is also a light on the background that is carefully barn-doored so that it falls off in intensity as it goes up the wall, reproducing the effect of a shaded table lamp.

In each of the close-ups, however, this lighting has been changed somewhat. In the shot of Kane, the side of his face that was originally well lit has now been made quite dark. This change was accomplished by using the back light, which is just to the right of his face, as the key, and by eliminating the previous key so that there is no fill. The result is a much higher lighting ratio, with sharp, dense shadows that emphasize the contours of his face, giving it a rugged strength. A pattern which simulates the effect of street light shining through a window has also been added to the background. This pattern lightens the wall so that he won't blend into it, while creating lines that lead our attention to his head so that the light wall doesn't become more important than his face.

Similar changes also take place in the close-up of Susan Alexander. The key light now falls on her face from directly in front of it, softening and smoothing her features so that the contours of her face are gently flattered. But this illumination has been tightly barn-dooored off her hair and one side of her to make it seem as if the light is still coming from the right, the direction of the previous key. The barn doors also keep the light from spilling onto the background. And while a strong back light still rims her head, simulating the effects of street light entering the window behind her, this window isn't the actual source of the back light. Instead, a separate light is used to softly illuminate the window. This low light level not only keeps the window dimmer than the back lighting but leaves the background essentially dark.

There is a logic to this lighting that ties it together without tying the cameraman to an absolutely fixed lighting setup. For one thing, every light has an apparent source. The illumination comes either from the table lamp in front of them, which we infer is there only from the shadowy lighting on the background of the first shot, or from the street light just outside the window, which is not revealed until shot 3. In addition, the relative intensity of these lights on both the foreground and the background remains about the same in every shot, keeping the appearance of the characters' surroundings the same from shot to shot. The result has a subtle logic that reproduces our everyday experience of light and so allows the cameraman to manipulate his lighting without losing a continuity of effect.

Lighting Styles

It is not only within the structure of a scene or even a group of scenes, but within the spell of an entire film that the lighting must be consistent. More often than not it is the look of a film, a compelling tone created through lighting, that bonds the surface of that film to the story it tells until the two are indistinguishable. The conceptualization of a film story in terms of the way it is lit fashions a solid vessel to carry and so shape our final impressions of that film.

Charles Higham, in the excellent introduction to his *Hollywood Cameramen,* captured the excitement that this feeling for light created as it was developed in the 1920's to deepen and extend the already flowering range of emotions that films could touch.

> It was in the mid twenties, at about the time of the development of panchromatic film in 1924, that strongly individual styles began to emerge. John F. Seitz began to use Rembrandt's north light in films made with Rex Ingram, and the results were markedly individual. Victor Milner and Lee Garmes took up the mode, and transformed it into separate and personal styles. In Garmes' lovely *The Garden of Allah,* directed by Ingram, the north light bloomed superbly, isolating hands and portions of faces, casting deep shadows, making the whole film richly alive.

> . . . It was in *Sunrise,* though, that the cameraman really came into his own as a creative artist: Charles Rosher and Karl Struss, both portraitists and both stamped with the same attitude to cinema, together created a work dazzling in its innocent enchantment, creating a whole romantic world as complete as Renoir's.

The beginnings of this use of light can be seen in that revolutionary German film, *The Cabinet of Dr. Caligari,* made at the dawn of the 1920's. Because the studio had a limited amount of power and lights, the film's enterprising producer suggested that lighting effects should be painted on the sets. These effects took shape, in the hands of three gifted artists, as a jagged, sharp-pointed complex of patterns. According to Siegfried Kracauer, whose book *From Caligari to Hitler* explores the psychological pressures underlying the German films of this period,

> . . . the ornamental system in *Caligari* expanded through space, annulling its conventional aspect by means of painted shadows in disharmony with lighting effects, and zigzag delineations designed to efface all rules of perspective. Space now dwindled to a flat plane, now augmented its dimensions to become what one writer called a "stereoscopic universe."

These disorienting patterns of painted light and shade infuse the film with a malaise that ultimately dominates the meaning of the action. They constantly make us aware that the mad, power-hungry doctor and his murderous somnambulist are not simply aberrations loosed upon an otherwise normal world. Rather, they are the legitimate offspring of a setting in which nothing is as it seems to be or as it should be, a setting that mirrors those personal and social dislocations which make us distrust our usual perceptions and so leave us without defenses.

The pressure of circumstances has also played an important role in creating and defining those other styles of light we have long associated with certain types of movies. For instance, because the first motion-picture film stocks were so slow, it was cheaper and easier to make westerns and serial dramas that could be shot outdoors in direct sunlight. This light, as mentioned at the beginning of the chapter, lent an unambiguous, often mythic quality to the action in these films. As a result, this quality of light became so much a part of the style of these films that, even after film-making moved into the studios, the climactic scenes of westerns and other action-adventure films still had to take place outdoors in bright, hard sunlight.

Newsreels and documentaries, too, have had their effect on styles of light. Since spontaneous events don't wait for ideal lighting conditions, these types of films are usually shot with whatever light is available. Thus, the extreme contrast of available light, both indoors and out, and the pronounced grain of high-speed film have become synonymous with the actuality of an event, a guarantee of the reality of what was recorded on film. Later, these documentary qualities were carried over into feature film-making as a touchstone for the veracity of emotions expressed on the screen. This quality of light was most notable in *Breathless* and the other works of the New Wave French directors of the 1960's, though it has been widely used since.

More often, however, the stylization of the lighting to build an emotional context for the action is more delicately constructed. It tends to form a pattern that subtly accumulates throughout the film rather than finding concrete expression in each and every scene. As a result, the audience rarely becomes conscious of the ways in which the film-maker is using light until some contrasting quality in the lighting makes the pattern apparent.

Courtesy: JANUS FILMS, INC.

In *The Seventh Seal,* for instance, Bergman alternates between high- and low-key lighting. This alternation, while it isolates those who are doomed by the plague from those who will be saved, also creates a dark setting of doubt and fear within which the simple, trusting faith of an itinerant juggler and his family can become a bright oasis in the knight's search for the meaning of life. But it is only through the slow repetition of these changes in the quality of the light that we eventually become aware of the lighting scheme as anything more than a background to the action.

This same alternating pattern can be seen in a still simpler form in the changes in the quality of light used to illuminate the heroine in Robert Bresson's *The Trial of Joan of Arc.*

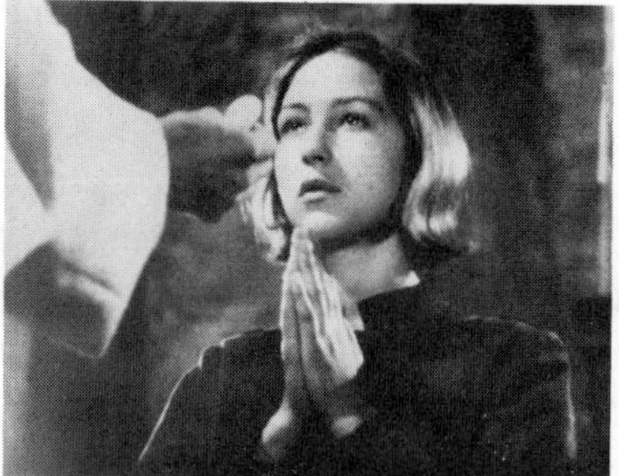

Throughout the film, whenever Joan is on trial she is pinned in sunlight whose harsh brilliance rigidly molds her confession of faith to the hard contours of her public ordeal. Yet, when she returns to the dimly lit privacy of her dungeon cell, the intensely personal shape of her simple faith is allowed to emerge in the gentle modeling of a softly diffused, almost iridescent infiltration of daylight.

Probably the most subtle evolution of the light in a film occurs in the slowly changing use of light and shadow on the face of each character. Throughout *The Blue Angel,* Sternberg does little to change the nature of the light on the settings. But in the first half of the film he fully illuminates the face of the professor so that

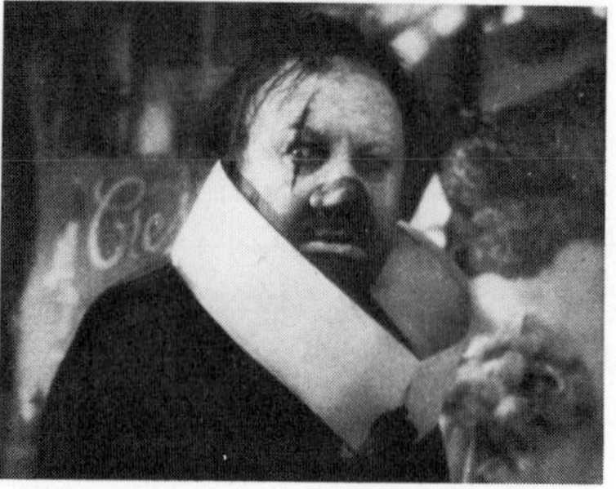

the intensity of the light clearly sets him off from the tawdry, worn walls of the nightclub. By the second half, however, his shadowy features begin to merge into the surrounding dimness. This change captures the dissolution of his imposing self-assurance under the erosive domination of Lola-Lola and makes his unwilling role as stooge and clown only the final stage of his slowly unfolding destruction.

These are just a few of the ways that the light which pervades a film can be molded to shape the film's meanings. Since light is infinitely varied and flexible, it can be given as many forms as there are film-makers sensitive to its subtly changing values. But regardless of how light is used, its qualities become one of the dominant themes in a motion picture. Not only does light bear the image that is impressed upon the film, it also determines how we will perceive that image. From moment to moment throughout the film its every nuance and shading convey the film-maker's meanings until this most evanescent part of the film-maker's craft becomes an indelible impression in the mind of each viewer.

Thus far we have looked at all the ways in which a film-maker creates images, first in their conception, then by using the camera, and finally by exploiting light and film. These powerful creative tools permit a full range of meanings and emotions to be captured and then conveyed to an audience. At one time they were all that the film-maker had to work with. Yet with little more than carefully edited images, the silent film reached wondrous peaks of expression, and many who grew up with them still lament their passing. Editing remains at the heart of film-making, even after movies have achieved a richness in their use of sound, while the advent of sound has opened up yet another creative world to the film-maker. These aspects of film-making—editing and sound—will be covered in the next section. They complete that complex process which first begins when a film-maker starts to bend reality to his purposes.

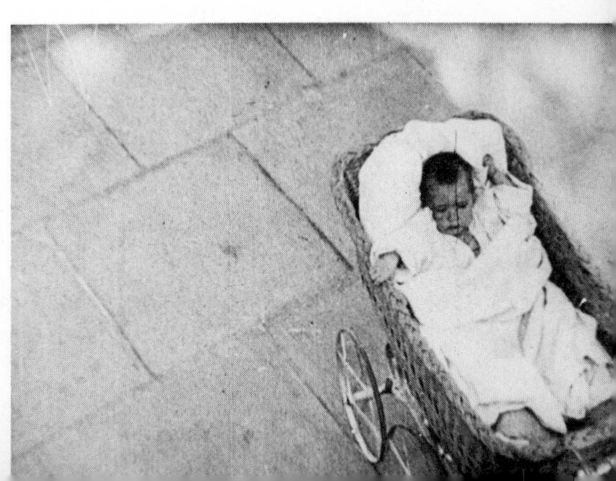

INTO FILM
SECTION II

Technique as Vision

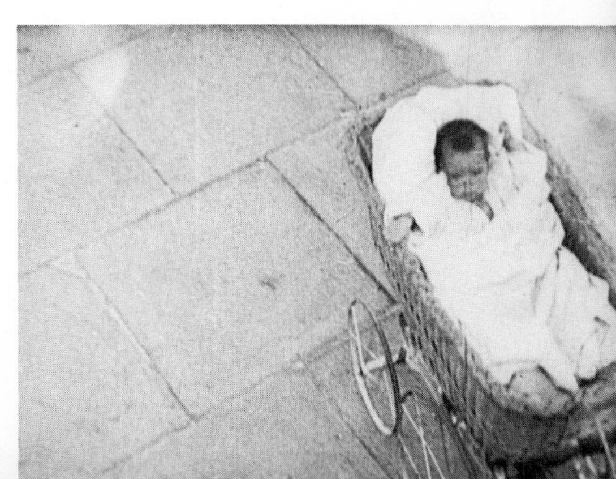

Contents

Section II

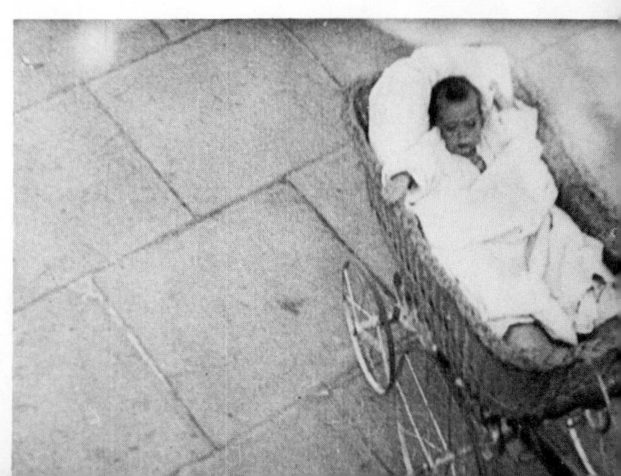

Chapter 6

Into Sound

Sound is another entire world in which the film-maker can express himself to the limits of his imagination. Like the limitless worlds of space and time in motion pictures, sound in films provides a unique, evocative, and necessary way to convey ideas. In building a sound track the film-maker can call upon all the traditional arts which appeal to our ears—that is, all of music and language—and adapt their resources to the pictures on the screen. He can also select from among all the naturally occurring noises randomly found in our surroundings; and if he still isn't satisfied, he can create electronically sounds that wouldn't otherwise exist.

But despite these voluminous resources, when we think of sound we usually think of the nonstop talk or overblown theme music which characterizes so much film-making. The fact is, talk is truly cheap compared to carefully staged action, and music can pass for emotion when emotions are not deeply stirred by the drama on the screen. Sound is plentiful and easy to obtain, but there is nothing so elusive

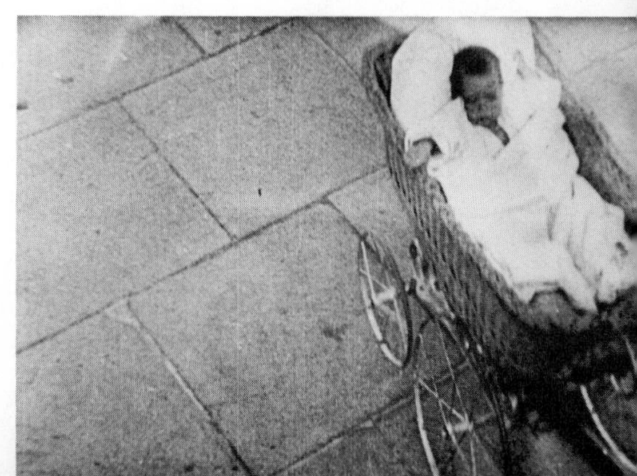

as the construction of a really well-made sound track. Like a good servant, a good track is working best when we notice it the least.

The sound track assumes this subordinate role because, in motion pictures, the sound takes on its full meaning only as it interacts with the images on the screen. We can and do have silent pictures but there is no such thing in motion pictures as pictureless sound. Although the track usually alternates with the pictures in carrying important information, most of the time the images dominate our attention. We become so swept up in the minute and freely changing detail of the pictures that we normally have little time during a film to concentrate on what we hear. Try just listening to a film without shutting your eyes. It takes the greatest possible effort. And when picture and track don't make sense together, we make them make sense by carefully following the action and forcing as many connections as possible between the pictures and the sound. In effect, we have a tendency to synchronize as best we can what we hear with what we see.

But even though films make their strongest appeal to the eye, their effect is ultimately the result of the eye and the ear working together. This interaction is particularly fascinating because the overall effect of sound and picture isn't necessarily inherent in either. In our daily experience we are enveloped by a confusion of images and sounds from which we must make a selection, if for no other reason than to preserve our sanity. But in motion pictures the choices are made for us by the film-maker. By narrowing and arranging our perceptions he frees us to build new connections between sound and picture far beyond what might be anticipated from either alone. The result is amazingly compelling, the product of our full participation with both senses.

Because the creation of a sound track is almost an art in itself, it is crucial to an understanding of film to recapture what the film-maker goes through in building a track. But it is clearly impossible to call up the complex interplay between sound and picture—their subtle drama—with nothing more than the isolated still pictures and descriptive phrases that serve as our examples. Nonetheless, there are sequences in almost every film that capture within a very few moments the essence of some technique for creating meaning with sound. Just as in the filming and editing of pictures, it is these techniques which determine the flexibility with which sound can be used and the insights which it can build. With close analysis of these sequences at least the techniques, if not the deeply moving effects, can be made available for inspection.

A particularly concise and effective example of how sound and picture work together occurs toward the beginning of the British documentary *Night Mail,* directed by Harry Watt and Basil Wright, with sound direction by Alberto Cavalcanti. The film is ostensibly about moving the mail from London to the north of England by train. But the film-makers wish to invest this rather prosaic process with the adventure of a journey. By focusing on the passage of the train itself they permit us to see beyond the slatted walls and pigeonholes of the mail cars and builds a rhythm and excitement rarely sensed by the mail handlers who inhabit the aisles of these cars.

After an introductory sequence in which the mail is loaded and we see the train pull slowly out of the station, we come to the short section analyzed below.

XCU = Extreme close-up	**MS = Medium shot**	**SFX = Sound effects**
CU = Close-up	**MLS = Medium long shot**	**NAR = Narrator**
MCU = Medium close-up	**LS = Long shot**	**MUS = Music**
	XLS = Extreme long shot	

	PICTURE	SOUND
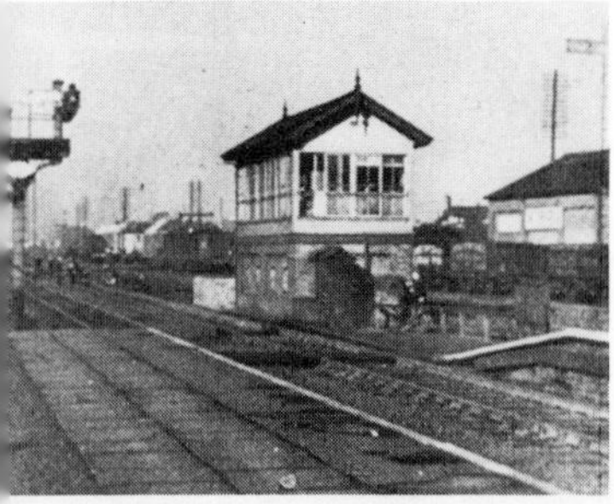	**1.** MLS, switching tower (2½ sec.).	SFX: Silence until just before cut, when we hear distant telegraph bell.
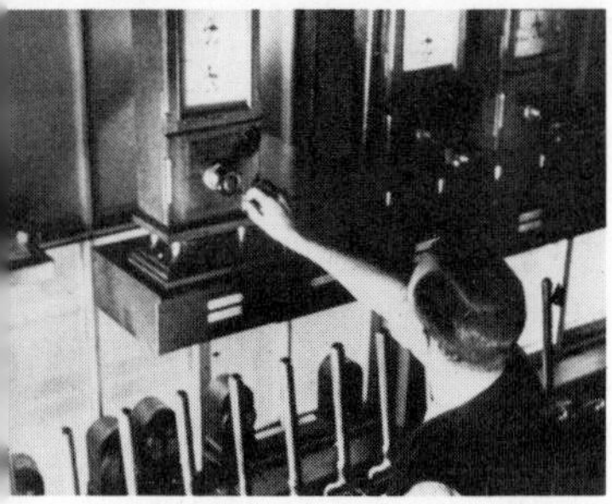	**2.** MS, switching handles in tower. Switchman enters R-L and reaches for key on telegraph (10¼ sec.).	SFX: Ringing of telegraph bell, fades under . . . NAR: Section B, this is Section C. SFX: Ringing, continues under . . . NAR: Can you do special? SFX: Clack of telegraph key as switchman responds, fades under . . .
	DISSOLVE	NAR: We'll take the special.
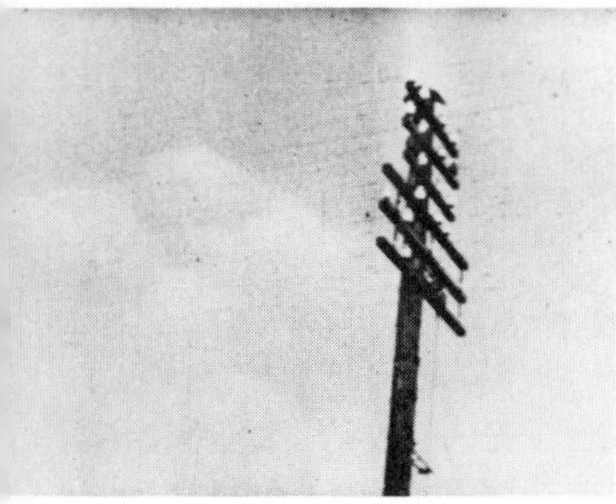	**3.** MLS, trucking R-L past telegraph poles and lines (2 sec.). *DISSOLVE*	SFX: One last clack over dissolve, then silence until ringing starts just before next dissolve.

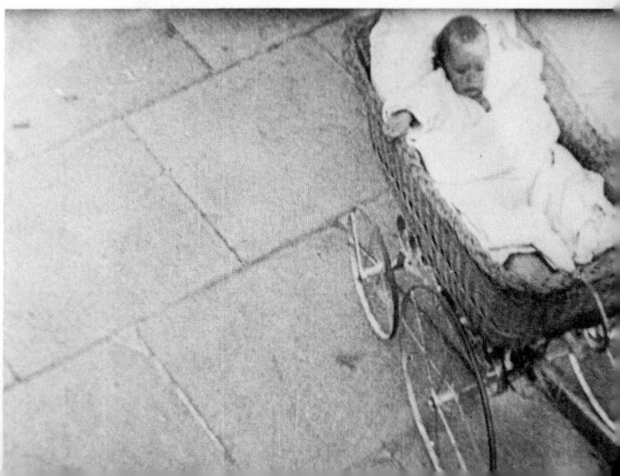

PICTURE | SOUND

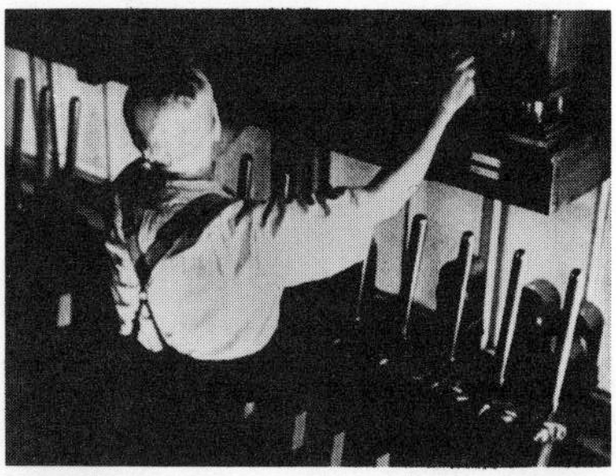

4. MS, interior of different switching tower. Switchman standing at telegraph (7¼ sec.).

SFX: Ringing of teleg bell, fades under . . .
NAR: Can you take p special?
SFX: Clack of telegraph as switchman responds, f under . . .
NAR: Line clear.

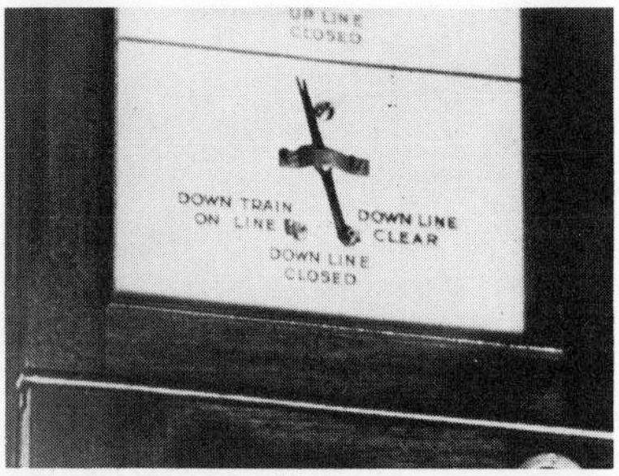

5. CU, switch indicator dial. It flicks over to "Down Line Clear" position (1¼ sec.).

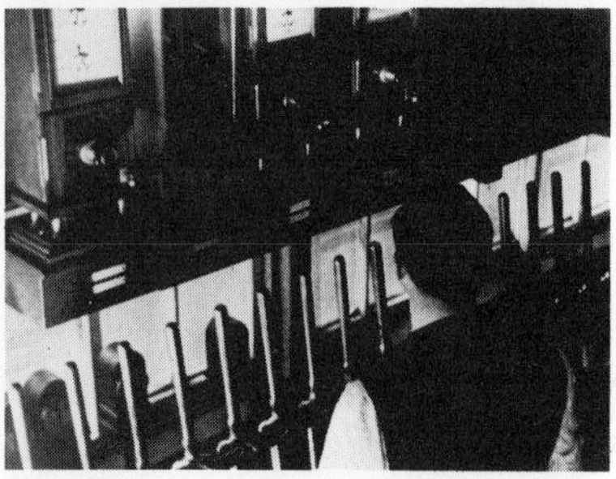

6. MS, same as shot 2. Switchman watching switch indicator (1¼ sec.).

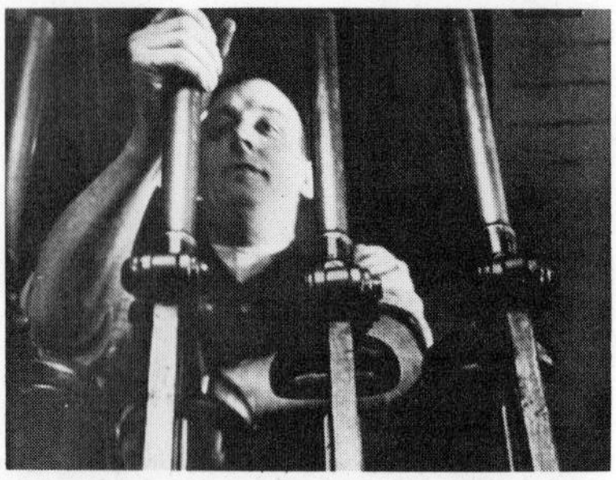

7. MCU, through switch handles. Switchman pulls one back and grabs second (4 sec.).

SFX: Clank-clang of ha being pulled.

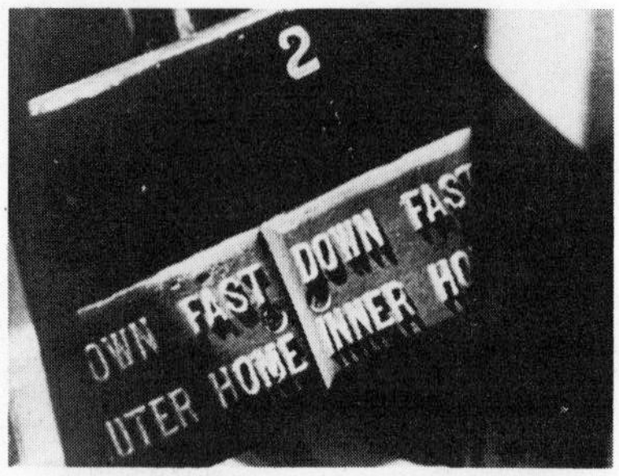

8. XCU, switch identification plate. Switch handle passes L-R through foreground (2 sec.).

SFX: Clank-clang of sec handle being pulled.

	PICTURE	SOUND
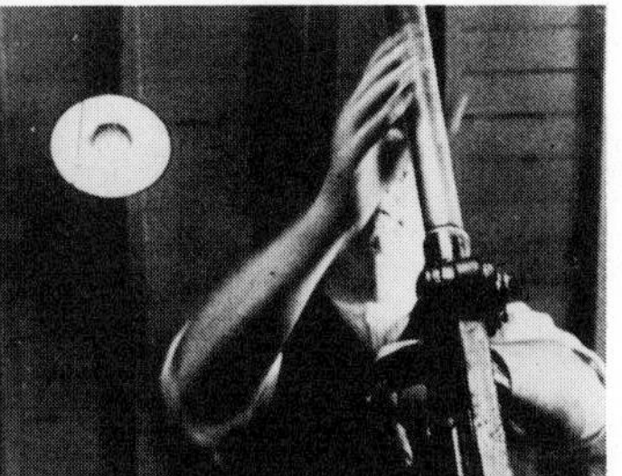	**9.** MCU, same as shot 7. Switchman grabs third handle and starts to pull (1¼ sec.).	SFX: First part of handle being pulled, clank . . .
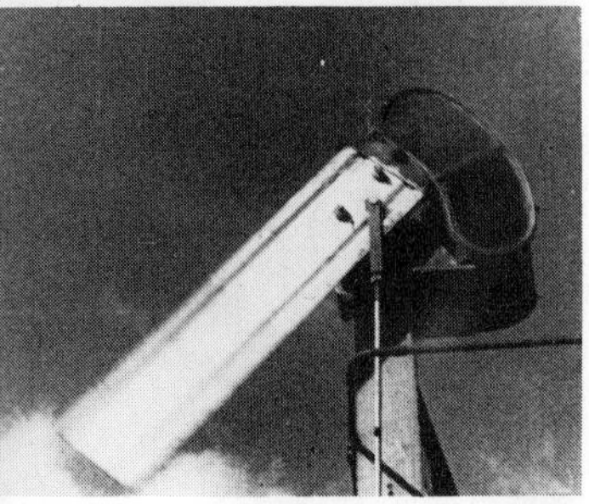	**10.** MCU, semaphore arm drops (2 sec.).	SFX: . . . bang, as arm drops.
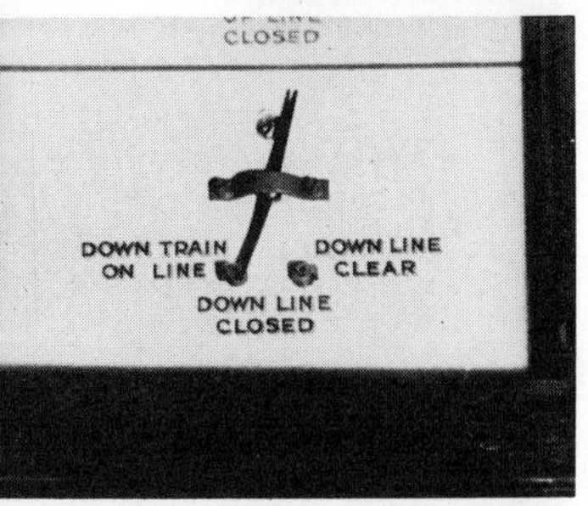	**11.** CU, same as shot 5. Indicator flicks back to "Down Train on Line" position (2½ sec.).	SFX: Silence until just before end, then roar of approaching train.
	**12.** LS, train passing behind switching tower, seen past silhouette of switchman. He waits, then operates telegraph key and starts to throw switch handle (9½ sec.).	SFX: Roar of passing train.

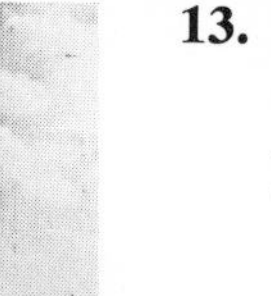

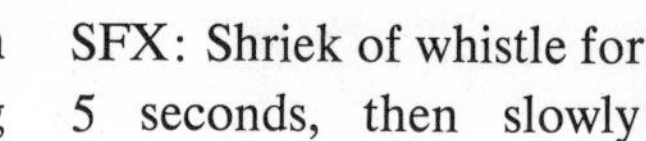

	PICTURE	SOUND
	13. LS, train rushing away from camera through switching yards (10½ sec.).	SFX: Shriek of whistle for 5 seconds, then slowly minishing roar of passing c

In less than a minute the film-makers suggest a train picking up speed without showing us the train. By the time we see the train in the final two shots of this sequence it is well underway, so its acceleration is totally a product of the rhythm of the editing. This rhythm is first established by means of a number of longish shots connected by dissolves (shots 2, 3, and 4) in which we are introduced to the routing arrangements. But once these arrangements are complete, the actual switching is accomplished with a series of close, quick shots of the apparatus in operation (shots 5 through 11), culminating in the rush of the train past the tower and out of the yards.

This tempo, however, would lose much of its effectiveness without the sound, because it is the sound that punctuates the editing. The first four shots are made to seem slower by being tied together into one long event by an almost continuous sound track; and the next seven shots are made to seem all the quicker through the further interruption of these shots by clean-cut, clearly isolated sound effects. It is through the sound that we also relate this changing tempo to the progress of the train. We know the train is coming because of constant references to it in the narration, and we are made aware that we are waiting for it to arrive by the silence over shots 5 and 6.

Our expectations are pulled taut here by the subtle interplay between the rhythms of sound and picture. While the pace of the cutting is beginning to accelerate, the sound is hanging back slightly, momentarily creating tension through conflict in tempo. This conflict is quickly resolved in the noisy haste of the switching operation, but the contrasting silence has simultaneously served to make this activity more intense and to rivet our attention on the telegraph dial, and through it on the progress of the train.

Sound is being used by Cavalcanti to do more than build pace and tension though. By using a narration rather than the actual voices of the switchmen to translate the clacking and ringing of the telegraph, he creates the impression of a disembodied presence shepherding the train through the yards. This sense of omniscient care, an impression reinforced by later sequences in the film, transforms the daily run of the mail train into an event. As the train's passage becomes a precisely choreographed sequence of widely separated activities, we come to feel that the most pressing duty of the railroad is to get this train where it belongs and keep it on time.

The careful and imaginative blend of sound track and picture in this sequence

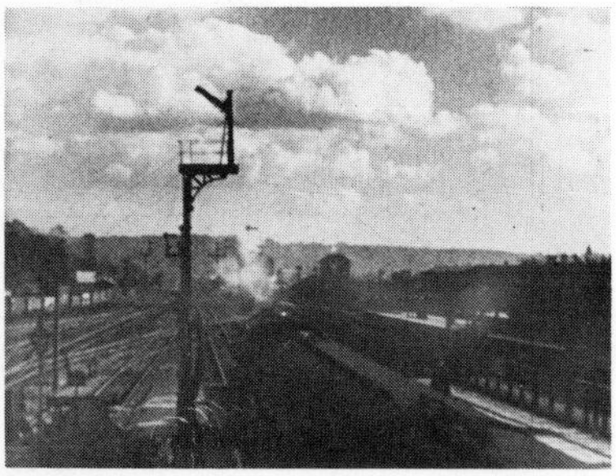

transforms each object and sound, giving them new meanings. Yet the techniques used to achieve these sophisticated results are among the simplest available to the film-maker. Even though the sounds closely match the pictures, there was no need to record them as the action was filmed. It would not, in fact, have been desirable to do so. A railroad yard is a busy place and all the extraneous noise would have cluttered up the sound track. Each important sound had to be isolated, and so the film was shot without sound and the sound effects were recorded later, in a quieter location. In other words, this is a synchronous sound sequence that was not filmed synchronously.

We commonly think of synchronous sound as the recording of sounds and actions simultaneously. But this isn't so. All the sounds contained in this example are synchronous. To be fully effective, each particular sound effect and picture had to match precisely, no matter whether the sound was prominent or simply in the background. And the narration had to fit exactly within the shots to which it made reference, not only to keep words and pictures together, but also to keep the speech rhythms from interfering with the very important rhythms of the cutting. And had there been any music or dialogue, the same considerations would have been applied to them as well.

To put it simply, all sounds in motion pictures are synchronous. They are intended to be heard as a specific frame appears on the screen. Because twenty-four frames appear on the screen every second, it is possible for the film-maker to control in great detail everything we see and hear from moment to moment throughout the film. Without this precise control neither picture nor sound can be fully coherent; with it, the film-maker can orchestrate the use of our senses to build meanings not fully expressed by sound or picture alone. It is this question of synchronization—how to keep the sound track in place opposite the picture, how to create sounds that match the pictures, and how to make sound and picture work together—that we should like to explore in the rest of this section on sound for films.

Sound Synchronization

Because sound and picture have to work together so closely, recording sounds for films is different from other kinds of sound recording. The film-maker must not only find sounds that match the pictures, but as we have seen, must also keep sound and picture in synchronization. Of the two problems, maintaining synchronization is actually the more difficult. But it is obviously not insurmount-

able. There are, in fact, a wide variety of solutions of gradually increasing complexity from which to choose. They range from the precise and sophisticated methods used to record lip-synchronous dialogue to such simple, semisynchronous techniques as playing a record while the film is projected.

As the film-maker progresses from the simplest to the most complex of these sound-recording techniques, he often relives the history of the medium. For instance, Edison played a Gramophone with some of his peep-show movies as far back as 1895. Similarly, the beginning film-maker could first experiment with sound by playing a record while showing his film. Next, he might try projecting the film with simple narration, music, or sound effects recorded directly on it. This would present him roughly the same problems as those encountered in the earliest days of sound films. And finally, the film-maker would become involved in the intricacies of recording and editing synchronously recorded sound. Here his efforts would parallel the evolution of present-day film sound recording.

Each step of the way the film-maker encounters many of the same problems faced by the early directors of sound films. But he does not have to invent his technology every time he is ready to take the next step. All the machines involved in the development of sound films, though modernized, are still in use in some form. Each can solve the same problems now as it did when it was invented. All the film-maker has to do is call upon the right machine.

In order to help you become aware of these problems and make the proper choices, we will sketch in over the next several pages the history of sound film-making. Each new development in sound for motion pictures seems more complicated than the last, but if we look at these developments historically, we can concentrate on a few pivotal techniques and understand why they are crucial. This is also the most interesting way to illustrate the connection between a variety of sound-recording techniques and the principles which are their basis. The principles themselves are relatively simple. Once they are understood, it is possible to improvise solutions to the numerous problems which inevitably arise in such a technological medium as film.

Early Sound Systems

Even in silent films sound was a problem because the so-called silent pictures were never really silent. As was the case with most important pictures, an elaborate orchestral score accompanied Griffith's *The Birth of a Nation* to major theaters throughout the country. And even the smallest theaters usually had a pianist who could improvise music and sound effects to suit whatever film happened to be showing. Many of the early experiments in film sound were aimed at a recording method that could substitute for this sometimes haphazard accompaniment. The director would then have complete control over the sound that accompanied his picture.

Just how badly this musical accompaniment could sometimes be butchered by poorly trained, underpaid musicians is indicated by F. H. Richardson in the 1910 edition of his *Motion Picture Handbook*.

> The music should follow the picture and the . . . musician absolutely must not be allowed to speak to anyone during the time a picture is running. How often

> have we seen a young lady piano player drumming out the music of a topical ragtime song, while at the same time industriously masticating a wad of gum and talking to her "gentleman friend" seated in the front row. The aforesaid topical song serves for the deathbed scene or the picnic party. She does not know what is on the screen, neither does she care.

By the mid-1920's a number of film sound systems were available, but the most ambitious use to which any of them was put was background music for the film *Don Juan,* produced in 1926. As Edward Kellogg, one of the inventors of this new medium, recalls:

> Many, even the most enthusiastic advocates of the sound-picture development, were not convinced that the chief function of the synchronized sound would be to give speech to the actors in plays. The art of telling stories with pantomime only (with the help of occasional titles) had been so highly developed, that giving the actors voices seemed hardly necessary, although readily possible.

It took *The Jazz Singer,* released the following year, to convince the major studios that they should make the expensive conversion to sound film production. This was the turning point. *The Jazz Singer* conclusively demonstrated the popularity of sound, especially dialogue. But the resulting scramble to produce feature-length sound films created a deluge of talk in a medium which until that time had shunned voices. Later films were billed as "All Singing! All Dancing! All Talking!" With a few brilliant exceptions, the film-makers as well as their public quickly forgot that meaning could be conveyed by other than words. Sound became synonymous with talking, and sound films were called *talkies.*

This preponderance of words was at least partially caused by the inflexible technical requirements of the early sound-recording systems. The sound for *The Jazz Singer,* for instance, was supplied by the Vitaphone system. This consisted of nothing more than a phonograph synchronized with the projector and one long-playing record for each ten-minute reel of film. Because this disc recording could not be edited after the film was shot, each sound take had to last the full ten minutes and every sound needed during that time had to be recorded as the action was filmed. As a result, films using Vitaphone sound were limited to materials in which the sound was relatively simple so the action could be filmed in large chunks. Theater pieces of all sorts were ideally suited to these requirements, and so a great many Vitaphone productions were remakes of plays, musical revues, and vaudeville sketches.

There were also in existence at this time several equally inflexible sound

systems in which the recording was made photographically, directly on the film. These systems were called *optical sound*. In the early years sound films were produced using both disc and optical sound equipment. If the theaters were to show all the new sound films which came pouring out of the studios, they had to have both. But in 1930 the movie industry dropped the Vitaphone system in order to standardize on optical sound because improvements in optical sound-recording equipment and techniques had made sound-on-film simpler and more flexible than discs.

Optical Sound-on-Film

This is the way optical sound works. A narrow slit of light is set to vibrating by the sounds picked up with a microphone. As the film moves through this vibrating light beam, a picture of the sound is photographically traced along one edge of the film, between the pictures and the sprocket holes. This sound track is then developed along with the pictures. For playback the track must travel through

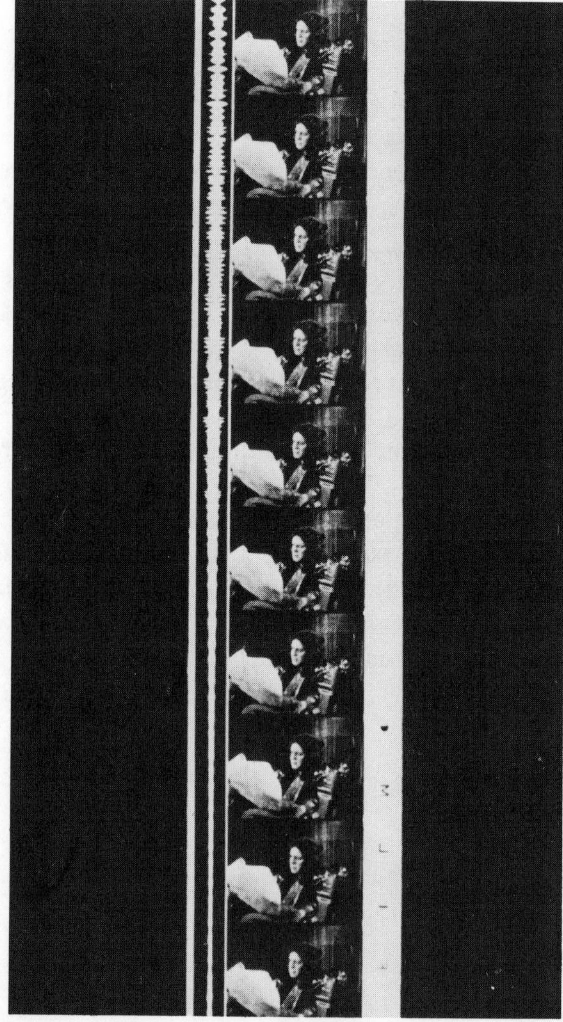

Optical sound track traced along the left edge of the film.

another steady beam of light. As this light passes through the film the variations from light to dark in the sound track set the light beam to vibrating, and these vibrations are then converted electronically back into the original sound.

The first commercially useful optical sound-recording system was the Movietone system. It was used to make newsreels, a kind of film-making which benefits from mobility. And Movietone sound cameras had a relatively compact mobility because sound and picture were exposed in the same mechanism, the camera. But mobility was not of such overriding concern when the studios began producing feature-length sound films. Under studio conditions it quickly became apparent that having the original recording of sound and picture locked onto the same strip of film was a serious drawback.

In fact, all the problems with single-system sound arose because sound- and picture-recording are different in their very nature. The movement we see projected on a screen is formed of discrete segments of time, each segment frozen onto a frame of motion-picture film. The film stands still in the camera aperture while being exposed; and then, while the shutter is closed, it is pulled down one frame for the next exposure. This stop-and-start motion, twenty-four times a second, creates an intermittent movement of the film through the camera.

But sound cannot be broken down into discrete frames. It must be recorded on the film at a constant rate of speed so as to avoid variations in pitch. A variation in pitch is what happens when you speed up or slow down a phonograph record while it is being played. When such variations are regular and very rapid, they are called *flutter*. When they are further apart they are called *wow*. They sound very much like the names given them and are easily detected by the ear.

The first requirement of optical sound-on-film, then, was that the film be driven through the camera at a constant speed so that variations in the pitch of the sound track would be avoided. This could be done only if the erratic hand crank of the silent camera was replaced by an electric motor. Although such motors had long been available, the crank was preferred by silent cameramen. Cranking had, in fact, become part of the art of the silent film. During active or comic scenes the cameraman could turn the crank more slowly, or *undercrank,* causing the action to speed up when the film was projected at the standard, and therefore relatively faster, projection speed. Conversely, the cameraman could *overcrank* when slow-motion effects were needed. For instance, both of these effects are used within the same example from *An Italian Straw Hat* (Section 1, Chapter Two). But such variations could not be tolerated with sound-on-film. Because sound and picture were locked onto the same strip of film, any change in the speed at which the pic-

ture was recorded would result in wild variations in the pitch of the sound track. Only an electric motor could assure the same pitch between and within shots.

Another limitation was that the sound track had to receive a standardized development in the processing laboratory. But since the sound was on the same strip of film as the picture, this requirement also affected the cameraman. When making a silent film he had been able to use under- and overexposure to create a variety of tonal effects in the picture because these variations could be compensated for in processing. However, if the picture were over- or underdeveloped the sound track would be just as over- or underdeveloped, and sound-on-film required a fixed development of the exposed strip of film for optimum sound quality. This lack of flexibility took control of tonality out of the processing laboratory and made it totally a matter of careful exposure and lighting.

The requirement that created the greatest difficulty, though, arose because the picture and its associated sound had to be simultaneously recorded on the same strip of film and therefore couldn't be exposed onto the film next to each other. If the sound-recording head had been mounted next to the aperture, the stop-and-start motion necessary to expose the picture would have also caused the film to jerk past the recording light. This would have made the sound quite incomprehensible. Instead, the sound- and picture-recording mechanisms were mounted a short distance apart and the intermittent movement of the film smoothed out in the space between them. This separation was eventually standardized at twenty frames, with the sound head advanced beyond the aperture.

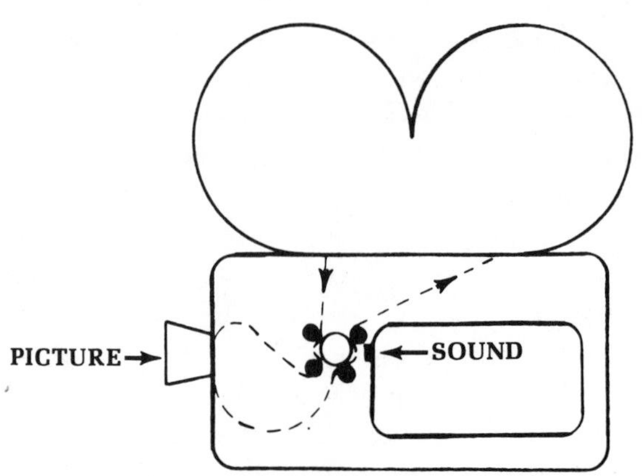

Single-system camera. The picture is exposed onto the film, L, at the same time that the sound is recorded to the right.

This separation of sound and picture made editing extremely difficult. The film editor couldn't cut into the picture and its sound in the same place. If he cut on the correct frame at the beginning of a shot, he cut off almost the first full second of sound; and at the end of the shot he was always left with almost a second of extra sound. If the shooting of the film could be laid out so that there was silence at the beginning and the end of each shot, smooth editing was possible. The editor could then leave a one-second pause on either side of each cut. But two seconds is a long pause even for normal conversation and definitely ruins the pace of filmed dialogue.

Double-System Sound

The answer to these problems was found in the principle behind the abandoned Vitaphone system. By using a phonograph to supply the sound, this system had shown that sound and picture, although separate, could be kept in close synchronization. The trick, then, with optical sound was to separate the recording of sound and picture onto two different strips of film at the time the movie was shot. Of course, each strip of film would have to run through its own separate machine, either camera or sound recorder, at the exact same speed. Unless this was so, when picture and sound were ready for editing the two strips of film would not match up, sprocket hole for sprocket hole, in exact synchronization.

The most efficient means found for keeping the machines running together was a special type of electric motor called, not so surprisingly, a *synchronous motor*. Electric clocks use this kind of motor because other types of motors do not always run at a constant speed and therefore cannot keep the proper time. The reason the synchronous motor always runs at the same speed is because it is sensitive to a characteristic of the electrical current called *alternation*. The current in a standard electrical outlet rises and falls in regular, carefully regulated peaks sixty times a second. Synchronous motors rotate in step with these controlled alternations of the current, so it is these alternations that keep electric clocks all running at the same speed. They are synchronized by the power companies.

It was this same characteristic that made possible the separate recording of optical sound and picture. All that was needed was to equip each camera and recorder with a synchronous motor. There need be no connection between the machines other than the power line. As with clocks, the electrical power itself would keep the motors running at the same speed.

Using separate strips of film for recording sound and picture had distinct advantages for everyone concerned. Because the picture now received separate processing from the sound track, the cameraman could again vary the exposure and the lighting with wide latitude. And since sound and picture were locked together only after editing was completed, he could go back to shooting all but lip-synchronous dialogue with a silent camera. Appropriate sounds could be added to this silent footage later, on the editing bench.

For the cameraman this separation of sound and picture also meant a return of much of his previous freedom to shoot in almost any manner he pleased. He could again move about without the encumbrance of a sound-recording crew and their equipment, and he could use any camera he needed without having to worry

about synchronization. As long as there was sufficient light, he was free to shoot wherever the director wanted him to. Sound ceased to be of primary concern.

As for the editor, he no longer had to worry about that twenty-frame displacement between sound and picture. Since each of the two was now on a completely independent strip of film, he could line up picture and associated sound opposite one another and cut them straight across. Or he could remove the original sound and replace it with some other sound, leave the sound and change the picture, add sound to silent footage, or produce any combination of sound and picture with as great freedom as he had had cutting pictures alone in the silent area.

Actually, sound-on-film was such a difficult system to use that it was part of feature-film production for only a very few years. The two-machine system, which for obvious reasons became known as double-system sound, was adopted as the standard studio technique as quickly as it was perfected. But the older sound-on-film, or single-system sound, is still widely used for making 16mm television news film, and there are even 8mm single-system cameras available. Also, sound-on-film is still the standard means for projecting sound films. Throughout the production of the film, sound and picture are separated as double-system sound; but once production is completed, sound and picture are printed onto a single strip of film. That way only one machine, the sound projector, is needed to show the finished sound film.

Basic Sound Synchronization

The principles behind double- and single-system sound still govern today's sound film recording and reproduction techniques. But principles are useless until they are embodied in machines. Without the expensive, specially designed cameras and recorders necessary to keep sound and picture in synchronization, the film-maker is left in almost the same position as Edison in 1895. To start out in sound film production he must improvise around the machinery available.

The easiest, most available alternative is to shoot silent footage and add a sound track later. At its simplest, this can be done as Edison did it, by showing the film on an ordinary projector while playing the sound on a phonograph or a tape recorder. Unfortunately, only a loosely synchronous sound track can be produced this way because ordinary movie projectors, record players, and tape recorders are not designed to start simultaneously or keep running at exactly the same speed. With a certain amount of practice it is possible to learn how to start these machines reasonably close together, but their speed is impossible to control because it is affected by too many variables.

How significant this variation in speed can become depends upon the quality of the machines used, their state of repair, and the length of the film. Take as an example an error of no more than 1 percent over thirty minutes of film. In this case the sound will gradually begin either to lead or to lag behind the picture until the final difference between picture and sound is eighteen seconds. Compare this to the discomfort you feel watching a movie in which there is only a fraction of a second between seeing lips move and hearing the sound. You will then realize the limitations in matching sound and picture closely by means of loose synchronization.

This acute awareness of lack of synchronization can be overcome in a loosely synchronized film only if it is taken into account when the film is scripted. For instance, accurately synchronizing people's voices with the movements of their lips is out of the question. But there are effective ways to compensate for this. If we see only the back of the speaker's head while we are watching the face of the person being spoken to, the semblance of lip-synchronous recording can be created. For the same reason, naturally occurring sounds cannot be closely matched to the specific actions causing them. The sound of a gun, for example, can be used on the sound track only while we are watching something to which this sound is indirectly related. If the audience hear a gun fired while watching the police rush to the rescue and then see the bandit holding a smoking revolver, they will make the necessary inference as to where the shot came from.

Although such techniques may seem like stopgap measures, they are actually quite efficient means for making sound and picture work together. In the dialogue example just mentioned we simultaneously hear the words and see their effect, whereas in the example using sound effects, the plot develops along two different lines at the same time. Because such economy of expression is the mark of imaginative film direction, we often find that professional film-makers shoot and edit film in this manner even when they are technically free to do otherwise.

For instance, early in the John Ford western *My Darling Clementine,* Ford wishes to demonstrate the courage of the hero, Wyatt Earp (played by Henry Fonda), without making him seem brutal. Earp, while getting a shave, is almost hit by the wild shot of a drunken Indian. When no one will go into the saloon to subdue the drunk, Earp volunteers, initiating the following sequence.

	PICTURE	SOUND
	**1.** MS, Earp, with shaving cream on face, talking to older woman and man.	SFX: Several shots and screams of fright. WOMAN: Young man, you be careful!

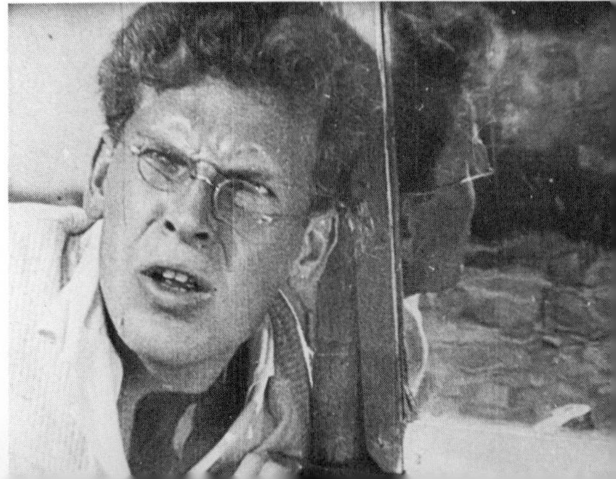

	PICTURE	SOUND
	**2.** MLS, front of saloon. Earp dashes toward saloon, darts L to pick up rock, dodging gunshot through window; kicks saloon door as he darts R, dodging second gunshot through window, and climbs exterior staircase.	SFX: Two gunshots.
	**3a.** MS, looking up staircase. Earp opens window and climbs in.	SFX: Feminine shrieks. EARP: Sorry, ladies.
	**3b.**	
	**4.** MLS, group of onlookers in doorway of nearby saloon.	SFX: Creak of saloon door.
	**5.** MS, three men watching.	MAN: I don't blame the ma shall. I wouldn't go in ther either (laughs).

	PICTURE	SOUND
6.	MS, same man and woman as in shot 1.	SFX: Long silence, then clunk of a blow and the thud of a body hitting the floor.
7.	MLS, front of the saloon. Earp drags out Indian by the heels.	SFX: Footsteps and scrape of body on wooden sidewalk.

Every shot in this sequence uses lip-synchronous dialogue or closely synchronized sound effects, all except for shot 6, the crucial moment when Earp actually captures the Indian. Here all we see is the reaction of a group of onlookers while we hear the clunk of the blow and the thud of the body. Not only do we make the right connection between sound and action in this context, but we are forced to imagine actions which, if shown, might look more sordid than heroic. After all, subduing drunks is not the most glamorous occupation in the world, particularly when the scene is being played in a mildly humorous vein. By filming and editing the most dramatic part of the action in this manner, Ford also manages to stress the reaction of the townspeople—who eventually hire Earp as sheriff—rather than the fight itself, an event of minor importance to the overall development of the plot. It is obvious, though, that had the director wanted to show us all the visual details of the fight, he could have done so, and in complete synchronization with the sound.

There is a big difference, of course, between the professional use of this technique for one shot in an otherwise precisely synchronized film, and its use in an

amateur production in which there is no way of ensuring exact synchronization anywhere in the film. But there are a number of ways to use sound throughout a film so that the audience is not aware of the lack of absolutely precise synchronization. When background music, for instance, and some kinds of generalized sound effects such as crowd sounds are combined with a narration, quite a complex sound track can be built using only loose synchronization.

And, even though the most that can be achieved with ordinary projectors and recorders is this kind of loose synchronization, the sound track need not be as hit or miss as the word *loose* would seem to imply. There are commonsense techniques which can be used to start picture and sound together so that they will stay in approximately the same relationship each time the film is shown. We would like to explain some of them as they apply to sound tracks of varying complexity. We have tried them and they work. Particularly with short films of from five to ten minutes, they can be very effective. But these are not the only ways for achieving a degree of synchronization and you should be able to devise other methods to deal with the specific technical and artistic problems encountered in your own films.

Using Recorded Music

Nothing would seem simpler, for instance, than to play a single piece of music as the background for an entire film. The only equipment needed are a projector and a record player. There is a trick, however, to using even these two machines properly. Attach a piece of blank white film, called *leader,* immediately ahead of the first picture in the film. Then, using a small-diameter paper punch, make a hole in the leader at one second and one half second before the first picture (the ninth and eighteenth frames at silent speed, the twelfth and twenty-fourth frames at sound speed). Start the record player, put the needle on the record a quarter turn ahead of the music, and hold the edge of the record so it won't turn. Now start the projector. The first flash at one second will give warning, and at the second flash let go of the disc. The reason for starting the machines in this order is that it takes almost a second for the projector to reach its normal operating speed. By starting the projector first, this lag is eliminated, and the chances of keeping sound and picture in the same relationship each time the film is shown are greatly improved.

Although a visually more complex film might need several different pieces of music to reinforce its changing moods, this variety is nearly impossible to achieve with discs. To change the music while projecting the film would require either changing records quickly or using a couple of phonographs. A better approach in this situation would be the use of a quarter-inch magnetic tape recorder.

First find the length of each section of the film. Then time the pieces of music to make sure they are long enough. Next, transfer the music, in the right order, from the discs to magnetic tape. In order to tailor the recording to fit the film, use the volume control to fade in at whatever point in the selection you want the music to start, and fade out again when the piece is the right length for its section of the film. This way, any part of a selection can be used regardless of its natural beginning or end. Finally, cut out most of the short, silent section of tape between each piece of music and join (*splice*) the music back together again.

Now the recording should be almost exactly the right length for the film, with the smooth fade-out, fade-in eliminating what would otherwise be crude jumps between the various pieces of music. Attach a piece of tape leader ahead of the first sound on the tape and align this splice with the playback head on the tape recorder. When the projector is started the flash of the first punch mark will give warning, and at the second flash start the recorder.

This technique too might seem a rather haphazard approach to using music, another stopgap for lack of proper equipment. But it is really no different from what is often done in professional film-making. For instance, the sound track for this short scene from *Ugetsu,* by Kenji Mizoguchi, consists of nothing more than some very simple music. Earlier in the film it is established that the potter, the central figure of the story, can sell at great profit as many pots as he can quickly make. Just before the scene starts the potter roughly reprimands his wife and young son for interrupting his work, saying that he must rush to complete as many pots as possible. Then comes the following sequence, accompanied only by the slowly accelerating beat of a small, hollow-sounding drum and the shrill wail of a reed pipe.

urtesy: JANUS FILMS, INC.

In this scene Mizoguchi not only wants to show how thoroughly the ancient art of potting organizes the lives of this family, but also how the inordinate haste in which the pots are being made is doing violence to the family's traditional way of life. As soon as the father turns away from his wife and son, the drum starts a moderately rapid beat, which slowly increases in tempo as the potting picks up momentum. By the middle of shot 3 the pipe adds its keening to the beat of the drum, amplifying the strain under which they are working, and finally, in shot 7, underlines the glance of avaricious pleasure which the men exchange as the last pots are put in the oven to be fired.

In this case the music evokes a feeling of anxiety and greed by catching and emphasizing the dominant atmosphere of the action. But music can also be used to work against the grain of the action, creating a whole new atmosphere. A good example of this is this fight sequence from Jerzy Skolimowski's *Le Départ*.

The hero, played by Jean-Pierre Léaud, while rushing to return a borrowed Porsche, knocks a cyclist off his motor scooter. Since the car was borrowed under false pretenses, it is quickly apparent that Léaud is desperately trying to settle the matter before the police arrive. But the scene becomes ridiculous because, out of an adolescent sense of honor, Léaud persists in arguing and wrestling with the enraged cyclist.

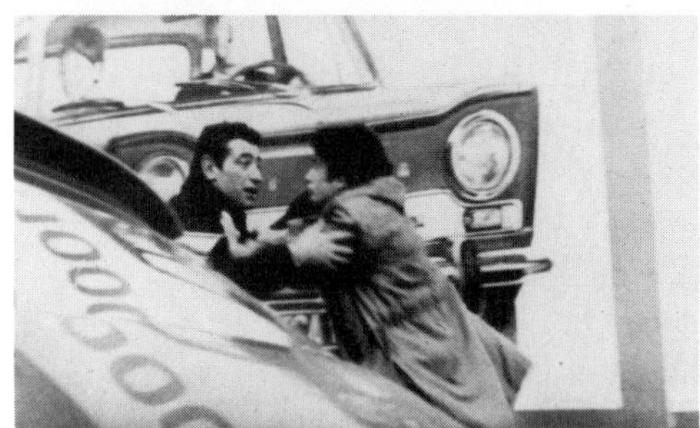

If we just look at the pictures the humor of the situation is not very apparent. While there are some funny visual elements, such as the cut-ins of the billboard and some of Léaud's expressions, the dominant impression of the footage is grim antagonism. But the fight is meant to be funny, and so the director chose to accompany it with a background of lighthearted, cacophonous music. In this way the music comments upon the action and quickly builds the ludicrous contradictions of Léaud's behavior. The director was also careful not to add dialogue and sound

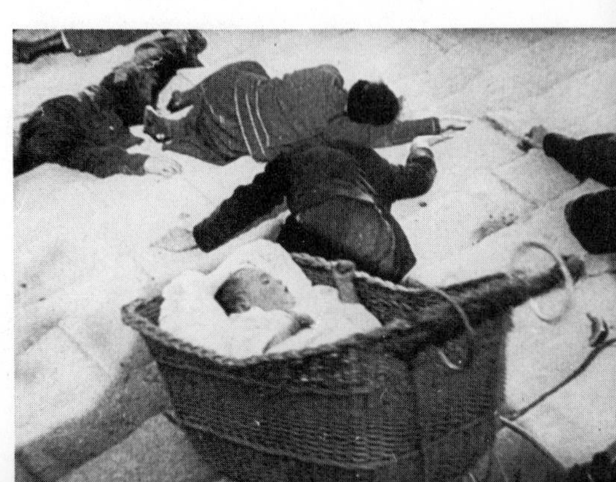

effects, since these would only have called attention to the fight itself rather than his ironic attitude toward it.

Narration

Even more common than a musical background is the use of narration alone to accompany a film. Unlike music, which comments only generally on the pictures, a narration can say some very specific things about what we see on the screen. And unlike synchronous dialogue, a narration can quite efficiently explain an idea or a situation because the words are not part of the ongoing action. This effect can be most easily seen by looking at the first four shots from François Truffaut's *Jules and Jim.*

PICTURE	NARRATION
1. MS, Jules and Jim playing dominoes.	It was 1912. Jules, a foreigner, ask Jim to get him into the Art Studen Ball. Jim got him a ticket . . .

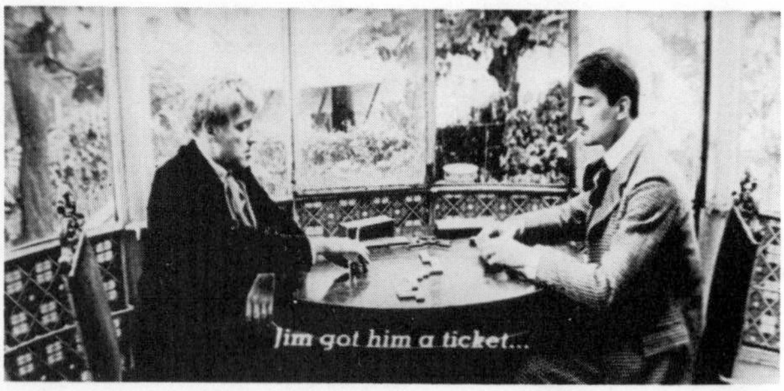

PICTURE	NARRATION
2. MS, Jules and Jim looking for a costume.	. . . and a costume. While Jules w hunting for a costume their friendsh was born. It grew as Jules watched t Ball with his warm, kind eyes.

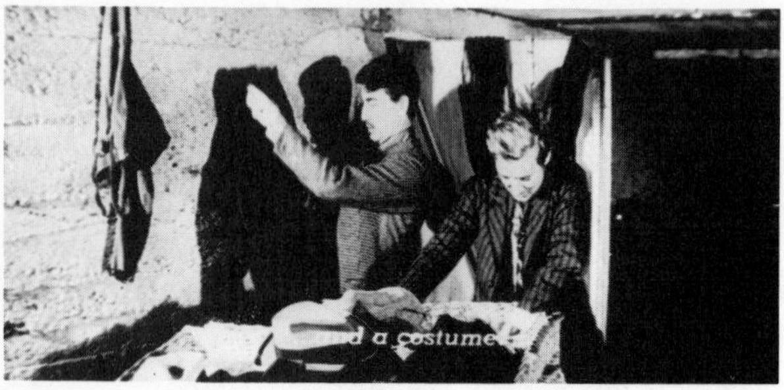

PICTURE	NARRATION
3. MS, Jules and Jim at a bookstall.	Soon they were seeing each other eve day.

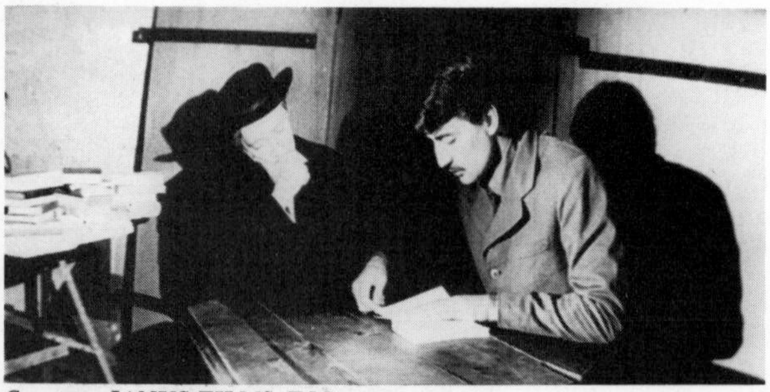

Courtesy: JANUS FILMS, INC.

PICTURE	NARRATION
4. MS, Jules and Jim walking.	Each taught the other his language. They translated each other's poetry. They shared a distaste for money. They talked—and they listened—to each other.

While Truffaut uses the pictures to set the scene quickly—the period, the dress, the manners, and the social and economic situation of the two leading characters—his narration expeditiously tells us who these characters are and what they are doing, and suggests the meaning this has for the rest of the film. Because the pictures carry only part of the meaning, they can be assembled in a rather shorthand manner. The narration gives them continuity by tying together their widely separated locations and disconnected activities with a common theme. The narration also quickly explains the meaning of a series of actions that would have had to run considerably longer had synchronous dialogue been used to convey the same information.

A narration is actually rather easy to create. Because words can be added, subtracted, and rearranged on paper before they are committed to tape, it is a fairly simple matter to fit the script to the pictures. And if the narration is recorded as the film is projected, the timing and inflection of the recording can be matched quite nicely to the pace and content of the action.

A certain amount of preparation and practice is needed before the narration can be recorded. First, time each section of the film, if this hasn't been done already. Then figure out how many words per minute can be read aloud by timing a section of the script. Next, adjust the script to fit the time available in each section of the film and read the whole thing aloud as the film is projected to see how closely script and picture match. Several more such script revisions and practice readings will be needed before the narration is ready to be recorded.

Once the reading feels right, use a grease pencil to make cue marks within the body of the film a half second and a second before the start of each major

section of the narration. These can be rubbed off when the recording is finished. If someone else is to record the narration, have them practice reading the script against the film at this point in order to refine the timing of words and pictures. If you are recording the narration yourself, make a trial recording before revising the script any further.

Since the narration will be recorded while the projector is running, steps must be taken to keep the projector noise as far in the background of the recording as possible. In professional sound studios this noise problem is usually overcome by the isolation of either the projector or the narrator in a soundproof booth. Outside the studio it is possible to keep this noise out of the recording if a window or a partially open door separates the narrator from the projector. Where this is not practical, at least put the projector at the other end of the room.

Editing the Narration

If there are errors in the delivery of a very short narration it is easier to do the whole recording over than to edit out the mistakes. But when an error occurs during a longer narration, stop the film immediately and back it up several feet. Then start over. As the picture which matches the beginning of the troublesome sentence comes on the screen, start reading again. The tape is now longer than the film because of this duplication, but the overlap is needed for editing purposes.

After the recording session is over, the narration must be put back in synchronization with the picture. To do this, simply match the first word of the sentence to be removed with that same word in the duplicate sentence of the new section and make a splice. After all the errors have been removed, time the pause between the start of the picture and the start of the narration. Then attach a piece of tape leader an equal amount of time before the first word on the recording. This splice can now be lined up with the playback head of the tape recorder and punch marks on the film leader can be used to start picture and sound in synchronization. This is exactly the same technique as was used earlier to synchronize background music with the film.

During playback certain sections of the picture and the sound track won't work together as well as they seemed to during the recording session. Because this is the first opportunity the film-maker has to step back from the details of production and see the entire film as an audience sees it, certain kinds of errors will become more readily apparent. For instance, a specific reference to the pictures will probably require that a close-up replace the medium shot which seemed adequate before sound was added. Or an action that didn't seem important before will occur either a couple seconds too soon or just not soon enough and throw off the pace of the narration. Or the narration would make better sense if the shots in one section were in another order.

If the change involves nothing more than shifting the sound in relation to the picture, it is usually easier to cut out or rearrange a few sentences or a paragraph than to alter the pictures. Of course, simply rearranging pieces of the track won't change its length; but if a portion of the track is removed, an equal length of silent tape must be inserted ahead of the next section of the narration in order to put the remainder of the sound track back into synchronization with the picture.

Where new materials must be added to the sound track it is definitely easier to re-record whole sections of the script than to try to add an isolated word or phrase. To fit these new sections into the existing track, simply record them while watching the film and then splice in the new recording in place of the old. Care must be taken, however, to keep the finished tape the same length as the film, so make sure not to remove any more or less of the unwanted part than is replaced.

In some cases it may not be desirable to alter the sound track since the weaknesses that have shown up are in the editing of the picture. Adding, subtracting, or rearranging shots is really not much more difficult than changing the sound and may make the visuals more coherent and interesting. If possible, though, do not make the reedited section of the film longer or shorter than before, or the picture and the track will be out of synchronization.

However, where changes in the picture alter the length of the film—or shift its emphasis by rearranging the way in which the action develops—changes in the sound track will also be necessary. Since changes in both sound and picture can get fairly complex, it is advisable to do only one section of the film at a time, each time checking to make sure that picture and track are still properly synchronized. Of course, if such changes become very extensive, it might be best to consider the track a trial run and do the whole narration over once the picture is reedited.

Wild Track

A less formal and often exciting way to create a narration is to use people's unrehearsed comments. Such candidly recorded material, called *wild track,* easily captures normal speech patterns and the natural sounds of the surroundings in which the recordings are made. As a result, this kind of sound track is usually quite vital, giving an authenticity and a freshness to the narration which can be obtained in no other way.

The sound of one or more voices can easily be recorded with a portable quarter-inch tape recorder, and then the comments can either be used separately, as individual statements, or be mixed together as a composite viewpoint. But it is difficult to say whether the voices should be edited to fit the pictures or the pictures cut to fit the finished narration. Both sound and picture have natural rhythms that keep the editor from cutting just anywhere, so it depends upon the material at hand. If the action must flow smoothly from shot to shot, it is best to cut the picture first; but if, as in the next example, there is little or no action, then the sound can determine how the pictures are assembled, and sometimes even how they're shot.

This sequence is from *The World of the Teenager,* an NBC documentary produced by Fred Freed. It is a good example of the variety of effects that can be created by means of wild track. As the camera slowly trucks through the halls and classrooms of a high school, we hear both the voices of the students and, as a background effect, a hollow-sounding, barely intelligible chorus of teachers.

	PICTURE	SOUND
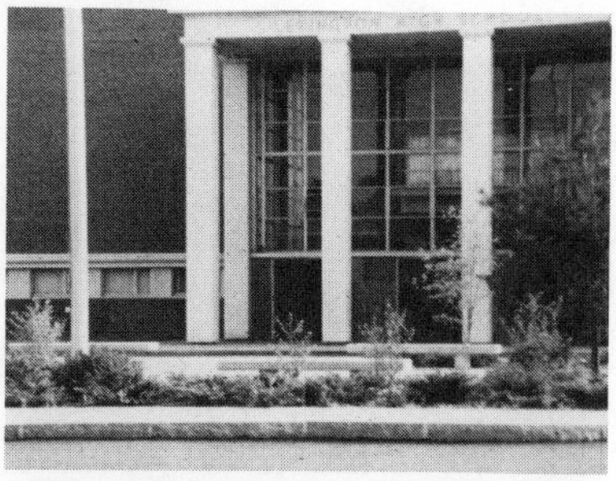	**1.** FADE IN FROM BLACK LS, front of high school; slowly zoom in to front door (7½ sec.).	MUS: Long trumpet n which slowly fades out w dissolve.
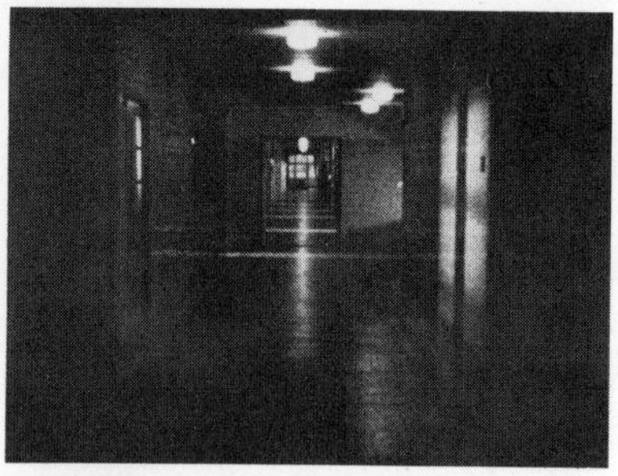	*DISSOLVE* **2.** XLS, empty corridor; slowly truck forward (14½ sec.).	SFX: Echoing sound of fem teacher's voice giving less fades under . . . MALE STUDENT I: I ca wait to get out of school ev day. SFX: Echoing sound of m teacher over dissolve, th voice of female teacher.
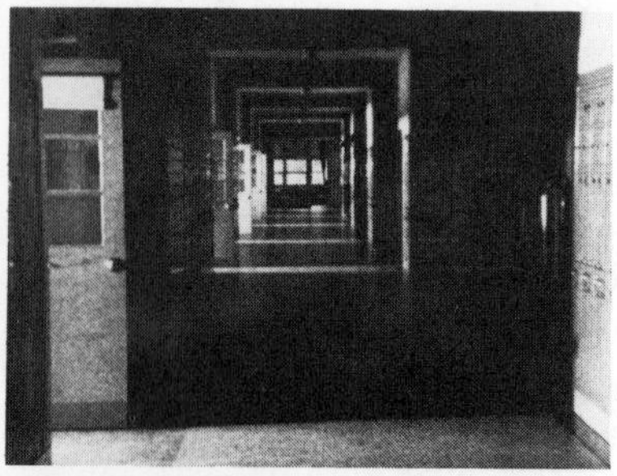	*DISSOLVE* **3.** LS, same corridor as shot 2; slowly truck forward (21½ sec.).	STUDENT II: The place is like a prison. SFX: Echoing voices contin at low level, slowly mix w ponderous, dreary orchest music, then fade under . . .
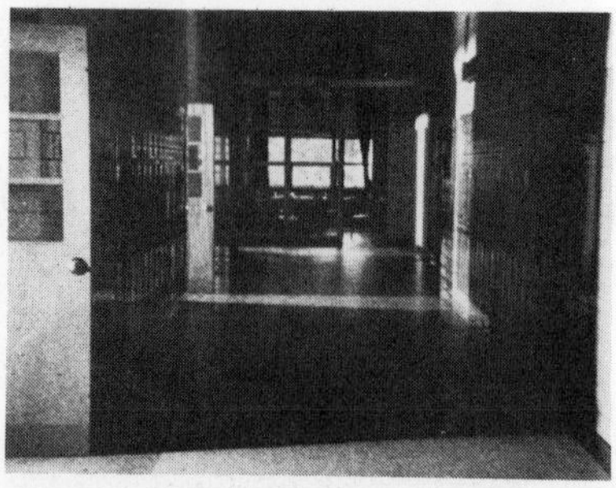	*DISSOLVE* **4.** LS, same corridor as shot 3, but further toward the end. Continue to truck slowly forward (28 sec.).	STUDENT II: You fe trapped in it. SFX and MUS: Continue low level, then fade under .

PICTURE	SOUND
DISSOLVE	
5. MLS, same empty corridor as shot 4; slowly truck forward (36½ sec.).	STUDENT III: You're always told, "You've got to do this!" You never get to do anything on your own. MUS: Continues at low level, then fades under . . .
DISSOLVE	
6. MS, same corridor as shot 5, but almost at end; slowly truck forward (44 sec.).	STUDENT IV: We don't have any freedom. It's more like a prison. MUS: Continues, then fades under . . .
 *DISSOLVE*	
7. MCU, looking out classroom window; then pan quickly R to blackboard (50½ sec.).	STUDENT IV: I sit in there and I daydream out the window. MUS: Continues, then fades under . . .
 *DISSOLVE*	
8. MLS, classroom, same blackboard as in shot 7; slowly truck back (1 min.).	STUDENT IV: Right now I have no desire to learn anymore. MUS: Two long, low, mournful horn notes, then slowly fade out.

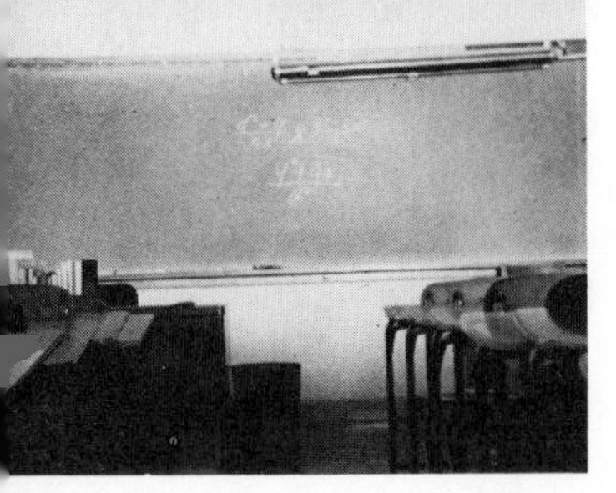

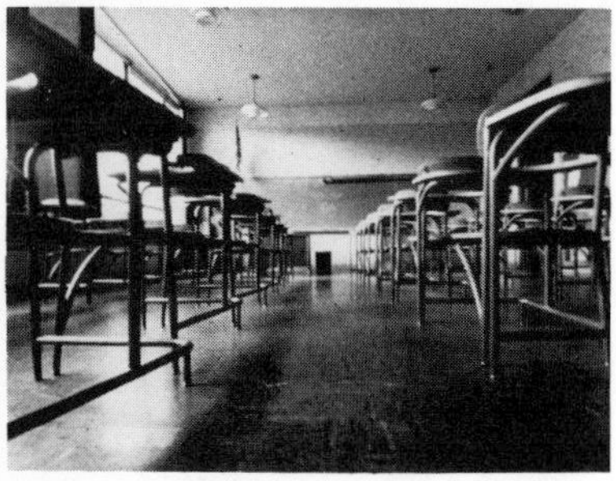

	PICTURE	SOUND
9.	LS, extreme wide-angle shot of empty classroom (1 min., 6 sec.).	TEACHER: Somehow v have not communicated children that the idea of g ing to school is not to g grades . . .
10.	MCU, teacher speaking in shot 9.	. . . or to pass, or to get in college, or to please t teacher. It's to learn.

Freed uses wild track not only to let us hear some teen-agers' complaints about school, but also to help us feel the meaning of these complaints by making us participants in the action. Although the feeling of emptiness was most strongly developed visually, it was made more palpable by the addition of the unreal recordings of the teachers' voices. These voices echoed through the deserted rooms and halls like a bad memory. The illusion becomes complete, though, in shot 7. Mimicking the student's words with the subjective movement of the camera places us in the classroom, and the slowly revealed emptiness sums up our expectation for what it holds.

Mixing a Sound Track

It is not unusual, as in this example, to combine a narration with music or sound effects. In fact, this sequence contains every kind of sound that can be used in a film. There is narration at the beginning and synchronous dialogue at the end, and these are combined with both music and the sound effect created by the teachers' voices. But despite its complexity, and with the exception of the last two shots, this same sequence could have been made by means of the synchronizing techniques we have discussed so far.

Combining a variety of sounds into a single sound track is not very difficult, only time consuming. Of course, if the various sounds do not overlap one another there is no difficulty at all. Each type of sound can then be recorded separately and the segments spliced together to make up the finished track. The procedure becomes more involved only if the sounds overlap, since they then have to be mixed together at the proper volume and with each in the right place.

In professional films sound-mixing normally involves the prerecording of each basic element of the sound track—voice, music, and sound effects—in synchronization with the picture but with each on its own separate track. These tracks are then played back simultaneously, in synchronization with the picture, and the sounds are mixed together electronically. The mixing is done by an audio control device with a separate volume control for each track. A master tape machine, also running in synchronization with the picture, records the composite sound track put out by this audio mixer.

This is a complicated process requiring a great deal of specialized machinery. But like everything else in film-making, there are alternatives. It is a fairly simple matter, for instance, to play a background of music or sound effects on a phonograph or tape recorder while recording the narration. Unfortunately, a continuous background makes the smooth editing-out of mistakes in the narration impossible. If exactly the same part of the music or the same kind of effect isn't behind the new narration as was behind the old, there will be a perceptible jump in the background sound. When a mistake is made under these conditions it is best to record the narration over from the beginning.

It is also possible to add bits of music or sound effects to a narration by having them ready on a record player or tape recorder, and starting and stopping this playback machine during the recording session as the additional sounds are needed. The advantage of this technique over a continuous background of sound is that the track can be mixed in segments. That way the whole track need not be done over when there is a mistake in one of the sections. This is a technique also used in professional sound recording when there is not enough time to prepare all the tracks before a mixing session. Because starting and stopping machines makes the session more complicated, the process has been justifiably and graphically designated a *flying mix.*

To blend the prerecorded music and sound effects smoothly with the narration, start the tape or record with the volume control on the playback machine closed. Then slowly turn up the volume to a proper background level (this can be determined only by trial and error) and turn it down again when the sound is no longer needed. But do not use the volume control to raise the level of the background further if the music or the effects must be used to fill a pause in the narration. It is much better to move the microphone slowly toward, and afterwards away from, the playback machine. This technique will have the same effect as a fade-up, fade-down. Turning the volume control way up introduces a great deal of distortion into the playback, and at full volume, the background sound becomes quite hollow because the playback machine is relatively distant from the microphone.

A stereo tape recorder with facilities for recording on each of its two channels separately is also quite useful for making a complex sound track. Record the narration on one channel while watching the picture. Then, while playing back this narration in synchronization with the picture, record the music and/or sound effects

on the other channel. Making the recordings in this order permits the narration to be edited without having to worry about cutting into an adjacent music and sound effects track. It also allows erasing and re-recording the music and effects as often as necessary without having to re-record the narration simultaneously.

Recording on a Magnetic Stripe

In some cases, using a quarter-inch tape recorder to produce a sound track will be the only alternative. But if a magnetic sound projector is available, the sound track can be permanently linked to the picture by recording it on a narrow magnetic stripe glued to the edge of the film. This stripe can be inexpensively applied by most film laboratories once the film is developed.

Magnetic stripe. The main stripe is on the top edge and a narrow balance stripe is on the opposite edge; the smaller stripe keeps the film flat in the camera and projector gates.

Because the quality is superior to optical sound, almost all commercially produced 8mm sound films are made with a magnetic stripe. And many 8mm and 16mm magnetic sound projectors not only play back this stripe, but record on it at either sound or silent speed. It is best, however, to anticipate using a magnetic sound stripe before any film is shot. Since film shot at sound speed will permit recording and playback of the sound track at a higher speed, and therefore with higher fidelity, shoot the whole movie at twenty-four frames per second.

The advantage of using a magnetic projector to record the sound track is that the track is no longer "loosely" in synchronization with the picture once it is recorded on the stripe. Of course, starting and keeping the various sounds in step with the picture during the recording session still depends upon the skill of the film-maker. But accurately playing back the recording itself is not a matter of chance when sound and picture are locked together on a single piece of film. As a result, making the recording on a magnetic projector permits both a greater range of precisely synchronized sounds in the finished track and synchronous projection of the finished film wherever another similar projector is available.

A relatively complex sound track can be easily constructed by means of a magnetic projector since most of these machines have facilities for electronically mixing the output of a tape recorder or a phonograph with a live narration. Before the track can be recorded, though, the film must be edited and sent out for striping. Since the stripe is applied only to the edited footage, this procedure saves money. It also results in a smoother sound track because there are no splices in the stripe itself.

Do not try to edit the stripe if a mistake is made during the recording session. Editing not only requires cutting into the picture, but means cutting into a picture many frames ahead of the picture to which the sound is synchronized. As was mentioned earlier, when sound and picture are on the same strip of film it is single-system sound. The sound leads the picture by twenty-eight frames in 16mm, fifty-six frames in standard 8mm, and eighteen frames for the majority of super 8mm projectors, and this displacement makes smooth editing nearly impossible.

When a mistake is made while recording a relatively simple sound track, do the whole thing over from the beginning. This procedure is necessary because starting over somewhere other than the beginning is only possible where there is a long silence in the track. Projectors take several seconds to reach their normal operating speed, and any sound recorded before the speed stabilizes will be radically altered in pitch. Also, starting the recording while the stripe is over the recording head will leave a loud electronic pop on the track. This noise can be removed only

by a complete erasure of that portion of the magnetic stripe with an audio head demagnetizer or some other kind of small electromagnet.

If the sound track can be recorded in segments, it is possible to remove mistakes by re-recording only a section of the track at a time. Attach several feet of film leader to the beginning of each section. The time needed for this leader to run through the projector will allow the projector speed to stabilize and the recording circuits to begin operating before the magnetic stripe reaches the recording head, eliminating problems of sound pitch and popping. But this is single-system sound, and each section will have to begin and end with anywhere from eighteen to fifty-six frames of silence, depending upon the gauge of the film, so that the sections can be smoothly joined together into a finished film.

Post-synchronized Dialogue

Recording the sound track in segments also permits the insertion of short sections of synchronous dialogue. If the dialogue is not too extensive it can be recorded by means of post-synchronization, or in other words, by having actors speak in synchronization with silent footage of the dialogue. This technique is often used in Europe. It originally was cheaper than filming synchronous dialogue, and, once it was mastered, the technique resulted in better performances. Every European director has had to use it, and some prefer it. This technique is also used in this country, but usually just to replace an unusable original recording.

Post-synchronous dialogue footage can be made with any camera and quarter-inch recorder. The scene is shot as if the dialogue were being recorded synchronously, but the recording is only an exact record of what was said, not a sound track. The number of each shot and the number of retakes of that shot should be indicated on a *slate;* this slate is photographed and the numbers read into the microphone at the start of each shot. There should also be a written record, called a *log,* of each shot filmed, the number of retakes, and which takes were best. After the footage is processed, this log will prove invaluable for selecting the takes and matching them to the sound recordings.

Before striping the footage, edit those sections of dialogue which consist of more than one shot. Where there are single shots containing dialogue, attach a short piece of film leader to each shot and splice these shots together also. Then have everything magnetically striped. The post-synchronizing session can be treated as if it were a narration. Use the quarter-inch recordings to prepare a script. Keep projector noise out of the recording. Attach film leader to each separate piece to be recorded and make punch marks a half second and a second before the first frame of picture.

If the dialogue sections are short enough, rewinding the film after each practice reading can be eliminated. Instead of running the film from the supply reel to the take-up reel during projection, bypass the reels after the projector is threaded and splice the end of the film to the start of the leader, forming a closed loop. There is now no need to rewind the film since it will circulate endlessly through the projector. The actors can practice reading their lines with only a short interruption for the leader, and after several passes they will be able to establish a rhythm to match the rhythm of the pictures. Press the "record" button when their delivery of the dialogue is satisfactory, and the dialogue will be recorded the next time around.

Because it is difficult for untrained actors to post-synchronize dialogue lasting more than thirty seconds, longer inserts should be shot synchronously. This is done on prestriped film stock using a single-system magnetic sound camera. A variety of these cameras are available in 16mm, and most of them can be rented as well as purchased. Such cameras are also available in both super and standard 8mm; and prestriped super 8 mm film stock is widely available. If possible, shoot each dialogue insert as one continuous shot, dollying and zooming to provide a variety of camera angles. One shot is preferable to a number of different shots which must then be edited together because, as has been mentioned several times, smoothly editing single-system sound is nearly impossible. Single-system is seldom used for professional sound film production for just this reason; and while television news departments often have to edit single-system footage, unless the cutting is quite simple they transfer the sound to double-system.

Double-System Sound Recording

Double-system sound, the recording of sound and picture on two separate but synchronous pieces of film, has been the standard professional technique almost from the beginning of sound film production. But during the past two decades the means for making the sound recording has undergone a significant change. Magnetic recording, because of its superior fidelity and greater ease of handling, has replaced the older optical method for almost all professional sound film recording.

Instead of the light-sensitive emulsion used for optical-sound recording, a magnetic oxide is now coated on the sprocketed film base. And instead of using a light to expose the sound track along one edge of photographic film, a magnetic head now records a quarter-inch-wide track along one edge of magnetic film. The two materials are used in exactly the same way, though. Like the photographic film it replaced, the magnetic film is recorded on a sprocket-driven machine and passes the recording head at twenty-four frames per second so that picture and sound can be matched up on the editing bench, sprocket hole for sprocket hole, in exact synchronization.

But, magnetic film recorders like optical recorders are too big and heavy for easy use outside a motion-picture sound stage, and magnetic film itself is expensive and cumbersome. For instance, a ten-minute roll of 35mm magnetic film is an inch

thick and a foot across; and while the same size roll of 16mm magnetic film is half as thick and runs three times as long, it too is still quite expensive. As a result, another, cheaper, more portable double-system magnetic recorder is now used by a majority of professionals for the original recording of synchronous sound.

This recorder is little more than a battery-operated quarter-inch tape machine that has been specially adapted for synchronous recording. Quarter-inch tape is nowhere near as bulky as magnetic film and is extremely cheap to use; and the easy portability of a quarter-inch recorder, coupled with a battery-operated camera, has permitted double-system filming under almost any circumstances. In fact, these units have proved so reliable that the cheaper quarter-inch system is now used even where portability is not a problem.

However, when a camera and a recorder are battery operated, their speed can no longer be regulated by the alternations of the current in the electric power lines. So the two machines are instead coordinated by a small electric generator built into the gears of the camera. When the camera is running, this generator produces a tiny electrical current, called a *control signal,* which is fed to an extra recording head on the tape machine. There this control signal is recorded on the tape as a narrow sound track, called a *control track,* parallel to the regular sound track.

Before editing, this quarter-inch recording must be transferred to either 16mm or 35mm magnetic film, depending upon the film gauge in which the picture was shot. But only the regular sound track is transferred. Because the control track serves as a kind of electronic sprocket hole, it is used only to maintain synchronization. When the film was shot, any variations in the speed of the camera or the tape machine were recorded as variations in the signal on the control track. As this control track is played back, these variations are sensed by electronic circuits, which alter the rate at which the tape is transferred to magnetic film so that afterwards the sound on the magnetic film will match the picture, frame for frame, in exact synchronization.

The one area in which synchronous sound recording is yet to develop to professional standards is 8mm. There was never any need for synchronous sound in standard 8mm since this was always considered a strictly amateur medium. But super 8mm holds promise of becoming professionally useful and has already stimulated a great deal of interest in systems for recording synchronous sound that are as portable and inexpensive as the super 8mm film and cameras. All the sound systems now available for super 8mm are double-system magnetic sound and are more highly portable and cheaper than those used in 16mm and 35mm. But, unfortunately, none of these new systems is currently as easy to edit and mix as those used in professional film-making.

The film-maker who has to work exclusively in 8mm is therefore restricted to sound-synchronizing techniques that are less flexible and accurate than the mechanically perfect methods of professional double-system sound. But even in its present state of development, 8mm does offer a reasonable guarantee that most of the effects the film-maker creates are what he planned in the first place and not merely the product of a chance relationship between sound and picture. As a result, the skill and imagination developed in the making of 8mm sound films can often be directly applied to professional film-making, and 8mm can play a significant role as an inexpensive, experimental prelude to the use of double-system sound in the making of bigger and more expensive 16mm and 35mm films.

Thus, the next step for the beginning film-maker, after he has mastered a few of these simple techniques for keeping sound and picture together, is to invest greater energy in the recording and editing of the sound itself. Unlike synchronization, which can always be done better if better machinery is used, the skills developed in using a microphone or in cutting a sound track can never be automated. The product of these skills must vary with the content of the film, and so the techniques used must always be open to innovation. We will explore the most basic techniques of double-system sound recording and editing, and the principles behind them, in the following chapters. These are techniques that have been developed and elaborated upon by professional film-makers, but there is no question that all of them can be usefully tried out in some form in 8mm or 16mm by the beginning film-maker.

Chapter 7

Sound Recording

Sound recording takes less technical skill than any other part of film-making. But the one thing it does require is a trained ear. A recording captures a complex body of detailed information, information that can make sounds as expressive, in their own way, as pictures. When we listen to someone speaking, for instance, we don't hear just the words, we also listen for the meanings contained in the pace, the tone, and the timbre of the speaker's voice. A good example of this is the closing paragraph of one of Winston Churchill's greatest wartime speeches.

> The battle of Britain is about to begin. Hitler knows he will have to break us in this island or lose the war. Let us therefore brace ourselves to our duty, and so bear ourselves that, if the British Empire and its Commonwealths last for a thousand years, men will still say: "This was their finest hour."

Although the words are simple and direct, and the language beautifully constructed, it is possible to grasp the full meaning of this passage only by listening to a recording of the original broadcast. The speech was made at the peak of the Nazi advance in Western Europe. Churchill needed to shore up the spirit of a nation which believed itself on the brink of invasion. He met this fear both by appealing

to national pride and resolve and by offering an example of personal strength. The deep, clear, gruff voice, the confident tone, the precise, clipped enunciation and phrasing all contributed to a feeling of leadership and character around which the British people could rally. And the people responded, but the power of the words lay in how they were spoken.

The meanings a sound can have are inferred not only from the sound itself, but also from the noise and echo which are part of its surroundings. These background sounds tell us where the recording was made, whether in a small, furnished room or a large, empty one; outdoors in the open countryside or in a narrow city street; amidst activity or in solitude. By placing the sound in a definite context, the quality of the background simultaneously extends the meaning of the sound and tells us how to feel about what we are hearing.

For example, look at the subtleties of mood and meaning Josef von Sternberg has built through sound effects alone in just the first two minutes of *The Blue Angel.* The film is set in pre–World War I Germany. An elderly high school teacher, Dr. Rath, betrayed by his schoolboy emotions, falls in love with a dance-hall singer and deserts his dull, bourgeois existence for a tawdry theatrical life that eventually destroys him. This opening scene sets the stage for his appearance by showing us two worlds, the one he knows and the one he is about to enter.

In the first three shots we see the town in which the film takes place. It is a jumble of lines and angles, a busy place in which the sound is rich and bright. The opening title music gives way to clucking chickens and honking geese, and these then mix with the sound of household chores. But we almost immediately learn that these are not the sights and sounds of Dr. Rath's world. Abruptly, starting with shot

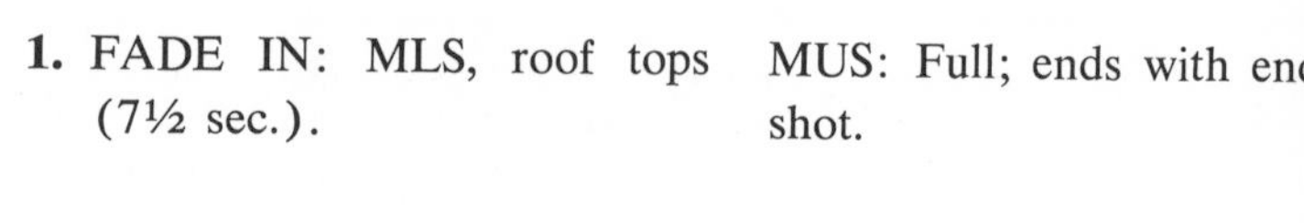

	PICTURE	SOUND
	1. FADE IN: MLS, roof tops (7½ sec.).	MUS: Full; ends with end shot.
	2. MLS, busy street. Woman in foreground is crating geese. Other woman enters street from shop in background (11½ sec.).	SFX: Clamor of honki geese.

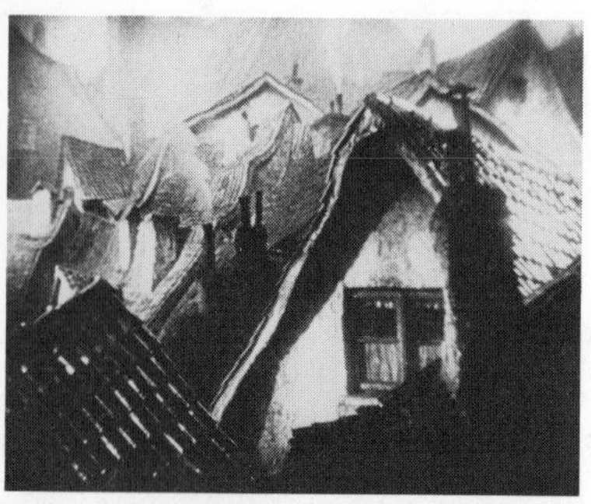

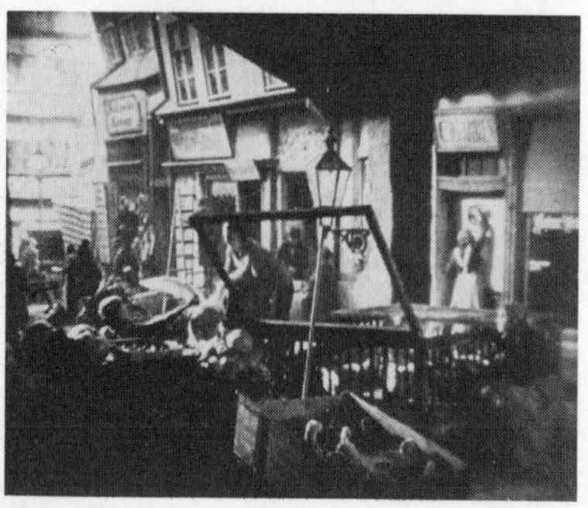

PICTURE	SOUND
3. MS, woman opens shutter over shop window to reveal poster of dance-hall singer "Lola-Lola." She throws pailful of water on window, then pauses to mimic poster (24½ sec.).	SFX: Clank of shutter being raised, then splash of water hitting glass. Geese, in background, slowly fade out at end of shot.
4. CU, door with nameplate, "Prof. Dr. Rath" (4 sec.).	SFX: Loud, hurried footsteps.
LONG DISSOLVE	
5. MLS, interior stairway and upper landing. Child is frantically running to get books and coat while mother watches. Child exits down stairs (10½ sec.).	SFX: School bell starts ringing with start of dissolve and continues over sound of child rushing about; ends as child is about to leave. Footsteps end at end of shot.
DISSOLVE	
6. MS, vestibule. Housekeeper crosses with tray and enters study (7 sec.).	SFX: Quick, firm footsteps; rattle of dishes on tray.

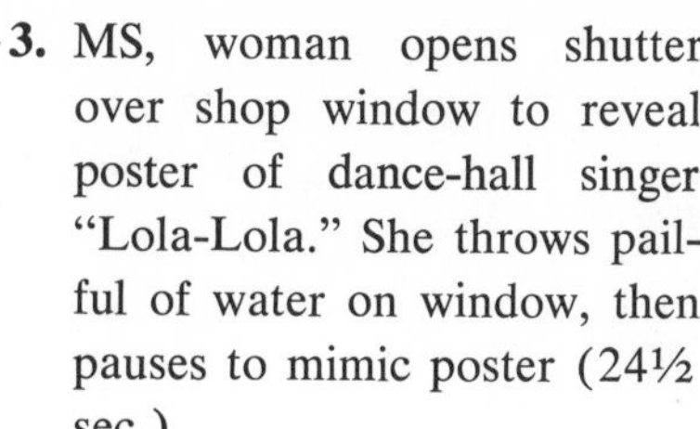

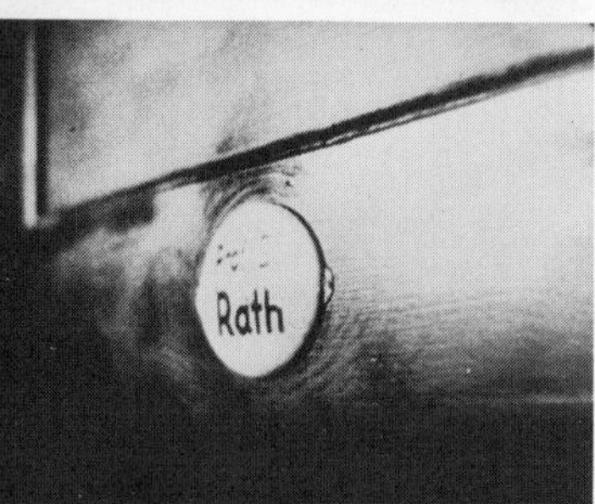

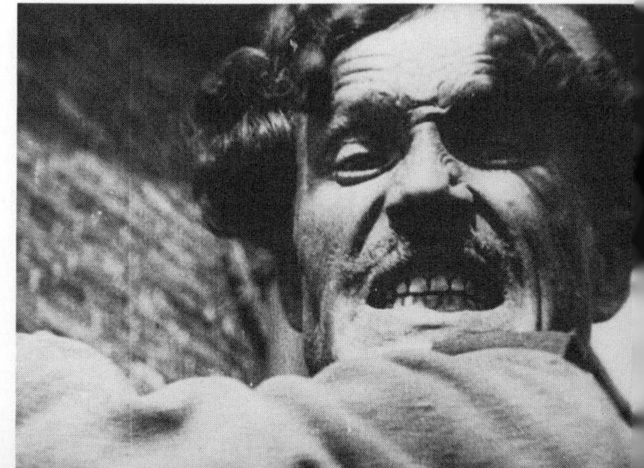

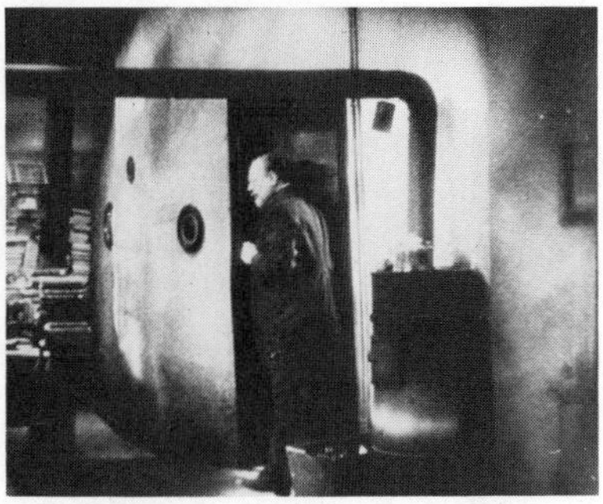

PICTURE	SOUND
7. MLS, Rath's study. Housekeeper enters R and camera pans L with her as she crosses to table, puts tray down, and calls him. She arranges food on table, then camera pans R as she leaves, holding on door to his bedroom as she exits frame. He enters through door, checking his pockets, and exits frame L (36 sec.).	SFX: Footsteps continue. HSKPR: Herr Professor breakfast (she mutters sof to herself as she sets table). SFX: Soft footsteps as enters.

4, the images become simple, even austere in their composition, and just before shot 4 the street sounds fade out.

Against a subdued and decorous background of silence, we first hear feet rapidly mounting a stairway somewhere inside the house. Then, over a long dissolve to the next shot, we hear the equally disembodied clangor of a school bell marking off the beginning of another well-regulated school day. When the dissolve ends we see that the footsteps are the result of a child scrambling to find coat and books before rushing off to school. These footsteps end as the child leaves, only to be replaced by the fast, firm steps of the housekeeper as she quickly crosses the vestibule, enters the study, and informs the professor that his breakfast is ready. Finally, with quiet but confident strides, Dr. Rath enters the study, ready to start his day.

The footsteps in these last four shots serve to differentiate the characters and tell us something about how they relate to each other. The pace and the sound quality are different for each character, and one set of footsteps never overlaps another. This device clearly separates these people from each other as well as from the outside world. But the various cadences and qualities of their steps are then rhythmically cut together to form one long ascent to Dr. Rath's apartment. This effect places him high above the others and makes his appearance the climax of the ascent. He is the focus of their attention and activity, and his world is a hierarchy in which they exist only to serve his needs. Thus, before we have even seen Dr. Rath, the director has created a specific sense of his character. These expectations are then borne out by his commanding appearance when we finally see him in shot 7.

It takes considerable skill and imagination to create as complex a track as this, but ultimately its success depends upon having exactly the right sounds in the first place. There is too much going on in a film for the audience to stop and figure out what it is they just heard. But if the sound is clear they can sense its implications even if they cannot fully grasp its logic. As a result, the film-maker must find the specific sounds which contain his meanings. He must overcome a natural tendency to screen out everything except what he'd like to hear, and instead learn to listen critically to the rich diversity of the sounds around him.

He must also learn to hear if he has accurately recorded exactly what he wants the audience to hear. That means that he must listen to the recording for sound qualities that are unlike anything we encounter in our everyday lives. Recording sound involves translating it into a new medium, and no translation is ever exact. Every recording distorts the sound both by altering its characteristics and by adding new sounds. If these distortions are not controlled they can make the sound unrecognizable, while if they are taken into account they can help the film-maker express a large amount of information clearly and succinctly.

Fortunately, magnetic recorders offer the tremendous advantage of immediate playback. This allows the film-maker to hear how the sound has been affected by being recorded and to correct any unwanted distortions before they ruin the next recording as well. But while distortions are easy to hear, they are not quite as easy to correct. Each particular distortion must be recognized and its cause identified. This is a skill that is acquired only through experience and through some understanding of the technical problems inherent in the process of recording.

Frequency Response and Dynamic Range

Every component of the recording system adds its own peculiar distortion to the quality of the sound, but the most basic kinds of distortion are caused by the recorder itself. To record and reproduce sound accurately, the recorder must take the broad range of sound pitch and intensity which we hear quite easily and adjust it to fit within the more limited capacity of the recording tape or film. To put it somewhat more technically, the recorder determines the two most fundamental qualities of recorded sound. One is *frequency response,* or the highest to the lowest pitched sounds which the recording can reproduce; and the other is *dynamic range,* or the loudest to the softest sound in the recording.

Frequency response is easy to deal with. The range of frequencies that can be recorded and reproduced is determined essentially by the speed at which the film or the tape passes the sound head. The higher the speed, the broader the frequency response. Most quarter-inch tape recorders offer a combination of several standard recording speeds: 15, 7½, 3¾, and 1⅞ inches per second (ips); but magnetic and optical-sound films are restricted to twenty-four frames per second. If the frames happen to be large, as in 35mm film, then quite a bit of film will be pulled through the projector each second. In 35mm the film runs at 18 ips; but in 16mm the film runs at only 7²⁄₁₀ ips, and standard and super 8mm run at about 3½ ips.

Each successively slower speed reduces the frequency response by decreasing

the amount of high-frequency sounds. These frequencies are extraordinarily important, however, because they give sounds their characteristic qualities. Without them music lacks brilliance, voices become dull and hollow sounding, and sound effects are hard to distinguish from background noise. As a result, a higher speed gives 35mm films a better sound quality than 8mm or 16mm, and the higher tape speeds produce better-sounding original recordings from which to make the finished sound track.

But even the lower quality of 8mm and 16mm optical sound requires full-frequency response in the original recordings. Some of the higher frequencies disappear each time a recording is duplicated, and the original recordings may have to be transferred from duplicate to duplicate at least four times before they are part of the finished film. First they are transferred from quarter-inch tape to sprocketed magnetic film for editing; then the separate magnetic tracks are combined into a composite magnetic master during the mixing session; next the magnetic master is converted to an optical-negative sound track; and finally this negative is printed alongside the pictures as part of the completed sound print. Each one of these duplicates is called a *generation,* and unless there is sufficient high frequency in the original recordings there will be nothing left to transfer by the third or fourth generation.

It is not worthwhile to increase the recording speed beyond a certain point, however, since not every sound reaches into the very highest frequency range. In most professional recording, 7½ ips is usually sufficient for everything except music, which is recorded at 15 ips. The top speed available on most home tape recorders is also 7½ ips. This is a good choice for recording sound for films unless convenience or economy dictates the next slower speed of 3¾ ips. This speed permits twice the recording time on the same roll of tape and is adequate for all but music recording. As for cassette recorders, their fixed slow speed of 1⅞ ips puts most music and high-pitched sound effects beyond their reach.

The frequency response of low- and medium-priced recorders is also often restricted by the poor quality of the microphones supplied with these machines. But these microphones can be replaced with better ones at no great additional expense; or for somewhat more money, the recorder can be custom fitted for a professional microphone, which will permit an inexpensive recorder to make surprisingly good voice and sound effects recordings even at low tape speeds, and excellent recordings at higher speeds.

Unlike frequency response, the other characteristic of a recording, its dynamic range, can be altered very little. The reason is that the extremes of loudness and softness that a recording can handle are determined by the overall design of the recording system, and particularly by the type of recording material. Optical-sound systems, for instance, have a narrower dynamic range than magnetic recorders, and some kinds of magnetic materials have a wider range than others. But no matter what the recording system or material, its dynamic limits are easy to recognize. When the sound is too loud it overloads the track and becomes fuzzy and hoarse; and when it is too soft it becomes buried in the electronic hiss and background noise which are part of every recording.

In order to keep the sound between these two extremes, every recorder has either a meter or a recording lamp that indicates when the volume control should be turned up or down. Some machines also have an electronic circuit which controls the recording volume automatically. However, any kind of volume control indiscriminately alters the level of all the sounds reaching the recorder. As a result, when the volume is turned up high enough for soft sounds, loud sounds overload and surrounding noise becomes quite audible. And when the volume is turned down for loud sounds, soft sounds and background sounds become inaudible.

There is simply no way, by use of the volume control alone, to record a soft sound without a lot of background noise, or a loud and soft sound simultaneously. To do either of these things, the sounds must be rebalanced by moving the microphone closer to the softer sound. Then the soft sound becomes louder without raising the level of all the other sounds. The effect of this is the same as one's hearing a sound better by leaning close to it.

This close microphone technique is also the best means for overcoming the most common problem in all sound recording—separating a sound from surrounding noise and echo. Unlike our hearing, the microphone has no psychological mechanism for screening out unwanted sounds. But if the microphone is kept close to a particular sound, that sound will be disproportionately louder than anything else the microphone picks up. And if, as a result, the volume control also has to be turned down, these lower-level sounds will become inaudible in the recording.

Types of Microphones

Exactly how close the microphone must be placed to achieve this sound balance depends upon the sensitivity characteristic of the microphone. Almost invariably, the microphone supplied with the recorder has a sensitivity called *omni-directional.* That is, it hears sounds equally well from all (omni) directions. Professional microphones, on the other hand, are made not only with an omni-directional pattern, but with a figure-eight and a cardioid sensitivity pattern as well. If the space around each type of microphone were divided into quarters, the omni-directional would pick up sounds in all four quarters, the cardioid would be most sensitive only to those sounds originating in the front quarter, and its figure-eight variation (double cardioid) would respond to sounds coming from only the front and back quarters.

The great advantage of this directional characteristic is that if sounds occurring toward the sides and the back of the microphone are suppressed, sounds coming from the front can be recorded at a higher level without an automatic in-

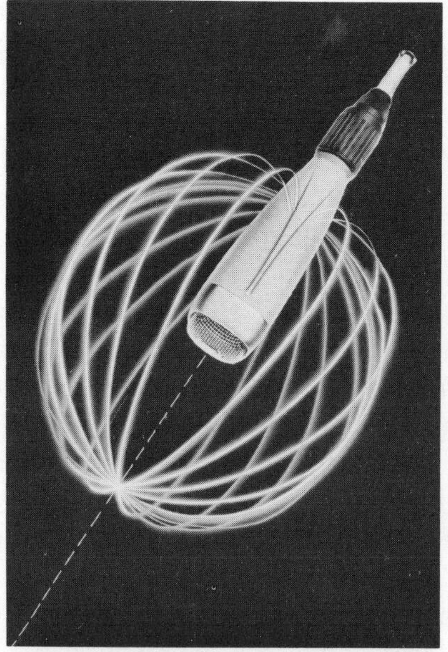

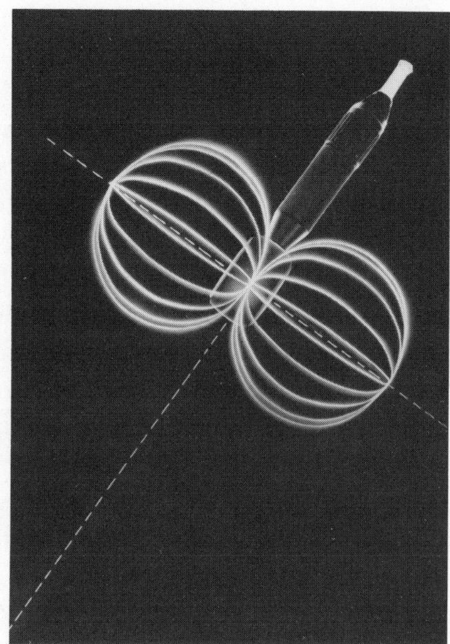

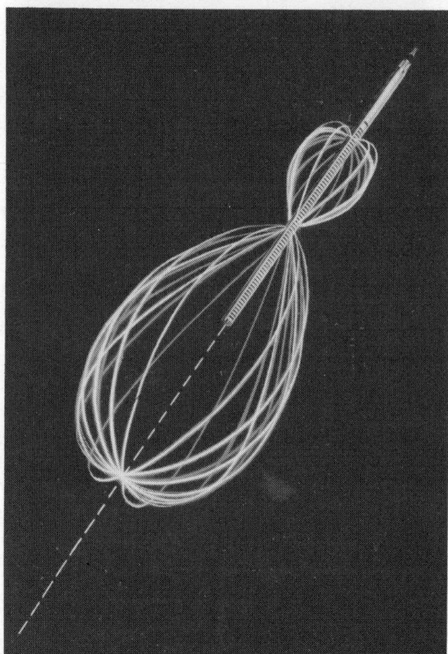

Above left: Omnidirectional sensitivity pattern extends equally on all sides of the microphone. Above: Figure-eight sensitivity forms two lobes extending from opposite sides of the microphone. Left: Super cardioid or shotgun pattern has its maximum sensitivity toward the front of the microphone.

crease in unwanted noise and echo. This is extremely useful when recording in a noisy or highly reverberant setting or when filming synchronous dialogue.

In dialogue recording it is not always possible to place an omni-directional microphone close enough to the actors to eliminate unwanted noise and echo and still keep the microphone outside of camera range. But a cardioid microphone, by suppressing sounds from other directions, permits a clear pickup of the dialogue even from a distance. In fact, eliminating extraneous noise is such an enormous problem in location filming that a type of super-cardioid or *shotgun* microphone has been developed. These microphones seem to reach out and pull in sounds from ten to fifteen feet away.

Controlling Background Sounds

The most selective microphone, however, will still pick up more of the surrounding sounds than we are used to hearing, even in settings in which these sounds don't seem excessive. As a result, no matter what type of microphone is used, some background noise and echo will get into the recording, giving the sound a distinct sense of the environment in which it was recorded. This atmospheric quality must be carefully controlled when recording sound for films. Each piece of sound must eventually work in conjunction with specific pictures, so it is not enough for a recording simply to reproduce the surroundings in which the sound actually occurred. The resulting sound quality must also be exactly what is needed to match the pictures.

This necessity leaves the film-maker only two choices. One is to record the sound under the appropriate environmental conditions in the first place, with the sound properly balanced through the careful placement of one or more microphones. Then the original recording will have most or all of the sound qualities needed for a particular sequence of pictures. The other choice is to record the sound in an isolated environment such as a recording studio, one with little inherent noise and echo. Or if that is not feasible, the sound must be isolated from its surroundings as much as possible by keeping a directional microphone close to the action. Then if any background sounds are needed, they are later added electronically during the mixing session.

An example of the first method, balanced sound, is this scene from the

WABC-TV documentary *Dong Xoai: The Town the Viet Cong Couldn't Kill,* produced by Arthur Alpert. The scene takes place in an army mess tent during lunch. The reporter, seated left, is questioning a group of soldiers about their impressions of serving in Vietnam. In this case the microphone was simply laid on the table—it can be seen near the forearm of the third person from the left. Because it is not particularly close to anyone, the recording volume had to be turned up. This higher volume raised the level of the background along with that of the voices, and the sound of this nearby activity helped lend authenticity to what might otherwise have seemed like a staged interview.

A typical example of the second method, highly isolated sound, is this brief segment from Robert Bresson's *The Trial of Joan of Arc.* The film is based on the actual records of Joan's trial for heresy. Bresson's interpretation is that her English captors used the trial as nothing more than a legal veneer for their lust for vengeance. The public had demanded her life and her every word was meant to incriminate her. The film goes beyond the bare record, however, to contrast her private doubts with her public assurance in the face of a rigorous ecclesiastic inquisition. As a result, a series of insidious maneuvers designed to catch and condemn her also become a very genuine test of her faith. The strength of her faith is searchingly probed in the sharp exchanges between Joan and the court, while a subdued murmur from the crowd behind her serves as a constant reminder of the political motives of her accusers. These two themes briefly come into sharp focus in the following piece of dialogue.

Bresson forces our attention to the dialogue by giving us little more to look at during the trial scenes than what we see here. This narrow focus of attention also

	PICTURE	SOUND
	1. MS, priest in charge of the proceedings. He addresses Joan and then quickly shifts his eyes to his right.	PRIEST: Are you in Go grace? SFX: Low buzzing of t crowd; stops abruptly as looks right.
	2. MLS, court clerks writing in large record books.	SFX: Slightly exaggerat scratching of their pens.

	PICTURE	SOUND
	**3.** MS, Joan looking at the clerks. She pauses a moment, then looks straight ahead and answers the question.	JOAN: If I am not, may God put me there. If I am, may God so keep me.
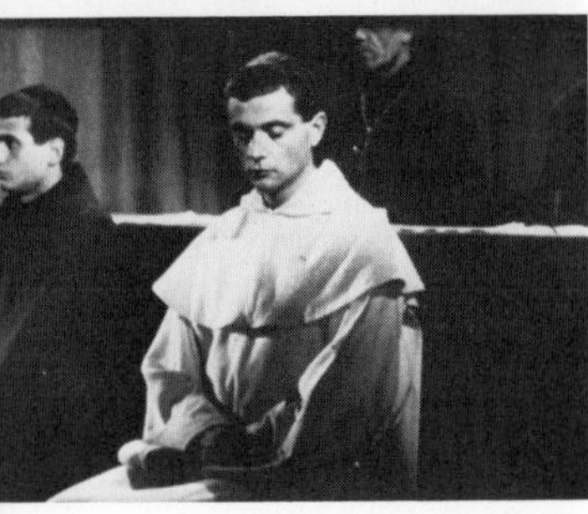	**4.** MLS, priest who is advising her. He glances toward the floor.	SFX: Slow fade-in of low crowd sound.

leaves him free to create what we never see—the rest of the courtroom—by means of sound alone. We know that the room is filled with a large hostile mob from the unremitting background of muted voices. This background must be precisely controlled, however, so that it is kept well below the level of the dialogue. It is, in fact, kept so low that we are barely aware of it until it stops. Then the contrasting silence behind the scratching of the pens makes us painfully aware of her terrible vulnerability because of the life-or-death quality both Joan and her adversaries place on her words.

This degree of control is possible only when the dialogue is recorded without a background, without the possibility of irrelevant noise or too much background sound's cluttering up the track. A separate background recording can always be added if needed, and the sound edited and mixed in at exactly the right places and at the proper level. But once unwanted sounds are part of the original recording they are nearly impossible to alter or remove without alteration of the whole track.

Because adding a background to an isolated sound is easier and more accurate

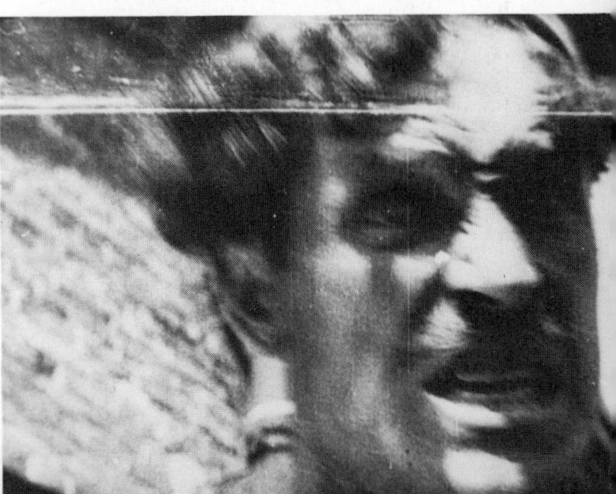

than trying to record a proper balance of all the sounds in the original recording, the tendency in most sound recording for films is to isolate each sound from its surroundings as much as possible. A great many sounds are recorded in a studio or on a sound stage, and on location the sound is usually recorded in the quietest setting available. Even in news film and documentaries, where spontaneous, authentic backgrounds are an asset, background sounds are greatly reduced by means of a highly directional microphone. This kind of microphone helps ensure a clear recording with a minimum of extraneous noise and echo; any additional background sounds that are needed can be mixed in later.

Background Sounds and Editing

Minimizing the background also makes the sound easier to edit. When a recording has a noticeable background, the level and quality of that background must be almost exactly the same in all the pieces that are to be joined together. Otherwise there will be an unnatural jump in the background sound every time there is a cut. There are some backgrounds, of course, such as traffic, crowd sounds, and construction noise, that have a random quality in which jumps are normal. But abrupt changes in even these backgrounds must occur at regular breaks in the sound or the cut will sound awkward. For instance, a cut which interrupts the sound of a passing truck, stops applause before it is finished, or breaks the regular rhythm of a jackhammer will call attention to itself no matter how smoothly the foreground sounds have been cut together.

Background sounds of any sort pose a special problem, however, in the recording and editing of synchronous dialogue. Like silent footage, sound film is shot in any convenient sequence and reassembled during editing. This makes it difficult to keep track of the exact quality of the background in shots which will be joined together but which may be filmed hours or even weeks apart. If the background of even one shot doesn't match that of the rest of the shots, there's going to be a jump in the sound where that shot is cut into the track. In fact, if even a random noise occurs during one of the pauses where a cut was planned, there is no way to avoid a jump in the background sound unless the cutting is changed. And, since words and pictures are tied together, if a piece of sound will not fit with the rest of the track, not only the sound has to be replaced but the picture as well.

In order to prevent such problems, synchronous dialogue is shot in as silent a setting as possible because silence is easier to judge and control than any particular background sound. Almost any background sound, even the most minimal, may be composed of several sounds (air conditioning, fluorescent buzz, traffic, etc.), any of which may disappear midway through a day's shooting. Since these sounds tend to mask each other, even the disappearance of several may never be noticed until the pieces of sound are joined together on the editing bench. Then there will be a noticeable difference in the backgrounds of shots made at different times of the day.

Similarly, if it is difficult to judge the quality of background sounds over the period of a day, to do so from day to day and from set to set is nearly impossible. But a standard that can be set for every location is silence. When the setting is extremely quiet it is easy to hear a new sound, no matter how soft, as soon as it occurs. And even though silence is not always a perfectly attainable goal, differences in the quality of a near-silent background can easily be masked by the later addition of a new background of sound effects or music.

Sound Perspective

A silent background is also important in synchronous recording because of the closely related problem of sound perspective, or how far a sound source seems to be from the microphone. In our everyday lives we judge the distance a sound has traveled not only by how loud it is but by how well it is able to compete with other surrounding noises. In other words, we infer its distance from the overall balance of sounds we are hearing at the time. But when we listen to sounds through a microphone, the relationship of the various sounds is exaggerated. Because even a directional microphone is unselective compared to our hearing, simply turning up the recording volume to pull in more distant sounds also greatly emphasizes surrounding noise and echo. For this reason, a sound source needn't be very far from the microphone for the sound to seem hollow and distant. Also, small changes in the distance of the actors from the microphone are much more noticeable in a recording than in normal hearing.

As a result, not only must the actors stay approximately the same distance from the microphone while each shot is being filmed, but the microphone must be placed at about the same distance from the actors from shot to shot. If the microphone is closer to the actors in close-up than in medium shot, there will be a distinct change in sound perspective when the shots are joined together. Under most circumstances, however, unless there is a big jump in the camera position we do not expect the sound perspective to change.

These requirements produce a conflict. If the microphone must be kept at a distance in order to be outside of camera range on medium and long shots, it must also be kept at a distance during close-ups. But even at relatively short distances the background of all but the quietest setting will be emphasized. The only solution is to compromise between the closest possible microphone position and a constant sound perspective, a compromise which is easier to accomplish when there is an absolute minimum of background sound.

The Sound Stage

Multiply all these problems by the hundreds of shots in the average feature film and it is not difficult to understand why film studios go to so much trouble and

expense to build sound stages. They are the easiest possible settings in which to record synchronous dialogue because almost perfect silence can be maintained throughout the filming. This silence, however, is more than just the result of filming inside a specially constructed building. It is also the product of a number of techniques that eliminate the noise which is part of the film-making process itself.

Of course, comparatively few film-makers ever get to work on a sound stage. But a brief outline of sound-stage techniques can be quite useful because these techniques are common to all synchronous-sound recording. And since, on a sound stage, the most elaborate precautions can be taken both to maintain silence and to record the dialogue clearly, it is the place where the standards for dialogue recording are set. These standards are then the basis for judging the effectiveness of the simpler techniques and equipment often used on location.

The most obvious function of a sound stage is to create a background of silence by excluding outside noises. But silence can be maintained only if inside noises are also controlled. One of the most basic of these inside noises is the sound of the room itself, its acoustics. Sound stages are usually barnlike structures, and unless sound-deadening materials are put on the walls, the dialogue will echo as if it were being recorded in an empty warehouse. This effect would not only make the dialogue hard to understand, but if the sets were a re-creation of several small rooms or other quiet, intimate surroundings, even a little echo would destroy the visual illusion. As a result, sound stages are acoustically overdeadened so that as much echo as possible is eliminated. The hard, flat walls of the sets add more than enough acoustic bounce to keep the dialogue from sounding dead, and if still more reverberation is needed, it can be added electronically after the track is edited.

Camera Noise

The next most important noise occurring inside the sound stage is that of the camera. When sound first came to motion pictures the cameras were quite noisy. There had been no reason for them to be quiet during the making of a silent film. In fact, their whirring was an asset. It told the actors and the director that the camera was still rolling even when their backs were turned to it. And the pitch of the camera mechanism helped indicate to the cameraman that he was cranking at the right speed even when he hadn't time to look at the tachometer.

But sound films forced the cameraman and his noisy camera inside a soundproof shed. They were immobilized inside an unventilated prison and had to view the action through a window. This arrangement precluded such simple camera movements as panning or tilting (the zoom lens was not yet perfected) and made each new camera setup an arduous undertaking. Rather than move the camera, directors first tried filming from several angles simultaneously, but this maneuver both ate up film and made it impossible to light properly for even one camera. When technology finally caught up it was in the form of quieter cameras and smaller, lighter soundproof shells that fit around only the camera itself. Now the camera could again be mounted on a tripod or a crane and so regained its mobility. But to this day these soundproof housings remain massive and unwieldy, and in tribute to their bulk are called *blimps*.

Even the best blimp won't make a camera perfectly quiet, so in practice the microphone is kept close to the actors and the camera kept away from the microphone. This relationship is not hard to maintain on long or medium shots but can be a problem on close-ups. If the camera is close enough to fill the frame with an actor's face, it is usually too close to the microphone, thus increasing the amount of camera noise in the recording and causing a jump in the background of the dialogue when the close-up is cut together with a medium or a long shot. One way that this mismatch is avoided is to make the close-ups with a long-focal-length lens. Then the actor's face will fill the frame even from a distance. Another way is to use a directional microphone. Its insensitive back side can be turned toward the camera, keeping down the amount of camera noise.

Mounting and Placing the Microphone

Another source of noise is the microphone itself. Because it has to remain approximately the same distance from the actors throughout the shot, it is usually mounted on the end of a long, mobile, overhead boom. This boom permits the microphone to be extended and retracted, swung about, and swiveled on its axis. That way it can both follow the action and switch back and forth as the dialogue shifts among the various actors. These movements often have to be quite violent, however, so the microphone is fastened inside a *shock mount*. This is a highly compliant suspension, such as a set of rubber bands, which floats the microphone inside a mounting ring. The shock mount cushions the vibration and jiggling of the boom movements and keeps them from being physically transmitted through the microphone and into the recording as a loud, crunching, thumping sound.

Mounting the microphone on a boom is also the simplest solution to the problem of perspective. To maintain perspective, the microphone is placed just outside of camera range for the widest shot containing dialogue, and approximately this same distance is then used for all the rest of the shots in the sequence. This distance is minimized, however, when the microphone is mounted overhead, because even in long shots the actor's head is usually close to the top of the frame. As a result, a boom microphone can be placed somewhere between six and ten feet from the actors and still kept out of the long shots. That distance is close enough for a good directional microphone to pick up the dialogue easily without unduly emphasizing random noises, camera noise, and echo.

It is also possible to conceal a microphone in the set or on the actors, a technique which is as old as sound films themselves. The earliest microphones had to be kept almost on top of the actors for the sound to be heard, so the players in these

early films often found themselves speaking into a microphone hidden in a bouquet of flowers or in that old favorite, a telephone receiver. In fact, some silent-film actors only made it into sound films because they were large enough to conceal the relatively big microphones then in use. Corpulent, gravel-voiced Andy Devine, for instance, first appeared in sound films as an extra—with his back to the camera and a microphone strapped to his chest.

Although microphones have since become far more sensitive, concealing the microphone is still a useful technique. When the shot is too wide for even a shotgun microphone to pick up the dialogue clearly, an easy alternative is simply to hide the microphone somewhere near the actors and keep the action close to it. Or if the actors must move around, several microphones are hidden in key locations and the actors speak only when close to one of them. However, if more than one microphone must be used, a microphone mixer is required. This is an electronic device that controls the volume of each microphone and combines all the sound into a single recording.

There is also a type of microphone small enough to be hidden on the actors. Called a *lavalier* or *neck microphone,* it is hung on a cord around the actor's neck. The microphone and the cable are then concealed inside the actor's clothing, behind a man's tie, for instance, or in a woman's blouse. This technique keeps the microphone extremely close to the person speaking without its being visible. It takes skill to conceal these microphones, however, since there will be a loud swishing or crunching sound if the microphone moves and rubs on the actor's clothing. It also takes skill and planning to move around while wearing one since it is easy to get tangled in the cable. And when more than one person speaks in the same shot, a microphone must be used for each of them and the sound combined by means of a microphone mixer.

The long cable that must be used to connect any microphone to a mixer or a recorder can also add noise to the recording if it is not properly handled. The studio floor is often a snake pit of power cables for the lights; if a microphone cable closely parallels one of these power lines for any distance, a low-pitched hum will be introduced into the recording. And every time the microphone or light is moved the hum level will change. As a result, microphone cables are kept away from power lines whenever possible, and if the two must cross, they are placed so that they cross at right angles. This angle keeps the hum to a minimum.

Noise on the Set

The action in any dialogue sequence inevitably creates a certain amount of noise. But such sounds as a newspaper rustling, chairs creaking, silverware rattling, etc., seldom add anything to the meaning of the track, and if they are loud enough they will distract from the dialogue. To prevent this from happening, the actors make as little noise as possible as the film is shot. And when certain noises can't be eliminated, they try instead to keep them out from behind the words. That way the editor can easily cut these unwanted sounds out of the recording without cutting into the dialogue. At other times, however, such natural sound effects as footsteps, or a door closing, are wanted in the track, but they do not sound right because they are *off-microphone,* that is, they occur too far from the microphone to be properly recorded. While an additional microphone can be used to pick up such incidental sounds, it is usually easier just to eliminate them or keep them out from behind the words. Then they can be replaced by sound effects which are later recorded and edited to fit the track.

A background sound which naturally continues throughout the dialogue presents a somewhat different problem. Such continuous sounds as those of a cocktail party, for instance, or of someone playing a piano, would make the dialogue impossible to edit because the quality and level of such sounds would have to be the same from shot to shot; otherwise there would be jumps in the background. And in the case of music, a specific note would have to fall on the cutting point of each of the shots to be joined together so that the music will flow without a break in the melody. To avoid these problems, it is necessary to eliminate any background sound as the film is shot. The actors or musicians go through the motions soundlessly, and if necessary, the ice is left out of the glasses, the actors take off their shoes, the strings are removed from the instruments, etc. These measures preserve the silence needed for editing the dialogue, and the background sounds which had to be eliminated are later added during the mix.

Even after all these precautions have been followed, however, there still remains a subtle form of noise called *room presence*. It is composed of a certain amount of residual outside noise, camera noise, the movement of air through the microphone, and electronic noise from the recording circuits. These sounds give a specific quality to the background of silence. At the end of each shooting session a minute or two of *presence* is recorded with everything quiet and the camera running. This recording is later used by the editor to replace unwanted noises or as filler whenever sufficient pauses haven't been provided. Since the sound of room presence is somewhat different from that of unrecorded tape, using it to pad out the track eliminates any possibility of even the smallest jumps in the background of the dialogue.

Recording on Location

These, then, are the problems involved in the recording of synchronous dialogue in the carefully controlled acoustic environment of a sound stage. It is obvious that few natural locations will match these conditions. But more and more films are being shot on location as directors demand, and lower budgets require, authentic surroundings.

Location filming presents the sound man with a whole new set of problems.

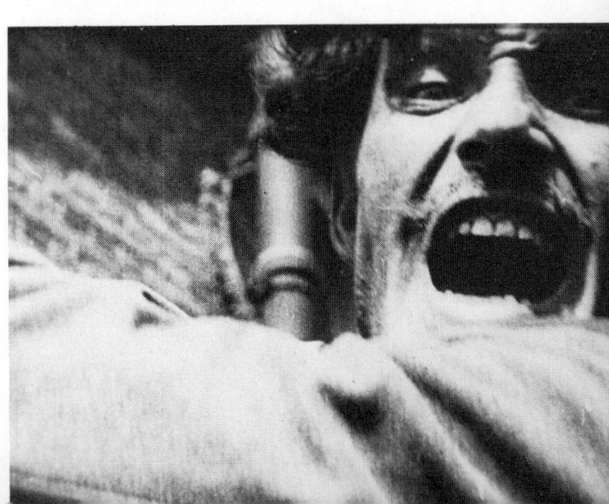

He must achieve the same results off the sound stage as on, but without the same close control over either sound quality or silence. Location recording also demands that he reduce the size and the amount of his equipment in order to move about freely. This is less of a problem in feature-film production because a separate sound van is often available, but it becomes a major consideration in news, documentary, educational, and independent film-making. In these kinds of films the sound man may be able to use little more than what he can load on his back and carry in his hands. Under such conditions, recording synchronous dialogue becomes a real test of a sound man's skill since ingenuity and a sharp ear must substitute for sophisticated equipment.

Even an experienced sound man, however, cannot guarantee good results under exceptionally noisy conditions. In some cases, such as documentaries and news film, as long as the voice is intelligible, not much else matters. And the interference of surrounding noise and echo may even be a plus under certain circumstances since the quality of the environment may be more important than what is said. Some of the best reporting from the battlefields of Vietnam, for instance, has been most effective because the only thing that could be heard was the enveloping roar of a fire fight. But whichever is to become more important, the words or the surroundings, depends upon the first decision—where the recording will be made.

Naturally Occurring Noises

Sounds are as critical a consideration as appearance when choosing a location. Noise and echo cannot be masked out of the sound track in the same way that unwanted parts of the setting can be framed out of the pictures; and, particularly outdoors, unwanted sounds can carry a long, long way. For instance, only the most modern idyllic love story could be filmed in a sylvan glen a half mile from a busy interstate highway. But the same setting much further from civilization would be filled only with the sounds of nature. These are appropriate to an idyllic mood and, as long as they are not at too high a level, can easily be controlled by means of a directional microphone.

But the microphone alone cannot control certain kinds of sounds. The wind is a typical example. It not only causes trees and grass to rustle, but it can cause a loud thundering noise of its own as it blows through the microphone. While this makes it impossible to record in a strong wind, in light to medium breezes this noise can be prevented by the use of a windscreen. These screens are commercially available for most professional microphones but they can also be quite easily made by loosely wrapping the microphone with an inch-thick piece of foam rubber or several layers of cheesecloth. This covering lets in the minuscule sound vibrations while breaking up the direct, strong pressure of the wind. Because a breeze can spring up at any time and ruin an otherwise good take, a windscreen is a normal precaution in all outdoor recording.

Another sound which is difficult to control is the large amount of echo found in any but the most heavily carpeted, drape-covered indoor settings. It cannot even be greatly reduced by means of a directional microphone since some of this echo is reflected into the sensitive front end of the microphone no matter which way it is pointed. As a result, the only way to make a significant reduction in the amount of echo in the recording is to alter the acoustics of the setting. This can be done by adding drapes, carpets, and overstuffed furniture. Or if that is impossible, either because such props would look wrong or because there isn't enough time to get them, blankets, drapes, or carpeting can be hung just outside of camera range. Either method reduces the amount of echo by absorbing some of the sound and by causing the rest to diffuse irregularly.

Camera Noise

Because the higher noise levels found on location tend to mask camera noise, it is possible to use simpler techniques to blimp the camera. Of course, if the setting is extremely quiet, a full-sized studio blimp can be used. But if this is too unwieldy, there are smaller, lighter aluminum and fiberglass blimps designed for location shooting that work almost as well. There are also self-blimped cameras available. These cameras were originally designed for shooting single-system news film, but in recent years they have been adapted for highly mobile double-system filming. Because the camera mechanism is specially designed for quiet operation, the camera body itself is sufficient insulation against noise. The result is a camera which is only slightly larger than ordinary cameras; and while not so silent as an externally blimped camera, it is still barely noticeable in a quiet room.

When the location is not particularly quiet, blimping is kept to a minimum. Sometimes all that is needed is a *barney*. This is a thickly padded quilt cut to fasten snugly around the camera without interfering with its operation. Or a real quilt or blanket is simply thrown over the camera. For many years this was all the Japanese did even on studio productions. And in a pinch, should nothing be available to quiet the camera, a cardioid microphone can be kept close to the action and a long enough lens used to keep the camera away from the microphone. While this procedure results in a relatively noisy recording, the dialogue will still be understandable. Of course, when the location is noisier than the camera, no blimping need be used at all.

Mounting and Placing the Microphone

Simpler techniques are also used to position the microphone when on location. On feature films, a large studio boom is often used even in the field; but where portability is a problem, a lighter version, called a *fishpole*, is preferred. This is a

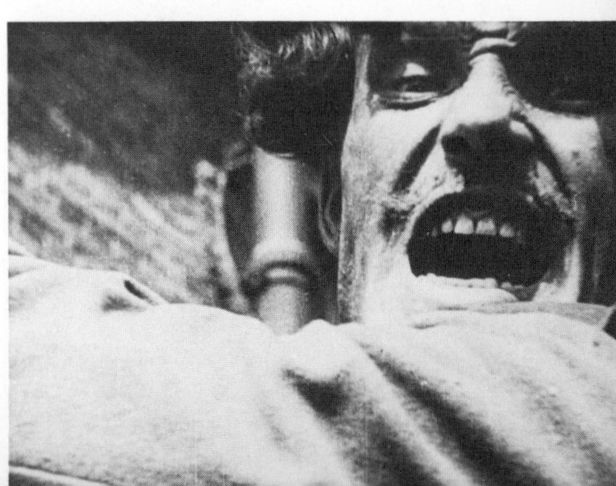

six- to ten-foot aluminum or bamboo pole (hence the name) used to suspend the microphone above the actors. But even a fishpole may be too cumbersome for truly mobile filming. Then the sound man usually hand-holds the microphone. Sometimes he does this by holding the shock mount, sometimes by simply holding the microphone itself. Keeping the microphone in its mount is preferable, however, since even a slightly shifting grip on some microphones will cause what is called *handling noise.* The hand movements are transmitted into the recording as a loud scraping, thumping noise.

But when recording the dialogue for a long shot in a noisy setting, none of these techniques will work. They simply do not permit even a shotgun microphone to be placed close enough to pick up the words clearly. Instead, a microphone has to be hidden somewhere near the actors. And if the noise level is high enough, or if there is a great deal of movement in the shot, it would be better yet to have the actors wear microphones. But even this isn't the complete answer since the cable on a lavalier presents two problems—it restricts the action and is difficult to conceal.

These problems are so common in location shooting that there is a special *wireless microphone* designed to overcome them. It consists of a lavalier connected to a tiny radio transmitter which is also hidden in the actor's clothing. This transmitter eliminates the cable by broadcasting the sound of each actor's voice to a special radio receiver connected to the microphone mixer. Depending upon the surroundings in which it is used, the receiver can pick up the sound from a wireless microphone over a quarter mile away.

The wireless microphone is the only type of microphone which stays close enough to the actors to minimize surrounding noise effectively while still allowing them great freedom of movement. It is also the only microphone which can be used in a barren, open setting (since there is no cable to conceal), or in a very busy location, such as a street or a crowded room (because there is no cable to interfere with the surrounding activity). In fact, wireless microphones would be a perfect solution for most location sound problems except that they are erratic. Because they are more complicated than the standard microphone they break down more easily. As a result, they are usually used only where the sound cannot be picked up by a more reliable conventional microphone.

Background Loops

Because location sound is highly unpredictable under even the best of circumstances, the last thing done before leaving each location is to make a separate recording of just the background sounds. This procedure is similar to the recording of room presence except that later the sound is mixed into the dialogue to mask small jumps in the quality of the background. It is usually enough to record only four or five minutes of this sound because the recording can be spliced into a continuous loop, which is then endlessly run through a loop recorder and faded in or out as needed during the mix. The loop may run full circle several times during the same scene, however, so it is important to exclude any distinctive sounds, such as a loud birdcall or an auto horn. The audience will begin to recognize these repetitive sounds and they will no longer blend into the background.

Synchronization and Slating

Synchronization also becomes a special problem on location because nearly all lip-synchronous dialogue is now recorded double-system. This means synchronously recording sound and picture on separate machines. Keeping these two machines running together is not normally difficult, but there is no way to check their synchronization until after the film has been processed. Then it is too late. At best, *out-of-sync* footage can be corrected only by the most arduous efforts, and sometimes not at all. Unless the camera and recorder can be counted upon to maintain synchronization accurately and reliably, solving every other sound-recording problem is a waste of time.

In the studio and in conventional location filming, the two machines can easily be synchronized by simply locking them to the same power line. Or if both machines are battery operated, they can be kept together by a synchronizing signal generated in the camera and fed to the recorder through a cable. But it is impossible to work at the end of a power cord or synchronizing cable when shooting news, documentary, and some kinds of independent films. Both the camera and the recorder must be able to respond quickly and freely because the action is often unpredictable.

The synchronizing techniques which have been devised for these particular kinds of situations are more flexible, but they are also more complicated. One such technique is to transmit the synchronizing signal from the camera to the recorder by radio, a system similar to that used in wireless microphones. Another ingenious method involves a pair of identical tuning forks or tuned crystals, one in the camera and the other in the recorder. These act like extraordinarily accurate electric clocks, timing the operation of the two machines so that they automatically and independently run in exact synchronization. Both these systems allow the cameraman and the sound man to move about unhindered by any physical connection between their two machines. But neither system is quite as reliable as conventional synchronizing methods because more things can go wrong with a complicated device than with a simpler one.

A procedure closely related to synchronization, called *slating,* also becomes more complicated on location. Because double-system sound and picture are

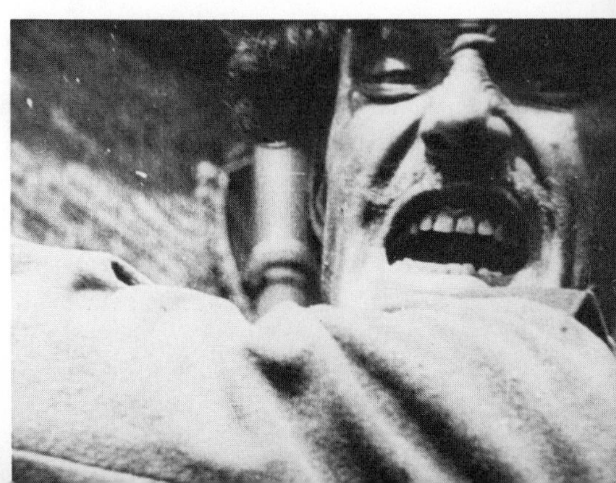

recorded separately, a slate is used to identify the film and tape for each shot and to record an exact point at which the two are clearly in synchronization. This information later helps the editor sort the good shots from the bad, match each piece of sound to the appropriate picture, and accurately synchronize all the hundreds of shots which eventually make up the finished film.

The slate itself is a small blackboard with a stick, called a *clapstick,* hinged to one corner. On the blackboard are written the name of the film, the shot number, and the number of times the shot has been taken. As soon as both camera and recorder are rolling, the slate is held up in front of the lens and the information on it read into the microphone. This simultaneously records the same identification on both film and tape. Then the clapstick is banged shut against the edge of the slate.

Courtesy: JANUS FILMS, INC.

These two frames are from the introduction to one of the sequences in Max Ophuls's *La Ronde.* The slate is held by the central figure in the film, a combination master of ceremonies and narrator. It was included by the director as an ironic comment on both the persuasiveness and the artificiality of the medium he is using. We have included these shots simply because they are more interesting to look at than those of the assistant who normally holds the slate. They show how the clapstick appears just as it closes. When it hits the edge of the slate, it also makes a sharp bang on the sound track. In the editing room this bang is matched with the first frame in which the clapstick is obviously shut. From that point on the pictures are in exact synchronization with the sound track.

This is the simplest way to slate each shot so it is used both in the studio and for most types of location filming. But there are also a number of alternative methods. For instance, when it is impossible to anticipate the start of the action, the end of the shot is slated with the slate upside down. This tells the editor that the slate applies to the previous shot and not the one immediately following. And when slating will consume too much time, interrupt the action, or attract attention to the camera, the slate is skipped altogether. Instead, the microphone is held in front of the lens and the end lightly tapped with a finger. This is done either at the beginning or at the end of the shot. The tap makes a sharp pop on the sound track that corresponds to the first frame in which the finger touches the microphone.

None of these slating methods may be feasible, however, when the camera and the recorder are not physically connected. The sound man may be too far from the cameraman to know when to slate the shot or even to know when the camera is running. As a result, some of the radio- and crystal-operated systems also use a radio signal to start the recorder automatically, and to slate both film and tape, every time the camera is started. In addition, the most sophisticated of these systems provide a separate radio channel for communication among the director, the cameraman, and the sound man. This permits the sound man to find out what is being filmed so that he can keep himself out of the shot.

Crystal-synchronized automatic-slating systems are also well adapted for multiple-camera location filming. In this technique several cameras running in synchronization with the recorder simultaneously provide different views of the same sequence of dialogue. It is a technique which is often used to film unusual events or action that is hard to repeat. For instance, several cameras, an automatic synchronizing system, and wireless microphones were used to film dialogue sequences on the streets of Hong Kong for the television series *I Spy*.

In a multicamera setup, one camera and the recorder run continuously to provide a master long shot and sound track. In addition, one or two other cameras take medium shots and/or close-ups, but these cameras run only when needed, thus saving film. Whenever one of the cameras starts, it transmits its own coded slating signal to the recorder. These signals are recorded on the tape and later used by the editor to synchronize the various shots with the appropriate sections of the sound track.

Post-synchronization

Sound quality and synchronization can become so difficult to control on location that sometimes the dialogue is created by means of post-synchronization. This involves filming the dialogue double-system, but with the sound used only as a record of exactly what was said. Later, in a sound studio, the actors re-record

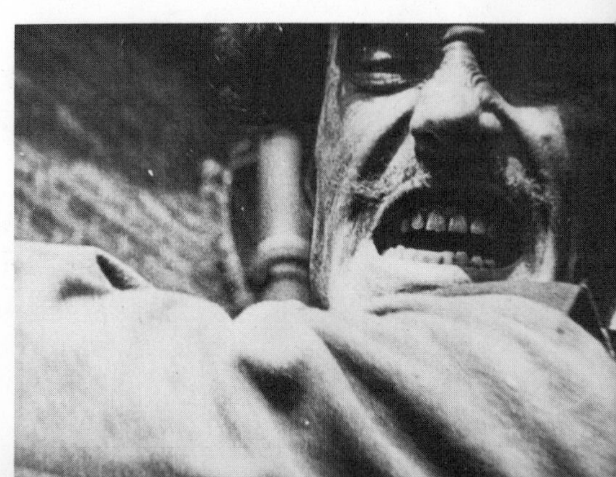

the voices while watching the footage and synchronizing their words to the lip movements on the screen.

This is an easy way to record the dialogue in crowd scenes, or for such extremely active scenes as fights, sports, or combat—situations in which even staged action is sometimes too confused and volatile for the sound to make much sense. And when synchronously recorded dialogue has been ruined by noise and echo, or a faulty synchronizing system, the quickest and cheapest way to save the footage is to post-synchronize new dialogue. But post-synchronization is more than just an emergency or stopgap technique. It is much more flexible, especially on location, than double-system recording because sound quality and synchronization are never a problem.

A good example of this is this brief scene from Jean-Luc Godard's *A Woman Is a Woman*. The film is a loving study of a richly simplified woman—one who wants a child (anyone's) and simultaneously wants to be in a musical comedy (why not?). She is determined that if her husband won't get her pregnant, she'll get her husband's bachelor friend to oblige. The friend, played by Jean-Paul Belmondo, is a natural piccolo player routed to the bassoon section. Like sour notes that set off sweeter melodies, gags punctuate the film in a burlesque of musical comedy styles. The following sequence is one of those gags.

Belmondo walks down a busy street. From out of nowhere, in one of those coincidences that have traditionally held together pulp novels and classic comedies, a hotelkeeper appears, to whom he owes a long-overdue bill. The man attacks, hoping to get the money by publicly embarrassing Belmondo. But Belmondo defends in the best Gallic tradition—counterattack. Insult follows insult in a growing crescendo of abuse. Finally all reason is lost in a dizzying game of joyously escalating invective. End scene.

PICTURE	SOUND
 **1.** Camera pans L with Belmondo.	HTLKPR: Louse! BMDO: Slob!

PICTURE		SOUND
	**2.**	HTLKPR: Chiseler!
	**3.**	BMDO: Leach!
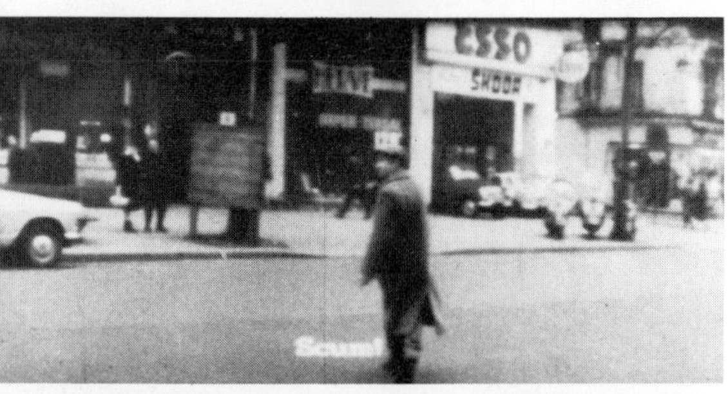	**4.**	HTLKPR: Scum!
	**5.**	BMDO: Pervert!

The humorous quality of this incident largely depends upon where and how it was shot. The busy street both emphasizes the unexpected nature of their meeting and provides a public arena for their shouting match. And having them walk away from the camera in shots 2 through 5 makes their futile argument become sillier and sillier. This is because each successively longer shot increases the distance between them. As this gap widens they must strain harder and harder to make themselves heard, so they both appear slightly more petulant and ridiculous each time we see them.

All these shots were simple to film and edit, but shots 2 through 5 would have required the toughest kind of synchronous-sound recording. Because the scene depends upon passing traffic and pedestrians to give the location its most important characteristics, surrounding noise would make it difficult both to hear the words and to keep the background sounds at the same level from shot to shot. To minimize this noise, the microphone would have had to be kept close to the action. But crucial parts of the scene are too distant for the use of a directional microphone from outside camera range, and the open space around the men precludes the hiding of a microphone or even the cable from a lavalier. About the only thing that would have worked well is a wireless microphone, and that would have required a lot of extra equipment for only a few words of dialogue.

When the track is post-synchronized, however, these problems never occur because both dialogue and background sounds are added later, under perfectly controlled studio conditions. In addition, the film can be shot as if it were silent—in any location, with any camera, a smaller crew, and no retakes for sound. And even after the footage is shot, new voices or new words can be used. If the director doesn't like an actor's voice, or if nonactors are cast in speaking roles, he can get a skilled dialogue actor to provide a new voice for a good face. Or if he doesn't like the old dialogue once he's seen the footage, new lines can be matched to the old lip movements. As long as the new words or sentences have about as many syllables as the old, it is nearly impossible for an audience to tell that the sounds being formed by the lips are not the same as those they are hearing.

This technique makes it possible to post-synchronize the dialogue in a whole new language, a great advantage in Europe, where feature films must be distributed in several different languages in order to make a profit. It also permits American film companies to shoot abroad with foreign casts, or to change the language of domestically made features for foreign distribution. In fact, post-synchronization is an inexpensive way to create all of the dialogue needed in a low-budget feature. It thus permitted many young European directors to make their early films. But this technique is not as widely used in this country. Because our major films are shot mostly or entirely on sound stages, it is easier to record the dialogue clearly in the first place than to re-record it, a shot at a time, for the two hundred or more shots in the average feature film.

Recording Narration

Regardless of how the dialogue is recorded, however, the sound effects, the music, and the narration in a film are normally post-synchronized. These types of sound are recorded either by projecting the film and recording the sounds as they are matched to the actions, or by editing the recording to fit the pictures. Like the post-synchronization of dialogue, this technique makes both sound and picture easier to record and edit. In addition, these sounds are usually fewer and less continuous than dialogue and more loosely matched to the action than words are to lip movements, thus making their post-synchronization faster and less demanding than re-recording dialogue.

A narration is usually the easiest kind of sound to record. If the script is read as the film is projected, the recording is done in a studio with a soundproof window between the narrator and the projector; while if the narration is recorded without the film, any small studio or quiet room will do. In either case, the microphone is placed about a foot in front of the narrator, and is suspended at eye level or mounted on a stand about shoulder high. Either position keeps the narrator from speaking directly into the microphone and thus prevents popping *p*'s and hissing consonants. The microphone itself should be omni-directional so as to allow the narrator to move his head without moving outside the microphone's area of maximum sensitivity.

Several special voice effects can be created by the changing or moving of the microphone. To deepen the voice, for instance, an older style cardioid is used in place of the omni-directional microphone. When placed within two feet of the narrator, these directional microphones exhibit what is called a *proximity effect,* a gradual increase in low-frequency response as the microphone gets closer to the sound source. Or if a more seductive sound, a thought voice, or a whisper is needed, it can be created by moving the microphone closer and speaking more softly. The closer the microphone, the more breathy and intimate the vocal quality. At such short distances, however, popping and hissing become a particular problem, so a windscreen is used to keep them under control.

There is also a form of narration called *on-camera narration.* It is most commonly used when a reporter introduces a TV news story or a documentary. Here the narrator appears before the camera for part of the narration and then records the rest of the script in the same setting, with the same microphone in exactly the same position. It is necessary to record the narration in the same way as the synchronous portion because, if the voice-only part were later recorded somewhere else, there would be an abrupt change in the sound quality.

Still another kind of narration can be created from interviews. These interviews can be done either on camera or by recording only the voice and can be made either in a studio or, as is more often the case, on location. Interviews, however, present the same kinds of editing problems as synchronous dialogue. As long as

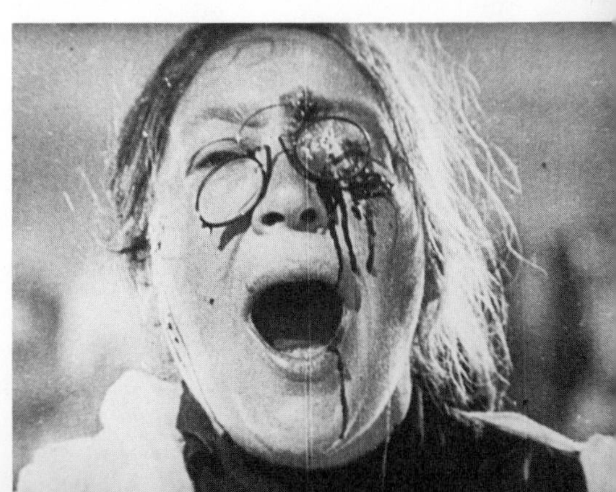

they are recorded in a studio or another quiet setting, it is relatively easy to cut together different parts of the same interview, or even several different interviews, without any noticeable jumps in the quality of the background sounds.

But the background needn't always be silent if the background sounds are chosen carefully. Surrounding noise can tell us as much about the person as the interview itself. And if the strongly differing backgrounds of two or more interviews are abruptly cut together, or even used close to each other, the contrasting quality of these background sounds is emphasized. The conflicting backgrounds thus set off the voices and call our attention to their context, creating new levels of relationship between the people speaking, their words, and the pictures.

This is exactly the effect that occurs when interviews recorded in different locations are used together in the following sequence from *The World of the Teen-ager,* an NBC documentary produced by Frank DeFelitta and Joe Mehan. The film is about the pressures and constraints that envelop adolescents growing up in an average American community. In this scene a sympathetic adult's view of teen-agers is played against a teen-ager's own sentiments.

	PICTURES	SOUND
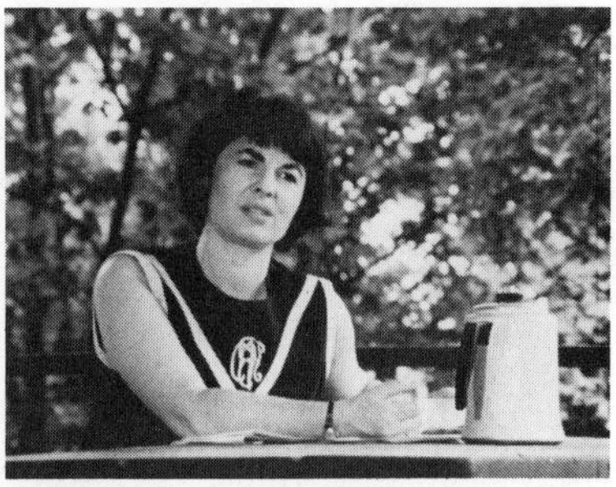	**1.** MS, woman talking (6½ sec.).	WOMAN: I don't—think t really mean to do harm. T just want to be noticed.
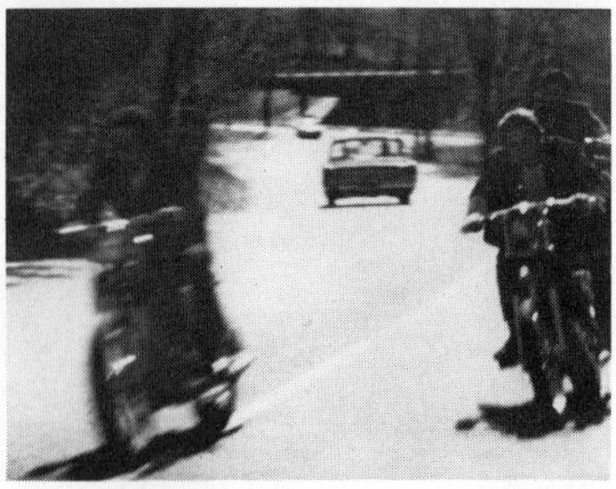	**2.** MLS, three motorcycles coming toward camera; pan L with them as they pass (3½ sec.).	MUS: Cut to fast coun and-western banjo music. SFX: Roar of motorcyc fades out as they pass.
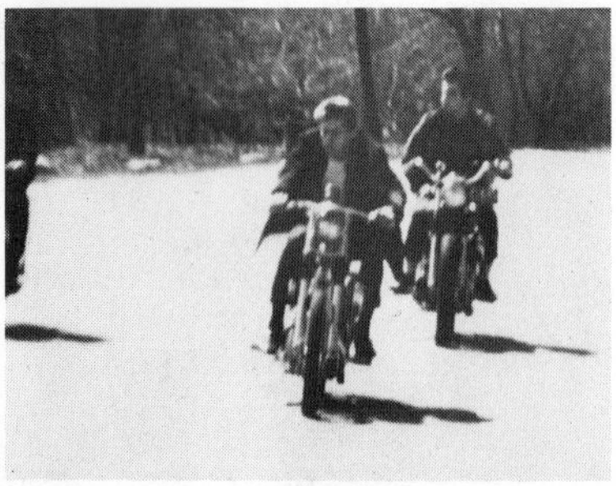	**3.** MLS, three motorcycles coming toward camera; truck back with them (4½ sec.).	MUS: Up and then under lowing: BOY: . . . feel like a k when you're on your b You know you've got power right in your hand

	PICTURES	SOUND
	**4.** MCU, lead motorcyclist coming toward camera; trucking back with him (2½ sec.).	BOY: . . . and you can just —if anybody looks at you . . .
	**5.** MS, three motorcycles pass camera, R–L, one at a time (2 sec.).	SFX: Roar of each motorcycle as it passes camera.
	**6.** MLS, same as shot 3 (10 sec.).	MUS: Under and then fades out. SFX: Roar of motorcycles under following: WOMAN: I think this is the period of the individual. They are taking a "notice me" attitude. Notice . . .
	**7.** MS, lead motorcyclist coming toward camera; trucking back with him (2 sec.).	WOMAN: . . . me as an individual.

	PICTURES	SOUND
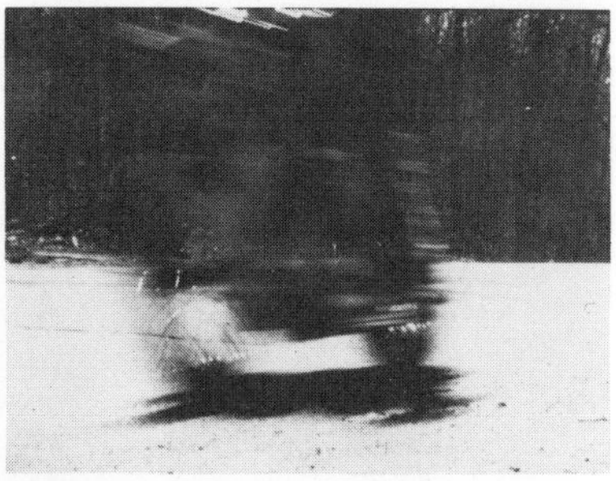	**8.** MS, low angle of one motorcycle passing camera, R–L (⅔ sec.).	SFX: Roar of motorcycle.
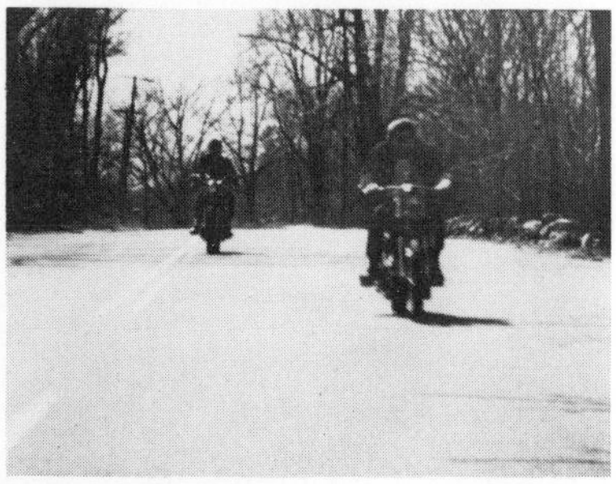	**9.** MLS, two motorcycles coming toward camera; pass camera on either side (1½ sec.).	SFX: Roar of motorcyc fades out as they pass. WOMAN: They want to .
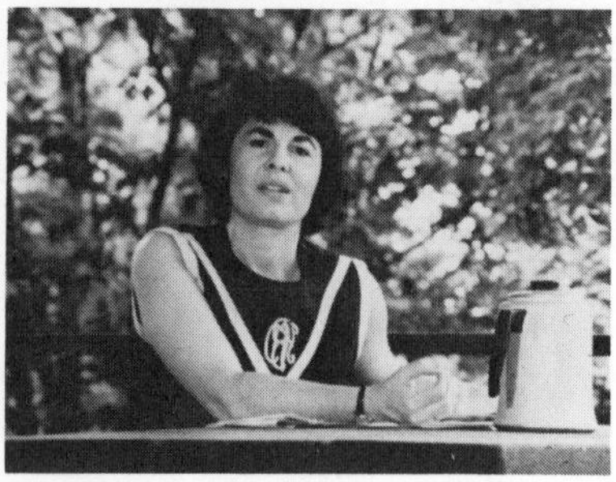	**10.** MS, same as shot 1 (13 sec.).	WOMAN: . . . take par they want to be part of t world. And I think they ne guidance—along this to— realize exactly how they c give, and I think this perh is where the community l fallen short.

The words alone would all seem to support the woman's conclusions. Both the community and its children really want the same thing, so all that is needed is a little more awareness and compassion. But the contexts of the interviews tell us quite the reverse. Each of these people is firmly embedded in a completely different culture and any changes will be hard won.

This contradiction is implicit in both sound and pictures. The woman speaks quietly in the tranquil privacy of her yard, while the boy's voice is heard against a background of other voices, plus the motorcycles and fast music which were added later during editing. It is this contrast which makes us feel what their words alone cannot express—how very differently they live. The teen-ager's world offers little stability. It is one in which he must compete for his identity but can do so only in marginal ways, such as riding a motorcycle. And the woman, insulated and secure in a world of her own, is unaware of how fierce this competition is or how strongly pressures from the adult community force these boys to cling to whatever roles they can find.

Finding and Recording Music

Compared to finding the voices, getting the right music can be much more complicated. In the previous example, the budget provided by NBC was large enough to cover an original score composed and recorded by The Blues Project. But music from a prerecorded tape or disc could have been used just as easily because every broadcaster has a blanket license to use any music from the vast repertoire of copyrighted recordings now available. This kind of license, however, is not available for any other kinds of films. As a result, other film-makers who want to make a profit from their work, or even just show it publicly, must first obtain a separate clearance for every piece of copyrighted music they wish to use. Each clearance involves getting separate permission from the composer, the music publisher, the musicians' union, and the record company. It also usually means paying each of them a fee and there is no set scale for these fees. They each charge what they think they can get, except that the musicians' union charges per performer.

This licensing problem can be avoided if the music is taken from a record library. These are collections of prerecorded music which are sold through commercial sound-recording studios. As much music as is needed can be purchased for a flat fee, but the fee depends upon the particular collection, the amount of music used, and the size of the audience for the film. The music in these collections is rather stereotyped, but it does run the gamut of musical styles. It includes everything from old favorites, such as "Turkey in the Straw" and the "Blue Danube Waltz," to classical, country-and-western, blues, and rock, plus selections specially written to evoke certain moods, such as "fast and active," "pensive," "playful," etc. There are also bridges and endings. These are short pieces and single notes which can be used to end a scene, provide a transition between scenes, or punctuate certain actions. The longer selections are written with the same melody in a number of different tempos and keys so that the same tune can be used in several scenes. They also have prolonged, repetitive endings so that there are a number of places to end the music, making it easier to cut the music to fit the pictures.

When more than just a couple of pieces of music are needed, it is usually easier for the film-maker to use an original score. This can vary from something as simple as having a musician improvise some music as he watches the film to having a score for chorus and orchestra specially composed and recorded. Anything more than just improvisation, however, requires a certain amount of preparation. The music must be written, and writing music for a film is not like composing any other

kind of music. Not only must the composer constantly keep the pictures in mind, he must also know how his score will fit with the rest of the sound track. This means that the music cannot be finished and recorded until after the film is edited. But the composer should still become acquainted with the film as early in the production as possible. That way he is given enough time, as the film is being shot and cut, to complete the equally difficult and expressive task of writing the music. This procedure also allows the film-maker to take into consideration the composer's musical ideas and requirements so that the music can mesh coherently with the finished footage.

Multitrack Recording

Music recording can be done in two very different ways. The more complex of these is a recently developed technique mainly used to record popular music. But since the same sound studios that do this recording also record motion-picture sound tracks, the technique is used for film music as well. It involves a tape machine that can simultaneously record eight, sixteen, or twenty-four separate tracks across the face of one-half-, one-, or two-inch-wide tape. The music is recorded in a very large, dead studio with the various instruments widely separated and isolated from each other by sound-absorbing screens. Each instrument is picked up by a separate, closely placed cardioid microphone, and each microphone is fed to a separate track on the recorder. In this arrangement the musicians can hear each other, but each microphone can pick up only its own particular instrument. As a result, each track contains only one instrument recorded as fully and cleanly as possible.

There are a number of advantages to this obviously elaborate technique. One is that the final sound quality and balance can be determined at leisure. After the recording session is over, the separate tracks are mixed down to a single track, and as this is done, the instruments can be rebalanced in a number of ways simply by the turning up of one track or the turning down of another. It is also possible to create new sound perspectives by electronically adding varying amounts of echo to some instruments and not to others, filtering out certain frequencies on some instruments, distorting others, etc. In other words, many things that create new sounds can be tried without keeping high-priced musicians sitting around waiting.

Another advantage is that the various instruments can be recorded at different times. Once the basic tracks are recorded, they can be played back into earphones for other musicians as they perform their part of the music. This flexibility allows new instruments to be added to the original recording if the music director feels that it lacks fullness. It also permits a small group of performers to be backed up by a full chorus, for instance, without having to have everybody in the studio at once. And it even makes it possible for the same performer to play several different instruments, or several different parts on the same instrument, within the same piece of music.

Conventional Recording

The other, more traditional, technique for recording music is less flexible but much simpler. It too involves multiple microphones, but during the recording session the sound from each is immediately combined by means of a microphone mixer so that a single recording can be made on quarter-inch tape using a standard tape recorder. As a result, the sound quality and balance are determined at the recording session. The first requirement of this technique is to use a studio or a concert hall that has *brighter,* meaning more reverberant, acoustics—a more pleasing sound than a dead studio. The musicians sit as an ensemble, with a separate microphone predominantly, but not exclusively, picking up each major section of instruments. The sound balance is then set both by moving the microphones and by adjusting the volume of each microphone with the separate volume controls on the mixer. But the quality of the sound is largely determined by the room itself. Because the microphones are not extremely close to the performers, they also pick up the room's acoustic qualities. These characteristic qualities color and blend the sound from each instrument, giving the recording its overall feeling of clarity and balance.

A simplified version of this technique requires only one microphone, a standard quarter-inch tape recorder, and a room with the proper acoustics. When the music must have a close, intimate quality, a small, rather acoustically dead room is used and the microphone kept close to the performers. While if the music must have a more spacious, imposing sound, a larger, brighter studio or concert hall is used and the microphone kept farther away. It takes more skill to balance the sound with only one microphone, but this technique does makes it possible to record even large groups with a minimum of equipment.

Timing the Music to Fit the Action

Although original music is written to the right length, it must still be performed at the right tempo if it is to fit the edited footage. When this timing doesn't have to be absolutely accurate, the music can either be performed as the film is projected, or just played to last a predetermined length of time. But if the music is very complicated, or must closely match certain actions, the timing must be more carefully controlled. An example is the music behind this shot from Kurosawa's *Yojimbo.* A samurai, played by Toshiro Mifune, is playing two corrupt families against each other. Here he brings one of the families news that two of their henchmen are captured and have confessed to a crime against the Emperor. As he talks to some underlings, he senses the leader of the family coming down the stairs behind him. He decides to test the man's intentions by offering the family a way out of their dilemma if they hire him. The leader slows his steps and then hesitates. He

wants this particular warrior on his side but is afraid of the cost. His uncertain steps betray his anxiety, and this irregular rhythm is emphasized by altering the beat of the background music to mimic his faltering movements. Then he suddenly makes up his mind, and the quickening tempo of both the action and the music foreshadow the success of the samurai's scheme.

This kind of scoring requires that the music reach the right point at exactly the right time and then accurately change its rhythm to match the new rhythm of the action. This match can only be made with the help of an electronic metronome called a *click track,* a tape on which the changing rhythms have been recorded as a certain number of clicks per minute. The tape is synchronized with the film during the recording session and played back to the conductor through a pair of earphones. The clicks allow him to concentrate on the performance rather than on the projected images by automatically telling him the right pace for the music.

When a song or dance number is used in a film it is usually easier to let the music control the tempo of the action. Then the post-synchronizing procedure is reversed; the music is recorded first and the action later synchronized to it. The recording is played back as the film is shot, and the cast sings along with the recording and/or goes through the dance routine in time with the music. The shooting and editing have to be very carefully laid out in advance, though, since there is very little leeway when the cuts have to match the rhythm of the music.

Recording Sound Effects

The techniques used to obtain sound effects are generally the same as those used for both narration and music. Many sound effects can be gotten from records and tapes available through sound-recording studios. But since we are surrounded by the raw materials from which to create a sound-effects track, it is usually easier just to record what is needed. The simplest way to understand how this is done is to come full circle and look once again at the opening sequence from *The Blue Angel.* The techniques used to record the many sound effects in this sequence are the same ones used in almost all sound-effects recording.

These sound effects had to be particularly well done; in this sequence, they carry the burden of the meaning. Therefore, the sound quality of each effect, including the type of sound, the acoustics of the location, the nature of the background sounds, and the placement of the microphone all had to be calculated exactly. But in order to regulate all of these elements the sound man first had to analyze the script and then organize the recording according to the practical problems in each shot. For instance, the first sound effect in the sequence (shot 2) is the honking of geese. Since these fowl were included in the shot, and the shot was filmed on a

	PICTURE	SOUND
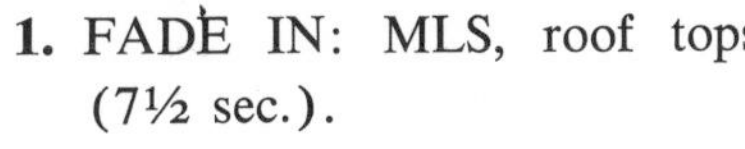	**1.** FADE IN: MLS, roof tops (7½ sec.).	MUS: Full; ends with end of shot.
	**2.** MLS, busy street. Woman in foreground is crating geese. Other woman enters street from shop in background (11½ sec.).	SFX: Clamor of honking geese.
	**3.** MS, woman opens shutter over shop window to reveal poster of dance-hall singer "Lola-Lola." She throws pailful of water on window, then pauses to mimic poster (24½ sec.).	SFX: Clank of shutter being raised, then splash of water hitting glass. Geese, in background, slowly fade out at end of shot.

	PICTURE	SOUND
	**4.** CU, door with nameplate, "Prof. Dr. Rath" (4 sec.). *LONG DISSOLVE*	SFX: Loud, hurried footstep
	**5.** MLS, interior stairway and upper landing. Child is frantically running to get books and coat while mother watches. Child exits down stairs (10½ sec.). *DISSOLVE*	SFX: School bell starts rin ing with start of dissolve a continues over sound of chi rushing about; ends as chi is about to leave. Footste end at end of shot.
	**6.** MS, vestibule. Housekeeper crosses with tray and enters study (7 sec.).	SFX: Quick, firm footste rattle of dishes on tray.
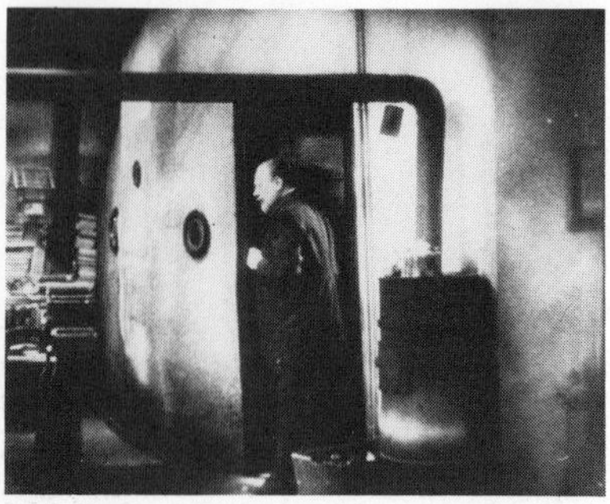	**7.** MLS, Rath's study. Housekeeper enters R and camera pans L with her as she crosses to table, puts tray down, and calls him. She arranges food on table, then camera pans R as she leaves, holding on door to his bedroom as she exits frame. He enters through door, checking his pockets, and exits frame L (36 sec.).	SFX: Footsteps continue. HSKPR: Herr Professor- breakfast (she mutters soft to herself as she sets table). SFX: Soft footsteps as enters.

sound stage, it was probably easiest to record the effect synchronously, along with the pictures. Animals, however, don't always cooperate by providing enough noise at the right time, so this same sound effect might have also been recorded a second time, after the shooting was over. Then the two recordings could later be mixed together to give a more intense feeling to the action.

The sounds of the shutter opening and the water hitting the shop window (shot 3) were also probably recorded synchronously because this shot too was made on a sound stage. And the background sound of geese honking was simply extra sound carried over from the previous shot. Similarly, in shot 4, the sound effects were also probably carried over from another shot. Since nothing we see in this shot would cause what we hear, the sound of footsteps rapidly mounting the stairs was no doubt part of the sound recorded with the next shot. However, this sound could also have been recorded after the film was edited. It is a simple effect that can be done in any small studio by recording someone running up a short flight of wooden steps. Echo could then have been added to this recording later, during the mix.

The school bell at the end of this shot could also have been recorded in a studio. But finding exactly the right bell is sometimes difficult unless the recording is made on location. Then the recording would have had to have been made during some quiet period, such as in the evening, so that the sound could be recorded without any competing background noise. Regardless of where the sound was recorded, however, it was extremely important to keep the microphone close to the bell. A distant microphone would have made the bell seem deeper and more resonant, while keeping the microphone close would capture the sharp urgency that was needed in this shot.

The child's footsteps in shot 5 were also probably recorded synchronously since it would have been quite a job to post-synchronize the sound to match the action. But the footsteps in the next shot needn't have been recorded with the pictures since we never see the housekeeper's feet. As a result, this shot was probably filmed without sound, and the sharp, quick sound of her feet crossing the wooden floor recorded in a small studio. However, this sound could have been recorded synchronously if the microphone had been placed below the frame line and close to her feet. Although the quality of the sound might not have been exactly right, it would still have been possible to correct it electronically during the mix.

But these options were not available in the last shot (shot 7). Since this shot contains the first dialogue in the film, the microphone had to be above the frame line to pick up the woman's voice. This position thus placed all the footsteps a considerable distance off-microphone. Nor could synchronously recorded effects have been altered electronically without a change in the quality of her voice as well.

This is the first frame of a flip sequence from Godard's Breathless. *It is designed to be seen at twelve frames per second. The sound track for this sequence can be found in Chapter Four, pages 209 & 210.*

So in order to achieve the right sound quality, the footsteps had to be re-recorded. And during the shooting the dialogue had to be kept clear of the footsteps so that these unwanted sound effects could be removed from the dialogue track without the editor's cutting into her words.

Isolating Each Sound Effect

Every one of these sound effects presents its own special recording problems. If these problems had to be multiplied by the number of shots in the film, the job of recording sound effects would be prodigious. In practice, however, the number of different effects that must be recorded is minimized. Whenever possible, each specific effect is recorded in isolation from every other sound so that there is no longer any way to tell from the sound quality or background sounds where the effect was recorded. This isolation permits the same effect to be used in a number of different places and makes it easier to edit it in different ways for different shots. It also allows the sound quality of an effect to be changed without a simultaneous change in some other sound in the recording.

In fact, such isolation even makes it possible to create a quite different sound effect from an existing recording. For instance, when a shot of a plane taking off is shorter than the sound effect available on a record, the effect can be shortened by an increase in the speed of the turntable from 33 rpm to 45 rpm. This change in speed also increases the pitch of the sound, but when the higher frequencies are electronically filtered out, the speeded-up recording sounds like a shorter takeoff. Or if the sound of a wheelbarrow dumping stones is slowed from 7½ ips to 1⅞ ips, the decreased speed and pitch of the sound produces the effect of a truck dumping boulders. Several isolated effects can also be mixed together to form still other effects. For instance, the sound of a railroad train can be re-recorded and the two recordings combined to produce the sound of two trains passing. Or the regular thump of a staple gun can be mixed with the low-pitched hum of an electric motor to create a background of imaginary machine noise, or an imaginary sound for shots of a real machine. The possibilities are almost limitless.

When sounds are recorded in isolation they are immensely flexible. In the hands of a skilled editor, any sound can become something else. Voices can become sound effects; music, voices; and sound effects, music. They can be cut apart, rearranged, altered in their pitch and pace, mixed and filtered, and then they can be cut together to form sequences with a structured, almost musical quality that extends the meaning of the film beyond what is contained in the words and pictures alone. But even the most skilled editor must have sounds which are clear and precise, and that begins with knowing what sounds are needed, how to listen for them, and how to isolate them accurately on tape. Although the recordings are just the start, it is the start which determines the quality of the finished sound track.

Chapter 8

Picture Editing

Editing is at the heart of film-making. In its most basic sense it is the physical manipulation of pieces of sound and picture—arranging and rearranging their order, length, and synchronization until the pieces form a sequence and rhythm that conveys the film-maker's meanings. The editing process, however, actually begins long before the film reaches the cutting room. The effects that are created during editing often have to be anticipated in the script and implemented during shooting in order for the editor to bring them to fruition on the editing bench. In this sense, then, editing is more than just a matter of cutting and splicing; it is the final step in an imaginative process that ultimately defines how the film will look and feel.

Because editing decisions can be made at any stage in a film's production, it is difficult to define the editor's role in creating the final product. In some cases, particularly in feature film-making, the shooting can be so carefully controlled that little more is shot than is needed in the finished film. This reduces the editor's job to joining pieces of a set length in a predetermined order. More often, however, the action is filmed from several different angles, so the editor must choose among the shots and determine where the cuts will be made. This gives the editor a major

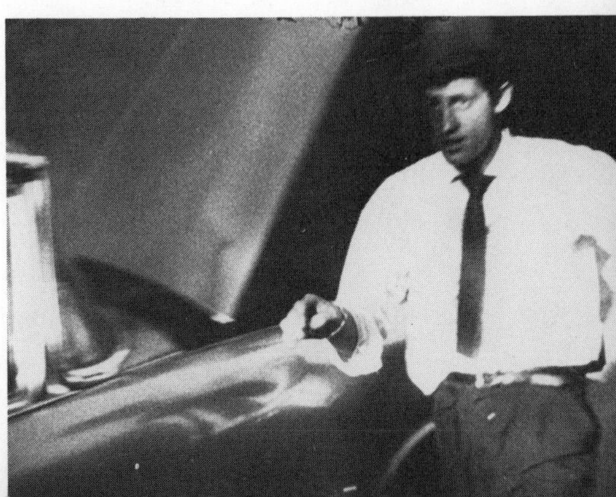

role in the film's creation. And at editing's most creative extreme, such as in films made from random footage, the entire film is concocted on the editing bench.

Over the next two chapters, editing will be defined as those film-making techniques that depend for their effect primarily on joining picture and sound in a specific order and with a particular rhythm, no matter at what stage in the production this order and rhythm originate. Regardless of the film-maker's original intentions, once the action is isolated in the frame and on the track, it begins to take on a life of its own. Freed from the confines of real space and time, it not only looks and sounds different from the way it did during the filming, but it begins to suggest new meanings or new ways of shaping its original meanings.

Thus, even in those situations in which the editor's role would seem minimal, there is still a range of editing decisions to be made since it is the editor who eventually has the best perspective from which to judge how the film should be assembled. At the very least, this means that the editor must decide whether the material can be edited in the way that was originally intended, and if not, how it should be cut. And at its best, editing means being aware of, and fully exploiting, all the many possibilities inherent in the footage. Therefore, no matter how widely the editor's opportunity to shape the film may vary, his responsibility for its final effectiveness remains equally great.

Assembling the Pictures

There is no rule concerning what should be cut first, picture or sound. Because double-system sound keeps the two on separate pieces of film, either can be done first, depending upon the nature of the movie. And in the case of lip-synchronous dialogue, because picture and sound are linked to each other from their very inception, the two are cut simultaneously. Generally, though, it is the sequence and length of the shots that determine the basic rhythms of the film, so the pictures are at least roughly assembled before the sound is cut. For this reason, the picture assembly process will be described first, and then, in the next chapter, the editing and mixing of the sound tracks.

The technical skills required to sort out the shots and then splice them together, probably the simplest in film-making, haven't really changed much since the earliest days of the silent film. Here is how Allan Dwan, who worked in films almost from their very beginning, describes editing his first pictures; the quote is from *Allan Dwan, the Last Pioneer,* an extended interview he gave to Peter Bogdanovich.

> Q. Did you physically cut the footage yourself?
>
> A. Yes, we didn't have cutters. And we didn't have any instruments or machines—we did it by hand. I would take the reels and run them through in front of a light. I could read the negative. Wherever I wanted to end a scene, I'd just cut it with a pair of scissors and that'd be a scene. Then I'd get the next scene I wanted and we'd glue it together.

Picture editing has remained essentially a hand process, and the editing procedure still consists of running through the film in front of a light and then gluing it together. However, a few simple machines are now generally used to cut the picture, both because editing techniques have become much more complicated and because the 8mm or 16mm image is so much smaller than that in 35mm. These basic tools are rewinds, a splicer, and a viewer.

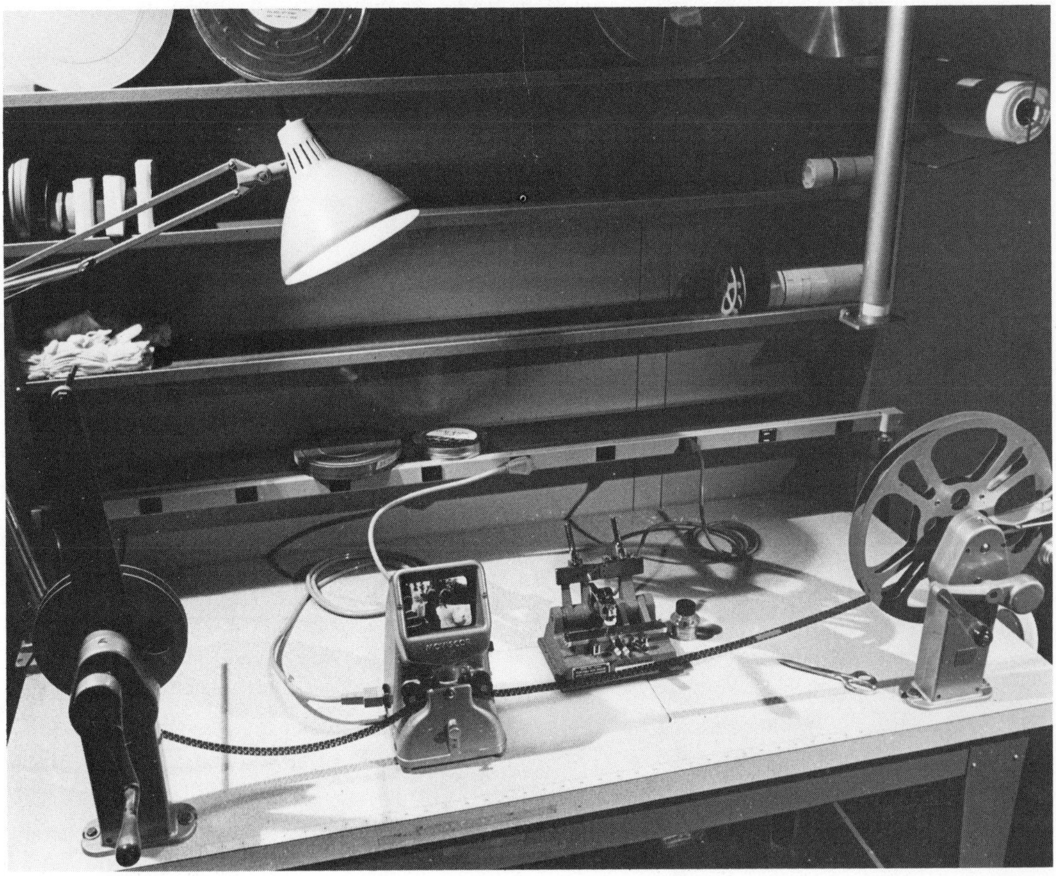

Editing bench set up for cutting picture only. From the left: rewinds, film viewer, picture splicer.

Rewinds are nothing more than rotating shafts on which reels of film can be easily unwound and rewound by means of hand cranks. And a splicer is basically a mechanical jig that aligns the ends of two pieces of film while they are being glued

together (types of splicers and how they are used are discussed in Chapter Ten). Only the viewing apparatus is somewhat complicated. A film viewer is, in essence, a small projector, with a lamp, a shutter, a lens, and a built-in viewing screen—but without a drive motor. Instead, the film is pulled through the viewer by means of the rewinds, causing the shutter to rotate so that one frame at a time is flashed on the viewing screen. This process both magnifies the image and lets the editor see it move.

Hand cranking the film through the viewer permits the motion to be viewed at any speed, making it easy to pick out exact cutting points. But since hand cranking doesn't allow the editor to see the action at exactly the same speed as it will appear in the finished film, a projector is a necessary addition to this basic equipment. It permits the editor to view the cut footage periodically on a large screen so that he can see whether he has missed any significant details and whether the pace of the cutting is right.

Simple editing can easily be done with little more than this basic equipment. But when picture and sound are edited simultaneously, or when several sound tracks are cut at the same time, it is more efficient to do the cutting on a motor-driven editing machine. This is because, while the picture can be viewed at any speed, sound has to run at a set speed in order to be intelligible, and it is much easier to control the speed with a motor. These editing machines will be described in detail in the next chapter because, although they are useful for cutting just picture, their greatest advantage is in sound editing.

Pre-editing Procedures

The preparation of the footage prior to editing is also somewhat more complicated now than it was in the earliest days. All Dwan had to do was simply cut his original negative. Of course this is still done and is even easier now than in his day because reversal original eliminates the need to "read" a negative. But cutting original has become the exception rather than the rule and is generally restricted to 16mm news film and 8mm amateur footage. Now the normal procedure in professional film-making is to make a print of the original and cut that.

There are several advantages to cutting this *workprint* instead of the original. For one thing, handling the original during editing results in dirt, scratches, and other damage that become a permanent part of the image. In addition, since cutting a shot apart and then splicing the pieces back together inevitably produces a jump in the image, every cut in the original commits the editor to using only that much of the shot or less. A workprint, however, can be handled as roughly as necessary and can be cut apart and reassembled as often as the editor desires without having the least effect on the original. Then, once the final, edited version of the film is decided upon, the original can be cut to match the edited workprint and any number of clean, undamaged prints made from this cut original (the details of this process are covered in Chapter Ten).

Of course, only those takes of the original are workprinted that have been marked as acceptable in the shooting log or on the dope sheet. After each day's footage has been processed, either the editor or the laboratory must identify the *print takes* by means of the slates, pull them from the rolls of original, and splice them together into printing rolls. Since the print is usually ready for the director and the cameraman to view a day or two after the original footage was shot, it is called the "rushes" or the "dailies"; but once it has been seen by them it becomes the editor's workprint. The rest of the original, consisting of *out takes,* is also spliced into rolls. These are carefully put aside for future use in case a good take is damaged during matching or printing.

The preparation of the workprint also involves one other procedure. Since even a short film may contain dozens of shots, matching the original to the workprint can become quite complicated unless there is some method for finding each piece of original and then aligning it to the workprint, frame for frame. This is done by the use of *edge numbers.* These are four- or five-digit numbers printed along the edge of the film at six-inch or one-foot intervals, with the number increasing by one each time it is printed.

Edge numbers. Upper, print through; lower, inked edge numbers. 1A0011, the next inked edge number, would appear 40 frames further toward the end of the roll of film.

There are two types of edge numbers. One type, the *print-through edge number,* is exposed onto the original by the manufacturer, giving every roll of camera stock a series of numbers that can later be printed through onto the edge of the workprint. But these numbers are only on 16mm and 35mm original; evidently if they were made small enough to fit along the edge of 8mm they would be too small to be useful. There are also *inked edge numbers.* These are somewhat larger, clearer numbers printed by the laboratory onto the edge of both the workprint and the original. These numbers are still not widely available in 8mm, though new types of 8mm edge numbers are currently being developed.

Inked edge numbers are generally preferred by professional film-makers, even though they involve an additional expense. Not only are print-through numbers sometimes hard to read, they also randomly vary from one roll of original to the next. As a result, when shots from several different rolls of original are spliced together to form a printing roll, there is no way to tell from the print-through edge numbers which printing roll contains which pieces of original. But with inked edge numbers, a specific series of numbers can be assigned each printing roll so that just by looking at the edge numbers it is possible to figure out how far down into which printing roll a particular piece of original will be found.

The last step before editing can actually begin is the rearrangement of the workprint so that all the shots in each scene are grouped together and in order. When there is a script, this generally means arranging the shots according to the slate numbers; with an unscripted film, such as a documentary, it usually means arranging the sequences in the order in which they were filmed. Once this is done, the editor can start to cut the picture.

Picture Editing

Picture editing is that part of the film-making process in which all the bits and pieces of the action must again be made to coalesce. Up to this point the film-maker's efforts have been directed toward dissecting the action so that each salient detail can be isolated on film. Now all these various parts must be brought back together to form a coherent whole. This coherence is usually achieved by assembling the shots so that they follow a narrative line; that is, so that they tell a story, describe a chronology, or illustrate a process. But the eventual shape of this narrative is more than just the result of stringing together segments of action to form specific events. It is also the result of that sensuous play of movement that is produced by the constant alteration and reorganization of the space and time in which the events occur.

The possibilities for reshaping space and time in the narrative film are as diverse as the events portrayed and the sensibilities of the film-maker who portrays them. On one extreme, they extend to the staccato rhythms of films like *Breathless* and the work of the New Wave directors that followed. These are films in which we are supposed to be highly aware of, and involved in, the often complex permutations of space and time because our perception of the characters' psychological experience of events is as much the subject of the film as the events themselves.

At the other extreme is that infinitely larger body of films that compose the mainstream of feature and documentary film-making. These pictures are characterized by their ability to mask almost completely the alterations in the basic space/time dimensions of the film. In most cases the scenes take place in what seems to be uninterrupted space and time, and only when the action is punctuated by some conventional signal, such as a fade or a dissolve, do we become aware of the liberties the film-maker must take to tell his story. As a result, while our perception of the events in the film is affected by the shape they are given, this is such a subtle pressure that we may never consciously recognize it.

It is this tradition of seamless cutting to which we are accustomed and against which we instinctively judge as "radical" those innovations which characterize many contemporary films. In fact, all films are structured by the same body of editing techniques. These techniques are based on the premise of *continuity;* that is, that the viewer's attention should be held by an unbroken flow of movement and detail from shot to shot. But even though the techniques remain the same, the filmmaker is still free to decide how he will use them: when he will carefully observe the rules of continuity in order to hide his manipulation of space and time, when he will violate them so as to create those irregularities in the procession of images that, by catching our attention, reveal the inner structure of the film, and when he will abandon them altogether in order to produce some more unconventional structure that will tell his story better.

Continuous Space

The easiest way to understand the problems of continuity is to look at those sequences in which the continuity is the most obvious. These are the sequences in which the action appears quite normal because it seems to occur in continuous space and time. We have already discussed, in the chapters on camerawork and lighting, the techniques which are used to produce footage that can be cut together in this way. But these techniques, by themselves, don't create continuity; they only ensure that the editor has what he needs to join the shots together smoothly.

In other words, editing the shots to create a sense of continuous space and time is more than just a matter of mechanics. Any cut, even one that is barely noticeable, is still an instantaneous jump through space, and therefore a jump through time. But, because of the very nature of film, the effect each cut has on our perception of time is different from that on our perception of space. Unless we are given some indication to the contrary, we accept shots that follow one another in sequence as representing continuous time. However, the spaces that are isolated in each shot are not seen as parts of a whole unless something in the shots connects one to the next.

These connections between the shots are supplied by points of reference—people, objects, and actions around which the audience can place everything else in a scene no matter how the viewpoint shifts from shot to shot. A point of reference can be as general as a similarity of setting from shot to shot, or it can be as specific as a particular object that appears in every shot. However, the more specific the point of reference, the more the procession of shots tends to create a sense of screen geography. This is a cumulative impression of the total space in which the action occurs, regardless of how fragmented it is from shot to shot. Once this screen

geography is firmly established, the spatial connection between shots is no longer very important because the audience will be able to place each shot according to what they have already seen. Thus, the film-maker is allowed to manipulate space and time freely without his audience's losing track of either.

Establishing Shots

The simplest way to create points of reference is to introduce the audience to the action a step at a time, first with a long shot, and then with progressively closer shots, until the most important details are isolated in close-up. That way, the initial long shot, or *establishing shot,* shows all the most prominent details of the setting at the same time. Then, when one of these details is isolated in the next closer shot, the audience knows how it fits into the whole. And this shot, in turn, reveals further details that can then be isolated in still closer shots without the audience's losing its sense of spatial connection.

This technique of slowly moving in on the action can be seen in a short sequence from Eisenstein's *Battleship Potemkin.* In this scene the townspeople

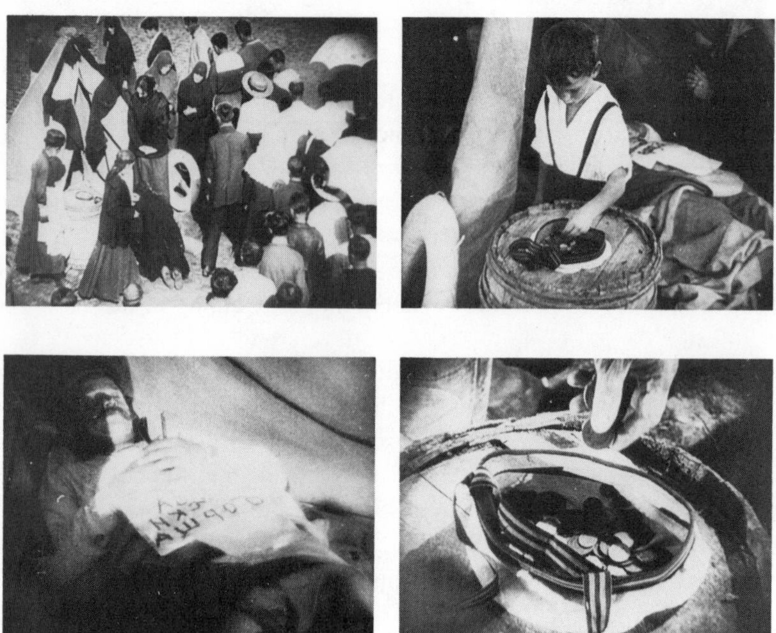

show their support for the rebellious sailors by paying their respects to a sailor killed in the mutiny. His body has been placed under a small tent at the end of a jetty, and as the people file past they place coins in his hat to help pay for his burial.

Despite some rather obvious technical and temporal discontinuities, the scene still seems to take place in continuous time and space. For example, from one shot to the next the lighting on both the barrel with the hat and on the body varies from bright to shaded; also, the young boy in shot 2 is not seen in the first shot, while the hand in shot 4 is that of an older person we haven't seen step up to the tent. But these inconsistencies never disrupt the spatial continuity because there are points of reference that smoothly lead us deeper and deeper into the action. We locate the barrel with the hat in shot 1, and this in turn indicates the location of the body, which we don't see until shot 2. As a result, when the body and the hat are each finally isolated in close-up, they have a clear spatial relationship both to one another and to the scene as a whole.

After we have been shown these close-ups, Eisenstein slowly begins to move back in space. In increasingly wider shots he first shows the crowds lining the jetty, and then mobs of people flooding through various parts of the town, until he ends

on this aerial view of the jetty jammed with people waiting to pass the tent.

This careful construction of space not only captures the meaning of the sequence in the close-ups and then expands the impact of that meaning in the subsequent long shots, it also structures the spaces so that we are never lost. Once the tent and the jetty have been firmly established in continuous space, we immediately know where the crowds are heading, so Eisenstein is free to cut together shots made in a series of unconnected locations. And by the time we see the final long shot, it is easy to envision a still larger mass of humanity pressing toward the jetty from every direction to show their solidarity with the fallen sailor.

This classically simple means for developing spatial continuity has its origins in the cutting that was first done in the earliest silent films. In those days filmmakers were accustomed to showing all the action from the theatrical point of view of the best seat in the house; that is, in long shot. It seemed only natural, then, once they started using closer shots, to insert these close-ups into the wider views. The result was a technique that has been used ever since because it clearly develops

the spatial connection between the shots while building the dramatic intensity of the action.

Continuous Action

But this technique is only one of several that can be used to create a sense of continuous space. For instance, instead of showing the entire setting at the beginning of a sequence, it is sometimes preferable to reveal the details of the action in isolation before establishing their connection. Then the film-maker must depend upon continuity of action, created by match-action cutting and screen direction, to build up points of reference that guide the viewer from detail to detail.

Here is an example of this technique; it is the closing sequence from René Clement's *Forbidden Games.* A child whose parents were killed in the war has been taken from the farm family who first took her in and placed instead in a refugee center. But we are only dimly aware of the size of this place, and therefore of the overwhelming dimensions of her predicament, because, until the very last shot, we are shown only close shots of the action.

At the start of the scene we see the girl all alone, seated stiffly on a bench. A nun comes up to her, hangs an identification tag around her neck, and tries to offer her some reassurance. But the child's face registers nothing until she hears a woman shout, "Michel!" This is the name of the farmer's young son, the girl's closest companion until they were separated. When she hears his name she jumps down from the bench (shot 1), and softly repeating "Michel, Michel," she starts into the crowd (shot 2). Then we see that the woman was only calling a man with whom she is now reunited (shot 3). Undaunted, the girl begins running and calling out

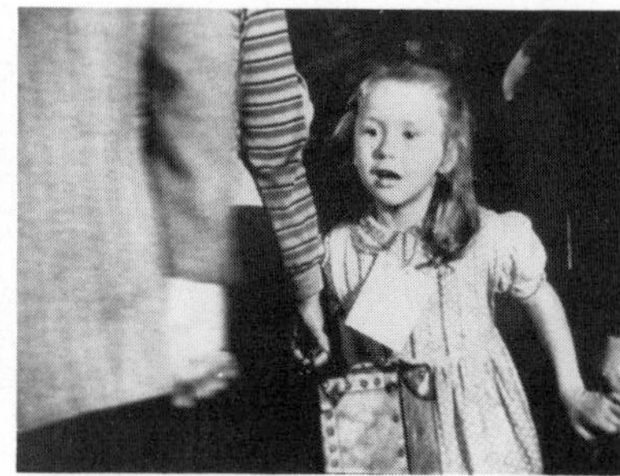

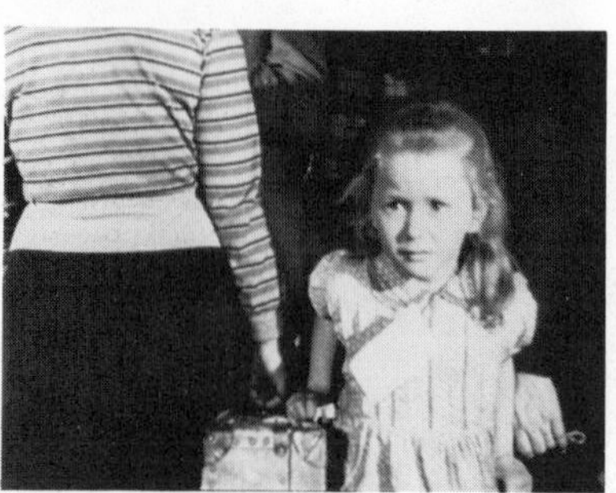

Courtesy: JANUS FILMS, INC.

"Michel"; and as she is swallowed up by the crowd, the camera slowly pulls up and back (shot 5) to show how utterly lost and alone she now is.

While we aren't shown where the girl is located in the overall setting until the last shot, her movements serve as our point of reference. Because the cuts are matched, and because she always moves in the same direction, each shot logically extends the movement in the previous shot, so we can easily follow her from shot to shot without having to reorient ourselves in space. Screen direction also furnishes a point of reference when her movements are interrupted by the cut-away to the woman in shot 3. Although the woman could be anywhere in the hall looking in any direction, she seems to be looking toward the girl and the girl toward her because they are looking across the screen in opposite directions; this eye-to-eye contact seems to locate them opposite one another.

Screen Direction

The cut-away in the previous example illustrates how a shot that is not otherwise connected to the action either by an establishing shot or by match-action cuts can still be tied to the sequence through screen direction alone. This power of screen direction to create spatial continuity was also demonstrated in the example from Robert Bresson's *The Trial of Joan of Arc* (Chapter Four, p. 161). In that case screen direction served as the sole point of reference throughout the sequence. Because Joan and her inquisitors were isolated in separate shots, they could con-

A similar use of screen direction also occurs in the first brief encounter between the central characters of Nikos Koundouros's *Young Aphrodites.* At the beginning of the scene a young shepherd wanders down to a tiny inlet in search of

water, unaware that it is seawater and undrinkable. After choking on his first mouthful, he looks up and sees a young girl with a pitcher of fresh water on the far bank. Wordlessly, she pours some of the water into a bowl and tries to float it across to him. At first the bowl won't move, so he tries to create a current by pulling at the water with his hand. When this doesn't work, she wades out and gives the bowl another push. Once he has it, she waits only an instant to see him drink. Then she quickly runs away, leaving him to cool himself by pouring the rest over his head.

Courtesy: JANUS FILMS, INC.

Koundouros has purposely kept his characters isolated in separate shots in order to emphasize all the things that keep them apart—the intervening water, the fact that they are strangers, a natural shyness, and their modesty when confronted by someone of the opposite sex. Against this isolation he then plays a normal adolescent naïveté and curiosity that holds them together long enough for her to offer him a gift of water. But the connection between them is no more solid than the fragile movement of the camera as it pans with the bowl floating across the water. As soon as he accepts the gift the spell is broken, and she flees back to her world, leaving him to his.

While the opening long shots would seem to establish the water as a point of reference, the relationship of the boy and girl is at first ambiguous. Although he enters shot 1 from left to right, and she enters shot 2 going in the opposite direction, right to left, they could as easily be moving toward each other on the same bank of the inlet as approaching opposite banks. But once he looks across the water in shot 3, we assume he is looking toward her, not away from her. We automatically place them opposite one another, and therefore on opposing banks of the inlet, because they are facing across the screen in different directions.

Recurrent References

Another way to connect characters isolated in separate shots is to use a recurring point of reference, an object around which the rest of the action can be placed because it appears in several successive shots. This technique can be seen in a sequence from Jean-Luc Godard's *Breathless.* The last part of this scene has been reproduced as a flip sequence on the lower corners of the pages of this section. However, before flipping through this sequence, look at the following frames. They

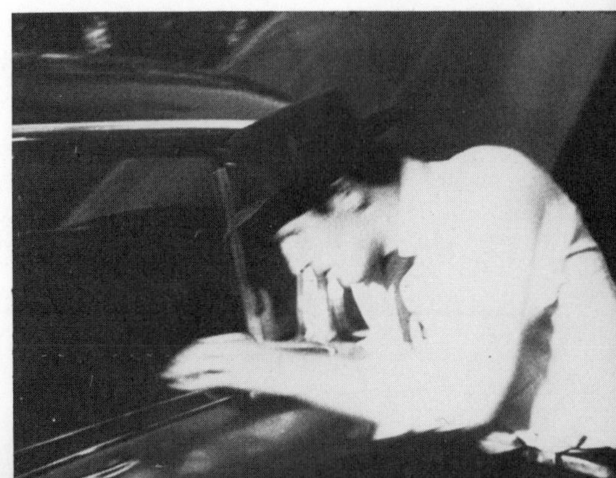

are from the shots that immediately precede the flip. Because there was only enough room to reproduce the final ten seconds of the scene as a flip sequence, we have had to include these shots separately.

This sequence forms the end of a chase scene in which Belmondo is being pursued by two motorcycle cops. He is driving a stolen car, and they are trying to stop him for speeding. At this point he has just evaded them by suddenly turning the car into a side road and stopping. When he looks back he sees the first motorcycle cop speed past the entrance to the road, and after he gets out to check the engine, he sees the other one pass. But just when he thinks he's safe, the second cop returns. Belmondo dives for his gun, and even before he gets a reply to his warning, he shoots the man.

Godard helps set the impersonal tone of this killing not only by keeping the characters isolated in separate shots but also by reversing Belmondo's screen direction so that he doesn't even seem to be facing the cop when he shoots him. It's as if he's dispassionately striking out in any direction at anyone who stands in his way. However, even though killer and victim are not connected in space by their screen direction, we still know that they are only a short distance apart because the entrance to the side road has established their position relative to one another. Since we see Belmondo pull only a short way onto this road, when the cops ride by the entrance we know they are passing close by him. And then, when the second cop turns in the entrance and rides down the road, the two of them have to be within a few feet of each other.

Organizing Time

Of course, the reorganization of space in a film is also a reorganization of time. Every shot contains a fragment of time as well as space, so depending upon the length of the shots and the order in which they are joined together, each cut expands, contracts, or rearranges time. However, in motion pictures there are really two kinds of time to be manipulated. First of all, there is our experience of time as it passes while we watch the film. This is time without tenses. Because we experience the events portrayed on the screen as if they were actually occurring before us, we perceive them not as having already happened, or about to happen, but as happening *now,* in a continuously unfolding present. Upon this filmic *present* is then superimposed *narrative* time. This is time with tenses, that past, present, or future which we assign to events according to the order in which we are told the characters, or objects, in the film experience them.

In essence this means that we must reconcile two different and usually contradictory kinds of time—a filmic present which, like real time, moves inexorably forward without interruption; and narrative time, which can not only switch from events in the character's present to those in their past or future, but which, even when it just moves forward, can freely expand or contract the time usually needed for those events to take place. We are rarely aware of this difference, however, because we are so used to these shifts in the flow of narrative time. They are a convention of the motion picture to which we have long been accustomed, and we can accept even radical jumps in the developing action as long as events connect logically from one shot to the next.

This connection is partly based on always knowing where we are in narrative time, in clearly understanding whether we are seeing events in the characters' past, present, or future. This subject has already been discussed in the chapter on time (Section 1, Chapter Two) and will be covered again shortly. The connection is also based on the fact that, once we've located ourselves in narrative time, we

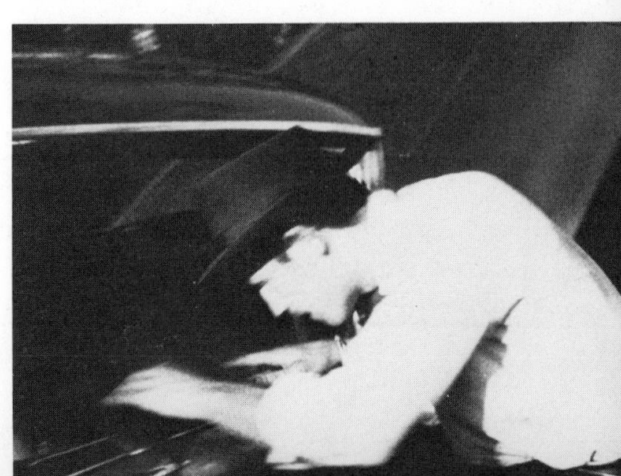

always see the action as again moving forward in the filmic present. At that point, however, we are not usually conscious of how time is being altered because we have no objective way of judging the actual passage of time. All we are aware of is the rate at which the present seems to pass, and this rate is controlled by the rhythms created during editing.

These editing rhythms are produced by a subtle interplay between the apparent speed of the action (whether it is shown in long shot or close-up), the speed of camera movements, the frequency of the cuts, and the flow of motion from shot to shot. The result is a shifting cadence that ties the shots together, no matter how the cuts expand, contract, or rearrange time. As long as the action develops within a rhythmic structure, each shot seems inevitably connected to the next. At the same time, however, these visual rhythms make the action seem to stretch out or pass quickly, regardless of how long an event is on the screen. Thus, the editor not only builds the rhythms that hold events together, but in rhythmically shaping those events he helps to determine their meaning by controlling our response to them.

It is easiest to understand the problems of rhythmic continuity, and its effect on the meaning of the action, by looking at several sequences in which the continuity is most obvious. These are sequences in which the action is supposed to occur in a semblance of continuous space and time. Then the spatial continuity keeps us firmly anchored in the present while the rhythmic structure of the editing continuously moves us forward through that present.

Long Shots and Close-ups

The apparent speed of any action is significantly altered by how greatly it is enlarged upon the screen; that is, by whether the action is shown in long shot or close-up. This, in turn, affects both the pace at which the action develops and its meaning. One example, the Canadian Film Board's documentary *Runner,* has already been discussed in the chapter on time (Chapter Two, pp. 74 to 76). The film is about a long-distance runner preparing for and then winning an important race. It starts out by showing his long hours of cross-country running in slow-moving long shots. Then, during his trial heats around the track, medium shots and medium close-ups are used to increase his tempo. Finally, close, rapid panning shots fill the frame with his driving speed during the race itself. The effect is to give each section of the film a distinctive rhythm while gradually increasing the apparent pace of the action so that the film builds to a rhythmic climax.

This same technique can also be used to alter the pace and meaning of the action within a scene. For instance, in the following sequence from Jerzy Skolimowski's *Le Départ,* the humor of the situation is created by his first cutting from a long shot to a close-up to speed up the action and then cutting back to the long shot to slow it down.

In this scene, the young hero of the film (played by Jean-Pierre Léaud) becomes involved in an argument, and then a fight, with his best friend. The friend has helped Léaud defraud an auto dealer of a new Porsche; by donning a turban, he was able to pass himself off as a wealthy Indian diplomat so that he could demand to use the car before buying it. Actually, Léaud needs the car to compete in a big race the next day. But the car turns out to have defective brakes, so Léaud tells his friend to take their boss's pickup truck and meet him on the edge of town. Then they can take the license plates off the Porsche and put them back on the truck before returning the car to the dealer.

We first see them, in extreme long shot, as they drive up to the appointed spot and almost collide. After Léaud leaps from the Porsche and berates his friend for nearly damaging it, the friend tells him that he has had enough of this crazy scheme. But Léaud won't give back the license plates unless his friend will help him return the car. The friend, angered, flings the turban at him and reaches for the plates. Léaud retreats, his friend grabs hold of him, and, both now enraged, they wrestle each other to the ground.

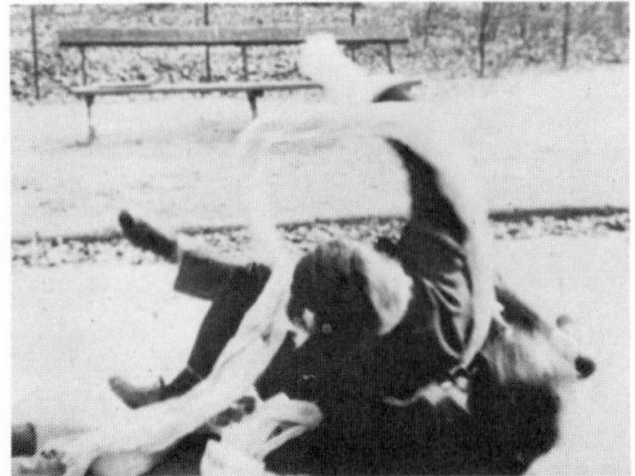

At this point, Skolimowski cuts to a medium close-up. This magnifies the growing intensity of their anger by filling the screen with their flailing arms. But just as the fight is becoming surprisingly fierce, Skolimowski again cuts to the extreme long shot. Suddenly, instead of seeming deadly serious, they appear slightly ludicrous, a pair of quarrelsome adolescents whose fight, muted by distance and the bleak indifference of the still landscape, seems to drag on interminably. Finally, they just give up and drive off in opposite directions; but by then we know that they are so involved with their bruised egos that they've obviously forgotten why they were fighting in the first place.

Camera Movement

The speed at which the camera itself moves also affects the rhythmic development of the action. For instance, in the opening sequence of the NBC documentary *Battle of the Bulge,* subtle changes in the speed of a series of camera movements

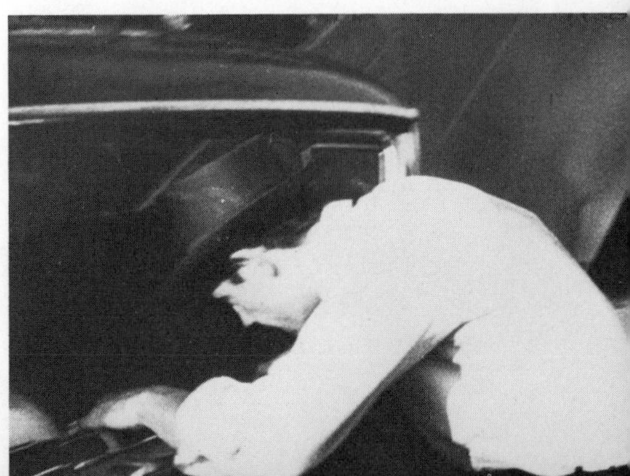

re-creates both the rapid pace of the Allied advance across France after D-Day and their sudden halt in the face of a German counteroffensive at Bastogne.

	PICTURE	SOUND
	**1.** MLS, trucking forward down highway (3 sec.).	SFX: Grinding clank rapidly moving half-track.
	**2.** MS, trucking past roadside trees and telephone poles (2½ sec.).	Half-track continues.
	**3.** MCU, camera trucks toward cluster of signs, momentarily holds, and then swish-pans L (2½ sec.).	Half-track continues.
	**4.** MS, truck past "Houffalize" sign while panning to hold it in frame (2½ sec.).	Half-track continues.

PICTURE	SOUND
5. XLS, camera trucks up to cluster of road signs until they fill frame, then stops (11 sec.).	SFX: Artillery, gunfire, and explosions fade up over half-track as signs fill screen.
6. XCU, "March-Bruxelles," rapid tilt down and R to "La Roche," swish-pan R (4 sec.).	SFX: Large explosion, close by.
7. MLS, swish R to signs, rapid zoom in to close-up of "Clervaux," then swish R (4½ sec.).	SFX: Machine-gun fire and several nearby explosions.
8. MLS, "Bastogne" (1½ sec.).	SFX: Explosion begins on cut to each of the following shots.

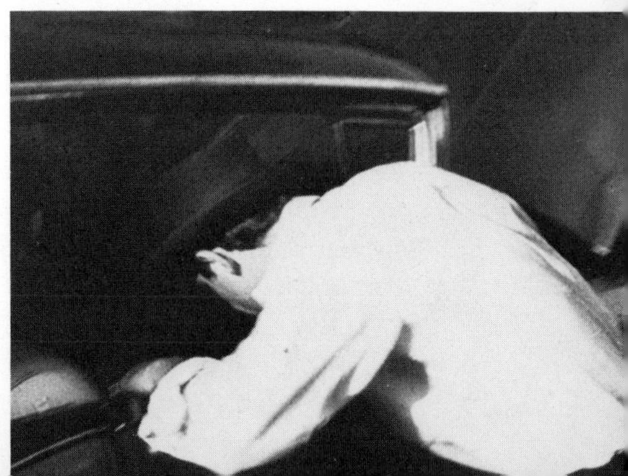

PICTURE	SOUND

9. MS, "Bastogne" (1 sec.).

10. MCU, "Bastogne" (¾ sec.).

11. CU, "Bastogne" (⅔ sec.).

12. XCU, "Bastogne" (½ sec.).

In this case the only subjects are roads and road signs, and these are all static, so it is principally variations in the speed of the camera movements which control the pace and meaning of the action. This camera movement starts at a brisk pace with a fast trucking shot looking straight down a main road. The pace is then accelerated slightly as nearby trees and telephone poles slip quickly through the frame; then the pace is slightly retarded as the camera trucks up to the first sign, holds it briefly in medium close-up and rapidly pans away from it. In the next shot, however, the pace slows even further. As the camera trucks forward, it holds the sign in the frame by panning backward, thus reducing the feeling of forward motion. Then the pace slows to a halt as the camera trucks from extreme long shot into a medium close-up of a cluster of signs—and stops.

At this point the sound track indicates the renewed enemy resistance by shifting from the rumble of a half-track to the percussion of gunfire. But while the advance itself is slowed, the pace of battle is not. So, as the volume and intensity of the gunfire swell on the sound track, the visual tempo is increased by the camera's zooming, panning, and tilting from one sign to the next in nervously jerky close-ups. Then, in a sequence accompanied by the beat of a series of explosions, the shots move in closer and closer on the sign that indicates where the Allies were eventually forced to stop.

Shot Length

The pace of the action is also controlled by the length of time each shot is on the screen. To put it simply, the shorter the shots, the faster the pace. For instance, at the end of the previous example, progressively shorter shots accelerate the tempo even though the camera is no longer in motion. This same effect can also be seen if you flip again through the sequence from *Breathless* reproduced on the pages of this section. Here the tempo gets faster not only because the shots get increasingly closer, but because the shots themselves become shorter and shorter. The first shot lasts five seconds, the next three and one-half seconds, and so on until the two shots of the gun going off are only one and one-half seconds each.

Actually, it takes Belmondo longer to kill the cop than it does for the cop to ride down to where the car is parked. The three shots in which Belmondo tells him to stop and then shoots him last a total of five seconds on the screen, while that of the cop turning onto the road lasts only three and one-half seconds. Yet we experience the killing as happening faster than any of the other action; because this action is broken up into three shots, the increasing frequency of the cuts accelerates its pace.

Of course, if short shots increase the tempo of the action, lengthy shots slow it down. Here is an example, a sequence from *Nanook of the North* in which Flaherty uses five lengthy, relatively static long shots to stretch out a race between

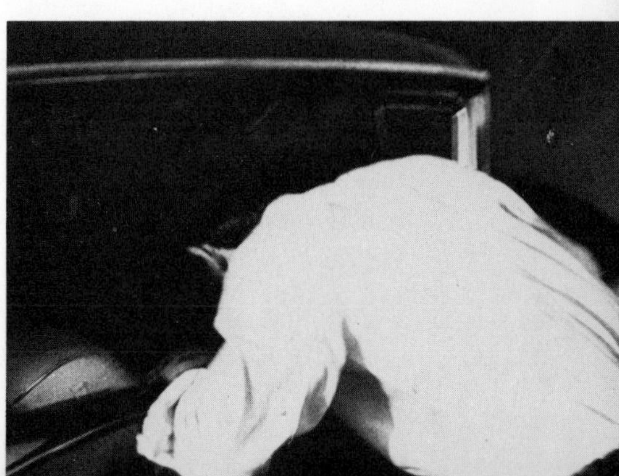

Nanook and his family and an encroaching Arctic storm. In this case the effect of the cutting on the rhythm of the scene is exactly the opposite of that in the previous example. Instead of expanding the time needed for fast action—a shooting—and then making it pass quickly, Flaherty condenses a long process, a journey, into a few minutes and then makes time seem to pass slowly by using shots that linger on the screen.

Screen Direction

Flaherty also does one other thing that both expands the action into a journey and slows its pace even further. He carefully maintains the same screen direction from shot to shot so that the movement in each shot seems a logical continuation of the movement in the previous shot. He thus prolongs the drama of their race against an invisible antagonist by locking the action into a single sweep.

In the first shot we see the Eskimos leave their fishing grounds, moving right to left as they head for the safety of their igloo. But as they pull away from the camera and diminish into the distance, they seem to move ever more slowly across the endless field of snow. Next, they again move from right to left as they slowly pick their way across the broad expanse of the frame, but now their tiny figures seem to make little headway over the vast waste spread out before them. In the third shot, however, while their screen direction continues from right to left, they grow in size as they approach the camera, and we sense that they are gaining on the storm. This feeling is then reinforced in shot 4. Again they start small, but they pass very near the camera, and that seems to signal the end of their journey. In the final shot this assumption is confirmed as they pull past the igloo and stop in the foreground.

In *Nanook* maintaining the same screen direction extended the flow of action and thus slowed its pace. But again, just the opposite effect can be obtained by sudden reversals of screen direction as can be seen in the flip sequence from *Battleship Potemkin* in Section 1. Here the baby carriage begins its journey by consistently moving from right to left. However, as the tempo of the scene accelerates, the shots not only get shorter but the screen direction of the carriage changes from shot to shot.

The first change we see is when the student, horrified, follows the progress of the carriage by turning his head from left to right while the carriage itself continues to move right to left. Then, as the carriage gains momentum, we see the baby, in close-up, pass through the frame from left to right, the carriage wheels going right to left, and the baby again moving left to right. Finally, as the Cossacks fire and the student screams, two short shots of the carriage careening back and forth through the frame bring the action to a peak by wildly flinging our attention about the screen. Thus, without actually changing the speed of the carriage this series of increasingly shorter, sharper reversals of screen direction seem to propel the baby more quickly and perilously down the steps.

Match-Action Cutting

In all the previous examples the editing rhythms have been created by the use of cuts to vary certain mechanical properties of the shots: the magnification of the action, camera movement, shot length, and screen direction. As a result, the rhythms produced by the cutting are superimposed upon the natural rhythms created by the action itself. But the subject's own movements can also be made part of the rhythmic structure of the editing by means of match-action cutting. Then the cuts create an uninterrupted flow of movement from shot to shot that, by interacting with the other editing rhythms, helps control both the tempo and the meaning of the action.

This interaction can be seen in a sequence from Chaplin's *The Gold Rush.* In this scene the Tramp is forced to leave Black Pete's cabin, his only refuge from a raging Alaskan blizzard. But the wind is blowing so fiercely that the harder he tries to get out the door, the further back into the cabin he is pushed. Then, just as he steps aside to rest, another prospector, Lucky Jim, is blown through the cabin and out the back door. Without thinking, the Tramp looks to see where Jim has gone and he too is sucked out the back door. However, persistent to the end, the Tramp crawls back into the cabin and then uses the wind to get rid of Black Pete. This

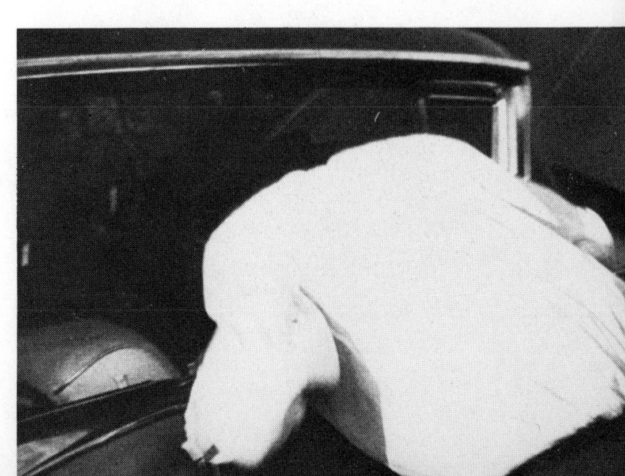

leaves him in sole possession of the cabin, free to gnaw on a bone, the only food around and his first meal in days.

PICTURE

1. Black Pete shoves the Tramp out of the cabin; but before Pete can shut the door, the wind blows the Tramp back. The Tramp then runs forward as the wind blows him backward (8 sec.).

2. Lucky Jim being blown along before the wind, his tent acting like a kite (2 sec.).

3. Lucky Jim being blown through front door of cabin (1½ sec.).

4. Lucky Jim blown through cabin (1¼ sec.).

PICTURE

5. Lucky Jim being blown out rear door of cabin (1 sec.).

6. Tramp turns to look out rear door and is blown out too (2 sec.).

7. Tramp being blown out rear door of cabin (¼ sec.).

8. Black Pete slowly pushes front door shut (2½ sec.).

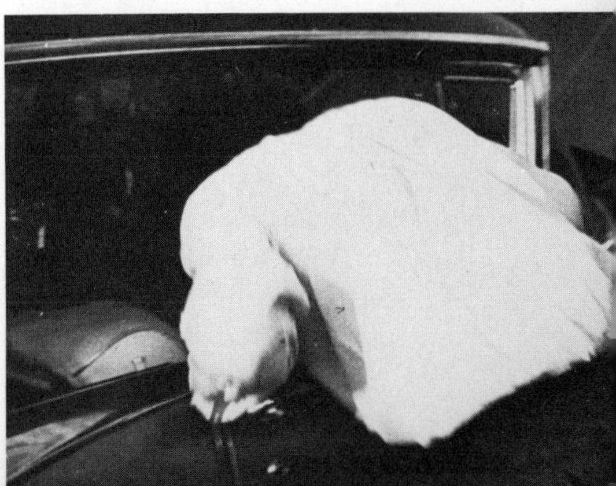

9. Tramp slowly crawls back toward cabin (5 sec.).

10. Tramp crawls into cabin, slips behind Pete, and opens door so that Pete is blown out (11½ sec.).

11. Black Pete being blown out rear door of cabin (¾ sec.).

12. Tramp shuts front door, then gets old bone and starts gnawing on it (12 sec.).

Here the mounting suspense and humor of the situation are created by the linking of groups of shots with match-action cuts so that the tempo of these sections builds the action in stages. At first the extraordinary force of the wind is depicted by the Tramp's unsuccessfully fighting against it, a struggle that is prolonged in an uninterrupted shot lasting 8 seconds. Then the tempo picks up in the shorter second stage as Lucky Jim is blown through the cabin in four progressively shorter shots tied together with match-action cuts. These cuts connect his movements in one continuous surge through the cabin that seems to increase in speed from shot to shot. Next, in the third and shortest stage, the Tramp makes the mistake of looking out the back door and he too is whirled out of the cabin. In this case the match-action cut between a longer and a shorter shot exaggerates his sudden exodus by slightly prolonging it without slowing its pace.

Up to this point, although the cutting has varied within each section, the sections themselves have gotten progressively shorter as they built toward the Tramp's defeat by the forces of nature. As a result, when Black Pete strains to shut the door, the slow pace of this uninterrupted shot seems to indicate that he has finally disposed of the Tramp. But then we see the Tramp crawl back into the cabin, his slow, careful movements stretched out into painful suspense by a match-action cut and the increasing length of the shots. Suddenly, he slips behind Pete, who has just succeeded in closing the door, and flings the door open again. Pete is instantly swept from the cabin, and in one last match-action cut, dances briefly away into the wilderness. At last the cabin is the Tramp's, and in a long, peaceful shot he settles down to enjoy his hard-won meal.

Jump Cuts

Obviously, the effectiveness of match-action cutting depends upon its smoothness. If, from one shot to the next, there are noticeable jumps in the flow of action, the movements lose their rhythmic continuity and the action may even seem to leap about in time (as, for instance, in *Breathless*). While the causes of such "jump cuts" have already been analyzed in the chapter on camerawork (Chapter Four, pp. 232 to 237), it is useful to discuss them here again because, in editing, there are not only techniques for avoiding jump cuts, but ways for using them expressively as well. First, however, how to avoid them.

There are three causes of jump cuts. The first is a noticeable mismatch in the action, either an overlap or a gap between the movement in one shot and that in the next. The second is too small a change of camera position from shot to shot. Then the actions match, but the small jump in position of everything on the screen looks more as if the camera was jerked than like an intentional cut. And lastly, if the change of camera angle is too great, the position and direction of everything on the screen is instantaneously reversed from one shot to another.

In the case of a mismatch, either shortening or lengthening one of the shots by a few frames will usually smooth the cut. While if the jump is caused by either

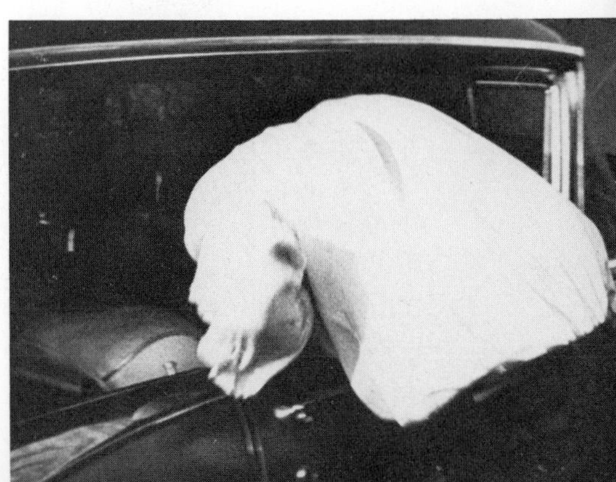

too large or too small a change of camera angle, the best remedy is to cut to a different shot of the same action. However, if the jump is the result of inadequate footage, the only alternative is to use a cut-away. Then, even though this interrupts the flow of movement, the cut itself is smoothed by momentarily diverting our attention from the ongoing action.

Cut-aways

The easiest way to create a cut-away is to insert a shot of someone or something not directly involved in the ongoing action. Examples of this have already been discussed in the chapter on time (Chapter Two, p. 49), and the chapter on camerawork (Chapter Four, p. 237). There is another method, however, that diverts our attention without the use of an extra shot. That is to hold one of the shots on the screen for a moment either before the action enters the frame or after it has left the frame. This creates a brief pause that masks a mismatch or a change of screen direction without adding the extra beat of an additional cut; as a result, the cut-away actually helps maintain the thrust of the action.

For example, here is a sequence from Ermanno Olmi's *The Sound of Trumpets* in which both a mismatch that jumps us forward in time and a repeated reversal of screen direction are smoothed over by just a slight lengthening of a couple of shots. The scene simply shows a boy, who is applying for a job in a large company, going for lunch during a break between tests. He enters a restaurant, and after he sits down, he discovers another applicant, an attractive young lady, also seated at his table. In order to show how these shots are edited, the frames from either side of each cut are grouped together.

1a

1b

2a

Courtesy: JANUS FILMS, INC.

2b

In the first shot we see him enter the restaurant and look around for a seat. After he leaves the frame, however, Olmi momentarily holds on the waitress bustling about in the foreground. She diverts our attention from his movement so that when we see him in the next shot (2A), already in the back of the restaurant, he has jumped forward in time without our being aware of it. But not only does this cut-away speed up the action by slightly truncating it, it maintains the flow of action by transferring our attention to the harried waitress. Her activity, too, is then smoothly jumped forward by a momentary hold on the boy before she hurries into the frame (2B) to clear a place for him.

Once the boy is seated and waiting to be served, we see him in medium long shot, stranded at the far end of the table, small and lost in a crowd of strangers. Suddenly the man in the foreground snaps, "Pass the paper!" as he brusquely reaches out and tries to take it (1B). This action causes the boy to look to his right,

1a

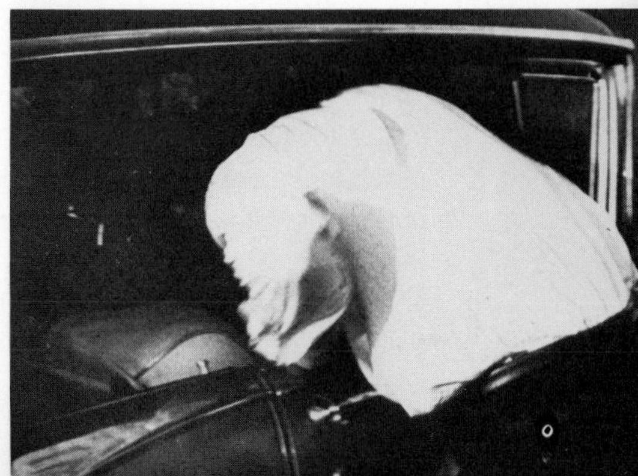

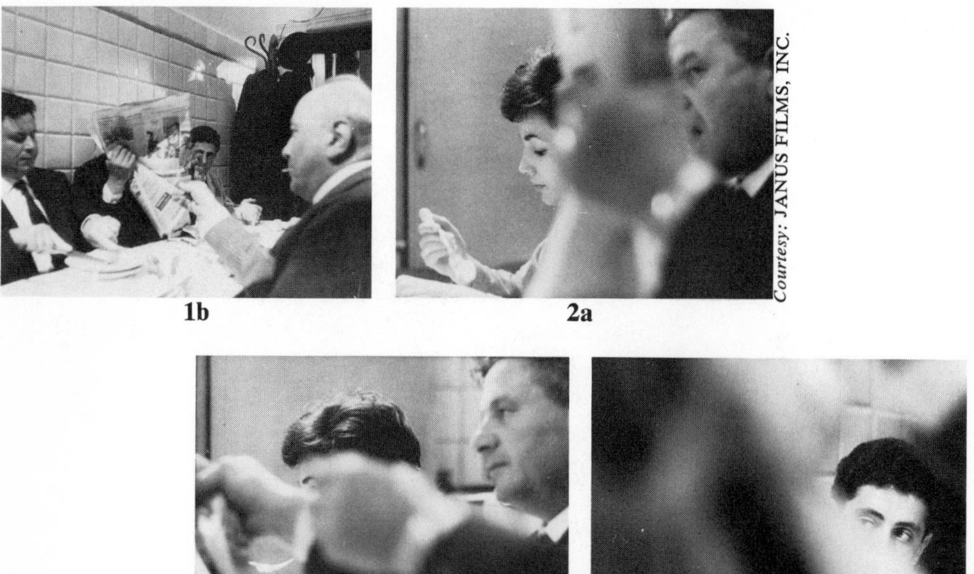

Courtesy: JANUS FILMS, INC.

1b 2a

2b 3a

3b

and because the next shot (2A) then reveals the girl, we discover her at the same time and in the same way he does. But in the process the newspaper has unaccountably hopped to the opposite side of the frame. This discrepancy is smoothed over both by focusing sharply on just the girl and by starting the shot several frames before the man with the newspaper begins to surrender it. As a result, our attention is momentarily diverted to the girl so that when we again notice the paper, we've forgotten that it's moving in the wrong direction.

The newspaper is next used to reveal a close-up of the boy intently staring past it toward the girl. Now, however, the screen direction of the paper is reversed in the middle of its passage across the table. But again, the newspaper is, in effect, removed from view, first because shot 2 ends after the paper has left the frame, and then because shot 3 starts with only the boy in sharp focus. Again, our attention is diverted from the movement of the newspaper just long enough so that we never really notice the change of screen direction.

Expressive Jump Cuts

While jump cuts are usually avoided, they can sometimes be used expressively. Then they alter the natural rhythm of events by noticeably shoving the action forward or backward in time. This effect has already been demonstrated in the chapter on time with a sequence from Roman Polanski's *The Lean and the Fat* (Chapter Two, p. 76). The film is a political allegory in which the fat master cunningly offers to free his lean servant by giving him a personal possession—he chains him to a goat. Inevitably, the goat becomes a nuisance and the servant begs to be released from it. As soon as the servant is unshackled, a series of jump cuts makes him leap about without consideration for the time needed to get from one part of the setting to the next. His actions are thus speeded up, and he seems to be everywhere, doing everything, in an illogical frenzy of joy at being returned to his original condition of servitude.

But, just as the action can be accelerated by being clearly jumped forward in time, it can as easily be slowed by noticeably overlapping the movements from shot to shot. For instance, in the following sequence from *Battleship Potemkin,* Eisenstein uses jump cuts to expand time and slow it down. In this scene the rebellious sailors take revenge against the ship's doctor by throwing him overboard. He had previously approved putrid, maggoty beef for their meals, and it was this callousness that sparked their mutiny. But Eisenstein prolongs the doctor's fall, making him float through the air and into the water. This approach turns what would otherwise seem quick, offhand vengeance into a firm, just act of retribution and gives the doctor's immersion a terrible finality.

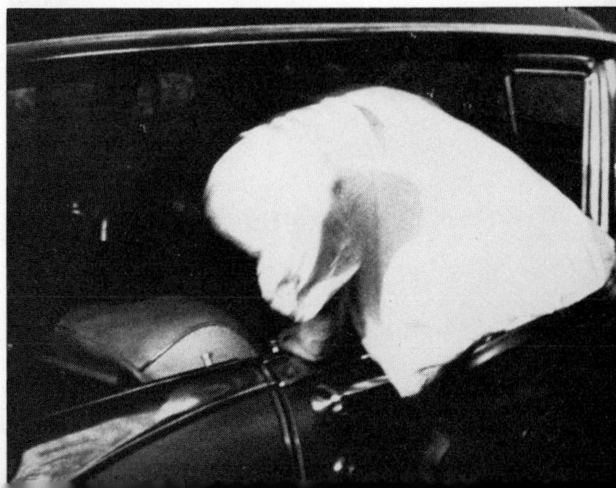

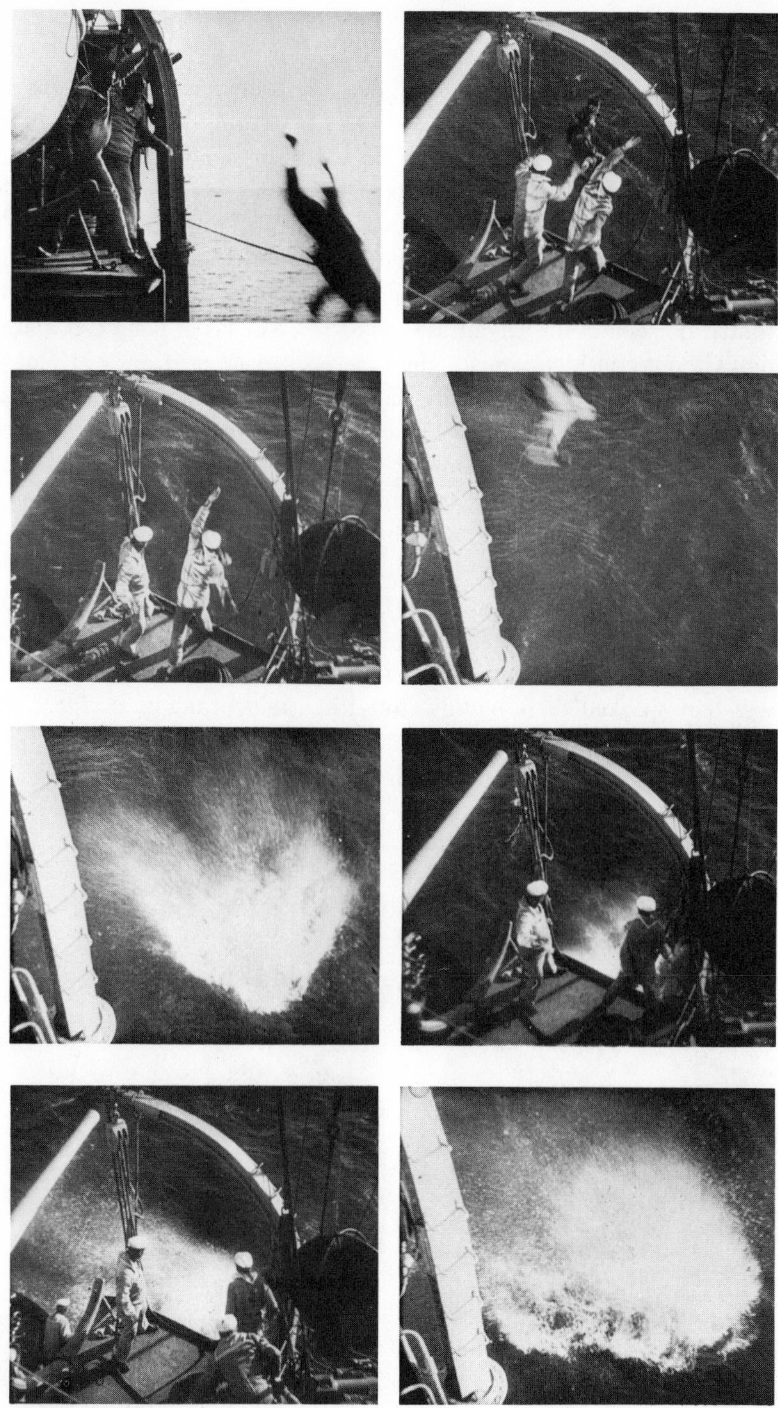

Building the Rhythms

So far we have covered those individual elements of the editing which rhythmically structure the action while building its meanings by varying the pace.

But these elements rarely occur one at a time, nor are they always very apparent. In most cases they are so woven into the texture of the narrative that it is impossible to distinguish between the story and the way in which that story is told. As a result, even when an editor has a carefully laid-out script to follow, he still constructs the rhythms of the editing as much by intuition as design.

Some of the complexity of this process can be seen if we look at a sequence from the final scene in Kurosawa's *Yojimbo*. In this scene a lone samurai is arrayed against a small band of hired killers. The samurai has successfully pitted against each other the two corrupt families that dominated the town, and now he is intent upon destroying the last vestiges of the only remaining family, the Ushi-tora. This group is led by the family's youngest son, who is arrogant and cocksure of himself because he has the only gun, a six-shooter. However, the battle develops within the same rigid framework as the film's chivalrous model, the American western. The adversaries face each other down a long, dusty street, and as they slowly advance toward one another, every movement becomes a play in a contest of wits. The Ushi-tora, apparently safe in their superior numbers and weapons, are unsure of themselves in the face of the samurai's unswerving confidence; while the samurai, on the offensive from the start, has to remain in control until he can get within striking distance with his knife and sword.

PICTURE	SOUND
1. LS, samurai at end of street; he stops and waits (10½ sec.).	MUS: Horns and drums.

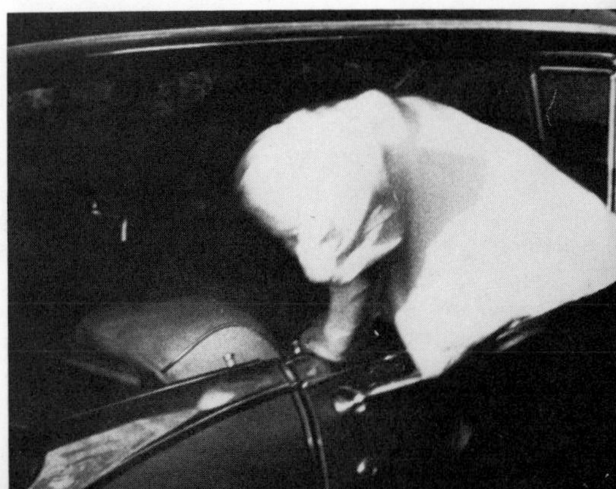

PICTURE	SOUND
2. XLS, samurai in distance, guards playing cards in foreground. Local constable runs into street, calls out time, sees samurai and reacts with a grunt. This alerts guards, who run into house (pan L) and bring out rest of gang (pan R) (44 sec.).	MUS: Gives way to SFX: Wind. CONSTABLE: Grunts.

PICTURE	SOUND
3. LS, samurai stands and waits (same as shot 1) (3 sec.).	SFX: Wind. MUS: Slow beat of cymbal starts t ward end of shot.

PICTURE	SOUND
4. LS, Ushi-tora; leader starts forward near end of shot (5 sec.).	SFX: Wind continues throughout rest of scene. MUS: Cymbal beat continues.

PICTURE	SOUND
5. MLS, samurai in foreground, Ushi-tora in background; he starts forward. (8½ sec.).	MUS: Continues.

PICTURE	SOUND
6. LS, Ushi-tora (same as shot 4); under-taker starts across background (9½ sec.).	MUS: Continues.

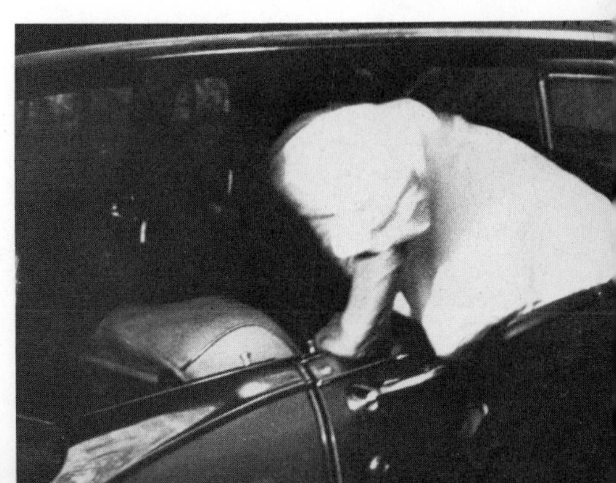

PICTURE	SOUND
7. MS, undertaker; pan R until he stops stops and sees innkeeper; he turns and goes toward him (4½ sec.).	INNKEEPER: Grunts. MUS: Continues.

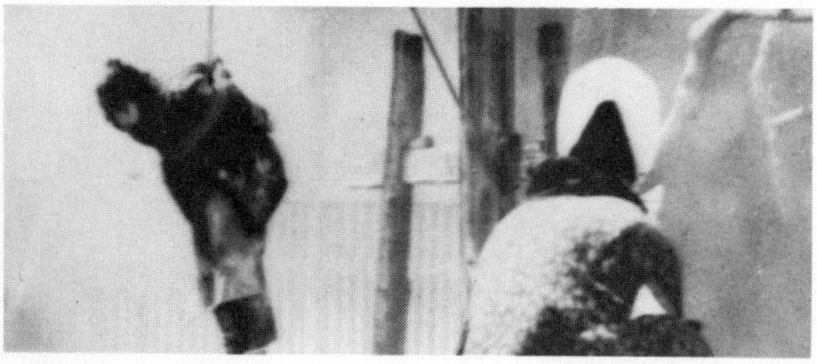

8. MLS, Ushi-tora, samurai in background; slowly walk toward each other (8½ sec.).	MUS: Piano chord added to slo beat of cymbal.

9. MS, undertaker lowers innkeeper to ground; both start toward camera, then stop and stare (21½ sec.).	MUS: Fades under. SFX: Fade under. UNDERTAKER: Get away whi he's fighting Ushi-tora and his men. INNKEEPER: You told him? Yo stupid meddler!

PICTURE	SOUND
10. MS, Ushi-tora, samurai in background; gang starts to pull swords toward end of shot (5 sec.).	MUS: Swells slightly in volume.

PICTURE	SOUND
11. MLS, samurai; gang in background finish pulling swords (4½ sec.).	MUS: Continues.

PICTURE	SOUND
12. MLS, Ushi-tora; leader pulls gun (9½ sec.).	MUS: Continues.

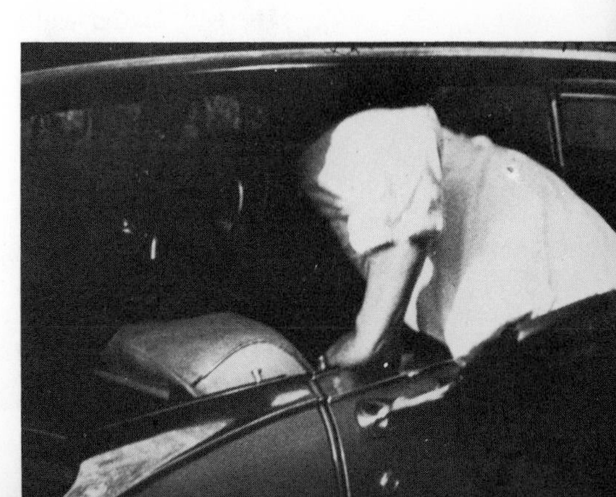

PICTURE	SOUND
13. MLS, samurai; he walks slowly forward (7½ sec.).	MUS: Continues.

PICTURE	SOUND
14. MS, leader; he walks slowly forward (5½ sec.).	MUS: Continues.

PICTURE	SOUND
15. MS, samurai walking (7 sec.).	MUS: Continues.

PICTURE	SOUND
16. MS, leader walking (same as shot 14) (4¼ sec.).	MUS: Continues.

PICTURE	SOUND
17. MS, samurai walking (same as shot 15) (4¼ sec.).	MUS: Continues.

PICTURE	SOUND
18. MS, Ushi-tora in foreground, samurai in background (4 sec.).	MUS: Continues.

PICTURE	SOUND
19. MS, leader (same as shot 16); stops (3 sec.).	MUS: Stops. LEADER: Don't come too close!

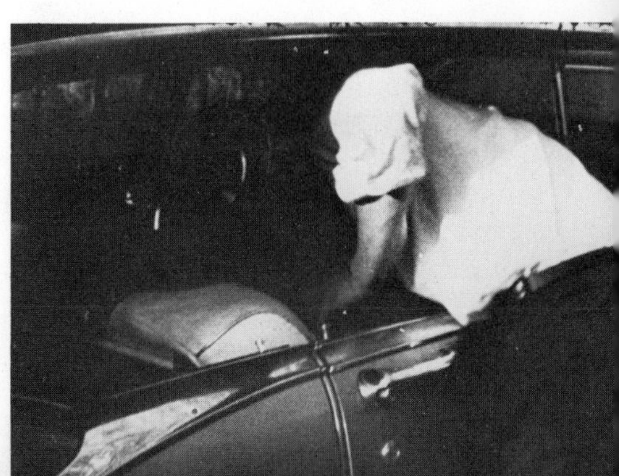

PICTURE	SOUND
20. MS, samurai (same as shot 17); he walks a little faster, smiles, gives a slight shrug (2½ sec.).	MUS: Rapid drums, trumpets.

PICTURE	SOUND
21. MS, leader (same as shot 19); he tenses (1 sec.).	MUS: Continues.

PICTURE	SOUND
22. MS, samurai (same as shot 20); his hands emerge from under his kimono and he darts R (½ sec.).	MUS: Continues.

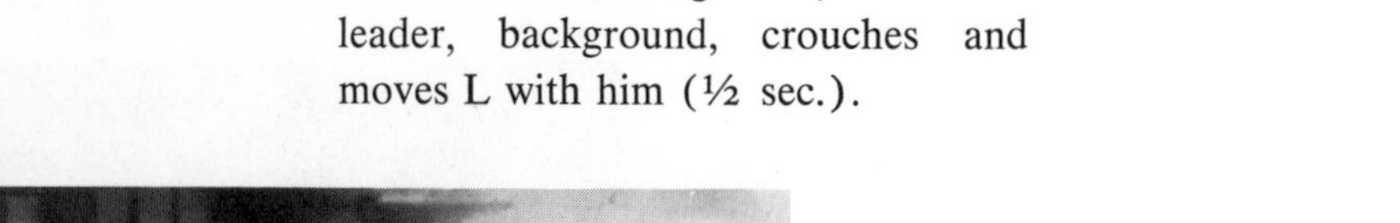

PICTURE	SOUND
23. MLS, samurai, foreground, darts L as leader, background, crouches and moves L with him (½ sec.).	MUS: Continues.

PICTURE	SOUND
24. MCU, leader; camera pans L with him as he cocks gun (¾ sec.).	MUS: Continues.

PICTURE	SOUND
25. MCU, samurai; camera pans R with him as he pulls knife and raises it (⅔ sec.).	MUS: Continues.

PICTURE	SOUND
26. MLS, leader (same as shot 23); background, shoots and misses; samurai, foreground, throws knife and hits his gun hand (1 sec.).	MUS: Continues. SFX: Gunshot.

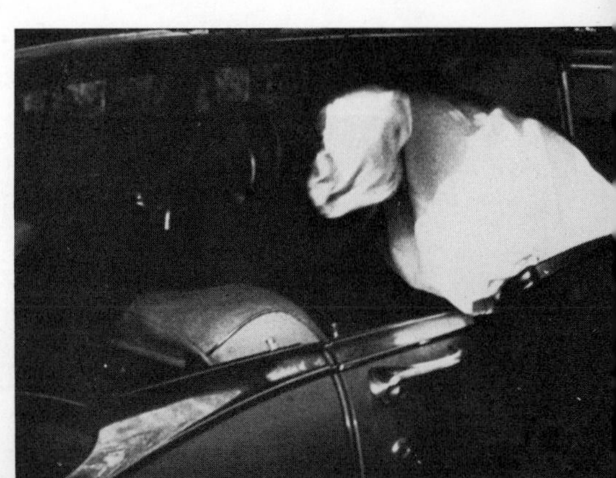

PICTURE	SOUND
27. MCU, leader, knife in arm; he starts turning to the R (1 sec.).	MUS: Stops. LEADER: Grunts in pain.

PICTURE	SOUND
28. MLS, leader and samurai; leader turns R as samurai runs toward him, pulling sword (1 sec.).	

PICTURE	SOUND
29. MCU, leader (same as shot 27); turns R as he fires gun in air, then pulls at knife (2 sec.).	SFX: Gunshot.

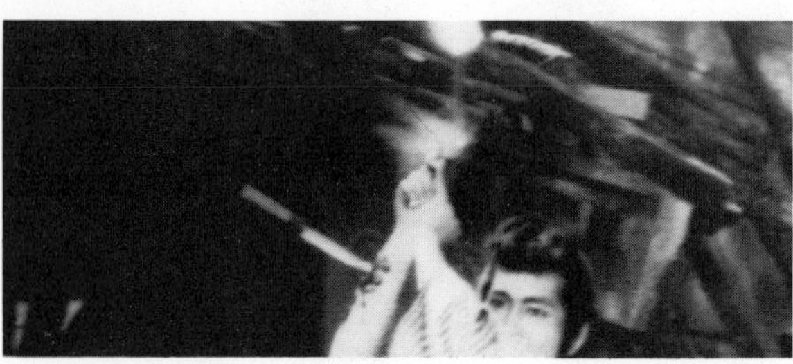

PICTURE	SOUND
30. MLS, leader and samurai (same as shot 28); camera follows samurai as he cuts down leader and members of gang, each with one or two swipes of his sword (10 sec.).	SFX: Grunt as each man falls.

PICTURE

As in any western, the outcome of the scene is never in doubt, so it is not really the story that holds our attention. Nor is it the excitement created by the action, since the action mainly consists of almost three minutes of walking. Yet an intense feeling of suspense is pulled taut by the cutting, which slowly increases the pace of the action while the action itself continues to develop at the same speed. Of course, the sound track too plays a role in shaping this rhythmic structure. The music, mostly a simple piano and cymbal, punctuates the shots with a regular beat that marks off the unseen footsteps; and the unceasing wind, which increases the samurai's mysterious powers by wrapping him in a cloak of dust, fills the silences in the music with its long, plaintive moaning. But as important as these sounds are, they only reinforce the basically visual structure of the rhythms that slowly but inevitably draw the warriors into their final confrontation with the samurai.

The growing tension of the scene is almost imperceptibly built by a subtle interplay between the increasing screen size of the protagonists, small changes in their movements, and the length of the shots. The scene is first set by a long shot of the samurai, poised at the end of the ravaged village street, his mere presence announcing his challenge. Immobile and silent, he stands there for ten and one-half seconds before Kurosawa cuts back to an even longer shot showing the deserted street stretching between his distant figure and the two henchmen in the foreground. They are playing cards to pass the time while torturing the innkeeper, who knows where the samurai has been hiding. This shot too hangs on the screen until, after twelve seconds, the local constable runs into the street to announce the time. It is his grunt of surprised recognition that alerts the guards, who then run into the house to call out the rest of the men. But this action is developed without a cut, just a slow pan and hold on the dangling figure of the innkeeper, and then a slow

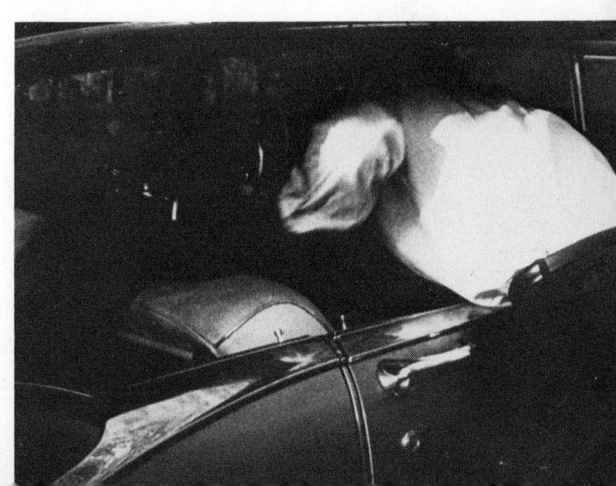

pan back to show the Ushi-tora and the samurai facing one another down the street.

Once these two slow-moving shots have established both the field of battle and the rhythmic context of the action, Kurosawa picks up the pace with a short repeat of the opening long shot accompanied by the slow beat of a wire brush on a cymbal. He then begins to build the suspense by maintaining this pace over the next several shots. He does this by carefully balancing the increasing amounts of action with increments in the length of the shots. For instance, in shot 4, even though the young leader (in the center of the group) starts to move forward, his action is slowed because this shot is almost twice as long as the previous one. Similarly, in shot 5 the samurai is larger and also moving forward, and in shot 6 the whole gang is in motion, but the tempo of the action is held steady because each shot is progressively longer.

At this point the undertaker, a friend of the innkeeper and the samurai's only other ally, starts to cross the background of this long shot, and Kurosawa uses this movement to increase the tempo just a slight bit more. First we see the undertaker, in a short medium shot, turn toward his friend; next, as we see the antagonists moving toward each other from the innkeeper's point of view, piano chords are added to the beat of the cymbal. These ominous notes then give an urgency to the action and dialogue in the following shot, shot 9, the second longest in the sequence. As a result, even though our attention is diverted from the main action for over twenty seconds, the music, plus the tension reflected in their hurry to escape, and the horror in their faces as they finally move into medium close-up, all further increase our suspense about the offscreen action while indirectly accelerating its pace.

This increase then carries over into the next three shots, both because the figures are larger than when we last saw them and because the action picks up as the Ushi-tora draw their swords. But then the suspense is stretched out a moment longer by the balancing of this jump in the action with a match-action cut between shots 10 and 11 that maintains the pace of the cutting by tying these shots into a unit that is exactly the same length as shot 12. Now, however, the Ushi-tora are armed and ready, so the pressure quickly begins to mount. The next five shots either get shorter, or closer, or both, and this constant increase in the pace of the action makes them seem to approach one another quite rapidly. Then, in shot 18, they appear in the frame together, suddenly confronting each other at point-blank range.

In the following shot the leader stops and, realizing what is happening, tells the samurai, "Don't come too close!" But the samurai has gained the advantage now, and as he begins to move in on them, the cutting accelerates and the music swells in volume and tempo. He shrugs his shoulders, the man with the gun tenses, the samurai darts forward. Here, Kurosawa steps back slightly to show the samurai throwing the gunman off balance; but at the same time he reverses the screen direction of their movements so that the matched action doesn't smooth over the first of a series of staccato cuts. With the pace of the action at its peak, the camera sweeps left and right, following each of them in turn. Finally, Kurosawa again steps back and reverses their screen direction as the first shot misses and the samurai impales the gunman's arm with a knife.

The leader's agonizing paralysis is then emphasized in three short shots that overlap his slow, twisting movement. In shot 27 we see him, knife in arm, start turning to the right; he repeats the turn in 28 as the samurai begins to charge forward, pulling his sword; and in 29 the leader turns again as he vainly fires his second shot into the air. This frozen moment then stands in sharp contrast to the final ten seconds of furious action. In a single moving camera shot we follow the samurai as he wildly rushes from one adversary to the next, completing his victory by cutting down the leader and his stunned men, each with one or two swipes of his sword.

It is evident that the rhythms of this sequence could not have been created in the editing room alone. First the film-maker had to know what effects he wanted and how to produce them. Then the camera had to be placed, and the action carefully framed, so that later each shot would fit into the overall plan for the scene. But this much of the film-making process still provided the editor with little more than a mass of footage. It was up to him to finish building the rhythms, a shot at a time, until each nuance of the original conception was revealed in the action developing on the screen.

Thematic Cutting

The same rhythmic devices that structure continuous space and time can also be used to tie together shots that are made in a variety of places and that have no particular relationship in time. Then, however, instead of these rhythms' shaping a semblance of actual events, the rhythmic structure builds a purely imaginative event—a theme. This theme emerges from those elements, such as mood, setting, objects, or actions, which are common to the series of shots. But since this relationship is not at first apparent, it is the rhythm of the cutting that catches us with its beat, carrying our attention from shot to shot until, through repetition, the thematic connections between the shots are established.

In some cases this theme is little more than a series of impressions, with each shot simply showing us another aspect of some central subject. An example is Charles Braverman's *An American Time Capsule*. This is a three-minute film in which each shot represents a different stage in America's historical development. These shots, most of them lasting less than five seconds, are cut to the beat of a fast-moving music track. The result is a rhythmic flow of images whose thematic relationship accumulates as the shots quickly succeed one another on the screen.

More complex themes can also be developed in this way. In *Cosmic Ray,*

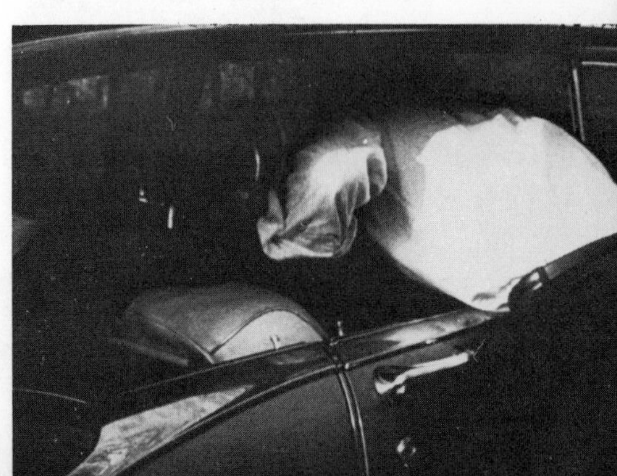

Bruce Conner freely cuts together or superimposes a shifting arrangement of such diverse images as TV commercials, Mickey Mouse cartoons, fireworks, film leader, theater marquees, war footage, and a nude go-go dancer. These are then cut to the beat of Ray Charles's "On My Mind." Here, for instance, is half a second of the film, and this is typical of all the rest. Ultimately, the kaleidoscopic im-

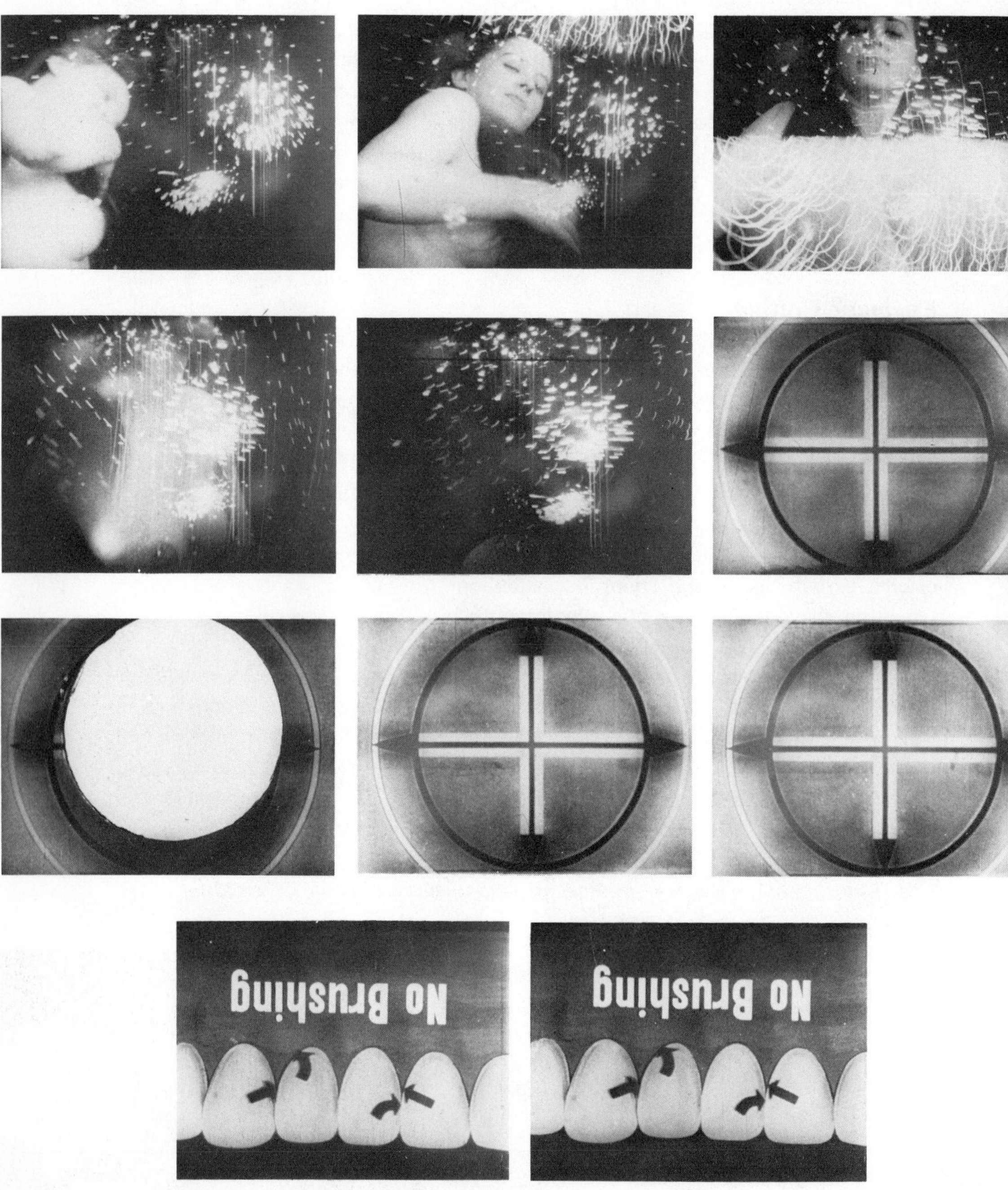

pression produced adds up to an acerbic comment on the American public's confusion between the reality of war and the mass media images of war served up for the vicarious gratification of our more aggressive sexual fantasies.

Cutting on Movement

Another use for thematic cutting is to distill a central idea within a narrative. In Hollywood feature films this is often done with a *montage,* a transitional sequence in which such things as the flipping of calendar pages denote the passing of time, or a succession of street scenes is used to characterize a particular time or place. Like the previous examples, the theme of the sequence is developed by the repetition of the same, or similar, subject matter in each shot; then the shots are tied together through the use of cutting rhythms in conjunction with the beat of a music track.

Montage of this sort has become hackneyed, a storytelling device that is closely associated with an earlier era of slick feature film-making. Now thematic cutting is woven into the narrative much more subtly, as can be seen in a sequence from Ermanno Olmi's *Fiancés*. It is a brief flashback in which the theme is conveyed, not only by the subject of the shots, but by the rhythmic flow of movement created by the cutting. In this scene a mechanic, who has been transferred from Northern Italy to a project in Sicily, calls home to speak to his fiancée. During their conversation we momentarily see his memories of their first meetings, shots which give his trite and halting expressions of loneliness a painful immediacy.

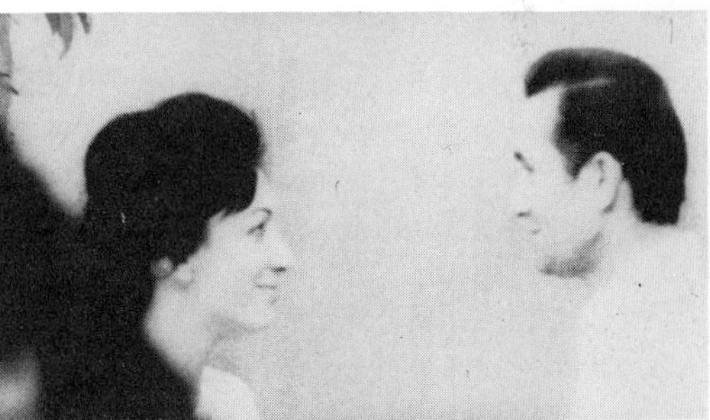

Courtesy: JANUS FILMS, INC.

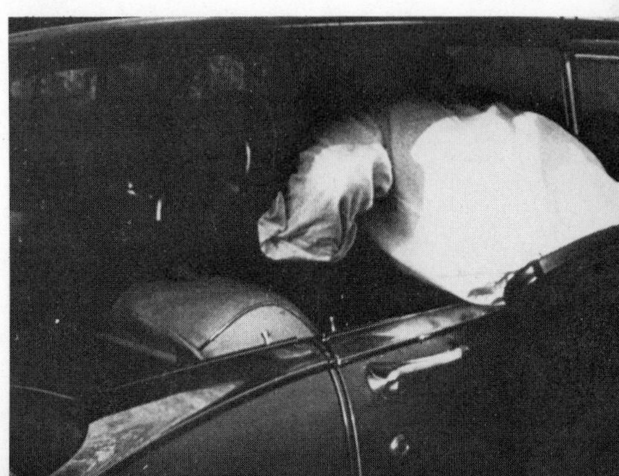

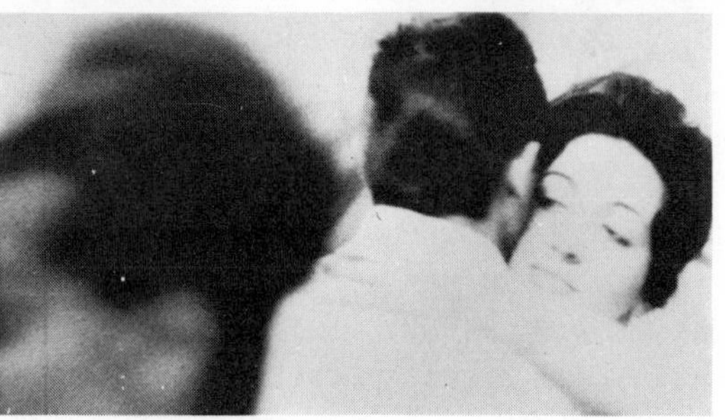

Here the cutting joins the movement in one shot to that in the next. This is much like match-action cutting except that there is no need either to match their movements exactly or to maintain their screen direction. All that is important is the similarity of movement from shot to shot. The rhythmic cutting of this movement then becomes part of the theme. It slowly draws the two of them toward each other until they meet and briefly cling to one another, thus creating a sense of coming together that poignantly sums up his longing for the joy they shared simply by being in each other's company.

Cutting on Shape

Thematic cutting can also be woven into the rhythms of the narrative if the shape of the objects in one shot is related to the shape of the objects in the next shot. This is what was done, for example, to build the opening sequence of Hiroshi Teshigahara's *Woman in the Dunes*. The film itself is a semiallegory about man's alienation from his rightful place in an otherwise harmonious natural order. It is the story of a young botanist who is tricked into living at the bottom of a sand pit that has no exits. Together with his only companion, a woman who has elected to live there, he fills baskets of sand in return for the food and water lowered to them by the townspeople living around the pit. At first he tries to escape, but eventually he reconciles himself to his role by accepting this as his ordained place in nature.

The theme of man's destructive effect on nature is first developed in the opening sequences, a series of shots of sand made unrecognizable by the magnification of the subject upon the screen. Because we cannot identify what we are seeing, our attention is instead focused and held both by the regular beat of the cuts and by the subtly modulated play of shapes from shot to shot.

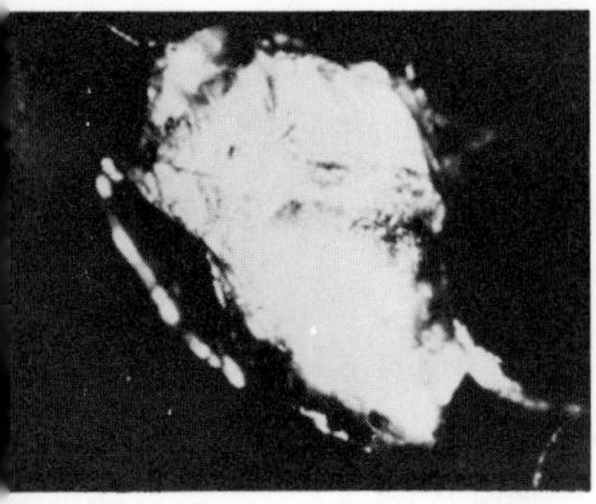

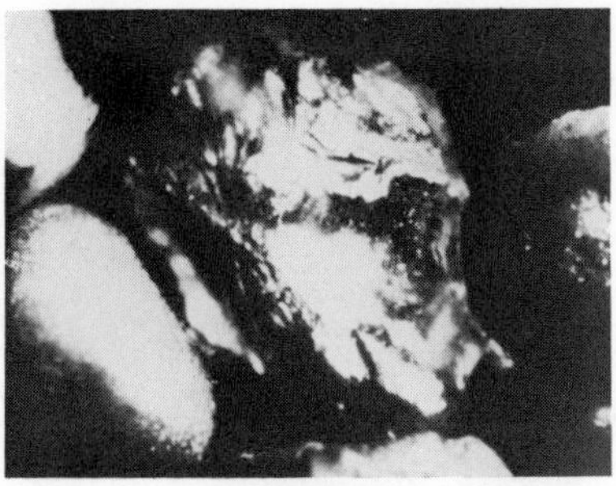

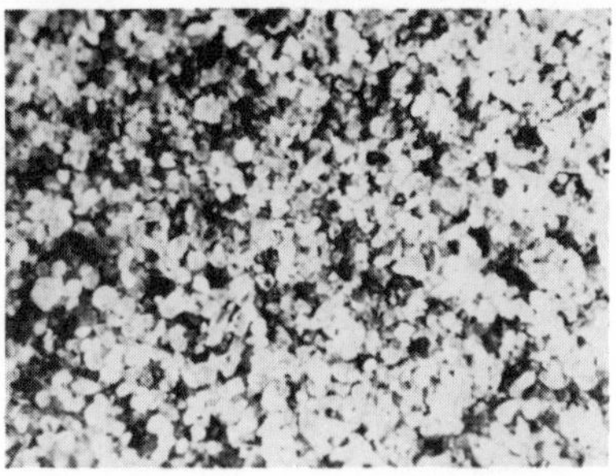

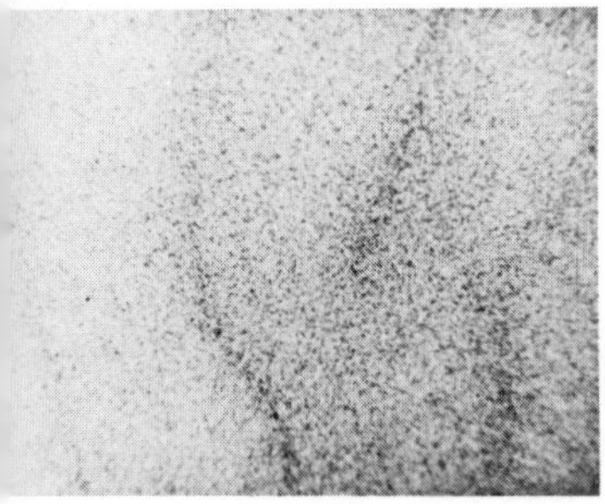

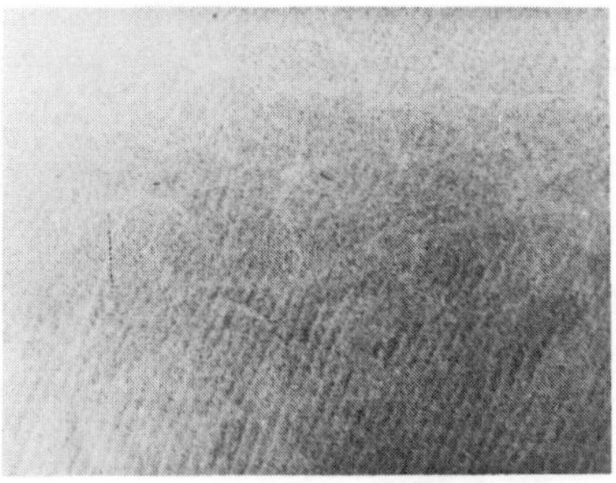

At first we seem to be looking at a misshapen rock set in darkness; but this dissolves to the same-shaped rock surrounded by others. Next, these rocks become a patch of stones, and in shot 4 the stones become part of the grainy surface of a field of sand. This graininess then connects shot 4 to the coarse, rippled texture of the following shot, and these ripples, in turn, form part of the even, fingerprintlike pattern of shot 6. At this point, however, this slowly evolving series of shapes is suddenly violated by the figure of a man, the central character of

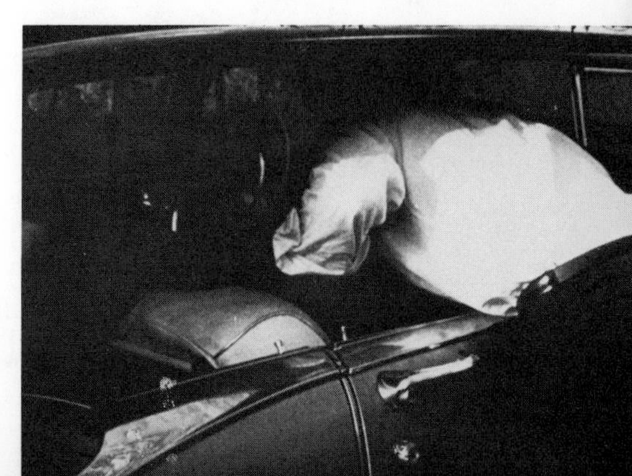

the film. Here, his mere entrance into the frame immediately sets him in opposition to the theme of the sequence, the organic relationship which integrates the various parts of the world through which he so carelessly travels.

Visual Transitions

When there is a significant shift in the narrative, such as when the action jumps forward or backward in time, or when it moves to a new location, the change can momentarily disorient the viewer and disrupt the rhythm of the film, unless there is some kind of warning. Traditionally, this warning has taken the form of an optical effect, a clearly recognizable visual transition which tells us that time and space are no longer continuous. Then, through long habit, we immediately search for whatever clues will identify the new time or place—and thus relocate us in narrative time—so that events can once again move smoothly forward in the present.

These optical transitions can take many forms: wipes, ripples, flips, revolves,

Optical-effects chart. This chart includes only commonly available wipes; there are many other effects, including some that can't be shown graphically.

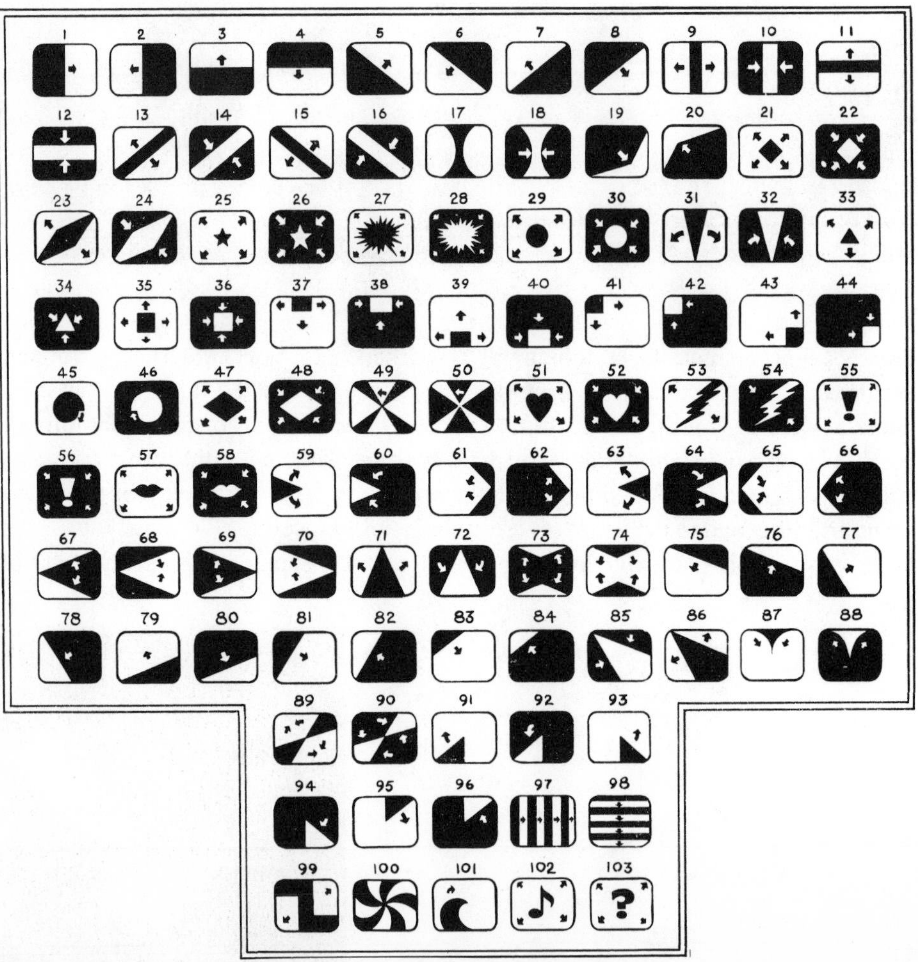

going out of focus, etc. In fact, the specialized laboratories, called *optical houses,* that produce such effects, routinely make available the following 103 different effects. The choice of effect depends upon a number of things. Sometimes a particular one is used because it naturally fits the flow of action. In *Yojimbo,* for instance, most of the transitions are wipes (see figures 1 and 2) that follow the samurai as he crosses the screen. At other times an effect is used because it makes an appropriate comment on the action, for instance, explosions (figures 27 and 28) or hearts (figures 51 and 52). Most of the time, however, a transition is used that can easily fit a variety of situations without calling attention to itself. Then one of the two most neutral and easily produced effects is used—either a dissolve or a fade.

Fades and Dissolves

These two effects are quite similar. In a fade the last shot in the scene *fades out,* that is, it slowly dims to black; then, in the next scene, the first shot *fades in,* that is, it slowly comes up from black to normal brightness. In a dissolve, on the other hand, as one shot fades out the next fades in, briefly superimposing the two images. Because of this small difference, however, there is a difference in the transitional effect each produces. In a fade the screen momentarily goes black, bringing the action to a temporary halt; while in a dissolve the images blend together, carrying the action in the first shot over into the second. As a result, dissolves help maintain the pace of the action.

This blending effect also makes dissolves useful within a scene. Then they ease the action forward in time while imperceptibly slowing its pace by eliminating the need to punctuate the flow of movement with cuts. This technique, and its effect on the meaning of the action, can be seen in an unusual double dissolve which is part of a scene in Bergman's *The Seventh Seal.* In this scene a long line of penitents suddenly invades a town whose inhabitants are in mortal fear of the plague. The leader of this procession, a monk preaching hellfire and brimstone, exhorts the townspeople to mend their ways before God singles them out to die. Finally, the penitents, scourging their flesh and rending the air with their wails and groans, wend their lugubrious way out of town. As they leave, we first see a monk, straining under the weight of an immense cross, lead the procession across the frame; next there is a dissolve to the stragglers who bring up the rear; and last of all a dissolve to just their tracks in the bare earth.

These shots were probably filmed as one static shot, with the sections be-

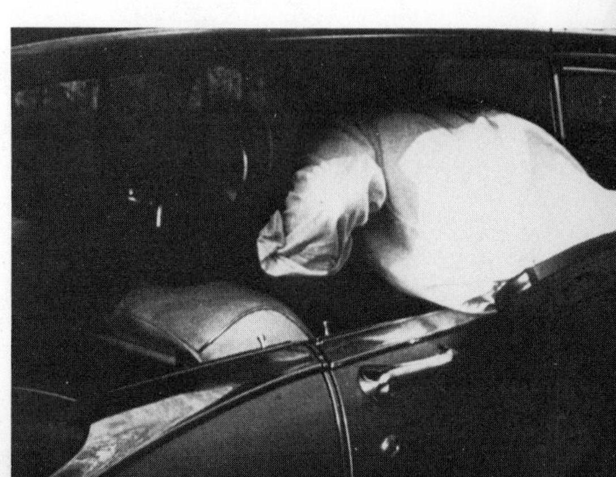

Courtesy: JANUS FILMS, I

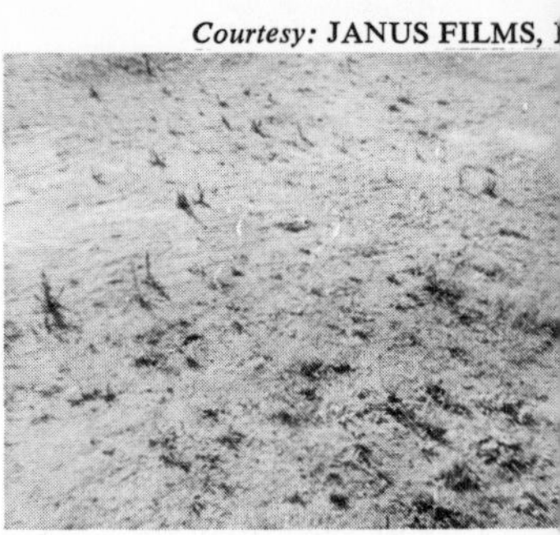

tween the dissolves removed during editing. As a result, the beaten ground remains the same from shot to shot while the penitents are only briefly superimposed upon it. This technique makes them disappear from town as quickly as they had descended upon it, but without making them seem to rush. And in the process, Bergman switches our attention from the procession itself to the effects of their passage. Like a cloud of locusts, they roil the earth and then leave nothing behind but desolation and anguish.

Length and Pace

It is also possible to vary the length of a fade or a dissolve between sixteen and ninety-six frames, and this too has an effect on the pace of the film. At one extreme, fades and dissolves of only sixteen frames last less than a second on the screen and are barely noticeable. They operate more like a slightly blurred cut and help propel the action across the effect. At the other extreme, opticals of ninety-six frames are so long that they have a lingering, almost languid effect no matter what the pace of the action. In general, however, an intermediate length of forty-eight frames, or two seconds, is most commonly used because it produces a noticeable transition without greatly affecting the pace of the scenes on either side of it.

Although these effects can be created in the camera, they are now usually produced by the laboratory when the final prints are made (the details of both techniques are discussed in Chapter Ten). This means that when an effect is to

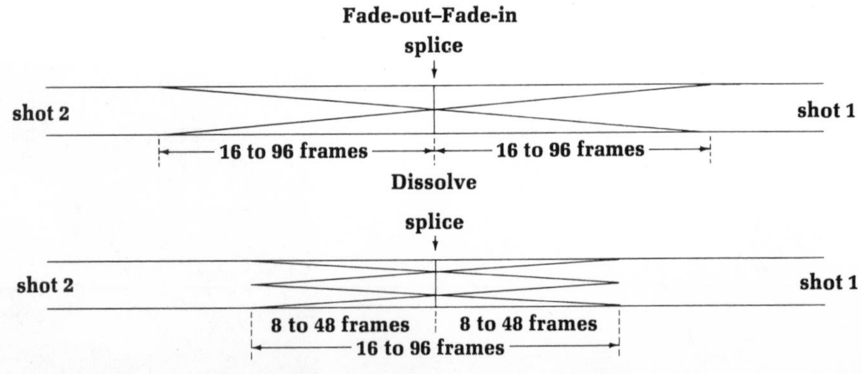

be added later, the editor has to indicate the effect by marking it on the workprint with a grease pencil. Since the effects are similar, the marks are also similar.

Straight-Cut Transitions

There are also times when optical effects are avoided entirely and each jump through time or space is simply made by means of a straight cut. The cut thus maintains the pace of the action by eliminating the interruption of a noticeable visual transition. But since these jumps are made without warning, they can easily be confusing unless some other means is used to alert the audience to the fact that they must relocate themselves in space and time.

One way to do so is by altering the rhythm of the action. An example of this, a scene from René Clair's silent classic *The Italian Straw Hat,* has already been discussed in the chapter on time (Chapter Two, pp. 55 to 60). In this scene the action alternates between the hero's wedding reception and his lurid anticipations of how threats to wreck his house might be carried out. However, these "flash forwards" are clearly set off from his present because they are filmed first in slow motion and then in fast motion. Clair then wove them into his hero's present by slowly increasing the pace of all the action so that the accelerating tempo of the scene matches the growing intensity of the man's anxiety.

The use of straight-cut transitions has been greatly simplified, however, by the advent of sound. Now all that is often needed to make the transition is just a line of dialogue. In *Breathless,* for instance, Seberg and Belmondo go looking for a friend. When they can't find him at his favorite hangout, they ask the bartender where he has gone and they are told, "He's in Montparnasse." When the next shot shows their car pulling to the curb, we immediately know that they have gone to Montparnasse.

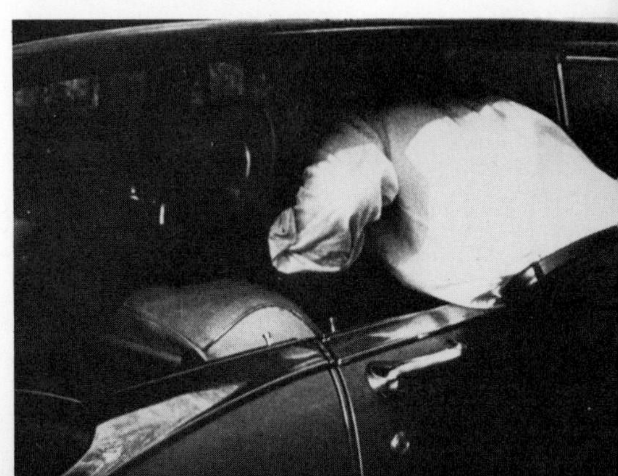

Music and sound effects, either singly or in combination, also play similar roles in helping the audience make these transitions; a number of examples have already been discussed in the chapter on time. But because the nature and timing of these sounds play such an important part, not only in making the transition, but in creating its meaning, these effects will be discussed in the following chapter, along with the many other details of sound editing.

Chapter 9

Editing Sound

It's not surprising that silent film-makers felt little need for a synchronous sound track. Over the years they had developed a rapport with their audience that turned their pictorial vocabulary into a fully expressive art form. Nevertheless, under the duress of competitive pressures the major film studios suddenly accepted recorded sound. At first the inclusion of sound was artistically stultifying because the process of recording and editing it was so inflexible; but once the industry perfected double-system sound, a whole new creative dimension opened to the film-maker. Now sound could be shaped to meet his exact demands, and he could make us hear just as easily and precisely as he had been able to make us see.

The great virtue of double-system sound is that the sound track can not only be recorded independently of the pictures, but sound and picture can then each be edited separately, yet kept in complete synchronization. Until they are locked together on the finished print, sound and picture remain on independent, parallel strands that can be manipulated almost at will. This means that sounds, as easily as pictures, can be cut apart and added, subtracted, or rearranged before they are finally mixed together to form the finished sound track.

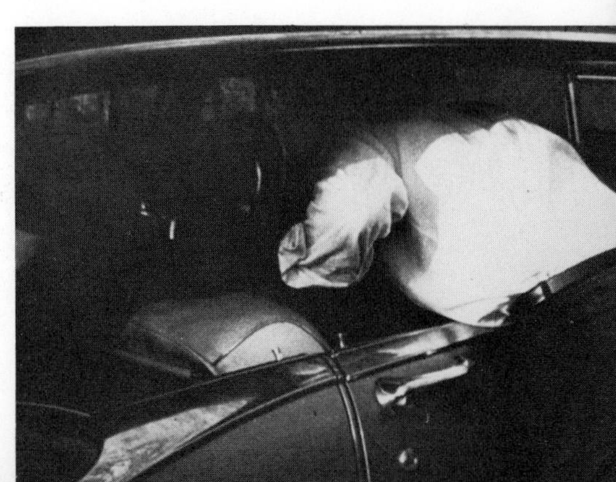

At the heart of double-system editing are the pieces of magnetic film on which each sound is recorded. Since these pieces of magnetic film run at the same speed as the pictures, and have the same kind of sprocket holes, once picture and sound are matched together sprocket-hole-for-sprocket-hole, they remain in synchronization until one or the other is purposely moved. As a result, the editor can systematically work his way through the film, locking each piece of sound in place as he goes. In addition, he can edit each type of sound—voice, sound effects, or music—independently, putting each on a separate but synchronous track. This permits him to build the complex interactions of sound and picture a layer at a time and then later, during the mix, minutely control the sounds as they are blended together.

This layering technique can best be understood if we look at an example. It is a brief sequence from Jean Renoir's *Grand Illusion* in which just the accumulation of sounds creates an ominous, but unseen, battalion of enemy soldiers. At the start of the scene the French prisoners are standing around their barracks talking about their lives before the war. Suddenly their conversation is interrupted by the military cadence of a fife and drums outside in the courtyard.

PICTURE	SOUND
1. MCU, one of the Frenchmen; as he speaks, he walks toward the camera. The camera trucks back until we see all the men clustered around the window (17 sec.).	MUS: Military fife and drums. 1st MAN: Something about it gets you.

PICTURE	SOUND
2. MCU, slow truck R–L past men in window (16 sec.).	2nd MAN: I detest fifes. MUS: Fife and drum stop. SFX: Thud of marching feet fades up through end of music. 1st MAN: Anyway, it gets you. 3rd MAN: What gets you is not the music, but the thud of marching feet.

Courtesy: JANUS FILMS, INC.

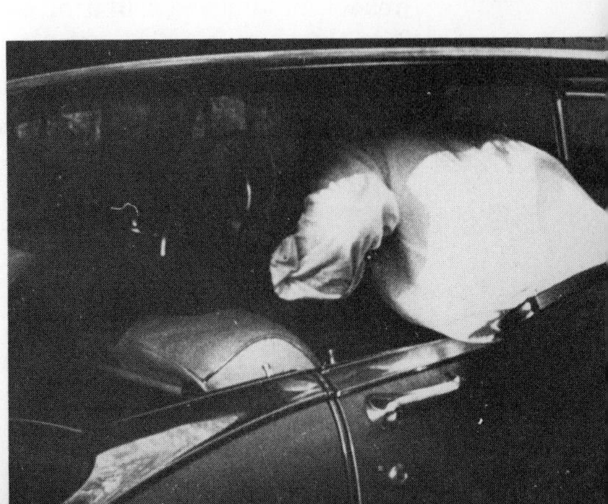

	PICTURE	SOUND
3.	MLS, the same as the end of shot 1; the men stand and listen as the camera slowly trucks toward them.	SFX: Marching continues.

In this case the first layer of sound is the lip-synchronous dialogue. This was recorded when the shots were filmed; then it was edited to form a roll of sound that ran parallel to the pictures. Next, the marching feet were recorded as *wild track,* that is, independently of the pictures. This track too was then matched to the pictures, only it was cut into a second roll containing just sound effects. Finally, the third layer, the fife and drum music, was recorded to fit the edited footage and cut into a third roll of just music. All these sound tracks were then played back in synchronization with the picture, and the various sounds faded in and out or mixed together as they were recorded on a master sound track.

Preparing the Footage for Editing

The mechanics of sound editing start immediately after the original is ready for workprinting. This is because, in the scenes in which there is lip-synchronous dialogue, sound and picture are linked from their very inception, so all the separate strips of film on which the two are recorded must first be locked together in synchronization before either can be evaluated.

The first step in this process is to pull out all the sound takes that go with the workprinted original. Then, regardless of whether the original recording was made on sprocketed film or quarter-inch tape, the original is duplicated on magnetic film. In the case of a sprocketed original, this duplicate serves as a *safety,* a backup copy that can be used if the original is somehow damaged during editing. In the case of a quarter-inch original, however, a sprocketed duplicate is an absolute necessity since it is impossible to edit unsprocketed tape synchronously. The transferring process is then called *resolving.* As was mentioned previously, this involves using the control track on the tape—the "electronic sprocket holes"—to guide the magnetic film copy so that it exactly matches the pictures sprocket-hole-for-sprocket-hole. After it is duplicated, the quarter-inch original becomes the safety from which any number of additional copies can later be made.

Of course, all post-synchronously recorded narration, music, and sound effects must also be recorded on magnetic film in order to be edited. But this needn't be done before editing starts. If a magnetic film recorder is readily available to the film-maker, recording post-synchronous material is relatively simple and can be done as the sound is needed during editing. This, in fact, is often preferable since sounds that are recorded as the editing proceeds can be more easily matched to the pictures. And narration and music are usually recorded after the entire picture is cut so that the tempo and feeling of the original recording can be tailored to the visuals.

Sorting the Takes

Once the dialogue is transferred and the workprint made, the next step is to match each sound take to its associated picture. This means that the editor must identify each take by listening to the slate recorded at the beginning, a task that requires the first of several basic pieces of sound-editing equipment—a *sound reader*. A sound reader is nothing more than a magnetic playback head and amplifier that make the sound on the magnetic film audible. In other words, it is a magnetic playback machine, much like any other magnetic recorder, except that there isn't any transport mechanism for moving the magnetic film past the head.

Instead, the magnetic film is slid over the head either by hand or by the cranking of the rewinds. This makes it easy to locate a particular sound since the track can be moved both forward and back at will and at any speed. In addition, the editor can find the exact cutting point by rocking the sound back and forth over the head, the same as he does when using a viewer. After the sound is located, it is positioned over the head and that spot is marked on the track with a grease pencil. However, since the sound track can be moved at any speed in either direction, the result is often a horrible din, and this has earned the sound reader its nickname of *squawk box*.

The sound reader is used to break down the takes into separate rolls. As each slate is read the shot and take numbers are noted on a small piece of masking tape that is later used to identify the roll. Then the first sound of the clapstick, or other slating device, is located over the magnetic head and the frame marked. This frame is next punched with a small, round hole so that the synchronizing point is clearly and permanently indicated. The take is then wound up *heads out,* that is, with the beginning of the sound to the outside, and the loose end is secured with the marked tape that identifies the roll.

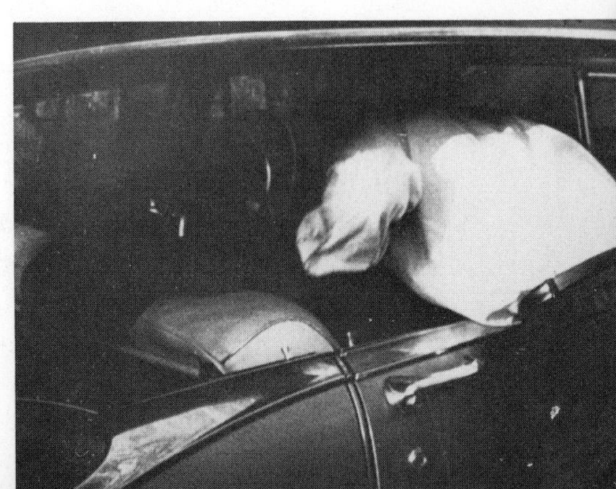

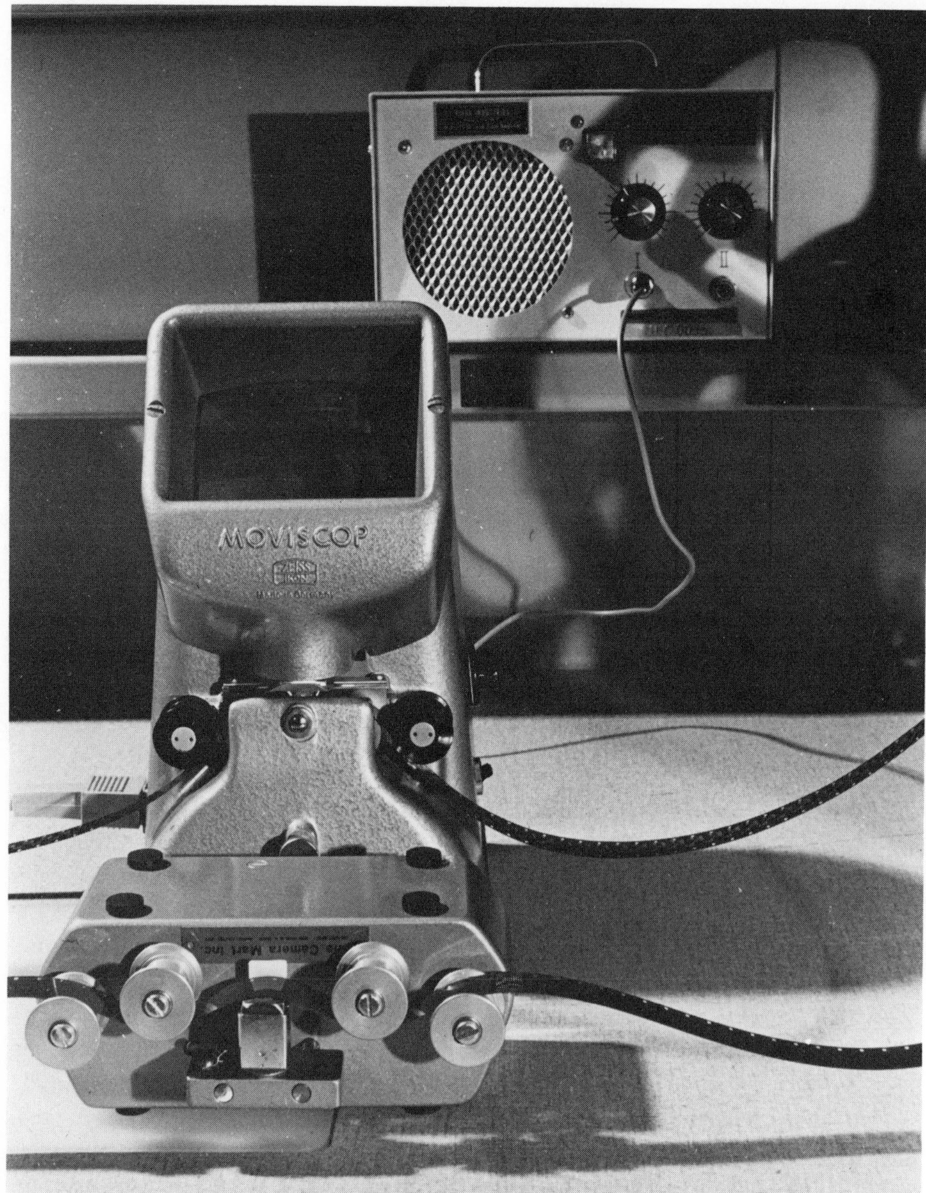

Sound reader. The sound head is mounted in front of the film viewer, foreground, and connected by a cable to the squawk box, rear.

These separate pieces of sound can either be wound on reels or, as is more often the case, spooled on *cores*. A core is just a small plastic hub that fits between the two metal flanges of a *split reel*. That way the reel can be taken apart after the film is wound on the core and a new core used for the next piece of film. This is much cheaper than using a separate reel for every one of the hundreds of pieces of sound and picture used in a film; and once the film is tightly wound on the core, there is little chance of its slipping off.

A similar procedure is also used to identify, punch, and segregate each piece

Split reel. On rewind, front, and split apart, rear. Film on a core is placed on the hub of one-half of the reel and the two halves are then screwed together.

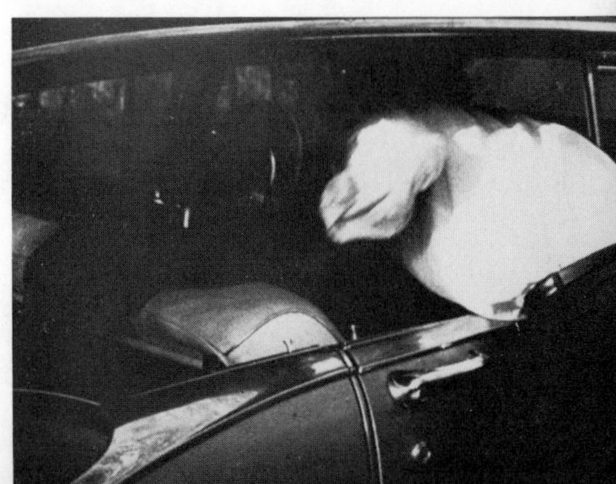

of workprint for which there is synchronous dialogue. The punch marks are placed where the clapstick first appears closed, or where some other slating device first indicates a synchronizing point. The separate rolls of sound and picture are then grouped so that each piece of sound is with its associated roll of picture.

Synchronizing Sound and Picture

Synchronizing requires two other pieces of equipment that are basic to sound editing—a *synchronizer* and *gang rewinds.* A synchronizer consists of two or more wheels with sprocket teeth on them. These sprocket wheels are fastened to a common shaft so that they all automatically rotate together and at the same speed. As a result, when sound and picture are locked in the synchronizer with

Synchronizer and gang rewind. The magnetic sound film, foreground, is locked together with the picture, rear, by the sprocket-toothed wheels of the synchronizer; the two strips of film are then taken up together by locking the reels onto the long shaft of the gang rewind.

their sprocket holes engaged in the teeth on the wheels, pulling one of them through the synchronizer automatically pulls the other at the same rate, thus keeping the two in step sprocket-hole-for-sprocket-hole. These wheels are also designed so that one full rotation equals a foot of film, that is, sixteen frames of 35mm, forty frames of 16mm, or seventy-two frames of super 8mm. These rotations are then read out on a footage-and-frame, or minute-and-second, counter that is geared to the common shaft.

The other piece of equipment, gang rewinds, is simply a pair of rewinds with long shafts. They permit several reels of film to be unwound or rewound simultaneously. They are a necessity in editing sound since at least two reels, one each of sound and picture, must be edited at the same time.

The first two rolls of sound and picture to be synchronized are locked into the synchronizer so that the punch marks are opposite each other. Then a twenty-foot piece of black film, called *leader,* is spliced to the beginning of each roll and the two rolls are wound through the synchronizer onto two separate take-up reels. Just before the end of these rolls the wheels of the synchronizer are locked in place, and if the rolls are not the same length, a piece of leader is attached to the shorter of the two. When the picture is shorter, this *slug* is just spliced in as if it were another piece of picture. But if the sound is shorter, another kind of leader and a different splicer are used.

The sound track can be slugged with either clean scraps of magnetic film or blank leader, whichever happens to be available. When leader is used, however, it must be turned over so that, instead of the photographic emulsion, the hard backing material rides over the magnetic head. Otherwise the head will scratch off the soft emulsion, and this will clog the head, causing the sound to deteriorate. In addition, the splices should be made with mylar tape and a demagnetized pair of scissors or a nonmagnetic (brass and aluminum) splicing block. This is necessary because the film cement used to make picture splices will damage the sound, which often continues over a splice, while a tape splice, which is applied to the backing of the magnetic film, has no effect on the sound side. Secondly, the splicer must be nonmagnetic, or demagnetized steel, or the metal will magnetize the splice. Then the splice will make a loud pop every time the track is played back.

Once the *tails* of the first two rolls have been evened out, the punch marks in the next two rolls are laid on top of each other in the editor's hand. Then these two strips of film are carefully pulled through his fingers so that the sprocket holes stay together. When the head of one of the rolls is reached, the two strands

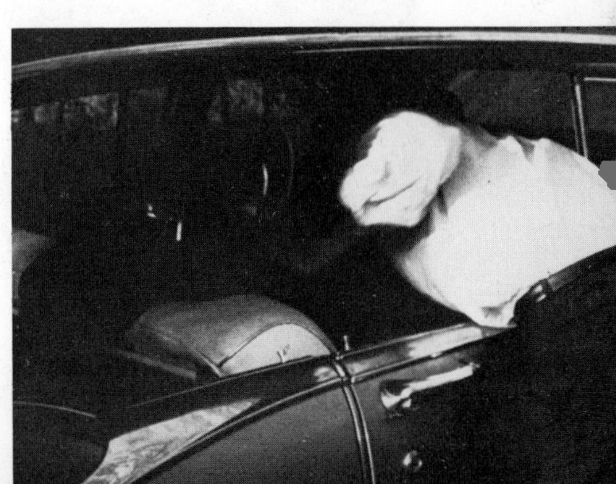

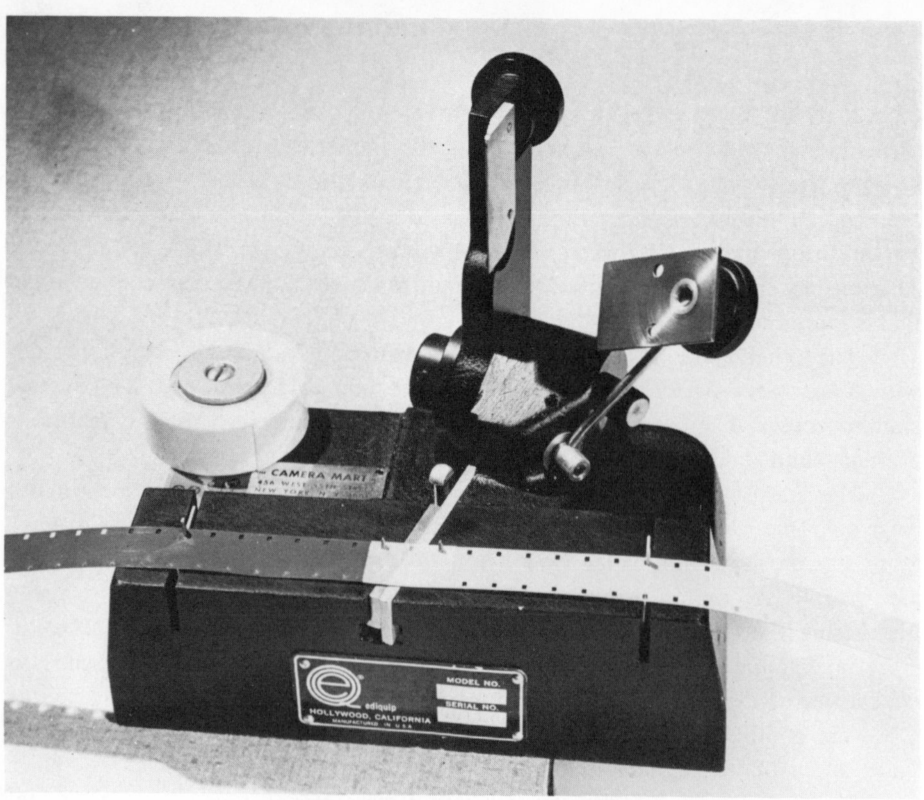

Sound splicer. This particular model makes diagonal splices; the mylar splicing tape sits on a knob at the rear of the splicer.

Editing bench set up for cutting picture and sound together. From the left: rewinds, picture splicer, sound splicer, film viewer and sound reader, synchronizer.

are cut straight across and each roll is spliced to the tail of one of the rolls locked in the synchronizer. Now these two new rolls are wound into the synchronizer and the punch marks checked to make sure that they are still opposite each other.

This whole process is repeated until all the sound and picture for the shots with dialogue are spliced in order. In some cases, a few silent shots are also included in the picture reel so that they are conveniently located for editing. Then, however, the reel of track must be slugged with the same amount of blank leader. When the take-up reels are full, a twenty-foot piece of leader is spliced to the tail of each roll and a synchronizing mark, labeled "tail sync," punched in each leader six feet from the end. And after the reels have been rewound through the synchronizer, a similar mark is also punched six feet from the beginning of each head leader and labeled "head sync." Later, these beginning sync marks will be used to position the rolls in the projector and sound reproducer when picture and sound are *interlocked,* that is, played back in double system.

Sound-Editing Equipment

The actual editing of the sound tracks can be done any number of ways. But the simplest way is to set up an editing bench with just the basic, hand-operated equipment described so far—gang rewinds, synchronizer, film viewer, sound reader, and film and tape splicers. Although only one sound track at a time can be edited on this equipment, it is adequate for most simple sound film-making. In fact, many small studios and most television news film facilities use no more equipment than this.

There is, however, one major drawback to this kind of setup. If the editor wants to evaluate his work under something approaching normal viewing conditions, he must periodically interlock sound and picture on a double-system projection system. This means that he must edit each sequence largely by instinct and then shuttle the film back and forth between the editing bench and the projector until all the bugs are worked out of the editing. And even then, depending upon the flexibility of the playback system, he is usually able to interlock the picture with only one sound track at a time.

Because this procedure is too inefficient for anything but short films, most professional editing is done on an editing machine. These machines expedite double-system editing by replacing the hand rewinds with a motor-driven transport that automatically interlocks sound and picture at 24 fps. At their most sophisticated, such machines permit up to three sound tracks and two picture tracks to

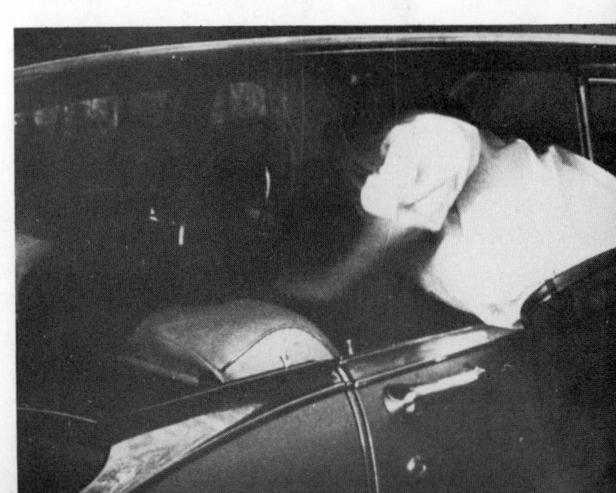

Moviola vertical editing machine. The picture head is on the right, the sound head on the left.

Horizontal editing table. This 6-plate model can play back the picture and two sound tracks.

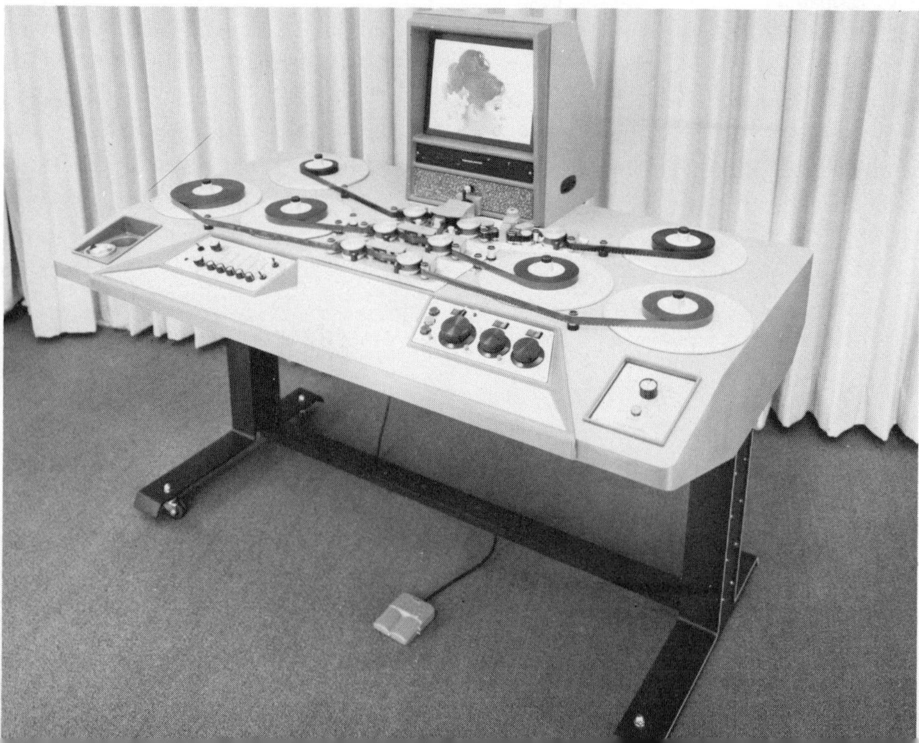

be locked together at sound speed, or run either forward or in reverse at any speed. In addition, any combination of track and picture can be edited and played back without disturbing the rest of the material on the machine, or each individual sound or picture track can be edited separately.

Editing machines come in two basic types—vertical and horizontal. The older, vertical machines are so called because the reels are mounted on the machine vertically. One example of this type of machine is the *Moviola,* a name that is used for most vertical editing machines even though it is the brand name of just one. These machines are still widely used, but they are less flexible than the newer, horizontal *editing tables.* For one thing, because the film is mounted horizontally, it is held in place by gravity, so it can be left on cores. These tables have also been designed so that the sound and picture tracks simply drop into slots instead of having to be threaded through a complex array of sprockets. As a result, editing tables are now the preferred means for editing sound films.

However, one further step has recently been taken, and that is to computerize the editing. This is done with a hybrid editing machine that combines film, video tape, and computer operation to automate the sorting and joining of the various bits and pieces of sound and picture that go into the finished film. In essence, the computer permits a video-tape copy of the sound and the picture to be arranged and rearranged nearly instantaneously by electronic means until the final version of the film is arrived at. This version is then read out of the machine as instructions for printing the film. The vast increase in speed and ease of handling is most useful in the production of filmed television series; but so far only the large volume of work involved in television film production can justify the tremendous expense of a computerized editing machine.

Editing Dialogue

No matter how the editing is done, though, by hand, machine, or computer, the sound-editing process itself is still the same. The film-maker must build up the track a layer at a time and then blend these sounds into a final version that is locked onto the edge of the finished print. In most professional film-making this process starts with the creation of a dialogue track as the basic track around which all the other sounds are built. This procedure is followed because lip-synchronous dialogue is tied to specific pictures, and cutting the pictures also necessarily requires that the sound associated with those pictures be cut at the same time.

However, pictures and dialogue together can't be cut quite as freely as

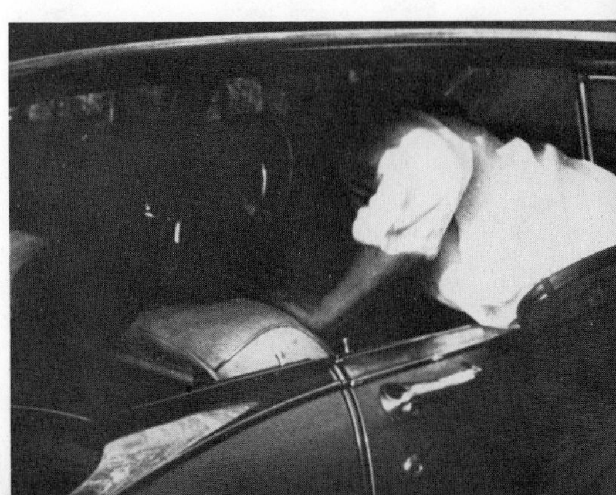

just pictures alone. While the action in the pictures can be assembled in any number of ways, the words must follow one another in sequence. But this doesn't indelibly link the sequence of the pictures to the order of the words. Since, in double system, words and pictures are on separate pieces of film, the dialogue can be made to fall over any picture. In practical terms, this means that a piece of dialogue can continue on the track even after the pictures have cut away to another part of the action. For example, we quite often see a shot of someone listening while someone else goes on talking. This kind of flexibility makes it possible to assemble the dialogue in order and still build the action through a carefully controlled variety of shots.

At its simplest, this can involve nothing more complicated than cutting away from the dialogue with one of those standard reaction or insert shots that have already been discussed. This is what was done, for instance, to build the meaning of the following dialogue sequence in Alfred Hitchcock's *Suspicion.* The scene takes place during a dinner at the home of a woman mystery-story writer; it involves just a brief exchange between a central figure in the film, John Aysgarth (played by Cary Grant), and the writer's brother, a coroner. Aysgarth's wife, Lena, also present, suspects that her husband wants to murder her, so when the conversation turns into an argument about how to commit the perfect crime, she is both afraid and anxious to hear her husband's response. After he declares that a murder should be done simply, she interrupts to ask, "How would you do it simply?"

	PICTURE	SOUND
	**1.** MS, John.	JOHN: Oh, I don't kno dear. But I would use th most obvious method. Th most important thing is tha no one should suspect me. LENA: (offscreen) For in stance? JOHN: For instance, poison.
	**2.** MS, Lena. She looks up from her dinner.	JOHN: Just use the first o that came to my mind, um . . . say arsenic.

	PICTURE	SOUND
	3. MS, Dr. Sedbusk. He is talking and eating at the same time.	DR.: Ah, arsenic. I remember . . .
	**4.** CU, his dinner. He is vigorously cutting into a chicken.	DR.: . . . in Gloucester, where we exhumed a body four years after . . .
	**5.** MS, Doctor (same as shot 3).	DR.: . . . there was still enough poison in the fingernails and hair.
	**6.** MS, John (same as shot 1).	JOHN: Yes, but did you get the murderer? DR.: Let me see . . . ah. No, I don't think we did.

urtesy: JANUS FILMS, INC.

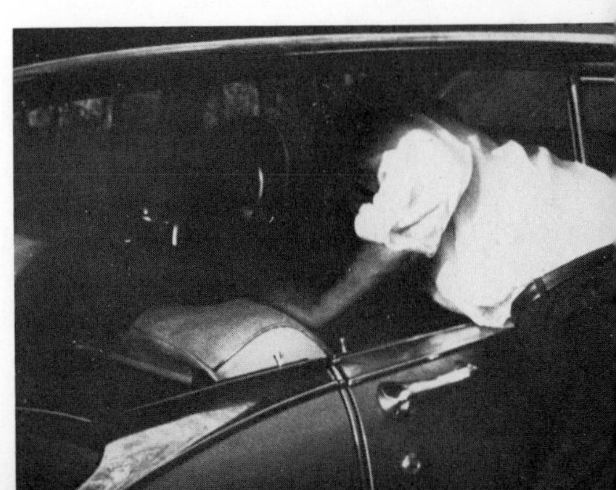

The cut-aways, shots 2 and 4, force us to vacillate between accepting Lena's increasingly hysterical fears, `or accepting the discussion as essentially innocent table talk. In shot 2, the reaction shot, Lena's nervous pause expands her husband's preference for arsenic into a scenario for her own murder. But then, in the insert shot, shot 4, her anxiety is made to seem exaggerated, and finally trivial, as the coroner slices up a roast chicken while discussing an autopsy. At first we can only see the bird as Lena does, as her own dead body consigned to the doctor's knife. But we simultaneously realize that the gusto with which he cuts into the fowl is also just a gruesome little joke. It simply implies that he gets as much enjoyment from dismembering his dinner as he does from his professional concerns. This bit of macabre humor then makes Lena's response to the conversation seem slightly ridiculous. But only until John forces the doctor to admit that the murder had indeed gone unsolved. In the end we are left feeling as ambiguous about John's intentions as Lena does.

The Interplay of Meanings

Here the effect of the cut-aways is quite incisive. Just read the dialogue without reference to the pictures. What a different scene this would be if we had only been shown each person talking. Even allowing for the actors' delivery of the lines, there would be none of the innuendo, suspense, and humor, and the scene would not have pushed us even further into Lena's obsession. Before the scene starts, Lena already believes John wants to poison her, so when she glances up as he says "poison," we know that she feels confirmed in her suspicions. However, this counterpoint of words and picture also invests the rest of his sentence with such enormous power that it is hard for us, from that point on, to hear his words as anything but those of a murderer toying with his victim.

Yet, just as we expect the doctor to confirm her, and our, suspicions, we get the other cut-away, a shot that tells us not to take her any more seriously than the film-maker does. This shot, which is Hitchcock's comment on the dialogue, takes us outside the action and makes us laugh at it. It momentarily puts us in the position of a somewhat jaundiced viewer, and by thus allowing us to step back to look at the conversation objectively, gives us a chance to discount her, and our, anxiety. As a result, the scene can be edited normally from this point on because the cut-aways, by setting up all the implications of the dialogue, have told us how to react.

Now we take in the last part of the doctor's statement as the sane analysis of a rational authority. John's suggestion is just a silly scheme, one that no intelligent man would ever attempt. Then, however, John disabuses us of the doctor's authority by quickly proving that this particular scheme has already worked. And so we are left just a bit more perplexed than when we started and slightly less sure of our ability to discern John's motives. In the process, however, we have not only been tested, but the suspense has been prolonged and the noose pulled just a little bit tighter. All this from action that is so tightly coiled around two cut-aways that when Hitchcock frees us from them, the tension in that coil can shoot through all the rest of the dialogue.

The Counterpoint of Rhythms

Besides the interplay of words and pictures' creating new meanings, meanings can also be built through a rhythmic counterpoint of the dialogue and the pictures. Although the natural sequence of the words gives the dialogue a flow that is based on the habitual pace of spoken language, this pace can be kept quite separate from that developing in the pictures. In other words, double-system sound permits the pictures to be edited so that their pace sometimes reinforces that of the dialogue, and at other times plays against it. And that effect too is achieved by means of cut-aways.

This technique can be seen in its subtlest, but most common, form in a sequence which opens the trial scene in Fritz Lang's *M*. Here the words and pictures have been cut in such a way that the dramatic intensity of the scene is built not only by the developing action but also through an interplay between the rhythm of the dialogue and that of the pictures. This is accomplished by editing the scene so that the words in some shots either begin over the previous shot or flow into the shot to follow. This technique converts into a cut-away the part of each shot in which there is overlapping dialogue.

ɔurtesy: JANUS FILMS, INC.

PICTURE	SOUND
1. MLS, stairs leading into abandoned brewery. A man swings the door open and two others shove M, coat over head, through the door and down the steps (5 sec.).	M.: (offscreen) Bastards! 1st MAN: Let him go. M: Grunts. SFX: Bumping footsteps as he half falls, half stumbles down the steps.

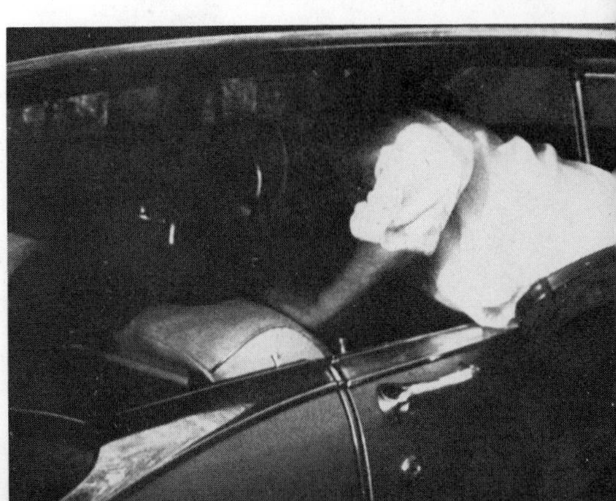

	PICTURE	SOUND
	**2.** LS, steps. M pulls coat from over his head and starts yelling at attackers. Then he turns and freezes in frightened surprise at what he sees (6½ sec.).	M: Bunch of bastards! W do you want with me? W do you want?
	**3.** LS, interior of brewery. Camera pans R over huge crowd of criminals, prostitutes, and beggars to table at which are seated Shranker, leader of the underworld, and several of his henchmen (30 sec.).	Long silence. M: (at end of shot) Help!
	**4.** LS, stairs (same as shot 2). M turns and starts up stairs, his voice becoming increasingly shrill as he tries to pass the two men who block his way (6 sec.).	M: Help! Help, let me go! want to get out! I want get . . .
	**5.** MLS, Shranker and henchmen at table (6 sec.).	M: . . . out! Let me out! SHRANKER: You will n get out of here.
	**6.** MS, stairs. M descends stairs as he speaks, and camera trucks toward him; when camera stops he continues to walk toward it until he is in close-up.	M: But gentlemen . . . pleas I don't even know what yo want me for. I beg you, s me free. There must be som mistake . . .

PICTURE	SOUND
 As he talks a hand enters the frame, feeling around in the air near his head. Then the hand falls on his shoulder and he starts as if struck by a blow.	M: . . . a mista . . . BEGGAR: No, no . . . no mistake. Impossible, there's no mistake. No, no mistake.
 Camera trucks back as M turns toward beggar. When beggar is finally revealed, he is holding balloon that is like one we've seen earlier.	M: But . . . what do you mean? BEGGAR: Remember this? It's a balloon like the one you gave little Elsie Beckman . . .
M flinches at girl's name; the beggar lets the balloon rise to the end of its string (47½ sec.).	
 **7.** MLS, reverse angle. Balloon rises immediately in front of the lens and floats there. M, terrified, his eyes fixed on it, backs away from the camera (10½ sec.).	BEGGAR: . . . a balloon like that. M: El . . . El . . . Elsie . . . El . . . Elsie. . . . No— No— No. SHRANKER: Where . . .

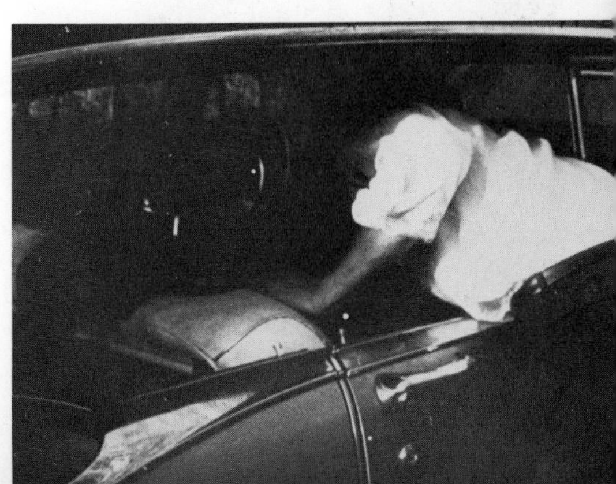

	PICTURE	SOUND
	**8.** LS, reverse angle. M, back to camera, turns abruptly when he hears Shranker (1½ sec.).	SHRANKER: . . . did yc bury . . .
	**9.** MS, Shranker. He leans forward belligerently (3 sec.).	SHRANKER: . . . litt Martha, you dog?
	**10.** MS, M. He walks toward camera, pleading (10½ sec.).	M: But . . . I never . . . never even knew her.
	**11.** MS, Shranker (same as shot 9). He waves a picture in the air (7½ sec.).	SHRANKER: So—you didn even know her. And wha about this one?
	**12.** MS, M (same as shot 10). He quickly backs away in fright (1 sec.).	Silence.

	PICTURE	SOUND
	**13.** CU, first photograph. Shranker drops it out of frame and then lifts up another (3 sec.).	SHRANKER: And this one?
	**14.** MS, M (same as shot 12). He gnaws at his fingers as if to repress a scream (1½ sec.).	Silence.
	**15.** CU, photograph (same as shot 13). Picture of third child (3 sec.).	SHRANKER: And this one, you didn't know her either, eh?
	**16.** MS, M (same as shot 14). Crazy with fear, he turns and rushes toward the exit (2 sec.).	SFX: Woman's scream.

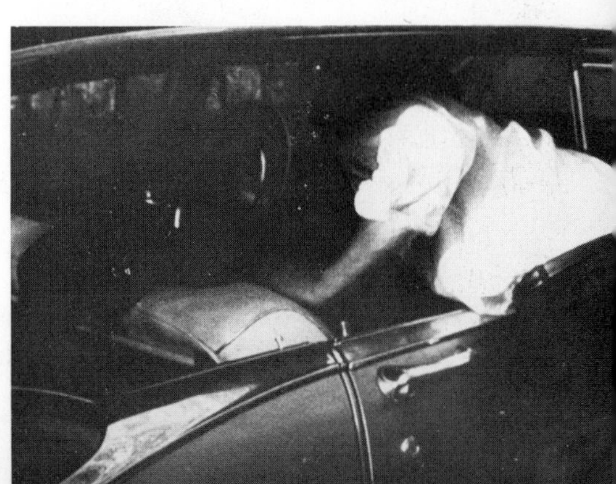

	PICTURE	SOUND
	**17.** LS, crowd. They jump to their feet and start after him (2 sec.).	CROWD: Stop him! S him!
	**18.** MLS, M (same as shot 16). Man sitting at foot of stairs jumps up to bar his way (2½ sec.).	CROWD: (shouting hyst cally) Don't let him get aw Get him! etc.

Courtesy: JANUS FILMS, INC.

At the beginning the slow pace of the cutting matches M's halting realization of the danger he is in. This rhythm is the result of both the longish shots and the overlapping of the dialogue from shot to shot. First the two opening shots are linked by a match-action cut and the sound of M's outraged demands. Then, after shot 3 has silently hung on the screen for almost thirty seconds, shots 3, 4, and 5 are tied together by the overlapping of all of them with M's futile screams for help. Finally, this slow beginning culminates in the extended trucking movement of shot 6, the longest-running shot in the sequence. Here the nearly imperceptible dollying of the camera first isolates the murderer and so makes his pleading seem to dominate the action, and then as it moves away, leaves him exposed and defenseless as the case against him is revealed.

Now he knows that he is trapped, and the increasing tempo of both track and picture reflect his mounting terror. But the pace at first builds slowly. Although each line of dialogue, and therefore each shot, gets shorter, the shots are initially tied together because the dialogue in shot 6 laps into shot 7, that in 7 into 8, and 8 into 9 so that the cuts in the pictures alternate with the breaks between either the voices or the words. This technique subtly escalates the pace of the cutting by holding the shots together while giving them two opposing rhythms. The heightened pace is then reinforced in shots 10 through 15 because both the cuts and the breaks between the lines coincide. This pulls the action taut by punctuating it at a steady but progressively faster pace until, as inevitably as the ticking of a clock, M is forced to confront each of his victims. Then, when his self-control collapses, pictures and dialogue break into little pieces. A scream pierces shot 16, staccato shouts fill 17, and in 18, pursued by the murderous frenzy of the crowd, he desperately rushes for the heavily guarded door.

The Mechanics of Cut-aways

Besides shaping the pace and meaning of a sequence, cut-aways also serve the mechanical function, mentioned previously, of bridging gaps in the action so that the shots flow together in a semblance of continuous space and time. This function is particularly important with lip-synchronous dialogue, however, because a cut-away simultaneously permits lines to be dropped or rearranged. Then, although the pictures too must be rearranged since they are linked to the dialogue, visual continuity can be maintained if the breaks in the action are covered with cut-aways.

While this technique is useful for smoothing out the changes that occur in even the best-planned dialogue sequences, it is central to the editing of the unplanned lip-synchronous footage used in news film and documentaries. Here the events filmed are largely spontaneous, so the shooting, which is at best piecemeal, produces a mass of dialogue from which relevant segments must first be excerpted before picture and sound can be arranged into a coherent whole. Yet, even though the action which accompanies this dialogue rarely connects from shot to shot, cut-aways make it possible not only to build continuous action, but to control the interplay of meaning and rhythm within the sequence.

The best way to understand how this is done is to look at a sequence from William Jersey's *cinéma vérité* documentary *A Time for Burning*. The film is a record of a St. Louis minister's efforts to integrate his church. This scene takes place at the barbershop of a black man to whom the minister has turned for criticism and advice. The shop is a neighborhood gathering place, and the conversation of the men in the shop illustrates how impatient they have become with the whole idea of integration.

The construction of this sequence hinges on the cut-aways, particularly those of the boy getting a haircut. For instance, over shot 3, the first shot of the boy, the barber answers the statement made by the man in shot 2. But this reply was probably delivered either as the man went to get the coat he puts on in shot 4, or even during some other part of the discussion. Because this man's action, and all but the last part of his response to the barber, were unnecessary to the sequence, they were dropped and the cut-away used both to bridge the gap in the action and to provide room for the barber's statement. The cut-away to the boy in shot 6 was also probably used for a similar purpose, only here it also serves as a bridge to shot 7, a reaction shot. In shot 5 the man listening is looking left, while in shot 7 he is looking to the right. This reversal is due to the

	PICTURE	SOUND
	1. CU, 1st Man.	1st MAN: Why should he over there and fight the Vi namese, they've done nothi to him? But right in his ov country he can go places a he can't even get in a hot (voice off: Right!) I mean and he can drive into a pla and might not even be ab to get gas if the people do look at your license plat and see where you're fro That's what he's talkin' abo
	2. MCU, 2nd Man.	2nd MAN: Have you ev been in Hawaii? What do th think about you? (Yeah They're black as you are a I am, right? (Yeah.) C then, what a bottle of be cost you? Eighty cents, do it? Will they speak to yo (That depends.) Becau they got long pretty hair.
	3. CU, Boy getting haircut.	BARBER: (offscreen) Yo know the white man got the and contaminated them. 2nd MAN: You can't go places . . .
	4. MS, 2nd Man putting on coat.	2nd MAN: . . . in Japa man! (general shouting a disagreement).

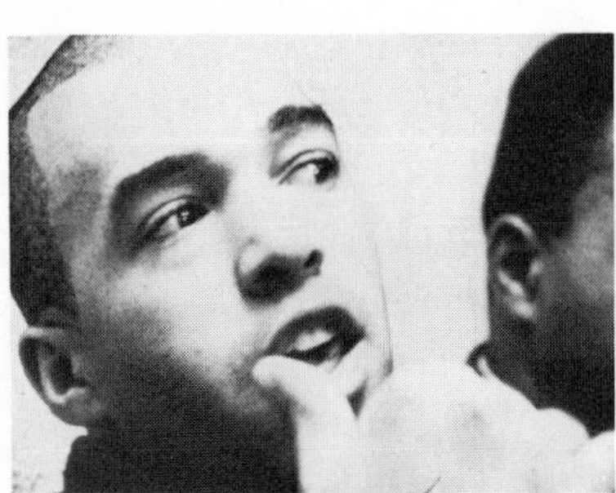

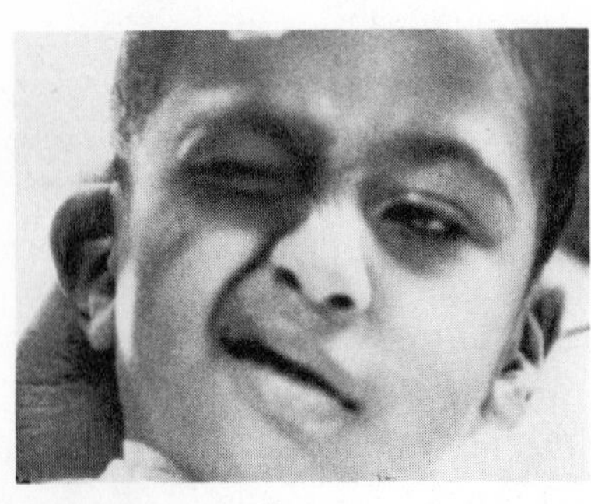

	PICTURE	SOUND
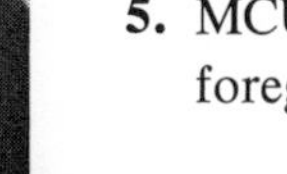	**5.** MCU, 3rd Man, 2nd Man in foreground, listening.	3rd MAN: Let me say this now, even if you go somewhere over there and they mistreat you . . .
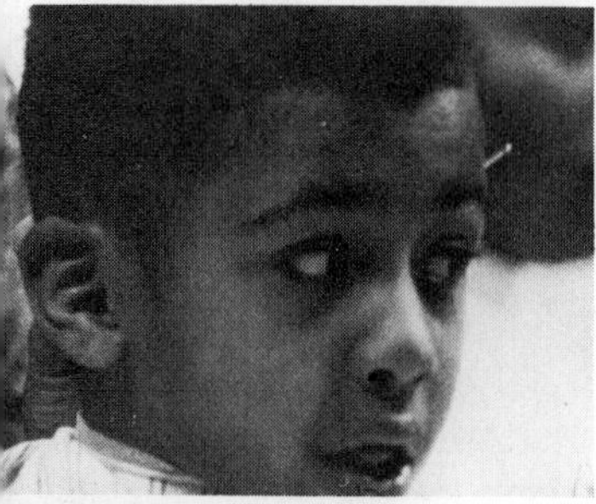	**6.** CU, Boy (same as shot 3).	3rd MAN: . . . well you can't just feel so bad because it's not like your home. But if it comes to your own home and . . .
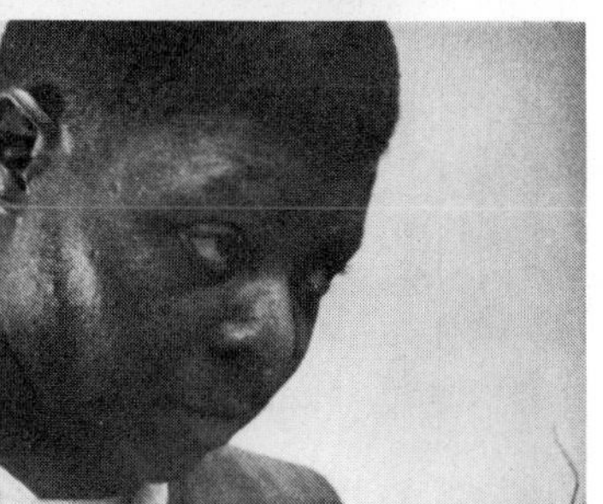	**7.** CU, 2nd Man listening. He looks up slowly.	3rd MAN: . . . then you really feel mistreated . . .
	**8.** MS, 3rd Man.	3rd MAN: . . . and this is my home here, and it's been worst right here. (Amen.) You know what I mean? Why go over there and fight?

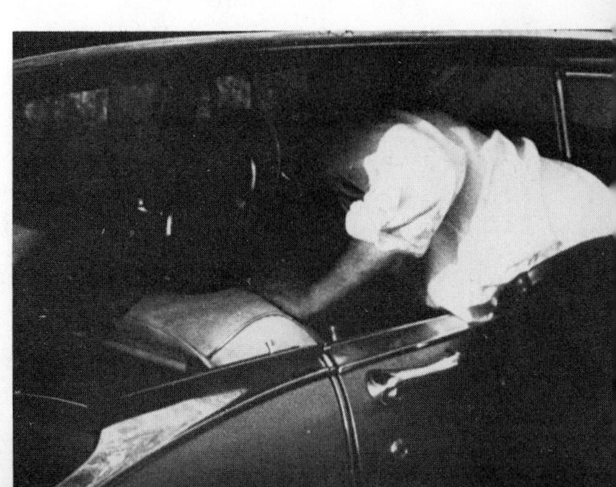

PICTURE | SOUND

9. CU, 4th Man, listening.

BARBER: (offscreen) A one here been turned aw from a hotel by a Viet . . .

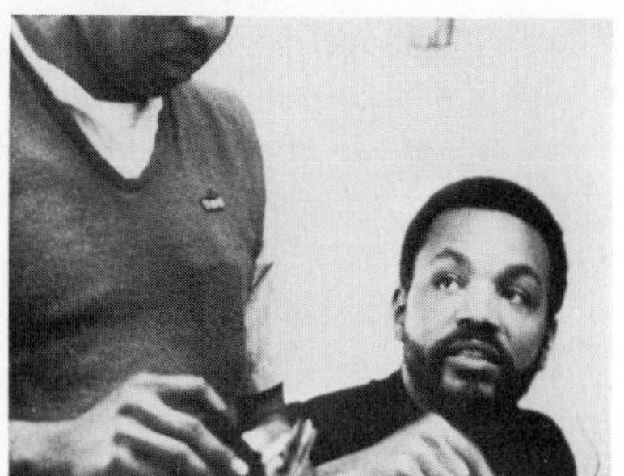

10. MCU, Barber.

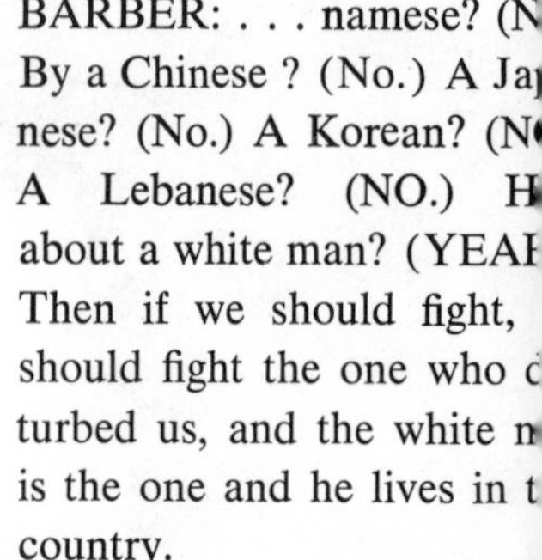

BARBER: . . . namese? (N By a Chinese ? (No.) A Ja nese? (No.) A Korean? (N A Lebanese? (NO.) H about a white man? (YEA Then if we should fight, should fight the one who d turbed us, and the white m is the one and he lives in t country.

fact that shot 7 is probably a piece of a shot made earlier, before the man put on his coat. But joining 7 directly to 5 would have meant abruptly changing his screen direction. The cut-away thus avoids the momentary confusion that would have been caused by the reversal of the direction of the action.

However, as crucial as these mechanical functions are to the shape of the sequence, they are no more important than the aesthetic functions served by the various cut-aways. The insert shots of the boy, shots 3 and 6, expand the meaning of the conversation to include an unspoken responsibility these men feel for the world they wish their children to inherit. And the reaction shots, shots 7 and 9, evidence at least a tacit acceptance of the arguments by all present that eventually reinforces the impact of the barber's ominous concluding statement. These cut-aways also break up the rhythm of the rather longish statements so that the pace of the cuts interacts with the accelerating pace of the discussion to create a growing feeling of agitation and involvement. This acceleration gives us a sense that they are discussing not just petty grievances but the bitter injustice of shared wounds.

Assembling the First Layer

Actually putting together the first layer of dialogue is the most technically complicated part of double-system sound editing. Because the dialogue is linked to specific pictures, sound and picture must be edited at the same time. And every time either the pictures or the sound change length as they are being cut, even if it's only by one frame, there must be a corresponding change in the other track if the two are to remain in synchronization.

The procedure for cutting pictures and dialogue is similar to that used in synchronizing the sound takes to the workprint. If the cutting is done on an editing table, the tracks are placed to the left and threaded through the sound and picture heads of the machine. If it is done by hand, the reels of sound and picture are placed on the left-hand rewind and then threaded through the viewer and sound reader and onto take-up reels. Next, the tracks are synchronized by locking the punch marks in the head leaders opposite each other in the synchronizer, or if the cutting is done on a machine, by centering them over the sound and picture heads. Then both tracks are rolled through the machine or synchronizer from left to right, past the slates, to the first frame of the shot, and the frame line is marked on each roll with a grease pencil. The splices will be made on these marks.

Because all the cutting and splicing are done to the left of the point where the tracks are locked in synchronization, the rolls are next wound back until the slates are to the left of either the synchronizer or the sound and picture heads of the machine. Now the slates are ready to be cut off. However, this means cutting off the only exact sync point in the shot. So, unless some other sync mark is placed within the shot, there is no way to check the synchronization of sound and picture once the tracks are cut. The editor must therefore create some other sync point before the slate is removed.

There are two methods for supplying additional sync marks. The most efficient but more expensive and complicated method is to print the same edge numbers on the original, the workprint, and the sound track. That way, every edge number is also a sync point. This type of numbering requires that, before the original is sent out for workprinting, the sprocketed magnetic track be synchronized with it. Then, after the workprint is made, all three rolls can be printed with the same set of inked edge numbers, producing identical numbers at the same point on each strand of film.

The other method is cheaper and simpler but less efficient than using edge numbers. It involves punching small notches into the edge of each piece of sound and picture used in the film. The point at which to make the notch is found by rolling the tracks forward through the synchronizer or editing machine past the first word on the dialogue track. Next, a frame of sound and picture that are opposite each other is marked with a grease pencil. Then, before the slate is cut off, the edge of each of these marked frames is notched between the sprocket holes with a small punch. These notches serve as an indelible sync point once the slate is removed.

If sound and picture are edge-numbered, or after they're notched, the slates

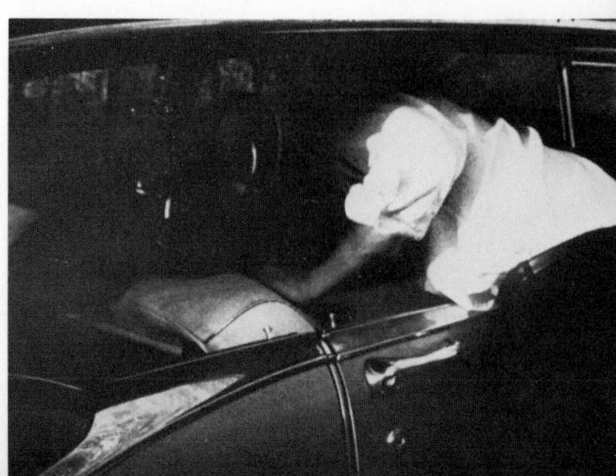

can be cut off at the point previously marked on each track, and the first frame of picture can be spliced directly to the leader. Now, however, the picture is shorter than the sound, so the same amount of sound track has to be removed. This is done by first rolling the picture splice back into the synchronizer, or over the picture head, and marking its position on the corresponding frame of sound-track leader. Then the sound leader is cut at this point and spliced to the frame that was previously marked on the sound track. Although sound and picture should automatically be back in synchronization, the easiest way to check is to roll the tracks through the synchronizer or over the heads of the editing machine to see whether the notches, or edge numbers, are still aligned.

The same procedure is now used to cut all the rest of the dialogue—except where the sound in one shot overlaps into one of the adjoining shots. Then the sound cut is usually made first and the picture adjusted to the proper length. This adjustment is made by first marking in grease pencil the cutting point for the picture on both the picture and the sound tracks. Next, the notch, or the nearest edge number, of the following shot is aligned with its section of the sound track and the mark on the track is transferred to the corresponding frame of picture. Now the shots can be joined at the point indicated by these two grease-pencil marks, and the notches, or edge numbers, should be in sync when the tracks are rolled back into the synchronizer or through the editing machine.

Unless the tracks are edge-numbered, there are several other situations in which notches must be used to indicate the synchronization of sound and picture. It is important, for instance, to notch both the pieces of picture which are removed when a cut-away is inserted and those sections of dialogue which are replaced either by new dialogue or the overlapping dialogue from another shot. This notching permits these extra pieces to be reinserted accurately should the editing of the sequence change. In addition, when a shot is cut apart and used in sections, it is necessary to make several sets of notches so that each section has its own sync point. Also, storing any un-edge-numbered leftovers, called *outs* or *trims,* requires a certain amount of care since there is no way to tell from the notches which piece of picture goes with what piece of sound. To avoid confusion, keep the pieces together, either by hanging them on the same pin in a cutting bin, or by rolling them up together on a reel of outs.

After each sequence is *rough-cut* it is interlocked, either on an editing machine or in double system, so that the synchronization can be checked and all corrections and refinements noted. These changes are then made by recutting sound and picture together. That way, both will remain the same length, and therefore in sprocket-hole-for-sprocket-hole synchronization.

The Second Layer

The next layer of sound contains either voice-over or narration. *Voice-over* (v.o.) usually means hearing just the voice of someone we have already seen speaking synchronously, while *narration* refers to the voice of an unseen narrator. This is a small difference, however, since both are cut in the same way. Because the words are free of any lip-synchronous connection with the pictures, the film-maker is able to create an interplay of meaning and rhythm, not only between words and pictures but between the pictures and a variety of voices.

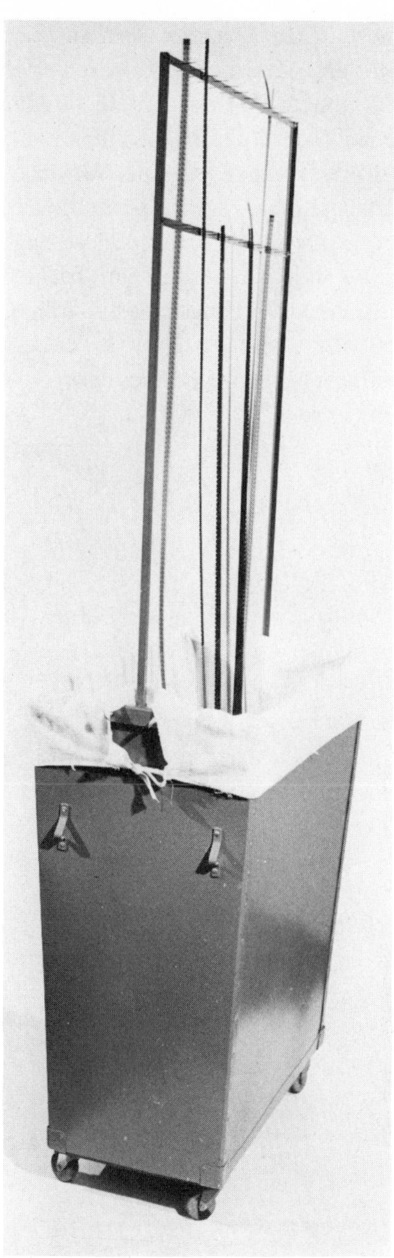

Cutting bin. The sprocket holes of the film fit over pins projecting from the metal frame, top.

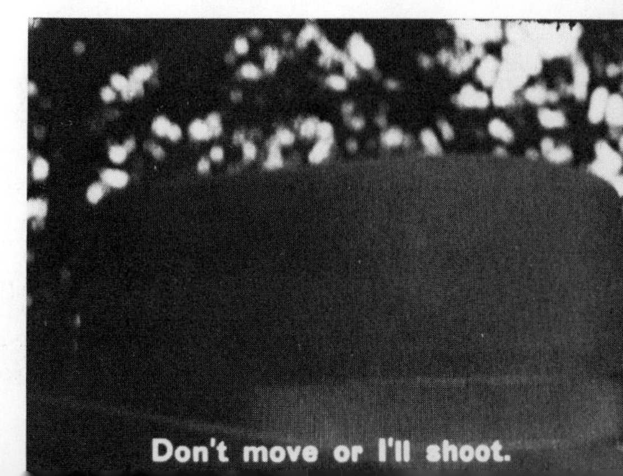

For example, in the following sequence from François Truffaut's *Jules and Jim,* lip-synchronous dialogue, voice-over, and narration are woven together to build the meaning of the scene. The film is about two friends, both of whom love, and live with, the same woman. This scene occurs late in the film. In the usual convoluted fashion of a *ménage à trois,* Catherine has left Jules for Jim, only to find him both unfaithful and unable to father a child. So she sends Jim away and returns to Jules, but not before she and Jim give their love one last, halfhearted try. Then, after Jim has taken up with an old and faithful girl friend, he unexpectedly gets a letter telling him Catherine is pregnant. What follows is an exchange of letters in which their love slowly revives, only to be crushed again when she has a miscarriage. This is the first part of their correspondence.

PICTURE	SOUND
1. MLS, Jim and Gilbert. The camera dollies in as Jim reads letter.	GILBERT: Your medicine . . . a letter. JIM: Thanks. CATHERINE: (v.o.) I'm going have a child. Come. Catherine. JIM: Gilbert, please give me sc writing paper.

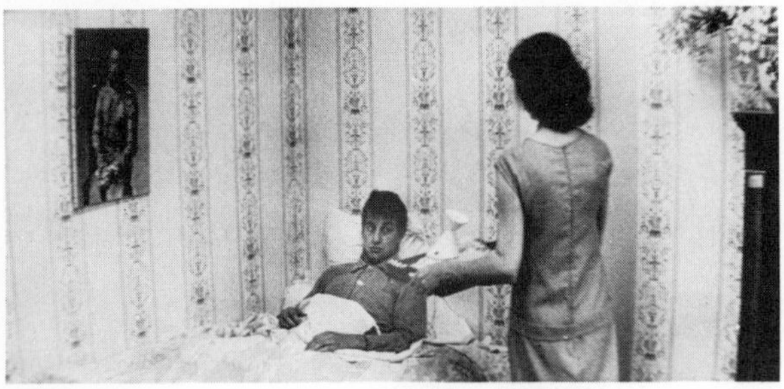

DISSOLVE

PICTURE	SOUND
2. CU, Jim, writing.	JIM: (v.o.) Catherine, I'm in bed very ill. Besides, I doubt that y child is mine. One night could not s ceed where love failed.

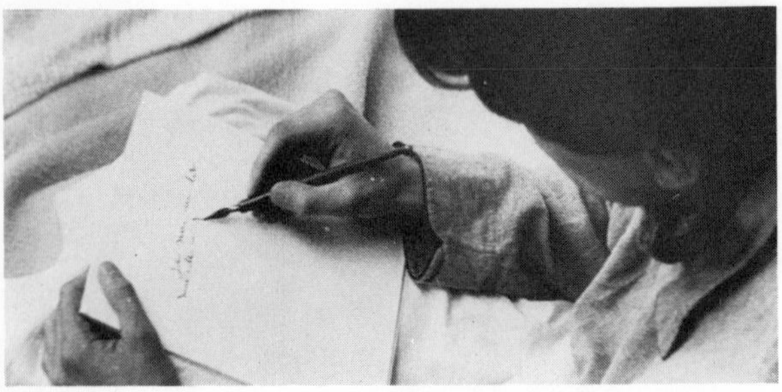

PICTURE	SOUND
3. MLS, Jules and Catherine. Jules reads the letter, then turns to desk and starts to write.	JULES: "Where love failed." Yo right. That illness is a joke. I'll w and say you want to see him. (v Dear Hypochondriac, come as soo you can. Catherine awaits a let Write in big letters for her eyes tired . . .

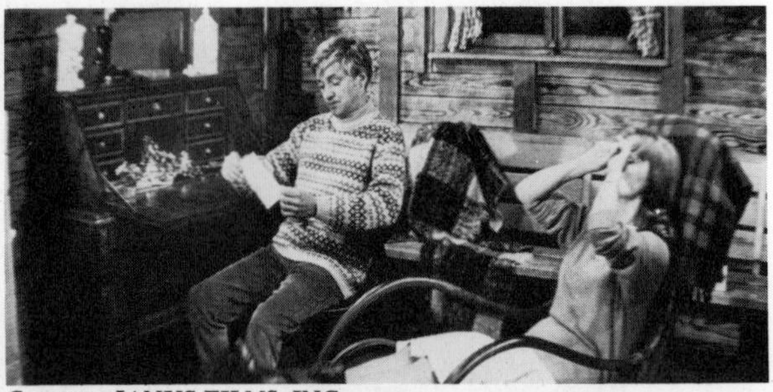

Courtesy: JANUS FILMS, INC.

PICTURE	SOUND
4. MS, Jim. He lies in bed reading letter. Then he crumples the letter, picks up pad, and starts to write.	JULES: (v.o.) . . . and she cannot read small handwriting. JIM: (v.o.) She doesn't think I was ill. I don't think she is pregnant. I doubt that I'm the father. I've got reasons to doubt: our past . . . Albert . . . and the rest.

PICTURE	SOUND
5. MLS, Jim (same as shot 1). Gilbert enters R and takes letter from Jim. Camera pans with her as she leaves room and goes to front door, where she picks up another letter. Camera continues to follow her as she reenters room and hands letter to Jim; then camera dollies in to Jim as he opens letter.	JIM: When you go out, mail this letter please. GILBERT: Certainly. JIM: Thanks. GILBERT: Oh, there's a letter for you. (pause) I'm late. See you later.

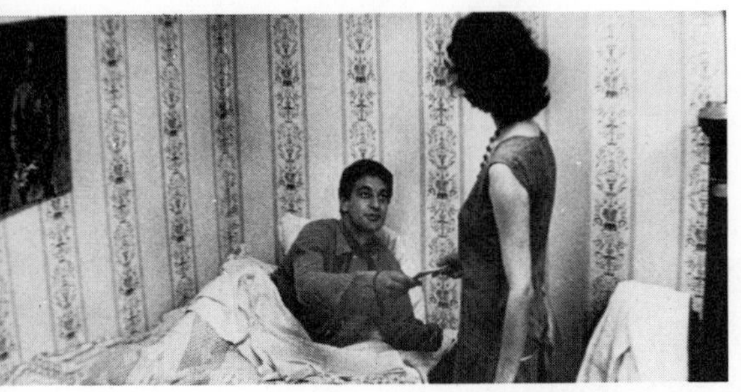

PICTURE	SOUND
6. LS, aerial trucking shot of countryside, with Catherine's face superimposed over it.	CATHERINE: I love you Jim. So many unbelievable things turn out to be true. I'm going to have a child. Let

PICTURE | SOUND

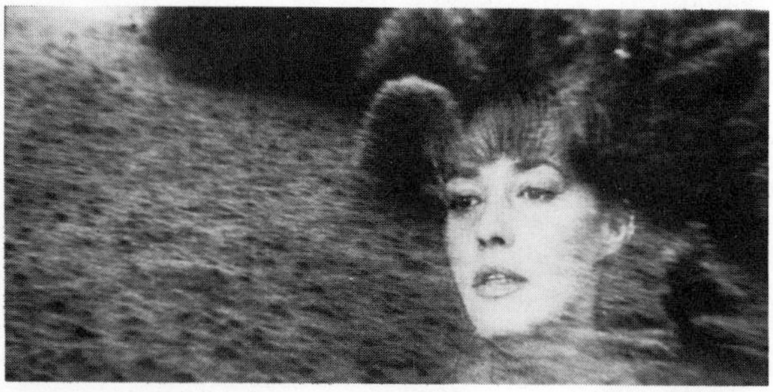

us thank God, Jim. I am sure you the father. I beg you to believe Your love is now alive within You must believe me. This paper your skin. This ink is my blood.

7. MLS, Jim (same as shot 5). He goes to window and tries to catch Gilbert; then he turns and starts to dress.

JIM: (shouts) Gilbert!

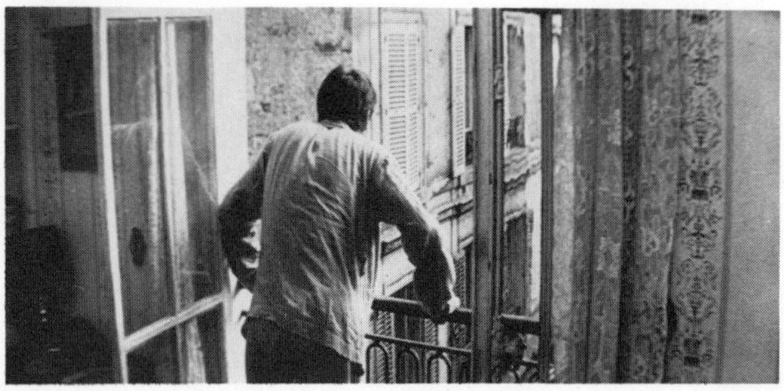

DISSOLVE

8. MS, Jim. He is seated on a balcony, writing.

JIM: (v.o.) Darling, I believe you am going to you. All that is go within me comes from you.

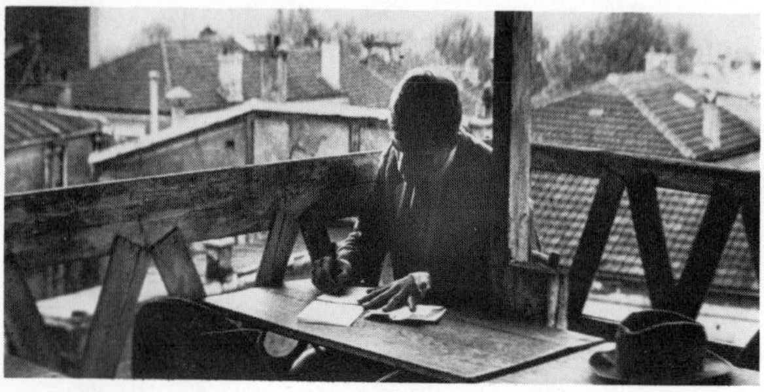

NAR: They never telephoned. Th feared disembodied voices . . .

9. MS, Catherine. She is seated at a desk, reading a letter. When she finishes, she starts to write.

NAR: . . . The post took three da Their letters crossed.

CATHERINE: (v.o.) "I've got re sons to doubt: our past . . . Alb . . . and the rest." I will stop thin ing of you. You disgust me. But th is wrong. Nothing should ever be d gusting.

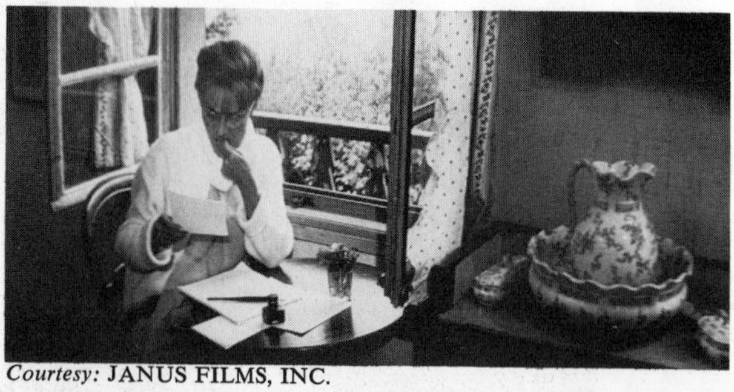

Courtesy: JANUS FILMS, INC.

Truffaut uses this scene to pull together the various strands of the film. His characters are essentially romantics who defy the world, not by reacting to it but by ignoring it as much as possible. This puts them at the mercy of those changes in their circumstances that most people would attempt to alter or control. Yet they are also out of phase with each other, unable to find consolation or support in their shifting associations and dalliances. Now Catherine has one last chance to recapture Jim by bearing the child they both feel will cement their love. But her desperate fear and hesitation are reflected in the reluctance and fragility of their confrontation. They speak to one another only haltingly and indirectly by giving voice to feelings expressed in letters, rather than directly, either in person or by telephone. They are afraid of disembodied voices, yet with deliberate irony the film-maker uses their disembodied words to show how isolated and disconnected they really are.

The psychological distance between them is mirrored in the physical distance that separates them, and this is emphasized by the embedding of the voice-over narration in lip-synchronous dialogue. Since this dialogue is as much a part of the places they are in as the walls or furniture, it helps establish the reality of their separate locations. The interspersed narrative voices are thus each firmly caught within the filmic space of these clearly separate places. This sense of distance slowly dissolves, however, as a line in shot 2 is repeated in shot 3, and a line from 3 continues into 4. Each voice begins to lap over into the other's surroundings and so becomes somewhat detached from its own.

Then Catherine's thought voice and presence are blended in a lip-synchronous shot of her disembodied features floating over the idyllic landscape in which she and Jim first came together. Now her voice, given the solidity of synchronization, seems to speak to him directly. This gives her feverish declaration of love a vividly imagined reality that almost literally transports her to him through her words. The intensity of this sudden fusion of thought voice and synchronization also gives us a sense of the impact with which she overrides all Jim's doubts and complaints. He leaps out of bed and with one shouted word—"Gilbert!"—he dismisses his surroundings and his illness and rushes to join Catherine.

However, before he can do much more than start his journey, the flat voice and clipped sentences of the narrator intervene. Throughout the film Truffaut has used this narrator to describe those events surrounding their lives that have conspired to influence their feelings toward one another. This terse voice also gives us an objective view, a sense of omniscience that places us outside the action. So now, by forcing us to see them from the narrator's viewpoint, Truffaut im-

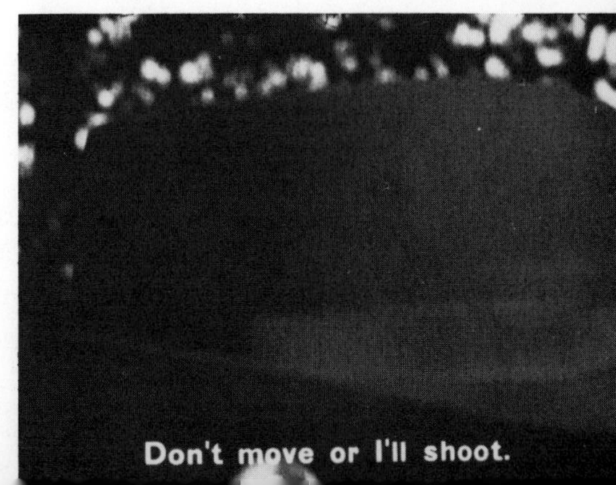

mediately implants a premonition that yet another small but implacable circumstance will inevitably work to keep them apart. From here on the love that they would will into existence quickly disintegrates in the crush of events.

Like most sequences, this one depends as much upon how the words and pictures are arranged as it does upon what is said or done in each shot, making the effectiveness of the scene ultimately dependent upon the editing. But because of the precise relationships between all the various pieces of sound and picture, the editing necessarily had to be carefully scripted in advance. That means that about all an editor would have had to do to cut the sequence would have been to assemble the materials given him to fit a predetermined pattern. Even this requires skill, however, because it is the editor who refines the rhythm of the scene. He not only cuts the pictures so that the action flows from shot to shot but also times the cuts and dissolves so that they punctuate the flow of dialogue and narration to build the pace of the action.

In addition, editing the various types of voice tracks in this kind of sequence is almost as complicated as cutting lip-synchronous dialogue alone. Because the level and quality of the voices are easier to control during the mix if each type of voice, lip-synchronous or narrative, is kept on a separate roll, the editor usually has to cut a roll of picture and two rolls of sound simultaneously. There are, however, different ways to go about doing this. One is to cut the lip-synchronous dialogue first, slugging in spaces where the voice-over and the narration are supposed to fall. This procedure permits the narrative voices to be recorded after the picture is assembled. But it also means realigning the rolls of picture and dialogue as the roll of narration is *laid in,* that is, cut to fit. Another way is to cut all the tracks at the same time. Then the pictures and the dialogue can be accurately cut on the first pass. In the previous example, since none of the voices overlaps, it would have been easiest to cut all the sounds into one track. This reduces the complexity of the creative part of the editing and requires that only one roll of sound be interlocked with the pictures for the results to be checked. The different voices can then be segregated onto separate rolls later, before the mix.

Cutting Narration Alone

When narration is the only voice track that has to be matched to the pictures, the editing is much simpler. Then the narration, rather than the dialogue, becomes the basic sound track around which all the other sounds are assembled; and the editing consists of first arranging the words and pictures so that they make sense together and then refining their rhythmic structure. This last step, refining the rhythm, is accomplished by changing the length of the shots, by changing the length of the pauses between words or sentences, or both. Again, however, the final product is as much the result of scripting as editing since either the narration is written to fit the pictures or the pictures are filmed to fit an already existing narration.

The first of these alternatives, recording the words to fit the pictures, has already been discussed in the chapter on sound recording (Chapter Seven, pp. 384 to 388). This procedure reduces the editing to laying in the track and then making any small adjustments needed to refine the timing of words and pictures.

But the second alternative, shooting and cutting the pictures to fit a narration, is much more dependent upon editing for its effectiveness because it is harder to script pictures than words. An example of this kind of editing is this first-person narrative sequence from Frank DeFelitta and Joseph Mehan's NBC documentary *Battle of the Bulge*. The scene is a re-creation of the World War II Ardennes massacre as told by a survivor while visiting the site.

	PICTURE	SOUND
	**1.** MCU, survivor (4¼ sec.).	V.O.: . . . when I heard some shooting which sounded like machine guns.
	**2.** LS, open field. Camera slowly zooms into trees (10 sec.).	Pause for 2½ seconds. V.O.: We saw some movement—uh—of German infantrymen in the woods in back of the farmhouse.
	**3.** CU, survivor's eyes (2 sec.).	V.O.: I took cover behind a . . .

	PICTURE	SOUND
	**4.** Hand-held camera ducks down behind woodpile, then stands up and walks toward road (26½ sec.). *DISSOLVE*	V.O.: . . . pile of logs. had nothing but side a and rifles. We were forced give up because at that pc I was looking down the b rel of an 88, mounted or German tank. I threw rifle down and crawled b onto the road. They lined up on the road . . .
	**5.** Hand-held camera walks down road, then turns L and crosses field (23½ sec.). *DISSOLVE*	V.O.: . . . and marched back towards the crossro and assembled us near a fie I was one of the last ones be shoved in the field. (ca era lurches to the left) stood there with our ar raised wondering what v going to happen next.
	**6.** Hand-held camera pans back toward road, holds there, then zooms in until tree line fills the frame. Just before cut tilts up and quickly zooms into sky (18½ sec.).	V.O.: The German tanks w lined up on the road. One the German tank drivers sto up on top of his tank and pulled out his pistol. He fi a shot into the first row group.
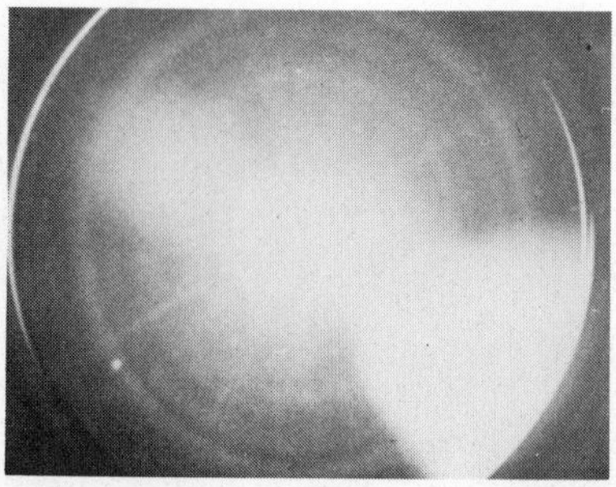	**7.** CU, spotlight lens. Camera rapidly zooms in (¾ sec.).	SFX: Burst of machine-g fire.

PICTURE	SOUND 
8. CU, nameplate on Ardennes memorial. Rapid zoom in and hold (4 sec.).	SFX: Machine gun ends with end of zoom. V.O.: One of the boys dropped. He'd shot him in the head.
9. CU, survivor's eyes (same as shot 3) (2¾ sec.).	V.O.: Then the machine guns opened up.
10. CU, spotlight lens, out of focus against dark background. Camera pans rapidly back and forth, causing a bright flare each time it is head-on to light (2½ sec.).	SFX: Deep, hollow, monotonous machine-gun fire.
11. CU, nameplate on Ardennes memorial (same as shot 8). Quick zoom in (¾ sec.).	SFX: Pause for cut, then machine gun continues.

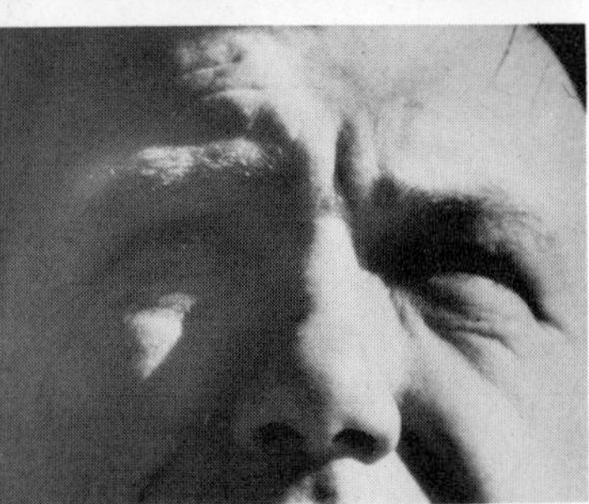

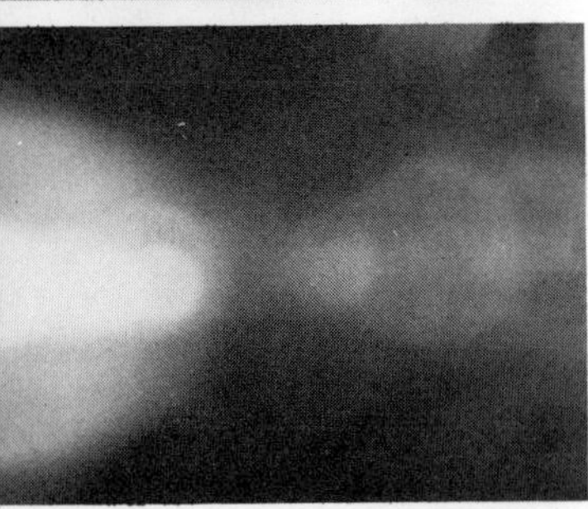

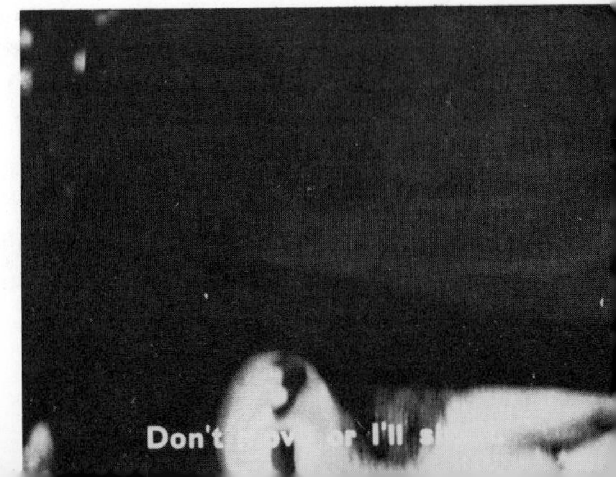

	PICTURE	SOUND
 12.	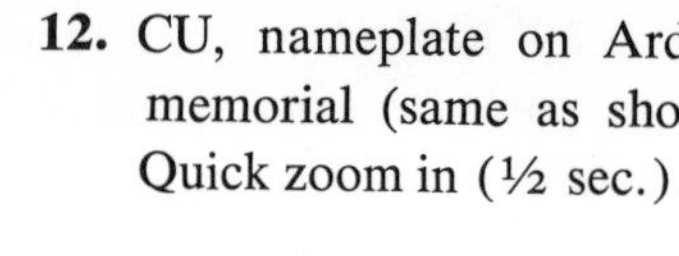 CU, nameplate on Ardennes memorial (same as shot 11). Quick zoom in (½ sec.).	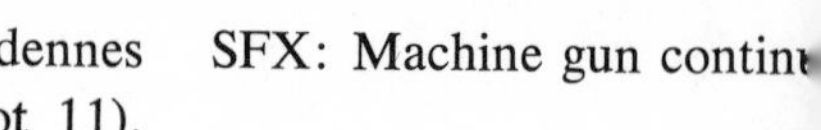 SFX: Machine gun contin

In this case the camera plays the role of a participant, showing us, step by step, what this survivor would have done and seen before and during the massacre. But while the resulting connection of words and pictures gives substance to the bare bones of his description of events, it is the varied pace of the editing that builds our sense of his helplessness and horror. First, his inability to spot the enemy is re-created by the insertion of a two-and-a-half-second pause in the narration at the beginning of shot 2. This gives the camera time for a slow zoom into the trees, as if peering into the distance. This sense of straining to see is then reinforced by the cutting back to a close-up of his eyes.

This shot, however, is also a cut-away. It serves to collapse the time the Germans need to cross the field in shot 2 and reach the woodpile in shot 4, thus emphasizing the swiftness with which the survivor's position was overrun. Next, his suspense while waiting to learn his fate is drawn out by the stringing together with dissolves of several long-running hand-held shots in which the camera movements carefully mimic his description of his actions. Finally, as he, and we, stand facing his captors, the scene explodes in a series of quick cuts and camera movements that are matched by the staccato pace of the short sentences with which he ends his description.

There is nothing complicated about the editing of this scene. What it did require, though, was a sure sense of what the man had experienced so that his feelings could be carried through the shooting of the footage and then pulled taut in the cutting. This meant first editing the recording so that his words re-created the pace of the action. For instance, in shot 4 the sentence, "I threw my rifle down and crawled back onto the road," and in shot 5 the words, ". . . one of the last ones to be . . ." and ". . . with our arms raised . . ." could easily have been deleted without destroying the sense of what he was saying. But that would have significantly speeded up the pace of the action in the opening of the sequence. Parts of his description were also probably dropped in order to accelerate the tempo toward the end of the scene. Next, the shots had to be filmed to match his description of the action and then the whole thing cut so that the interplay of words and pictures built a rhythm that echoed his unspoken feelings. Thus, words and pictures together were given an immediacy and impact that neither alone would have been able to provide.

Sound Effects

The next layer is usually the sound effects. One example of how they can be used, the sequence from Josef von Sternberg's *The Blue Angel,* has already been discussed in the chapter on sound recording (Chapter Seven, pp. 360 to 362). There a succession of slightly differing sound effects was built into the prime vehicle for carrying the meaning of the sequence. There are, however, many less evident but equally important roles played by more generalized sound effects. One of the most common is as a continuous background to the action. Then the sound effects give each scene a fuller sense of realism while tying the shots together by becoming a thread that characterizes all of them. And, as was mentioned previously, a continuous background can also be used to conceal small jumps in the quality of the lip-synchronous dialogue.

In some cases, however, a generalized sound effect can be so central to the meaning of the action that it dominates a scene, or even the whole film. In *Black Orpheus,* Marcel Camus uses the throbbing of drums throughout the picture. The film is a modern version of the tragic myth of Orpheus and Eurydice, transferred to Rio de Janeiro during Mardi Gras. So, whenever we see shots of the festivities, these drums pace the action, and in almost every other scene the background is permeated by at least a vestigial ticking of this beat. The drums thus become an all-pervasive metronome insistently marking off the hours remaining before the inevitable death of the hero and the heroine of the film.

A similar effect is also created by the hoofbeats in a western chase, the snarl of engines in an auto race, or, in the final scene of King Vidor's *Our Daily Bread,* by the regular thunk of picks and shovels digging into the earth. This film, which takes place during the Great Depression, is about a group of unemployed city people who drift onto the newly acquired farm of the film's hero. Under the pressure of their common predicament they agree to farm the land cooperatively. But just when it seems that they have made the farm a success, a severe drought threatens to destroy their crops unless they can immediately dig an irrigation ditch cross-country to the nearest water. This means coordinating their efforts so that they can work night and day, without a break, to survey the right of way, clear a path, and dig the ditch.

Here is a series of shots from near the beginning of the scene. First we see a crew of men starting to dig, and next a group that is ahead of them heaving boulders out of the way. Then, in a wider shot, we see the last of the boulders removed as a crew approaches that is breaking the ground with picks. This same

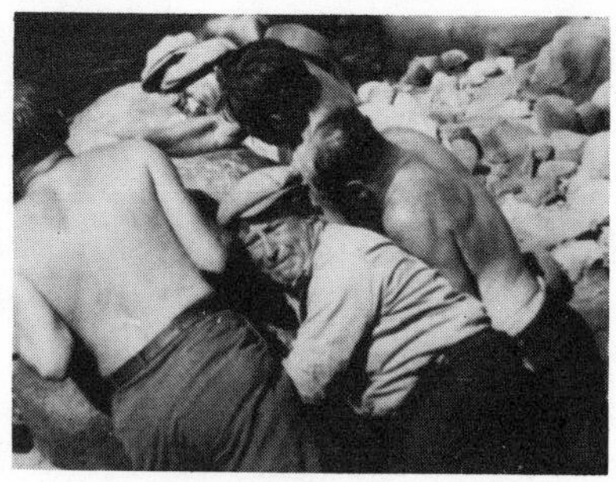

Courtesy: JANUS FILMS, INC.

crew is next shown in a closer shot, and then we see another group, still further on, laying out the right of way. Again, in shot 6, we see the men with picks, and finally, in shot 7, the men with shovels following after them.

At the most basic level this seemingly disjointed series of shots is tied together by the regular beat of the picks and shovels. Each cut falls on this beat, and at every cut the level of the sound goes up or down to indicate how far we are from the digging. But like the throbbing drums in *Black Orpheus,* this beat not only links the action from shot to shot, it also catches us in the meaning of the action. The product of their cooperative labor is greater than the sum of their individual efforts, and it is exactly this social element that is conveyed by their work rhythm. At first it represents the power of many men working together, and then, as it permeates the scene, it becomes the means by which each individual recognizes this power and is inspired to still greater efforts.

Laying in the Background Sounds

Because each cut in the previous example was accompanied by an abrupt change in the level of the background, the sound had to be cut to fit each shot.

That can be done in one of two ways. The first is to record the background for each shot at the proper level and then lay in each piece of sound opposite the corresponding shot so that the background forms one continuous roll of sound. The other is to alternate pieces of the same background recording between two sound rolls. Then the level of the background for each shot can be adjusted during the mix. The first method makes the recording and editing more difficult, while the second complicates the mix; but either way, the cuts in both sound and picture are synchronized so that the sudden changes of level accurately match the changes in the shots.

When the background sounds are more generalized, however, they can often be provided by a sound loop. This has already been discussed in the chapter on sound recording (Chapter Seven, p. 378). It is an endless sound track which, because it runs continuously, can be faded in and out as needed during the mix. A continuous background can also be provided by a separate roll containing one long recording of the background sound for each scene. This provides a more varied background than a loop. But sometimes both are used. Then the two tracks can be superimposed to form an even more complex sound background. Two tracks also permit what is known as a *segue* or *cross-fade*—a sound dissolve in which one background sound fades out as the other fades in. This is used when the transition from one background to the next should go relatively unnoticed.

Sound Transitions

There are times, however, when abrupt changes in the background sounds can serve as an important transitional device, one that not only indicates the contrasting nature of each setting, but, by calling attention to the change, tells us something about the characters' relationship to their surroundings. That is how Bergman has used the background sounds in the opening scenes of *The Silence.* At the end of the first scene we see a young boy peering out a train window at a freight train passing on the next track. This is accompanied by the clack and rumble of the two trains. The next shot then shows the boy looking out the window of a hotel room, and the background abruptly changes to the rush of street sounds. This change immediately tells us that the boy is in a different setting, even before we are shown, in the following shot, what the boy now sees from his new perch. Finally, Bergman cuts to a shot from inside the room just as the boy's mother tells him to shut the window. He reluctantly does as she asks,

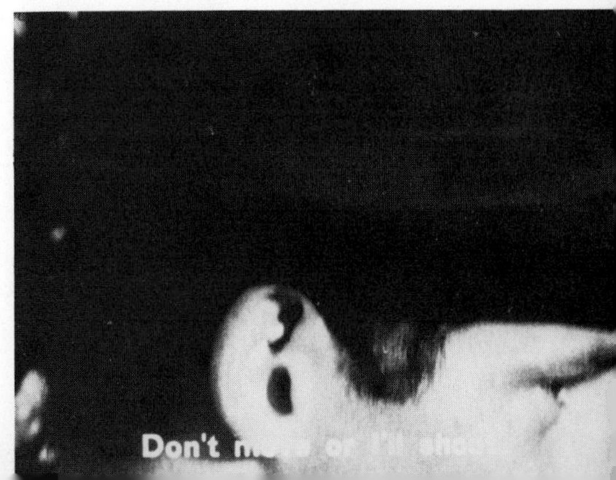

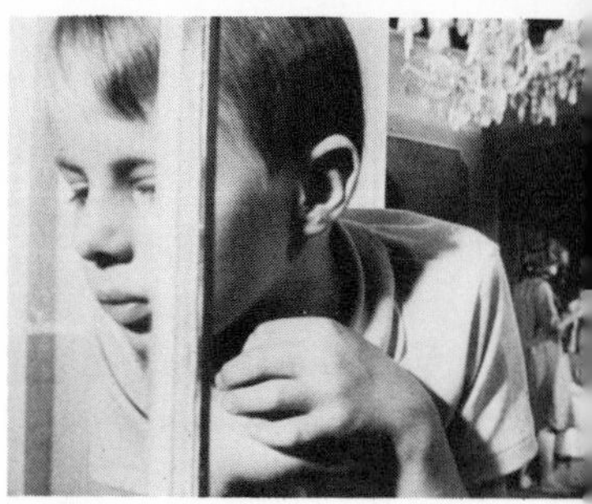

Courtesy: JANUS FILMS, INC.

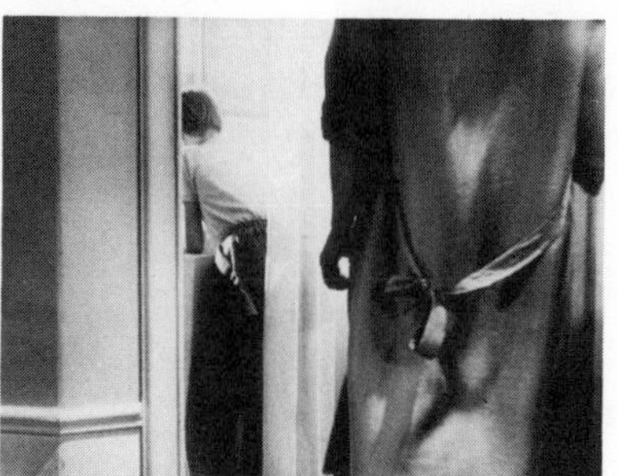

and then she walks over and pulls the curtains. But in this shot the background—even before he shuts the window—is complete silence.

The first of these abrupt changes in the background sounds seems natural because it is accompanied by an obvious change in the setting. However, its very abruptness calls our attention to the background so that, when there is no background sound in shot 5, we are immediately aware of the unnatural silence. The window is still open and our everyday experience tells us that we should continue to hear the street noise, even softly. This happens so early in the film, though, that this seemingly unmotivated change is more puzzling than revealing. But it does alert us to the way in which the characters will develop. Their relationship to the world is mirrored in how they hear the sounds around them. While the boy's mind is still open, and he is curious to see and hear everything, his mother has shut out the world. For her these sounds no longer exist because she doesn't wish to hear them. She has willingly, though subconsciously, cut herself off from her surroundings because she can no longer cope with them.

Just how self-imposed this silence is is then revealed a short time later in the film. Now it is the boy's aunt, their traveling companion, who steps to the window. Unlike her sister, she has knowingly shut out the world and so can come back to it if she wishes. Here, as she turns toward the window without opening it, the radio playing in the background quickly fades out and the street sounds fade in. This sound is not something that is being forced on her consciousness because, even though the window is closed, it continues at full volume all the while she stands there. Then, as she turns from the window at the end of shot 4, the fade-out–fade-in is reversed and we immediately hear the radio again. Only now she has

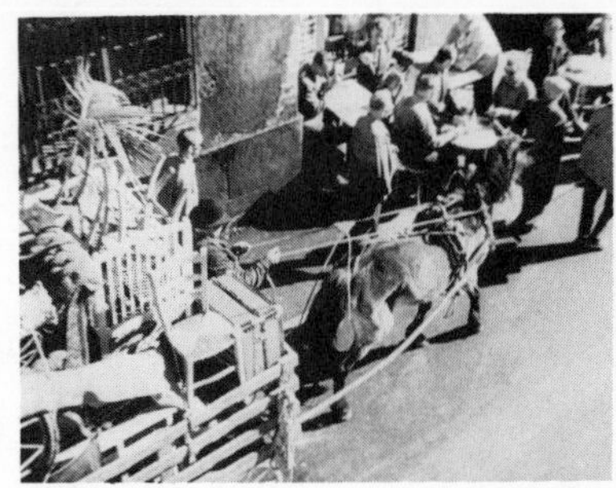

urtesy: JANUS FILMS, INC.

willingly returned to her inner silence and the radio is an intrusion. So we see the radio in close-up as she turns it off.

Isolated Sound Effects

Individual sounds, as well as generalized backgrounds, can also acquire a tremendous weight of meaning, especially when they are surrounded by silence. This is what happens to the sound of a hand-cranked mimeograph machine that fills an otherwise quiet office at the end of Ermanno Olmi's *The Sound of Trumpets.* The young hero of the film has just reached his most coveted goal—a clerk's desk in the office of a large firm. The film has followed him as he weathered an entrance exam, served an apprenticeship, and finally achieved a permanent position. But along the way we also see how the work has narrowed the lives and deadened the feelings of his fellow employees. And even he, by the time he reaches this post, has renounced his few small ambitions in life and is ready to

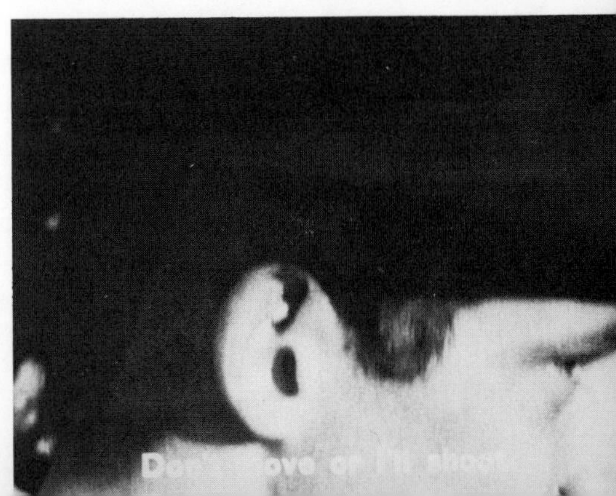

settle for what he can get. Now he waits at his new desk, without an assignment,

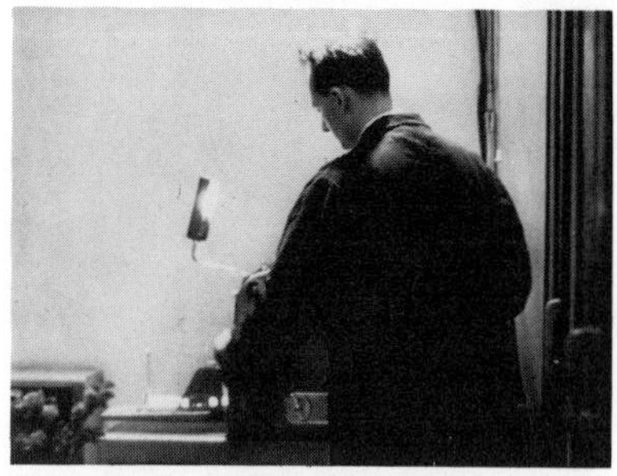

not knowing what to expect. Suddenly, out of the cloying silence emerges the grindingly monotonous clack of the mimeograph, churning out page after mechanically perfect page. As the sound of the machine swells in volume, the camera dollies in to a close-up of his still, blank face, and we know that this sound, more than any other, describes what he can expect to become here.

Music

The final layer of sound is the music. As was mentioned in the chapter on sound recording (Chapter Seven, pp. 389 to 392), the music is often written and recorded to fit the pictures. Then the editor's job is reduced simply to laying in each piece of music so that it starts in the right place. However, when prerecorded music, such as selections from a music library, is used to score the film, the editing is more complex. If the music is to fit the film, alterations must usually be made in the length of the music, the pictures, or both.

It is generally easier to alter the music than recut the pictures. In fact, when the shots are connected by match-action cuts, if all the action is shown in just one shot, or when there is synchronous dialogue, the mechanics and rhythms of the picture editing often leave little or no room for change. But the length of the music is not all that difficult to change, particularly if the piece of music is too long. Then the music can be laid in so that it either starts or ends at an appropriate point and the excess removed by simply fading in or out during the mix. Or, if there is no definite beginning or ending to the piece, it can be started with a fade-in and ended with a fade-out.

On the other hand, if the selection is too short, or if it suddenly changes character, either all or part of the piece can be repeated, or two different selections can be used. Then the editor has the option either of joining the pieces of music with a cut or of fading from one to the other. Cutting is the more difficult choice because if the cut interrupts a melodic phrase or misses the beat it will be painfully apparent. And similarly, in the case of two different pieces of music, all but the most carefully worked-out changes in the musical key or tempo will automatically produce an awkward cut. When the cuts work, though, the editor is, in effect, creating a new piece of music, and this makes cutting music an art in itself.

As a result, the easiest way to deal with this problem is just to segue from one selection to the next. This is possible if each piece of music is put on a separate roll of sound so that, during the mix, one track can be faded out as the other is faded in. The effect is similar to that of a dissolve; while there is less continuity to the musical rhythm than with a direct cut, momentarily blending the two pieces together eases the transition.

Musical Rhythms

In addition to the mechanical problem of fitting the music to the length of the scene, there is also the aesthetic one of fitting the rhythm of the music to the visual rhythms of both the action and the cutting. It has already been shown, in the chapter on the types of sound (Chapter Six, pp. 340 to 344), how the mood of the music can affect the meaning of the action by playing either with or against the mood of a scene. The same thing is also true of the rhythm of the music. At its simplest, this means that music with a rapid tempo can make a slow scene speed up or quicken a fast one, while music with a slow tempo will have just the reverse effect.

There are also, however, more complex interactions between the pictures and the music in which their rhythms work together either to emphasize the meaning of particular actions or to create meanings that picture or sound alone could not convey. An example of the first of these is the sequence from *Yojimbo* discussed in the chapter on sound recording (Chapter Seven, p. 391). In this scene the impact of the samurai's bad news is emphasized by the matching of the beat of the music to the irregular rhythm of his new master's footsteps on the stairs behind him.

Another example is the following sequence from Hitchcock's *Suspicion*.

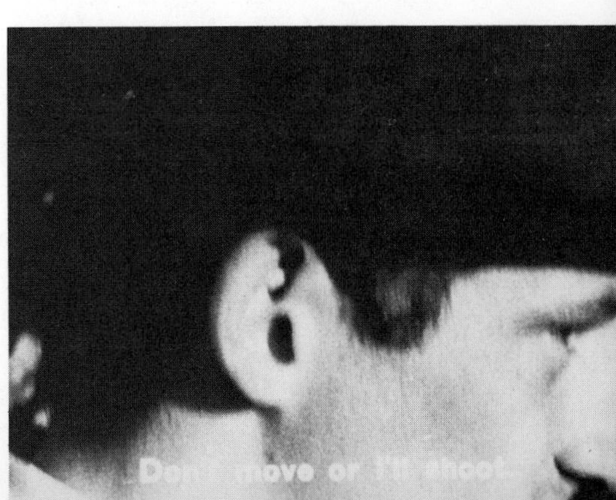

Here, by timing the opening chords of a piece of background music to coincide with his heroine's movements, Hitchcock both emphasizes her feelings and explains their meaning. Just prior to this scene, John, her husband, takes their friend Beeky for a ride in the country to inspect a site for a real estate development. Then, a short while later, because she is afraid that John wants to murder Beeky to get his money, she also goes to the site. But when she arrives the only sign that they have been there are tire marks leading to the edge of a towering cliff. Now thoroughly alarmed, she quickly returns home. At the start of the following sequence she enters the foyer and hears John, seemingly alone in the living room, absentmindedly whistling a Strauss waltz. This song, which they had danced to when they first met, recurs throughout the film.

	PICTURE	SOUND
	1. MS, Lena. She enters door and camera trucks back with her as she heads toward living room. When she hears whistling, she stops and winces, then camera pans L as she peeks into the living room (51½ sec.).	SFX: Door closing softl then silence. JOHN: Tentatively whistl opening of Strauss waltz, the repeats entire phrase.
	2. MLS, John. He is fiddling with the phonograph, trying to make it work (2½ sec.).	JOHN: Whistling waltz.
	3. MCU, Lena. She is looking at John rather coolly (2½ sec.).	JOHN: Continues whistlin

Courtesy: JANUS FILMS, INC.

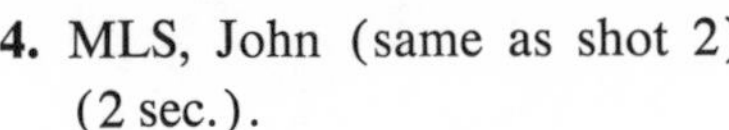

PICTURE	SOUND
4. MLS, John (same as shot 2) (2 sec.).	JOHN: Finishes whistling phrase and says: This ought to do it. Put in the plug now.
5. MCU, Lena (same as shot 3). She slowly peeks around corner of door (1½ sec.).	
6. MS, Beeky. He is stooping to put in plug (2½ sec.).	BEEKY: Umm . . . uh . . . how's that, old bean?
7. MCU, Lena (same as shot 5). She looks toward John, greatly relieved (2½ sec.).	

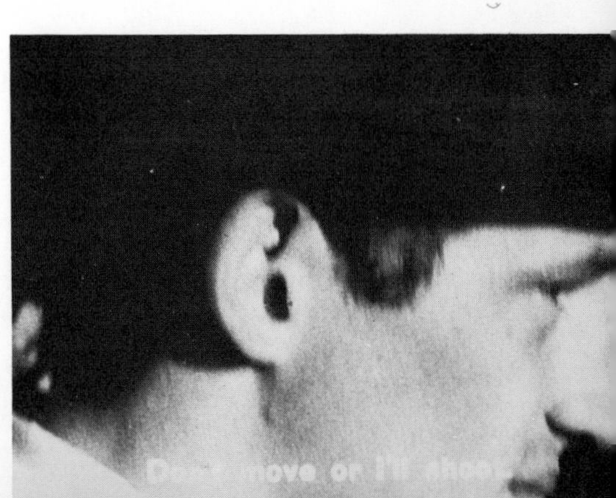

	PICTURE	SOUND
	**8.** MS, Beeky (same as shot 6). Camera pans L to follow him as he crosses room to join John at phonograph; then both notice Lena standing in doorway (6½ sec.).	SFX: Footsteps as he cros room. BEEKY: Oh, hello, old girl. JOHN: Hello, darling.
	**9.** MCU, Lena. Camera trucks back with her as she starts into living room, taking off coat as she goes (5 sec.).	MUS: Opening chords of f orchestral version of wa John was whistling.
	**10.** LS, living room. Lena drops her coat on chair and almost runs across room into John's arms (6 sec.).	MUS: Melody begins just she drops her coat.

Courtesy: JANUS FILMS, INC.

At first the seeming innocence of John's off-key whistling is an ironic comment on the distaste she now feels for him; then it begins to grate on her nerves, putting an edge on the anxiety she feels about confronting him with her knowledge of his crime. This anxiety also builds visually in shots 3 through 6 as the progressively shorter shots increase the tempo of the action while stretching out her growing fear and hesitation. However, after we see Beeky in shot 6, both the longer shots and the few dry lines of dialogue begin to loosen the tension. Finally, satisfied that her suspicions are absurd, she abandons her natural reserve and rushes to embrace her husband.

At this point Hitchcock uses the music to make the feelings expressed by her movements almost palpable. He switches to a full orchestral version of the waltz, seemingly coming from the phonograph. This sumptuous music, in sharp contrast to John's thin, scratchy whistling, not only underlines her change of heart, but, because it is synchronized with her actions as she crosses the room, also makes us almost literally experience the surge of relief that floods over her. As she starts toward her husband, in shot 9, the first few introductory beats of the waltz pick up the quickening rhythm of her steps. Next, a match-action cut carries her movement across into the following long shot; and then, as she drops her coat to the chair, the melody begins, its long, graceful opening notes accenting her impetuous sweep forward into his arms.

Besides using the rhythm of the music to emphasize the meaning of certain actions, it is also possible to create totally new meanings by making the musical rhythms interact with those of the cutting. An example is the following sequence from Humphrey Jennings's *Listen to Britain,* a World War II documentary that chronicles the stoic determination and sense of purpose which kept the British fighting despite the overwhelming odds against them. In this, the climactic scene of the film, a Mozart piano concerto accompanies shots of some of the most diverse segments of British society. Through the synchronization of the cuts to the beat of the music, Jennings builds a rhythmic continuity which unites pictures and sound in a common theme: the British, by defending their way of life, are preserving the accumulated culture of Western civilization.

The scene, a noontime concert in a London art museum, starts with the beginning of the last movement of the piano concerto. During the orchestral introduction we are shown shots of the soloist, various instrumentalists, and the audience, including both members of the royal family and ordinary men and women in uniform. Then the cutting moves further afield. After the soloist begins playing, shots made in other parts of the museum are intercut with those of the musicians. We see women in uniform seated on the museum steps having lunch, the bomb damage to the roof of the museum, the empty frames of paintings removed for safekeeping, and soldiers and sailors wandering about the galleries. Finally, as the melody swells in both volume and intensity, the cutting takes us outside the building, and we are shown the everyday life of the British people, their landmarks and public buildings, monuments to their history, and the men and women defending this long, proud tradition, all woven together and moved by the beat of the music.

Here the thematic unity of the sequence is maintained both by cutting on

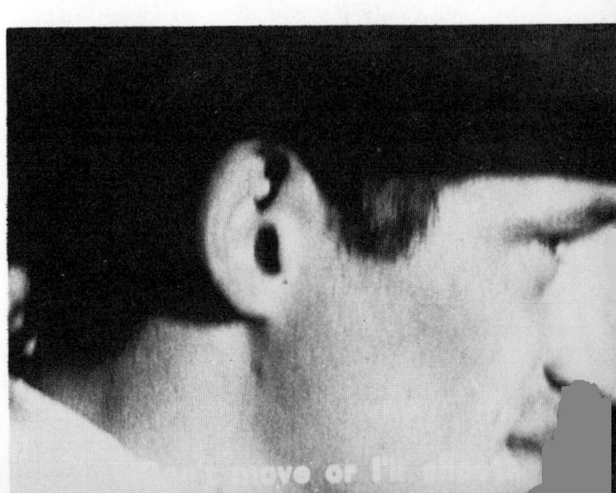

	PICTURE	SOUND
	**1.** MS, Dame Myra Hess, piano soloist (8 sec.).	MUS: Mozart piano concer
	**2.** MLS, nurse reading (2½ sec.).	MUS: 6 beats.
	**3.** MS, blowing leaves (1⅔ sec.).	MUS: 4 beats.
	**4.** LS, people sitting on steps of building (2½ sec.).	MUS: 6 beats.
	**5.** MLS, woman leaning on railing (3½ sec.).	MUS: 8 beats.

	PICTURE	SOUND
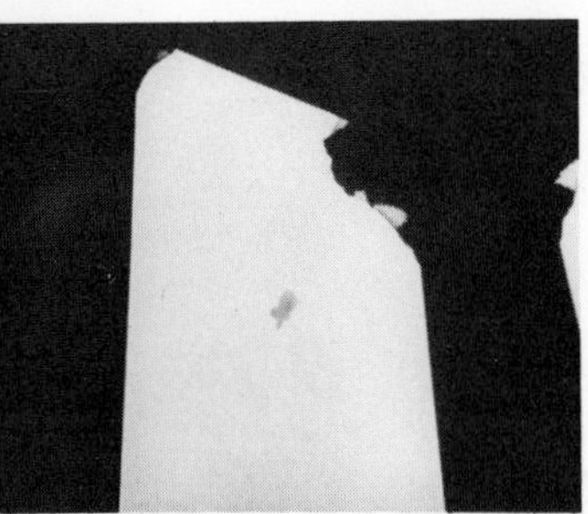	**6.** MLS, columns. Barrage balloon in distance (1⅔ sec.).	MUS: 4 beats.
	**7.** XLS, street. Buses pulling up to and away from curb (3½ sec.).	MUS: 8 beats.
	**8.** LS, people getting off bus (3½ sec.).	MUS: 8 beats.
	**9.** LS, emblem (1⅔ sec.).	MUS: 4 beats.

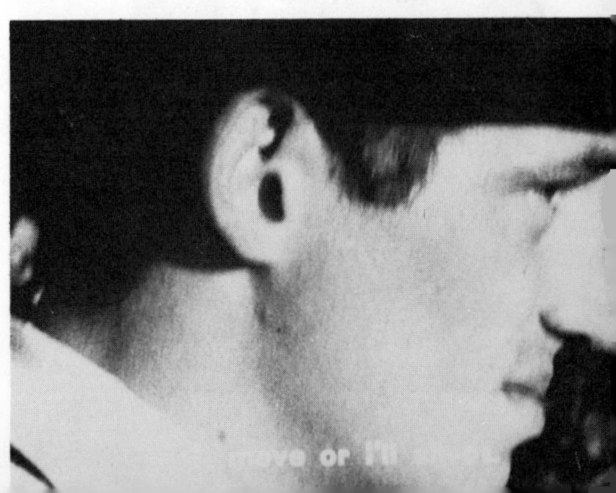

	PICTURE	SOUND
	**10.** LS, people getting on and off buses (1½ sec.).	MUS: 3 beats.
	**11.** XLS, Nelson monument over rooftops (1⅔ sec.).	MUS: 4 beats.
	**12.** MS, Nelson monument (1½ sec.).	MUS: 3 beats.
	**13.** MS, Sailor leaning on railing (1⅔ sec.).	MUS: 4 beats.
	**14.** LS, stone lion silhouetted against building (3½ sec.).	MUS: 8 beats.

	PICTURE	SOUND
	**15.** XLS, cranes and factory chimneys silhouetted against sky. Barrage balloon floats in distance (4½ sec.).	MUS: Speeds up in tempo and pitch; 12 beats. SFX: Fade in factory noises.
	**16.** MS, man using hand tool (4½ sec.).	MUS: 12 beats. SFX: Factory sounds louder.
	**17.** MLS, men guiding tank turret into place on chassis (3 sec.).	MUS: 7 beats. SFX: Louder.
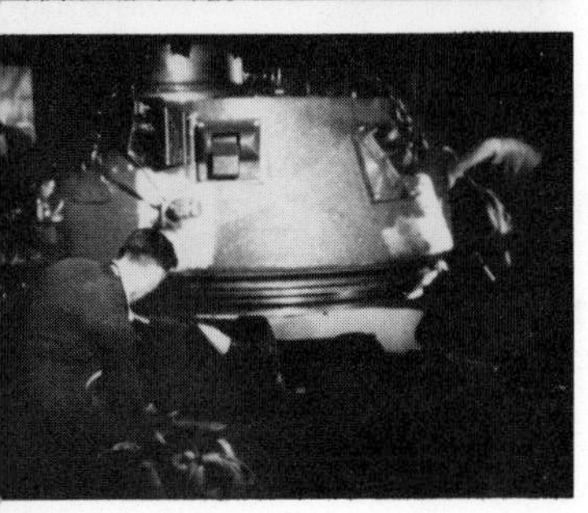	**18.** MS, men securing tank turret (3 sec.).	MUS: 7 beats. SFX: Begins to override music.

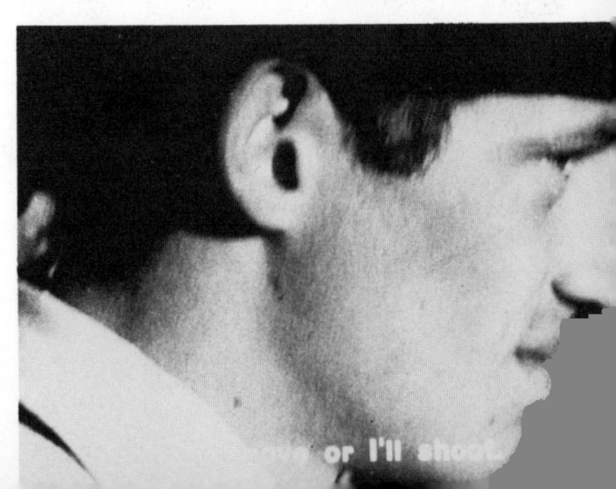

	PICTURE	SOUND
	19. MCU, woman operating lathe (3¼ sec.).	SFX: Slowly accelerat pounding emerges from ba ground of factory sounds.
	20. MCU, woman operating drill press (3 sec.).	SFX: Pounding continues.

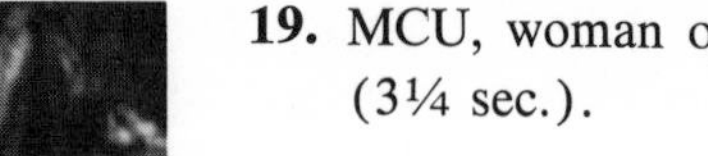

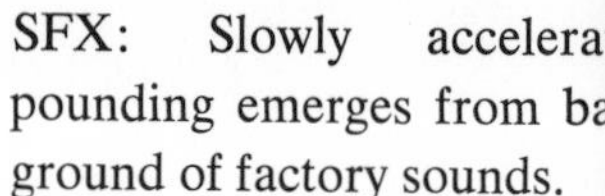

shape, that of the majestic columns which mark the façade of London's official buildings and monuments, and by placing the cuts so that they match the rhythmic shape of the music. In this case this kind of cutting is not hard to do because there are no match-action cuts to restrict either where the shots can be joined or how long each must remain on the screen. As a result, the cuts fall at regular intervals on the fourth, the sixth, or the eighth beat of the music.

However, at shot 9 the music starts moving toward a crescendo, so the pace of the cutting accelerates and the cuts begin to fall on either the third or the fourth beat. This change is also matched by a slight shift in thematic emphasis—from the people to the imposing setting through which they move. First there is the royal crest of empire (shot 9); then a monument to the victorious tradition which built that empire, the statue of Admiral Nelson perched atop a tall column in Trafalgar Square (shots 11 and 12); and lastly, the stark shadow of the British lion brooding over the historic edifice of government in the background (shot 14).

Then, as the music climaxes in a long, involved piano solo, these stately artifacts are directly joined to the gangling towers and awkward shapes of modern Britain's industrial might. At the same time, however, the connection between these sharply contrasting scenes is cemented by the beginning of both a change of tempo and a segue to the throbbing and pounding of the factories. Thus, the music not only merges with the sound effects but also speeds up to match their increasingly faster, more strident beat. That beat maintains the rhythm of the cutting across this transition so that, even after the music has given way to the roar of wartime production, the shots continue to have a regular cadence. This makes the pictures, the music, and the sound effects all part of one long, rhythmic crescendo.

While the means used to develop this sequence are relatively simple—nothing more than a compounding of rhythms—the results are quite complex. In addition to the cutting rhythms, which tie the music to a broad sense of the lifestyle in which that music is embedded, there is the rhythm of the sound transition, which joins the music to the never-ending cycle of work that dominates life in this besieged island. It is this rhythmic development, then, which both creates and explains the relationship of these diverse elements by forming them into the ends of a spectrum that ultimately defines the limits and meaning of the struggle for existence in wartime Britain.

Refining the Rhythms

The last step in editing the sound track is to refine the timing of the various sounds so that they not only match the rhythms of the pictures but also form a clear rhythmic pattern of their own. That means adjusting the rhythms of the narration, the sound effects, and the music tracks so that, where these sounds overlap, their various rhythms don't interfere with one another. This is a delicate process, one that involves playing back all the tracks in synchronization with the picture and, where necessary, sliding one of the pieces of sound forward or back a few frames until the overall rhythm of the scene feels right.

An example of the role played by this kind of rhythmic clarity can be seen in a sequence from Gustav Machaty's *Ecstasy*. In this scene the heroine's lover unknowingly accepts a ride with her husband. The husband, though, is aware of their relationship and in a moment of jealous desperation decides to destroy both himself and his passenger under the wheels of a freight train. In the first part of the sequence the distant clack of the train and its impatient whistling, the quick beat of the music, and the shadows of passing trees rapidly sweeping across their faces all work to accelerate them toward the railroad crossing. And then, after the car abruptly stops, the husband's heavy breathing and the steam escaping from the locomotive interact with the slow rhythm of the music to release the tension of the scene.

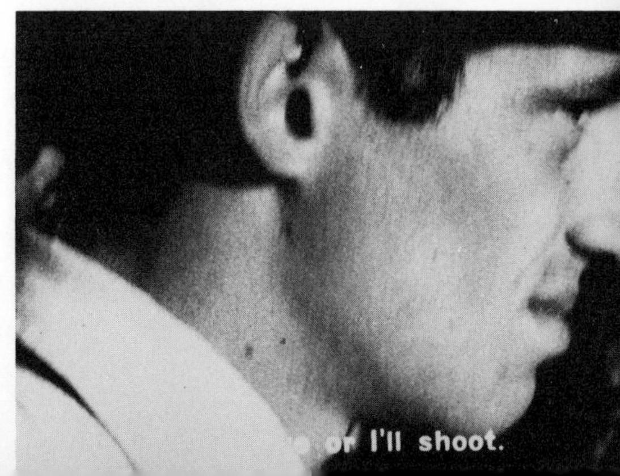

	PICTURE	SOUND
	**1.** MS, husband and lover in car. Their faces regularly go dark as they pass through the shadows of trees along the road (15½ sec.).	MUS: Fast and impatient. SFX: Clack of train whe and sporadic whistling, in d tance.
	**2.** CU, husband. He stares straight ahead (2½ sec.).	Music and sound effects cc tinually grow louder throu shot 13.
	**3.** CU, lover. He turns toward husband with worried look toward end of shot (2½ sec.).	
	4. CU, husband (same as shot 2) (4½ sec.).	
	5. CU, lover (same as shot 3) (4½ sec.).	

PICTURE	SOUND
6. MS, rapid truck past fence posts along the side of road (3½ sec.).	
7. MCU, trucking down railroad tracks (4½ sec.).	
8. CU, tire and road (1¼ sec.).	
9. MS, trucking past trees, then tilt down to fence posts (same as shot 6) (1½ sec.).	

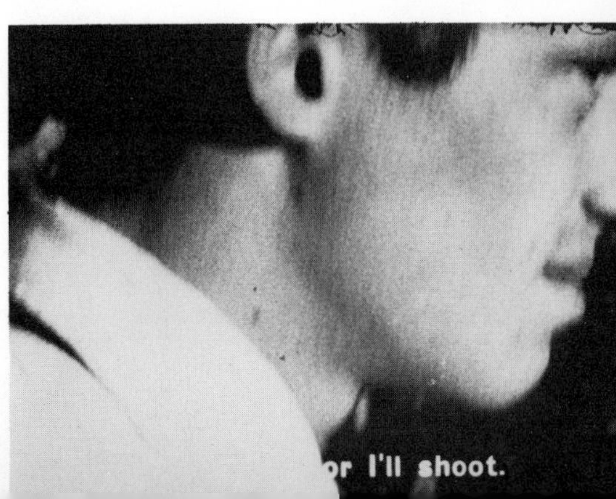

	PICTURE	SOUND
	**10.** Slow zoom in on freeze frame of crossing guard rail (2 sec.).	
	11. CU, husband (same as shot 4) (1½ sec.).	
	12. CU, lover (same as shot 5) (1¼ sec.).	MUS: Stops abruptly.
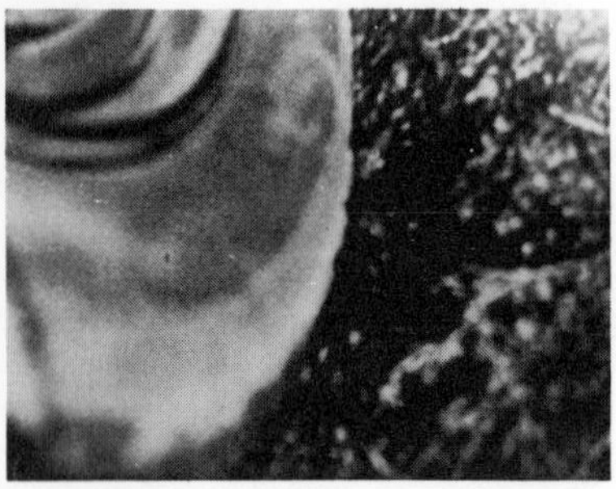	**13.** CU, tire (same as shot 8). Comes to sharp stop (1½ sec.).	SFX: Screech of brakes, t silence.
	**14.** MLS, guard rail. Train races over crossing (8 sec.).	SFX: Short, sharp whis then roar of train.

PICTURE	SOUND
15. MCU, husband. He is breathing heavily (7½ sec.).	MUS: Slow and mournful; it continues through shot 22.
16. MS, train wheels. They pull into frame and stop (2½ sec.).	SFX: Rush of steam escaping from cylinder.
17. CU, husband. He takes deep breath (4½ sec.).	SFX: Intake of air.
18. CU, cylinder of locomotive (2 sec.).	SFX: Rush of steam.

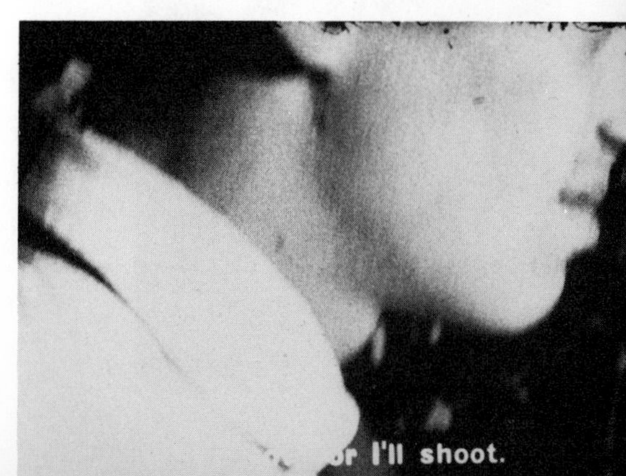

	PICTURE	SOUND
	**19.** CU, husband. He takes another deep breath (3 sec.).	SFX: Intake of air.
	20. CU, cylinder of locomotive (same as shot 18) (1½ sec.).	SFX: Rush of steam.
	**21.** CU, husband. He takes deep breath (5 sec.).	SFX: Intake of air.
	22. CU, cylinder of locomotive (same as shot 20) (2¾ sec.).	SFX: Rush of steam.
	**23.** CU, husband (same as shot 21). Halfway through shot his head slumps forward onto his chest (8 sec.).	Silence.
	**24.** XCU, cylinder.	Silence.

Since we never see the car and the train together in the same shot, it is both the cutting and the sound track that create the illusion of a potential collision. This means that not only the cuts but the various sounds had to be carefully orchestrated so that the pace of the action was developed by the unfolding rhythms. The train whistle, for instance, is placed over the ends of the musical phrases in order to keep the tempo pushing forward; and the sound of the train wheels is synchronized with the beat of the music in order to emphasize the musical rhythms, and through them the rhythm of the passing landscape. In addition, as these sounds get progressively louder, they increasingly accent the beat of the action, which helps build the growing intensity of both the husband's determination and the lover's anxiety.

Then, when the car screeches to a halt, the music stops, so that there is an instant of silence separating the sound of the brakes from that of the train lunging over the crossing. This silence, just a beat before the whistle and roar of the train bring the rhythm to a climax, emphasizes how narrowly they have missed death. In the next section, as the stunned husband begins to realize what nearly happened, the beat of the music is used to reinforce the lengthening rhythm of both the cuts and the sound effects. This helps decelerate the tempo of the scene slowly but continually until it reaches his final, helpless silence.

It is obvious that the complex process of refining and clarifying the rhythms of the sound track is greatly simplified if the sound is cut from the very beginning on a multitrack editing machine. Then the editor can listen to the tracks he has already laid in as he cuts each new track. And even when the tracks are cut one at a time with just a sound reader and a viewer, an editing machine can still simplify the making of the final cut. But if an editing machine is not available, these fine adjustments can be made only at the last moment, after the first run-through at the mixing studio.

The Mix

Mixing, dubbing, and *re-recording* are all names for the same process—combining all the edited sound tracks on a master track. This is done by playing back each track on a separate sprocketed sound reproducer, or *dubber,* running in synchronization with the picture. The sound from each dubber then goes to a separate volume control on an audio control board so that the sound engineer, or *mixer,* can control the level of each sound as the tracks are combined. In addition, these boards are usually set up so that the sound from each track can be run through a

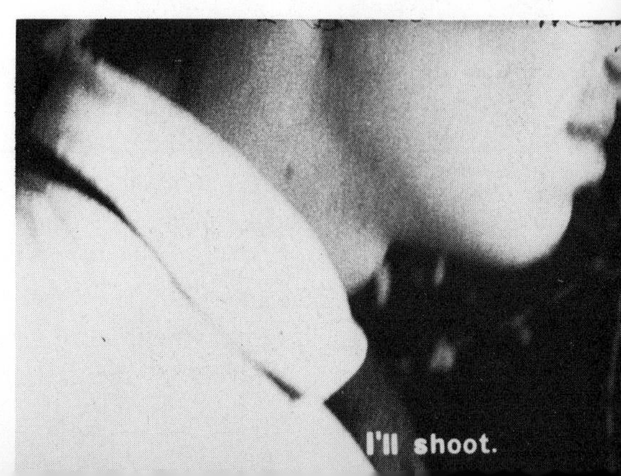

variety of filters, equalizers, echo chambers, and limiters, which permit the quality of the various sounds to be altered as they are mixed. Finally, this board combines all the sounds into a single, composite sound track that is recorded on a master sprocketed recorder which also runs in synchronization with the picture.

There are several ways to go about mixing the sound track. When the finished track is relatively simple, it is possible for each roll to contain all there is of each type of sound. Then the mix is limited to fading in or out and finding the proper levels for only three rolls of sound. As a result, the mixing can usually be completed in just one session. However, if the track is more complicated, it is not unusual for each type of sound to be placed on several rolls. Then these rolls are *mixed down* into a single roll before the various types of sound are combined in the final mix. This permits the mixer to make complicated electronic alterations and do other involved mixing a step at a time over several sessions, rather than having to mix a large number of tracks (sometimes twenty or more) all at once.

Preparing for the Mix

A number of mechanical procedures must be completed before the tracks are ready for mixing. First, the editor must make sure that at least a twenty-foot leader is attached to each roll of sound. This is used to thread the dubber. Next, one frame of sprocketed magnetic film recorded with a 1,000-cycle tone, or *beep,* is spliced into each sound leader exactly two seconds (forty-eight frames) before the first frame of picture. (If the sound starts before the pictures, the beep should be placed two seconds before the first sound on the composite track.) A similar point on the leader of the workprint should also be marked by a large *X* with the center punched out.

Now the *X* on the workprint and the beep frames should all be aligned in the synchronizer and the leaders rolled toward their heads so that the original sync marks can be checked to make sure they are all still aligned. Later, during the mix, the twelve feet or more of leader between the head sync and the beep allows the speed of the dubbers to stabilize before the mixing actually begins. Then, just before the first sound, the beeps should all be heard simultaneously, and at the same time the punch mark in the workprint should flash on the screen, both confirming that everything is still in synchronization and placing an accurate sync point on the master track.

Cue Sheets

The last step is to prepare a *mixing sheet* or *dubbing cue sheet.* This sheet is laid out in graphic form, with each roll of sound assigned to a separate vertical column. These columns tell the mixer on which track to find each sound. The footage at which each sound starts and stops is then marked down the left margin of the sheet. Later, these footage numbers will tell the mixer when to expect each sound as he watches a footage counter running in synchronization with the projector.

The editor prepares the cue sheets by first locking the rolls of sound and workprint in a synchronizer or in sync on an editing machine. Next, the footage counter is *zeroed* at the first frame of picture or sound—whichever comes first.

Then, as the tracks are slowly rolled forward, the sound on each track is noted in the appropriate column, and the footage at the beginning and the end of each sound is indicated to the left of all the columns. Each sound is also marked according to whether the sound cuts in or out, or fades in or out, whether there are any electronic alterations to the sound, and whether the sound should be especially loud or soft.

Here is an example of a possible cue sheet for a brief sequence from Hitchcock's *Suspicion.* While this is a relatively complex scene in terms of the sound track, the mixing itself is comparatively simple. In this scene Lena first begins to suspect that her husband wants to kill Beeky. During a game of Scrabble Beeky remarks that *er* would turn the word *murder* into *murderer;* at the same time Lena looks carefully at a picture her husband is holding of the site he wishes Beeky to inspect the next day. Suddenly the sheer, towering cliffs in the picture suggest a simple means for doing Beeky in, and as her imagination runs away with the possibilities, Hitchcock shows the foul deed and the hapless victim flashing through her mind's eye. Then, overwhelmed by a sense of horror, she slumps to the floor in a dead faint.

urtesy: JANUS FILMS, INC.

	PICTURE	SOUND
	1. CU, Scrabble game (3⅔ sec.).	BEEKY: Now if I had an *er,* I could make that *murderer.* MUS: Low, discordant note fades in behind dialogue.
	2. MCU, Lena. She looks up from table toward her husband (1 sec.).	

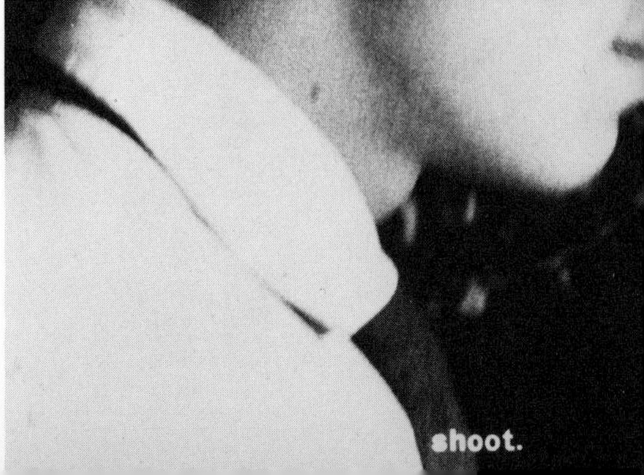

	PICTURE	SOUND
	3. MCU, John. He is speaking to Beeky (3¼ sec.).	JOHN: The earlier the bet I'd say about 7 o'clock . .
	4. MCU, Lena. She looks back down at table (¾ sec.).	JOHN: . . . There won't so much . . .
	5. XCU, word *murder*. Camera tilts up and L to photo John is holding (3½ sec.).	JOHN: . . . traffic on road. BEEKY: At that hour . I'd say in a pig's tail. MUS: Deep, sharp bass n then woodwinds swell beh dialogue.
	6. CU, Lena (1¼ sec.).	JOHN: In a pig's tail?
	7. Zoom in to XCU of photo; at 2¼ sec. CU of Lena (same as shot 6) and scene of John pushing Beeky off cliff are superimposed. Then fade out photo with John and Beeky (6¼ sec.).	BEEKY: That's too early, early. Pig's tail, pig's (laughs hysterically). MUS: Loud, long, clangorc note submerges dialogue.

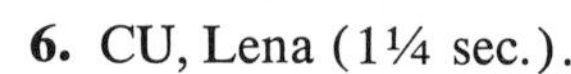

PICTURE	SOUND
8. CU, Lena (same as shot 6); after 1½ sec. superimpose MCU of Beeky falling down cliff (3 sec.).	MUS: Continues loud and strident. BEEKY: Laugh becomes shouted, hollow, tortured cry.
DISSOLVE	
9. MLS, wave breaking over rocks at base of cliff (1½ sec.).	MUS: Continues. SFX: Beeky's cry merges with sound of waves breaking.
DISSOLVE	
10. CU, Lena. Camera dollies back as she faints and falls to floor (8½ sec.).	MUS: Cuts off sharply. SFX: Cut off sharply; then soft thump as she hits floor, and men's footsteps.
FADE OUT	

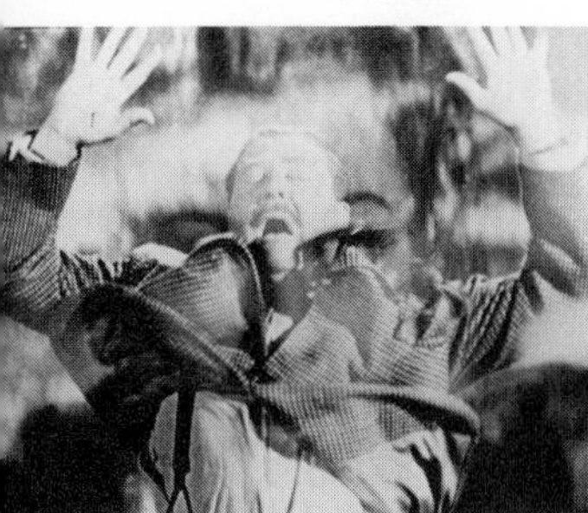

rtesy: JANUS FILMS, INC.

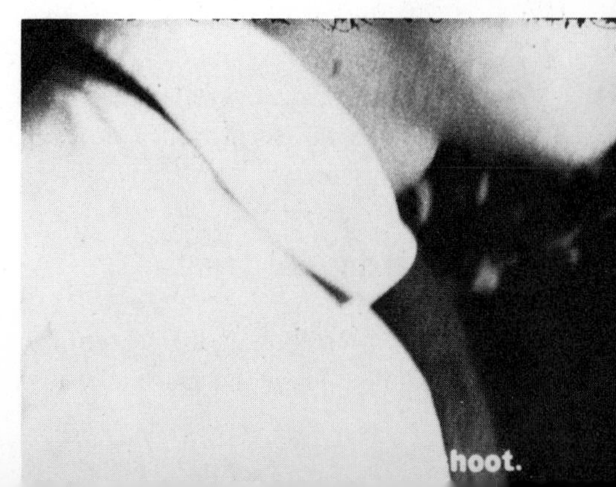

hoot.

That's the scene; now here's how this complicated mélange of sound might be reduced to the simple notations required to mix the tracks.

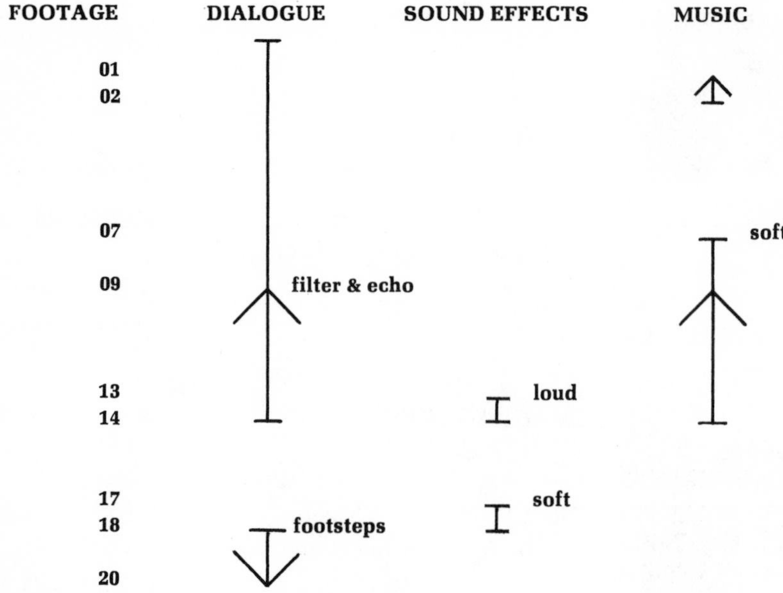

Since the dialogue starts at a normal level and continues for fourteen feet, a *T* is marked at the beginning of the dialogue column, and the vertical leg of the *T* is extended to fourteen feet. A straight line is also placed in the music column starting at one foot, but because this music fades in, an inverted *V* is placed at the top of the line. The music then stops abruptly at two feet, so the end of this line is marked with an inverted *T*. Similarly, the music starts softly but cleanly at seven feet, so at that point another straight line is begun with a *T*. Next, at nine feet, both the dialogue and the music get louder, so both columns are marked with an inverted *V*, and the dialogue is also marked for a filter and echo.

At fourteen feet, the start of the last shot, all the sounds stop, so all the columns are marked with an inverted *T*. This silence then continues for three feet, as the camera slowly dollies back from Lena's falling figure, until at seventeen feet a soft thud cuts in on the effects track. Immediately after that we hear the footsteps of the men rushing over to pick her up. This last sound effect has to be moved to the empty space in the dialogue track so that, if necessary, the level of the thud can be set separately from that of the footsteps. Finally, the footsteps fade out as the scene fades out, so the dialogue column ends with an upright *V* at twenty feet.

Mixing the Tracks

As soon as the mixing sheets are prepared the film can be taken to a mixing studio. There the film-maker can either mix the tracks himself or turn the operation of the audio board over to a sound engineer. Except for a very simple mix, however, it is usually preferable to let a professional engineer do the mixing. Then the film-maker can listen to the overall results rather than being preoccupied with technical details. In addition, an experienced sound engineer develops an intuitive ability to operate the board and can quickly mix segments that the film-maker might require many practice runs to master. At fifty dollars an hour and up to rent the studio, this kind of practice can easily run into a lot of money.

If an error is made during the mix, it is no problem to erase the magnetic master, rewind the tracks, and start over. But if it is just a small error, it may be preferable to complete the mix and simply redo only the bad section. Then this new piece can later be cut into the rest of the master. It is also possible to mix several slightly different versions of the track. This permits the film-maker to listen to them at his leisure, when he has a better perspective on the film, and then choose one, or several different sections of each, as the master.

Because the mix is the closest the film-maker gets to seeing the finished film before it is printed, it may become apparent during the mix that certain alterations or additions are needed to produce a satisfactory sound track. If this simply means adding or changing background sounds or music, the sound studio normally has the necessary resources to produce the change. Then, as the tracks are mixed, a prerecorded sound effect or piece of music can be inserted at the proper time. However, when the new sound has to be exactly synchronized with the action, or if other detailed reediting of the tracks becomes necessary, it is usually cheaper and easier to stop the mix. This permits the film-maker to return to his editing bench and make the corrections without having to worry about accumulating studio rentals.

After the mix the sound and pictures are locked onto two separate but synchronous strips of film that the film-maker must entrust to the processing laboratory for printing. Unlike mixing, this is not a process which he can evaluate as it takes place. But even here the film-maker plays a role because he must tell the laboratory exactly how he wants the picture to look. And in some cases, particularly with a small or low-budget film, he may want to do a part of the post-production work himself. It is therefore necessary to know some of the technical details of this finishing process, and these will be covered in the next chapter.

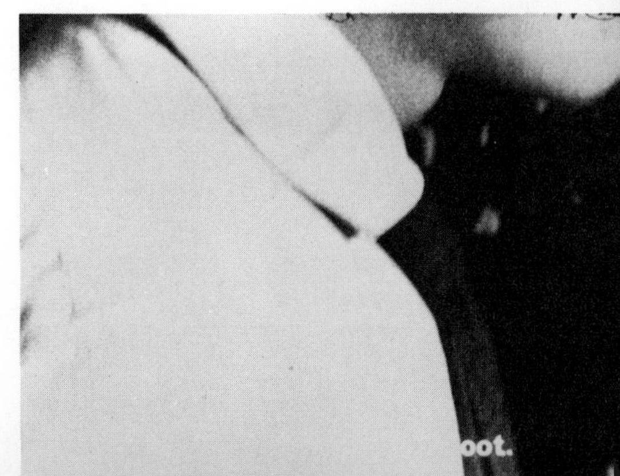

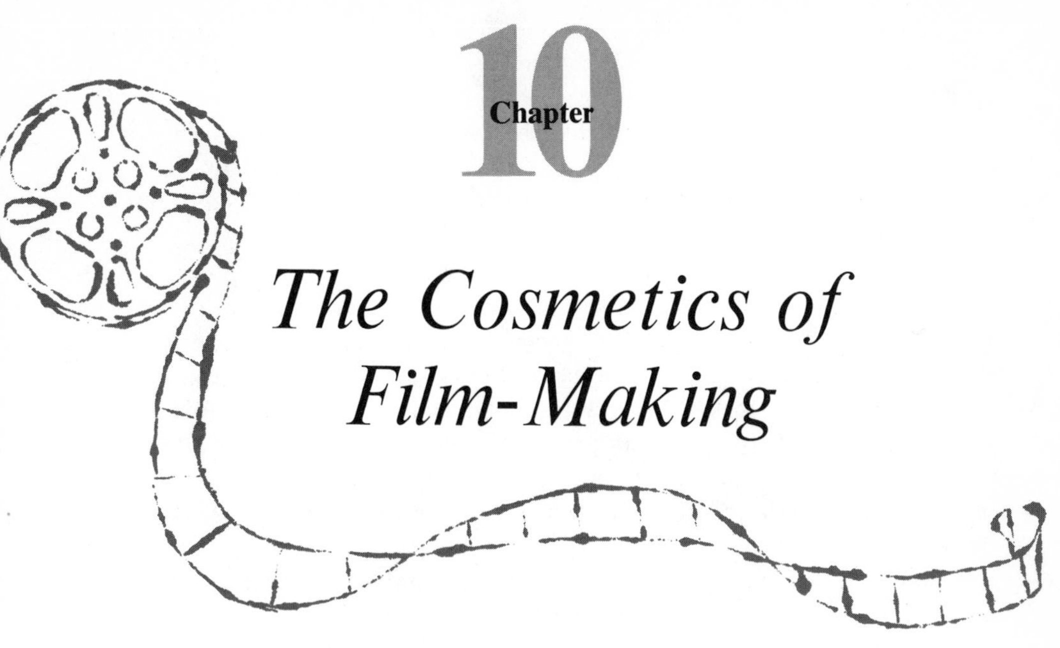

Chapter 10

The Cosmetics of Film-Making

Once the sound track is mixed, the last creative decision in the film-making process has been made. Now the film has to be readied for the largely mechanical task of printing. This final step in the making of a film is one in which neither art nor craft are as important as sheer precision and technical skill. The object is to reproduce both picture and sound as clearly and accurately as possible in a form which is suitable for public showing. In most cases this means converting the magnetic track to optical sound and preparing the original camera footage so that both sound and picture can be printed together on the same strip of film—the projection print.

In its simplest form, printing a motion picture involves nothing more than sandwiching together processed film and some raw stock and moving the two past a light so that the image is transferred from one piece of film to the other. In the earliest days of motion pictures the camera was used for this purpose. It already doubled as a projector, so all that was needed to turn it into a printer was to feed raw stock through the film gate along with the processed footage. The projection lamp would then expose the image onto the new piece of film.

This technique is still in use. It is called *contact step printing,* both because the processed film and the raw stock are in contact with each other and because

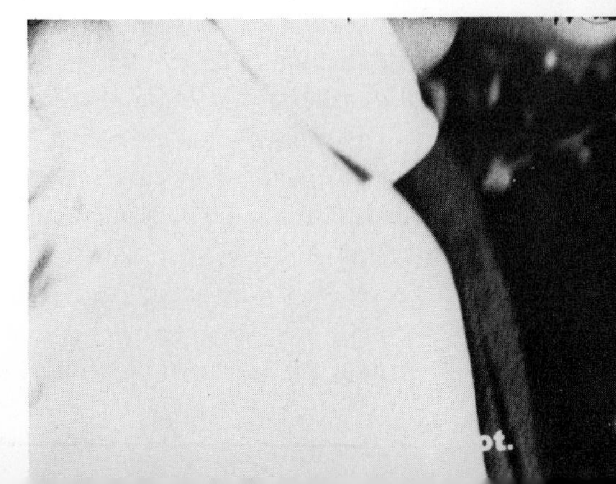

they are exposed one frame (step) at a time. This is a very accurate but relatively slow way to make prints and has largely been replaced by *continuous contact printing*. In printing there is no need to stop the original and the raw stock in the gate for each exposure since, unlike photography, printing doesn't involve freezing a moving world onto static frames. The image in the processed film is already frozen, so all that is needed to transfer that image is to move the processed film, along with the raw stock, past a slit of light.

Because continuous contact printers eliminate the lens and the shutter, the devices normally used to control exposure, there is instead a mechanism for altering the intensity of the printing light. This mechanism allows the lab technician to compensate for errors in the original exposure of the various shots as the image is being exposed onto the raw stock. It also permits him to match up the density of shots that are supposed to cut together smoothly. In fact, these adjustments have become such a delicate art that determining the proper printer light, called *timing* the print, is usually done in the larger motion-picture laboratories by a separate, skilled professional *timer*.

However, before the print can be timed, the film originally shot in the camera has to be prepared for printing. If the editing was done with the camera original instead of with a workprint, all that need be done to ready the original for printing is to clean it. But if, as is most often the case, the editing was done with a workprint, the camera original must be edited so that it matches the workprint frame for frame. This process, variously called *matching, conforming,* or *negative cutting,* is also such a delicate and specialized part of professional film-making that negative cutters too form a separate profession within the film business.

Matching the Original to the Workprint

The key to high-quality matching is cleanliness. Every fingerprint, scratch, and dirt particle on the original will be permanently printed onto all the copies and then greatly enlarged upon the screen. And since the emulsion on the camera original is softer than that on any other kind of film stock, handling an original requires an extraordinary amount of care. In the best professional negative-cutting rooms the atmosphere is exactly the same as that in the white rooms used for assembling lunar rockets. The air supply is filtered and all airborne dirt excluded by means of positive air pressure, that is, the air pressure in the room is higher than normal so that air blows only out of the room. The personnel wear special white coveralls and lintless, soft, white linen or cotton gloves. All equipment and work surfaces are kept immaculate, and of course, smoking is strictly prohibited.

While it is impossible to re-create these rigorously controlled conditions outside the film industry, as long as the work area is kept clean, it is possible for the film-maker to do quite acceptable matching. After all, the matched original can still be professionally cleaned before it is printed. However, the only things that can't be removed by careful cleaning are scratches. So, to prevent scratches, gloves should be worn whenever handling original materials and the original handled as little as possible. Also, keep the original firmly wound whenever it is not in use to prevent what are called *cinch marks,* scratches caused by dirt between the layers of spooled film. Because there is some slight play in all but the most tightly wound roll of film, the layers of film will shift every time the roll is unwound and rewound.

And every time the film shifts, any dirt between the layers gouges out a tiny scratch.

If the original is loosely spooled, do not tighten the roll by pulling on the end of the film. This will cause the worst posssible cinching. Rewind the roll instead, using, if possible, a device called a *tight wind*. This is a special kind of rewind on

Tight wind. This particular model is an attachment to a standard rewind.

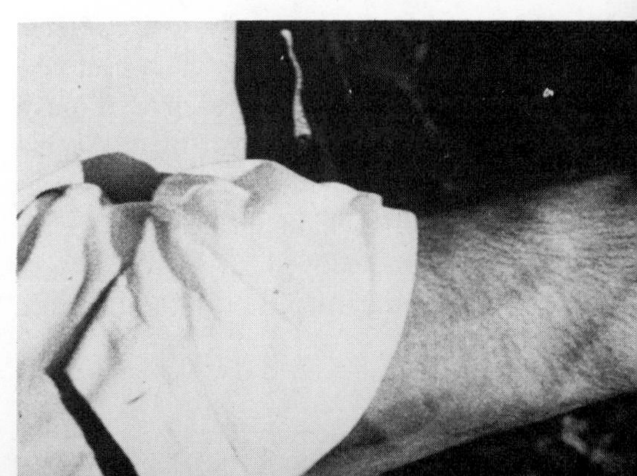

which is mounted either a shaft, or a spring-loaded arm, and a heavy roller. The roller rides on the film, keeping it taut as it is spooled onto a core.

The first step in matching is called *pulling* the original. Only a small percentage of the shots workprinted usually appear in the finished film, and the original of these shots must be separated from all the other, unwanted takes that make up the rolls of original from which the workprints were made. To begin the pulling, note the first edge number of each shot in the workprint and then list the numbers in ascending order. That way, no matter what order the shots appear in in the workprint, they can be pulled from the rolls of original in the order in which they appear. This procedure minimizes the number of times the negative cutter has to reel through the original to find each shot.

Each entire shot is cut from the roll of original and spooled on a separate core. It is rolled in emulsion to protect the end of the shot from dirt and scratches, the end is taped down with a narrow piece of masking tape and the first and the last edge numbers for that shot are written on the tape. These rolls of pulled original are then either stored in large film cans or stood on edge, with the tape facing forward, in a core rack. A core rack is like a shallow bookshelf except that the shelves are trough-shaped instead of flat so that the cores won't roll off. The cores can then be rearranged on the shelves so that they are in the same order as the shots in the workprint.

Checkerboarding 8mm and 16mm Originals

Next the original is cut to match the workprint and the pieces spliced together for printing. This is a relatively simple matter with 35mm film, but somewhat more complicated in 8mm and 16mm. In 35mm, the large size allows plenty of room for splices between the frames without the splices overlapping into the picture area. Therefore, the 35mm original can be spliced into a single roll and printed without any splice marks showing in the print. In 8mm and 16mm, however, each splice must extend into at least part of one frame in order for the splice to be wide enough to hold together. As a result, a special technique must be used to conceal the splices when printing 8mm and 16mm originals. The first step in this technique is to alternate the shots between two printing rolls. This is called *checkerboarding* the original because when there is a shot in one roll, the other contains black leader. In other words, when a shot ends, it is spliced to black leader and the beginning of the next shot is spliced onto the black leader in the other roll, directly across from the end of the previous shot. This way the splices can always be made to overlap into black leader instead of into a frame of picture.

These rolls, called *A* and *B* rolls, are then printed, one after the other, onto the same strip of film. But wherever there is black leader in one of these printing rolls no light can pass through to expose the printing stock. Therefore, after the *A* roll is printed there are blank, unexposed spaces on the print stock that are exactly as long and in the same position as the shots on the *B* roll. The *B* roll is then printed into these spaces and the black leader in it fits exactly over the shots already printed from the *A* roll, preventing these areas from being further exposed to the printer light. Each printing roll thus provides every other shot; and since the black

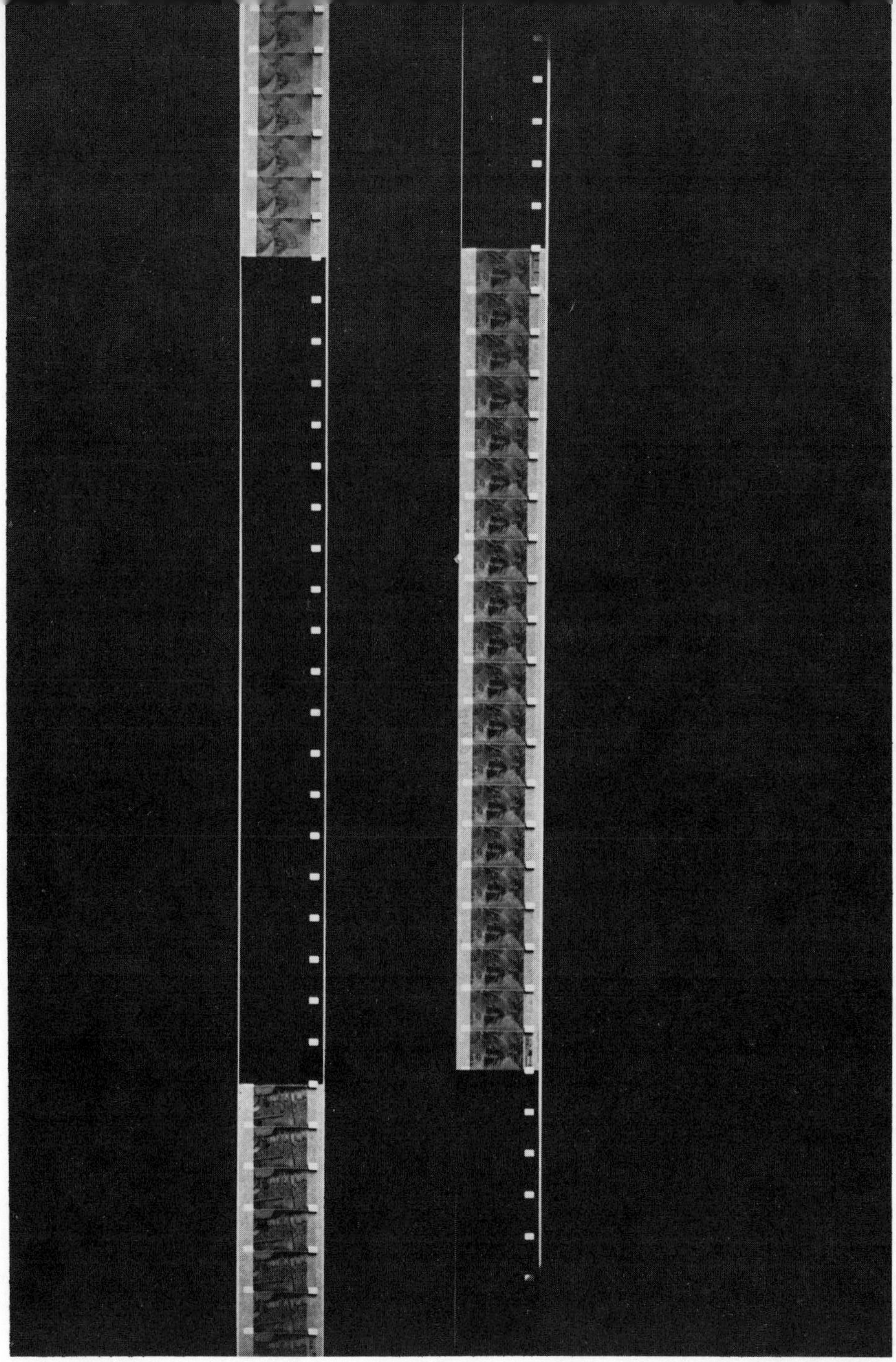

A&B roll checkerboard.

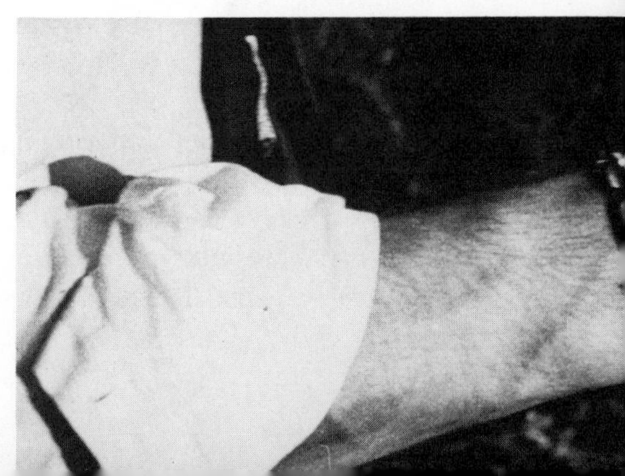

leader doesn't pass light, the splices, which overlap into this leader, can't be seen in the finished print.

A&B-Roll Optical Effects

A&B-roll printing also offers the tremendous advantage of simple and inexpensive dissolves and superimpositions. These are optical effects in which one scene overlaps another, either for the entire length of the shots in a *super,* or only briefly, in a dissolve, as the end of one shot fades out and the other simultaneously fades in. In single-roll printing, such as is done in 35mm, these optical effects must be produced by rephotographing the overlapping footage with a special optical printer. The new footage is then cut into the single printing roll in place of the original camera footage. This is not only an expensive process, but causes some reduction in the image quality of the finished effect because rephotographing footage places the new footage a generation or two away from the original.

While this change in image quality is not terribly noticeable in 35mm, it is quite apparent in 16mm and totally unacceptable in 8mm. But *A&B*-roll printing permits these common optical effects to be produced directly from the original during the printing process. For instance, all that need be done to produce a super is to place the overlapping shots, one on each printing roll, so that they are directly opposite each other. Then they will both be exposed onto the same part of the finished print. The same thing is done to produce a dissolve except that only the end of the shot on one roll overlaps the beginning of the next shot on the other roll. Then, when one roll is printed, the end of the first shot in the dissolve is faded out. And when the other roll is printed, the overlapping portion of the next shot is faded in.

This is such an economical way to produce simple optical effects that it is now used in some 35mm printing as well as in most 16mm prints. It is also becoming available for super 8mm prints because the quality of super 8mm camera stock has improved to the point where acceptable duplicates can now be made in that size also. In fact, setting up *A&B* printing rolls in any of these film sizes is so similar that we will describe just the techniques used in 16mm. The only difference between what is done in this size and in 35mm is that there is no need to checkerboard the straight cuts with the larger film because there is no need to hide the splices. There is also a small difference between 16mm and 8mm techniques in that there is no way to produce fades on some 8mm printers. Then the 8mm optical effects cannot be produced through *A&B*-roll printing but must be done in the camera. We will discuss how this is done in the latter half of this chapter.

Preparing the A&B Rolls

The following section of this chapter may not be of immediate interest to all our readers. Although setting up *A&B* printing rolls is not terribly difficult to do, it does take a certain amount of concentration to understand how it is done. Unless you have to set up some *A&B* rolls of your own, it may be difficult to focus on the many details that make the procedure both interesting and useful. If that is

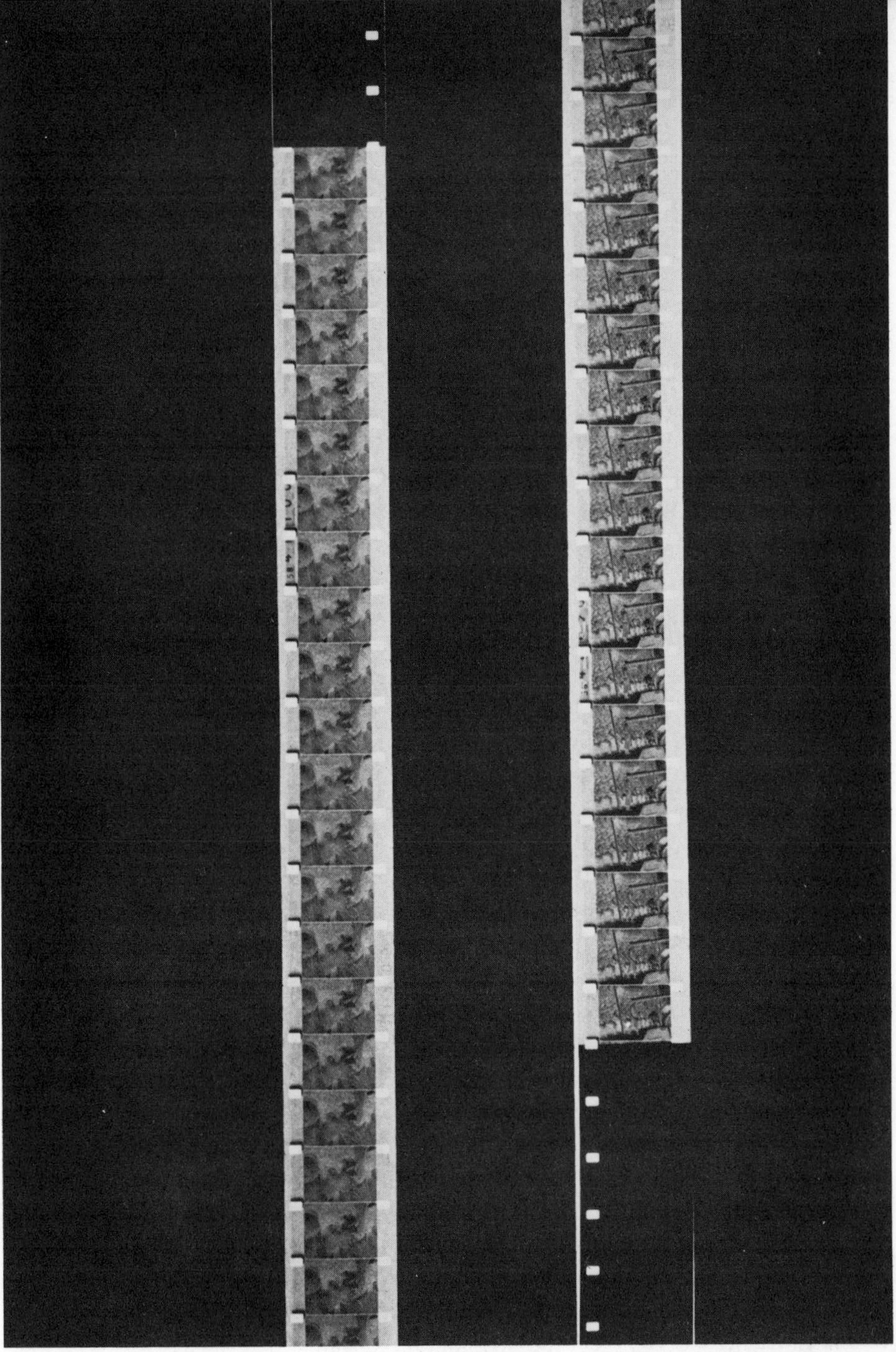

A&B roll dissolve.

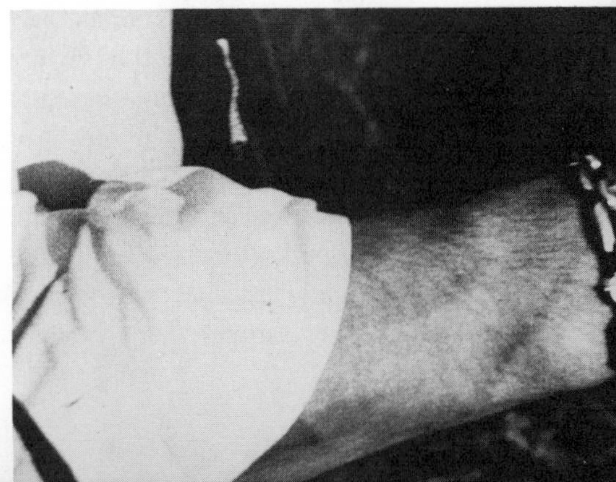

the case, skip ahead to page 545, the beginning of the section on in-camera optical effects, and come back to these pages at some later date when *A&B*-roll matching looms as a concrete problem that must be mastered.

A&B-roll matching requires only the same few simple pieces of equipment that are used for any other kind of editing: an editing bench with a pair of gang rewinds, a three- or four-gang synchronizer, and a splicer. To prepare for matching, first thread the workprint from the left-hand rewind through the rear gang of the synchronizer and onto a reel on the right-hand rewind. There should be approximately twenty feet of white leader on the workprint with a punch mark about six feet from the head of this leader. Two similar leaders, each with a punch mark, should also be threaded through the next two gangs of the synchronizer so that all the punch marks line up. These leaders are then taken up on reels just inside the one for the workprint on the right-hand rewind. These last two leaders will eventually be used to thread the printer, so their exact length should be checked with the laboratory that will do the printing.

The leader for the printing rolls should be threaded through the synchronizer with the emulsion side up. Then all the original cut into these rolls will also be spliced together with the emulsion side up. That way, when the original goes slack during splicing, only the tougher backing material of the film will drag across the surface of the editing bench. In 16mm there is also a choice of leader perforated along one or both edges. Only in this film size are both kinds available. As a general rule, use only single-perforated leader unless the whole film has been shot on double-perforated stock. Otherwise, the lab technician may inadvertently thread the printer with the double-perforated leader wrong side around and the sprocket teeth will punch a new set of sprocket holes in the first piece of valuable, single-perforated original they come to.

The procedure for checkerboarding B&W or color, negative or reversal, 8mm or 16mm film is exactly the same. Place a reel of black leader on the left-hand rewind, inside the reel of workprint. This should be fresh leader that is very dense. (The outline of a 60-watt bulb should just be visible when viewed through the leader.) Splice a piece of this black leader onto the leader for each printing roll two to three feet before the start of the first picture in the workprint. Next, count the number of frames from the start of the first shot in the workprint to the nearest edge number and measure off that same distance from the corresponding edge number in the original. Then add one more frame and cut the original across the middle of this extra frame. *DO NOT* cut the original on the frame line because the extra half-frame is needed to make the splice. Also, be careful to save the piece of original that has been cut off. It may be used somewhere else in the film, especially if it is six inches or longer. Place an empty reel on the right-hand rewind, tape together the unused pieces of the original, and wind them up in order.

Now the original is ready to be cut into one of the printing rolls. It doesn't matter which roll, but whichever one is used first usually becomes the *A* roll. Place the first frame of the first shot in the workprint opposite the arrow on top of the synchronizer and mark the middle of that same frame in one of the black leaders. Then pull all the leaders to the left until the mark is well out of the synchronizer, and cut the leader on the mark. The piece of black leader to the right, the one threaded through the synchronizer, is then spliced to the original.

Splicers and Splices

There are several different types of film splicers available. For instance, some splicers use film cement and some use transparent adhesive tape. An adhesive splice is all right in a workprint but only a cement splicer should be used to join the original into the printing rolls. There are several reasons for this. When the original is tightly wound, a tape splice tends to ooze adhesive out from under the backing material and this sticks to the next layer of film. This ooze then picks up loose dirt, both at the splice and somewhere in the adjacent shots, and any solvent used to remove this extra adhesive will also weaken the splices. Adhesive splices also dry out and stretch. Once this happens, the sprocket holes are no longer properly aligned at the splices, so the image jiggles every time a splice is printed.

Cement splicers are of two types: positive and negative. As its name implies, a positive splicer is basically designed for splicing prints (positives). It makes a splice which is wider, and therefore stronger, than a negative splice. But in 8mm and 16mm a positive splice overlaps two frames, one on either side of the cut. This makes a positive splicer useless for preparing *A&B* rolls, since no matter how the splice is made, it is bound to overlap into a frame of picture. The narrower, negative splice, however, overlaps only one frame, so it can always be made to lap into the black leader.

Cement splicers are also available in *hot* or *cold* models. Either of these can be used for splicing the original. The only difference between them is that the hot splicer has a heating element that speeds the drying of the cement. This is very useful when a great many splices have to be made since it cuts the drying time from thirty to ten seconds. There is also a type of hot splicer called a *pedestal* or *pedal* splicer. This is a massive machine mounted on its own pedestal and partially operated by foot pedals. These machines are very expensive and extremely fast, and they are used to make the strong, accurate splices needed in professional film work. Pedal splicers are, in fact, so ruggedly constructed that some of those used to make silent films are still in use today.

In *A&B*-roll splicing the original is always clamped into the left-hand side of a negative splicer and the black leader into the right-hand side. They are both placed emulsion up. The emulsion is then scraped from the extra half-frame of the original that is left sticking out of the left-hand side of the splicer, thus exposing the backing material under the emulsion. Cement is applied to this scraped area and then the black leader is firmly clamped on top of it, gluing the backing material of one piece of film directly to the backing material of the other. Since film cement is

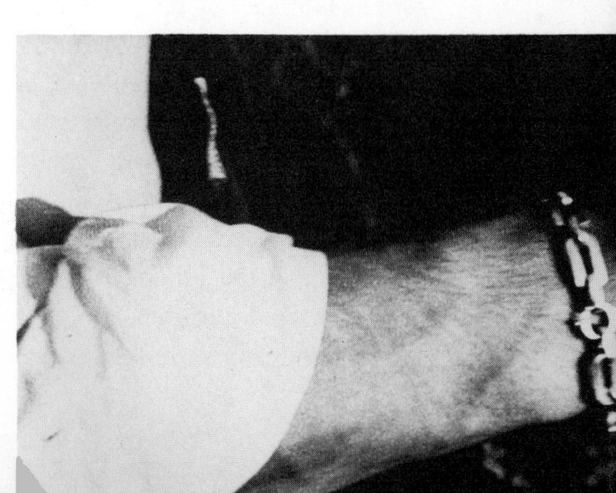

a powerful solvent, the backing of each piece of film is softened, and when the cement evaporates, the two pieces fuse into a new, double thickness of film backing that is actually stronger than the backing material on either side of the splice.

Checking the Splice

Once the splice is made, roll all the leaders to the right, back through the synchronizer, until the first edge number in the workprint is opposite the arrow. Then check the original to make sure that exactly the same edge number is in the exact same position. If the numbers line up, everything is in order and the work can proceed. If they don't, roll all the leaders to the left until the splice in the workprint is opposite the arrow. Then, if the black leader was cut to the wrong length, the splice in the workprint and the one in the printing roll won't line up; while if it was the original which was cut wrong, the splices will line up.

When the black leader is the wrong length, go six inches ahead of the old splice and splice in or cut out the appropriate number of frames of leader. This correction cannot be made by breaking the splice between the original and the leader because every time a splice is broken and then remade a frame on each side of the old splice must be used to make the new one. Therefore, breaking this first splice would result in the loss of a frame of the original.

When the original is too long, simply cut it to the right length. Then cut into the black leader several inches ahead of the old splice, splice on a new piece of leader, make a new mark, and splice the original back into place. Little can be done, however, if the original is too short. Splicing back the needed piece of original will cause a jump in the action when the scene is printed because at least one frame of the original has already been used to join the original to the black leader. As a result, the only remedies are to lengthen the shot at the other end, to find another good take to substitute for the ruined original, or to recut the workprint and the sound track to conform to what is left of the original.

Preparing a Straight Cut

When the first shot cuts straight to the second, place the first frame of the second shot in the workprint opposite the arrow on the synchronizer. Then make a mark in that same frame on both the original and the black leader and again pull everything to the left until the marks are well out of the synchronizer. Cut both the original and the black leader on these marks. Now measure the distance from the cut at the head of the second shot to the nearest edge number in that shot and cut the original for that shot to this same length plus one-half frame. Then splice this original to the piece of black leader threaded through the synchronizer. This procedure will place the second piece of original in the *B* roll.

The loose end of the roll of black leader is then spliced to the tail of the original for shot one. However, this splice cannot be made in quite the same way that shot two was spliced to its leader. The original must always be placed in the left-hand side of the splicer for the splice to fall in the black leader, but the end of shot one is now on the right. So shot one must be looped around to the left side of the splicer and the black leader pulled over to the right side. That places them in the correct position for an invisible splice. Once this splice is made, the edge numbers in the original and the workprint for the second shot can be checked and any corrections made as outlined above. This whole process is then repeated for every straight cut in the film.

Fades and Dissolves

The fades and dissolves in a film must be handled somewhat differently from straight cuts. They are created by means of a mechanical shutter, called a *fader,* that can be set to open or close over 16, 24, 32, 40, 48, 64, or 96 frames. Although some of the newer *A&B*-roll printers can produce effects of varying length within the same print, the fader in most printers can operate at only one predetermined speed throughout the entire print. This means that it is necessary to choose a standard length for all the effects in each film.

If a scene starts with a fade-in, splice the first shot into the printing roll in the same way as a straight cut. Then, if the film is being printed from an original that is B&W or color reversal film, a small paper label is stuck to the black leader just ahead of the splice and marked *FI.* This tells the lab technician to start printing that shot with the shutter closed. Since, with reversal materials, an absence of light produces a dark area, the closed shutter keeps the printer light off the print so that the first few frames will be black. When preparing the roll for printing, the technician also cuts a notch into the black leader or pastes a shiny foil sensing-tab to one edge. This notch or tab automatically activates the fader mechanism so that the shutter slowly opens over the remaining frames of the fade-in, thus allowing more and more of the printing light to strike the print until the image reaches its proper exposure.

A somewhat different procedure must be followed, however, when the original is B&W or color negative film. Since a negative always works the opposite of reversal materials, keeping the shutter closed and the light off the print will make the start of the fade-in clear film. Only exposure to light will create a fade-in that starts from black. As a result, when printing from a negative, a fade-in starts with a very bright light. This is then slowly decreased over the length of the fade.

To create a fade-in on negative film, a clear leader of forty-eight frames, or some other standard length, is cut into the *B* roll directly opposite the section of original in the *A* roll that is supposed to contain the fade. The *A* roll is then printed normally; but when the *B* roll is printed the printing light is turned all the way up and the shutter opened fully at the start of the fade-in. This intense light completely

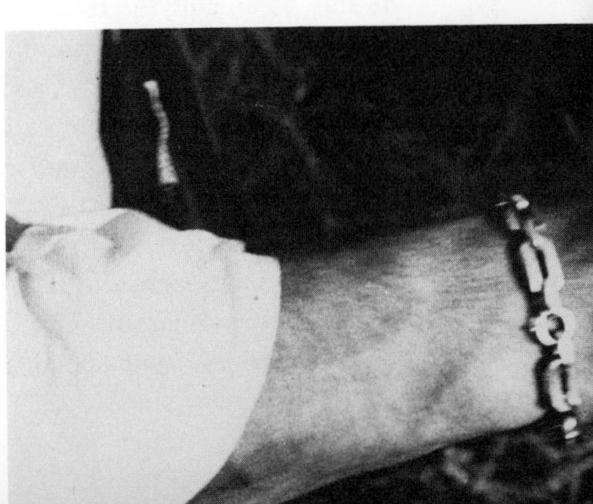

reexposes the print to light, blackening the previously exposed image from the *A* roll for the first few frames. Then, when the notch activates the fader mechanism, the shutter slowly closes, allowing the properly exposed image from the *A* roll to emerge from darkness.

Another common optical effect is a combined fade-out–fade-in within the body of the film. This effect is accomplished by running the fader through a complete open and close cycle. In the case of reversal materials, the two pieces of original on either side of this optical effect are cut together in the same printing roll with the splice at the exact midpoint of the effect. This splice is then labeled *FO–FI*. When this section of the roll is printed, the shutter is slowly closed over forty-eight frames (or some other standard distance) before the splice, and slowly opened for the same number of frames after the splice.

With negative materials the shutter cycle is reversed. The negative original is joined together in the same way as a reversal original and a piece of clear leader is cut into the other printing roll directly opposite the place where the effect is to occur. This leader is labeled *FO* at the head end and *FI* at the tail end. When this piece of clear leader is run through the printer, the printer light is turned all the way up and the shutter slowly opened over a standard number of frames and then closed over the same number of frames. This second exposure superimposes the fade-out–fade-in over the image printed from the original in the other roll.

Because a certain amount of time is required for the fader mechanism to reverse direction, a FO–FI sequence is always anywhere from twelve to thirty-two frames longer than the opticals in the rest of the film. The exact number of extra frames depends upon the laboratory doing the printing. This means that for the printing of negative materials, the clear leader must be from twelve to thirty-two frames longer than the standard length adopted for the other effects in the film. Otherwise, the fader won't complete its cycle before the clear leader ends and there will be a jump from a partially completed fade-in to properly exposed footage. However, no such adjustment is required for the printing of this effect from reversal materials. Because the fader is operated while the roll containing the original is printed, the extra frames needed to recycle the mechanism are automatically available at each end of the effect.

It is possible, when printing from reversal original, to shorten a FO–FI to the same length as the opticals in the rest of the film by splicing the two shots into alternate rolls, just like a straight cut. Then, when the shutter is closed at the end of the first shot, it can recycle over black leader. And when the other roll is printed, the shutter can be closed over the black leader immediately preceding the shot containing the fade-in. Then it is ready to open as soon as the first frame of original is over the printer gate. This arrangement also allows the next shot to pop on without a fade as soon as the first has faded out; or for the first to end with a straight cut and then the second to fade in.

With both negative and reversal materials, a dissolve is printed in almost the same way as the FO–FI just described. In a dissolve, the second shot starts to fade in as the first shot begins to fade out, so the only way to overlap the shots is to have each in a different printing roll. In the workprint this overlap is indicated by a grease-pencil mark. The two pieces of workprint are spliced together at the exact middle of the dissolve and half the overlap marked off on

TAIL Splice HEAD

Workprint

← 24 fr. →← 24 fr. →

A Roll FO

2 1

B Roll FI

either side of the splice. During matching, the original for the first shot is extended to the end of this mark (to point 2 on the diagram). This means that, for a 48-frame dissolve, the original for the first shot is spliced to the black leader twenty-four frames after the splice in the workprint.

In the other printing roll just the reverse is true; the original for the second shot has to start at the beginning of the mark (at point 1 on the diagram). Since this piece of original is not yet locked into the synchronizer, measuring off the exact number of frames is a little tricky. First, count the number of frames from the splice in the workprint to the first edge number in the second shot. Next, add twenty-five frames to this number—twenty-four for the overlap and one for the splicer. Then measure off this distance from the same edge number in the original and cut across the middle of the last frame.

The black leader to which this original is spliced is cut across the middle of the first frame after the start of the dissolve mark (the first frame after point 1 in the diagram). Once the original is spliced to the black leader it will start with the dissolve mark, and its edge numbers will line up with those in the workprint, when everything is rolled to the right through the synchronizer. After the splice is made and the edge numbers checked, stick a paper label to the black leader ahead of the second shot and to the leader after the first. Each of these is marked *DIS*. This label indicates to the lab technician that he must set up the original so that the first shot fades out and the second fades in.

The Problems of A&B-Roll Optical Effects

There are certain limitations regarding how closely the optical effects can be spaced in *A&B* rolls. When two dissolves follow one right after the other,

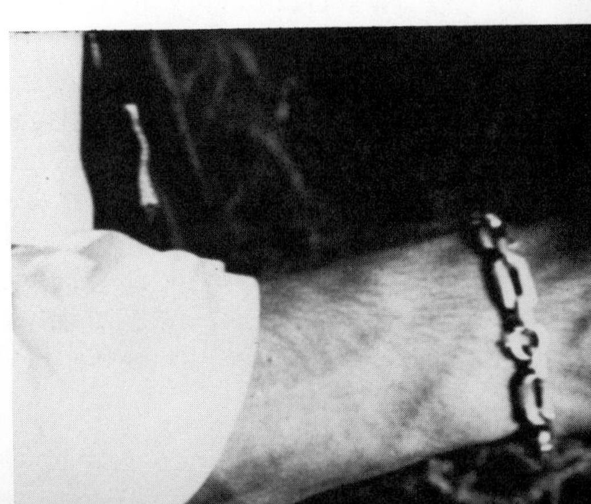

there will have to be a fade-in and a fade-out in the same shot. Then the shot must provide anywhere from 12 to 32 frames between these effects for the fader mechanism to reverse direction (the exact number of frames depends upon the laboratory doing the printing). In other words, when 48-frame effects are used in a film, a shot containing an effect at either end must be at least 108 to 128 frames long (48 + 12 to 32 + 48). This means that in the workprint there must be at least 60 to 80 frames between the splices at either end of the shot.

DIAGRAM 1

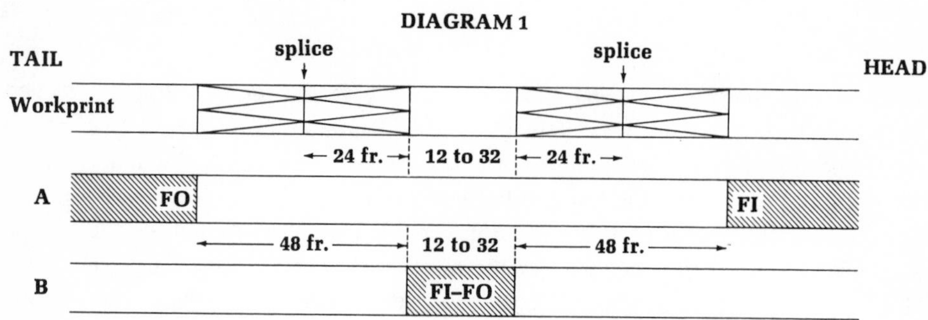

There are also limitations when any effect except a FO–FI on the same printing roll is preceded or followed by a straight cut. A typical example is a 48-frame fade-out followed by a 48-frame fade-in which is set up on separate printing rolls, with a straight cut at each end of the effect.

DIAGRAM 2

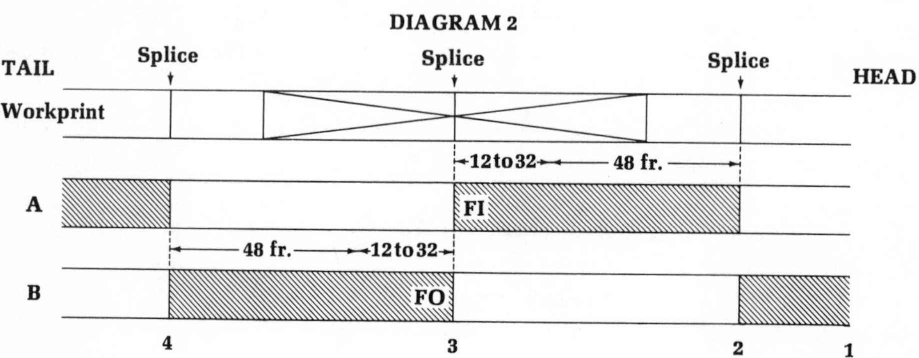

When the *A* roll is printed, the shutter must be fully open to expose the shot between points 1 and 2 (Diagram 2). Then, between points 2 and 3 the shutter must close (forty-eight frames) and reverse direction (twelve to thirty-two frames). This means that at least sixty to eighty frames of black leader are required before the fade-in. That is the minimum needed for the shutter to close and recycle so that it is ready to open at point 3. The same is true if, instead of fading out, the shot before the fade-in simply cuts to black. Either way, the shot in the workprint immediately before the fade-in must be at least sixty to eighty frames long.

A similar situation arises after point 3 in the *B* roll. At point 3 the shutter is fully closed. So, between points 3 and 4 the shutter must reverse direction (twelve to thirty-two frames) and reopen so that the shot starting at point 4 gets a full exposure. This means that the leader following the fade-out must be at least sixty to eighty frames long. This is also true if, instead of fading in, the shot after the fade-out simply pops directly onto the screen. In either case, the shot in the workprint immediately following the fade-out must be at least sixty to eighty frames long.

The problem is the same when a dissolve is preceded or followed by a straight cut. Here is a diagram of a typical 48-frame dissolve with a straight cut on either side.

DIAGRAM 3

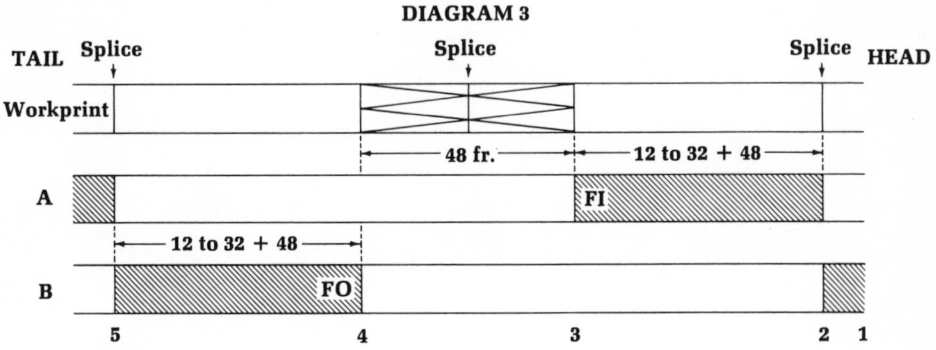

When the *A* roll is printed, the shutter must be fully open to expose the shot between points 1 and 2 (Diagram 3). Then, between points 2 and 3, while the black leader is passing through the printer, the shutter must close (forty-eight frames) and reverse direction (twelve to thirty-two frames) so that it is ready to fade-in at point 3. The same thing is true after point 4 in the *B* roll. At point 4 the shutter is closed, so it must reverse direction (twelve to thirty-two frames) and reopen (forty-eight frames). Then the shot starting at point 5 will get a full exposure. So, whenever there is a straight cut on both sides of a 48-frame dissolve—and this is usually the case—in the workprint each shot in the dissolve must be at least 84 to 104 frames long (48 + 12 to 32 + 24).

C&D Rolls

These limitations are somewhat complicated, but they needn't be confusing if the marking and cutting of the workprint is checked, and any errors corrected, before matching starts. If, however, simple corrections are not possible, the film will have to be printed with an additional roll, called a *C* roll. Then the shot that immediately precedes a fade-in on the same printing roll, or immediately follows a fade-out, is transferred to this *C* roll. When this is done, the space normally occupied by this shot in the *A* or *B* roll is filled in with black leader. This extra leader provides the necessary frames for the shutter to complete its cycle.

Setting up a *C* roll may seem like a lot of extra work for only one or two shots, but in fact, this extra printing roll is useful for several other things as well. For instance, when the opening title of a film must be superimposed over two or more shots, the background shots occupy both the *A* and the *B* rolls, so the only place to put the title original is in the *C* roll. And when two titles connected by a

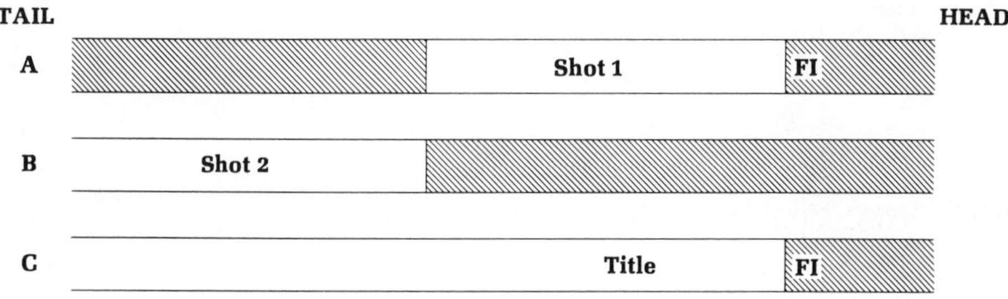

dissolve each extend over two or more shots, the only way to create the dissolve between the titles is to prepare a *D* roll. Then the background shots alternate between the *A* and *B* rolls, while the dissolve is created by the alternation of the titles between the *C* and *D* rolls.

TAIL HEAD
A FO Shot 1 FI
B Shot 2 FI
C FO Title 1 FI
D Title 2 FI

Extra printing rolls also permit rather complicated superimpositions to be created within the body of the film. For instance, in *The World of the Teenager,* an NBC documentary produced by Frank DeFelitta and Joe Mehan, there is a long sequence portraying the agony of the Scholastic Aptitude Test, a three-hour ordeal which is used to determine which high school students are college material.

PICTURE	SOUND
1. MCU, clock. Second hand swings straight up (2½ sec.).	SFX: Bell rings as second hand reaches 12.
2. MS, girl looking at test (2 sec.).	Bell continues.
3. MCU, same girl. She looks down and camera follows, tilting down to test on table (4½ sec.).	Bell stops. MUS: Music starts, apprehensive and heavy, played by piano and xylophone.
DISSOLVE	
4. MCU, same test on table. Camera tilts up to show same girl pondering test (5½ sec.).	Music continues to end of shot, then stops abruptly on cut.

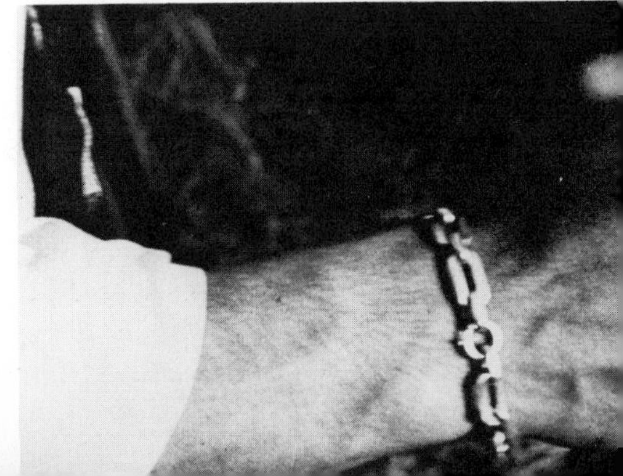

	PICTURE	SOUND
	**5.** CU, boy looking at test. Camera zooms back slowly to show other students (7 sec.).	Music starts again, slow a eerie, played by piano a horns. (This music contint through shot 13.)
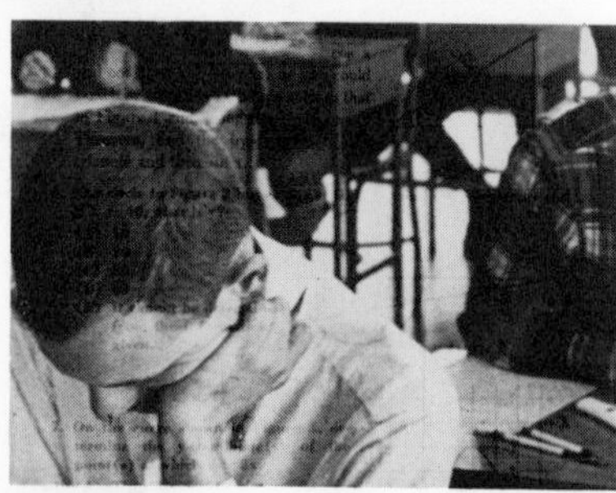	**6.** LS, room full of students taking test (2 sec.).	
	**7.** CU, boy concentrating. Fade in super of test, camera slowly tilts down test page. First shot pans R to shot of another boy (3½ sec.). *DISSOLVE*	
	**8.** MCU, girl writing. Super of test from previous shot continues (3 sec.). *DISSOLVE*	
	9. MCU, another girl writing. Dissolve in new super of later part of test with dissolve to this shot (3 sec.). *DISSOLVE*	

PICTURE	SOUND
10. MCU, boy thinking. Dissolve in super, still photograph of clock stopped at 10:13, along with dissolve to this shot (3 sec.).	

DISSOLVE

11. CU, girl's hand, writing. Dissolve in super of test with dissolve to this shot (2½ sec.).

12. CU, boy looking down. Camera zooms back to reveal that he is holding his hand up (4 sec.).

13. MS, teacher helping same boy (3 sec.).

DISSOLVE

PICTURE	SOUND
14. MCU, clock. This shot dissolves almost immediately to:	Music becomes somew faster and pulsating.

15. MLS, room full of students. As soon as dissolve ends, super of test question fades in (3 sec.).

DISSOLVE

PICTURE	SOUND
16. LS, reverse of previous shot. Super of test from previous shot continues to end of this shot (4 sec.).	Music becomes still fast louder, and more urgent.

17. MLS, boy, seen through exam-room door. Camera zooms in (5 sec.).

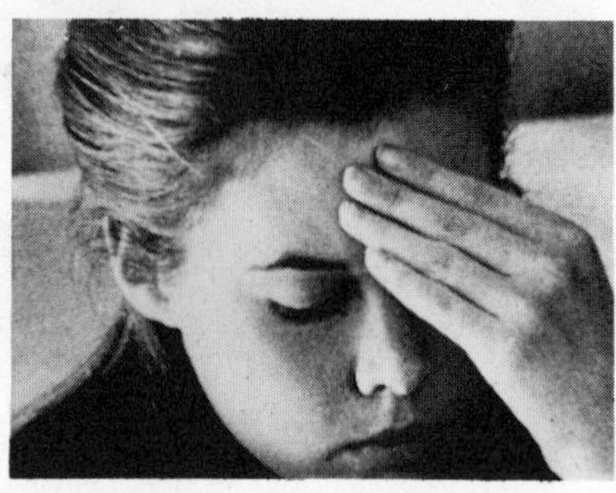

18. CU, girl concentrating. Camera zooms in (2 sec.).

PICTURE	SOUND
 **19.** CU, still photograph of clock. Camera zooms in (2 sec.).	
 **20.** MCU, girl writing (1½ sec.).	
 **21.** MCU, girl writing (1½ sec.).	
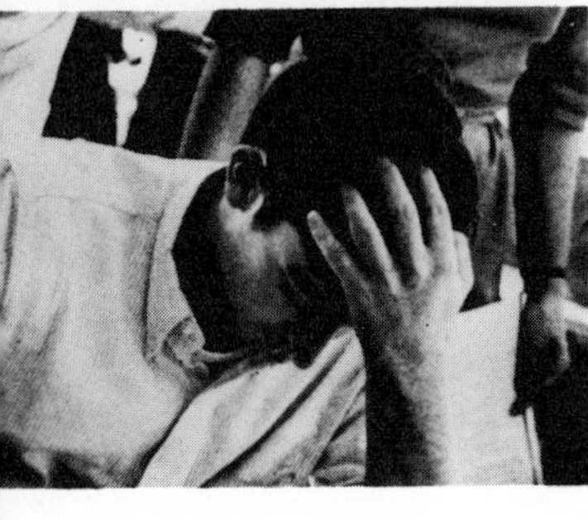 **22.** MCU, boy, hand on head (1½ sec.).	Music reaches a crescendo of dissonant horns which holds through shot 28.

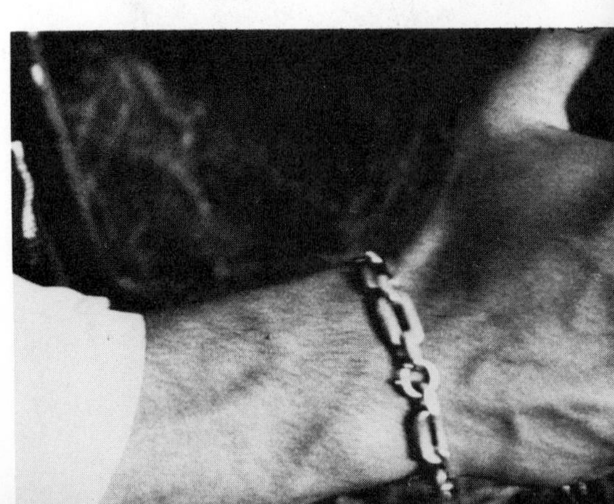

PICTURE		SOUND
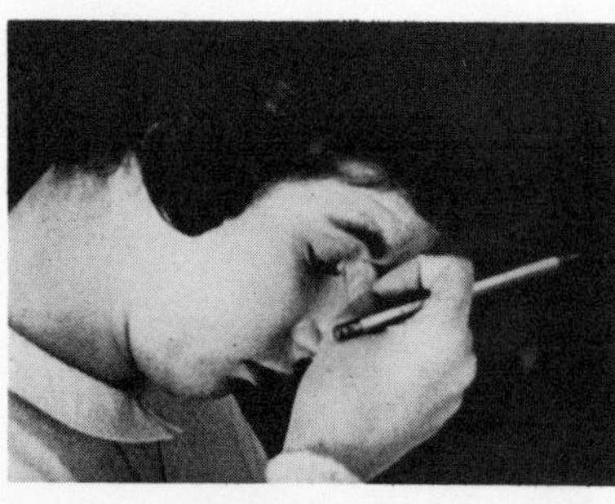	**23.** CU, girl's hand on test. Camera tilts up to her face, hand on nose, thinking (2½ sec.).	
	**24.** MCU, boy writing (1 sec.).	
	**25.** MCU, girl writing. Camera zooms in quickly (¾ sec.).	
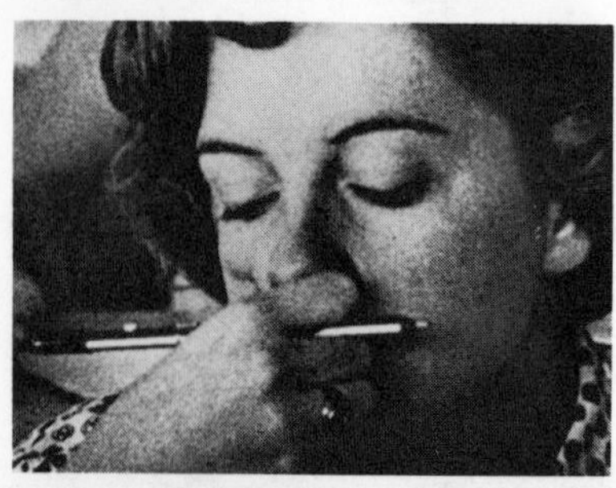	**26.** CU, girl thinking. Camera zooms in quickly (¾ sec.).	
	**27.** MCU, boy thinking. Camera tilts down quickly to show girl thinking (2 sec.).	

	PICTURE	SOUND
	28. CU, boy thinking (1 sec.).	
	**29.** XCU, clock as second hand swings straight up (4 sec.).	Music fades out as second hand approaches 12. SFX: Bell rings as second hand reaches 12.
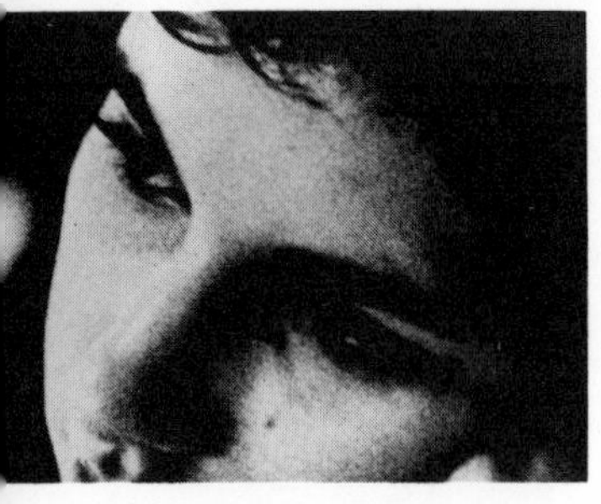	**30.** CU, girl gazing into space. Camera zooms back slowly to MCU as she begins to talk (6 sec.). *DISSOLVE*	Bell slowly changes to long, low, pensive note, then fades under: GIRL: Everybody realizes how important these are . . .
	31. MLS, students leaving the school.	. . . and when they leave they tend to look rather brow-beaten and harried.

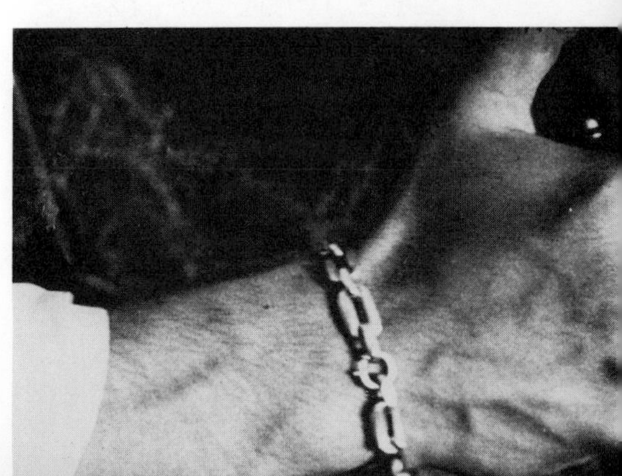

DIAGRAM 4

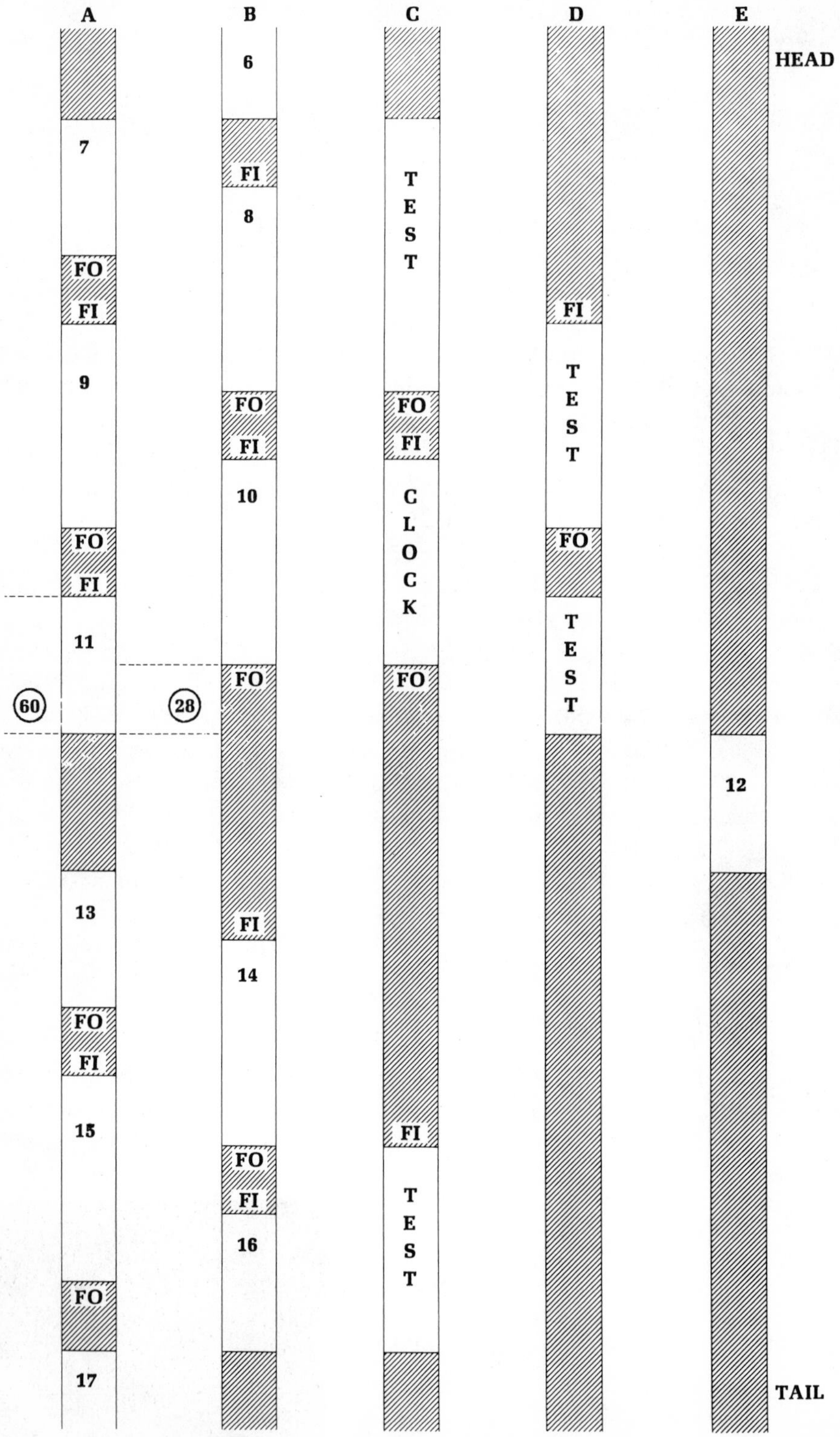

A	B	C	D	E
	6			HEAD
7	FI	TEST		
FO	8		FI	
FI				
9	FO	FO	TEST	
	FI	FI		
FO	10	CLOCK	FO	
FI				
11 (60)	FO (28)	FO	TEST	
				12
13	FI			
	14			
FO				
FI				
15	FO	FI		
	FI	TEST		
	16			
FO				
17				TAIL

To create a sense of what the students are going through during the test, the producers superimposed over the shots of students taking the test images of the test itself and of time passing on the exam-room clock.

This sequence contains a fairly complicated series of optical effects, but they are all effects which can be easily created with multiple printing rolls. The only trick is to know where in each roll to put each shot. The simplest way to figure that out is to analyze the sequence using a schematic diagram. The sequence would then break down as follows:

The test starts and the students get down to work in shots 1 through 6; these shots cut or dissolve between the *A* and *B* rolls in a normal manner. Then, after shot 6 has established that all the students are totally involved in their work, shot 7 introduces the first super, a tilt down the face of the test they are taking. This super continues over two shots, and then time begins to move ahead slowly and regularly. As each new background shot dissolves in and out on the *A* and *B* rolls, a new super of either a later portion of the test, or of the clock, dissolves in and out on the *C* and *D* rolls. Each set of dissolves is in step with the other, creating a monotonous rhythm of dissolves that matches the slow march of time in the early part of the test.

This rhythm is also reflected in both the music and the sameness of the medium close-ups that serve as the background up to shot 11. Here the closer angle signals an abrupt change of rhythm as shot 11 cuts to shot 12, and 12 to 13. There are no supers here as this section is meant to be a slight break, just as asking the question breaks the early monotony of the test. Then time plunges forward as dissolve follows on dissolve in the *A* and *B* rolls. There is also only a single super in the *C* roll, but instead of fading in as shot 15 dissolves on, it fades into 15 after the dissolve from 14 has ended. This helps maintain the quickening rhythm of this section by adding another beat to shot 15, a rhythm which is also caught in the music and the extreme changes of angle between the shots. Straight cuts, and shorter and shorter shots, then complete the sequence, rushing the test to its conclusion.

This was not a hard sequence to set up in terms of the matching involved. In almost every case, the shot to be superimposed fades in or out at the same time as the background shot. As a result, whenever there is a splice in the *A* roll, there is a splice directly across from it in the *D* roll; and when there's a splice in the *B* roll, there is a parallel splice in the *C* roll. This alignment of the splices is the result of confining all the background shots to the *A* and *B* rolls, and the supers to the other, additional printing rolls. That makes the matching quite orderly and

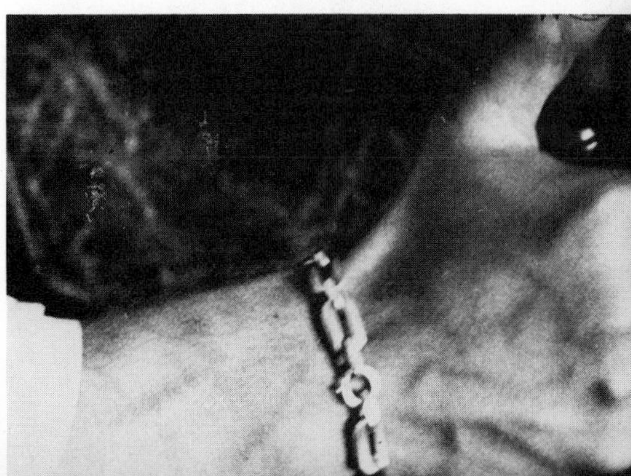

simplifies the checking of each piece of original against the workprint after the matching is completed.

An important exception, however, is shot 12. This shot had to be placed in yet a fifth, or *E,* roll because the straight cut at the beginning of this shot was too close to the dissolve leading into shot 11. The effects in this sequence are thirty-two frames long. But shot 11 has only sixty frames (circled on diagram on page 542), and thirty-two of these are overlapped by the dissolve from shot 10. Had shot 12 been put in the *B* roll, there would have been only twenty-eight frames of black leader (also circled in diagram on page 542) between the end of the fade-out in shot 10 and the straight cut to 12. This is not enough leader for the shutter to re-open and give shot 12 a full exposure from the start. Normally, shot 12 would then be moved to the *C* or *D* roll, but there is also no place for this shot in either of these rolls. At this same point in the *C* roll the shutter is still partially closed from the previous fade-out, and in the *D* roll there already is another piece of original. So an *E* roll is necessary if shot 12 is to be printed with a full exposure from the start and without any splice marks showing.

Completing the Matching

These, then, are all the many considerations involved in *A&B*-roll matching. While these procedures may at first seem complicated, they are not difficult to master with a little practice. And once they are understood, it is a great deal easier to plan simple optical effects and mark them into the workprint. Then the matching can proceed with full confidence that the marks in the workprint are an accurate guide to what must be done with the original.

When the matching is completed, attach the same kinds of leaders to the tail of each roll as were put at the head. First add two to three feet of black leader to each roll, then sixteen to twenty feet of white leader. Next, punch a synchronizing mark about six feet from the end of each white leader and label this punch mark "tail sync." The long leader and the punch mark are necessary because the laboratory will print some of the rolls from the tail to the head. This procedure eliminates having to rewind the raw stock after each roll is printed.

At the very end of the white leader, also write in the name of the roll (*A, B, C,* etc.), the type of original (B&W or color, negative or reversal), and the name of the film and the film-maker. These markings will identify the roll if it is left wound tails out. The information should be written on the emulsion side of the leader with either a standard fountain pen containing waterproof ink or a felt-tip pen specially designed for this purpose. These special pens can be obtained from most motion-picture suppliers. However, the writing must be on the emulsion side. If it is on the base side the ink can't soak in and it will be removed the first time the film is cleaned.

The final step in the matching is to check each piece of the original against the workprint. While slowly rewinding the printing rolls back through the synchronizer, make sure that the edge numbers on the original and the workprint match, that all the straight cuts line up, that the optical effects aren't too close to the straight cuts, and that all the fades and dissolves are labeled. When the rolls are completely rewound, label the punch marks in the head leaders "head sync"; then write all the same information on the beginning of each head leader as was written on the tail leader. Now the picture rolls are ready for printing.

Creating Effects in the Camera

A&B-roll printing from 8mm originals is still not very common. Instead, the most widely distributed 8mm films are reduction-printed from 16mm or 35mm originals. This procedure permits a wide variety of professional camera and editing equipment to be used throughout the production, and a large-size original gives the best possible image quality in the finished print. As a result, there simply isn't a large enough volume of work in 8mm for most laboratories to own an 8mm printer that can produce optical effects. Any 8mm printer can print an 8mm original that has been checkerboarded to conceal the splices, but a printer must have a fader mechanism to produce fades and dissolves.

However, a film-maker needn't abandon the lower costs and greater convenience of 8mm production if he wishes to use optical effects in his film. He must just use the techniques that were used to create optical effects before our present, highly sophisticated printers were developed. That is, the effects must be created in the camera. In fact, every effect we now create in the printer was once created in the camera. The only difference is that, if a mistake is made when an optical effect is created in the printer, only the effect need be done over. The original itself is not affected. But when an error is made while an effect is being created in the camera, both the effect and all the rest of the original in the shot must be repeated. This duplication can be difficult and time consuming if the shots in a dissolve, for instance, take place in widely separated locations—and impossible if the events cannot be repeated at all.

In-Camera Fades

The simplest possible effect to create in the camera is a fade-out or a fade-in. These effects can be created with any camera on which the *f* stops can be set manually. Then all that need be done is to stop down the lens to create a fade-out or open it from the stopped down position to create a fade-in. This technique is easiest to use when shooting with the lens almost wide open, since there will then be a great decrease in exposure when the lens is at its smallest *f* stop. Conversely, this kind of fade will be almost impossible outdoors in bright sunlight, since even

with very slow film the lens will already be stopped down at least halfway. Under such bright conditions the image will darken but won't go black.

If the camera is equipped with a variable shutter, a fade-out or a fade-in can be made under any light conditions. No matter what the *f* stop, as long as the shutter is completely closed, no light can reach the film. Slowly opening or closing the shutter will then provide a smooth transition into or out of darkness. Some cameras with variable shutters also have mechanisms that automatically close or open the shutter over a predetermined number of frames. These devices can usually be set to give fades of various lengths.

Another alternative, especially when shooting in bright sunlight with a camera that has a fixed shutter, is to pan from brightly lit action to a very deep shadow. Since the exposure is set for the bright area, no details will register when the camera is pointing into a dark area. This same effect is used in a shot from the experimental film *Terminus* by Walter Pfister and Richard Mansfield. When the hero of the film gets lost on the New York City subway system, we look over his shoulder as he stares out the front window of the train while it starts its plunge underground.

In this case the screen goes dark as soon as the train enters the tunnel, creating a transition to a dream sequence in which the man imagines his own death on the streets of New York.

A fade-out or a fade-in can also be created by means of the iris effect so popular in the old, silent films. One example is this irised close-up, which is used to isolate the central figure in the early German silent classic, *The Cabinet of Dr. Caligari.* This effect is created by placing a photographic diaphragm, also called

an *iris,* immediately in front of the lens so that it registers on the film as a circular, out-of-focus shadow. This diaphragm is exactly like the one used inside the lens to control the amount of light reaching the film. It can be completely closed and then slowly opened until it is outside the field of view, creating an iris-in; or it can be slowly closed at the end of a shot to create an iris-out. This sort of effect has to be used with care, however, since years of use in silent films have left it indelibly associated with the sentimental stories of that period. Of course, if the object is to evoke the feelings of those early films, as in François Truffaut's *The Wild Child,* the effect can be used to advantage.

In-Camera Dissolves

A somewhat more complicated optical effect is the in-camera dissolve. The effect is created by fading out the first shot in the dissolve, and then backing up the film to the start of the fade-out and fading in the second shot. Obviously, this technique requires a camera with a device for winding back the film and a frame counter so that there is some way to know exactly how far the film has been backwound. Until recently, only a few 16mm cameras had such equipment. Now, however, some of the more expensive super 8mm cameras have automatic mechanisms that close the shutter and count the length of the fade-out so that, once the film is wound back, the shutter can be reopened over the same number of frames.

A dissolve not only serves as a transition between two different shots; it can also be used to make people or objects appear or disappear within the same shot. In *Potemkin,* for instance, there is a shot in which Eisenstein wished to show the quiet, early morning streets of Kiev quickly filling with people going to work. He did this by means of a long, in-camera dissolve. First he made a shot of a steep flight of empty steps, with a long fade-out at the end of the take. Then, without the camera's being moved, the film was wound back to the start of the fade and the exact same shot faded in as a crowd descended the steps. This frame is from the center of that dissolve.

In the film this dissolve serves as a pivotal transition between shots of empty streets and shots of crowded streets. It could not have been made in a printer, though, because the two halves of the dissolve might not have overlapped perfectly due to slight changes in the size of the film during processing. This change in film size would cause a slight shifting of the image of the steps during the dissolve and ruin the illusion. But as long as the camera remained firmly anchored in place, there

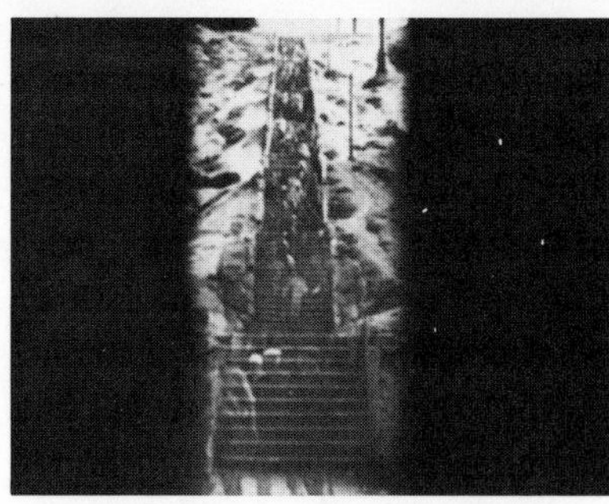

could be no shift in the image. The same piece of film run through the same camera mechanism would overlap, or *register,* the images perfectly.

In-camera dissolves become especially difficult when the overlapping shots occur in widely separated locations or at widely separated times. In such cases, the camera may be tied up for a long period until the dissolve is completed. These effects are also difficult because the dissolve must be completed before any retakes can be made. And any mistakes will not show up until after the film is processed. These problems can be eliminated, however, if each half of the dissolve is shot as a simple fade-out or fade-in. Then, when the original is made up into *A&B* rolls, the fade-out can be overlapped with the fade-in to create the dissolve. This process eliminates the need for an 8mm printer with a fading mechanism and simplifies the creation of the dissolve.

Superimpositions

Since a dissolve is really nothing more than a short superimposition, these same techniques can also be used to create longer supers by means of double exposure. When a super is created in the camera, the whole shot is backwound after the first exposure and then reexposed to another scene. However, both shots in the super must contain light images against a dark background. If the film is exposed to light from the background, a second image will not register clearly because the whole frame has already been exposed to light. Also, if the images overlap, each shot will have to be underexposed so that the total exposure for both shots doesn't exceed the normal exposure for only one of them. Otherwise, the areas of overlap will be badly overexposed, having received twice the normal amount of light.

In-camera supers offer all the same drawbacks as in-camera dissolves, plus the additional problem that it is nearly impossible to know where particular actions fall in the unprocessed footage, so synchronizing the two images becomes extremely difficult. As a result, it is usually much easier to shoot the super on separate pieces of film; then they can be *A&B*-printed on top of each other. This procedure also eliminates exposure problems since each shot can be fully exposed in the camera and the exposure then rebalanced in the printer by a reduction of the printing light. In addition, if the film is being shot with a cartridge-loading super 8mm camera, double exposure in the printer offers the only way to produce long superimpositions since super 8mm cartridges cannot be backwound more than ninety frames.

However, double exposures can be made in the printer only if the scenes to be superimposed are shot in certain ways, and those, in turn, depend upon the camera stock being used. When the film is shot on a reversal original, the lightest areas are clear and pass the most light. Therefore, when a print is made from a reversal original a very light area will saturate the print with light to the point where nothing more can be printed into that area of the frame. In a negative original just the reverse is true. Light areas are dark in a negative and dark areas clear. This means that when a negative is printed the dark areas pass the most light, saturating the print with light to the point where nothing else will register in that area of the frame.

In other words, when printing a super with a reversal original, any light image can be printed into a dark area, but no image will register in a very light area. And as would be expected, with negative originals any dark image can be printed into a light area, but an image will not register in a very dark area. The practical effect of this difference can be seen in two examples of superimposition from two different films. The first is from *Cosmic Ray,* an experimental film shot by Bruce Conner on color reversal film. In this shot a woman's torso against a black background has

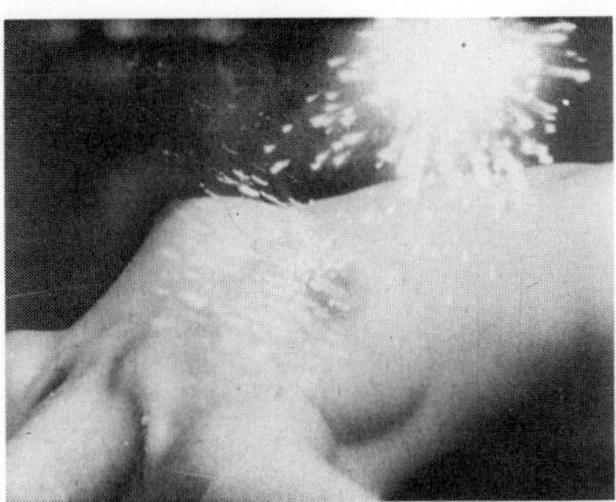

been double-printed with fireworks against a night sky. Since the light images passed the most light, they printed into the dark areas of the frame. And where the two images overlap, the lighter one, that of the fireworks, dominates. In the other example, a dissolve from the NBC documentary *Battle of the Bulge,* the reverse effect can be seen. This film was shot on B&W negative. As a result, where the shot of the general's face overlaps the snow in the other shot, his features and the dark background dominate. But where he overlaps the darker soldiers, they dominate.

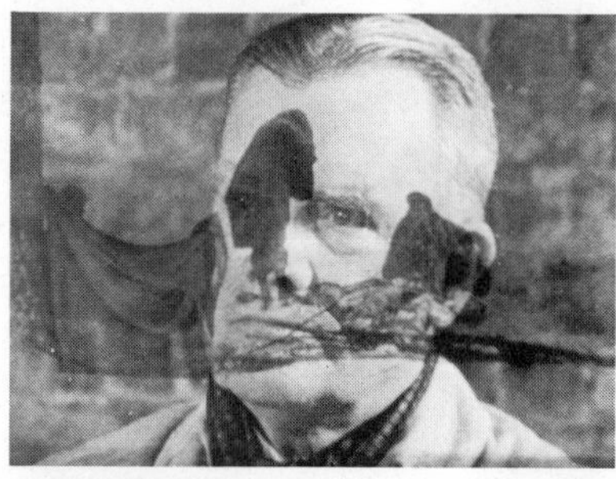

In this dissolve the relationship between light and dark worked out quite effectively. The general was talking about the plight of his troops and the brief superimposition makes them literally seem to be on his mind. However, if this same dissolve had been printed from a reversal original, his features would have first appeared only within the dark areas represented by the soldiers and the tent, with the shape of his head not appearing until the very end of the dissolve. This would not have been so powerful an effect as the one that in fact occurred.

The Optical Bench

Fades, dissolves, and superimpositions are basic to most film-making because they are relatively easy to create both in the camera and in a printer. But they hardly exhaust the range of special optical effects used in professional motion pictures. There is, in fact, no limit to the variety of optical effects that can be created, given the time and skill, on an optical bench. While little understood and rarely talked about outside the industry, optical bench photography is central to a great deal of professional film-making. It is used to create the many unusual transitions and trick effects which professional directors have come to depend upon as part of their art.

At its simplest an optical bench is little more than a horizontal animation stand on which original footage can be rephotographed a frame at a time. At one

Optical printer. The projector, left, illuminates the original, which is rephotographed by the camera on the right.

end of the bench there is an animation camera and at the other a projector. The camera lens is precisely aligned with and focused upon the projector gate, and the two machines are synchronized so that each time a frame of processed film is pulled into the projector gate, another frame of raw stock is pulled into the camera gate, ready to be exposed. The result is a form of camerawork halfway between animation and printing.

With this basic equipment it is possible to change or correct original footage by rephotographing only part of each frame, by zooming in on or out from a detail in a scene, by straightening or tilting a shot, by reshooting the footage last-frame-first so as to reverse the action, or by repeatedly photographing the same frame, called *freeze-framing,* in order to stop the action. It is also possible to use this equipment to combine several different pieces of original into new images. This can be done in the form of transitions (dissolves, wipes, flips, etc.) or by the multiple

Courtesy: JANUS FILMS, INC.

printing of the images to form a new shot. Multiple printing produces such effects as this split-screen multiple image from the NBC documentary *Confrontation;* the superimposed titles, including this director's title, from *The Lady Vanishes;* or this nearly impossible-to-detect double printing of a bird in a scene from *Citizen Kane.*

Almost every feature film has several shots that were done on an optical bench, and this kind of camerawork is becoming common even in 16mm documentary, commercial, and educational films. But only a few major studios own their own optical benches. Because even a basic bench is expensive, and the skills required to use it quite complex, most optical camerawork is taken to an independent optical house in the same manner as processing and printing are taken to a film laboratory.

Other In-Camera Optical Effects

However, any number of simple effects normally done on an optical bench can also be done in the camera. Take, for example, this shot of the heroine of Robert Bresson's *The Trial of Joan of Arc.* It is filmed from the point of view of a man who is spying on her through a hole in the stone wall of her cell. While the shot of the man was made by placing the actor behind a hole cut in the

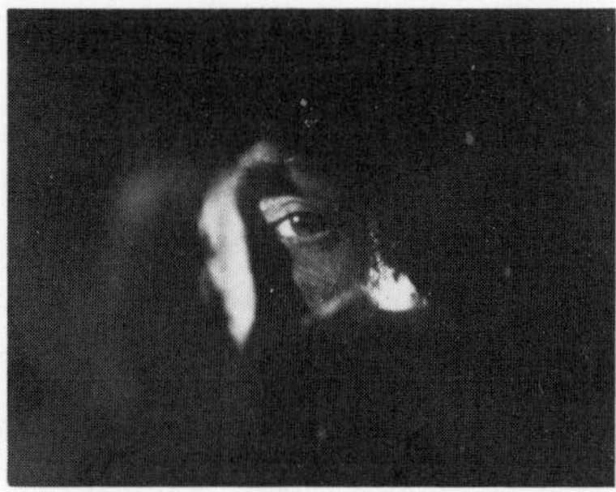

wall of the set, the other shot was probably made by filming the girl through the same shape cut in a black card mounted immediately in front of the lens. Because the card is so close to the lens, it produces a black, out-of-focus silhouette around her image on the film. This black card is called a *matte,* and many professional cameras still have a *matte box,* a slot just behind the sunshade into which these mattes can be inserted.

Mattes can also be used to produce two different images in the same frame. An example of this is this double image from the end of D. W. Griffith's silent classic *The Birth of a Nation*. In this shot the hero, finally reunited with his true love, happily tells her his golden dreams for the future of the war-ravaged South. The image of

the two of them talking was filmed through a semicircular matte cutout. Then the film was rewound and the rather exotic image of a rebuilt city filmed through another matte with a cutout in the opposite corner of the frame. Each matte thus

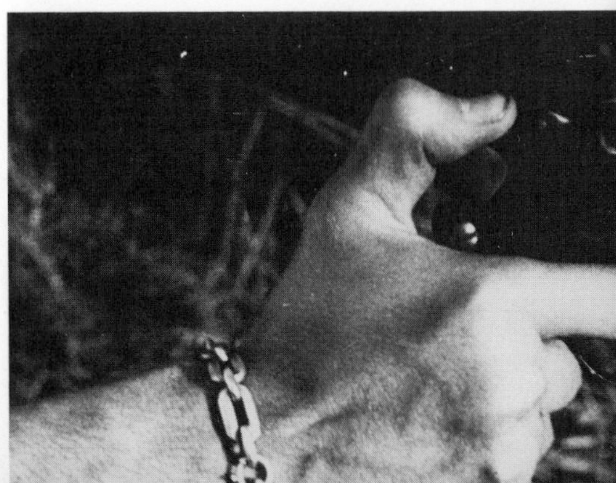

allowed a selected part of the frame to be exposed to light while covering the rest of the frame.

This same technique can be used to create a *split screen*. This is used, for instance, to show both ends of a telephone conversation simultaneously. However, the difference between this double image and the previous one is that here each image fully occupies half the screen. This effect is created by using the same, straight-edged matte to alternately mask a different half of the frame as each image is exposed. After the first exposure the film is rewound and the matte carefully moved to the other side by pivoting it on the edge that splits the frame. Then the second image will butt up against the first without overlapping it.

Exactly the same split-screen technique can also be used to film such trick shots as someone holding a conversation with himself. Because the out-of-focus edge of the matte creates a blurred junction between the two halves of the image, if the camera is kept firmly anchored in place for both exposures, the background will be continuous across the junction. This illusion can be further perfected if the actor doesn't reach or cross over into the matted part of the frame and if the matte edge is aligned with some vertical object that stretches across the frame—with the corner of a room, for instance, or a tree trunk.

Title Mattes

Mattes can be used to create somewhat more complicated effects, such as superimposed titles, if just the image created by the matte itself is shot on a separate piece of film. This produces a high-contrast B&W image of the matte that can be superimposed over any normal piece of B&W or color original by means of *A&B*-roll printing. Mattes created by this method are a form of what is called a *traveling matte*. These are mattes that both travel through the printer with the original and also sometimes travel around within the frame, masking off different parts of the image from frame to frame.

This traveling-matte technique is most commonly used to superimpose titles over a background scene. The matte itself consists of clear letters on a black background. When this matte is printed over the image from the background scene, only the clear letters pass any light. But these clear letters pass so much light that the image of the letters saturates the print and bleaches out the details of the background scene; these are called *burn-in* titles.

There are a number of ways to shoot the mattes for burn-in titles. One way is to film black letters on a white card using high-contrast B&W negative film. The exposure should be set so that the white area of the title card is overexposed by about one *f* stop. This overexposure, in conjunction with special high-contrast processing, will result in a very dense black background. And since there will be no detectable exposure from the black letters, they will end up as clear areas.

It is also possible to film the title mattes on any normal B&W reversal film. However, instead of filming a black card with white letters, have the titles produced on a transparency as clear letters on a black background. This process is routinely done by any print shop that provides titles and overlays for the advertising industry. The transparency is then filmed while it is in front of a light box. This is much easier than filming a black card because a card has to be illuminated from the front and any dirt or dust on it is lit along with the letters. The dust or dirt then shows up as white specks on the black background. But with a transparency the light comes from behind so the surface dirt is never illuminated and only the clear letters have to be kept clean.

In order to have enough flexibility in positioning the titles when shooting on negative, have the title cards printed so that there are very wide borders all around the lettering. Then the title can be positioned in any part of the frame without the frame line's extending beyond the edge of the card. Size is less of a problem when a transparency is shot on reversal film, however, because the transparency only has to be big enough to cover the face of the light box. And since just the letters are lit, it doesn't matter if the edge of the frame extends beyond the edge of the transparency. When that happens, just darken the room so that blackness surrounds the edges of the light box.

When title mattes are printed into a film shot on B&W or color reversal original, the letters print white; and when they are printed into a film shot on B&W or color negative, the letters print black. This means that when the background scene is shot on reversal materials, the titles must be framed so that they fall into a dark area, and on negative in a light area. Look, for instance, at how the titles are positioned in *Fairground,* a student film by Victor Nunez. The main title fades in

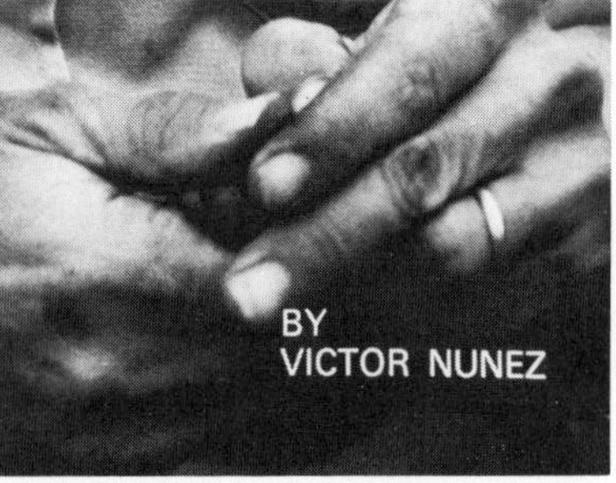

over a shot of a woman putting on a dark sweater over a white blouse. Since the film was shot on reversal stock, the titles print white. Therefore, until her sweater is on, not all the letters are visible. This problem doesn't occur with the director's title, however, because it has been positioned in the dark area below the hands.

Other Matte Techniques

The same matte technique used to produce titles can also be used to superimpose other shapes. For example, in this shot from Adolfus Mekas's *Hallelujah the Hills,* a rectangle was printed around the film's two protagonists. This rectangle simultaneously creates two different senses of the space they occupy. One, created

Courtesy: JANUS FILMS, INC.

by the normal frame line, is of distant and insignificant figures in an open landscape; the other, created by the rectangle, focuses our attention on two characters whose presence and actions are more important than their surroundings. The matte from which this effect was printed contained a clear rectangular outline on a black background. When this matte was printed over the image from the original negative of the background scene, the rectangle printed black. Since it was superimposed in a medium-to-light area of the scene, it shows up quite clearly.

In another part of the same film, Mekas also uses a matte to alter the shape of the frame. In this case, the effect simulates the proportions of a wide-screen spec-

Courtesy: JANUS FILMS, INC.

tacular in order to heighten the humor of playing banderillero to a herd of cows. He created this new shape by shooting a matte with a solid black rectangle across the middle of the frame. When this was superimposed over the image from the original negative, the upper and lower edges of the image were blacked out. This effect can be obtained only with negative originals, however, since printing a matte over the image from a reversal original would produce glaring white borders. But at least with negative originals this technique opens up the possibility of using mattes to create a dynamic frame. In other words, various-shaped mattes can be used throughout the film to give the frame any shape or proportion the film-maker desires.

Animated Titles

All of the matte effects discussed so far can also be made to move. This movement is created by using simple animation techniques. Animation, however, requires a camera with a single-frame mechanism, a device for accurately exposing and advancing the film one frame at a time. This device permits the material in front of the camera, and/or the camera itself, to be moved slightly after each exposure so that when a series of these single frames is projected there is the effect of continuous motion.

Animation also requires a camera mount that permits the camera to point straight down. Then objects can be moved in front of the lens without having to be fastened in place for each exposure. The force of gravity keeps them where they belong. In addition, the camera mount must be quite steady. If the camera makes any unplanned movements between exposures, objects which are supposed to remain stationary from one frame to the next will jump about erratically in the finished footage. Both these conditions can usually be met, however, by mounting the camera on such inexpensive and readily available devices as a still-camera copy stand, a photographic enlarger from which the enlarging head has been removed, or even just a tripod firmly fixed in place over a low table.

Single-framing is relatively simple because it is entirely mechanical. What can become quite involved, though, is designing the movements between each exposure. In full-fledged animation these movements are usually complicated. This complexity is what makes animation such a technical art. But animation need not be complex to be effective, and simple animation can be designed with little more than common sense and some basic arithmetic.

The simplest kind of animation involves nothing more than having things pop on or off the screen instantaneously. This technique can be used to build both regular and superimposed titles a word or a letter at a time, to superimpose moving objects or shapes within a shot, or to create simple animated sequences. This technique is the basis, for instance, for one of the more humorous transitional sequences

in the children's television series *Sesame Street*. In this sequence dots appear, one at a time, to the beat of a simple march until the screen is filled with rows of dots. However, each time the sequence is repeated one of the dots finds a different way to break the rhythm, thus poking gentle fun at clever dots that can't behave themselves.

This kind of *pop-on* animation is produced by putting the first word, letter, or object in place and shooting a number of single frames, then putting the second in place and exposing another series of frames, and so on until everything is in place. The exact number of single frames to shoot for each item depends upon how fast the action should develop. For example, in a four-word title each word might pop on at one-second intervals and then the whole title remain on the screen for an additional three seconds. This means that, for a film that is supposed to run at 24 fps, the shutter must be released twenty-four times for the first word, then the second word put in place and the shutter released another twenty-four times, and so on through the first three words. The fourth word is then shot seventy-two times to give the final three seconds of the completed title.

In somewhat more complicated animation, letters, words, shapes, or objects tumble, drift, or slide into place. These effects are filmed in the same manner as pop-on animation except that the movements and their calculation are more complex. For instance, with the same four-word title the words could slide left, one at a time, across the screen and into position. In other words, the first word would be slid slightly to the left after each exposure until it was in place, then the same thing with the second word, and so on through all four.

If this piece of animation was supposed to last the same six seconds as the previous example, the movement itself would take only four seconds. This would leave two seconds for the completed title to remain on the screen at the end of the shot. To calculate the distance each word would have to be moved between each single frame, divide the distance all the words were supposed to move by four seconds times 24 fps, or 96. That means that if the total distance to be covered by all the words was thirty-six inches, each word would have to be moved left three eighths of an inch between each single frame. Calculating the movements in this way gives a constant speed to the movement of the words. As a result, some words will take longer to cross the screen than others. For instance, a word that has to move twelve inches will require thirty-one frames, or about one and a half seconds, to cover the distance, while one that has to move only six inches will require half the number of frames, or three quarters of a second.

The speed of the words can be varied in a predetermined way, however, if each word is allotted one second, or twenty-four frames, to move into position. Then a word that must move twelve inches will have to move twice as fast as one that moves only six inches during the same twenty-four frames. This means that the word which moves twelve inches will have to be moved left one-half inch between each frame if it is to cover the distance in one second ($12/24 = 1/2$); while the word that has to move only six inches will be moved only half as far, or one-quarter inch, between frames if it is to take the same twenty-four frames to cover half as much distance. This, in turn, will make its speed half that of the previous word.

To sum this all up then, if the speed of the movements is to vary, divide the distance covered by each separate movement by the time allotted for it to occur;

and if the speed is to be constant, divide the total distance of all the movements by the total time allotted them.

Reverse-action Filming

The most difficult part of animating words and letters, or any other objects that are supposed to end up in a straight line, is getting them all properly aligned at the end of the shot. Even if each is properly positioned after its movement is completed, it can still inadvertently shift as the other words or objects are being animated. This problem can be minimized, however, if the animation is shot in reverse. This is done by turning either the artwork or the camera upside down and doing all the animation backwards, last movement first. Then the completed title or design can be carefully aligned and lightly rubber-cemented in place before the shooting starts.

Of course, the action must again be reversed, and the image turned right side up, when the animation is printed into the film. This is done by turning the original head for tail and splicing it into the printing roll last frame first. This procedure, however, creates the further requirement that the animation be shot on double-perforated camera stock. Turning single-perforated footage end for end would place its sprocket holes on the opposite edge from those in all the rest of the printing roll, and this odd piece of original would then get chewed up in the printer. Since there is no such thing as double-perforated 8mm film, reverse animation cannot be done in 8mm.

This same technique can also be used to reverse live action. While such reversals are usually done by rephotographing the action, last frame first, on an optical bench, they can just as easily be done in-camera. Simply load the camera with double-perforated film, turn the camera upside down when the film is shot, and then turn the footage around for printing. And if it doesn't matter if the printed image is upside down, any normal piece of double-perforated footage can be reversed this way too. For instance, in the nightmarish wedding dance sequence from René Clair's *An Italian Straw Hat* (Chapter Two, p. 60), the climactic shot is of the hero's house collapsing. What Clair needed, however, was not just the collapse but the resulting cloud of dust. Then he could dissolve through the dust to a shot of the hero's acute distress at his imagined misfortune. The shot Clair used was one in which a collapsing doorway created a great dust cloud. But using it right way around would have shown the densest dust-fall at the beginning, just as the arch gives way, and not at the end, where the dissolve occurs. So, since the shot is short

and the details obscured by dust, Clair ran it upside down, placing the dust cloud at the end.

This reverse-action technique can also be combined with a matte effect, as was done in this shot from Mekas's *Hallelujah the Hills*. In this case the two effects combine to make the man diving for cover behind the tombstone look as if he were being blown out of his hiding place. Mekas probably had these effects pro-

Courtesy: JANUS FILMS, INC.

duced on an optical bench. But they could also have been created by first filming the action with the camera upside down, and then applying a commercially prepared stick-on effect to a series of frames. Since these opaque designs keep the printer light from reaching the part of the print immediately behind them, the effect prints black on reversal originals and white, as it does above, from negative originals. This is the reverse of an effect exposed from a traveling matte.

All the techniques mentioned so far can be combined, as they were in the previous example, to create any number of interesting and unusual optical effects. And even these combinations do not exhaust the possible number of ways that optical effects can be created without an optical bench. But there are still limits to what can be done in the camera and in a printer; and there are also much more mechanical uses for an optical bench for which there are no substitutes.

Optical Printers

One of the more important of these mechanical functions is to enlarge 8mm original to 16mm, and 16mm to 35mm. Then shots made in 8mm and 16mm can be cut into films made on larger-sized materials, or whole films can be enlarged so that they can be shown in a theater. This has become relatively common with 16mm originals since it greatly reduces the cost of film and processing during the original shooting without too great a reduction in the quality of the finished film. As a result, there are optical benches specifically designed for making enlargements called *optical step printers*. These printers are usually fitted with what is called a *liquid gate,* a special film gate on the projector that circulates a colorless fluid around each frame of original as it is being rephotographed. This liquid fills in the scratches and eliminates the dirt that would otherwise be printed into the enlarged copy and greatly magnified on the screen.

Optical step printers can also be used to reduce 16mm or 35mm originals to 8mm or 16mm. Then prints of films originally shot on large-size materials can be sold more cheaply and shown on the small projectors commonly available outside the theaters. Of course, reduction printing is a lot less delicate than enlarging. Since the smaller prints are seldom projected on as large a screen as big prints, small printing defects are not easily noticed. Therefore, continuous optical reduction printers have been developed. While not quite as accurate as step printing, continuous optical printing has the same advantage as continuous contact printing—far greater speed.

As its name implies, a continuous optical reduction printer simply runs the

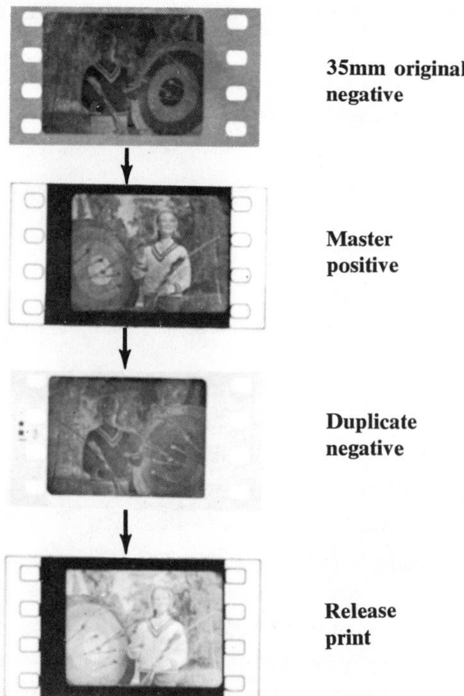
35mm original negative
Master positive
Duplicate negative
Release print

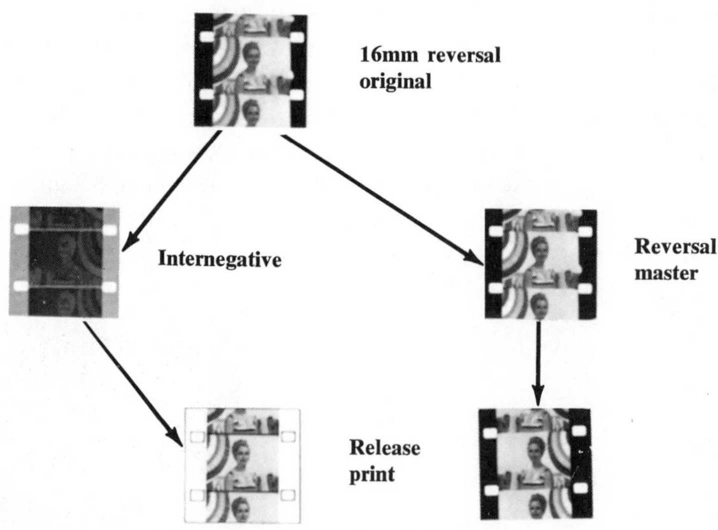
16mm reversal original
Internegative
Reversal master
Release print

original through the printer gate without stopping it for each frame. The light coming through the original is then gathered by a lens system and relayed to another part of the printer, where it is focused down onto a smaller piece of film running at the same number of frames per second as the original. In its simplest form, a reduction printer makes one row of smaller frames from a single strip of larger ones. This process is very inefficient, however, when a large number of prints have to be made, so the newer reduction printers produce two or four rows of smaller frames across a wide piece of raw stock each time the original is passed through the printer.

Duplicating Materials

This kind of multiple-rank printing offers the great advantage of cutting printing and processing time by a half or three quarters. This, in turn, not only reduces the cost of the prints, but saves wear and tear on the valuable original from which the prints are made. However, yet another step is introduced into the printing procedure when a particularly large number of prints are to be released, because wearing out the original becomes a real possibility even when the prints are made four at a time. This additional step involves making an *internegative* or a *reversal master,* a duplicate of the original that can be used to make the prints in place of the original.

These intermediary copies, called *duplicating materials,* are made of all originals from which a large number of prints must be produced. Of course, making prints from a copy doesn't produce as high-quality results as making prints from the original. But once an original is worn out, nothing more can be done, while if a duplicate wears out, another copy can always be made. Because of the loss of quality, making duplicating materials is an art in itself and there are almost as many ways of making them as there are types of film stocks. Typically, however, a feature film shot on 35mm negative original is copied onto a master positive. This positive contains all the optical effects and corrections in the color balance and density of each shot. The positive is then used to make as many duplicate negatives as are needed to print the film. This makes the release print the fourth generation.

A somewhat different procedure is followed with 16mm originals because they cannot stand as many duplications. Since most 16mm films are shot on reversal original, either a reversal master is made on reversal duplicating film or an internegative is made on negative duplicating stock. The reversal master is then printed onto a reversal release-print material or the internegative onto a positive

release-print stock. Either way, the final print is then only two generations away from the original.

Quality considerations also govern the choice of duplicating materials used in reduction printing from 16mm and 35mm originals. One can generally obtain the best results by keeping the duplicating materials as large as possible until the final print is made. This means making full-sized intermediate copies and then reduction-printing as the final step. However, such rapid advances are being made in this area that it is now also possible to reduce the size of the original directly to a multirank 8mm or 16mm internegative by optical printing. This can then be continuously contact-printed to produce the release prints with great savings in both time and money.

The size and type of audience for which the film is designed will determine the procedures used to print the film. But these procedures can only be arrived at in consultation with the laboratory that will actually do the work because, just as there are film studios that specialize in certain kinds of film-making, so are there laboratories that specialize in certain kinds of printing and processing. While most laboratories can make workprints and continuous contact prints, only some have the equipment and skilled personnel necessary for optical blowups or reduction printing. And even within these specialized areas, one laboratory will use one procedure for which it has the equipment and experience, and another will follow quite another procedure that it has perfected. The film-maker has to learn for himself what he can expect from each laboratory and then determine his own quality standards for the finished prints.

Preparing the Sound Track for Printing

Along with the printing procedures, the laboratory will also determine how the sound track must be duplicated and printed. If the magnetic master is to be transferred to optical sound for printing alongside the pictures, the laboratory will normally provide the exact specifications for this optical track and see to it that the transfer is made to their specifications. Then all the film-maker need do, once the transfer is made, is punch a synchronizing mark in the head leader of the optical-sound original.

This is a very simple operation. The thousand-cycle tone at the head of the magnetic master will reproduce as one frame of squiggly lines in an otherwise straight line at the beginning of the optical-sound original. This synchronizing point is in the same position in the track as the punch mark in the head leader of the workprint. But this sync point is not used to print the track because an optical sound track has to be advanced twenty frames in 35mm, twenty-six frames in 16mm, or twenty-two frames in super 8mm for the track to be synchronized with the pictures when the release print is projected on a standard projector. So, in order to get the track ready for printing, count the required number of frames back from the thousand-cycle synchronizing "beep" and mark the frame with a grease pencil. Next, lock the optical-sound negative and workprint in a synchronizer so that the marked frame is aligned with the sound-sync punch mark in the workprint. Then roll both strands toward the head until the "head sync" of the workprint is in the synchronizer. At this point punch the optical-sound negative and mark it *Printer Sync* so that the lab technician will know that the punch mark is the correct synchronizing point for printing the optical sound track.

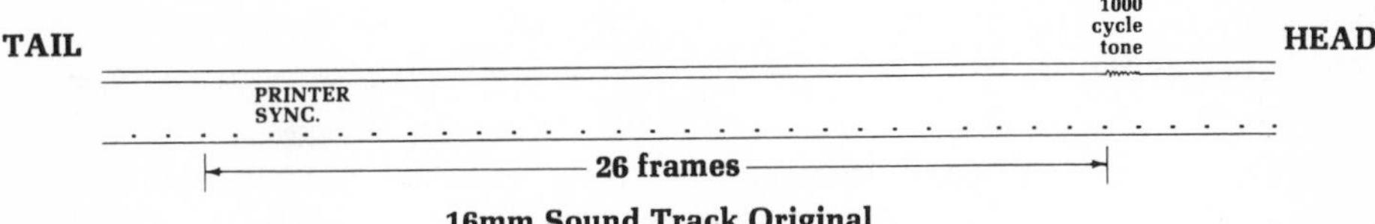

16mm Sound Track Original

It is also possible for some laboratories to make an optical sound track from the magnetic stripe on a workprint. Of course, the quality of the sound on a stripe is not as good as that on a sprocketed magnetic master, but it is still better than optical sound and will make an acceptable optical track. An increasing number of laboratories are also able to make an optical sound track from a quarter-inch magnetic tape by playing back the tape on a variable-speed recorder. Once the filmmaker has determined exactly how long the optical track should be, the lab technician can set the recorder to play back the tape at a speed which will result in an optical track exactly the correct length. This may change the speed of the tape, altering the pitch of the sound somewhat; but except in some of the music, the change will not be noticed.

When only one or two prints are to be made, instead of having the sound transferred to a separate optical sound-track original, it is usually easier and cheaper to have the track *electroprinted* directly onto the finished prints. In electroprinting the images are exposed onto the raw stock in a regular printer, but the magnetic track is converted to optical sound by next running the unprocessed print through an optical-sound recorder. Then picture and sound can both be processed at the same time, thus avoiding the time and expense of transferring the sound to a separate optical original.

So far, most of the sound tracks on 8mm prints are on a magnetic stripe, and a few 16mm prints are still released this way. These prints are made on prestriped raw stock with the sound transferred directly to the stripe from the magnetic master. In 16mm the distance between magnetic sound and the picture is always twenty-eight frames, and the lab technician will automatically record the sound this far in advance of the picture. But there are as yet no set standards for the sound

advance in either standard or super 8mm. While the distance between magnetic sound and picture is usually fifty-six frames in standard 8mm and eighteen frames in super 8mm, these distances can vary, especially among some of the 8mm cartridge-loading projectors. As a result, the spacing of 8mm magnetic sound and picture should always be specified in advance by the film-maker.

The Answer Print

The first print to come from the laboratory is called the *first trial print* or *answer print*. The origins of the term answer print are obscure, but it is only half-jokingly said that the name comes from the fact that this is when everyone connected with the film has to answer for his mistakes. Actually, this is the first print in which the film-maker gets to see exactly how his film will look to an audience. The laboratory usually charges 50 percent more to make the first print; this charge pays for timing it in case only a few more prints are ordered. But the laboratory will also usually pull a second answer print free of charge if they are responsible for any major errors the first time around.

The answer print is used to check the timing, the color balance, and the sound quality. In most instances mistakes in these areas can be corrected by small changes in the printer lights, the filter combinations, and the exposure given the sound track in subsequent prints. The answer print will also reveal mistakes in matching and scratches or excessive dirt on the original. Unless the laboratory did the matching or the film-maker can prove that the dirt and scratches are the laboratory's fault, these problems must usually be taken care of by the film-maker himself before more prints are made. In the case of dirt and scratches, there are specialized firms that clean the film and remove scratches, but this can get quite expensive. Last of all, the answer print may reveal weaknesses in the general concept of the film that should have been caught much earlier in production. If these are to be corrected, the workprint and the sound track will have to be recut and remixed, and a new optical-sound original made, before further prints can be pulled. That is obviously an expensive and time-consuming business, but it sometimes cannot be avoided.

As soon as the answer print has been approved, or the mistakes corrected and a second answer print accepted, the printing can begin. If an internegative is involved in the final printing, or if a large print run is contemplated, there may be further approvals involved. But these approvals must usually be stipulated by contract or the laboratory will simply go ahead and make the prints according to their own best judgment. A good laboratory will normally not do this blindly, though, and will spot-check prints throughout the print run, or even check all the prints, in high-speed inspection projectors. Once the prints are approved and delivered, and all the bills paid, the laboratory will return the original to the film-maker. He can then store this original in some safe place of his own or leave it with the laboratory for storage in their film vault. The latter is often preferable because it ensures proper storage conditions and keeps the original handy should more prints be needed in the future.

This, then, completes the film-making process. Even at its simplest, this process involves a multiplicity of skills, all of which are dependent upon a great deal of care and attention to detail. But meticulous work in the early stages of production becomes meaningless if the original is not properly handled in the final stage, the preparation of the release prints. There simply is no way to shortcut the printing process without impairing the quality of the finished product. Although this work is largely in the hands of the laboratory, ultimately it too must come under the filmmaker's control. He must learn how images are treated in the laboratory just as he learns how to create images in the camera or to assemble them in the editing room. Only then can he demand and get the results he set out to achieve.

Appendix A

Choosing and Testing a Camera

It is often difficult for a film-maker to choose among the wide variety of movie cameras now available. But making the right choice can be critical since not every camera is adaptable for shooting the various kinds of footage the film-maker may need. There are, however, systematic means both for choosing a camera and for evaluating the quality of the footage it can produce.

Film Size

Like every other decision in film-making, it is the type of footage and the style of the film-maker which determine the choice of camera. For instance, take the size film the camera must handle. If the footage is to be shown theatrically, the large size of the projected image dictates that the film be shot in 16mm or 35mm; while if the audience, and therefore the image, is to be smaller, either 8mm or 16mm will be adequate (the reasons for this are discussed in Chapter Five, pp.

282 to 283). Thus, the maximum size of the projected image almost automatically restricts the film-maker to a camera designed for the appropriate film size.

But portability is often equally as important as image quality, and the smaller the film size the smaller the camera. Given recent improvements in the quality of motion-picture film, 16mm has now become the best all-around film size for both nontheatrical and standard-format theatrical production. However, these same improvements have also led to the rapid development of super 8mm as an even more flexible alternative for small-screen professional production.

Film Length

The next consideration, after film size, is the length of film the camera should hold. This length controls both the amount of shooting that can be done before reloading and the ease with which the camera can be loaded. Most super 8mm cameras, for instance, are designed to hold a 50-foot cartridge. This length provides only two and one-half minutes of filming at 24 fps, or three and one-third minutes at 18 fps. But even though a cartridge-loading camera has to be reloaded quite often, a cartridge is still the quickest and easiest way ever invented to load a movie camera. Because the film is sealed inside a lighttight plastic shell, the camera can be reloaded anywhere—even in bright sunlight. And because the film is prealigned within the cartridge, there is no need to thread the film through the camera mechanism. All the film-maker has to do is shove the cartridge into the camera and start shooting.

Super 8mm cartridge and 16mm daylight spool.

However, in order to permit longer-running shots, some of the more complex and expensive super 8mm cameras now available use either 100- or 200-foot daylight-loading spools. Like cartridges, film on daylight spools can be loaded into the camera in normal room light since the solid metal sides of the reel keep the light from reaching the film. But daylight spools are not as easy to use as cartridges. First, the film on the spool has to be threaded through the camera mechanism, and this takes a certain amount of skill even if the camera has an automatic threading mechanism. Second, the film is protected from light only as long as it is tightly wound on the spool and there is a tendency for the film to unwind as the spool is being loaded into the camera.

Loading is further complicated if the camera uses daylight spools of double super 8mm film. Double super 8mm, while perforated with standard super 8mm sprocket-holes, is 16mm wide in order to accommodate two rows of images side by side. The first time through the camera 8mm-wide pictures are exposed along one edge of the film; then the film is run through the camera again, in the opposite direction, so that 8mm-wide pictures can be exposed along the other edge. Later, after the film is processed, the two rows of pictures are slit apart.

The advantage of double super 8mm is that twice the amount of filming can be done with the same length of film. But having two rows of images creates yet a third hazard when using daylight spools. If the film is misthreaded or somehow jams in the threading mechanism, it can scratch, tear, or jerk through the camera. And if this happens during the second pass of the film through the camera, not one, but two sets of images are apt to be damaged.

Although there are still some cartridge-loading 16mm cameras around, most of the lower-priced 16mm cameras now available use 100-foot daylight spools. This length provides three minutes of filming at 24 fps, or four and one-half minutes at 16 fps. While the small size of these spools keeps down the cost and weight of the camera, small spools also mean frequent reloading. Therefore some daylight-spool loading cameras, and all studio cameras, use the closest thing to a cartridge now available for shooting in 16mm or 35mm—the external film magazine. These magazines are large film chambers that clamp to the outside of the camera. They are designed to hold 200-, 400-, or 1,200-foot rolls of film.

Unlike a cartridge, a magazine is not purchased loaded with film. The magazine is bought empty and the film is loaded and unloaded for each day's shooting. Once the magazine is loaded, it can be attached to the camera, and the film threaded through the camera mechanism, in normal room light. But the magazine itself must be loaded and unloaded in complete darkness because the rolls of film used in

magazines are not usually supplied on spools. Instead, the film is tightly wound on a small plastic hub, or *core,* with its edges exposed. As a result, the film's only protection from light is the metal can in which it is shipped or the magazine in which it is eventually sealed, and opening either in the light will ruin the film.

However, having to load and unload the film in complete darkness is not as

Film magazine. The lighttight cover is open to show the film feeding off the left-hand core, into the camera, and then back onto the take-up core, right.

much of a problem as it might sound. If there is no darkroom available, the loading can be done in a changing bag—a large, lighttight cloth bag with elasticized, self-sealing armholes. Because a changing bag permits the magazines to be reloaded anywhere, two magazines are usually sufficient for a day's shooting. After the first one is finished, it can be reloaded as the other one is being used.

The Motor

The next most important factor, after film load, is the type of motor on the camera. Camera motors are of two kinds—either electric or spring-powered. Of these, the simplest and most reliable is the spring drive still used on a few small

16mm cameras. A spring motor can provide a wide range of frame rates, including single frame; it also permits the camera to be used in those locations in which electric power is not available for recharging the batteries of an electric motor. There are, however, a number of drawbacks to a spring drive. First, a spring can drive only eighteen to thirty feet of film through the camera on one wind, thus restricting the length of each shot. Second, the spring must be rewound after each shot or the motor may inadvertently run down and stop in the middle of a shot. And third, a spring motor doesn't run at a constant enough speed for lip-synchronous sound filming.

Because of these shortcomings, instead of using a spring drive, most movie cameras now are powered by an electric motor. These motors are of various types. The simplest, called a *DC wild motor,* is widely used on super 8mm cameras. It is a battery-driven motor that, like a spring motor, can operate over a wide range of frame rates, including single frame. In addition, one set of batteries, or a full charge on reusable batteries, will usually run the camera all day. And because of the light weight of a 50-foot super 8mm film load, even these simple motors can drive the camera at a constant enough speed for sync-sound filming.

With 16mm and 35mm cameras, however, the greater weight of the film load requires that the camera be driven by one of a number of stronger, more specialized electric motors. Again, the basic motor is a DC wild motor since this type of motor permits filming at a variety of frame rates. But the speed of these motors is not stable enough for lip-synchronous filming, so sync-sound is shot either with a *DC constant-speed motor* or, where standard electric power is available, with an *AC sync motor.* Finally, there are special motors and motor controls for single-frame or time-lapse filming.

The closest thing to a universal motor now available for 16mm and 35mm cameras is a DC constant-speed motor with crystal control. In this camera drive system the crystal provides both a highly constant speed for sync-sound filming and variable speeds over a wide range of frame rates for silent shooting. However, even this type of motor drive doesn't provide for single-framing, so 16mm and 35mm cameras with DC constant-speed motors must still have motor mounts that permit the motor to be changed if the same camera is also to be used for animation or time-lapse work.

Lenses

The hardest part of choosing a camera is picking the lens. This difficulty is

partly due to the fact that most super 8mm cameras have the lens permanently attached, so a poor quality lens can destroy the value of the entire camera. But it is a problem to evaluate a lens because this evaluation is largely a matter of subjective judgment. The only properties of a lens which can be objectively judged are focal length and maximum lens opening, and these tell nothing about the quality of the image. Nor is the most expensive lens, usually the one with the widest *f* stop, necessarily the best-quality lens. The demands made by an extra *f* stop or two of light can force serious compromises in the design of the lens. These compromises can be discovered, however, and they will be discussed shortly, in the section on testing the camera.

There are also a number of other features besides image quality that must be considered when choosing a lens. For instance, many super 8mm cameras minimize the disadvantages of a permanently mounted lens by using a zoom lens. Many of these zoom lenses are now quite as good as fixed-focal-length, or *prime,* lenses for all but extremely large screen projection, and they offer considerably more flexibility than prime lenses. The range from wide-angle to telephoto, or *zoom range,* now extends up to 20 to 1 in the most expensive zoom lenses; and even moderately priced super 8mm cameras may have 10mm to 80mm, or 7mm to 56mm (8 to 1) zoom lenses. Some of the zoom lenses now available also have a very small minimum focal length. This shorter focal length provides a wider field of view that is particularly useful when shooting in tight quarters. It is preferable for hand-held shooting since longer focal lengths magnify camera shake.

An unusual feature of some zoom lenses is *macro* focusing; that is, the ability to focus on objects that are very close to the lens. Close focusing is often desirable since it simplifies the filming of titles, animation, and an incredible variety of extreme close-ups. There are, however, two types of macro zoom lenses: one type focuses continuously from infinity to about five or six inches; the other focuses from infinity to about one foot, and from there on a separate lever is used to focus on objects that come as close to the camera as the front element of the lens itself. While it is much easier to focus on a moving object that comes right up to the camera with the continuously focusing type of lens, a dual-focus lens offers some interesting split-focus possibilities. For instance, if the two separate focusing mechanisms are used to focus on both near and distant objects, the focus can be snapped either forward or backward so that one object pops out of focus as the other becomes sharp.

Lens Mounts

Although zoom lenses are beginning to eliminate the need for shooting with a variety of lenses, a camera with a removable lens still offers several advantages. For instance, if the lenses are interchangeable, it is possible to use macro lenses, which focus closer than most zoom lenses, or prime lenses with focal lengths that are either longer or shorter than those on a zoom lens. Interchangeable lenses also make it possible to use a number of different prime lenses to shoot the critically sharp images needed for large-screen projection.

On some older-style cameras changing lenses is simplified by mounting the lenses on a *turret,* a rotating metal plate which holds from two to four lenses at a time. This arrangement allows each lens to be swung into place as it is needed. However, a movable turret is not as precise and durable a way to mount a lens as fastening the lens directly to the camera body. As a result, most studio cameras have a *hard front;* that is, one lens at a time is mounted directly to the camera itself. Also, most of the new, interchangeable-lens cameras are made without a turret because top-quality zoom lenses have eliminated the need for frequent lens changes.

Lens mounts. The threads on the "C" mount lens, L, screw into the turret of the camera on the left; the bayonet mount of the lens, R, lock into the body of the camera on the right.

There is, however, one problem. There are a number of different lens-mounting systems, so the lens must have the same type of mount as that on the camera. On 8mm and 16mm cameras the most common mounting system is the *C* mount, a standard-size threaded hole into which any lens with the same size barrel and thread can be mounted. But the *C* mount, although it furnishes adequate support for any normal size lens, is not usually strong enough for large zoom and telephoto lenses. Therefore, many top-quality cameras have specially designed, heavy-duty lens-mounting systems that are unique to each make of camera. Despite the variety of mounting systems, lenses with different types of mounts can sometimes be fitted to a particular camera by means of lens-mount adapters. These adapters also permit still-camera lenses to be used on a movie camera.

Viewfinders

The two types of viewfinders currently available are the side- or top-mounted monitor finder and through-the-lens viewing. Monitor finders, although much less precise than through-the-lens viewers, are sufficiently accurate for simple cameras and are usually found on those less-expensive super 8mm cameras which have fixed-focal-length and fixed-focus lenses. Monitor finders are also used on some of the new low-light-level super 8mm cameras because, under poor lighting conditions, the simple optical design of a monitor finder produces the brightest possible image in the viewer.

Through-the-lens viewfinders are of two types: those which use a mirrored shutter and those which use a beam splitter. In a mirrored-shutter arrangement, when the shutter is closed its silvered front surface reflects all the light from the lens into the viewfinder; and when the shutter is open the finder goes dark because all the light passes to the film (there is a diagram of this system in Chapter Four, p. 221). The resulting viewfinder image, while quite bright, flickers on and off 24 times a second. With a beam splitter, on the other hand, there is no flickering, because part of the light from the lens is continuously diverted into the viewfinder by a half-silvered mirror or prism. Of course, since only part of the light from the lens enters the viewfinder, the finder image is never as bright as with a mirrored shutter; nor is there as much light available to expose the film. This light loss can be critical if a great deal of footage must be shot at low light levels.

While through-the-lens viewing permits the image to be focused quite accurately, the great depth of field of super 8mm lenses makes them inherently more difficult to focus. Therefore, through-the-lens viewfinders on super 8mm cameras often include some kind of focusing aid. The most common of these aids is a split image in the viewfinder. This device shows objects which are out of focus as two slightly offset images; these images merge when the object is brought into focus. Another focusing aid is the *micro prism,* a fine pattern of tiny prisms cut into the surface of the ground-glass focusing screen. Micro prisms, in effect, defeat the depth of field of the lens by causing objects to pop in or out of focus quickly. Yet a third type, which is also found in 16mm and 35mm cameras, is a high-powered magnifying lens which can be swung into the viewfinder. This magnifier greatly enlarges part of the viewing screen for more critical focusing.

Through-the-Lens Exposure Meters

Through-the-lens viewfinder systems also incorporate a number of other features. They include exposure meters, battery-life indicators, running lights, and end-of-film indicators. While all these features are useful, only the operation of the exposure meter has any critical effect on the flexibility of the camera. A dependable, built-in meter can greatly simplify the sometimes difficult job of making uniform, accurate exposure readings.

The first consideration in judging a built-in metering system is where the meter is placed. Some built-in meters don't work through the lens at all, but are instead mounted on the front of the camera. They thus read a fixed area regardless of the field of view of the lens. But those meters which are built into the through-the-lens viewing system read the light actually passing through the lens. Therefore, through-the-lens meters measure the changes in the value of the light that result from changing the field of view of the lens. It is obvious that this is quite important when using a zoom lens. In addition, through-the-lens metering automatically compensates both for the loss of light inherent in a complex zoom lens and for the light losses that result when making extreme close-ups.

Through-the-lens meters are of two types: *full-field* meters that read the entire image, and *center-weighted* meters that give more importance to the central third of the frame. Of the two, the center-weighted meter tends to be more accurate. While a full-field meter can be easily thrown off by an exceptionally light or dark background, the center-weighted type discounts the background in favor of the subject, which is usually located toward the center of the frame.

Some built-in meters also set the *f* stop automatically while others require the cameraman to open up or stop down the lens until a needle is centered in an indicator in the viewfinder. This operation, too, affects the accuracy of the meter. Although an automatic meter is fast and convenient, it is easily fooled. For instance, when some extremely light or dark object enters the frame, an automatic meter will react by over- or underexposing the rest of the image. Or, when there is an abrupt change in light level, an automatic meter can't always react quickly enough. As a result, the shot momentarily becomes too light or too dark. Because of these problems some automatic metering systems also provide for manual control of the *f* stops. But in a *match-needle* system these problems don't arise. The exposure is set before the shooting begins by rotating the *f* stop ring until a needle in the viewfinder lines up with an index mark; from then on the exposure remains the same unless the *f* stop is changed by the cameraman.

Shutter Angle

One last area for consideration is the camera's shutter mechanism. Here the basic option is the *shutter angle*. The size of the opening in the shutter controls the amount of blur in the image: the smaller the shutter angle, the less the blur. But shutter angle also affects exposure since every decrease in the shutter angle also reduces the amount of light reaching the film. Shutter angle is thus a compromise between acceptable blur and adequate exposure.

On most cameras this compromise has resulted in a shutter angle of between 130 to 180 degrees. These angles produce exposures ranging from one forty-eighth to one sixtieth of a second (at 24 fps). But some 16mm and 35mm studio cameras, and the new low-light-level super 8mm cameras, have shutter angles of up to 235 degrees, producing a maximum exposure of up to one thirty-seventh of a second (at 24 fps). There is, in other words, a 25 percent increase in exposure at the same frame rate. While this may seem like a small increment, even this increase in exposure can be crucial when shooting sync-sound with slow color film in a situation where light is at a premium.

Another, closely allied attribute is the ability to vary the opening in the shutter. With a variable shutter, instead of stopping down the lens to reduce exposure, the cameraman can cut the light by reducing the shutter angle—a technique which is used to produce shallow depth of field in a brightly lit scene. A variable shutter also facilitates in-camera fades and dissolves (this technique is covered in detail in Chapter Ten, pp. 545 to 548). However, these optical effects also require that the camera have a frame counter in addition to the footage counter that is normally part of every camera. This frame counter gives the cameraman an exact indication of where he is as he creates the effect. And in-camera dissolves require that the camera have some means for backwinding the film so that the incoming and outgoing shots can be superimposed.

Animation

If the camera is to be used for shooting animation as well as for live action, some of the facilities that have been mentioned as options become necessities. First, and most obvious, the camera must provide a single-frame mechanism. But this mechanism need not be built in if it can be added on in the form of a special animation motor. Second, the lens must focus down to a foot or less. However, this too can be either built in or added on by means of an interchangeable lens or a closeup attachment. Third, the camera must have through-the-lens viewing. Accurate framing and focus become critical in closeup work, and these are most consistently done with a through-the-lens viewfinder. Fourth and last, there has to be a frame counter. Again, however, if this isn't built into the camera it will usually be found as part of the animation motor. Given these four basic elements it is possible to use any camera for a wide range of animation.

Sync-Sound

Lip-synchronous sound filming also requires certain specialized facilities.

Most essentially, the camera must have a constant-speed motor—either an AC sync motor or a crystal-controlled DC motor. Or, if the camera has just a regular DC constant-speed motor, it must also have a sync generator. This generator produces a sync signal which is recorded along with the sound track and later used to put picture and track into exact synchronization (the details of this process are covered in Chapter Six).

A secondary, but still important consideration in sync-sound filming is camera noise. The quieter the camera, the lower the background noise in the sound track. Camera noise can be controlled in one of two ways. One way is to use a self-blimped camera; that is, a camera which is designed to operate almost noiselessly. Another way is to put the camera into a separate blimp. Although a separate blimp always makes the camera larger and heavier, it is to be preferred when there is only a small amount of sync-sound to be shot. Then, since the blimp is not an integral part of the camera, it can be removed for the silent shooting. The unblimped camera will therefore weigh much less, and be easier to handle, than a similar self-blimped model.

Testing the Camera

Once the camera has been chosen it should be put through a series of tests. These tests, while not exhaustive, will at least indicate whether or not the camera's most basic components—its optics and film-advance mechanism—are working properly. And since these tests require little or no special equipment, they can be done easily and quickly even by a beginning film-maker.

Focus

The first step in testing a camera is to determine whether the lens focuses properly. This test primarily involves finding out whether the footage scale engraved on the barrel of the lens actually matches the point at which the lens focuses. In addition, if the camera has through-the-lens viewing, it is important to know whether the footage scale and the viewfinder both focus the lens on the same point, and if not, which of the two is the more accurate.

This test requires a long corridor or other large space 75 to 100 feet in length, in which the light is uniform and just sufficient for an exposure at the lens's widest *f* stop. A uniform light level is important because it permits the same *f* stop to be used for all the tests, from the nearest to the farthest focus settings. And using the

widest *f* stop is necessary because the point of critical focus is easiest to determine when the image has the least depth of field.

If more than one lens is to be used with this camera, the test should be shot on color film. Then the pieces of film shot with each lens can also be compared for color match. If only one lens is to be used, the test can be shot on either B&W or color film. In either case, however, the test should be made on slow film so that the grain structure of the film won't interfere with the evaluation of image sharpness.

To make the test the camera should first be securely mounted on a tripod. Then short segments (three feet or so) should be filmed with the lens focused on a slate placed at the following distances:

1. Infinity (usually seventy-five feet and beyond)
2. Thirty feet
3. Ten feet
4. Minimum focus (between three and six feet)

In each case the distance from the film plane to the slate should be measured with a tape measure. The film plane is usually marked on the camera body by the symbol -⊖-. If there is no such symbol, use a grease pencil to mark the position of the camera's aperture plate on the outside of the camera body.

If the distance scale on the lens is to be compared to through-the-lens focusing, the following test should be run as well. First, carefully focus the viewfinder eyepiece on the focusing screen; then, place a focusing target next to the

Focusing target.

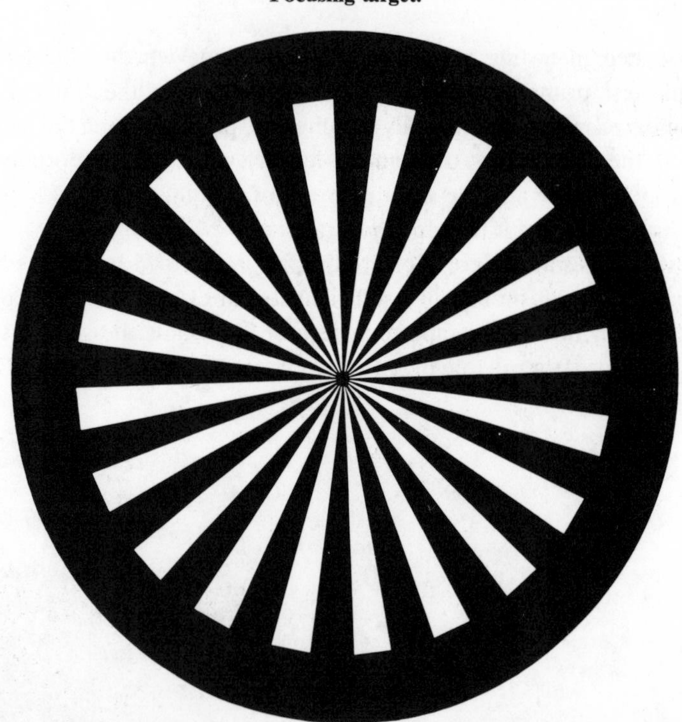

slate used to mark off the distance. This target provides an accurate focusing point because it tends to snap in and out of focus. After filming each tape-measured distance, mark the slate with a *V,* refocus the lens through the viewfinder, and film another short segment. Later, the two pieces of film can be compared for accuracy of focus at each distance.

A somewhat different procedure is followed when testing a zoom lens because most zoom lenses don't have index marks that show the exact point on the footage scale for each distance. Therefore a zoom lens cannot be tested for absolute focus, but only for through-the-lens focus and *tracking.* A zoom lens tracks when it holds the same point in focus throughout its entire zoom range. The test is run by first focusing on the target with the lens at its longest focal length; then, as the film is being shot, the lens is slowly zoomed to its shortest focal length. This procedure is repeated for each of the four distances—infinity, thirty feet, ten feet, and minimum focus.

Registration

Another test that is easy to make is a check of *registration.* Registration refers to the accuracy of the pulldown mechanism in placing each frame of film in front of the aperture. When the film is misregistered, each successive frame is seated in a somewhat different position relative to the opening in the aperture plate. As a result, when the film is projected, the image weaves from side to side, or up and down, on the screen.

Registration is tested by filming a double exposure of the grid pattern shown on the following page. This grid is produced by simply marking a piece of graph paper with a cross in the center and with brackets in the corners to indicate a three-by-four aspect ratio.

To make the test, securely lock the camera in place and frame the grid so that the brackets touch each corner of the viewfinder. About five feet of the grid is then filmed. However, because the grid must be filmed twice, the exposure has to be reduced one *f* stop. Otherwise the film would receive double the normal amount of exposure. Next the lens is capped, or the variable shutter closed, and the film is backwound to the start of the test. Then the camera is shifted slightly so that the center mark is half a grid division to the right and below center and a second exposure is made over the first.

If the camera doesn't have a backwind mechanism, there are other ways to rewind the film for a second exposure. One way is to shoot the test in a darkroom.

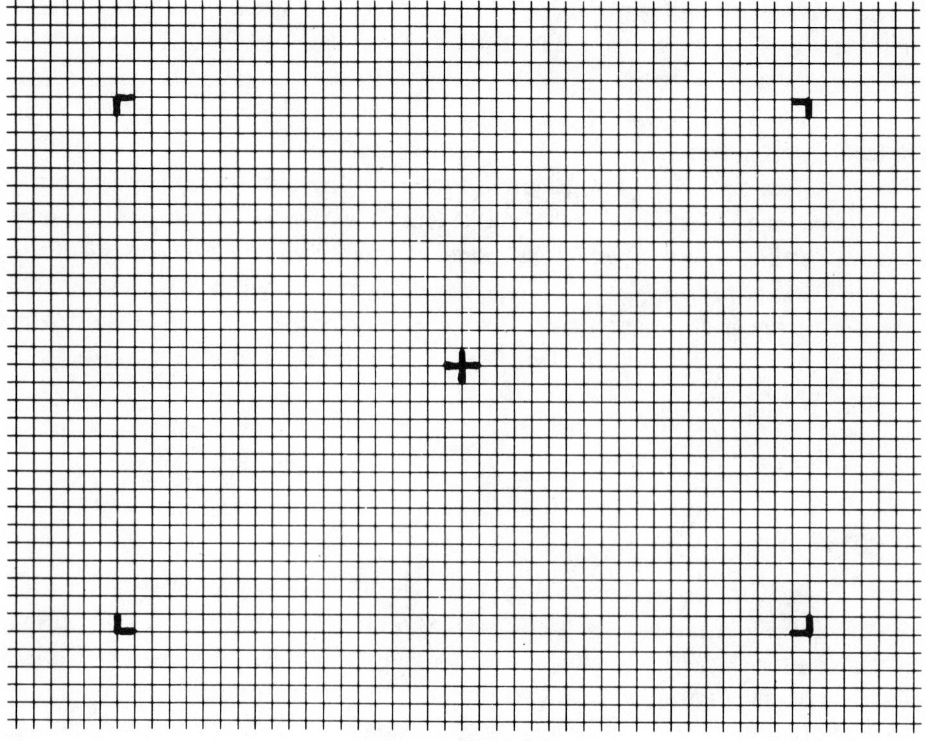

Registration test grid.

Then the camera can be opened after the first exposure and the film rewound by hand without exposing it to light. However, this technique can be used only with spool-loading cameras or those with external magazines. If the film is in a cartridge, it can be rewound only if it doesn't take up properly in the first place. In other words, the take-up spool in the cartridge has to be jammed so that instead of being neatly spooled, the film just piles up in the take-up side of the cartridge. This is done by putting some tape across the take-up gear on the outside of the cartridge. Then, after the first exposure, the cartridge can be taken into a darkroom and the film slid back manually into the supply chamber.

Evaluation

After the test footage has been processed, it is evaluated in two ways: first by physically inspecting the film and then by projecting it. The physical inspection tells whether there are any troublesome scratches. Any scratching can be seen by looking at both sides of the original with a strong magnifying glass. Scratches normally show up as very fine lines running the length of the film. It is important, however, to differentiate between the scratches made during processing and the scratches made by the camera itself.

Processing scratches (and those made by the camera guide rollers) show up as continuous marks along the edges of the film. As long as these marks stay outside the image area they are of no concern. The scratches that indicate trouble, though, are short, repetitive marks that occur within the image area. These intermittent scratches are usually produced in the camera aperture. Of course, continuous scratches within the image area are also a problem, but more often than not they are the result of processing.

The second part of the evaluation consists of projecting the film on a screen at least four feet wide (a smaller image will not show up defects, while a larger screen should be used to evaluate film that will be shown theatrically). The following qualities then can be determined simply by looking at the image on the screen:

1. Whether or not a sharp image is produced at all the points at which the lens is focused.
2. Whether the image is sharper when the lens is focused with a tape measure or through-the-lens.
3. If a zoom lens was tested, whether it tracks.
4. Whether there is any weaving between the superimposed sets of graph lines.

In addition, the corner brackets in the registration test will indicate the accuracy of the viewfinder. Since these brackets were aligned with the corners of the viewfinder, they should appear in the corners of the projected image. There is another problem, called *breathing,* that should also be looked for during projection. This defect, which is most easily seen during the registration test, shows up as a regular, frequent softening of the entire image.

If more than one lens was tested, there is one other evaluation that should now be run. This check consists of intercutting pieces of footage from the focus test of each lens. These alternating pieces of footage will then indicate the color match of the lenses and their relative sharpness.

If the camera fails any of these simple tests, return it to the dealer or rental house for correction or replacement. Or, if more definitive checks must be made, information on further test procedures can usually be gotten from the camera manufacturer or distributor, or from any company that specializes in camera testing and repair. However, more detailed analysis normally involves special charts and expensive test equipment, so the work should probably be left to a professional.

Appendix B

Film List and Picture Credits

Film Rental Sources

Almost: 1970 Kodak Teenage Movie Awards

Alphaville: Contemporary Films

Anderson Platoon, The: Contemporary Films

Avventura, L': Janus Films

Battle of the Bulge: NBC-TV

Battleship Potemkin: Contemporary Films, Janus Films, The Museum of Modern Art

Beauty and the Beast: Janus Films

Birth of a Nation, The: The Museum of Modern Art

Blue Angel, The: Contemporary Films, Janus Films, The Museum of Modern Art

Breathless: Contemporary Films

Cabinet of Dr. Caligari, The: Contemporary Films, Janus Films, The Museum of Modern Art

Citizen Kane: Janus Films

Confrontation: NBC-TV

Corral: International Film Bureau

Cosmic Ray: The Museum of Modern Art

Day in the Life of Two Hoods, A: 1969 Kodak Teenage Movie Awards

Départ, Le: Contemporary Films

Ecstasy: Contemporary Films

Excedrin—"Tax Audit": 1968 CLIO Awards

Fairground: Victor Nunez Films

Fat and the Lean, The: Janus Films

Fiancés, The: Janus Films

Fire Rescue: NBC-TV

Forbidden Games: Janus Films

400 Blows, The: Janus Films

Gold Rush, The: Contemporary Films, Janus Films, The Museum of Modern Art

Grand Illusion: Janus Films

Grapes of Wrath, The: The Museum of Modern Art

Hallelujah the Hills: Film-maker's Cooperative

Hiroshima Mon Amour: Contemporary Films

Informer, The: Films Incorporated

Iron Horse, The: The Museum of Modern Art

Italian Straw Hat, An: Contemporary Films

Jour Se Lève, Le: Janus Films

Jules and Jim: Janus Films

Kanal: Janus Films

Lady Vanishes, The: Janus Films

Listen to Britain: Contemporary Films, The Museum of Modern Art

Ludens—"Big Squeeze": 1968 CLIO Awards

M: Contemporary Films, Janus Films, The Museum of Modern Art

Magnificent Ambersons, The: Janus Films

Monika: Janus Films

My Darling Clementine: The Museum of Modern Art

My Life to Live: Contemporary Films, The Museum of Modern Art

Nanook of the North: Contemporary Films, The Museum of Modern Art

Night Mail: The Museum of Modern Art

Nosferatu: Janus Films, The Museum of Modern Art

Our Daily Bread: Janus Films, The Museum of Modern Art

Pas de Deux: Learning Corporation of America

Passion of Joan of Arc, The: The Museum of Modern Art

Rashomon: Janus Films

Ronde, La: Janus Films

Rules of the Game: Janus Films

Runner: McGraw-Hill Text Films

Seventh Seal, The: Janus Films

Shoot the Piano Player: Janus Films

Silence, The: Janus Films

Sound of Trumpets, The: Janus Films

Spies: Janus Films, The Museum of Modern Art

State Farm Auto Insurance—"Egg and You": 1968 CLIO Awards

Suspicion: Films Incorporated

Time for Burning, A: Contemporary Films

Trial of Joan of Arc, The: Contemporary Films

Trip, The: 1969 Kodak Teenage Movie Awards

Troublemaker, The: Macmillan/Audio-Brandon Films

Ugetsu: Janus Films

Volkswagen—"Mr. Jones": 1968 CLIO Awards

Whirlpool—"Cashiered": 1968 CLIO Awards

White Sheik, The: Contemporary Films

Wild Strawberries: Janus Films

Woman in the Dunes: Contemporary Films

Woman Is a Woman, A: Contemporary Films

World of the Teenager, The: NBC-TV

Yesterday, Today and Tomorrow: Macmillan/Audio-Brandon Films

Yojimbo: Macmillan/Audio-Brandon Films

Young Aphrodites: Janus Films

Addresses

Contemporary Films/McGraw-Hill

East Coast: Princeton Road
Hightstown, N.J. 08520

Midwest: 828 Custer Avenue
Evanston, Ill. 60202

West Coast: 1714 Stockton Street
San Francisco, Calif. 94133

This is a large collection that includes both feature films and documentaries. The films cover a broad time span, from the silents to the present, and represent the work of directors from almost two dozen countries. The catalogue descriptions for each film are quite complete, and further information, including rental rates and availability, can be gotten from any of their three offices.

Janus Films
745 Fifth Avenue
New York, N.Y. 10022

This is primarily a small collection of classic feature films from around the world. In addition, Janus has put together programs of carefully selected short films and special collections of English and French feature films. Their catalogue includes a story synopsis and critical comments for each film. Further information, including rental rates and availability, can be gotten from their New York office.

The Museum of Modern Art
Department of Film
11 West 53rd Street
New York, N.Y. 10019

Since 1935 the museum has been building an unusually varied collection of films on the history and art of the motion picture. Designed primarily for study purposes, the films are rented only to schools, universities, colleges, museums, libraries, and other accredited educational institutions. The films

can also be viewed at the museum, by appointment, by bona fide scholars. Their catalogue is small but detailed and can be purchased from the museum. Rentals are arranged through their New York office.

CLIO TV Library
30 East 60th Street
New York, N.Y. 10022

Eastman Kodak Company
Audio Visual Service (Dept. 396)
343 State Street
Rochester, N.Y. 14650

Film-Maker's Cooperative
175 Lexington Avenue
New York, N.Y. 10016

Films Incorporated
1144 Wilmette Avenue
Wilmette, Ill. 60091
(also five regional offices)

International Film Bureau
332 South Michigan Avenue
Chicago, Ill. 60604

Learning Corporation of America
711 Fifth Avenue
New York, N.Y. 10022

Macmillan/Audio-Brandon Films
866 Third Avenue
New York, N.Y. 10022
(also five regional offices)

McGraw-Hill Text Films
1221 Avenue of the Americas
New York, N.Y. 10020

NBC-TV
Room 914
30 Rockefeller Plaza
New York, N.Y. 10020

Victor Nunez Films
227 Westminster Drive
Tallahassee, Fla. 32304

Picture Credits

ABC News
Appalachian Poverty Program

Century Precision Cine/Optics
Focusing Target (Permission to reproduce given by Century Precision Cine/Optics, North Hollywood, Calif. 91601; Zoom Lens Repair Specialists, Mfg. Precision Tele-Lenses)

Columbia Pictures
Claire's Knee (A scene from the Columbia Pictures presentation of a film by Eric Rohmer, *Claire's Knee,* starring Jean-Claude Brialy with Aurora Cornu, Beatrice Romand, Laurence de Monaghan, © Columbia Pictures Industries, Inc.)

Conner, Bruce G.
Cosmic Ray (Distributed by The Museum of Modern Art, 11 West 53rd Street, New York City)

Contemporary Films/McGraw-Hill

Alphaville
The Anderson Platoon
Breathless
My Life to Live
Nanook of the North
Night Mail

Le Départ
Ecstasy
Hiroshima Mon Amour
An Italian Straw Hat
Listen to Britain
Pierrot le Fou
The Trial of Joan of Arc
The White Sheik
Woman in the Dunes
A Woman Is a Woman

Doyle, Dane, Bernbach Inc.
Volkswagen of America-VW Sedan *Mr. Jones*
Whirlpool *Cashiered*
Eastman Kodak Co.
Motion Picture Prints from Color Originals (Reproduced with the permission of Eastman Kodak Company)
Janus Films, Inc.

Ashes and Diamonds
L'Avventura
Beauty and the Beast
The Fat and the Lean
Fiancés
Forbidden Games
The 400 Blows
Grand Illusion
Hallelujah the Hills
Le Jour Se Lève
Jules and Jim
Kanal
The Lady Vanishes
M
Monika
Our Daily Bread
Rashomon
La Ronde
Rules of the Game
The Seventh Seal
Shoot the Piano Player
The Silence
The Sound of Trumpets
Spies
Suspicion
The Troublemaker
Ugetsu
Wild Strawberries
Young Aphrodites

Kodak Teenage Movie Awards

Almost
A Day in the Life of Two Hoods
The Trip

NBC News

Battle of the Bulge
Confrontation
Fire Rescue
Singing Salesmen
The World of the Teenager

National Film Board of Canada
Photos from the National Film Board of Canada's production of:

A Chairy Tale
Corral
Pas de Deux
Runner

Needham, Harper and Steers
State Farm Auto Insurance *Egg and You*
Nunez, Victor
Fairground (Victor Nunez Films, 227 Westminster Dr., Tallahassee, Fla. 32304)
Paramount Pictures Corp.
Avco Embassy Pictures Corp.
Sands of the Kalahari (Copyright © 1965 by Paramount Pictures Corporation and Avco Embassy Pictures Corp.)
The Philadelphia Agency
Ludens *Big Squeeze* (Produced by The Philadelphia Agency, Inc., through Gryphon Productions)
RKO General, Inc.
Pictures from *Citizen Kane* and *The Magnificent Ambersons* used by courtesy of RKO General, Inc.
Sostar, S.A.
Yesterday, Today and Tomorrow
Toho International, Inc.
Yojimbo (Produced by Toho Company Ltd., Japan)
Twentieth Century-Fox Film Corp.
The Grapes of Wrath (© 1940, 20th Century-Fox Film Corporation. Renewed 1967. All rights reserved.)
The Iron Horse (© 1924, William Fox. All rights reserved.)
My Darling Clementine (© 1947, 20th Century-Fox Film Corporation. All rights reserved.)
Videart, Inc.
Optical Wipe Chart (Courtesy of Videart, Inc.)
WABC-TV News
Dong Xoai: The Town the Viet Cong Couldn't Kill
Young and Rubicam
Bristol-Myers Excedrin *Tax Audit*

Glossary

A&B Rolls (also: **Checkerboarding**): A technique used to prepare original camera footage for printing. The shots alternate between two printing rolls, with black leader filling in the space between every other shot (hence the name *checkerboarding*).

Anamorphic lens (see: **Aspect ratio**): An optical device that permits a normal camera lens to squeeze an area more than twice as wide as it is high within a standard frame. A similar device is used during projection to unsqueeze this distorted image, producing an aspect ratio of 2.35:1.

Animation (see: **Single framing**): A technique in which the film-maker creates the action by photographing either animate or inanimate objects one frame at a time (*single framing*). After each exposure the object is moved slightly; when these small movements rapidly succeed each other on the screen, they create the illusion of continuous action.

Answer print (also: **First trial print**): The first print of the completed film which incorporates both the optical sound track and the picture with color corrections, exposure corrections (*timing*), and A&B roll optical effects.

Aperture, Lens (see: **F stop, Iris diaphragm**)

Aperture plate (see: **Aspect ratio, Gate**): A metal plate with a rectangular cutout mounted between the lens and the film in a camera or projector; the front part of the *gate*. In a camera, the cutout determines the

shape (*aspect ratio*) of the image exposed onto the film. In a projector, the cutout masks off the area of the film to be projected.

Aspect ratio (see: **Anamorphic lens, Aperture plate, Frame**): The ratio of frame width to frame height. Traditionally these dimensions have a relationship of 4 to 3, producing an aspect ratio of 1.33:1 for standard 8mm, super 8mm, and regular 16mm and 35mm frames. The aspect ratio can be altered by changing the shape of the cutout in the aperture plate, or by using an anamorphic lens.

Axis (see: **Screen direction**): An imaginary line drawn through the dominant action. Crossing the axis from one shot to the next causes the action to reverse its direction on the screen.

Background lighting: Lighting which highlights areas or objects in the background of a shot, or which forms patterns of light in the background that reinforce the feeling of a particular time or place.

Background sound (see: **Room presence, Sound effects**): The surrounding, secondary sounds that create a sense of a particular time or place. These sounds include both the echo and noise that naturally occur in the background of dialogue recording and the sound effects that are added to the background during the mix.

Back light (see: **Back lighting**): A light placed behind the subject and pointed toward the camera.

Back lighting (see: **Back light**): Lighting in which the principal source of light is behind the subject, thereby throwing the subject into silhouette.

Base (also: **Backing, Support;** see: **Emulsion**): A smooth, thin, transparent film onto which is coated a light-sensitive emulsion or magnetic recording material. This backing or support material is usually cellulose triacetate.

Base illumination: An overall light level, usually provided by soft, overhead lights, that permits the film to record some details in even the deepest shadows.

Batch number (also: **Emulsion number**): A serial number used to identify all the film produced by a manufacturer at one time. The film in each batch has identical sensitivity and color characteristics.

Beep (see: **Sync marks**): An audible tone, usually 1,000 cycles, used to synchronize the sound track with the picture during editing, mixing, and printing.

B&W: Abbreviation for black and white (film, image, print, etc.).

Camera angle: The position of the camera relative to the subject being photographed. This angle is expressed either as a comparison with a normal, eye-level view of the subject (high, low, near, far) or as a comparison between various shots of the same subject (higher, lower, closer, further).

Camera log (also: **Log, Shooting log;** see: **Dope sheet**): A list of the shots, and the number of takes of each shot, on each roll of film.

Camera speed (see: **Frame rate**)

Cardioid (see: **Shotgun microphone**): A type of microphone that responds more strongly to sounds coming from the front than to those coming from its sides or back.

Checkerboarding (see: **A&B Rolls**)

Cinch marks: Short, straight, parallel scratches caused by the rubbing together of loosely wound layers of film.

Clapstick (see: **Slate**): A stick hinged to the upper corner of a slate. At the beginning or end of a shot the stick is clapped against the top edge of the slate to create a visible and audible synchronizing point in both the picture and the sound track.

Close-up (also: **Close shot, CU**): A shot which includes only a small part of the subject; i.e., a shot of just a person's head or hands.

Close-up lens (also: **Diopter lens, Plus lens;** see: **Split-field lens**): A supplementary lens which, when mounted in front of a regular camera lens, permits the camera to focus more closely than normal.

Color balance (see: **Color temperature, Conversion filter**): The difference in response built into indoor and outdoor color film to correct for the difference in color content (*color temperature*) between daylight and incandescent illumination. Also, the relative distribution of the colors in an image.

Color-balancing filter (see: **Color temperature**): A colored filter that is mounted in front of a light source to change the color content (*color temperature*) of the light.

Color-compensating filter (also: **CC filter;** see: **Color temperature**): A colored filter that is mounted in front of the lens to compensate for small changes in the color content (*color temperature*) of the light to which color film is exposed.

Color-conversion filter (see: **Conversion filter**)

Color match (see: **Color balance**): A set of lenses that all have the same effect on the color content of light. The lenses thus produce images with the same color balance.

Color temperature (see: **Color balance, Color-balancing filter, Color-compensating filter**): A measure of the color content of a light source; i.e., the relative distribution of the spectrum of colors within what appears to the eye to be white light. This distribution is measured in degrees Kelvin (°K): the lower the Kelvin temperature, the redder the light; the higher the Kelvin temperature, the bluer the light.

Composite print: Any print in which sound and picture are on the same strip of film.

Conforming (see: **Matching**)

Contact printing (see: **Optical printing**): A process for transferring an image from one piece of film to another in which the two strands of film (processed film and raw stock) are sandwiched together as they are exposed to light.

Continuity: A premise underlying most film-making: the viewer's attention should be held from shot to shot by an unbroken, or carefully delineated, flow of movement and detail.

Contrast: The brightness range of a scene or the range of tones in an image. A contrasty scene has bright highlights and dark shadows; a contrasty image has few shades of gray between its lightest and darkest areas.

Contrast filter: A colored filter used with B&W film to increase the contrast between equally bright objects of different colors. Objects the same color as the filter become a lighter shade of gray, while objects of a complementary color become a darker gray.

Contrast range (see: **Lighting balance**): The difference in brightness between the lightest and darkest parts of a scene. Also, the ability of film to record details in both the lightest and darkest parts of a scene.

Control signal (see: **Control track, Crystal sync**): An electronic pulse, produced either by a generator in the camera or a crystal in the sound recorder, that is recorded on the control track. This pulse is later used to keep the sound track in synchronization with the pictures.

Control track (see: **Control signal**): The area on a magnetic tape in which the control signal is recorded.

Conversion filter (also: **Color-conversion filter;** see: **Color balance**): A colored filter that is mounted in front of the lens to convert daylight-balanced color film for use with incandescent light, or to convert indoor film for use in daylight.

Cool image (see: **Warm image**): A bluish image, produced either by the color content of the light, the tendency of the lens to absorb the red end of the spectrum, or the addition of blue during printing.

Core: A small plastic or metal hub on which film or tape is wound.

Cover shot (also: **Master shot**): A long shot that includes all the action in one scene.

Crabbing (see: **Dolly**): Any irregular dolly movement. Crabbing can only be accomplished when all the wheels of the dolly can be steered simultaneously.

Critical focus (see: **Depth of field**): That point in front of the camera at which the lens is focused. Objects behind or in front of that point will be out of focus to varying degrees, depending upon the depth of field.

Cross-cutting (also: **Intercutting**): To cut back and forth between shots from two or more scenes. This rapid alternation suggests that all the action is occurring simultaneously.

Cross fade (also: **Segue;** see: **Fade**): To fade out one sound as another fades in.

Crystal sync: A method for maintaining the synchronization of sound and picture in which the camera and recorder are each kept at the correct speed by means of an internal, crystal-controlled timing device.

CU: Abbreviation for *close-up*.

Cue sheet (also: **Dubbing cue sheet, Mixing sheet;** see: **Mixing**): A set of instructions prepared by the editor for the sound mixer. These sheets detail in graphic form the type of sounds on each track, where the sounds start and stop, how each should begin and end, their proper levels, and any other special requirements.

Cut: An instantaneous transition from one shot to the next created simply by joining two shots together. Also, to edit a film. The command given to stop the camera, recorder, and actors.

Cut-away (also: **Insert shot, Reaction shot**): A cut to a close shot of someone or something not directly involved in the ongoing action. Cut-aways are used to show related details (*insert shots*) or reactions that comment on the principal action (*reaction shots*); they also serve as a technical device to preserve continuity and/or establish cutting rhythms.

Dailies (see: **Rushes**)

Day-for-night: A technique for filming in normal daylight a scene that is supposed to occur at night.

Deep focus: A style of film-making in which everything in the frame, from the farthest background to objects immediately in front of the camera, is kept in sharp focus.

Degrees Kelvin (also: **°K;** see: **Color temperature**)

Depth of field (see: **Critical focus**): The zone of acceptably sharp focus behind and in front of that point at which the lens is critically focused. The depth of this zone varies with the *f* stop used and the focal length of the lens.

Diffusion lens: A supplementary lens which, when mounted in front of the regular camera lens, softens the image.

Diopter lens (see: **Close-up lens**)

Directional microphone (see: **Cardioid**)

Dissolve (also: **DIS;** see: **Fade**): To fade out one shot as the next fades in (similar to a *cross fade* in sound). A dissolve is usually used as a transitional device that connects two scenes.

Dolly (see: **Crabbing**): To move the camera toward or away from the subject, or to move the camera so that it follows behind or in front of a moving subject. Also, a wheeled camera mount which can be moved about during a take.

Dope sheet (see: **Camera log**): A description of the shots on each roll of film. A dope sheet is used when filming unscripted shots for a documentary, or when shooting news film.

Double exposure (also: **Superimposition;** see: **Super**): The successive exposure of the same strip of film to two different scenes.

Double key (see: **X lighting**)

Double-system sound: A synchronous sound system in which the sound is recorded on a different piece of film or tape from that on which the picture is recorded.

Dubber: A machine used to play back sprocketed sound film.

Dubbing (see: **Mixing, Post-synchronization**): To make a duplicate of a sound recording. Also, another name for mixing the sound tracks or post-synchronizing voices to match the pictures.

Dubbing cue sheet (see: **Cue sheet**)

Dynamic range: The difference in level between the softest and loudest sounds that can be recorded.

Edge numbers (also: **Code numbers**): Identical sets of four- to six-digit serial numbers printed at six-inch or one-foot intervals along the edge of the original, the workprint, and (where applicable) the lip-synchronous sound film. Edge numbers are used to synchronize sound and picture during editing, and to match the workprint to the original during conforming.

Editorial sync (also: **Edit sync;** see: **Printer sync, Sync marks**): Sync marks which place the sound track immediately opposite its corresponding frame of picture. Editorial sync is used throughout the editing and mixing of a motion picture.

EI: Abbreviation for *exposure index*.

Electro-printing: An electronic process for transferring the master magnetic track directly to the optical sound track on a finished print.

Emulsion (see: **Base**): The light-sensitive coating on photographic film.

Establishing shot: A long shot used at the beginning of a sequence to establish the spatial relationships of the details shown in subsequent closer shots.

Exposure index (also: **EI;** see: **Film speed**): A rating of a film stock's sensitivity to light (*film speed*) when the film is exposed and processed under specific conditions. The EI for the same film stock can vary from movie to movie.

Extreme close-up (also: **XCU**): A shot that includes just a small detail of the subject; i.e., a shot of an eye, a finger, a shoe, etc.

Extreme long shot (also: **XLS**): A shot in which the subject is quite small in the frame; i.e., a shot in which a human figure is dwarfed by its surroundings.

Fade: The gradual disappearance of an image into blackness (a fade-out), or the reverse, the emergence of an image from blackness (a fade-in). Similarly, in sound a gradual reduction in level until the sound disappears, or the gradual emergence of a sound from silence. A combination fade-out–fade-in is often used as a transitional device that clearly separates two scenes.

Fader (see: **Fade**): The mechanism in a motion-picture printer that produces fades by gradually increasing or decreasing the amount of light reaching the film. Also, the control used to adjust the level of sound.

Fast film (see: **Film speed**): Film with a relatively high sensitivity to light.

Fast lens (see: **Lens speed**): A lens with a relatively large maximum aperture.

Fast motion (see: **Frame rate, Projection speed**): Faster-than-normal movements created by filming the action at a slower-than-normal frame rate (*undercranking*) and then projecting the film at the relatively faster standard projection speed.

FI (see: **Fade**): Abbreviation for *fade in*.

Figure eight (also: **Double cardioid**): A type of microphone that responds more strongly to sounds coming from its front or back than to those coming from either side.

Fill light (see: **Contrast range, Lighting ratio**): Light directed into the shadows to reduce the lighting ratio and

therefore the contrast range of the image.

Film speed (see: **Exposure index**): A film stock's sensitivity to light. This sensitivity is rated according to ASA numbers: the lower the number, the less sensitive (slower) the film. ASA numbers are used to select a film stock, but the actual exposure is determined by the exposure index.

Film transport: The mechanism in a camera or projector that moves the film from the supply reel, through the machine, and back onto the take-up reel.

Filter factor: A numerical factor used to calculate the exposure increase required to compensate for the light absorbed by an optical filter.

Final cut (also: **Fine cut;** see: **Workprint**): The final version of the edited workprint.

First trial print (see: **Answer print)**

Flare: Spots, streaks, or an overall haze in the image caused by light reflected from the internal surfaces of the lens and camera.

Flashback: A break in the chronological progression of the narrative either to repeat a scene that has already been shown or to show a scene that is supposed to have occurred prior to the one into which it has been inserted.

Flashing (see: **Contrast, Film speed**): To give film an overall exposure to a small amount of light before it is processed. Flashing decreases image contrast and increases film speed.

FO (see: **Fade**): Abbreviation for *fade out.*

Focal length: The distance from the optical center of a lens to the film when the lens is focused on a very distant object. For any given frame size the field of view of a lens is in inverse proportion to the focal length; as focal length increases, the field of view narrows.

Fog filter: A supplementary lens similar to a diffusion lens which, when mounted in front of the regular camera lens, creates a foglike atmosphere by softening and veiling the image.

Follow focus (also: **Rack focus;** see: **Critical focus**): To change the point of critical focus during a shot in order to keep the subject in sharp focus.

Follow f stop: To change the exposure during a shot to compensate for extreme changes of brightness as the camera moves from a light to dark area or a dark to light area.

Footage: A general term for any exposed and processed film, or recorded sound film.

Forcing (also: **Pushing;** see: **Film speed**): To increase film speed by underexposing and overdeveloping the film.

Foreshortening: The exaggerated perspective that is created when an object close to the camera extends toward the lens.

FPS (see: **Frame rate**): Abbreviation for *frames per second.*

Frame: An individual picture on a strip of film. Also, the area outlined by the camera viewfinder.

Frame line: The area between each frame on a strip of film. Also, the edges of the area outlined by the camera viewfinder.

Frame rate (also: **Camera speed, Projector speed**): The rate of movement of the film as it passes the lens of a camera or projector, usually expressed in frames per second (fps).

Frequency response: The highest- and lowest-pitched sounds that can be accurately reproduced by a sound system.

F stop (also: **Aperture, F number;** see: **Iris diaphragm, T stop**): Numbers used to indicate the size of an adjustable circular opening (*aperture*) in an iris diaphragm located inside a lens. These numbers indicate the amount of light that can pass through the lens; the larger the *f* number, the smaller the opening. The *f* stops are marked on a ring on the outside of the lens.

Gate (see: **Aperture plate**): The assembly in a camera or projector that aligns the film with the lens. The gate consists of a fixed aperture plate and a movable, spring-loaded pressure plate.

Generation (see: **Original**): A designation of the number of copies intervening between an original picture or sound recording and each successive duplicate.

Graduated filter: Any supplementary lens or filter that gradually changes in character from one side to the other.

Grain: The microscopic particles of silver that clump together during processing to form the photographic image.

Graininess (see: **Grain**): The extent to which the granular structure of the film is apparent in the image when the film is projected.

Hard light (see: **Soft light**): Light which has little tendency to spread or scatter. Hard light, such as sunlight or spotlighting, creates dense, sharp-edged shadows.

Head (see: **Tail**): The beginning of a piece of film or tape. When a roll of film or tape has the beginning on the outside, the roll is said to be *heads-up* or *heads-out.*

Heads, Magnetic (see: **Dubber, Magnetic film**): Small box- or can-shaped devices in the threading path of a sound recorder or dubber. Magnetic film or tape must pass over the heads in order to make a recording or to reproduce the sounds already recorded.

High-key (see: **Lighting ratio, Low-key**): A style of lighting characterized by an overall lightness of tonality. High-key lighting is created by using light-colored costumes, a low-contrast lighting ratio, and a well-lit background.

Hyperfocal distance (see: **Critical focus, F stop**): A combination of critical focus and *f* stop that produces an acceptably sharp image from half the distance of critical focus to as far as the eye can see.

Indoor film (see: **Color balance, Color temperature, Outdoor film**): Color film that is balanced for exposure to incandescent light. Type B color film is balanced for light at 3,200°K; Type A for 3,400°K light.

Insert shot (see: **Cut-away**)

Intercutting (see: **Cross-cutting**)

Interlock (see: **Double-system sound**): To play back double-system sound and picture in synchronization.

Intermittent (see: **Gate**): The stop-and-go movement of the film through the gate of a camera or projector. Also, the mechanism that pulls the film through the gate one frame at a time.

Internegative (see: **Original, Negative, Reversal film**): A duplicate negative made from a reversal original.

IPS: Abbreviation for *inches per second.*

Iris diaphragm (also: **Aperture, Diaphragm, Iris;** see: **Matte**): A mechanical device used to produce an adjustable circular opening. An iris located inside a lens controls the amount of light passing through the lens; an iris placed in front of the lens creates a circular matte. Slowly opening a closed iris produces an *iris in;* slowly closing the iris, an *iris out.*

Jump cut (see: **Continuity**): A break in continuity from one shot to the next caused by a mismatch of setting and/or action.

Key lighting: The dominant light source in a scene.

Latitude: The degree to which film can be over- or underexposed and still produce a satisfactory image.

Lavalier (also: **Neck microphone**): A small microphone designed either to be hung from a cord around the actor's neck or to be clipped on or under an actor's clothing.

Leader (see: **Base**): Blank film base. *White leader* has a uniform white coating; *light-struck* leader is undeveloped film and has a grayish-white ap-

pearance; *black leader* is film developed to a highly opaque black; and *clear leader* has no coating. SMPTE Universal leader is film printed with standard identification marks.

Lens speed (see: **F stop, Iris diaphragm, T stop**): The maximum light-transmitting power of a lens. Lens speed is expressed in terms of the *f* or *T* number that indicates the maximum opening in the lens diaphragm.

Lighting balance (see: **Contrast range, High-key, Low-key**): The difference in intensity between the light illuminating the foreground and that on the background of a scene.

Lighting ratio (see: **Fill light, Key light**): The ratio of the light striking the highlights to that striking the shadows. In studio lighting, the ratio of key plus fill to fill light alone. With B&W film, the ratio is kept to 5 to 1 or less, whereas with color film it is kept below 3 to 1.

Limbo: A setting that tells the audience nothing about a character's location —usually a pure black background.

Lip-synchronous dialogue (also: **Lip sync**): Shots of people speaking, in which the recording of the words is in exact synchronization with the movements of the speakers' lips.

Log (see: **Camera log**)

Long lens (also: **Telephoto lens;** see: **Focal length, Normal lens**): A lens that is longer than the normal focal length for any particular frame size. A long lens has a narrower-than-normal field of view.

Long shot (also: **LS**): A shot that includes the entire subject and much of its surroundings; i.e., a shot in which a person's figure occupies less than half the height of the frame.

Low-key (see: **High-key, Lighting ratio**): A style of lighting characterized by an overall darkness of tonality. Low-key lighting is created by using dark-colored costumes, a high-contrast lighting ratio, and a dimly lit background.

LS: Abbreviation for *long shot.*

Luminaire: A general term covering all the various types of lighting units used in film and television production.

Magnetic film (also: **Full coat, Mag film, Sound film;** see: **Base, Magnetic oxide**): Film base coated with a magnetic oxide. Sound recorded on magnetic film is synchronized with the images by matching the perforations in the sound film with those in the workprint.

Magnetic master (see: **Mixing**): The magnetic recording that is made when the sound tracks are mixed.

Magnetic oxide (see: **Base**): The magnetically sensitive coating, usually iron oxide, on recording tape and sound film.

Magnetic sound track (see: **Optical sound track**): A sound recording in which changes in the pitch and volume of the sound are reproduced as minute variations in a magnetic field that runs the length of a piece of magnetic film or tape.

Magnetic stripe (see: **Magnetic oxide, Release print, Single-system sound**): A thin strip of magnetic oxide glued along one edge of motion-picture film. A magnetic stripe is used to record single-system newsreel sound tracks and to produce the sound tracks on super 8mm release prints.

Master long shot (also: **Master shot;** see: **Cover shot**)

Match-action cutting (see: **Continuity**): An editing technique used to maintain continuity, in which an action started in one shot is continued in the next.

Matching (also: **Conforming, Negative cutting;** see: **Original, Workprint**): The process of cutting the original to match the workprint. Matching permits the final prints to be made from the cleanest, best quality images—those on the camera original.

Matte (also: **Mask;** see: **Traveling matte**): An opaque mask with one or more areas cut out of it, which is mounted either in front of the camera lens or immediately in front of the film. The cutout(s) in the matte restricts the image to a corresponding part of the frame.

Matte box: A device used to hold mattes and filters in front of the camera lens.

MCU: Abbreviation for *medium close-up.*

Medium close-up (also: **Loose close-up, MCU**): A shot in which a detail of the subject doesn't quite fill the frame; i.e., a person's head and shoulders.

Medium long shot (also: **Full shot, MLS**): A shot that includes the entire subject; i.e., a shot in which a person's figure fills the frame.

Medium shot (also: **Half shot, MS**): A shot that includes about half the subject; i.e., a person from the waist up.

Mixer (see: **Dubber**): An electronic device for combining several sound sources, either microphones (*microphone mixer*) or dubbers (*dubbing console*). Also, the operator who controls the mixing of the sounds.

Mixing (also: **Dubbing, Re-recording**): The process of using a mixer to combine several sound sources while controlling their volume and tonality.

Mixing sheet (see: **Cue sheet**)

MLS: Abbreviation for *medium long shot.*

Modeling: Those qualities of light that give a two-dimensional image an appearance of depth and texture.

Montage: Another name for editing. Also, a short, impressionistic sequence used to show the passage of time, or to characterize a particular place or period.

Movement (see: **Intermittent**)

MS: Abbreviation for *medium shot.*

MUS: Abbreviation for *music.*

NAR: Abbreviation for *narration.*

Narration (also: **Commentary, NAR;** see: **Voice over**): A voice on the sound track for which there is no corresponding source in the pictures. A narration can be read by a professional narrator or actor, or it can be composed of spontaneous interviews.

Negative film (see: **Reversal film**): Any film that produces an image in which the light values are reversed: light areas record dark and dark areas, light. Color negative film also records every color as its complement.

Negative cutting (see: **Matching**)

Neutral angle (see: **Camera angle, Screen direction**): Any camera angle in which the dominant action takes place directly toward or away from the camera and so has no screen direction.

Neutral-density filter (also: **ND filter**): A neutral gray filter that is used to reduce the intensity of light without changing its color.

Night-for-night (see: **Day-for-night**): Night scenes that are shot at night. Also, a technique for lighting night scenes shot at night.

Normal lens (see: **Focal length**): A lens with a focal length that is twice the diagonal of the frame size with which it is being used. A 50mm lens is normal when shooting a standard 35mm image, a 25mm lens with 16mm, etc.

Off-microphone (also: **Off-mic**): Sounds that occur either at too great a distance from the microphone or toward the dead side of a directional microphone.

Omnidirectional (also: **Omni**): A type of microphone that is equally responsive to sounds coming from any direction.

On-camera narration (see: **Voice over**): The part of a *voice-over* narration during which the narrator is shown speaking lip-synchronously.

Optical effects (also: **Opticals;** see: **Continuity**): A general term for all the unusual visual effects that can be created in the camera (double exposures, split images), during printing (fades, dissolves, superimpositions), or on an optical bench (wipes, flips, freeze frames, etc.). In addition to a wide variety of trick

images, optical effects create those visual transitions used to maintain continuity.

Optical printing (see: **Contact printing**): A process for transferring an image from one piece of film to another, in which the light passing through the processed film is transmitted to the unexposed raw stock by means of a system of lenses. This intervening optical system permits the duplicate image to be made either larger or smaller than the original.

Optical sound track (see: **Magnetic sound track**): A sound recording in which changes in the pitch and volume of the sound are reproduced as variations in a long, thin photographic image that runs along the edge of a piece of film.

Original (also: **Camera original;** see: **Generation**): The first recording of the picture or sound. Each successive duplicate of the original (called a *generation*) has a progressively poorer image or sound quality.

Orthochromatic film (also: **Ortho film;** see: **Panchromatic film**): A type of B&W film that is more sensitive to bluish-green light than it is to the reddish-orange end of the spectrum.

Outdoor film (see: **Color balance, Color temperature, Indoor film**): Color film that is balanced for exposure to daylight; i.e., light with a color temperature between 5,500°K and 6,000°K.

Out takes (also: **Outs, Trims**): Shots and pieces of shots that are not used to produce the finished film.

Overcrank (see: **Slow motion)**

Pan: To pivot the camera horizontally.

Panchromatic film (also: **Pan film;** see: **Orthochromatic film**): A type of B&W film that is almost equally sensitive to the whole spectrum of visible light.

Parallax: The difference in the field of view between a camera lens and a viewfinder which is mounted either above or to the side of the lens.

Perforations (also: **Sprocket holes**): Holes punched in photographic and sound film along one or both edges (*single* or *double perf*). These accurately spaced *sprocket holes* are used to position each frame in the gate and to move the film through a camera, printer, or projector; they are also used to keep two or more rolls of film in synchronization.

Persistence of vision: A quality of our vision in which an image tends to persist for a moment after it has been removed from sight. This residual image fuses the discrete frames that make up a motion picture into an impression of continuous motion.

Plus lens (see: **Close-up lens)**

Positive film (see: **Negative film**): A negative film stock designed for the production of positive prints from negative originals.

Post-production (see: **Pre-production**): All the work done on a film after the original footage is shot; i.e., the editing, dubbing, printing, etc.

Post-synchronization (also: **Dubbing**): The addition of synchronous voices and sound effects after the picture has been shot. Also, the addition, during editing, of narration, music, and sound effects to form precisely timed relationships with the images.

Practicals: Lamps and other electric light sources that appear in the image.

Pre-production (see: **Post-production**): All the work done on a film prior to shooting; i.e., the scripting, casting, testing, etc.

Presence (see: **Room presence)**

Print (also: **Positive**): Any positive copy of another piece of film.

Printer (see: **Contact printing, Optical printing, Raw stock**): The machine used to expose onto a piece of raw stock the image from a piece of processed film. Also, the technician who operates the printer.

Printer sync (also: **Projection sync;** see: **Editorial sync, Sync marks**): Sync marks which place the sound track a set number of frames ahead of the corresponding frame of picture. This sound advance permits prints of the film to be shown on a standard movie projector.

Printing roll (see: **A&B Rolls, Optical sound**): A roll of picture or sound track that is designed to be run through a motion-picture printer.

Projection speed (see: **Frame rate**): The standard frame rate used for projecting films: 24 frames per second for sound films, 18 frames per second for silent films.

Proximity effect (see: **Cardioid**): A characteristic of cardioid microphones:

they accentuate the lower frequency sounds when the sound source gets close to the microphone.

Pulling (see: **Matching, Original**): The process of sorting the original prior to matching, in which the original to be used in the final version of the film is separated from what will not be used.

Pushing (see: **Forcing**)

Quarter-inch tape (also: **Audio tape, Magnetic tape**): A quarter-inch-wide magnetic tape that is used for both synchronous and nonsynchronous sound recording.

Raw stock: Unexposed and undeveloped film; also, unused magnetic film or tape.

Reaction shot (see: **Cut-away**)

Reduction printing (see: **Optical printing**): A type of optical printing in which the size of the image on the original is reduced to fit a narrower film stock.

Registration (see: **Gate, Movement**): The ability of a camera or projector movement to position each frame of film accurately and to hold it steady in the gate while it is being exposed or projected.

Release print (see: **Composite print**): A final composite print intended for general distribution.

Re-recording (see: **Mixing**)

Resolving (see: **Control signal**): The process of transferring to magnetic film a lip-synchronous sound track originally recorded on quarter-inch tape. The control signal recorded on the quarter-inch tape is used to maintain synchronization during the transfer.

Reversal film (see: **Negative film**): Any film that produces an image in which the light values (and colors) are the same as in the photographed scene.

Reverse angle: A shot from a camera position that reverses the point of view of the preceding shot.

Room presence (also: **Presence, Room tone**): The residue of background noise that is present in even the most quiet setting. A recording of this slight amount of sound is used during editing to fill in silent passages in the sound track.

Rough cut (see: **Workprint**): A preliminary assembly of the workprint.

Rushes (also: **Dailies**; see: **Take**): A print of selected takes from each day's shooting that is viewed by the director and the cameraman before the start of the next day's shooting.

Saturation: The intensity of the colors in an image. Colors with poor saturation appear washed out, whereas oversaturated colors are dense and muddy in appearance.

Screen direction (see: **Axis**): The direction in which the action moves across the screen. Continuity of screen direction is determined by the position of the camera relative to an imaginary line, or *axis*, drawn through the dominant action in each shot.

Script breakdown: The rearrangement of the script so that all the shots made in the same location are grouped together. Filming the shots in this order is usually more efficient than shooting them in the order in which they appear in the script.

Segue (see: **Cross fade**)

SFX: Abbreviation for *sound effects*.

Short lens (also: **Wide-angle lens**; see: **Focal length, Normal lens**): A lens that is shorter than the normal focal length for any particular

frame size. A short lens has a wider-than-normal field of view.

Shot (see: **Take**): In a script, each piece of action that is to be filmed from the same camera angle. During shooting, the length of film exposed between each start and stop of the camera (sometimes called a *take*). Also, the pieces of film that are joined together to form the edited print.

Shotgun microphone (also: **Super cardioid;** see: **Cardioid**): A type of cardioid microphone that is especially sensitive to sounds coming from in front of it. A shotgun microphone can be used at a distance of up to 12 feet from the subject.

Shutter: In a camera, a mechanical device which alternately closes while fresh film is pulled into the gate, and then opens a set length of time to control the exposure given the film. In a projector, the shutter controls the length of time the light passing through the film remains on the screen.

Shutter angle: The size of the opening in a camera shutter. Since the shutter opening in a movie camera is wedge-shaped, the opening is measured in angular degrees.

Shutter speed: The length of time the shutter allows light to pass, usually measured in fractions of a second.

Silent speed (see: **Projection speed**)

Single framing (see: **Animation, Time lapse**): Exposing the film one frame at a time.

Single-system sound (also: **Sound-on-film**): A synchronous sound system in which sound and picture are recorded on the same strip of film.

Sky filter (see: **Contrast filter**): A graduated contrast filter used with B&W film to darken just the sky.

Skylight: Sunlight reflected from the sky; skylight is considerably bluer and more diffuse than direct sunlight.

Skylight filter: A pale pink filter that is used to absorb ultraviolet light when shooting B&W or color film outdoors.

Slate: A small blackboard on which are written the shot and take numbers, the name of the film, and other information. The slate is recorded at the beginning or end of each take in order to identify each piece of film shot.

Slow film (see: **Film speed**): Film with a relatively low sensitivity to light.

Slow motion (see: **Frame rate, Projection speed**): Slower-than-normal movements created by filming the action at a faster-than-normal frame rate (*overcranking*) and then projecting the film at the relatively slower standard projection speed.

Slug: A piece of leader used in a workprint in place of a missing shot; or the pieces of blank sound film used to fill in the spaces between each sound in the rolls used to mix a sound track.

Soft focus: A style of film-making in which the image is softened by diffusing the light and reducing the sharpness of the lens.

Soft light (see: **Hard light**): Light which tends to spread and scatter. Soft light, such as indirect sunlight or floodlighting, produces a gradual shading between highlights and shadows.

Sound effects (also: **SFX**): All sounds other than synchronous voices, narration, and music. However, these sounds, too, become sound effects when they are made part of the background, distorted, mixed with other sounds, or used in some other unusual way.

Sound-on-film (also: **S.O.F.;** see: **Single-system sound)**

Sound perspective: The apparent distance between the sound source and the microphone.

Sound speed (see: **Frame rate**): The standard frame rate used for shooting and projecting sound films: 24 frames per second.

Sound track (also: **Track**): The narrow area along the edge of a print within which the sound is recorded. Also, any sound recording used in the production of a motion picture.

Splice: The point at which two pieces of film or tape are joined. Also, to join the ends of two pieces of film or tape.

Split-field lens (see: **Close-up lens**): A lens which is half close-up lens and half plain glass. When mounted in front of a regular camera lens, a split-field lens permits the regular lens to focus both on a point that is close and on one that is more distant at the same time.

Sprocket holes (see: **Perforations)**

Stop down (see: **Aperture, F stop**): To use a small aperture; also, to use a lens at less than its maximum *f* stop.

Super (also: **Double exposure, Superimposition**): To expose two images, one over the other, onto the same strip of film.

Swish (Pan or **Tilt**): A pan or tilt in which the camera moves so rapidly that the entire image is blurred.

Sync marks: Marks that indicate the point at which two or more rolls of sound and/or picture should be locked together so that they may be in synchronization.

Synchronizing signal (also: **Sync signal;** see: **Control signal**): An electronic pulse produced by a generator in the camera, which is recorded as a control signal on the sound track.

Synchronous sound (also: **Sync sound;** see: **Lip-synchronous dialogue, Postsynchronization**): Sound recorded in synchronization with the pictures—usually lip-synchronous dialogue. Also, all sounds in the finished film, whether recorded "in sync" or postsynchronized, are in a synchronous relationship to the pictures.

Tail (also: **Foot;** see: **Head**): The end of a piece of film or tape. When a roll of film or tape has the end on the outside, the roll is said to be *tails-out.*

Take (see: **Shot**): The length of film exposed between each start and stop of the camera. Also, when the same shot is filmed more than once, each repetition is called a *take.*

Telephoto lens (see: **Long lens)**

Tilt: To pivot the camera vertically.

Time lapse (see: **Single framing**): A technique used to speed up actions that would otherwise occur too slowly to be observed. In time lapse the action is photographed with single-frame exposures made at set intervals; when the film is shown these intervals are eliminated because the projector runs at 24 frames per second.

Timing (also: **Grading**): The first step in printing a film: the process of determining the correct exposure and color correction, and the location of all fades and dissolves.

Track (see: **Zoom range**): The ability of a zoom lens to remain focused on the same point throughout its entire zoom range. Also, the ability of a wheeled camera dolly to retrace a straight-line movement. Another name for *trucking.*

Traveling matte: A strip of film, used in printing, that serves as a repetitive or variable mask. Since the matte image consists of clear areas in an opaque field, the printer light can pass through only the clear areas. These areas are then either superimposed on another image, or used to control where parts of several other images appear in the frame.

Trims (see: **Out takes)**

Trucking (also: **Tracking**): To move the camera and camera mount past the subject horizontally, or to move the camera alongside a moving subject.

T stop (see: **F stop**): A system of lens openings that indicates the actual amount of light passed by a lens. Because of the light losses caused by the complex construction of some lenses, *T* stops are a more accurate indication of exposure than *f* stops.

Two shot: A shot of two people, usually from the waist up.

Undercranked (see: **Fast motion)**

Variable shutter: A camera shutter in which the size of the opening can be changed. Decreasing the size of the opening decreases the length of the exposure given each frame.

Viewfinder: An optical device on the camera that is used to show the exact area being photographed. On some cameras the viewfinder is also used to focus the lens.

V.O.: Abbreviation for *voice over*.

Voice over (also: **V.O.;** see: **On-camera narration**): A type of narration in which the voice of someone previously shown speaking lip-synchronously is heard.

Warm image (see: **Cool image**): A reddish-yellow image, caused either by the color content of the light, the tendency of the lens to absorb the blue end of the spectrum, or the addition of red and/or yellow during printing.

Wide-angle lens (see: **Short lens**)

Wild track: Sounds not recorded in synchronization with the picture.

Workprint (see: **Original**): The first print made from the original. The workprint is edited into the final version of the film.

XCU: Abbreviation for *extreme close-up*.

X lighting (also: **Double key;** see: **Back light, Key light**): A simple technique for lighting two people speaking to one another. In X lighting the key light for one person simultaneously serves as the back light for the other.

XLS: Abbreviation for *extreme long shot*.

Zoom: To change the focal length of a zoom lens during a shot.

Zoom lens (see: **Focal length**): A lens of variable focal length. Changing the focal length of a zoom lens produces a continuously changing field of view.

Zoom range: The difference between the shortest and longest focal lengths of a zoom lens.

Bibliography

Some Useful Books and Articles

Baddeley, W. H. *The Techniques of Documentary Film Production.* New York: Hastings House, Publishers, 1969.

Balázs, Béla. *Theory of the Film.* New York: Dover Publications, Inc., 1970.

Bazin, André. *What Is Cinema?* Berkeley and Los Angeles: University of California Press, 1970.

Bluem, A. W. *Documentary in American Television.* New York: Hastings House, Publishers, 1965.

Bluestone, George. *Novels into Film.* Berkeley and Los Angeles: University of California Press, 1961.

Bogdanovich, Peter. *Allan Dwan, the Last Pioneer.* New York: Praeger Publishers, Inc., 1971.

Brownlow, Kevin. *The Parade's Gone By. . . .* New York: Alfred A. Knopf, 1969.

Burder, John. *The Technique of Editing 16mm. Films.* New York: Hastings House, Publishers, 1968.

Cameron, Ian, ed. *The Films of Jean-Luc Godard.* New York: Praeger Publishers, Inc., 1970.

Clarke, Charles G. *Professional Cinematography.* Hollywood: American Society of Cinematographers, 1968.

———, and Strenge, Walter, eds. *American Cinematographer Manual.* Hollywood: American Society of Cinematographers, 1973.

Corliss, Richard. "The Hollywood Screenwriter." *Film Comment* (Winter 1970–1971), pp. 4–7.

Happé, L. Bernard. *Basic Motion Picture Technology.* New York: Hastings House, Publishers, 1971.

Higham, Charles. *Hollywood Cameramen: Sources of Light.* Bloomington, Ind., and London: Indiana University Press, 1970.

Holm, Wilton R., ed. *Elements of Color in Professional Motion Pictures.* New York: Society of Motion Picture and Television Engineers, 1957.

Jacobs, Lewis. *The Emergence of Film Art.* New York: Hopkinson and Blake, Publishers, 1969.

Kellogg, Edward W. "History of Sound Motion Pictures." *Journal of the Society of Motion Picture and Television Engineers* (June, July, August 1955), 46 pp.

Kracauer, Siegfried. *From Caligari to Hitler.* New York: The Noonday Press, Inc., 1959.

———. *Theory of Film: The Redemption of Physical Reality.* New York: Oxford University Press, 1965.

Lindgren, Ernest. *The Art of the Film.* New York: The Macmillan Co., 1968.

Lipton, Lenny. *Independent Filmmaking.* San Francisco: Straight Arrow Books, 1972.

MacCann, Richard Dyer. *Film: A Montage of Theories.* New York: Dutton Paperbacks, 1966.

MacGowan, Kenneth. *Behind the Screen.* New York: Delacorte Press, 1965.

Mascelli, Joseph. *Mascelli's Cine Workbook.* Hollywood: Cine/Graphic Publications, 1973.

Montagu, Ivor. *Film World.* Baltimore, Md.: Penguin Books, Inc., 1964.

Ogle, Patrick. "Deep Focus Cinematography." *Filmmakers Newsletter* (May 1971), pp. 19–33.

Patterson, Richard. "The Photography of 'I Walk the Line,' Part I." *American Cinematographer* (November 1970), pp. 1072–1075, 1095, 1133, 1136.

———. "The Photography of 'I Walk the Line,' Part II." *American Cinematographer* (January 1971), pp. 62–65, 69–71, 74–76.

———. "Highlights from the History of Motion Picture Formats." *American Cinematographer* (January 1973), pp. 40–43, 64–65, 84–90.

Perkins, V. F. *Film as Film.* Baltimore, Md.: Penguin Books, Inc., 1972.

Pincus, Edward. *Guide to Filmmaking.* New York: The New American Library, 1969.

Pudovkin, V. I. *Film Technique and Film Acting.* New York: Bonanza Books, 1959.

Reisz, Karel, and Millar, Gavin. *The Technique of Film Editing.* New York: Hastings House, Publishers, 1968.

Richie, Donald. *The Films of Akira Kurosawa.* Berkeley and Los Angeles: University of California Press, 1965.

Roudabush, Byron, ed. *Recommended Standards and Procedures for Motion Picture Laboratory Ser-*

vices. Alexandria, Va.: The Association of Cinema Laboratories, 1972.

Sarris, Andrew. *Interviews With Film Directors.* New York: Avon Books, 1967.

———. *The American Cinema.* New York: Dutton Paperbacks, 1968.

Silver, Sidney. "Synchronous Recording Techniques." *db—The Sound Engineering Magazine* (July 1970), pp. 25–29.

Smallman, Kirk. *Creative Film-making.* Toronto: Collier-Macmillan Canada, Ltd., 1969.

Spottiswoode, Raymond, ed. *The Focal Encyclopedia of Film and Television Techniques.* New York: Hastings House, Publishers, 1969.

Stephenson, Ralph, and Debrix, Jean R. *The Cinema as Art.* Baltimore, Md.: Penguin Books, Inc., 1968.

Walter, Ernest. *The Technique of the Film Cutting Room.* New York: Hastings House, Publishers, 1969.

Wollen, Peter. *Signs and Meaning in the Cinema.* Bloomington, Ind., and London: Indiana University Press, 1969.

Young, Freddie, and Petzold, Paul. *The Work of the Motion Picture Cameraman.* New York: Hastings House, Publishers, 1972.

Youngblood, Gene. *Expanded Cinema.* New York: Dutton Paperbacks, 1970.

Zavattini, Cesare. *Zavattini—Sequences from a Cinematic Life.* Englewood Cliffs, N.J.: Prentice-Hall, Inc., 1970.